D0850821

A Rereading of Romans

A Rereading of Romans

Justice, Jews, and Gentiles

Stanley K. Stowers

Yale University Press   New Haven & London

Set in Berkeley and Template Gothic types by Marathon
Typography Service, Durham, North Carolina.

Printed in the United States of America by Edwards Brothers, Inc.,
Ann Arbor, Michigan.

Library of Congress Cataloging-in-Publication Data
Stowers, Stanley Kent.
    A rereading of Romans: justice, Jews, and gentiles
        p. cm.
    Includes bibliographical references and index.
    ISBN 0-300-05357-6 (alk. paper)
    1. Bible. N.T. Romans—Criticism, interpretation, etc.
I. Title.
BS2665.2.S864 1994
227'.106—dc20   94-1249
                                                        CIP

A catalogue record for this book is available from the British
Library.

The paper in this book meets the guidelines for permanence and
durability of the Committee on Production Guidelines for Book
Longevity of the Council on Library Resources.

10 9 8 7 6 5 4 3 2 1

Contents

Preface & Acknowledgments

I have consciously adopted a rhetorical stance in writing this book, although the development of that stance has a considerable history. I am grateful to Katherine Hall and Luke Johnson for reading an earlier version of this book in 1983. Their criticisms together with their encouragement to seek publication emboldened me to revise my style of argument. Experience in presenting aspects of my reading to the public convinced me that I had to formulate my arguments in a sharper and more forcefully contrastive way over against accepted readings. Otherwise I found that my audiences naturally tended to assimilate my proposals to the larger schemes of more conventional readings. Thus I talk much of "traditional readings" and "accepted views" to which I contrast my arguments. In using this language, I believe that I represent conventional readings accurately on various levels of generality. In a real sense, the book contains a series of arguments against ways that I have read Paul's great letter, an argument with myself. I, of course, do not believe that my former reading was idiosyncratic but indeed representative of a dominant Western tradition.

I owe debts of gratitude to many, but especially to those who read portions of the work and freely gave of their critical insight. These include my colleagues at Brown, Wendell Dietrich, Shaye Cohen, Giles Milhaven, Saul Olyan, and John Reeder. Susan Garrett, Luke T. Johnson, David Balch, and Troels Engberg-Petersen gave me lively debate and insightful readings of chapters. Michael Foat did a splendid job on the indexing. I owe a special debt to Kristin Kalajainen, who collaborated with me as an UTRA fellow and did much to aid in getting the manuscript finally to Yale University Press. I would also like to thank the National Endowment for the Humanities and the Woodrow Wilson International Center. I was an NEH fellow in 1991 and at the Center during 1992. At points this project overlapped substantially with my project for the NEH and the Center so that their support aided the final work on this book.

Because it has been such an important standard, I have made comparisons with the *RSV* throughout. The book was also essentially complete before the appearance of the *NRSV*.

I have sometimes translated *ta ethne* as "gentile peoples" or "gentile nations" in order to stress the collective and ethnic implications, even though these translations are literally redundant. In general, I have also tried to avoid translating the same passages and phrases in exactly the same way every time, in order to reflect the range of semantic possibility and nuance. Unless otherwise noted, all quotations of the Hebrew scriptures are my translations of the Septuagint (LXX).

Abbreviations

Most of the references to ancient sources appear in the body of the text. I have followed the abbreviations for ancient works for the most part from the *Oxford Classical Dictionary,* 2d ed. (Oxford, 1970), and for periodicals and reference works from the *American Journal of Archeology* 69 (1965): 201–06. Abbreviations for ancient Jewish and Christian sources have been taken from the *Journal of Biblical Literature Membership Directory and Handbook* (Decatur, Ga., 1992) and *A Greek Patristic Lexicon,* ed. G. W. H. Lampe (Oxford, 1961). I have also adopted the following for frequently cited works:

Cranfield, *Romans*   C. E. B. Cranfield, *Epistle to the Romans,* 2 vols. (ICC; Edinburgh: T. & T. Clark, 1979).

Diatribe and Romans   Stanley K. Stowers, *The Diatribe and Paul's Letter to the Romans* (Chico, Calif.: Scholars Press, 1981).

Dunn, *Romans*   James D. G. Dunn, *Romans: Word Biblical Commentary,* 2 vols. (Dallas: Word Books, 1988).

Käsemann, *Romans*   Ernst Käsemann, *Commentary on Romans* (Grand Rapids: Eerdmans, 1982).

Letter Writing   Stanley K. Stowers, *Letter Writing in Greco-Roman Antiquity* (LEC 5; Philadelphia: Westminster Press, 1986)

OTP   *Old Testament Pseudepigrapha,* 2 vols., ed. J. H. Charlesworth (Garden City, N.Y.: Doubleday, 1985).

Paul and Torah	Lloyd Gaston, *Paul and the Torah* (Vancouver: University of British Columbia Press, 1987).
"Paul and Torah"	Lloyd Gaston, "Paul and the Torah," in *Anti-Semitism and the Foundations of Christianity*, ed. A. Davies (New York: Paulist Press, 1979), 48–71; repr. in *Paul and Torah*, 15–34.
Paul and the Law	Heikki Räisänen, *Paul and the Law* (Philadelphia: Fortress Press, 1983).
PLJP	E. P. Sanders, *Paul, the Law and the Jewish People* (Philadelphia: Fortress Press, 1983).
PPJ	E. P. Sanders, *Paul and Palestinian Judaism* (Philadelphia: Fortress Press, 1977).
"Righteousness of God"	Sam K. Williams, "The Righteousness of God in Romans," *JBL* 99 (1980): 241–91.
Sanday and Headlam, *Romans*	W. Sanday and A. C. Headlam, *A Critical and Exegetical Commentary on the Epistle to the Romans*, 5th ed. (ICC; Edinburgh: T. & T. Clark, 1902).
Schlier, *Römerbrief*	Heinrich Schlier, *Der Römerbrief* (HTKNT 6; Freiburg: Herder, 1977).
"Use and Abuse of Reason"	Stanley K. Stowers, "Paul on the Use and Abuse of Reason," *Greeks, Romans and Christians: Essays in Honor of Abraham J. Malherbe*, ed. D. Balch, E. Ferguson, W. Meeks (Philadelphia: Fortress Press, 1990)

A Rereading of Romans

1   Toward a Rereading of Romans

The thesis of this book is easy to state but difficult to prove: Romans has come to be read in ways that differ fundamentally from ways that readers in Paul's own time could have read it. More than any other writing of earliest Christianity, Romans, especially in the West, came to bear the major economies of salvation. These systems of sin and salvation reshaped the frame of reference that determined the reading of the letter. My challenge consists of attempting to imagine how readers in Paul's time might have read the letter while also keeping in view the ways that later Christian communities reshaped it.

It lies far beyond the scope of this book and my capabilities to provide a history of the letter's interpretation. Yet rereading Romans requires some sense of that history. Furthermore, rereading will require an investigation of rhetorical conventions, generic conceptions, and cultural codes that Paul's readers might have used in order to make the letter intelligible.

The Tradition and Rumors of Contradiction

Paul's letter to the Romans is one of the most influential writings in the past fifteen hundred years of Western culture. One thinks first of the great interpreters of the letter and of the social, political, and religious movements associated with them.[1] Foremost is Augustine, who stands at the threshold between the ancient and medieval worlds and who has been called the first modern man.[2] After him, and partly because of him, uncounted numbers of penitents and monks forged their senses of guilt, fear of God, and gratitude for God's mercy on the verses of Paul's greatest letter. For Aquinas and the schoolmen, Romans was the most systematic exposition of Christian theology in scripture. Romans was, of course, the text of texts for Luther, Calvin, and the Protestant Reformation. To a great extent, the same can be said of the English Puritan and continental Pietist cultures.

The revivalist movements in the English-speaking countries associated with George Whitefield, the Wesleys, and others offered an interpretation of religious experience focused through the lens of Romans. The characteristic evangelicalism of the nineteenth century shared much of this focus. The sources of twentieth-century existentialism find some of their strongest roots in Søren Kierkegaard, who was above all an interpreter of the Lutheran-Augustinian-Pauline tradition to which Romans is the key. In the early twentieth century, the theological revival called dialectical theology and neo-orthodoxy was ignited by the publication of Karl Barth's commentary on Romans.

All of this is quite clear. Yet, in thinking of the letter's influence, I also mean something deeper and broader. More than any other book, Romans has been the forge of the Western psyche. This was especially so when Romans was read together with the Psalms. As a historian, I cannot imagine a Freud without an Augustine first. I cannot imagine the Augustine we know without Romans, through which he interpreted and shaped the experience of his life. The West is marked by an introspective and psychologically oriented individualism. The road to this way of being human was marked by many momentous steps. One was the invention of the will as a distinct faculty, for which Augustine holds much responsibility.[3]

No text was more important to Augustine's discovery than Romans 7, which he took as a description of the human will in the abyss of sin. In his early theology he believed that the chapter depicted the unregenerate human; later he came to identify Paul's words with his own struggles. The chapter became a paradigm for the Christian life of agonizing struggle against sin, the believer in desperation continually throwing himself upon the grace of God. Augustine's *Confessions* is the first introspective and psychological autobiography. In it, Augustine models his interior narrative upon his understanding of the Pauline narrative; a history of Augustine's life from the perspective of his feelings. In some ways the book is very modern.

In the long cultural revolution promoted by the Christians of late antiquity, the focus of meaning gradually shifted from the heavens to the soul. Whereas previous cultures had projected what was meaningful onto the cosmos, now the focus of meaning shifted to a metaphysics and cosmology inside the head. The result was modernity. Romans more than any writing of the Christian West seemed to make the intense spiritual struggle normative. In this reading of the letter, the first chapters described the depth and horror of the human turning from God and fall into depravity. Through these chapters and chapter 7, Adam's experience was shown to be every person's experience. The reader knew, however, that the abysmal darkness of the soul depicted in 1:18–3:20 opened dramatically to the sweet light of salvation in Jesus Christ at 3:21–26. Chapters 6–8, then, described sanctification, or the life of good works in Christian charity.

Augustine is the first person whom we know to have put all the components of this interpretation together. His reading of Romans shaped the understanding of his own conversion, and his experience in turn shaped the way he understood the letter. In the *Confessions*, written years after the events, Augustine movingly describes how God's mysterious grace overpowered and turned round his life. "All the darkness of uncertainty vanished" when he read the famous words from Romans 13 (*Conf.* 7.12.29). But one finds nothing of this particular conversion narrative in Augustine's writings from Cassiciacum, which follow that experience.[4] At Cassiciacum in 386, his conversion is to philosophy, to a Neoplatonic interpretation of Christianity. The pursuit of philosophical progress reflected in these dialogues differs radically from his understanding of how God's grace suddenly transformed his heart some eleven to fourteen years later when he wrote the *Confessions*.

What altered his account of his conversion between 386 and 397–401 was his encounter with Paul's letters, an encounter stamped by self-searching and bitter polemic. When Augustine returned to North Africa and became bishop, he faced the Manicheans, who had claimed Paul as their own. The new bishop's task was to show that Paul's teachings supported orthodox catholic doctrine rather than the radically deterministic and dualistic Manichean philosophy. In this process, Augustine repudiated his earlier understanding of grace, free will, sin, the law, and human motivation. As he reinterpreted his life through his new understanding of Paul, and especially of Romans, he came to see his past as we now read it in the *Confessions*. He still read Paul through the Neoplatonic myth of the soul's fall and return to God, but now from the psychological perspective of the divided will. Humankind is the fallen child of Adam totally enslaved by sin. The law now takes a form that no Jew could recognize. It expresses God's terrible though just moral demands, and yet no unredeemed person can do good at all. God gave the law to show humans the futility of attempting to do good themselves. Only God's overpowering grace can effect any good. Only God can cause a person to want to do good.

Even if the church did not as a whole accept all of Augustine's theology, his fundamental model for reading Paul and understanding the Christian life made the deepest impression. Hand in hand with concomitant social and economic changes, the Augustinian-"Pauline" understanding of the self was a crucial factor in the creation of modern man. Antiquity and the medieval world, for example, did not know childhood as we know it. Childhood as a time for individual development set apart from the adult world of work evolved as a regular institution in bourgeois Protestant households in the sixteenth and seventeenth centuries.[5] But Augustine's understanding of his own childhood as the stage of preparation for his conversion anticipates modern childhood in many ways. His account of childhood also reflects the Pauline sense of being set apart and prepared from birth for God's purposes. It is no accident that childhood and the modern bourgeois family first appeared in staunchly Calvinistic and Lutheran cultures. There, the faithful venerated Paul's Romans and Augustine's *Confessions*. The bourgeois family, which focused on the education and development of the child with an intensity previously unknown, produced the individuals and individualism characteristic of modernity. The preceding account, vastly oversimplified but essentially correct, illustrates what I mean when I say that the impact of Romans has been broader and deeper than the overt religious use of the letter by the Christian church.

But what if Romans had never become part of the church's sacred scriptures? What if the letter had lain in a ruin for nineteen hundred years before being discovered by some twentieth-century excavator? How would the scholars who studied the roll of papyrus—a long scroll filled from side to side with unbroken and unpunctuated lines of Greek letters—unlock its secrets? In Paul's day, periods, question marks, exclamation marks, commas, paragraph divisions were unknown. There were not even breaks between words or sentences. It all ran together. Nor would scholars have any of the great Christian interpreters and their commentaries to help them. On almost every level the text would be uninterpreted. The only guide for scholars would be their knowledge of the syntactical, literary, and rhetorical patterns of other writings from the same age as the Romans scroll. Scholars would have to compare and contrast Romans to other writings of the first century to gain an overall picture of how it fit together and what type of literature it was.

The historian of early Christian literature must imagine what it would be like to come upon Romans for the first time while also recognizing the impossibility and undesirability of forgetting the nearly two thousand years of interpretation. The historian must realize that the church shaped the letter in ways unforeseen by the apostle and learn from the struggles of earlier interpreters. I shall offer another reading of Romans both because I have learned from numerous interpreters and also because I have tried to imagine reading Romans afresh as a writing of antiquity. If I challenge the historical accuracy of some standard intepretations of the letter, it does not mean that I intend to denigrate the contributions of its great commentators. But my purposes as a historian of early Christian literature differ from the purposes of the theologians and churchmen.

A thorough rereading of Romans is timely and vital because the traditional model for understanding Paul's letter has begun to disintegrate under the weight of its own contradictions. Such disintegration is illustrated, for example, in the recent work of three scholars who have approached Paul with great candor and consistency. J. C. O'Neill's commentary has shocked and infuriated readers.[6] O'Neill argues that 1:18–32; 5:12–21; 7:14–25; 9:14–23; 10:16–11:32; 12:1–15:12, and other texts are later interpolations in Paul's letter. Sometimes O'Neill's arguments are weak and his decisions seem arbitrary, but he is one of the very few who have consistently looked behind the received translations and texts of Romans that tend to smooth out the difficulties. O'Neill, perhaps wrongly, insists that Paul be consistent in his thought. When the received way of reading the text or construing the genre of Romans proves inconsistent, O'Neill concludes that one side of the contradiction must be an addition. In the process, he loses large parts of the letter.

E. P. Sanders also has seen the contradictions.[7] Like O'Neill, he accepts with modification the traditional model for construing the letter. But Sanders rejects the normal way of smoothing things over by importing systematic thought on law, grace, sin, and so on from later theology. He thus admits the contradictions. He writes, for example, "Paul's case for universal sinfulness, as it is stated in Rom. 1:18–2:29 is not convincing: It is internally inconsistent and it rests on gross exaggeration."[8] Sanders explains Paul's thought by arguing that the apostle's beliefs are independent of and prior to the reasons and explanations that he gives for them. Paul came to believe in Christ, assumed that Christ and the law were mutually exclusive, and so invented all kinds of arguments to show why Judaism and the law should be rejected. Or, as Sanders himself puts it, "In short, this is what Paul finds wrong in Judaism: It is not Christianity."[9]

Heikki Räisänen has written about the contradictions in the traditional understanding of what Paul says about the law.[10] Räisänen discusses anomalies in Paul's thought about the law, including the following: (1) Paul's concept of law varies between the Torah given to Israel and something else such as a principle of salvation or moral law; (2) Paul assumes that the law is an undivided whole and yet often virtually reduces it to the moral law; (3) Paul says both that the law has been done away with for Christians and that they must fulfill its requirements; (4) he argues that no one can fulfill the law and yet says that some nonbelieving gentiles do fulfill it and that Christians must; (5) the law was given to bring life, and yet Paul denies that it could possibly bring life; (6) if the law brings forth and multiplies sin, as Paul says, why is it not the same for Paul's own community rules and paraenesis? Räisänen concludes that "almost any early Christian conception of the law is more consistent, more intelligible and more arguable than Paul's—whether you take Matthew or Luke, Hebrews or James, Marcion or Justin."[11] Räisänen's solution is to first agree with Sanders that Paul works backward in his theology from conclusions to arguments. Paul had a case and then looked around for arguments to prove it. He concludes that Paul is contradictory and incoherent concerning the law and then suggests psychological explanations for Paul's beliefs.

These scholars have thought rigorously, but they have not questioned their fundamental model for reading Paul's letters, including Romans, and for construing his thought. They accept the received scholarly view with certain modifications and point out the contradictions. Then they try to provide explanations for Paul's inconsistency and incoherency. At some point the explanations become so ridiculous, however, that one has difficulty imagining a historical Paul. Räisänen's replacement, for instance, of systematic theological harmonizing by psychological speculation is a jump out of the quagmire into the quicksand.

The work of many scholars, beginning with the pioneering essay by Krister Stendahl on Paul and the West's introspective conscience, suggests the need for a persistent questioning of the traditional readings of Paul's letters on a much more elemental level. Attempts to read Romans afresh must be guided by rhetorical and literary patterns from Paul's own time. The more one learns and understands about the world of the Roman empire and Jews in the Greek East, the more difficult it becomes to imagine the Paul known from modern scholarship in that world. The Paul of traditional theological scholarship seems to have dropped directly out of heaven. Our programmatic question, then, is, "How can one read Romans afresh as a letter from the Greco-Roman world of the first century C.E.?"

Reading as Markup and Text as Interpretation

Modern scholars tend to treat critical editions and ancient manuscripts of the Pauline letters as if they represent given, or noninterpreted, texts. Furthermore, this blind spot supports readings of the letters that present the ancient church's appropriation of Paul as Paul. Scholars of early Christian literature always work with some implicit understanding or theory of text, language, and literature.

Language is always prior to the individual speaker. A language belongs to a particular human community. Languages have their meanings because they are grounded in the social practices, shared meaningful activities, of particular communities. Texts belong to languages and therefore also derive their meanings from social practices rather than, say, the intentions in the heads of authors, supposedly prelinguistic experiences, or objects that words are supposed to name. The shared meaningful activities of communities constrain the meanings of texts in both a wider and a more specific way. An author may extend the meaning of the word "tiger" to refer to a certain person, but this extension is made possible by the fact that there is a deep agreement among speakers of English that "tiger" means a certain kind of large cat. That agreement has been formed over many centuries of an English and Western tradition of communities that relate to animals in certain ways, for example, domesticate some, hunt others, classify by species, print pictures of and tell stories about animals they have never actually seen. Social practice also constrains meaning in a narrower sense. This narrower context of social practice includes what is often described as historical situation, authorial intention, implied audience, and genre. The one who uses "tiger" for a person might be writing poetry, something meaningful to moderns in the context of aesthetic appreciation, or teaching an English class about simile and metaphor. Practical contexts (for example, worship, planting seed, eating food, playing games) seem to be almost limitless, and each person in society participates in many of these "language games." Texts serve many different purposes—think of a hymn, a stop sign, a law, a grocery list—but depend for their meanings upon both a wider history of meaningful activity and the more specific practical context of the texts' composition and use.

In order to read a text, a person must understand both the wider language and a specific practical context. Thus a text is not objective in the sense that it is ever given or noninterpreted. The markings on the paper are meaningful only because they constitute conventions of a particular community. In different contexts of social activity the same markings might have different meanings. In another culture the same markings might mean something different or nothing at all. Texts are objective only in the sense that a community agrees deeply about a text's meaning. Their interpretation is relatively determinate most of the time because they play certain fairly stable roles in various social practices. Communities, however, are always changing, and the shared meaningful activities that constrain the meanings of texts also change. The traditions of communities consist of oral and written texts that have continued to be made meaningful by shared activities.

Since the practical contexts change as the communities change, the meanings of the texts change. The original practical context of Paul's letters is not the same as the practical contexts of the letters as scripture in the worship, moral instruction, and doctrinal controversy of the fourth-century imperial church. To approximate the readings given to a text in the first or fourth centuries, modern scholars must grasp the codes of meaning belonging to the practical social activities of the time and place in question. The marks on the page do not magically jump into the mind and force a meaning upon the reader. The text is a set of socially agreed-upon cues from the wider language that the reader constructs into a pattern of meaning according to the codes (for example, generic expectations, preunderstandings of words, webs of belief) of the corresponding practical social context.

Talk of communities, shared meaningful activities, traditions, and deep agreements should not be taken to imply lack of conflict and absence of domination by certain groups of people over others in the communities to which texts belong. The deep agreements are mostly unconscious and very basic to the society: "The sky is blue," "People differ from rocks in significant ways," "In our language S has a certain sound," "People do not eat slugs," "Men are more rational and less emotional than women." In fact, the massive fundamental agreement in cultures allows people to communicate, to wield language as a tool of power, and thus to fight and disagree.

When communities appropriate a writing like Paul's letter to the Romans and place it at the center of their discourse, there is usually a power struggle over who is to control its interpretation. Christianity before Constantine consisted of a diverse family of overlapping communities. Scholars have not yet adequately described this diversity and interconnectedness, being largely dependent upon categories (for example, gnostic, catholic) inherited from those groups that won the power struggle. In order to read Romans as a first-century reader, I must have at least some sense of later readings that I have inherited and of how dominating groups establish control over the reading of "authoritative texts." Here recent literary theory proves most helpful.

Roland Barthes has stimulated much illuminating thinking and debate about the nature of texts. He writes, "We now know that the text is not a line of words releasing a single 'theological' meaning (the 'message' of an Author-God) but a multi-dimensional space in which a variety of writings, none of them original, blend and clash. The text is a tissue of quotations drawn from the innumerable centers of culture." Barthes then emphasizes the centering role of the reader: "There is one place where this multiplicity is focused and that place is the reader, not, as was hitherto said, the author. The reader is the space on which all the quotations that make up writing are inscribed. . . . A text's unity lies not in its origin but in its destination."[12]

Although the direction of the debate and consensus among literary scholars cannot be easily anticipated, certain points seem clear. Writers do not magically create texts out of nothing, and readers *must* bring a stock of other texts and cultural codes to bear upon a writing in order to read it. In Barthes's words, "The text is a tissue of quotations drawn from the innumerable centers of culture." Romans manifests numerous fragments of earlier texts imbedded to different degrees and in different ways. The most obvious fragments are those from Jewish scriptures that the authorial voice explicitly calls to the reader's attention. Paul thereby identifies himself with a Jewish tradition of the prophetic reinterpretation of the sacred writings for new situations. He does not write this way in all of his letters (for example, 1 Thess). References to scripture are also often more allusive and shade into what one might call the discourse of scriptural language.[13] Certain letters of Paul, above all Romans and Galatians, privilege scripture by explicitly drawing attention to the connections between the discourse of the letter and earlier authoritative texts. But the language of the letters also contains many unacknowledged precursors. I will argue, for example, that Rom 7:7–25 contains allusions to words made famous by Euripides' Medea. The words had gained such cultural importance that Paul's readers can only with difficulty be imagined to have missed the echo of the Medean saying. A suppressed intertextual connection might be just as powerful as one thrown into the foreground in the form of an explicit quotation. As professional advertisers know so well, what is overheard or subtly suggested often carries more credibility than what is bluntly told.

By a "tissue of quotations," however, Barthes means more than quotations of or allusions to other written texts. A competent reader must share realms of discourse and cultural codes with the author. Paul's letters, for example, make extensive use of the language of Greek athletic competition. To read this language so as to understand how Paul's contemporaries might have read, one must understand the logic and substance of Greek athletics and how philosophers appropriated the language of athletic competition as a discourse for thinking about the development of self-mastery and the life of the sage.

Much scholarship assumes that a text exists "out there" that is objective in the strong sense but that intepretations are subjective.[14] Such an assumption leads to treating the text as neutral or noninterpreted at certain levels. I wish to argue that the problem of interpretation is acute even at what scholars suppose to be the most basic level of the text, namely, word division, punctuation, indicators of sense units, transitions, textual arrangement, and generic identification.

As noted, Paul, like all writers in his time, composed his letters without punctuation, divisions between words, paragraphs, or chapter divisions.[15] He or his scribe wrote in *scriptio continua,* unbroken lines of capital letters from margin to margin. He may have assumed that the very specific sociohistorical contexts in which he anticipated that the letters would be read would make their meanings clear. In that case, the written scroll would have been the cue for someone who would know well both the writer's and hearer's side of the practical social context. The carrier of the letters might even have a memorized text to use in reading the scroll.

The oldest extant manuscripts of Paul's letters are already edited and have a definite interpretive shape. As I have said, a change in the context of shared meaningful activity in which a text is used means a change in the codes of its interpretation, a change of genre. The most obvious change of genre for Paul's writings in the ancient church is that from occasional letters of various sorts to that of scripture addressed to the universal church or to humanity rather than to individual congregations at specific times and places. One way that ancient Christianity dealt with the problem was through the theory of seven letters to seven churches.[16] The theory held that Paul had written to seven churches because the sacred number seven was symbolic for the whole church. Romans was also generalized in much more violent ways. In the first or early second century some person or persons excised the addresses to the gentile believers in Rome (1:15, 17) and removed chapters 15 and 16 with their historically and locally specific materials.[17] With this material removed, Romans could be read quite easily as a general letter to Christendom. The influence of this form of Romans was far-reaching and affected all branches of the textual tradition.[18] Romans became a theological treatise about humanity and Christianity. Paul's situation as a Jewish "sectarian" who preached the redemption of the gentiles became incomprehensible.

The letters of Paul that survive from antiquity take the form of letter collections, or "New Testaments." These should be viewed not as copies of autographs but as literary genres that have substantially reshaped the letters.[19] They represent so-called orthodox Christian intepetations of Paul. Merely to select a certain group of letters and to arrange them in a certain order is an interpretation in itself. One collection that originated and was most influential in Egypt consisted of Romans, Hebrews, 1 and 2 Corinthians, and Ephesians.[20] The intent of this collection seems to be the presentation of a generalized and departicularized Pauline theology. Romans and Hebrews stood next to each other. The use of one to interpret the other was apt for Platonizing Egyptian theology. In contrast, imagine a collection that consisted of only Romans and Philemon. What a different Paul! In addition to selection and arrangement, one finds such things as introductions, headings, subtitles, punctuation, conflations, the elimination of addresses and greetings, and editorial insertions at key points.[21] Seemingly minor changes can facilitate completely different readings of whole sections of a letter.

A more subtle and equally significant editing of the text took place with the introduction of paragraph and chapter divisions and punctuation.[22] Divisions always impose interpretations upon the text. Whatever criteria are used to divide the text into paragraphs and chapters are necessarily related to what the editor believes about the genre of Romans. The division of Romans in this way forms a kind of outlining according to a certain perception of the argumentation, rhetoric, and contents of the letter. If the editor conceives of Romans as a document to instruct Christians in right doctrines, then that assumption will be reflected in the way that the editor introduces paragraphs. The very concept of a paragraph or a chapter is foreign to Paul's way of writing and obscures his rhetoric. The effect of this obscuring on Romans was radical. Paul wrote in dialogical exchanges, ring compositions, transitional false conclusions and rejections, various rhetorical figures, speech-in-character, and so on. A poetic text arranged according to meter would read quite differently if paraphrased in prose and divided into paragraphs and chapters. A scholar with a knowledge of poetic practices contemporary with the poem's writing might have to study it intensively in order to show that it should be read poetically. A similar editing has happened to Paul's letters, especially Romans.

Placed in a collection of sacred writings, Romans was homogenized. *Codex Vaticanus,* for example, numbers the chapters of all the Pauline letters continuously, as if they were one book. The homogenization of the letters into the New Testament also appears in the use of colometry in many manuscripts.[23] Colometry divides a text into *kola* and *kommata,* or clauses and phrases, respectively. A *comma* was usually said to have not more than eight syllables and a *colon* nine to sixteen syllables. Although the divisions were supposed to be made according to sense, the arbitrariness of such editing is obvious. Applied to the whole New Testament, a mass homogenization of an extremely diverse body of literature occurred. The effect on Romans was as if someone had taken a panel of deeply carved marble relief from an ancient Greek temple that depicted an epic scene of gods and heroes and had sanded the features, the emotions of the faces and bodies, down to a flat outline of the scene. Now new details could be carved into the outline and a different scene would appear.

I will illustrate this process of the leveling of Paul's rhetoric and the subsequent appearance of another reading by the development of the chapter division at 2:1. There Paul suddenly shifts from his description of the vices into which the gentile peoples have fallen to a vocative address in the second person singular: "Therefore you are without a defense, Sir, like anyone who judges." As I have shown elsewhere, this authorial device of turning from the audience to an imaginary individual is important in the rhetoric of the diatribe and the literature influenced by its style.[24] Both the apostrophe in 2:1–5 and the dialogue in 3:27–4:1 that I discuss below were known in Paul's time as speech-in-character.

The teacher giving the diatribe speaks to an imaginary person who represents a certain vice. The apostrophe characterizes this type of person, and the sharp censure of the teacher against this fictitious person is actually a censure for students in the audience who fit the type. The teacher, who has been speaking abstractly of this type of behavior, uses the apostrophe to drive the message home in a sharp but indirect way that criticizes any hearers to whom the indictment is applicable. These apostrophes are hortatory and were used in such practical social contexts as that of teachers molding the characters of their disciples according to certain patterns.

Paul's use of this rhetoric in 2:1f. is stylistically and rhetorically characteristic. He depicts the hypocritical judge or the pretentious moralist familiar from Hellenistic philosophical literature. The whole point of the device is lost when 2:1 is understood to begin a new section with a different subject and implied audience.[25] Among the vicious types of people Paul lists in 1:29–31 are the insolent (*hubristēs*), the arrogant (*huperēphanos*), and the pretentious (*alazōn*). The imaginary person censured in 2:1f. characterizes precisely these vices. The intended effect must have been something like that in Nathan's parable to David about the poor shepherd (2 Sam 12:1–7), when at the parable's end Nathan says, "You are the man."[26] Paul graphically describes the decline of the gentiles into sin (1:18–32). Just as the audience is at the point of saying, "Amen, the world is sinful, brother Paul," he says, "When you judge another, mister, you judge yourself." One loses the whole point when 2:1 becomes a new subject.

The oldest chapter divisions, the *kephalaia majora* and a system in *Codex Vaticanus,* have no break at 2:1. Both mark off 1:18–2:12 as a section. That division highlights what I take to be one of Paul's major themes: God judges both Jews and gentiles impartially according to their works.[27] Patristic commentators gave various opinions about who was being addressed in 2:1ff., but there was not a strong emphasis on a break between 1:32 and 2:1 until Augustine. Origen thought that the apostrophe was aimed at ministers of the church.[28] Chrysostom first says that the text applies to civil magistrates, then allows that its message is meant for all people.[29] Pelagius understood 2:1–5 to be addressed to morally arrogant gentiles.[30]

But another tradition eventually became dominant in the West. *Codex Fuldensis,* a manuscript of the Latin Vulgate copied between 541 and 546, has a major division at 2:1. *Codex Amiatinus,* regarded as the best Vulgate manuscript, has the same system of chapter divisions. The chapter divisions of today were introduced into the Vulgate early in the thirteenth century by Stephen Langton, later archbishop of Canterbury. Augustine best illustrates the theological reasons for reading the text with 2:1 understood as a new section. In *The Spirit and the Letter* (44), he gives the view that would become dominant.

Speaking of 2:1–5, he says, "Then he goes on to those who judge and yet do the things which they condemn. This no doubt refers to the Jews, who have boasted in the law of God; though he does not at first name them explicitly."

Augustine notes that Paul explicitly turns to the Jews in 2:17, but he is nevertheless certain that the hypocritical judge in 2:1–5 refers to Jews. As we have seen, Paul's diatribal rhetoric does not refer to a Jew but to those who fit a certain vice. Furthermore, the effect is to censure his gentile audience. Paul's rhetoric can be amply illustrated from pagan literature. Plutarch certainly was not referring to Jews when he wrote the diatribal apostrophe in *De curiositate* 515D: "Why do you look so sharply on other's evils, malicious man [*anthrōpe baskanōtate*], but overlook your own? Shift your meddling from things without and turn it inwards; if you enjoy dealing with an account of evils, you have much occupation at home. . . . so great a quantity of sins will you find in your own life, of passions in your soul, of oversights in your duties."

And Seneca does not depict the hypocritical Jew when he turns the tables on those who criticize philosophers for inconsistency: "But you, do you have the time to search out other's evils and to pass judgment upon anybody? 'Why does this philosopher live so luxuriously?' 'Why does this one dine so sumptuously?'. You look at the pimples of others when you are covered with sores" (*Vit.bea.* 27.4).

No evidence exists to show that the character of the hypocritical and arrogant judge was ever applied to Jews until after Paul's time, and then by Christians. Why is Augustine so certain that Rom 2:1–5 depicts a Jew? First, long before Augustine's time, the relation between the church and Judaism had radically altered. The situation that had existed in Paul's time was no longer comprehensible. The normative Judaism of Augustine's time did not exist when Paul wrote.[31] When Paul wrote, the church was still fundamentally one of the sects within the diverse Judaisms of the second temple period. By Augustine's time, Christianity and Judaism were not only distinct religions but religions with a history of hostility toward one another. Second, the church had developed a theologically motivated stereotype of Judaism. The characterization of the Pharisees in the canonical gospels, especially Matthew, had become the stereotypical view of the Jew. Jews were legalists who rejected human mercy and God's grace. When combined with a view of the Jews as Christ-killers disinherited by God, this characterization often became powerfully anti-Jewish. Christian writers who had never seen a Jew felt that they knew all about Jews and Judaism. Third, Augustine himself, notably in his anti-Pelagian writings, developed a way of understanding the gospel and of reading Romans that made the Jew the archetypal sinner and rebel against God's grace.

Augustine internalized, individualized, and generalized such Pauline concepts as justification, sin, law, works, salvation, and election. As Krister Stendahl says, "The Law, the Torah, with its specific requirements of circumcision and food restrictions becomes a general principle of 'legalism' in religious matters."[32] Whereas for Paul the censure of boasting forms part of an attempt to respond to a concrete historical situation, for Augustine pride becomes the fundamental sin of all humans, epitomized by the legalistic, self-asserting Jew. The aim, the very generic conception of Romans is thus transformed. Augustine says, "The apostle aims to commend the grace which came through Jesus Christ to all people, lest the Jews exalt themselves above the other peoples on account of their possession of the law" (*Spirit. et Lit.* 9). For Augustine, to defend the gospel of God's grace means also to attack the Jew. The arrogant pride epitomized by the Jew becomes a central human problem with which all must wrestle. Every human has an evil inside called the Jew. Augustine writes, "Paul . . . fights zealously and fiercely on behalf of this grace of God, against the proud and arrogant who presume upon their own works. . . . Truly then is he clear and eager above all in the defense of grace. . . . And in the letter to the Romans he is concerned almost solely with this very matter; fighting with such numerous arguments as to weary the reader's will to follow: yet such weariness is beneficial and salutary, training rather than weakening the various aspects of the inner person" (*Spirit. et Lit.* 12).

Augustine has partially individualized and psychologized the understanding of Romans as polemical and apologetical. Paul defends God's grace. The acceptance of grace crushes human pride, and God justifies the individual on the basis of faith. Paul attacks human pride, epitomized by Jewish attempts to justify themselves by works.

The same understanding of Romans occurs in Luther. He agrees with Augustine that 2:1–5 is an attack on the Jew. In his lectures on Romans, he cites the summary for 2:1 from his printed New Testament text, which had been derived from the glosses of Nicholas of Lyra (d. 1340): "The apostle refutes the faults of the Jews, saying that as far as their guilt is concerned they are the same as the gentiles and in a certain respect even worse."[33] On 2:1–5 he says, "With this sickness the Jews are afflicted more widely than all the gentiles. Therefore he mentions at the very beginning of the chapter that he is directing his verbal attack against the Jews."[34] Luther also cites the text from Augustine given above concerning how Paul fights against the proud and profitably wearies the reader in Romans.[35]

The chapter division at 2:1, then, reflects an understanding that not only obscures Paul's diatribal rhetoric but assumes a different understanding of Romans as a whole. Augustine and Luther view Romans as both an attack on human pride, epitomized by Jewish keeping of the law, and a defense of the gospel of God's grace. Romans has become a polemical theological treatise about humanity in which Jews and gentiles serve only as examples of human depravity. The division at 2:1 is a way of arranging the text that reflects a certain reading of Romans, and that reading in turn supposes a generic conception of the letter. Whereas for Paul the gentile (that is, the non-Jew) was the historical ethnic-religious other, for Augustine the Jew is the archetypical religious other.

If the chapter division at 2:1 first of all illustrates the later church's understanding of Judaism, the division at 4:1 represents criteria for textual arrangement foreign to Paul's rhetoric. I have shown elsewhere that 3:27–4:2 is a dialogue between Paul and the imaginary Jewish teacher introduced at 2:17.[36] I have argued that it should be arranged and read as a dialogue with a series of questions and answers (see chapter 8). If my reading is correct, what has come to be the standard textual arrangement has completely obscured Paul's rhetoric. The division at 4:1 cuts the dialogue in half. Moreover, the choice of prose paragraphs has hidden the dialogue. What happened? Some understanding of Paul's diatribal rhetoric persisted among well-educated Christians. Origen and John Chrysostom both note that Paul carries on discussions with a fictitious interlocutor in Romans.[37] At the same time they have little grasp of Paul as a Jew living before the destruction of the temple and find it difficult to understand the substance of Paul's discussions about Jews and gentiles. *Codex Ephraemi rescriptus* (*C*) employs capitals set into the margins and stops in 3:27–4:2.[38] This gives the sense of a dialogue. *Codex Amiatinus* has a new chapter beginning at 3:31 rather than at 4:a. Considerations of rhetorical form and not just content are patently reflected in the text's arrangement. *Amiatinus* uses sense lines, stops, and marks indicating a question and its answer.

If these traditions of arrangement persist so late, why did the division at 4:1 and the prose paragraph become standard? The answer can be found in the contexts of practical activity that gave meaning to the text. In the later church's moral and doctrinal instruction, the biblical texts were treated more and more as information. A text is read as information when the reader has accepted the truth of the text before reading it.[39] The ruling criterion for textual division and arrangement became content. Rhetorical form was not important: moral and theological ideas were. Theological topics about sin and salvation became the criteria for arranging the text. Thus 4:1 introduces Abraham, who is an example of justification by faith. The dialogue disappears and a new topic, "Abraham's saving faith," appears. The genre of the text ceases to be diatribal argument and becomes doctrinal information. Not surprisingly, even today some scholars persist in describing Romans as a theological treatise.

The theory of text sketched above suggests that it is misleading to think of the church first as transmitting a text in which Paul's meaning was fully and objectively present and then, secondarily, appropriating and applying that meaning in light of its own circumstances. That some of "Paul's meaning" was understood is clear. "Interpretation," however, occurred at every level. To have a meaningful text at all is a constructive activity, and practical social context determines the generic patterns for making a text meaningful.

I have chosen examples of text editing to illustrate my point because the text seems most objective on that level. Objectivity, however, really means broad tacit agreement that the editing presented in critical editions, based largely on manuscript traditions, represents Paul's meaning. Text editing is not just a matter of punctuating sentences. The way one edits a text corresponds to the editor's larger generic conception of the work, whether that conception be explicit or an unrecognized set of assumptions. Without diminishing the helpfulness of critical editions, I suggest that scholars also ought to work with a text in *scriptio continua*. Then it will be more difficult to forget that to have a text at all is an act of interpretation.

Tactics and Strategies of Rereading

In my arguments for a reading of Romans, I will stress four perspectives. First, I will attempt to read with some sense of the way that Romans was read in different places and different periods in the later church. Here I cannot hope to have a specialist's competence of such a broad field of knowledge, but I will attempt to be aware of how certain influential interpreters read Romans at key points. Second, I will attempt to read Romans in light of rhetorical conventions and generic conceptions available to readers in Paul's time. Third, I will try to discover cultural codes and interrelated texts available to Paul's readers that make the best sense of the text's discourse. Fourth, I will try to show how the audience and the author are textual strategies in Romans. I am convinced that the way one construes audience and author in the rhetoric of the letter is the decisive factor in determining the reading one will give to the letter.

Speech-in-Character: Toward Reading Anciently

The imaginary conversation that I have suggested for 2:1–5 and 3:31–4:2 appears also in 3:1–9, 7:7–8:2, and other texts in Romans. A major burden of my argument will be to show that Romans is best read with this ancient rhetorical technique of speech-in-character. Speech-in-character (προσωποποιία) is a rhetorical and literary technique in which the speaker or writer produces speech that represents not himself or herself but another person or type of character.[40] Cicero, Quintilian, and the *progymnasmata* (elementary rhetorical exercises) of Theon, Hermogenes, and Aphthonius provide the best evidence from the rhetorical tradition for προσωποποιία in the early empire.[41] For Theon, probably writing in the first century C.E., speech-in-character consists both of cases in which one invents the *ēthos* (that is, character by means of words) of a known person (*prosōpon*) and also of cases in which one invents both the *ēthos* and the person. In the latter case, the invented person is a type: a husband, a general, a farmer, or the person prone to anger. The later writers Hermogenes and Aphthonius employ the term ἠθοποιία to mean approximately what Theon does by προσωποποιία.[42] Origen and other ancient Christian writers identify passages in Paul's letters that employ *prosōpopoiia*, including Romans 7, and use the technique for exegesis.[43] In all of these writers, *ēthos* means using words to portray a person's character, "including presentation of moral choice embodied in words and arguments."[44] Cicero, Quintilian, Theon, the grammarians, Origen, and perhaps the *Rhetorica ad Herennium* seem to follow a common tradition somewhat different from that followed by Hermogenes, Aphthonius, and the later rhetorical writings.[45]

On general grounds, even before one observes Paul's use of speech-in-character, the level of education reflected in the letters makes it likely that Paul received instruction in the subject. Paul's Greek educational level roughly equals that of someone who had primary instruction with a *grammaticus*, or teacher of letters, and then had studied letter writing and some elementary rhetorical exercises.[46] Speech-in-character was important at two points in the kind of education that Paul had. First, as I discuss in connection with the grammarians, learning how to read ancient Greek texts involved the identification of characters and persons. Second, speech-in-character was one of the elementary exercises related to learning prose and poetic composition.[47] Theon and Nicolaus point out that the exercise was also used for training in letter writing.[48] The teacher would ask the student to compose a letter by imagining what a certain person would say to a certain addressee on a certain occasion. The exercise consists of speech-in-character because it involves the creation of speech that fits the character of some legendary, historical, or type of person. Paul's ability to read and to write letters, even if not in the tradition of high literary culture, makes it all but certain that he had been instructed in προσωποποιία.

The modern form of writing and printing removes one of the most important phases of ancient education from the elementary curriculum and reflects our great distance from the oral culture of the Greco-Roman world. Ancient students, unlike moderns, had to learn how to identify and interpret all of the basic units of sense beyond the letters of the alphabet. As we have seen, Greek and Latin books and writing had virtually no punctuation, sense units, or meaningful textual arrangement. Lines of letters not even broken into words extended from margin to margin. The elementary teacher taught his pupils to impose the interpretive conventions of formal oral speech upon the written texts.[49] First came the identification of words and syllables in the text. Then came instruction in other sense units. Whether the text was poetry or prose, conventions of rhythm, inflection, and emphasis were taught as the means of interpretation. Quintilian speaks of teaching boys when to take a breath, when to place a sense pause into a line, how to indicate where units of sense begin and end, how to modulate the voice, to speed or slacken one's reading (1.8.1). Above all, he says, the number one rule is that the students practice these things so as to understand what they read (1.8.2). The widely influential grammar book by Dionysius Thrax reflects this process, and papyri from Egypt show how students put marks in texts in trying to find word divisions and other units of sense.[50]

The identification of the speaking voice and characters formed another aspect of this elementary education in reading. In every passage the student had to ask, "Who is speaking?" Homer, for example, was the favorite text for elementary instruction, although many others were also used. Sometimes Homer speaks in the authorial voice; sometimes one character or another speaks but often without the poet specifically indicating that such and such has begun to speak except by keeping the words in character with the speaker. The problem of identifying speakers occurs in most types of literature, being especially acute in drama, philosophical dialogue, and narratives that have speeches and dialogue.[51] Quintilian complains about the excessive dramatization taught by some elementary teachers when giving instruction in the identification of προσωποποιία: "Neither is it good, like some teachers, to indicate speech-in-character [*prosōpopoeia*] in the manner of a comic actor, even though one ought to make use of some modulation of voice [when reading] in order to distinguish speech-in-character from where the poet is speaking in his own person [*persona*]" (1.8.3).

Comic actors interpreted their characters by means of exaggerated parodies of the character's speech. Quintilian wants to avoid this but nevertheless recognizes that speakers and readers must distinguish characters. This passage forms part of Quintilian's discussion of the most basic aspects of reading taught to beginning readers. In order to read ancient texts at all, Paul must have known how to identify instances of *prosōpopoiia*.

Those grammarians who wrote about the interpretation of texts discuss speech-in-character in connection with the exegesis of difficult passages. The great Alexandrian scholar Aristarchus of Byzantium developed the principle of judging a passage by τὸ πρόσωπον τὸ λέγον (the character speaking) for exegesis and textual criticism.[52] Earlier grammarians had emended many passages in the Homeric epics, the Bible of the Greeks, that they considered too immoral for Homer to have written. Aristarchus restored many of these by emphasizing that words spoken by persons in the narrative represented their views and not necessarily Homer's. One solution to contradictions and anomalies in the text was by character (λύσις ἐκ προσώπου).[53] Sometimes, for example, Homer speaks from his own character and at other times from a heroic character. Instances in which the poet or a speaker seems to contradict himself or speak out of character may mean that the words have been attributed to the wrong person. Thus the grammarians speak much about the appropriateness of words to the person (ἁρμόζειν τῷ προσώπῳ). The reader and critic determine who is speaking by criteria of appropriateness. Do the words fit the moral habits and inner dispositions (ēthē, ēthos) of a person or type of person? Do the words reflect the individual's peculiar history (idiōma)? Are the words worthy of a particular station in life (axion)? Does the subject matter fit the person? Above all, the reader must look carefully for changes of speaker (enallagē/metabolē), which are often signaled by dissonance in relation to preceding speech (diaphōnia). The discussions of the grammarians reveal not only the use of a powerful analytical tool but also the degree to which an understanding of prosōpopoiia was essential to ancient reading and why it had such a basic place in the schools.

Paul would also have received instruction in prosōpopoiia when he learned to compose letters. Theon's elementary exercises represent the kind of information that a teacher would have provided for his students. Theon defines speech-in-character as "introducing into the discourse" a character (prosōpon) with "words appropriate both to the character and the subject matter" (2.115.10–11). He then gives examples of the prosōpopoiia both of types and of known figures; words that a husband would say to his wife as he is about to set off on a journey or a general to his troops before battle, in the first instance, and the words of Cyrus advancing to Massagetae or from Darius to Datis after the defeat at Marathon, in the second. One must consider the speaker's character and the person to whom the words are addressed. Regarding appropriateness one need consider such things as the character's age (young and old speak differently), social status (for example, slave or free), gender, vocation, ethnicity (Laconians speak concisely and lucidly, Attics fluently) and moral-psychological disposition (someone in love versus someone with self-mastery).

The author should take into account the occasion, but as Theon's last example shows, the rhetoricians construe occasion broadly. Thus moral and psychological states count as occasions. Indeed, portrayals of such states appear frequently because speech-in-character served as a technique for moral instruction and exhortation. Some of the sources emphasize speech-in-character's power not only to portray moral habits but also to depict and elicit emotion. The *ad Herennium* notes its effectiveness in appeals to pity (4.53.66; cf. Quint. 6.1.25–26). Such examples show why *prosōpopoiia* was often in the first person singular. Speech-in-character, however, could take the form of monologue, soliloquy, address, and dialogue or a combination of these. Thus Quintilian explains,

> A bolder figure, which Cicero thinks more difficult, is *fictiones person-arum,* or προσωποποιία. This technique adds wonderful variety and animation to oratory. With this figure we present the inner thoughts of our adversaries as though they were talking with themselves. . . . Or without diminishing credibility we may introduce conversations between ourselves and others, or of others among themselves, and give words of advice, reproof, complaint, praise or pity to appropriate persons . . . peoples may find a voice . . . or pretend that we have before our eyes things, persons or utterances. (9.2.30–33)

This variety of forms persuades me that not only the first person speech of Rom 7 but also the apostrophes in 2:1–16 and 2:17–29 and the dialogue in 3:1–9 and 3:27–4:2 ought to be considered types of speech-in-character. Quintilian places all these kinds of speech involving imaginary speakers, interlocutors, or addressees under *prosōpopoiia*. According to Quintilian's categories, almost all of the dialogical techniques characteristic of the so-called diatribe would be types of speech-in-character.

Quintilian further points out that the device may be introduced in a variety of ways, with or without explicitly identifying the imaginary speaker: "We may also introduce some imaginary person without identifying him, as when we say, 'Here someone says,' or 'someone will say.' Or the words may be inserted without the introduction of any speaker at all, as in, 'Here the Dolphian host fought, here fierce Achilles held forth.' This involves a mixture of figures, since added to προσωποποιία is ellipse, which here consists in omitting any indication of the one speaking" (9.2.37). Quintilian's example represents the words of some Trojan surveying the scene after the Greeks had departed.[54] Emporius, a fifth-century orator who compiled earlier materials, wrote a work on *ethopoeia* that gives examples of three ways to begin a characterization.[55] First, one may begin with the character starting to speak about herself or himself in the first person ("I have truly deserved it, and I will not try to minimize . . ."). Second, the speech may begin as an apostrophe, with the author addressing the fictional character ("O you of such great fame . . ."). Third, if one wants to emphasize the occasion, one should begin by introducing the circumstances (for example, "These solemn rites . . ." or "During the war with Argolis . . ."). Such speech-in-character that lacked explicitly named speakers provided many of the difficult texts over which the grammarians worried and, as I shall show, ancient exegetes of Romans discussed.

In sum, given ancient reading and writing practices, Paul's educational level, and the nature of Greco-Roman education and rhetoric, it is almost certain that Paul received instruction in and employed *prosōpopoiia*. I find it impossible to imagine Paul as a letter writer or an exegete of the Greek Bible not using speech-in-character. Paul does use the technique with great skill, and the recognition of this fact can illuminate the reading of Romans.

The Audience in the Text

Pauline scholarship is in great need of conceptual discipline regarding the question of audience or reader. Literary theory has developed several approaches to the problem of the reader,[56] but for my purposes it is unnecessary to introduce the complexities of such theory because my goal is a comprehensive reading of the letter. Three basic categories are compatible with a wide range of literary theories and approaches: the empirical reader, the encoded explicit reader, and the encoded implicit reader.

If we presume that the letter reached Rome and was read, those readers are empirical readers. I too am an empirical reader. Empirical readers can represent vastly different periods and cultural assumptions. The encoded explicit reader, on the other hand, is the audience manifest in the text. When Paul writes "all the gentiles, including you yourselves" (1:5) and "yes I am speaking to you gentiles, however" (11:13), this is the reader explicitly inscribed in the text. Other examples of the explicit reader in the text include direct address of the audience in the second person plural and direct reference in the first person plural as well as the expression "brothers." The encoded implicit reader in some ways resembles what scholars call the ideal or competent reader. One conceptualizes this reader by asking the question, "What assumptions, knowledge, frame of reference, and horizon of expectations does Romans implicitly assume in order to be well or fully understood?" The letter, for example, implies an audience that understands something about Jewish scripture and the logic of its use and authority in Judaism or certain types of Judaism. At some points this assumption about the audience's knowledge of scripture may become an aspect of the explicit reader, as would be the case if Paul means Jewish law in 7:1 when he says that he is speaking to those who know the law. Other implicit assumptions about the competent reader include knowledge of and attitudes toward Paul, an understanding of certain Greek, Roman, and Jewish cultural codes and institutions, a knowledge of various texts, a grasp of the generic literary and rhetorical conventions manifest in the letter, certain common beliefs about God and Christ, and an ignorance of Aramaic (for example, 8:15). Normally one expects continuity between the explicitly inscribed and the implicitly encoded reader. Both, however, must be sharply distinguished from empirical readers of any sort. The encoded audience is a feature of the text itself. I can know with certainty that the audience in the text is gentiles at Rome who know something about Jewish scripture and Jesus Christ, but I can only speculate about who actually read the letter, their assumptions, knowledge, and reactions to the letter. This is true even if Paul knew the empirical audience well—and we do not know this to be true—and even if he had consciously or unconsciously identified the reader in the text with the empirical reader. Our knowledge of the text of Romans qualitatively differs from our knowledge of what was in the mind of Paul as he wrote and what was in the minds of empirical readers as they read. Separating the encoded reader from the empirical reader helps one to see that the encoded audience is always a rhetorical strategy of the text.

The Audience in Traditional Ways of Reading Romans

James Dunn's commentary on Romans brings the best of historical critical scholarship to bear on the traditional reading of Romans.[57] His commentary is a good example of the traditional treatment of the letter's audience and is representative of the best critical commentators. His section on audience bears the title "The Recipients: The Origin and Character of the Christian Community in Rome."[58] Typically, commentaries have a section in the Introduction entitled "The Church in Rome" or "The Roman Church," thus assuming a simple identity between the encoded and empirical readers. Dunn seems on the verge of transcending this approach and acknowledging the primacy of the encoded audience when he says, " It is less clearly necessary on a priori grounds to set the letter to Rome against the background of the history of its recipients, the Christian community in Rome. Paul could, after all, have been writing without any thought whatsoever of the circumstances of the Christian groups in Rome, in which case exegesis could proceed without going into such matters."[59]

Nevertheless, Dunn claims that the letter itself shows that Paul knew the character and circumstances of the Christian groups in Rome. Here he refers to what he rather strangely calls "personal notes" (6:17; 7:1; 3:8) and the personal contacts of chapter 16. This allows him to plunge into a speculative reconstruction of the original empirical audience. As a further warrant for this procedure of reconstructing the empirical audience in Paul's mind when he wrote, Dunn says that Paul was obviously writing to gentiles. Here he follows scholarship of the past forty years that has, often grudgingly, come to acknowledge the letter's explicitness about its gentile audience. Amazingly, however, Dunn reimports Jewish Christians into the letter in the second half of the same paragraph when he explains that "Paul was aware of the ethnic composition of Christian groups in Rome" and that the letter provides counsel on "how gentile and Jewish Christians should perceive their relationship to each other."[60]

Dunn immediately begins a history of the Jewish community at Rome and an argument that the Christian community at Rome emerged from Judaism in Rome. He stresses the ambiguous legal status of Christian groups not yet fully independent from synagogues and the growing independence of an increasingly gentile church. The now well known hypothesis about Jewish Christian/gentile Christian conflict due to the supposed expulsion of Jews by Claudius in 49 C.E. plays a central role in Dunn's commentary. The hypothesis provides a construction of an empirical audience against which he reads the letter and a conflict model for constructing Paul's thought. The house churches in Rome would have become predominately gentile after the expulsion. If the edict was allowed to lapse after Claudius's death in 54, returning Jewish Christians, so the theory states, would have found it difficult to regain leadership roles in the gentile-dominated house churches. The theory seems to account for many features of the letter: for example, the theme of the Jew first and also the Greek; the theme of God's impartiality; the warning to gentiles not to feel superior to Jews (11:17–21); the discussion of the "weak" and "food laws" in chapter 14.

This typical approach of conflating the empirical and encoded reader allows scholars to replace a careful analysis of the audience in the letter with a conjectural reconstruction that actually pays only scant attention to the way that the letter itself depicts its readers. The problem lies not only in the highly speculative nature of such reconstructions. Rather, such reconstructions permit scholars to beg the most fundamental questions about audience. Commentators assume that "the church" in Rome and therefore the audience of the letter consisted of Jewish Christians and gentile Christians. Discussions then focus upon the proportions of each group and the nature of their relations with one another. All of this presupposes without argument that Paul's letters individually and collectively contain the concept of Christianity, the idea of the third race neither Jewish nor pagan. Occasionally scholars confess that Paul does not yet have the concept of Christianity, yet rarely do they consider the numerous possibilities for construing the relation of gentile believers in Christ, Jewish believers, and other sorts of Jews.

The canonical Christian reading continues to dominate even scholars who think of themselves first of all as historians. In the reading that has become traditional in the West, the audience of Romans consists first of Christians and second of humanity. According to this scheme, the human being is found in two significant forms, saved or Christian and lost or non-Christian. These are the fundamental categories for reading the letter. Jewishness and Greekness are mere ethnic attributes, matters of culture, not religion. The religion/culture antithesis has become a corollary of abstract individualism and of treating Christianity as if it transcended culture. This scheme serves as the basis for a system of sin, salvation, and church that the concept Christianity implies.

I propose that Romans not be read with certain a priori assumptions that control reading. First, that the concepts Christian and Christianity not be introduced unless the text requires them, and similarly that the term "Jewish Christians" not be brought into the discourse prematurely. Neither should Romans be prematurely assimilated to Paul's other letters. I am asking that readers become conscious of the circularity in the reading process so that it can be evaluated critically. Ruling metaphors and schemes of thought allow one to make sense of texts, but one rarely examines one's interpretations of texts on the level of such metaphors and schemes of thought. Again, E. P. Sanders provides a helpful illustration because he has pushed the logic of the system so far. I take issue with many things in the following quotation but draw attention only to the role of the concept of Christianity. The quotation comes from a larger argument attempting to show that Paul's thought contains the concept of the third race: "The crucial point is that Paul applied the entrance requirement 'faith in Jesus Christ' to Jews as well as to gentiles. Even Peter and Paul, who had lived as righteous Jews, had to do *something else* in order to be members of the people of God; they had to have faith in Christ (Ga. 2:15f.). Paul did not count people who were as Jewish as they could be (such as himself, Phil. 3:4–6) among 'the seed of Abraham.'"[61]

The way that Sanders frames the question presupposes a positive answer to his question of the third race. The phrases "entrance requirement," "to be members," and "the people of God" presuppose the concept of Christianity. Jews have to do something else to become members of the one universal body of those who are saved. "People of God" could be replaced with "the Church."

If there were a biblical text in which Jonah said, "I had to go and preach to the Ninevites in order to be righteous before God," interpreters would be unlikely to say that Jonah had to do something besides being a faithful Jew in order to gain membership in God's people. Assuming the concept of Christianity for the Pauline text but not for the Jonah text is what makes the difference. It, of course, comes as no surprise that Paul's letters are read in this way after some fifteen hundred years of their appropriation by Christianity. The assumption that Paul had a fully developed concept of Christianity, the third entity, lies close to the heart of Sanders's treatment of Paul, as his famous dictum implies: "In short, this is what Paul finds wrong in Judaism: it is not Christianity."[62] Naturally, then, Sanders, like most others who write about Romans, lapses into the terminology "Christians" when Paul speaks only of Jews and gentiles: for example, "In Rom. 8:3–4 Paul writes that the purpose of God sending his own son was that Christians 'would fulfill the requirement of the law.'"[63]

The easy assumption among scholars that Paul had a clear-cut idea of the new religion or true religion of Christianity connects closely with the persistence of traditional Christian constructions of Judaism in New Testament studies.[64] A picture of Judaism is, of course, an intrinsic part of Christian theology.[65] Judaism is supposed to be the shadow to which Christianity is the reality. Judaism is the inadequate and often perverted prototype of the fully revealed true religion. Judaism was God's preparation for the gospel and precursor of the church. If Christianity is a religion of salvation, so must Judaism also be. If Christianity centers around going to church and experiencing the sacraments and liturgy, then Judaism is about going to the synagogue and experiencing its shadows of the sacraments and liturgy. If Christianity has its ascetics and communities of monks in the desert, then Judaism had its monks on the shores of the Dead Sea. If Christianity sought to convert and save all humans, then Judaism had its own mission and sought to save gentiles by converting them to the true religion, and so on.

In the logic of this view, because Christianity is in some sense what Judaism should have been, the Christian critique of Judaism is justified. At this point the Christian tradition has, above all, drawn on its interpretation of Paul. The problem with Judaism is that it sought salvation through works of the law and legalism rather than through true inward and spiritual faith. New Testament scholars have acutely failed to recognize that ancient Judaism constituted, even considering its variety, a distinctly different religious system (or systems) from Christianity. In Paul's day, Judaism centered on a temple state with a hereditary priesthood whose religious system was constituted of a complex structure of purity and pollution relating to the temple and its animal sacrifice. As such, ancient Judaism is comparable to many other temple systems that practiced animal sacrifice.[66] The fact that large numbers of Jews lived as resident aliens outside of Judea does not transform Judaism into a religion of salvation like Gnosticism or Orthodox Christianity. Even Philo, Christianity's pet Jew, with all of his platonizing spirituality, does not evidence a negation of the temple system.

Not only the Judaisms of the second temple period but also the later Judaisms of the Mishna and Talmuds constitute distinctively different religious systems from all known forms of ancient Christianity. This is an important point because New Testament scholars have often imagined that the kinds of Judaism represented in the Mishna (third century C.E.) and Talmuds (fourth to seventh centuries C.E.) existed in the first century C.E. and were known by Jesus and Paul. Even Sanders, who has done more than perhaps any other contemporary New Testament scholar to dispel distortions of ancient Judaism, has tended to cast Judaism into the mold of Christianity. Thus Anthony Saldarini writes,

> Sanders's sketch of rabbinic religion coheres, but it derives from Christian theological interests rather than from second and third century Jewish religion. Certainly the rabbis read Scripture and accepted the covenant, but neither their practice nor their self-consciousness centered on it. As difficult as it is for modern scholars—Christian and sometimes Jewish—to understand it, first and second century rabbis shifted their attention and efforts to the development of halaka and in its observance they found their God and guidance for living. Halaka is not derived from covenant in any concrete way in Tannaitic literature; it is itself central and primary.[67]

The perception of Judaism as a precursor to Christianity plays a subtle but critical role in traditional readings of the audience in Romans. If Paul already knew in Judaism a religion of salvation very similar to Christianity, then one can easily imagine him with a system of Christianity. If Judaism addressed itself to the human predicament of sin, then how much more must the religion of Paul's letters be a universal system of sin and salvation. Romans, then, has an essentially undifferentiated universal audience. Indeed, in one influential reading, as idolatry is the vice pointing to the Adamic fall in pagans, so particularistic nationalism is the vice pointing to the fall in Jews. The very problem with Judaism is that it did not live up to the universalism that God wanted of Israel.

The modern version of the traditional reading trades heavily on the anachronistic concept of religion. The concept of religion was created in eighteenth-century European culture. Intellectual historians have shown that religion becomes the genus of which Christianity is a species only in the seventeenth century.[68] The modern concept of religion as an essentially private sphere of personal belief and activity separate from politics, law, economic activity, and ethnicity is an even later development. When the high priest was the nation's ruler and the Roman emperor was the *pontifex maximus* and the law of the Judean people was their sacred writings it is easy to see that religion, politics, and ethnicity are inseparable. Yet exegetes of the New Testament constantly employ the anachronistic category of religion in reading Pauline texts. In fact, assuming the postindustrial organization of Western society is one side of the universal address based on liberal individualism that modern interpreters find in Paul's letters.

Examples of interpreters employing the anachronistic distinction between religion and ethnicity are easy to find. G. B. Caird, for example, writes, "But his conversion persuaded him that he and his fellow Jews had radically misunderstood their own history, failing to recognise that the true son of Abraham is he who shares Abraham's faith (Rom 4:11–12; Gal 3:7), that the true Jew is he who is such inwardly, and the true circumcision is of the heart, directed not by written precepts but by the Spirit (Rom 2:29), and that to identify religion with patriotism and national privilege is to deny the central affirmation of the Old Testament faith, that God is one (Rom 3:29–30; cf. Deut 6:4)."[69]

W. D. Davies, commenting on the Ps. of Sol. 18:4, which speaks of God's mercy in chastising Israel, writes, "In such passages national and religious fervour blend."[70] Of Paul, Davies says, "The names 'Hebrew,' 'Israelite,' and 'Abraham' in Rom. 11:1f and Phil. 3:5 points not only to his ethnic but to his religious pride."[71] Discussions of Jews that build on the religion/ethnicity distinction often assume without qualification that pride or confidence is, on the one hand, a gross evil and, on the other, that Jews are more susceptible to it than other groups. The opposition, true inward religion (faith) versus particularism and ethnic pride, plays a central role in traditional readings of 1:18–4:20. There interpreters characteristically produce a reading based on the premise that "Paul's intended audience" would have had a picture in their minds of Jews as legalistic, particularistic, and viciously prideful. In other words, first-century readers could have understood what Paul supposedly intended only if they already viewed Jews as characteristically legalistic, prideful, and so on and if they already considered problematic pride in one's people, seriousness about keeping one's laws, and so on.

Dunn provides a recent illustration of this way of reading Romans 1–4. According to Dunn, for 1:18–3:20, "the principal focus of critique is Jewish self-assurance that the typically Jewish indictment of gentile sin (1:18–32) is not applicable to the covenant people themselves (2:1–3:20; cf. Synofzik, 87–88)."[72] He views 1:18–2:17 as a rhetorical trick to trap Jews in their "typical" presumption of moral superiority.[73] "All" in 1:18 "has a polemical edge, since Paul has in view his devout Jewish contemporaries who thought" that because they were just, "they were distanced from all" injustice.[74] Dunn can know what was in Paul's mind here because he assumes that Jewish arrogance would have been obvious in the first century. Paul argues against "his fellow Jews distorted understanding of their part within the covenant." Jews supposedly believed that they were justified merely by their membership in the covenant instead of by faith. "Failure to recognize the . . . objective of deflating Jewish presumption (that Israel's being the people of the law indicates God's predisposition in Israel's favor) is the root of the confusion among commentators over the purpose and theology of chap. 2."[75] The confused commentators Dunn cites are Sanders, Räisänen, and O'Neill. Even though the text specifically attributes the vices of 1:26–31 to idolators who have rejected a true knowledge of God, Dunn writes, "The prominence given in that list to sins of pride and presumption . . . may well already have had the Jewish interlocutor in mind, since it is precisely Jewish presumption regarding their favored status as the people of God which underlay so much Jewish disparagement of gentile religion."[76] One might well ask if it would not be equally presumptuous for Paul himself or Christians in general to disparage pagan religion. Dunn is certain, along with "most commentators," that the interlocutor in 2:1–5 primarily represents Jews because that is what Jews are like, as Paul himself supposedly confirms in 2:17f. and elsewhere.[77] Paul has been explicit about gentile idolatry only up to 2:1. The picture of the Jew as a hypocritical and arrogant judge would have to be so obvious to ancient readers that they could recognize the sudden, unsignaled shift at 2:1, or else Paul miscalculated and they would have to reread backward from 2:17f., if indeed they understood 2:17 to be a generalization about Jews.

Again and again, Dunn claims that Paul had some subtle point in mind that provides a polemical jab at "the typical Jewish attitude." When 2:2 says that God's judgment is "according to truth," "Paul may well be 'playing his imagined opponent along,' since a pious Jew would readily think of God's judgment 'according to truth' as judgment in which God displayed his choice of commitment to Israel."[78] Verse 2:4 turns the Jewish interlocutor's own central beliefs against him, namely, God's goodness, patience, and the concept of repentance.[79] Dunn agrees with Wilckens that "righteous judgment" in 2:5 implies "a polemical note" because Jews would assume that God's righteous judgment took place only for the benefit of Jews.[80] When Paul cites Ps 62:12 and Prv 24:12: "God will render to each according to his work," "The implication once again is that Paul intends the formulation as a critique of the narrower Jewish view which discounts the good done outside the covenant just as it discounts the unrighteousness committed by those within the covenant."[81]

My point is not that Dunn or Paul (if Dunn is correct) is unfair to Judaism, although that is true: Jewish writings are mined for choice passages that fit preconceived Christian molds; Judaism is distorted into an inadequate religion of salvation; standards are held out for Judaism that Christianity itself could never be expected to attain. Rather, my point concerns the historical implausibility of this traditional way of reading. None of these so-called criticisms of Judaism are at all explicit in 1:18–2:16. And while the discovery of allusion and implication is a legitimate enterprise, one must show that author and addressee could have shared the kind of knowledge (textual, symbolic, encyclopedic, semantic) necessary in order to make sense of the allusions and implications. Because the letter does not explicitly develop the picture of the Jew that Dunn supposes, such a picture would have to be part of the shared knowledge of author and addressee. But no evidence exists for such a picture of Judaism, and in fact the picture developed in later Christianity. In the absence of this picture of the alleged typical Jew, the traditional reading of Romans collapses.

Dunn's reading, for example, assumes as a patently explicit and obvious Jewish doctrine that God punishes gentiles severely but mercifully overlooks Jewish evil. I find the evidence vastly more complex and, on the whole, very different from Dunn's assumption. I find no Jewish texts explicitly saying that God will ignore Jewish sin because of the covenant. One finds numerous examples of confidence in God's justice and mercy and ultimate faithfulness to Israel. Many texts also unsurprisingly assume that Jews are typically more faithful and more pleasing to God than polytheists, but Christian and Moslem texts say the same thing about Christians and Moslems. God's justice and impartiality is also a pervasive theme in Jewish texts. Indeed, the most widespread view seems to hold that Jews are punished even more severely and held to a higher standard than gentiles, at least in this world.[82] As 2 Macc 6:14 explains, God shows his mercy to Israel by continually punishing Jews in order to keep them in line and in order that their sins might be continually atoned. One finds in ancient Jewish texts a persistent theme of reading Israel's calamities as severe punishments wrought out of God's love in order to discipline her, whereas God is frequently said to overlook gentile sin, allowing gentile liability to accumulate (see chapter 3). The evidence of Jewish texts betrays the implausibility of Dunn's presumed reader.

Jewish Christians Everywhere

The assumption of a Jewish Christian element in the audience forms another pillar in the traditional reading of Romans and of Paul's letters in general. The obsession with finding Jewish readers is so great that interpreters ignore or disallow the letters' explicitly encoded audience. Although the text explicitly addresses itself only to gentiles and nowhere explicitly encodes a Jewish audience, interpreters persistently speak of the predominantly gentile audience and the gentile majority. The logic of this nearly willful dismissal of Paul's encoded audience goes something like this: Because we know that there were Jewish believers in Rome and because Paul's subject matter at times seems fit for Jews, there must have been a Jewish Christian element in the audience in Paul's mind as he wrote. The best hypothesis for explaining this dismissal of the audience in the text seems to be the dominating power of the concept of Christianity. If Christianity is by definition a universal answer to a single universal predicament manifest in every individual, and the church constitutes all those who have been saved from this predicament, then the church must consist of all, both Jews and gentiles. Dogmatic rather than historical assumptions still dominate the reading of the letter.

One of my principles in reading the letter will be to take the explicit audience in the text literally unless strong reasons arise for subverting the encoded audience. Thus I will resist speculating about an empirical audience in Rome as a replacement for the reader in the text. I will also take seriously the progressive and initially linear nature of reading. Texts normally progress from a beginning to an ending. The reader's knowledge and understanding progress as the text provides information and allusions to cultural codes, other texts, and appeals to protocols of persuasion. Because Paul begins by explicitly describing his readers as gentiles, the interpreter can go step by step asking at what point the text introduces a new audience or subverts the explicit one. Even if I suspect that Paul "knew in his head" that Jews or Jewish believers would read the letter, I must still account for the audience in the text, asking why he would describe his readers as gentiles.

It was once fashionable for scholars to say that Romans was addressed to Jewish Christians, but owing to the objections raised by Johannes Munck and others this position is no longer plausible.[83] Nevertheless, almost all interpreters still insist on a Jewish Christian minority. W. G. Kümmel's *Introduction to the New Testament* can be taken as representative.[84] The obsession with finding Jewish Christians in the audience and the weakness of that position can best be illustrated by quoting Kümmel at some length:

> Rom manifests a double character: it is essentially a debate between the
> Pauline gospel and Judaism, so that the conclusion seems obvious that
> the readers were Jewish Christians. Yet the letter contains statements
> which indicate specifically that the community was gentile-Christian.
> The suppositions (a) that the Roman community was predominantly

Jewish-Christian, or (b) that Paul is trying to win over Jewish Christians to the gentile mission, or (c) that Paul is combating Jewish Christians who have returned to Rome in order to regain control there, can appeal only to Paul's lively controversy with Jewish arguments (cf. 2:17; 3:1; 4:1; 7:1, 4). But there is no text which depicts the Roman Christians as in the majority former Jews. Rather the letter characterizes its readers unambiguously as *gentile Christians*. In 1:5 Paul represents himself as the bearer of the apostolic office among all gentile nations, to which the Christians in Rome also belong. In 1:13 he expresses the wish to gain among the Romans "some fruit, just as [I have] among the other gentile people" and similarly in 15:15 ff.. In 11:13 he writes, "To you gentiles I say," and in so doing he addresses the readers as gentiles, as distinct from the unbelieving Jews. And in 9:3 ff; 10:1 f; 11:23, 28, 31, Paul speaks to non-Jews concerning his own people.

Any attempt to gain a picture of the readers of Rom must be made from this established point of view. Even 4:1 and 7:1 ff offer no hindrance to achieving that goal, since in 4:1 Paul presents himself in a debate with a Jewish opponent and identifies himself with him as a Jew. The supposed opponent is not to be sought among the readers of the letter any more than is the Jew addressed in a rhetorical aside in 2:17. In 7:1 he calls his readers "people who know the law." Since Paul undoubtedly means here the Law of Moses, he can simply presuppose this knowledge on the part of the gentile Christians. The OT was their Bible as well as that of the Jewish Christians, fully authoritative for them by reason of continual use in worship and instruction. Through death both gentile Christians and Jewish Christians (3:19 f; Gal 4:1 ff, 8 ff; 5:1, 13) are freed from the Law (7:4). The whole of pre-Christian humanity stands under the Law and through Christ is freed from it.

Even so the Roman community is *not purely gentile-Christian*. The story of the origin of the Christian community in Rome makes likely a Jewish-Christian strain in it, even though after the edict against the Jews under Claudius the Jewish-Christian minority would have been severely decimated. Nevertheless Jewish Christians could have returned after 54. Above all, there would be no point to the appeal for mutual acceptance, with its reference to the effect of the incarnation on Jews and gentiles (15:7 ff), if both groups were not represented in the church. Furthermore, the repeated reference to Jews and gentiles having the same responsibility before God (1:17; 2:9 ff, 25 ff; 3:29; 10:12) and the broad discussion of the ground for the unbelief of the majority of Israel, including the proclamation of God's ongoing redemptive goal for Israel

(9–11), would alike be incomprehensible if there were no Jewish Christians in the church at Rome.

Kümmel's first two sentences reflect the contradictions between traditional assumptions and the evidence of the letter itself. Because the tradition has been unable or unwilling to imagine gentile believers who had a fairly extensive knowledge of the law and for whom issues of the law and Israel's future would be relevant, it has seemed that Jews were the natural audience. Thus the letter has been construed as "a debate between the Pauline gospel and Judaism." Romans is Paul's argument against the Jewish understanding of salvation. All of this, however, flies in the face of the letter's description of its audience. Kümmel then reviews some of the overwhelming evidence for the gentile audience in the text and dismisses the most patently false arguments for Jewish readers.

In spite of having outlined the case for an exclusively gentile audience in the text, amazingly, Kümmel must assert the existence of a Jewish Christian minority, even stressing it with italics. At this point, Kümmel without notice shifts from his previous discussion of the encoded audience to the empirical audience in Rome. He appeals to "the story of the origin of the Christian community in Rome," a story he has already reviewed in a section entitled "The Beginnings of the Roman Community."[85] Here the key seems to be Acts read according to a later Christian ecclesiology. Kümmel takes the mention in Acts 28:15 of "brethren" from Rome meeting Paul as evidence that Christianity existed in Rome before Paul and the presence of a strong Jewish community probably through which "Christianity entered the capital" as evidence for a partially Jewish audience for Romans. Kümmel's case (and it is typical) contains two major logical problems. First, the presence of Jews or Jewish Christians in Rome does not allow one to conclude that Paul had them in his mind as an audience, much less to prove that the letter encodes them as readers. Second, the assumption of Christianity in Rome begs the most basic question. Precisely what we think we know but do not know is how the letter to the Romans construes the theological and institutional status of Jews and gentiles. It will not do to assume merely that some settlement of this issue after 70 C.E. is the case for Romans.

Kümmel marks what he takes as the most decisive argument for a mixed audience with "above all": It would make no sense for Paul to exhort his readers to accept one another and then appeal to Christ's self-giving (Kümmel's "incarnation"?) toward both Jews and gentiles if the readers were not also Jews and gentiles. Again logic fails. To use a contemporary analogy, the fact that in writing to the Israeli government the secretary general of the United Nations mentioned Arab states and used Albania as an example for some point would not require the conclusion that the letter was also addressed to Arabs and Albanians. Kümmel makes the same false assumption when he further argues that the several references to Jews and gentiles and also the discussion of Jews in 9–11 would "be incomprehensible if there were no Jewish Christians in the church at Rome." Again, a letter addressed to Israel, perhaps even in top secret, might repeatedly discuss the Arab states. The reader would know that the intended readers were Israeli officials because the explicit readers encoded in the letter would be Israeli officials. The authorial voice in Romans 9–11 speaks to gentiles about Jews.

Why does the traditional reading of Romans erase the gentile audience and replace it with "Christians, both Jews and gentiles?" The erasure is a hermeneutical move that facilitates reading the letter as canonical scripture of the orthodox catholic church. This move is analogous to the ancient church's theory that the letters of Paul, being a perfect seven in number, represent the whole church to which they are truly addressed and to the editions of Paul's letters that have removed references to particular churches and addressees.

Finally, I must stress that I do not need to throw out chapter 16 in order to maintain a gentile audience in the text. We know that Prisca and Aquila were Jews who believed in Christ and that at least three others mentioned in 16 were Jews. Ancient letters frequently send salutations to individuals who are not the encoded readers. But more important, I am not denying that either the encoded readers or any likely empirical readers associated with Jews and had Jewish followers of Christ among them. But knowing that certain gentiles associated with Jewish believers does not automatically reveal how Paul conceptualized relations between Jews and gentiles. Yet "Christians, both Jews and gentiles" is both anachronistic and inadequate to the letter's own language about Jews and gentiles. Even the language of 16 fits only with difficulty into the conception of the church implied by that expression. Not only Paul but "all the churches of the gentiles give thanks to Prisca and Aquila" (16:4). Furthermore, they have a church meeting in their house (16:5). Could Paul also speak of "churches of the Jews"? How would he conceive the relation between the churches of the Jews and the churches of the gentiles and the relation of both to Israel (the Jews) as a whole? Are Prisca and Aquila "just plain Christian" when working among gentile believers or are they Jews who serve as resident sojourners among their gentile comrades? We may be unable to answer such questions satisfactorily, but we will never even have a chance to answer unless we carefully study the letter's audience and the letter's own distinctions.

Defining Concepts: Law, Jew, Gentile

Study of Romans has led me to the conviction that the letter's major concepts have typically been given their meaning by being placed in the context of a larger Christian theological construct in which "law," "Jew" and "gentile" play roles different from anything possible for readers in Paul's time. In this Christian reading, the understanding that Jews and gentiles constitute "ethnic" categories recedes into the deep shadows of the background. Acknowledgment that gentile is the ethnic-religious other of Jews nearly drops out of the traditional reading. Just as the fundamental distinction for Greek identity is the division between Greeks and the barbarian peoples, so for Paul the fundamental distinction is between Jews and the gentile peoples. Interpreters, of course, are aware of these distinctions but the Christian categories allow them only the most minimal role in the letter. These categories, I will argue, are not mere vestigial hangovers from Paul's preconversion "Jewish nationalism." Neither are Jew and gentile "merely ethnic" categories. Rather, they constitute Paul's most central religious distinctions, although it is impossible to distinguish ethnic from religious in Paul's world.

The gentile is the ethnic-religious other of Jews just as the barbarian is the ethnic-religious other of Greeks.[86] Such constructions of the other say little about actual gentiles and barbarians but a great deal about the ideals of the groups that constructed them. Conceptions of the ethnic-religious other serve as aspects of the particular group's construction of the self. Greeks, for example, did not always have a concept of all other peoples definable over against Greekness. The concept of the barbarian arose only during and in response to the Persian wars and corresponds to a new Greek consciousness.[87] Similarly, a new conception of the Judean and the other peoples arose during the Maccabean period, setting the stage for the beginnings of Judaism. During the Persian wars, the non-Greek came to represent despotic tyranny over against the freedom-loving Greek. Barbarian religion, although a version of that practiced by the Greeks, tends to be cruel, inhumane, and bizarre. Above all, barbarian psychology and political order stand in contrast to the Greek ideal. Barbarians have poorly developed deliberative and rational faculties. They are controlled by passions and appetites. The strong passions of barbarians present dangers both to themselves and to Greeks: to barbarians they mean the need for tyrannical rule, to Greeks the threat of military and cultural aggression.

Jewish conceptions of the gentile exhibit many similarities with the Greek view of the barbarian but tend to focus upon idolatry as the cause of gentile psychology and social order. The correspondence between psychology and social order (what Greco-Roman thought knew as *politeia* or *politeuma*) is crucial for understanding not only Greek conceptions of the barbarian and Jewish conceptions of the gentile but also Paul's argument in Romans. The correlation of social-political-religious constitution and individual psychology seems to have been a constant throughout antiquity. Jewish, Greek, and Roman writers share the belief that the function of a good constitution, an effective code of law, is to control the passions and desires of the citizens. What moderns divorce as separate domains, political constitution and law, on the one hand, and individual psychology and ethics, on the other, closely interrelate in ancient thought. With the Western separation of church and state and the modern understanding of religion as a private, personal matter, it has been easy to think of the law in Paul's letters and more generally in ancient Judaism as being analogous to the Bible in modern Christianity. But Jews like Josephus and Philo viewed the law as the religious-social-political-legal constitution of the Jewish people, a basis both for the temple state in Judea and for the Jewish communities in the diaspora which also contained universally applicable teachings. I am convinced that Paul understood the law in the same general way. The apostle to the gentiles, of course, adds a much stronger prophetic dimension to his way of reading the scriptures, but he does not thereby throw out the basic understanding of the books of Moses as containing the constitution for the Jewish way of life. In chapter 2, I will show how Paul's discussions of gentiles and the law make sense in the context of certain Jewish and wider Greco-Roman understandings of law and moral psychology.

Josephus describes the Jewish law as the ideal constitution (*Ap.* 2.183–85). Other peoples ignore their laws, but "for us, on the other hand, the one wisdom and virtue consists in refraining absolutely from every action and thought that is contrary to the laws originally enacted. . . . Could there be a finer or more just polity than one which places God at the head of the universe, assigns the administration of its greatest affairs to the whole body of priests, and entrusts to the high-priest the leadership of the other priests?"

Jews were not alone in making claims for the superiority of their constitutions. Many other "barbarians" made similar claims. One example comes from Hecataeus of Abdera through Diodorus of Sicily. The Egyptian polity is superior because it best controls the passions of the rulers and the populace (1.71.3). Polybius writes that two things make a constitution worthy or unworthy of imitation and praise: "These are customs and laws. What is desirable in these makes the private lives of people pious and self-controlled and the common character of the city gentle and just. . . . So when we see that the laws and customs of a people are good, we also feel confident in declaring that the men also are good and the constitution good. . . . when people are covetous in their private lives and we see that their public acts are unjust, clearly we can say

that their laws, their peculiar customs and the whole constitution is bad"
(6.47.1–5).

I will argue that Paul, like other Jews, understood the law as the constitution for the Jewish way of life, including what we distinguish as religion, politics, custom, and morals. But he is also an ambivalent heir of a Jewish
tradition that presented the law as the ideal constitution from which gentile
peoples ought also to learn. Because this tradition focused upon what we call
religion and ethics, those areas most easily applicable to gentiles, and because
Paul writes to gentiles primarily about the limited gentile concerns with the
law, Paul has easily been understood to have a narrower Christian-like and
modern-like view of the law.

The Shape of the Reading

Because I must argue both against traditional readings and for my
own, both in detail and more broadly, I must struggle to keep the coherency of
the reading from getting lost in the detail. Therefore I will provide a sketch of
my reading at the beginning, emphasizing continuity of argument and stressing the most distinctive aspects of my interpretation.

Romans tries to clarify for gentile followers of Christ their relation to the
law, Jews, and Judaism and the current place of both Jews and gentiles in God's
plan through Jesus Christ. The readers manifest in the letter consist of gentiles
who have a great concern for moral self-mastery and acceptance by the one
God and believe (or might be tempted to believe) that they have found the
way to that goal through observing certain teachings from the Jewish law.
These readers also might be tempted to consider themselves (or perhaps themselves and fellow Jewish followers of Christ) God's only true people, the main-
stream of the Jewish people having rejected Jesus Christ and having been
rejected by God. Against these assumptions of the readers encoded in the letter, Paul develops a rhetorical strategy to persuade them that the acceptance
and self-mastery they seek is to be found not in following Jewish teachers who
advocate works from the law but in what God has done and is even now doing
through Jesus Christ.

Two instances of speech-in-character dominate the first part of the letter
(2:1–16 and 2:17–4:22) prefaced by an epistolary address to gentile believers
in Rome (1:1–17) and a description of gentile evil (1:18–32). Paul immediately announces (1:16–17) his confidence that the news about Christ and his
faithfulness provides the key to understanding God's plan for dealing justly
and successfully with both the Jews and Greeks. The apostle to the gentiles
then presents an account (1:18–32) of the sinful degradation into which the

non-Jewish peoples have declined owing to their worship of many gods and idols, alluding to the typical Jewish way of reading Genesis 4–11. Since they have refused to acknowledge him, the true God has punished these idol worshipers by allowing their enslavement to the passions (*pathē*) and desires (*epithumiai*) of their bodies. Thus they live in societies characterized by evil and vice.

Paul then speaks to an imaginary gentile (2:1–16), warning him of his precarious situation in the present historical moment (2:1–5) and promising him that God will judge both Jews and Greeks as an impartial judge by the standards of the law and Paul's gospel (2:6–16). God has mercifully delayed punishing the gentiles in order to provide time for repentance (2:4–5). Chapters 9–11 will explain how God has brought about this delay as an opportunity for the gentile mission. In 2:17, Paul turns to begin a long discussion (2:17–4:22) with a Jew who has taken upon himself the task of teaching gentiles (2:19–20, 24) to perform certain works from the law (2:20–23). The readers thus overhear a debate between Paul and his Jewish competitors for gentile hearts and minds. The audience learns that God's way of putting gentiles into a right relation through Christ's faithfulness is to be sharply distinguished from the message of Jews who advocate works of the law. The Jewish teacher does not understand God's just impartiality (2:25–29): gentiles ought to have the same opportunity as Jews to be right before God. Given the teacher's own difficulty in keeping the law, how dare he presume to improve gentiles? Moral betterment is not the answer.

In the ensuing dialogue (3:1–9), Paul assures the teacher that God will be faithful to the Jews even though some (like the teacher, cf. 2:24) have failed in heeding and proclaiming the promises of God (3:1–4). Through a series of questions anticipating chapters 9–11, Paul gets the teacher to affirm that it is not unfair that this unfaithfulness on the part of Jews and God's resulting anger actually play a part in God's plan for a just treatment of Jews and gentiles (3:5–9). In fact, this current unfaithfulness of Jews in the face of the promises and the state of the gentile peoples has produced an apocalyptic (3:10–18) sinfulness among all nations. This situation has been brought about by God himself (11:32, cf. 3:19–20) so that he can judge all peoples with parity and have mercy equally upon all (3:9, 19–20, 22–23; 11:30–32).

The teacher needs to understand that in the present moment God is effecting his just solution not through the Jewish law (3:19–21) but in the gentile mission based on Christ's faithfulness (3:22–26). [Subtext: Jesus showed his faith-faithfulness-trust-obedience toward God and his mission as messiah by allowing himself to be killed instead of bringing about Israel's final restoration, the last judgment, and the age to come. This he did out of love for the lost, including the gentile peoples. God accepted his action as a trusting and faithful enactment of his mission. He thus vindicated Jesus through the resurrection, postponing the great judgment and allowing time for a mission to the gentiles and the repentance of all Israel before Christ returns to complete his messianic mandate.] God's acceptance of Jesus' faithfulness was a great act of grace and forgiveness (3:24–25) enacting his justice toward the gentiles whose sins had been stored up for a terrible judgment because (unlike the Jews) they had no covenant or atonement (2:5; 3:25–26). Thus through Jesus' faithfulness, God has shown himself to be just by providing a way for the gentiles to be made righteous (3:25–26).

In an ensuing dialogue, Paul tells the teacher that no basis any longer exists for his condescending pride in teaching gentiles to observe works of the law (3:27, cf. 2:17–20, 23). If God really is the impartial God of all and not just of the Jews, he will use the heroic faithfulness of chosen individuals to bring about good for gentiles just as he did for Jews (3:28–30 with chapter 4 in view). Basing gentile justification on this faithfulness rather than on the moral betterment of individual gentiles through works of the law actually upholds the centrality of the law and is supported by the law (3:31, 4:1–25). God did not accept and forgive Abraham because he first fulfilled a list of works from the law but because Abraham faithfully committed himself to God and to his promise (4:1–8). God's acceptance of Abraham occurred while he was still a gentile (4:9–12). Owing to his faithfulness, God gave him the sign of circumcision, blessing his descendants, the Jews, with a covenant of grace (4:11–12). Likewise the promise that Abraham would be the father of many peoples (gentiles) and that his seed would inherit the world was based on his faithfulness, not on his keeping the law (4:13–15). God has based his relations with Jews and gentiles on Abraham's and Jesus' faithfulness rather than on human ability to keep the law so that it would be guaranteed to all as an irrevocable promise from God himself (4:16–17). Through the promise to Abraham now being fulfilled in Christ, all peoples share a kinship with Abraham as ancestor (4:11–17, 18–20).

The Jewish teacher fades away toward the end of chapter 4 as Paul for the first time since his opening address begins speaking directly to his epistolary audience. He assures these gentiles of their salvation from God's anger because Christ adapted himself to their need, dying for them when they were ungodly (5:1–11). The apostle then tries to further assure his readers by explaining how the actions of one person can dramatically affect many (or all) people and in this way how Adam and Christ are analogous (5:12–20). Through Adam the habit of sinning and its punishment by mortality entered the world and affected all (5:12). Paul emphasizes that the one/all analogy works but works only for the period between Adam and the giving of the law (5:13–14). All those between Adam and Moses inherited the penalty even though they, unlike Adam, did not disobey God's commandments. After the law, people became individually accountable for good and evil because it was now obedience or disobedience to God, and death was not simply inherited from the one person's actions but was a matter ultimately held open until the final judgment. God's mercy through Christ far exceeds the punishment due to Adam, even though the law increased the liability.

Chapter 6 explains how this freedom from the tyranny of sin works for the gentile readers. They have reenacted Christ's death and resurrection in the ritual of baptism (6:2 ff.). As Jesus allowed himself to die rather than follow the traditional messianic path and God made him pioneer of the new life, so the readers should have imagined themselves as submitting to death and rising anew with Christ. The result will be the resurrection life pioneered by Christ (6:5, 22). Paul describes the readers' past lives (6:17–22; 7:5) in the same terms he used in 1:24–28 to portray the bondage into which God delivered the gentiles and exhorts them to resist their passions (6:12–14). Again in an echo of chapter 1, the readers' passions and desires, through God's decree promulgated in the law, bound them to sin and condemnation (7:5–6). But in reenacting Christ's death and resurrection they are freed from the old conditions encoded in the law for the rebellious gentile peoples (7:1–6, cf. 1:24–32; 3:20; 4:15).

In 7:7f., we again meet an individual painted through speech-in-character. Given the representation of the gentiles in chapter 1, the descriptions of the audience's past lives, and several comments about their dilemma under the law, the imaginary speaker can only be a gentile describing his struggle to live by works from the law. The section constitutes Paul's most daring attack on the belief that gentiles can gain self-mastery and divine approval through works of the law. This person learned from the law both that God enacted the commandment against desire (*epithumia*) and that he was bound to desire through enslavement to sin (7:7–12). Gentiles who try to morally better themselves by the law learn that they are sinners condemned by God but cannot master their passions and desires (7:14–23). Paul quotes the proverbial Medean saying about weakness of the will (*akrasia*): The speaker wants to do good but actually does what he does not want to do because his body is mastered by passion and desire. In chapter 8, Paul tells this gentile the good news that Christ and the Spirit have allowed his release from enslavement to sin and the condemnation of the law (8:1–8) so that he can actually do what the law requires of him (8:4, 7). Thus Paul finally shows how God has brought gentiles the equality of opportunity for righteousness that he argued for to the Jewish teacher in 2:25–29; 3:28–30, and to the presumptuous gentile in 2:6–16. Through Christ, gentiles now have sonship (8:15–23, 29), as Israel has always had (9:4). The readers gain a kinship with God that is modeled after Christ's sonship (8:29) and that includes empowerment by the Spirit now (8:4–8, 12–17, 26–27) and a perfected body in the future (8:9–11, 23).

Chapters 9–11 are a tour de force. Here Paul reveals how God has dealt and will deal with Israel and the gentile peoples so as to justly save both. The section also constitutes a warning against gentile presumption in light of the current Jewish unbelief (esp. 11:13–25). Paul for the first time in the letter since the epistolary opening presents a full authorial persona that reveals his strongly Jewish identity. He would willingly give up his life in Christ for the sake of his own people (9:3). The basic pattern of argument in the three chapters is this: In God's way of shaping the larger course of history, he chooses some and rejects others not because of the works of the chosen or the rejected but for the sake of his larger purposes; God sometimes allows (or causes) individuals or groups to rebel against him in order to bring about the greatest good for all; the Jews have in large part been unfaithful toward God's plans through Christ, while the gentiles have shown enthusiastic belief. But gentiles must not make the mistake of thinking that God has forgotten his commitment to Israel as a whole. In fact, God himself is the one who has temporarily hardened these Jews so that he can show mercy to the gentiles. God's stalling of Israel's restoration and the judgment of the nations has permitted a time for the successful mission to gentiles, even though only a small remnant of Jews have carried the gospel to them. When the "full number of gentiles come in" (11:25), then Christ will return to Zion and restore a repentant Israel (11:26–27). The letter's gentile readers must understand this mystery lest they fall into an evil and damning arrogance (11:25, 17–24).

The first eleven chapters do not offer much specific moral and social content about the renewal of the gentiles. Rom 12:1–15:14 provides an exhortation to the practices of gentile renewal. The first three verses (12:1–3) tie the exhortations to Paul's earlier discussion. Instead of pursuing their former idolatrous ways, the readers are to worship God rationally and to renew minds corrupted by rejection of the true God (1:21, 28) so as to live rightly (12:1–2). This renewal includes a realistic self-conception (rather than arrogance toward Jews and others, cf. 1:30; 2:1–5; 11:17–25) based upon a "measure of [Christ's] faithfulness." Paul understands Christ's faithfulness as his adaptability to the needs of Jews and gentiles and makes it a principle of community for gentiles (12:3; 15:1–9). God entrusts each member of the new social body with differing virtues defined as abilities to adapt to the needs of others (12:3–21). This includes adapting positively to outsiders (12:17–13:7). The virtue of love epitomizes the whole ethic: When the readers exercise the virtue of love, they will actually be doing what the law requires of gentiles (13:8–10).

Chapters 14–15 assume a certain set of psychagogic practices among the readers and in the community that Paul envisages. Here also Paul represents the readers as having a concern for self-mastery and Greco-Roman practices of mutual correction and character building. Paul exhorts the readers to modify their practices while keeping the model of Christ's adaptability to the needs of others in view. The community will consist of members who are more and less rational in their dispositions and ways of life. Those whose beliefs are not so well grounded should resist condemning those who are less constrained by fears and restrictions (14:1–4, 10–12). Paul places the greatest burden on the strong, who should understand the weak, be sensitive to their false but strongly held beliefs, and adapt their behavior to meet the needs of the weak (14:13–15:2). Christ did not merely please himself by exercising his awesome messianic prerogatives but adapted himself to the varied needs of others, becoming a servant to the Jews in order to fulfill God's promises to Israel and to the gentiles (15:1–12).

I want to show how Paul was fully implicated in the values and discourse of his society, time, and social group and yet how he distanced himself from some interpretations of those values and some uses of that discourse. Furthermore I must illustrate the concrete and existentially palpable significance of this ethic of self-mastery for people in Paul's milieu and situate Jewish moralizing directed toward non-Jews within this context. A nuanced thick description serves as an antidote to the constructing of a pristine Christianity that dropped out of heaven or out of the Old Testament; cells of humans speaking a unique idiom that removed them from the politics, values, and shared humanity of the Roman world.

The theme of self-mastery would have loomed very large for ancient readers of Romans but is scarcely noticed by modern readers. It has receded deeply into the background for contemporaries because the concept of self-mastery has none of the powerfully loaded social and cultural meaning for us that it did for people in Paul's day. Even apparent similarities between self-mastery and the modern concept of self-discipline mislead because the ancient and modern conceptions of the person and society differ so greatly. The rhetoric of Romans pushes the theme of self-mastery, or the lack of it, into the foreground in three ways. First, Romans tells the story of sin and salvation, problem and solution, punishment and reward at its most basic level as a story of the loss and recovery of self-control. Second, the letter represents the readers as characters in this basic story that concerns self-mastery. Third, Romans relates this story of loss to the story of God's righteous action through Jesus Christ so that Christ becomes an enabler of the restored and disciplined self.

Paul annunciates the problem in 1:18–32: Those peoples who refuse to honor God and instead worship idols have lost the capacity for self-mastery. Later, in 7:7–25, Paul refigures his depiction of the problem in psychological terms. Other parts of the letter employ the general category of sin in order to discuss God's righteousness and impartiality toward Jews and gentiles, why the law is an inadequate solution, and how Christ's faithfulness is the solution; but no texts except 1:18–32 and 7:1–25 treat the basic problem in its social and psychological particularity. God's anger has been justly expressed toward all humans who have refused to worship the one God above all created things and who have instead set up idols in the form of animals and humans (1:18–23). God has punished these people who have glorified and honored statues rather than him by allowing them to become enslaved to their passions and desires (1:24, 26, 29). Only the Spirit of Christ, not the law, can liberate those enslaved to these passions and desires (7:1–8:8).

Self-mastery as a personal, social, and theological problem is the most palpable issue of chapters 1–8, a point not lost on the ancient interpreters of Romans.[1] The concreteness of this issue comes about above all because Romans explicitly identifies lack of self-control as the audience's problem. This failure has characterized their moral past and threatens their moral and religious futures if they seek righteousness through works of the law. Let me illustrate what I mean by the immediacy of this topic. The same passage in chapter 1 that purports to describe the readers' past enslavement to passions and desires also condemns their yet more basic error of idol worship. But the rest of the letter remains silent about their idolatry. In contrast to his treatment of the issue of self-mastery, Paul makes no attempt to warn them of the temptations to idol worship. Surely some of these former pagans suffered from such temptations. Yet Paul did not choose to write about this or other practical issues in Romans. Instead, self-mastery stands out as the issue that bears practical consequences and ties together what later interpreters have called ethics and theology.

The importance of self-mastery becomes clear when one precisely observes the construction of the encoded readers and the relation that the text establishes between them and Paul. Only in Romans does Paul employ the epistolary opening to describe his apostleship as a ministry to the gentile peoples. He is the apostle whose task it is to bring about the "obedience to faithfulness on behalf of his name among all the gentiles, among whom also you are" (1:5). The majority of commentators recognize that the last clause describes the readers as gentiles.[2] A few have suggested that the words serve only to place the audience geographically among the gentiles.[3] But this last suggestion makes little sense. Paul describes himself not as the apostle who works geographically among the gentiles but in no uncertain terms as the apostle responsible for the gentiles (for example, 11:13; 15:14–29; Gal 1:15–16; 2:7–9). He twice reminds his readers of this commission in the opening verses (1:5, 13–14) and then amplifies this self-description in two later key texts (11:11–14; 15:14–33). Moreover, 1:13–14 cannot be read in the geographical sense: Paul desires to be in Rome in order to strengthen his readers so as to "harvest some fruit among you as also among the rest of the gentiles." Because he has an obligation to Greeks and barbarians, to the wise and the foolish, he also wants to preach the gospel to his readers in Rome (1:14). "Greeks and barbarians, wise and foolish" is another way of saying gentiles. For Paul these categories encompass all of the non-Jewish peoples.

Rhetorically the letter's opening is most crucial for encoding a relation and attitude between author and reader. The author in chapter 1 manifests an attitude of confidence, authority, and benevolence toward his readers precisely as the apostle to the gentiles. He implies a knowledge of their needs (1:11–12, 15), and he directs attention to the relevance for them of his interpretive powers concerning the gospel (1:15–18ff.). After the opening, Paul launches into an account of gentile morals and religion (1:18–32) that later passages in the letter identify as having once also been characteristic of the letter's audience (6:17–22; 7:4–6; 8:1–17). The initial connection between the readers described as gentiles in 1:1–17 and the people depicted in 1:18–32 requires only the assumption that gentiles are characteristically idolators, an assumption that other texts from Paul's letters show was obvious to him. Thus, the letter makes the paradigmatic story, telling how gentiles lost their self-mastery and became enslaved to their passions and desires, also the audience's story.

Attempts to insert a Jewish audience into the text must first overlook the explicit representation of the readers established in chapter 1 and then appeal to Paul's address to an imaginary Jew in 2:17–29. Here interpreters have thought that Paul must be addressing Jewish readers. But as I will show, this Jew ought to be understood as a teacher of the law to gentiles. One should not confuse depicting a Jew with encoding a Jewish audience. Finally, the text may also be relevant to the topic of gentile self-mastery. This Jew confidently teaches ethical precepts from the Decalogue to gentiles. If some Jews advocated the Decalogue to gentiles as a means of acquiring self-mastery, then 2:17–29 may indeed prove relevant to the issue of the gentile audience's self-mastery.

The letter establishes the audience's relation to the theme of self-mastery also by making Christ an enabler of the mastery over self that the readers are already depicted as having by virtue of their new lives. The arguments in chapters 5–8 aim to change the readers' understanding of how they have attained mastery over their passions and desires: not through the law but through their identification with Jesus Christ. According to 6:1–7:6, Jesus' death is somehow a cause of the encoded readers' "death to sin," which means that the readers can now be free from enslavement to their passions and desires. Chapter 8 combines this motif of liberation from passions through the Spirit with the themes of freedom from condemnation and a filial relationship with God leading to future reward.

Until recently, New Testament scholars have not noticed that the concept of weakness so prominent in Paul's letters had its cultural home at the very heart of Greco-Roman discourse about the passions and self-mastery.[4] In this light, 14:1–15:13 appears neither as incidental ethical exhortations appended to Paul's theological reflections nor as an allusive set of suggestions for improving relations between Jewish and gentile Christians in the church at Rome. Rather, the chapters read as a hortatory distillation of Paul's advice to gentile converts who sought to learn mastery of their passions and desires through psychagogic practices within the community of Christ.[5] The obscure and puzzling lines of these chapters spring to life when one recognizes them to be packed with the vocabulary and concepts of Greco-Roman psychagogic literature. This literature contains illuminating discussions of the problems of the weak and of the attitudes that stronger comrades ought to have toward them.

A passage in Aristotle's *Nicomachean Ethics* (7,1150b) discusses *enkrateia*, a form of the same word Paul uses for self-mastery in 1 Cor 9:25. In that context Paul describes his practice of adapting himself to the needs of the weak (9:22). He thereby provides a model for how the supposedly wise Corinthians ought to adapt themselves to the condition of the weak (chapter 8). Aristotle shows how important currents in the culture related weakness to the passions and self-mastery. He first compares self-mastery to endurance (*karteria*) and discusses their opposites, lack of self-control (*akrasia*; cf. 1 Cor 7:5; Rom 5:3–4) and softness (*malakia*; cf. 1 Cor 6:9), respectively.[6] Enkrateia is more noble than endurance because endurance means only successful resistance to passions whereas enkrateia involves their mastery. Then Aristotle notes that softness and lack of mastery are sometimes innate, as, for example, in the royal house of Scythia or in the female sex. In Greek constructions of the ethnic other, as in Jewish constructions of the gentile, barbarians often lack self-control because of either innate weaknesses or inferior laws and constitutions.[7] Gender hierarchy lies close to the heart of the discourse of self-mastery. Life is war, and masculinity has to be achieved and constantly fought for. Men are always in danger of succumbing to softness, described as forms of femaleness or servility. In the ancient Mediterranean construction of gender, the sexes are "poles on a continuum which can be traversed."[8] To achieve self-mastery means to win the war; to let the passions and desires go unsubdued means defeat, a destruction of hard-won manliness. The centrality of this gender defeat explains why leaving assigned gender roles for same sex love serves as the illustration in 1:26–27 of the extent to which gentiles have succumbed to passions and desires.

Aristotle says there are two forms of unrestraint (*akrasia*), recklessness and weakness. Weakness (*astheneia*), the same terminology used by Paul, is worse than recklessness. "The weak deliberate, but then fail to keep their resolution because of their passions" (1150b 20). The weak here are like the weak in 1 Cor 8, who know that only one God exists and that idols have no reality (1–6) but succumb to the feelings and beliefs of their pagan past when faced with idol worship.[9] Ancient sources often describe the weak as having what we moderns might describe as superstitions or irrational scruples. Cicero defines weakness as "an unwholesome aversion and loathing for certain things" and adds that "the product of aversion moreover is defined as an intense belief, persistent and deeply rooted, which regards a thing that need not be shunned as though it ought to be shunned" (Tusc. 4.23, 26). For concrete examples, writers include fear or hatred of certain foods, wine, strangers, and women.[10] In Rom 14, the weak shun meat and wine and judge certain days to be more auspicious than others. Paul speaks to the gentile readers encoded there as if they were deeply concerned about these issues of self-mastery.

The importance of self-mastery is apparent: Paul ties this topic most intimately to his literary construction of the audience. He also labors to emphasize that his readers are gentiles and that he writes to them as the apostle to the gentiles. As modern readers trying to be aware of how we read ancient texts, we must ask why the theme of gentile self-mastery has been so little emphasized in modern interpretation and what significance it might have had for ancient readers.

The Significance of Self-Mastery in Greco-Roman Culture

Generations of classicists, preachers, and biblical scholars have labored intensively to make ancient literature relevant by stressing the similarities between ancient and modern society. This interpreting of the ancient in terms of the modern has in no area been stronger than in regard to ethics and morality. But we will not understand the importance of self-mastery in Romans unless we recognize how ancient morality and society differed from our own. The modern attitude toward desire is, "You have the right and the potential to aspire to anything you want as long as you do not directly harm someone else; your legitimate wants and the means to achieve them are virtually unlimited." We live in a capitalistic consumer world in which a constant bombardment of advertisements stimulates our desires and communicates the idea that our desires are good. From this vantage point, one has difficulty understanding ancient Mediterranean attitudes. The dominant view in Greco-Roman culture held that desires in themselves were not bad but dangerous, powerful, and prone to act independently of rational control. The ancient attitude said, "Desire no more than the limited goods appropriate to your station in life."

These differing attitudes toward desire correspond to different social and cultural organizations and to differing perceptions of the world's resources. Individuals in our society act as if the world's goods were infinite. Most people today know that the earth's supply of oil is limited and nonrenewable and that at the current rate of use will be exhausted in a few decades. In spite of this knowledge about oil and many other resources, few worry about the problem. People believe that by the time oil is exhausted, science will have discovered some other energy source. Part of our most basic mentality involves assuming that there will always be enough to go around. This attitude precludes worry about waste, overconsumption, future generations, and people who do not participate in the current affluence of Western industrial cultures. In stark contrast, the person of the ancient Mediterranean assumed that all goods were by nature finite and always in limited supply.[11] Some people might have more goods than others, but virtually all goods were available and distributed. To take more than the share of goods allotted to you by birth was to take something from someone else. If a person or family improved their lot, people assumed that it was at someone else's expense and represented a threat to the community as a whole.

Thus values revolved around an ethic of moderation and restraint. The goods might be land, children (labor and heirs), social standing (honor), food, or sexual rights but the ethic was the same as that recommended by the most ubiquitous ancient precepts: In nothing too much, Do not overreach, You shall not covet, Know the limits. Behind such prescriptions stood a social life characterized by steeply hierarchical social stratification and intense competition for goods. All gain, as noted, was perceived to be at the direct expense of someone else. Such zero-sum competition applied even to honor. As an anonymous sophist says, "People do not find it pleasant to give honor to someone else, for they suppose that they themselves are being deprived of something."[12] At the beginning of the Laws, Plato says that peace is a fiction; all states are perpetually at war with one another by nature. He goes on to say that this "life as warfare" applies equally to village against village, male against male, and self against self (625E–626E). The last, self against self, was a common way of speaking about the self throughout antiquity and refers to the struggle of reason to master the passions.

In the century after Paul, Galen, in a way that had been typical for centuries, stresses that self-discipline itself ought to be a competitive enterprise. In disciplining oneself with regard to food, drink, and sex, "We should not compare ourselves to the undisciplined; it is not enough to surpass them in self-control and moderation; rather we should first of all strive competitively to outdo people committed to the same moderation—for such competition is an excellent thing—and next we should strive to surpass ourselves."[13] Galen is writing for an upper-class audience for whom such competition in virtue was of special importance. With the major exception of the early Stoics, writers from the Greco-Roman world did not believe that one could eliminate these unruly appetites and passions that were the source of immoral behavior. Rather, one had to subdue them, as a ruler would subjugate a rebellious province or a master a belligerent slave. Michel Foucault writes,

> Ethical conduct in matters of pleasure was contingent on a battle for power. This perception of the hēdonai [pleasures] and *epithumiai* [desires] as a formidable enemy force, and the correlative constitution of oneself as a vigilant adversary who confronts them, struggles against them, and tries to subdue them, is revealed in a whole series of expressions traditionally employed to characterize moderation and immoderation: setting oneself against the pleasures and desires, not giving in to them, resisting their assaults, or on the contrary, letting oneself be overcome by them or being defeated by them, being armed or equipped against them.[14]

Paul can use this discourse of struggle against the passions in the most typical way. Perhaps the prime example is 1 Cor 9:24–27: "Do you not know that all those in a race compete but only one receives the prize? So run that you might win! Everyone who is an athlete exercises self-control [*enkrateuetai*] in all things. They do it to win a perishable wreath, but we for one imperishable. So then I pummel my body and subject it to slavery, lest after preaching to others I myself not meet the test."

Here the preaching of the gospel has something to do with self-control. Only the explicitly communal goals of Paul's exhortation distinguish this text from the typical Greco-Roman uses of such discourse. Indeed, Paul's language illustrates a vital point about the Greco-Roman discourse of self-mastery: Psychology mirrors the organization of society. Just as intense competition characterizes social life, so a violent competition within characterizes those who aspire to moral excellence and self-mastery. Just as a hierarchy that put everyone in the empire except the emperor under the rule of someone and made a small part of the population masters of others, so the soul was to be master of the body and reason over the passions. The Pauline discourse also mirrors society by using the imagery of strenuous and even violent athletic competition to describe the struggle with the body and by speaking of that struggle as a process of enslavement.

If one can believe the impressive amount of Greco-Roman literature in one way or another concerned with mastery of the body and passions, many ancients must have experienced the basic dynamics of their society as inward psychological realities. Perhaps psychology is a reflection of social structure in all societies. At any rate, there is reason to believe that this competition and hierarchy within was more meaningful for some people in Greco-Roman society than for others. Crucial questions in this society are Who controls whom? and Who are my friends and who my enemies? The psychology of reason ruling the lesser self could work as a principle of social hierarchy because some classes of people were deemed to have more capacity for reason and more ability to rule themselves than others. Indeed, slaves, women, and barbarians were generally thought unable to properly control themselves and thus needed someone with more reason to govern them. Classical Greece, at least as far as the extant written literature shows, first strongly articulated the principle that to rule others, one had to master oneself. In the *Alcibiades,* for instance, Socrates shows an ambitious young man that he cannot successfully enter political life until he has first learned to master his passions and desires. Both Greek and Roman values derive from societies that had been centered on military elites. The gymnasium continued to train boys in physical prowess, competitiveness, hardness, and insensitivity to pain and emotions long after the Greek cities lost military power. Maleness was defined by the values of men at war and seen as the opposite of the female nature. Xenophon articulates what would become a ubiquitous theme: If you want a general who will save the city or a guardian for your children or a manager for your farm, you will want someone who is "stronger than his belly," having subdued his appetite for wine, sexual pleasure, and sleep (*Mem.* 1.5.1–6). Clearly people with any ambition in life got the message that they had to acquire mastery of their passions and desires in order to achieve their social aspirations. Since the vast majority of slaves and women were denied such aspirations and thought to exemplify weakness, to fail in this inner contest was to act slavishly or womanishly with regard to passions and desires.

In Greek thought, the stomach represents the bestial, wild, needy, and passionately desiring part of the human. The idea also appears in early Christian and Jewish writers, as when Paul accuses competing teachers of serving (Rom 16:18) and worshiping (Phil 3:19) their bellies or Titus 1:12 quotes Epimenides' epithet about Cretans: "They are always liars, wild animals, lazy stomachs." Such discourse about the stomach enshrined and naturalized ideas about social order, gender, ethnicity, and the human place in the cosmos. When Greeks ate meat, that is, when they sacrificed, they ritually communicated such thought.[15] In Hesiod's foundation myth of sacrifice, Prometheus in connection with humans tries to trick Zeus at the first sacrifice by hiding the edible meat inside the disgusting stomach and offering Zeus the bones disguised in a covering of fat. But all-knowing Zeus has the last laugh because humans have thereby accepted a position between the animals and the gods in which they must continually fill their stomachs with the lifeless flesh of animals in order to live while the gods, in an act befitting their immortal and needless state, receive the smoke of the undecaying bones. The stomach represents the human loss of and distance from the incorruptible divine life. Furthermore, Zeus punishes men by sending "the beautiful evil," woman (*Theogony* 585). According to Hesiod, woman is like an insatiable stomach who leads to man's death.[16] If one does not marry, one can escape the miseries caused by the drain that woman's insatiable appetite for food and sex brings to men, but in that case the man will have no son to inherit his goods. No wonder that Greco-Roman writers constantly link the appetite for food and sex with the weakening of men. One of the *Golden Verses* (9–10) exhorts, "Master first of all the stomach, and sleep, luxury and anger." Hierocles' commentary on the verses explains: "The stomach, when it is too full, provokes a surplus of sleep and these two excesses together . . . incite one beyond measure to the pleasures of Aphrodite."[17] The connection between the stomach and sexual desire made it possible for some Jews to hold forth their food laws as a comprehensive means to the goal of self-mastery.

Another concept that helps us understand the values associated with self-mastery is luxury. The word *truphē* means softness, delicacy, daintiness, and luxury but also conceit and insolence.[18] Luxury and conceit may seem to be unconnected in our thought, but in the discourse of the ancient Mediterranean, to enjoy more goods and especially to exhibit more goods than normally expected of someone of your place in society was considered an act of violent pride (*hybris*), an act of overreaching (*pleonexia*). In connection with gender, *truphē* had a different meaning. Men, as it were, carried about the latent "disease of femaleness." *Luxury* was a code word for a whole range of such qualities as softness, weakness, being subject to emotion, uncontrollable desire, and lack of toughness and discipline that were supposedly characteristic of women. If a man went too far in relaxing his toughness through pleasure or ease, then through weakened resistance the feminine disease would run rampant, destroying both soul and body.

Modern writers have usually described Philo's polemics against same sex love as Jewish, failing to see that they embody principles utterly characteristic of ancient moralists who articulated the values of the ruling elites. Ethnic minorities throughout the Mediterranean world adopted this discourse from their overlords, first the Greeks, then the thoroughly Hellenized Romans, in order to describe their own ethnic dentity and to define otherness. The otherness within, of women, thus provided a scale for describing others, for example, non-Greeks, non-Romans, non-Jews, non-Syrians, and provided elites within these groups a language through which they could claim a place among the ruling classes of the empire. Philo's discourse is hardly unique, although his advocacy of the death penalty would have seemed bizarre to most. He writes, "[Such love] robs men of manliness, the virtue most valuable for life both in peace and war, produces the disease of femaleness in their souls and turns into a hybrid of man and woman those who should be disciplined in all the practices that lead to prowess and valour" (*Vit. Cont.*).

Philo goes on to say that such love damages bodies, souls, and property. Desire (*epithumia*) causes their bodies to waste away (61). Because such activity does not produce children, "the best kind of men become scarce" and whole cities become desolate (62). Similarly, those who mate with barren women are enemies of nature and of God. Sex with a wife who cannot have children is like copulating with a goat or a pig (*Spec. Leg.* 34–36). On the subjects of pederasty and childless women Philo reflects the Roman imperial politics of procreation.

Scholars who touch on these subjects have not usually made clear exactly what Philo objects to in male same sex love.[19] Like all of the ancient witnesses, Philo assumes that there is always a passive and an active partner.[20] Sexual mutuality and equality are inconceivable, and humiliating violence toward the passive partner is natural. Natural sex is by definition the penetration of a socially subordinate person by a socially superior person. According to Philo, the passive partner in male same sex love should be killed, not even allowed to live for an hour (*Spec. Leg.* 3. 37–38), because he has allowed himself to lose his manliness and to suffer the "disease of femaleness." The active partner should be killed, first of all, because instead of training his partner in strength and robustness he encourages softness and unmanliness (*Spec. Leg.* 3. 39) and, second, because the activity does not produce children. Women are the natural passive partners. Such passivity and subordination are natural for them but an abomination for men, who were made to rule their inferiors. Natural sexual activity must signify man's domination of woman and produce legitimate heirs for the man's power and property.

Finally, Philo's typical ruling-class strictures about sex fit the broader values of the ruling elites. When we see evidence from antiquity about such matters that reflects not elites self-consciously exercising power as moralists but unguarded common attitudes, the views prove quite different.[21] Philo held the unbiblical idea that pederasty was the sin of Sodom. He says that the cause of the Sodomites' sin was the lavishness of their land and quotes Menander, "The greatest source of evils among humans is goods in excess" (*Abr.* 134).[22] The land produced abundantly, and the Sodomites ate their fill of the finest foods. This stimulated their desire, causing unnatural sexual activity leading to the female disease of softness. If God had not annihilated the city and if Greeks and barbarians had learned of these practices from the Sodomites, city after city would have become deserted (*Abr.* 136). Elsewhere Philo attributes the prevalance of same sex male love in his day to the influence of non-Jewish religious practices (*Spec. Leg.* 40–41; cf. Rom 1). The Jewish, early Christian, and broader Greco-Roman focus on sexual behavior reflects not so much what we moderns like to think of as private and personal ethics as the social and cultural domination of male ruling elites and ethnic politics in the new order of post-Augustan Rome.

Rome and the Moral Politics of the Augustan Revolution

Self-mastery also appears prominently from an early time in Roman texts. Plautus, for example, wrote a play concerning self-mastery, and since 186 B.C.E. a statue of the austere Cato the elder with an inscription celebrating his self-control had stood prominently in Rome (Plut. *Cat* 19.3). But in the early empire, Paul's era, the connection between self-mastery and ambition seems to have reached its apex. Although written about the Antonine age, the following words of Peter Brown apply equally well to the first century of Roman rule : "If the life of the cities was to continue, the discipline and the solidarity of the local elites and their ability to control their own dependents had to be mobilized with greater self-consciousness than ever before. A sense of public discipline had to reach deeper into the private lives of the notables as a price for maintaining the status quo of an imperial order."[23]

The ruling elites would have to show that they exercised firm control over themselves, their families, and their dependents if Rome was to successfully rule the world. Local aristocracies and the ruling elites of ethnic minorities all over the empire vied to demonstrate to Rome their fitness to rule.

One simply cannot understand the moral world of Paul's era and the adaptation of Jews to that world without a grasp of the changes wrought by Octavian, later also called Augustus. These changes began with the propaganda campaign that preceded Antony's defeat at Actium. A passage from Plutarch (*Ant.* 60) nicely summarizes Octavian's interpretation of Actium: "When Caesar had prepared sufficiently, a declaration of war was voted against Cleopatra and to take away from Antony the authority to rule which he had given up to a woman. And Caesar added that Antony had been drugged and was not master of himself, and that the Romans would be at war with Mardion the eunuch . . . and Iras the hair stylist woman of Cleopatra."

Octavian's propaganda presented the struggle with Antony not as a civil war between Roman factions but as an epic conflict between ancient Roman values and the moral degeneracy of the East, where women and castrated men ruled.[24] Octavian's propaganda made Antony into a lesson of what would happen to Romans who succumbed to the decadence of the East. Above all, Antony had lost his self-mastery, allowing himself to take the subordinate position to a woman.[25] According to Dio (50.28.3), Octavian expressed his goal as "to conquer and rule all humankind, and to allow no woman to make herself equal to a man." The charges manufactured against Antony included drunkenness, sexual indulgence, a life of luxury, and abandonment of the ancestral traditions of Rome. Antony's relation with Cleopatra allowed Octavian to associate femaleness with foreignness, lack of self-mastery, and failure to master inferiors.[26]

Octavian created an ethic and an ideology of imperialism rooted in the ancient ethic of self-mastery. The stunning success of this ideology was due largely to the effective ways in which Octavian's followers disseminated the message and to the self-interest of local elites among the peoples conquered by Rome. Literature, religion, art, and legislation were the major vehicles of this program. The work of the Augustan poets and historians is well known.[27] More important, Greek writers in the provinces picked up and expanded on the themes of the Augustan writers. If few could read and literary production affected mostly the elites of the empire, iconography and religion affected everyone.[28] Greek and Roman gods were multifaceted figures that lent themselves to complex interpretation. Antony followed Alexander and earlier Hellenistic rulers in associating himself with Dionysus.[29] Dionysus could be interpreted as a god of furious victory in war and of prosperity in peace, but Octavian exploited the god's other side as patron of wine and revelry, portraying Antony as lost in a piety of drunken foreign and eastern debauchery. Antony tried to defend himself by writing a work on his sobriety.[30] Octavian also exploited to the utmost his own associations with Apollo, who could be presented as god of reason and traditional morality.[31] Dionysus versus Apollo could be read as mastery by foreigners, women, and passion versus self-mastery. Octavian attributed his victory at Actium to Apollo and built a magnificent new temple to Apollo on the Palatine connected to his palace.[32] Artwork from cameos to monumental sculpture and widely circulated coins appeared throughout the empire advertising Octavian's interpretation of Actium and his association with Apollo.[33]

Octavian then set out on his famous program to "restore" the religion and morality of Rome.[34] Writers, sculptors, and temple builders worked to create a new mythology.[35] In this story, the Romans uniquely preserved the virtues of their simple agricultural society. These virtues most prominently included such militaristic values as courage and ascetic self-discipline together with piety. The Romans are the most pious of all peoples toward the gods. The other peoples of the empire had long ago abandoned the simple golden age virtues. Except for Rome, the world had been in a massive decline into luxury and degeneracy, a loss of discipline. Rome had, through luxury and vice imported from the East, admittedly begun to join in this slide during the last years of the Republic, but Augustus, son of god, had appeared in order to restore Rome's virtue and piety. This restoration marked the inauguration of a long prophesied golden age in which the whole civilized world would be included by virtue of Rome's providential conquests.

One glaring anomaly challenged this myth: Rome clearly owed an enormous, almost overwhelming, debt to Greece. How could this unquestionable fact be fitted to the myth? The mythmakers resolved the contradiction by creating classicism.[36] The earlier Greeks had been virtuous, self-mastered, militarily potent, and culturally great, but recent Greek culture had slipped into decadence marked by luxury and softness. Rome's debt was to the earlier, classical age. Classicism appeared most publicly in art and rhetoric. Cool, idealizing sculpture representing the emperor as a model of self-control and piety replaced the realistic and emotional Hellenistic and republican styles. Augustus's men saw that the new art was chaste; not only modestly clothed but also conveying moral lessons. The ambitious in the empire quickly fell into line. Dionysius of Halicarnassus, who came to Rome shortly after Actium, wrote of the return to classical or atticising Greek language as a moral reform. The so-called Asianic style of the Hellenistic era was luxurious, dissolute, and uncontrolled; the Attic morally pure and controlled. According to Suetonius, Antony had been an ardent exponent of the Asianic style (*Aug.* 86).

Augustus, with his own resources and by stimulating emulation, led a massive movement to restore old temples and to build new ones throughout the empire. Local elites raced for honor through marble and sacrificial feast.[37] Virtually every city in the empire erected monuments advertising Augustus, the lessons of Actium, and the new moral tone. Jerusalem was an exception, but Herod made up for the peculiarities of the Judeans by constructing the city of Caesarea in homage to Augustus (Jos., *Ant.* 15.339; *Bell.* 1.408). Elites in the cities of the East took the initiative in establishing cults of Augustus through which they articulated their relation to this godlike benefactor.[38] Among all the power and emotion of the new world order, expressed in the most observed monuments and rituals of the empire, also stood the message of self-mastery. Above all, Augustus himself was a model for those fit to rule others.[39]

It would be misleading, however, to leave the impression that this moral message appeared only in the oblique media of art and ritual. On the contrary, Augustus became an ardent moralizer. He avidly read moral writings, copying choice precepts and examples that he would send to his governors in the provinces (Suet., *Aug.* 89). Augustus not only studied Greek philosophy himself but encouraged philosophers in a way that cemented the alliance between philosophy and the new ruling order. His compositions included "Exhortations to Philosophy" (Suet., *Aug.* 85).

The essentially religious Secular Games of 18 B.C.E. gave expression to the belief that the golden age, the "eschatological" reign of Saturn, had begun.[40] Augustus carefully prepared the public for this "epic making" event. First he celebrated the defeat of the Parthians as the triumph of Rome over the barbarian peoples. Next followed the purge of the Senate and then passage of laws on marriage and morals in 18 B.C.E.[41] These laws and the added laws of 9 B.C.E. were designed to discipline the elite classes.[42] The modern personalistic idea of morality should not be allowed to hide the patent social goals of the legislation. Some measures aimed to prevent the contamination of the ruling classes through intermarriage. Laws purportedly designed to encourage increased childbearing for military manpower were thinly disguised attempts to ensure that the aristocracy passed its property intact from generation to generation.[43] Because such goals depended upon the proper behavior of the outsiders inside, wives and daughters, the program reflected great anxiety about controlling their behavior. Dio Cassius relates a scene in which the Senate, discussing "the disorderly conduct of the women and young men," alluded to Augustus's own womanizing behavior. In defence Augustus said, "Your own obligation is to admonish and command your wives as you see fit; just as I do." When the Senate pressed him for specifics he made a few remarks about women's dress, adornment, their going out in public, and modesty (54.16). Although these laws and Augustus's legislation against luxury (Aul.Gell., *NA* 2.24.13–14) were widely ignored, they set clear expectations about the kind of behavior that would be rewarded and punished in the new order.

Readers in Paul's time could be expected to understand that a key to almost any aspiration or ambition was the cultivation of self-mastery. Roman rule intensified an ancient Mediterranean ethic of self-restraint and promoted the hope of reward for those "by nature and training" fitted for such discipline. Philosophy had become the science of self-mastery. Cynic philosophers may have taught self-mastery as an end in itself to the masses, and Epicureans wanted to form alternative communities for people who had chosen not to play society's power games of rule and self-rule, but most philosophy aimed its attentions at the ruling elites and claimed to teach them how better to do their job. This gospel for the highborn and ambitious was philosophy's primary role from Plato into late antiquity even if it also claimed that all humans are spiritually sick and in need of the philosopher's remedy for the passions. Again, Peter Brown's words apply also to the first century: "The role of the philosopher and of the moral ideas generated in philosophical circles in the second century must be seen against the tense background of a need for closer solidarity among the upper classes and for more intimate means of control over inferiors. The philosopher, 'moral missionary' of the Roman world, claimed to address humanity as a whole. . . . In reality, he was no such thing. He was the representative of a prestigious counterculture within the elite, and he originally addressed his elevating message to members of that elite."[44] The alliance of philosophy with the ruling elites should provide clues about the significance of Jewish and early Christian claims to having an affinity with philosophy.

Philosophy added one new twist to the societal value of mastery/self-mastery. At least since Socrates, philosophers had intensively elaborated a certain line of reasoning: If the true self is not the body or appetites or emotions nor dependent upon attachments to things and people in the world external to the mind, then one could free that true self from the mastery of everything and everyone outside that self by strengthening and detaching it. The philosopher's message said that the same training that made one most able to control oneself and others also made oneself free from the control of others. Again, these counter themes of freedom and control were played out in circles of the socially elite. Jews and Christians elaborated their own versions of these themes as they struggled for a place in the empire.

A Jewish Reaction to the Augustan Revolution

The Augustan ideology featured Rome's subjugation of foreign nations.[45] By granting victory, the gods ordained the new order. The temple of Apollo planned by C. Sosius upon his triumph over the capture of Jerusalem integrated the new myths.[46] The temple's pediment interpreted the meaning of Actium by depicting the Athenian defeat of the Amazons, a barbarian society of women. Actium was also likened to the Greek defeat of the Persians at Salamis.[47] Augustus even had the battle reenacted in an artificial lake (Dio Cas. 55.10.7). Everywhere one turned, symbols appeared celebrating Rome's triumph over the so-called eastern barbarians.[48] At Augustus's funeral procession, individuals paraded in native costume representing each of the peoples conquered by Rome and presumably including the Jews (Dio Cas. 56.34).

Egypt, however, stood as the supreme lesson for the eastern peoples. Octavian's propaganda saddled Egypt with the stigma of being an incestuous, effeminate nation drenched in luxury and wicked passion.[49] Egypt was denied self-rule, and Alexandria was humiliated by being denied even a city council. Augustus created a system of apartheid in Egypt that kept Romans, Greeks, and Egyptians strictly separated in a hierarchical order, with native Egyptians on the bottom.[50] The moral stigma did not quickly fade. More than a century after Actium the orator and philosopher Dio Chrysostom lectured to the Alexandrians about their vices, particularly blaming their love of music and spectacle (Or. 32). He contrasts them with the Spartans, who, for example, ejected a harpist rather than allow themselves to become enslaved to the "low-born and luxurious pleasure" of such music (32.67; cf. 60). Fortunately for the Alexandrians, God sent the Romans as rulers (51). Spartans differ greatly from Alexandrians. For while the Spartans "displayed the ability to rule, leading the Greeks for many years and always conquering the barbarians, you do not even understand how to submit to rule" (69). The Alexandrians are fortunate to have the Romans controlling them (70–72). Dio, like Laelius in Cicero's Republic, employs self-mastery in the justification of Rome's conquests.[51] Some people simply lack the discipline to rule themselves. It comes as no wonder that anti-Roman apocalyptic literature and narratives of anti-Roman martyrdoms flourished in Egypt.

Augustan ideology, with its lessons about Egypt and the eastern barbarians, both posed a threat and exerted a special appeal upon Jewish elites. These pressures focused attention upon the moral qualities of Jewish culture. Jews suffered a great disadvantage in comparison to other ethnicities in articulating their relation to Rome. While the aristocracies of cities and towns throughout the eastern half of the empire instituted sacrifices, erected statues, and built temples for the emperors, the Jews in these cities had to stand back from such enterprises. Jews would have to work extra hard and take different routes to displaying their loyalty and fitness for local self-rule. If Jews could not promote the imperial cult, they could ally themselves with philosophy and present themselves as a uniquely self-mastered people; a people with just the sort of virtues valorized in the Augustan ideology. It comes as no surprise, then, that Jewish writings from the early empire, in contrast to earlier Jewish sources, place great emphasis on an ethic of self-mastery and present the Jewish law as a means to that goal.

Philo of Alexandria, the politically prominent and immensely wealthy aristocrat, proves our most extensive and instructive source for this Jewish strategy.

His treatise against the emperor Gaius rewards attention regarding this strategy, as the work self-consciously claims to represent the Jewish attitude toward the empire. Philo first describes the nature of the Jewish people (3–7). An Israelite is one who sees God. If the sight of elders, parents, and rulers stirs emulation to a life of order and self-restraint how much more are those stirred who see God. Philo gives unrestrained praise to Augustus. He transcended human nature in his virtues (143). When the nations of Europe were pitted against the nations of Asia and the whole world was on the verge of self-destruction, Augustus became the earth's savior (144). The benefits wrought by Augustus continued through the reign of Tiberius so that when Gaius came to power every nation agreed to his sovereignty (8). Indeed, so great was the prosperity, well-being, and joy that the golden age of Saturn seemed truly to have arrived (13). The calamities under Gaius resulted from his loss of self-mastery. When the moral exemplar for the whole empire loses control, passion will run rife. The sovereign must not be conquered by jesting, song, or dance because he is shepherd and master of the flock (44). But Gaius turned to extravagance with luxurious eating and drinking, hot baths, and sexual excess so that he nearly died. Philo comments, "The wages of self-mastery are strength and health, but lack of mastery, weakness and sickness bordering on death" (14). Philo defends the interests of Jews against charges of failing to honor the emperor in sacrifice partly by taking the moral high ground with the ethical ideology of the Augustan revolution.[52]

Judaism as a School for Self-Mastery

At times, Jewish writers did indeed present Judaism as a philosophy for the passions, a school for self-control. Philo writes, "The law exhorts us to philosophize and thereby improve the soul and the ruling mind. Therefore each seventh day stand open thousands of schools, in every city; schools of wisdom, self-restraint [sōphrosynē], courage and all the other virtues (Spec. Leg. 2.61–62)." Philo's schools are, of course, what moderns would call synagogues. He emphasizes that these schools stand open not only to Jews but also to gentiles. Jews inhabit the whole civilized world because they have a mission to be to the whole world as the priest is to the whole Jewish people. According to Philo, this sacred office of the Jewish people is evident because they purify both body and soul, obeying the divine laws that control "the pleasures of the belly and the parts below it . . . setting reason as charioteer of the irrational senses and . . . the wild and extravagant impulses of the soul . . . with philosophical exhortations (Spec. Leg. 2.162–63)." Furthermore the Jewish people have this office because they "corrected" the worship of many false gods that the other peoples adopted (ibid., 164–67). Emotion and desire, like diseases, will take over and destroy the whole body unless arrested by cautery and amputation. The only physician that can thus stop the ravages of desire is "philosophical reason" (*Dec.* 150). The mission of the Jewish people consists above all in teaching the truth of the one God and the virtues that God has ordained when reason rules over the passions.

For Philo, the highest and most rational philosophical speech can be found in the Jewish law. In spite of the distinctiveness of the Jewish law, Philo's views would have been quite understandable to his Hellenistic contemporaries, and Philo himself compares the Jewish law to the laws of other peoples. Greeks and Romans had come to distinguish between the traditional laws of the cities and the laws of nature. The laws of nature could be used to criticize the laws of the cities. In addition, there were the codes of law produced by such philosophers as Hippodamus, Plato, Zeno, Chrysippus, and Cicero in their plans for the ideal state. The Jewish law includes the laws of nature and constitutes the ideal law that philosophers have sought. Moses was the best of all lawgivers.

Philo apparently knows claims of the divine origin of the Spartan and Cretan laws and argues that only the Jewish law is truly divine because, although the other laws have been challenged and altered, only the Jewish law has never been changed. But, says Philo, the ultimate proof is this: "Among Greeks and barbarians, no city honors the laws of any other and scarcely even continually keep their own . . . the Athenians reject the customs and the laws of the Lacedaemonians and vice versa: nor among barbarians do Egyptians observe the laws of the Scythians . . . nor Europeans those of Asiatics. . . . But it is not so with ours. They attract and win the allegiance of all, barbarians, Greeks, inhabitants of the mainlands and the islands, of peoples from the east, the west, Europe and Asia, of the whole inhabited world from end to end" (*Mos.* 2.18–20).

Why do the Jewish laws win such approval? What makes the law of Moses superior to other laws? "The law requires that all who live according to the sacred constitution [*politeia*] of Moses must be free from every unreasoning passion and every vice to a higher degree than those who are governed by other laws" (*Spec. Leg.* 4.55). The Jewish law is superior because it better produces self-mastery. In contrast, the idolatry-promoting laws of other peoples "nourish and increase" the passions and vices (*Sacr. Abel* 15).

Above all, the law for Philo solves the greatest of human problems, the treachery of desire (*epithumia*). Desire is a "treacherous enemy and source of all evils" (*Virt.* 100). "Moses put off emotion loathing it as the vilest thing and the cause of evils, above all denouncing desire as like a destroyer of cities to the soul which must itself be destroyed and made obedient to the rule of reason"

(*Spec. Leg.* 4.95). Desire causes relatives to become bitter enemies and is "why large and populous countries are decimated by civil wars, and both land and sea are constantly filled with new catastrophes caused by sea and land battles. For all the wars of Greeks and barbarians, among themselves and among each other, that are the subject of tragic drama, spring from one source, desire, desire for money, glory or pleasure. These are the things that bring destruction upon the human race" (*Dec.* 151–53). Desire and emotion serve as general explanations for human evil. Paul suggests the same logic in Romans 1 when he first explains that gentiles became enslaved to their passions and desires and then follows with a great list of vices that stresses enmity and antisocial behavior.

Philo, Paul, and 4 Maccabees all understand the tenth commandment as a prohibition of desire (*Dec.* 142–53; 4 Macc. 2.4–6; Rom 7:7; 1 Cor 10:6–13). Just as modern interpreters of the Bible unconsciously read modern psychology, values, and institutions into the text, so Jews in the Greco-Roman world saw their assumptions about human nature in the writings of ancient Israel. For Jews like Paul and Philo, the tenth commandment showed that the law was concerned with the Greco-Roman ethic of self-mastery. As one might expect, Philo, Paul, and the author of 4 Maccabees wrote from the perspective of male ruling elites in this ethnic subculture of the Greco-Roman world. The discourse of desire and self-mastery is the language of their social location. This discourse embodies not only the psychology of social and gender hierarchy but also the ideology of the ethnic other. Greek writings represent barbarians as being dangerously different; incapable of controlling passions and desires.[53] So gentiles, including Greeks, suffer the same depiction at the hands of Jewish writers.

For Philo and 4 Maccabees, the law is a uniquely effective means of obtaining and maintaining self-mastery, or, to be more precise, of obtaining the degree of self-mastery possible in virtue of a person's social level and gender. Paul believes that the law prohibits desire but does not seem to view it as a means to self-mastery, at least for gentiles. Philo writes, "The last commandment forbids desire since he knew it to be revolutionary [*neōteropoios*] and treacherous. For all the passions of the soul that move and shake it so as to pervert its nature and prevent its health are severe but the most severe of all is desire" (*Dec.* 142). Here one can see how psychology mirrors social values. The dominant metaphors in much Greco-Roman discourse about the soul are those of rest versus motion, changelessness versus change, rule versus revolt. Health occurs when the soul, undisturbed by the body and lower nature, lies still and changeless. The repentant one has "fled from the revolt (*neōteropios*) of the body to join forces with the soul" (*Praem.* 16). *Neoteropoios*, a word most commonly used for political or military revolution and insurgency, literally means "to make younger or newer." In our world newness is generally a positive attribute. Everyone wants the all-new model. In antiquity, to call something new is to criticize it. The values and sense of reality promoted in the discourse of ruling elites like Philo naturalize the status quo and the privilege of those who rule. This extends to psychology and ethics, the realms of "more intimate means of control." Aristotle attributes the causes of revolution (*neoteropoios*) to the desire for equality (*Pol.* 1266b). Analogously, for ancient moralists like Philo, desire is revolt itself in the soul. To desire means wanting to change the status quo.

Philo views the law as an antidote to desire in several ways. The commandments of the law serve as exhortations addressed to the rationality of individuals. The law also contains the constitution of the ideal commonwealth, in which all of the institutions and offices promote self-mastery. The tenth commandment "stops that fountain of injustice, desire [*epithumia*], from which flow the most lawless acts, both public and private, both small and great, sacred and profane, concerning both bodies and souls and things called external. For nothing escapes desire, and as I have said before, like a flame in wood, it spreads and consumes and destroys everything. Many parts of the law come under this heading which is for the admonition of those who can be reformed and for the punishment of those who rebel making a lifelong surrender to emotion" (*Dec.* 173–74).

Philo explains that the law prohibits eating the meat of certain animals because they are most appetizing. Eating them would encourage desire and pleasure, whereas abstaining develops self-mastery. Philo then notes that this policy shows more wisdom than the extreme austerity of the Spartan laws but avoids the laxness and luxury of the Sybarites (*Spec. Leg.* 100–05). Such prohibitions embody further symbolic meaning. Animals, for example, that crawl on their stomachs represent the life of the belly, that is, the passions (*Spec. Leg.* 113). Philo also describes (*Spec. Leg.* 4.92–100) the laws pertaining to marriage, food, and drink as laws of self-mastery (enkrateia) and restraint (sōphrosynē). In the third century B.C.E., Hermippus of Smyrna (Jos. *Apion.* 1.182) claimed that the philosopher Pythagoras had borrowed his food laws from the Jews, and in the second century C.E. Celsus (Origen, *C. Cels.* 5.43) noted the similarity of Jewish and Pythagorean dietary rules.

Scholars have long puzzled at gentile attraction to Jewish practices. But if we understand the enormous appeal exerted by the ideal of self-mastery and the powerful interpretation of the Jewish law as a means to it, then the popularity of Jewish practices among certain types of gentiles (see below, "A Sociohistorical Caveat") becomes understandable. Jews could be perceived as different from the other ethnic groups of the empire in certain ways, giving the appearance of a uniquely disciplined nation of philosophers to many pagans. Gentiles certainly were not attracted because they sought release from a sense of sin or because they sought salvation. Gentiles attracted to Judaism for other reasons might have eventually come to fear the judgment of the Jewish deity. But the overwhelmingly moral character of the extant Jewish literature concerning gentiles and stressing a Hellenistic interpretation of Judaism indicates the area where Jewish and larger Greco-Roman interests overlapped. Judaism did not consider itself a religion of salvation like later Christianity but did often hold itself obliged to teach about the one God and the demands of his law deemed universal. Jews like Philo and the author of 4 Maccabees genuinely believed that the law of Moses taught an ethic of self-mastery.

A kind of popular romanticism about the virtue of certain peoples deemed exotic by Greek and Roman standards made the task easier for Jews, who wanted to present their law as a philosophical polity. This ethnic idealization, some of which appears already in Herodotus, served the Greeks as a way of thinking creatively about possible forms of life by attributing utopias to peoples exotic and distant, in time, place, or culture. One figure extensively idealized as the sage of a noble people was Anacharsis the Scythian. Legends say that he visited Greece in the sixth century B.C.E. and compared the Scythian to the Greek way of life at the marked expense of the latter. Letters were forged in his name in the third century, one of which was translated by Cicero. Above all, Anacharsis was known for his *sōphrosynē,* self-restraint. Anacharsis criticized all Greeks except the Spartans, as they too were noted for their self-restraint. The Anacharsis legends are examples of traditions that implicitly and explicitly compare the ways of life of different peoples with the question of which produce the greatest virtue. These ways of life attributed to noble barbarians in reality serve to cloak debates and philosophical propaganda about Greek and Hellenistic values. Such propagandistic idealization of exotic peoples often featured the ethic of self-mastery. Ironically, writers like Philo and Josephus readily adopted this Greek and Roman game for the promotion of their own ethnic minority.

From among the Greek ways of life, the Spartans, in a powerful tradition that extends up to the exaggerated admiration of the Nazis for a mythical Sparta, were idealized for their stern virtue.[54] So great was the Spartan reputation for self-mastery that any attempt to claim similar virtue for another way of life was apt to include a comparison with the Spartan politeia. Scholars usually translate *politeia* as "constitution," but Elizabeth Rawson warns that *politeia* means the whole way of life in a city-state.[55] By heeding this warning one avoids importing misleading modern distinctions between law, custom, politics, and religion. Thucydides admits that the Spartan "constitution" has produced

a superior self-restraint (1.68–71). Critias, who violently promoted his aristocratic values and ambitions as a member of the Thirty Tyrants and associate of
Socrates memorialized by Plato, was fanatically pro-Spartan. He wrote at least
two works discussing the Spartan politeia and praising Spartan self-restraint.[56]
A whole tradition of works devoted to and discussing the Spartan politeia followed. Polybius credits their divinely given "constitution" with making individual Spartans self-controlled and manly (6.48.2–4). In the early Empire, Dio
Chrysostom follows numerous philosophers in praising their self-mastery. Dio
attributes their success as a nation to their self-control and faithfulness to their
ancestral law and links them to the Indians, who were widely regarded as
another nation of self-mastered philosophers.[57]

All of this helps one to understand what Jews meant when they described
their law and way of life as a politeia and when they stressed the virtues that the
law and way of life would produce. Both Philo and Josephus, in different ways,
both explicitly and implicitly, compare Moses to Lycurgus, the Spartan lawgiver, and compare the Jewish and Spartan ways of life. When gentiles heard
Jews talk about the advantages of and virtues produced by the law of Moses,
they were hearing a familiar topic. The remarkably viable life of a myth claiming Jewish and Spartan kinship underlines the power of this interethnic discourse.

The myth displays its own logic if one adopts certain assumptions deemed
plausible by a number of ancient writers. Does it not make sense that the
Greek and the barbarian nations most known for surpassing self-mastery
should be related? How did it come about that two peoples should have such
similar attitudes toward law and produce such similar ways of life? The origins of the legend are unknown but a letter perhaps forged in the second century B.C.E. and purportedly written by the Spartan king Areios to the high
priest Onias proclaims a common descent from Abraham and calls for a community of goods (1 Macc 12:5–23; Jos. *Ant.* 12.225–27). Abraham is father of
both Spartans and Jews! According to 2 Macc 5:9, the ousted high priest Jason
in 168 B.C.E. sought refuge in Sparta, appealing to common kinship. About
twenty-five years later, the high priest Jonathan sent an embassy to Sparta. A
spurious letter from him also proclaiming Spartan and Jewish brotherhood
together with a reply from Spartan officials appears in 1 Macc 12:5–23;
14:20–23. Soon afterward there is evidence of a Jewish community in Sparta (1
Macc 15:23). Herod made very generous gifts to the city and maintained a
friendship with the Spartan leader Eurycles.[58] Certain legends send Lycurgus,
the Spartan lawgiver, to India, where he studied philosophy with the gym-
nosophists, Brahmans regarded by Greek and Roman writers as philosophers
capable of astounding feats of self-discipline (Aristocrates in *FGH* 3b, 591).

Clearchus, the student of Aristotle, remarked on the self-restraint (*sōphrosynē*) and endurance of the Jewish way of life, deriving the Jews from ancient Indian philosophers (F. Wehrli, *Die Schule Des Aristoteles,* frg 6; Jos., *Apion.* 1.22; cf. Megasthenes in Clem. *Strom.* 1.15).

If noted Greek writers could regard the Jews as a nation of self-mastered philosophers, then Jewish authors like Philo were ready to sell the advantages of the Jewish politeia to gentiles on that basis. Philo offers gentiles who repent and give up their false gods membership in the best politeia (*Virt.* 175–78). Such converts will be accepted as kinsmen and friends, "immediately becoming self-restrained [*sōphronēs*] and self-mastered [*enkrateis*]" and generally virtuous (*Virt.* 179, 182). Although he welcomes proselytes, Philo felt no mission to convert the world to Judaism. When he interprets the promise to Abraham (Gen 28:14), "In you shall all the tribes be blessed," it becomes a promise to all that "fight the war against the emotions" that they shall be partakers of the "Rational Nature" (*Somn.* 173–76). Conversion for Philo means incorporation into the Jewish community. This he carefully distinguishes from the status of metic. The latter is the technical term that some Greek cities had used for resident aliens, people who permanently associated themselves with a particular city but did not become citizens. Many laws about their status, rights, and restrictions, including religious privileges and restrictions, have survived from Greek states.[59] Philo thinks of interested gentiles, what New Testament scholars have called godfearers, in this way. The modern concept of converting to a religion provides misleading analogies because the social, ethnic, and political dimensions have been virtually factored out.

Josephus also presents Judaism as a kind of philosophy offering a better way to self-mastery, although he downplays gentile conversion and adherence to Judaism for apologetic reasons in the *Antiquities* and the *War.*[60] In spite of his negative attitude in these works, he still betrays knowledge of gentile interest.[61] In the work *Against Apion,* however, in which he may be following an Alexandrian apologetic source, he quite forwardly advertises Judaism as being similar to philosophy in its moral teachings, requiring great discipline, and having a wide impact on gentiles who have adopted various of its practices. Whereas Greek philosophy addresses only the few, Judaism addresses the many (*Apion.* 2.168–71). Judaism is a *religious* philosophy for the masses (ibid., 170–71). Josephus stresses that gentile religious practices lead to a lack of self-control (ibid., 2.195) and what great discipline the Jewish law requires (for example, ibid., 234). Nevertheless, beginning with the Greek philosophers, gentiles have increasingly adopted Jewish laws, to the point that the masses throughout the world keep various Jewish practices (ibid., 282). The Jewish law demands more discipline than either the laws of Plato or those of the Spartans (ibid., 2.221–24, 225–35). In striking contrast to the Qumran writings, which display no interest at all in an ethic of ascetic self-mastery but instead have an ethic of purity and pollution, Philo and Josephus depict the Essenes as austerely self-mastered philosophers. "They shun pleasures as evil and consider self-mastery [enkrateia] and resisting the power of the passions as virtue. . . . They do not reject marriage on principle . . . but wish to protect themselves against the sexual depravity of women, being convinced that no woman ever remains faithful to one man" (Bell. 2.120–21). Similarly, but with less extremity, the Pharisees lead a simplified life and staunchly resist any concessions to luxury (Ant. 18). The accounts of the Essenes, Pharisees, and Therapeutai in Philo and Josephus undoubtedly serve as attempts to claim that Jewish philosophical groups outdo Greeks and others in their degree of self-mastery.

The works of Philo and Josephus and other Jewish writings from the period of the second temple, but especially the sources from the early empire, provide vital evidence for Jews who wanted to attract gentiles into a sympathetic relation with Jewish communities by advertising Judaism as a superior school for self-mastery.[62] Such attraction did not normally mean becoming a naturalized citizen of the Jewish commonwealth. Rather, Jewish teachers encouraged gentiles to learn applicable moral teachings and practices from the law of Moses. Much evidence also exists for early Christians presenting themselves as an even more disciplined people who could outdo both Greeks and Jews. Such ascetics are thought of as antisocial extremists, but they were living symbols of their society. They are like super athletes of today seen on television talk shows: they symbolize the values of rugged individual achievement, self-fulfillment, and the belief that "anyone can realize their dream if they want to hard enough and work at it." These ancient athletes of self-mastery also mirrored the dominant values of their society. Life was about ruling and being ruled. The human world, like the physical world, consisted of levels and degrees of quality. Nature's basic principle was to place the superior over the inferior. An ancient ethic said that this natural principle of human society, at base, depended upon the battle within the individual between the superior and inferior parts. Ancient heroes of self-mastery were living lessons in these principles. The majority of Jews in late antiquity eventually may have rejected the interpretation of Judaism worked out by people like Philo who understood it as a school of self-mastery. In Philo's and Paul's time, however, the question was very much a live one, and the relation of the new Christ sect to such an interpretation was an open question.

Audience, Opponents, and Self-Mastery in Paul

Although certainly not the most important theme in Romans, self-mastery may be the theme most poorly understood and underemphasized in modern interpretation. In my view, the theme allows a coherent understanding of Paul's discourse about the law, his opponents, and his audience. Scholars widely agree that Paul faced competitors, who were vying with him for the allegiance of gentiles and who were teaching gentiles to observe the law or certain aspects of the law. Scholars also agree that the primary constituency over which Paul and these other teachers vied ought to be located among gentiles who had already associated themselves with Jewish communities.[63] Great unclarity has existed, however, about the causes of gentile attraction to Judaism and the goals of Jews who sought to teach gentiles. Paul's letters show his opponents offering a way to moral betterment focusing on the promise of self-mastery. Moral improvement may not have constituted their entire message, but Paul's way of responding to these opponents implies that he believed the ethic of self-mastery to be a key issue in the struggle for the hearts and minds of gentiles. Furthermore, interpreters have had a notoriously difficult time explaining how the extensive ethical material in the letters concerned with the gentiles and the law fits with his discourse about the justification of the gentiles. Again, understanding the law as a means to self-mastery uncovers an essential piece of the puzzle that unites ethics, theology, and a historically plausible explanation of Jewish and gentile motivations.

Paul's depictions of the opponents provide clues regarding what he believed that he faced. The three letters most concerned about opposing the way of the law for gentiles are Galatians, Philippians, and Romans. All three contain allusions to Paul's rivals. Paul's response to the teacher in 2:17–29 goes something like this: "How dare you possess the arrogance to teach gentiles that they can obtain moral improvement through the law when you do not even keep the ethical teachings of the law yourself." Philo places stealing and adultery, the lawbreaking attributed to the Jewish teacher, under the rubrics of "laws of self-mastery" and "laws against desire" (*Spec. Leg.* 4.87, 96). If Paul can persuasively claim that the law does not guarantee self-mastery even to native Jews learned in the law, then he has effectively eliminated the central appeal for Judaizing propounded by his opponents.

After the list of greetings for people in Rome, one finds a carefully placed warning (Rom 16:17–20), before the final greeting from those who are with Paul.[64] The placement of warnings at the end of letters is a way of personally sharpening a point for the readers by juxtaposition with the greetings (cf. 1 Cor 16:13, 22; 2 Cor 13:11; Gal 6:12–13, 17). If the context of Paul's previous discourse in the letter means anything, then one would expect the people of whom he warns to be teachers of the law resembling the teacher in 2:17–29. The readers are to beware of people who cause doubt (*dixostasis* + *para*) and misunderstanding (*skandalon*) aimed against the teachings that they have learned (17). These opponents of Paul's gospel deceive by using reasonable and plausible speech and serve not Christ but their own belly (18). As shown earlier, the last term, frequently used by Philo and other moralists, refers to the passions and desires. As in Rom 2:17–24, Paul depicts opposing teachers who have noble-sounding messages but cannot master their own passions and desires.

One meets issues and language in Philippians 3 similar to those of Romans.[65] The chapter is much more explicitly polemical, however. It begins with a reference to "dogs" and "evil workers" who advocate circumcision. Two of the arguments Philo gives for the practice of circumcision are that it is practiced by the Egyptians, a people regarded as preeminent for their philosophy, and that it symbolizes the excision of pleasures (*Spec. Leg.* 3.8–9). Paul's attack on these opponents who taught judaizing practices to gentiles suggests that their appeal may have centered on claims that gentiles could learn self-mastery by association with the Jewish community and by adopting certain practices that were described as methods of self-mastery. Paul begins with his own example. Although a native Jew of the highest status, he has left behind all of the truly great blessings of Judaism to find justification through Christ's faithfulness instead of through the law (3:4–11). Like Philo, Paul's opponents surely claimed that the self-mastery obtainable through the law would make them acceptable to the one true God. Thus the issues of gentile righteousness before God and achievement of self-mastery were interrelated. Next comes an agonistic passage based on the figure of a footrace. Modern interpreters have underemphasized the extremely rich background of the language (12–16) in the ethic of self-mastery because they have been obsessed with reconstructing the theology of the opponents. But ponderous and unlikely theories that cast Paul and his opponents into the mold of sixteenth-century theological polemicists prove unnecessary.

Instead of attaining his own righteousness through the law, Paul has a righteousness by means of Jesus' faithfulness. He obtains this righteousness by reenacting the manner of Jesus' death in faithfulness to God and thus experiencing the same kind of "passions" that Jesus suffered (10). Any competent ancient reader would recognize Jesus' and Paul's behavior as examples of individuals who had shown extraordinary mastery over their passions in service of a higher purpose. The passions (*ta pathēmata*)—what moderns distinguish as emotions, appetites, and feelings—are intimately related to the experience of suffering in Greco-Roman thought. The faculties of the body or self called passions allow a person to feel physical pain and experience psychological suffering. The passions are the self's entryways for being passively acted upon, whether by attacks upon the body that cause pain or the allurements of sexual pleasure through the senses. Thus *ta pathēmata* can mean both the faculties and the experience. After citing the example of king David's suffering from extreme thirst, for instance, 4 Macc. 3.17–18 says, "For the self-restrained [*sophron*] mind is able to conquer the constraints of the passions and to quench the tormenting flames [= *epithumia*], to win the match with even extreme pains of the body, and through the nobleness and goodness of reason to reject the entire rule of the passions." The martyrs of 4 Maccabees die in "faithfulness" and "obedience" to God, and their deaths become an "expiation" for Israel's sin (17.20–22; 6.28–30). Above all, 4 Maccabees teaches that its readers can obey the law even under duress and suffering by emulating the faithful endurance of the martyrs.[66] The writing again and again refers to the psychological mechanism for such faithfulness, reason's mastery of the passions and desire, but only reason trained in the law. Paul would agree with some claims in 4 Maccabees and disagree with others, but both speak a similar language.

Paul emulates Jesus' faithful suffering and calls on the Philippians to imitate him (3:17). The final reward is invulnerability from suffering in a resurrection body like Jesus'. Paul, as numerous commentators have stressed, emphasizes that he has not yet reached the goal and that he still struggles and competes valiantly with the goal in mind. The athletic imagery of 3:12–16 reminds one of 1 Cor 9:24–7 and the Greco-Roman philosophical tradition that went under the motto, To live well is to practice dying.[67] Here living courageously by one's convictions and struggling to subdue the demands of the passions and the body become ways of anticipating victory in death. Paul exhorts those who are perfect or mature to "have a mind" that struggles in this life toward the victory in death (v. 14). After explicitly urging his readers to imitate the model that he has just outlined, Paul returns to the counterexample of the opponents (17–21). Instead of following Paul's example of reenacting Christ's passions, these people live as enemies of his cross. Their god is their belly; they practice shameful things, and their minds, in contrast to those of the readers, are focused on earthly things.

Again, the opponents who teach gentiles to practice parts of the law cannot control their own passions and desires. Paul may be mocking their claims to reason when he contrasts their mind to the mind he urges on the Philippians (3:15, 19). The apostle also contrasts their earthly focus with a commonwealth (*politeuma*) that is in the heavens (cf. 1:27, "to live as citizens"). This swipe would make sense if Paul's competitors were, like Philo and Josephus, claiming that gentiles could best train for the mastery of their passions and desires by associating with the Jewish commonwealth. Why is the most devastating explicit criticism that Paul can conjure against his opponents to claim that they cannot control their passions and desires instead of, say, to criticize their theology or their teaching methods or their interpretation of the law? Most likely because the focus of their teaching was on mastery of the passions through the law.

One can only guess what Paul's claims that the opponents live under the mastery of their passions might mean concretely. Ancient sources most often associate *belly* with the appetites for food and sex but it can refer to other passions and desires. Philo, following a scheme from Platonism, makes the chest the seat of anger and relegates all of the other passions to the stomach (*Leg. All.* 3.114f.; *Spec. Leg.* 1.206). He says that the belly signifies desire in scripture and calls it the foundation of desire. From the belly springs the source, then, not only of desire for food and sex but also for money and reputation. At the conclusion of Galatians, Paul says that the people who want the readers to be circumcised do not keep the law themselves. A base desire for applause together with a fear that they might otherwise be persecuted for their activity among gentiles drives these people to advocate circumcision (6:12–13). Paul, in contrast, boasts only in the cross. The cross means that he has died to the world; circumcision and uncircumcision do not count for anything but a new creation (6:14–15). One could read this in a traditional way: The opponents have not accepted the idea that Christianity has replaced Judaism as the way to God. But concepts associated with self-mastery make better sense of the passage.

The opponents seem to be people working the borders between traditional Jewish approaches to gentiles, like Philo's, and the approach to gentiles made by the new preachers of Christ. Convincing gentiles to practice certain parts of the law and to believe that the law of Moses affords a superior way to self-mastery count as positive achievements for Paul's competitors. In fact, Jewish communities in general would likely agree in evaluating this approach to gentiles positively. But Paul no longer does, although he seems to have once agreed (5:11). As Paul now sees it, such teachers have refused to acknowledge God's way of making gentiles righteous through the faithful death of Jesus Christ. Their motivation springs from a desire to enhance their reputation in the Jewish community and a fear that preaching Paul's message would bring opposition from other Jews. Paul would have his message replace an older approach that had long successfully won the admiration and friendship of gentiles for Judaism. Paul claims to have left behind their base desire for increased reputation. Perhaps the best commentary on his claim to have been crucified is

5:24, "Those who are of Christ have crucified the flesh with its passions and desires." Paul, not the teachers of the law, stands as a model of self-mastery.

The strongest argument for making the ethic of self-mastery central in reading Romans and Galatians comes from the explanation it provides for the ethical material in the letters. Modern scholarship has long struggled to explain the presence of this material.[68] The three types of solutions that have predominated are, in my view and the view of many other interpreters, quite inadequate. The first explanation treats Paul as a systematic theologian who assumes that the division of ethics belongs with and is logically based upon the division of theology.[69] These interpreters, of course, do not describe Paul in the language that I have just used, and they would consider his grasp of these departments as intuitive or imagine that he had picked them up from Judaism. Intellectual history, however, shows that these categories came to Christianity by way of Greek philosophy and are versions of the relation between physics, which included theology, and ethics. The systems of ethnic law and temple state regulated by the purity codes of Judaism are certainly not precursors. Philo's kind of Judaism, which is greatly indebted to Greek philosophy, does sometimes use something like this distinction but in that case we are back to the ethic of self-mastery. Not surprisingly, then, scholars have had great difficulty with a model that has Paul writing theology, even ad hoc theology, in Gal 1–4 and Rom 1–11 and ethics in Gal 5–6 and Rom 12–15. This reading has not succeeded in showing the logical and necessary connection between theology and ethics because its proponents must constantly resort to anachronistic formulations that do not adequately account for the letter's discourse.

A second approach, whose most notable exponent was Martin Dibelius, denies any necessary or logical connection between the supposed theological and ethical sections of these letters.[70] Rather, the ethical sections are appendices containing traditional moral exhortation that Paul added to his letters because it would be good for his converts and the practice was the custom. First, Dibelius misdescribed the Greco-Roman practice of moral exhortation, which does not have the kind of mindless, arbitrary traditional character that he believed it did.[71] Second, the letters do not have discrete hortatory sections but display numerous points of integration between ethical and nonethical materials.[72] Dibelius's much-criticized approach need not detain us.

Third, scholars have stressed the occasionality of the letters and explained the ethical materials on the basis of speculative reconstruction of events and theologies to which Paul is supposedly reacting.[73] Since Paul employs ethical material, he must have been reacting to people who were behaving unethically. On this reasoning, some have claimed that Paul reacts to Jewish legalists in the first part of the letters and to gnostic libertines or charismatic enthusiasts in the moral sections.[74] Some interpreters combine the two into moral libertines who advocate Jewish practices. Most basically, this approach fails because the only warrant for finding libertines in these churches is the need to explain the presence of the ethical materials. Moreover the approach ignores the logic of the kind of ethical literature represented in the letters and the corresponding cultural codes (see note 71 above). Above all, the letters explicitly describe their readers as being morally upright.

Some features of Galatians indicate that an ethic of self-mastery is at issue and imply that Paul's discourse responds to an approach to self-mastery advocated by teachers of the law. The features I will note, though necessarily inexhaustive, possess enough coherence to illustrate the connections between certain motifs in the letter. According to Galatians, the virtues required by God have come to the letter's gentile audience through the Spirit rather than through works of the law. This power of the Spirit for virtuous action came to the readers when they heard the story of Jesus' faithfulness proclaimed (3:1–5).[75] In light of their desire to take up certain works from the law, Paul asks his readers if what they suffered (*tosauta epathēte*) when they heard the story of Jesus' faithfulness was in vain (3:4). The language here describes the readers as having reenacted Jesus' faithful endurance of suffering, thereby acquiring capacities of the Spirit.

Paul goes on from 3:5 to explain that this gift of the Spirit had been planned by God from long ago as a way of making the non-Jewish peoples righteous (3:8): "Scripture predicting beforehand that God would make the gentiles righteous by means of faithfulness, announced the gospel before its time to Abraham, 'In you all the gentiles will be blessed.'" Chapters 3–4 assure the readers that they are indeed heirs of the promise to Abraham and therefore sons of God. The chapters say much about the readers' status before they became believers. They stood under a curse because rather than observe the law as a whole they only performed works from the law (3:10). In 5:3, Paul warns them that if they receive circumcision they will be bound to keep the whole law.

The readers should not return to the law. Such statements assume that they had been under the law before Paul converted them (5:1; 3:23–4:10). But exactly the same addressees also served idols and worshiped false gods before their conversion. This has bewildered commentators and forced them to resort to an absurd theory whereby Paul equates Jewish religion with gentile idolatry. A more plausible and economical theory (because in using it one does not have to explain a large number of contradictory statements about Judaism and the law) is to understand the readers encoded in the text as so-called god-fearers: gentiles who observed certain practices of the law selectively and who maintained some degree of association with a Jewish community while remaining gentile. Such a person might attend a birthday celebration at the temple of Apollo one day and abstain from eating pork or observe a Jewish holiday the next. Paul writes, "Formerly when you did not know God you served gods that are not really gods. But now that you know God . . . how can you go back again to things that are weak and to impoverished elementary teachings which you wish to serve again. You observe days, months, seasons and years" (4:8).

The reference to what the readers "wish to serve again" provides a point of anchorage for interpretation. Interpreters widely agree that the readers Paul depicts in the letter want to be circumcised or practice works from the law or both. The text cited above describes the readers' ambiguous status before they heard Paul's preaching and gave up both pagan gods and Jewish practices for righteousness through Christ. According to Paul's rhetoric, if they now begin to observe Jewish holidays, they will be returning to that dark no-man's-land situated between Judaism and paganism.

Earlier, Paul had reassured his readers: Christ had redeemed them from the curse incumbent upon those who only partially observe the law, "so that the blessing of Abraham might come upon the gentiles in Christ, in order that we might receive the promise of the Spirit through [Jesus'] faithfulness" (3:13–14). The goal of the argument comes down to the claim that the readers possess the Spirit that above all serves as the guarantor of certain virtues. In light of this role for the Spirit and the Galatian desire to practice teachings from the law, one might well conclude that the readers as presented by Paul were primarily concerned with ethics. That indeed serves as the destination of Galatians' discourse.

Chapters 5–6 seem to demote the ethic of self-mastery to a position below an ethic of soft and cooperative virtues that Paul advocates. "In Christ, neither circumcision nor uncircumcision has any power [ischuei] but faith(fulness) made effective through love" (5:6). Instead of making the tenth commandment "against desire" the chief ethical principle, Paul raises Lev 19:18, the command to love the neighbor. Like Philo and 4 Maccabees, Paul finds one commandment from the law to serve as the guiding principle for his whole ethic. The letter next sets up an antithesis between two types of desire: "Walk by the Spirit and you will not fulfill [teleo] the desire of the flesh. For the flesh desires against the Spirit . . . they are opposed to one another so that you cannot do what you want to do. But if you are led by the Spirit you are not under the law (5:16–18)." Expressing exactly the opposite of what Jews who advocated the law as an antidote for gentile desire were, Galatians suggests that works of the law stand on the side of the flesh's desires. After asking the readers whether they received the Spirit through hearing about faithfulness or by works of the law, in 3:3 Paul says, "Having begun with the Spirit do you now end with the flesh?"

As I shall show in my discussion of Romans 7, the clause at the end of v. 18 corresponds to a widely cited maxim concerning *akrasia,* the lack of self-mastery. According to Paul, the Spirit and the flesh have opposing desires so that the readers cannot do what they want to do. In other words, the flesh makes self-mastery impossible for the readers. What the readers want apparently has something to do with the law. Otherwise v. 18 would seem to be gratuitous. Paul seems to say that the readers cannot gain self-mastery by fulfilling works from the law because of the flesh. When Paul lists the works of the flesh, he mixes vices of the appetites with those that result in a breakdown of social cohesion. Other passages bracketing the juxtaposition of Spirit and flesh exhort the readers to social cohesion and warn of a breakdown in fellowship (5:13–15; 5:25–6:10). Here Paul places the cooperative virtues under the rubric of love. Paul's concern clearly lies with these virtues, which he places under the love command and attributes to the work of the Spirit. In a listing of the fruit of the Spirit, first come love, joy, peace, patience, kindness, goodness, faithfulness, and gentleness. Paul elsewhere elevates these virtues and relates them to love. Self-mastery (enkrateia) comes last on the list. Chapter 5 thus deemphasizes the ethic of self-mastery and denies that any of the virtues can be had through the performing of works from the law. Paul does not deny a place to self-control, but he does not, as his competitors were likely to have, center his ethic on self-mastery.

Verses 23–24 nicely sum up Paul's claim over against those who sought self-mastery of their passions and desires through circumcision and other works of the law: "The law does not oppose such virtues but those who are of Christ have crucified the flesh with its passions and desires." These words come practically in the same breath as the word *enkrateia* (self-mastery). Verse 23 is difficult to construe but makes sense in the context I have outlined. In a negative formulation, Paul grudgingly grants that the law does allow these virtues, but he denies that it can do for gentiles what reenactment of Christ's faithfulness can do. Through Christ, gentiles can obtain the self-mastery that even the teachers of the law mentioned in chapter 6 have not attained.

Finally, one may speculate with some warrant that the appearance of those who were teaching works from the law in Galatia exacerbated tensions between people of various social strata and statuses. The ethic of self-mastery constituted the dynamic heart of Greco-Roman society's psychological and moral dimension for those who ruled or aspired to rule. I am struck by the rather obvious but overlooked fact that the discussion in Galatians assumes that males are the norm and center of the law and ethics. The central issue concerns whether circumcision provides the key to moral and religious power for non-Jewish men. The affinities between circumcision, the epitome of a male rite, and the male-centered and male-power-supporting ethic of self-mastery are too obvious to ignore. The ancient discourse of the ethic of self-mastery is also closely tied to the distinction between slave and free. In theory, teachers who focused on this ethic would likely have bolstered the ambitions either of the ruling classes to subject inferiors to strict control or of inferiors to gain their freedom and rule others. Does the letter's language allude to such social competition? Are Paul's descriptions of his audience "biting and devouring one another" (5:15) and are his exhortations against envy, provocation, and conceit (5:26; cf. 6:2) to be seen against this background? Could the verse "There is neither Jew nor Greek, slave nor free, no male or female; for you are all one in Christ Jesus" (3:28) be a principle annunciated in response to claims that the Jewish politeia both brought one closest to God and also provided the most effective means to self-mastery for those who were able?

No clear answers exist for these questions. Nevertheless, it is crucial to articulate the kinds of questions that a sociohistorical understanding of issues pertaining to self-mastery might bring to the writings of an ancient moralist. Above all, the coherency derived from this way of reading Galatians and Romans warrants the reading. When one factors in issues regarding self-mastery to the discourse about the law, works of the law, gentiles becoming righteous, Christ's faithfulness, and the Spirit's virtues, the mix yields a logic that tightly binds these themes. The idea of distinct doctrinal and ethical sections ceases to make sense.

A Sociohistorical Caveat

While one must separate encoded from empirical readers as a methodological principle, one cannot afford to ignore social history when reading a text. Social history provides the interpreter access to a sense of what is and is not generally plausible for people in the society. To take the question of this chapter, for example: Is it plausible that the discourse of writers like Xenophon, Philo, and Paul concerning self-mastery carried an appeal for certain classes of people? Can one realistically believe that Paul addressed himself to gentiles in Rome who might have been concerned with such issues?

A prosopography of Pauline circles yields a list of nearly eighty names. Analysis of the names, of information given with the names, and of other types of evidence from the letters provides a strong basis for a social analysis of Paul's associates and the kind of readers to which he most explicitly addressed himself.[76] In his study of Paul's social world, Wayne Meeks has analyzed this evidence and concluded that "the most active and prominent members of Paul's circle (including Paul himself) are people of high status inconsistency (low status crystallization). They are upwardly mobile; their achieved status is higher than their attributed status."[77] One would find an interest in the ethic of self-mastery especially among these people with the potential for social mobility. Furthermore, those attracted to an interest in Judaism would most likely come from this population.[78]

Five of those greeted in chapter 16, including Prisca and Aquila, may be Jews and probably are.[79] Prisca and Aquila are Paul's fellow workers in the gentile mission now back in Rome after time spent in the East. Both Paul and all the assemblies (*RSV*, "churches") of the gentiles give thanks for them (16:4). According to Acts, they met Paul in Corinth and then traveled to Ephesus with him (18:2–21). Paul and the couple were also business associates, having the same trade. Both 1 Cor 16:19 and Rom 16:5 describe them as having an assembly (church) in their house. Their mobility, kind of business, patronage of gentile assemblies, and the very fact that they had their own houses large enough to host assemblies indicate that they were people of means.[80] Acts describes Aquila as being Jewish, but it is not clear that Prisca was. Both have been plausibly identified as freedpersons or children of freedpersons of the Acilius family.[81] M. Acilius Glabrio, consul in 91, was executed by Domitian with a group of nobles charged with practicing atheism and adopting Jewish customs (Dio Cas. 67.14). It seems likely that the Acilius household had associated itself with the Jewish community or with followers of Christ. The fact that Paul once and Acts twice places Prisca's name before her husband's indicates that she possessed a higher status.[82] This probably means that she was born free and a Roman citizen and, on the basis of her name, was probably not Jewish unless she was descended from Jewish slaves emancipated by the Prisca gens in the not-too-recent past.

Perhaps Prisca and certainly Aquila are Jews who devoted themselves to recruiting and organizing gentiles into associations of Christ-followers. Paul may have sent them to Rome as a vanguard for his gospel. Like Andronicus and Junia, whom Paul designates "notable among the apostles (16:7)," and the other apostles except for Paul (1 Cor 9:5), Prisca and Aquila worked as a husband and wife team. The phenomenon of Jewish couples preaching Christ to gentiles should be imagined as a new version of an old practice whereby Jews sought to define some kind of relation with gentiles on Jewish terms. Yet in the Pauline version, this activity actually alienated gentiles from forms of traditional association with Judaism. Prisca and Aquila may have been exiled from Rome for disturbances within the Jewish community caused by this novel approach to gentiles.[83] Such activity needs to be understood in a more sociological and at the same time more intimate way. Aquila and Prisca represent Jews who lived and moved in close relation with gentiles while maintaining the clearest sense of their Jewish identity. They probably are or come from freedpersons of a prominent gentile household. If freedpersons, they would have maintained strong ties to their former masters' house in the form of duties and patronal privileges and owed their prosperity at least partly to his patronage. Now having a household and business of their own, they would have gentile slaves and perhaps even freedpersons of their own. Do you try to make proselytes of your gentile dependents or teach them Jewish morals? What does one have the gentile dependents do on holy days or in regard to purity laws? If you think of your household as a unit in the politeia or *politeuma* of the Jews or Judeans in Rome or Ephesus, how do you understand your gentile dependents? Are they sojourners among Israelites? But you yourself belong to a gentile city and are the dependent of a gentile household as a freedperson. Your prosperity and social mobility are highly dependent on your intimate ties with a network of gentiles. The Pauline mission to gentiles found its Jewish sponsors among socially and economically mobile Jews whose close relations with gentiles produced ethnic-religious tension and ambiguity. In turn, the gentiles who became most active in Pauline communities fit a similar pattern of ethnic-religious ambiguity because of their association with Judaism and social mobility. Both Jewish sponsors and gentile followers possessed a high degree of status inconsistency exacerbated by ethnic-religious ambiguity. In the case of Prisca and Aquila, these tensions would have been heightened if their marriage was mixed.

In Phil 4:22, Paul sends greetings from saints in the household of Caesar. These believers were members of the imperial administration that Augustus and his successors organized by patronage and slavery as an extension of the emperor's household.[84] In the traditional view, Philippians was written from Rome, but in the past few decades a number of scholars have come to favor Ephesus. I agree with Wayne Meeks, John Fitzgerald, and other recent commentators that Rome seems most likely.[85] The whole question has been much simplified by recent epistolographic and rhetorical research that has discredited theories that would partition Philippians into fragments of various letters.[86]

If Paul mentions believing members of the imperial household in writing Philippians from Rome, then he probably greets some of these individuals in Rom 16. Indeed, the hypothesis that Paul greets members of the imperial household allows various bits of evidence to converge in a coherent fashion. Verse 10 greets "those who belong to Aristobulus." The Greek expression refers to a group of dependents, slaves and freedpersons, in the household of a certain Aristobulus. The name Aristobulus appears only twice in the many thousands of inscriptions in the *Corpus Inscriptionum Latinarum* volume for the city of Rome.[87] This Aristobulus likely was the grandson of Herod the Great and brother of Agrippa 1, who lived in Rome and apparently died there sometime after 45 C.E.[88] Since Aristobulus was a friend and client of the emperor Claudius (Jos., *Bell.* 2.221–22; *Ant.* 18:273–76; 20:13), J. B. Lightfoot's theory that the Aristobuliani (dependents of Aristobulus) would have been willed or ceded to the imperial household seems probable.[89] Customarily, dependents transferred to the household of Caesar kept the designation of their former master.[90] Thus we hear of Agrippiani, Germaniciani, and Maecenatiani being in the imperial household.[91] This identification is made more likely by the fact that Paul next mentions a certain Herodian, whom he describes as his kinsman. Since freedpersons carried their master's name, Herodian was either a slave or freedman of some part of the larger family to which Aristobulus, grandson of Herod the Great and brother of Herod Agrippa and Herod of Chalcis, belonged. Instances of the Latin equivalent of this name refer mostly to imperial slaves or freedmen (for example, *CIL* 6.9005).

Paul's descriptions of himself show that as a Pharisee "who advanced in Judaism more than others in his generation" (Gal 1:14) and as someone with the authority to persecute the church (Gal 1:13; Phil 3:5–6; Acts 9:1–2), he moved in circles that made possible contacts with leading Jewish households. To illustrate the small world of the Jewish aristocracy, Aristobulus's brother Agrippa made a trip to Alexandria and persuaded Philo's brother, Alexander, to loan him two hundred thousand drachmae (*Ant.* 18. 159). Agrippa later visited the Jewish community of Alexandria in August of 38 (Philo, *Flac.* 25–28; Jos., *Ant.* 238). One can plausibly imagine writings of Philo circulating among the dependents of Agrippa's and Aristobulus's households and Paul having gentile followers in their households. Agrippa's daughter Drusilla married Felix, the Roman governor of Judea who, according to Acts, studied with Paul. Agrippa was known for his piety and remembered positively by those who claimed the heritage of the Pharisees (Jos., *Ant.* 19. 294, 331; Mishna, *Sot.* 7.8).

The Pharisees were a political interest group who tried to influence social and religious policy mainly in Judea. They were primarily retainers, that is, cultured clients serving the ruling class as educators, legal experts, and administrators.[92] As a politico-religious interest group, the Pharisees, as Josephus's portrayal of them shows, could also act as loyal opposition to the ruling aristocracy. Paul was a Pharisee and almost certainly belonged to this retainer class during the time he persecuted followers of Jesus. In Greek and Roman cities, members of ruling elites like Philo, and in Judea, the traditional aristocracy, were under pressure from their Roman overlords to increasingly exert discipline both over themselves and over their subjects. Above all, socially mobile dependents belonging to Jewish aristocratic households and to men in the imperial household constitute a population in which one would find an attraction to a Jewish ethic of self-mastery. In the case of the Herodian dependents to whom Paul writes, there was considerable overlap between Roman and Jewish aristocratic households.

In v. 11, one meets the same expression as that concerning Aristobulus in v. 10, but now dealing with "those who belong to Narcissus." Scholars have long suggested that Narcissus here is the enormously wealthy and powerful freedman of the emperor Claudius.[93] Narcissus was forced to commit suicide shortly after Nero's accession and two or three years before Paul wrote Romans (Tac., *Ann.* 13.1). Narcissus's dependents passed into the possession of the imperial household as a unit and bore the designation Narcissiani, attested in Latin Inscriptions (*CIL* 3.3973; 6.9035, 15640). Narcissus was Claudius's personal secretary (*ab epistulis*). Juvenal cites the example of Narcissus when he wants to mock the lowborn who have suddenly risen to wealth and power (*Sat.* 14.329–31). Satirists like Juvenal and Petronius, with his character Trimalchio, reflect the aristocratic contempt for socially mobile slaves and freedmen. Romans 16 pictures a group of addressees that is predominantly of foreign origin and from slave backgrounds.[94] Claudius's Narcissus, perhaps the Narcissus of v. 11, epitomizes the massive ambiguity of freedpersons in general: because of his efficient dedication to his master, one of the wealthiest and most powerful people in the empire; because of his ineradicable slave origins, an object of hatred and contempt by the freeborn and noble.[95] On the one hand, freedpersons often gained wealth because their masters saw ambition and skills that the master could capitalize upon by setting the slave free with money for a business venture. On the other hand, law and custom denied freedpersons the respect that wealth might otherwise afford. Freedpersons could never forget their servitude because they were bound to a continuing relation with their former masters. Satirists and aristocratic writers seethe with contempt for freedmen who don the manners of the elites in desperate hope of gaining respect. Petronius's freedman Trimalchio is not only boorish and vulgar but also lacking the gravity and self-mastery of a true aristocrat. Therefore he is capricious master of others. Not natural reason but lust and passion mark his rule of his dependents. Trimalchio's instructions for his epitaph read, "C. Pompeius Trimalchio was pious, stout and trustworthy; he rose from nothing, left thirty million, and never heard a philosopher." The last expression ordinarily means that the person lived a virtuous life naturally although not formally educated in philosophy. Petronius, of course, thus tells the reader that this impudent freedman lacked the virtue and self-restraint that philosophy taught.

An analysis of Romans 16 shows that Paul greets primarily slaves and freedpersons. Some are also likely to have been members of the most socially mobile group in the empire. In addition to having the status inconsistency of freedpersons, the readers are foreigners, mostly Greeks, disproportionately prominent women, and they have associated themselves with Judaism.[96] One is right to imagine that these people, who had the ambition to advance but not the cultivation of the ruling class and who had wealth or potential for wealth but not the respect that wealth ordinarily brought, found both moral cultivation and respect in the politeia of the Jews. Philo says that such people will be welcomed as kinsmen into the most noble commonwealth and will gain self-mastery under the most noble constitution (*Virt.* 175, 179, 182). In this light, Romans is striking because it seeks to convince such people that the Jewish law holds neither hope of self-mastery nor righteousness before God.

For those who might yet doubt that ancient readers would take seriously Jewish and early Christian claims to teach self-mastery of passions and desires, I will introduce two excellent witnesses, one from inside the movement and the other from outside. Even those who globally disparage the historical reliability of Luke-Acts allow that the author presents socially and culturally typical portraits. Whatever the historicity of events, Luke for the most part paints realistic and plausible pictures of the society. In chapter 24 of Acts, Paul goes before the Roman procurator of Judea, Antonius Felix. The episode with Felix is so replete with motifs of social mobility and ambiguity and issues pertaining to Judaism and Christianity as schools of self-mastery that it almost reads like a parody. Felix was a freedman of Claudius's mother, Antonia, and brother of Pallas the freedman who headed the imperial treasury under Claudius and rivaled Narcissus in wealth, power, and the scorn of the nobles (for example, Pliny, *Ep.* 8:6). Felix's first wife was the granddaughter of Antony and Cleopatra.[97] He later married Drusilla, daughter of Agrippa 1, the brother of the Aristobulus previously discussed. Thus for the audience of Paul's teaching, Acts chose an extremely successful freedman of the imperial household who was intimate with Augustus's "moral victory" over Antony, who married a Jew, and who had a keen interest in the teachings of Jewish sects. Not surprisingly, Paul discourses with Felix about "justice, self-mastery [enkrateia] and the judgment to come." Felix becomes alarmed upon hearing the message and sends Paul away, but he continues to have frequent discussions with him over the course of two years (24:25–26). The ongoing instruction by Paul seems to be curiously underplayed or forgotten by commentators.

New Testament scholars generally read this episode through the lens of Josephus's and especially Tacitus's portrayal of Felix: Owing to Felix' immoral character, Paul's mention of enkrateia struck his conscience and caused him to drive Paul away. This reading runs into problems, however, when one realizes that this is Josephus's and Tacitus's portrait of Felix, not Luke's. For Acts, Felix is an open-minded gentile with at least an intellectual interest in the new Jewish movement. His vice, like that of almost all officials under Roman rule, is that he expected bribes and that he was never moved to make a commitment to the new way. Josephus generally depicts Felix fairly positively for a Roman governor. He does claim that Felix, seeing Drusilla's beauty, conceived desire (*epithumia*) for her. He then persuaded Drusilla to leave her husband, king Azizus of Emesa, by sending a Cypriot named Atomos to woo her (*Ant.* 20.141–44). Josephus and Philo wrote at a time when the emperors, beginning with Augustus's legislation, put enormous pressure on the ruling class throughout the empire to maintain stable aristocratic family and lineage and, above all, to control their women. Josephus takes every opportunity to say that Jews are stricter about morals and marriage than anyone else and that they are harder on their women. Whatever Felix's character, Josephus would have told the story to make the point that the couple had transgressed the strict Jewish marriage laws (*Ant.* 20.143).

Tacitus says that Felix, "with all brutality and lust [*libido* = *epithumia*], ruled as a king with the mentality of a slave" (*Hist.* 5.9). As historians generally recognize, Tacitus thought that imperial freedmen could do no good and depicted the problems under Claudius as due to the evil influence of women and freedmen. Tacitus believed both classes to be unfit to govern because they were incapable of controlling their baser passions. There is no reason to think that the Felix of Acts is not genuinely interested in Paul's message about justice and self-mastery. Although this episode may not reveal anything about the historical Paul, it does show that it was plausible for readers in Luke's day to envisage a Jewish follower of Jesus teaching the message of self-mastery to a person like Felix. Ambitious and mobile people from ignoble backgrounds wanted to gain that inner power that was the mark of the ruling class.

If our modern mentality requires more evidence that self-mastery had a remarkable appeal to certain kinds of people in antiquity, then the testimony of the physician Galen should suffice. Galen's well known but often misunderstood remarks about Christians and Jews come from about one hundred years after Paul.[98] Galen stands as a valuable witness to the way that certain Jewish and Christian groups could present themselves to educated pagans. Galen moved in elite Roman and Greek circles, was steeped in Greek philosophy, and spoke as a disinterested outsider. His references to Jews and Christians—in his language the *schools* of Moses and Christ—come as examples that he pulls out of the air with no particular interest in saying anything either positive or negative about the two groups. When he wants to make the point that intellectual groups depend too much on untested beliefs, he lumps the schools of Moses and Christ together with the Greek philosophical schools to illustrate his point. This demonstrates that Philo's and Josephus's depictions of Judaism as a kind of philosophy could be plausible to the most educated and critical outsiders. If Galen found such a depiction plausible, then how much more so would the typically less cultured gentiles who heard Judaism presented as a school of self-mastery. In the second century, numerous Christian teachers and groups were describing Christianity as a philosophy and as the means to the most powerful self-mastery ever imagined to be practically possible for ordinary people. When the Christian propagandists called their ascetics athletes, they were self-consciously claiming victory in the public arena among competitive rituals of strength and endurance. These writers knew that many people like Galen watched intently for the latest achievements in this self-potential movement that endlessly elaborated the theme of control. In a famous passage, Galen writes, "For their contempt of death and of its sequel is patent to us every day, and likewise their restraint from intercourse. For they include not only men but also women who refrain from intercourse all through their lives; and they also number individuals who in self-discipline and self-control in matters of food and drink and in their keen pursuit of justice have attained a pitch not inferior to those who genuinely practice philosophy."[99]

The later Christian rhetoric of the new religion's uniqueness and qualitative difference from everything pagan obscures the obvious in Galen's remarks. He and these ascetic Christians are in full agreement about the ideal of subduing the passions. Both hold to basically the same view of the person and the same social and moral values. What differs are the traditional philosophical and Christian means for obtaining the ideal. Even here, however, it would be false to stress only differences. Although Galen thinks the Christians inferior for attaining mastery through moral exhortation, exemplary tales, and sheer will power rather than reasoned arguments, he nevertheless classes them as philosophical. Clearly Jews and Christians who proffered their teachings and practices as powerful ways to self-mastery found a ready audience among certain types of their contemporaries.

The ethic of self-mastery had deep roots in the organization of ancient Mediterranean society. There arose in Greece a class of intellectuals, philosophers, who articulated a powerful discourse of self-mastery. They created a systematic organization of knowledge and practices concerning self-mastery that came to serve the needs of various elite classes throughout the Mediterranean world. The Augustan revolution appropriated and employed this ethic to a degree hitherto unknown, using it for political and social control. Jewish writings from the early empire show that some Jews also adopted the ethic and made it into a means for interpreting Judaism to non-Jews. The Pauline issue of whether gentiles should be trained to perform certain works from the law and the caricature of gentiles as lacking self-mastery best make sense in light of this Jewish appropriation.

Granting that one of the letter's major themes concerns gentiles' inability to control their passions and desires, then understanding the ethic of self-mastery should aid one's reading of Romans. Moreover, the ethic provides the necessary context for elaborating a hypothesis about why Paul opposes works from the law as a solution to the plight of the gentiles and for showing how Romans constructs an alternative to the law as a means to gentile self-mastery. The fact, for example, that Rom 12:3 employs one of the two most important words for self-mastery, *sōphronein*, in introducing the so-called ethical part of the letter should have new significance in this light. This understanding provides a solution to the old problem of relating ethics and theology in Romans. The discussions of the law, God's impartial justice, Christ's faithfulness, the Abrahamic promise and heritage, freedom from and slavery to sin, the empowerments of the Spirit, and the proper attitude of believing gentiles to unbelieving Jews hold a heretofore unnoticed coherence in light of this context.

But in addition, I have wanted to formulate a historically plausible and humanly palpable approach to reading Romans. Augustine's reading of the letter through the themes of human agency versus divine grace and Luther's through individual dependence on God's grace versus dependence on the human institutions of the church will not work because they suppose readers in the letter already formed by the institutions and doctrines of orthodox Christianity. In contrast, I have shown that the issues of why non-Jews are mastered by passions, why God has permitted such a situation, and how the crucified but faithful Jew Jesus holds God's answer to gentile self-mastery are issues that could have gripped readers in Paul's time. The readers greeted in chapter 16 turn out to be exactly the type of people for whom the ethic of self-mastery was so vital. We as modern interpreters can arrive at a more deeply human understanding of ancient Jews and Christians through the social psychology of the ethic of self-mastery. Paul responded to these values and practices in a situation laden with religious and ethnic ambiguities. He attempted to resolve the ambiguities between Jews and godfearing gentiles and the larger question of Jews' relation to gentiles by interpreting the contemporary situation through a certain reading of the Jewish scriptures and of the story about Jesus Christ. Paul used Christ and scriptures to think about basic social and psychological realities.

Gentile Culture & God's Impartial Justice (1:18–2:16)

Since antiquity, interpreters have supposed the underlying myth of Romans 1–3 to be the story of the human fall in the Garden of Eden. But Paul intended—and his readers would have read—a quite different story in 1:18–32. The exchange of one myth for another in the reading of this text proved one of the crucial transformations as Romans became the primary scriptural carrier of the orthodox economy of salvation. What Christian exegesis came to read as the consequences of the fall of humanity in the Garden of Eden, Paul read as the corruption of the non-Jewish peoples. The first story explains how human nature got to be the way it is; the second concerns the religious and ethnic other of Jews, how the gentiles became alienated from God and from Israel. Human nature and ethnic other are quite differing subjects answering divergent kinds of questions.

Modern readers of Romans share a broad consensus about the function of Rom 1:18–32. It forms the first part of Paul's argument, concluding in 3:20, intended to demonstrate the sinfulness of humankind. Paul describes the problem so that he can announce the solution of righteousness by faith in Jesus Christ. Recently certain scholars have argued with force that if Paul meant to demonstrate universal sinfulness, he did not succeed in his task. E. P. Sanders has written that "Paul's case for universal sinfulness, as stated in 1:18–2:29, is not convincing: it is internally inconsistent and it rests on gross exaggeration."[1] Sanders and especially Heikki Räisänen have raised the criticisms of "internal inconsistency" and "gross exaggeration" in the sharpest way.[2]

Sanders rightly chides scholars for speaking of Paul's "empirical description": "The acceptance of Rom. 1:18–2:29 as an objective, inductive statement of the human condition, however, shows that we have become too accustomed to thinking of Paul as stating not only the truth of the gospel, but also the gospel truth."[3] For Sanders, 1:18–2:29 is a "gross exaggeration" because Paul argues that "everyone has been guilty of gross and heinous sins."[4] Sanders's statement of Paul's purpose certainly accords with traditional Western readings of Romans. Yet a modification of the traditional reading itself is needed.

In the debate over whether Paul's language constitutes empirical description, one side lauds the apostle's deep factual insight into the human condition, while the other side criticizes his lack of objectivity and his rhetorical exaggeration.[5] Both sides pose the question in an epistemologically naive way. Such facile talk of empirical description and inductive knowledge has been decisively discredited. These interpreters of Paul speak as if a person could by careful, objective observation give the bare facts about the human condition. The question, then, becomes, How successful was Paul in this enterprise? Any number of distinguished contemporary philosophers counter the assumptions of this approach. Hilary Putnam, for instance, writes:

> Any choice of a conceptual scheme presupposes values, and the choice
> of a scheme for describing ordinary interpersonal relations and social
> facts, not to mention thinking about one's own life plan, involves,
> among other things, one's *moral* values. One cannot choose a scheme
> which simply 'copies' the facts, because no conceptual scheme is a mere
> 'copy' of the world. The notion of truth itself depends for its content on
> our standards of rational acceptability, and these in turn rest on and presuppose our values. Put schematically and too briefly, I am saying that
> theory of truth presupposes theory of rationality which in turn presupposes our theory of the good. 'Theory of the good,' however, is not only
> programmatic, but is itself dependent upon assumptions about human
> nature, about society, about the universe (including theological and
> metaphysical assumptions.)[6]

Historians of early Christianity ought to be trying to understand the conceptual schemes and value systems that generated accounts like Rom 1:18–2:29 rather than asking whether it matches the facts. In this light, one can see the importance of comparing Paul's text to analogous accounts from his culture. The charge of exaggeration should be rephrased: would Paul's language have seemed an exaggeration in his own time? if so, by whom? and how would such language have functioned and been understood?

Räisänen and others have emphasized the contradiction between what Paul says about gentiles in chapters 1 and 2.[7] In chapter 1, the gentiles are all horrible sinners. In chapter 2, some gentiles keep the law. What Paul says about gentiles keeping the law in 2:14–15, 26–27 contradicts his argument about universal sinfulness. Räisänen has little trouble in showing the inadequacy of traditional attempts to reconcile the chapters. Recent studies have concluded that Paul argued inconsistently and poorly. In my view, however, these studies actually call into question the standard readings of 1:18–2:29. Clearly a reappraisal of the traditional readings of these texts is called for.

Decline of Civilization Narratives

In Greco-Roman antiquity, stories about the decline of civilization form part of the larger phenomenon of primitivism, which looked to humanity's distant past or beginnings in order to explain the present state of society.[8] Primitivism was a major characteristic of Greek and Roman thought in general. The vast majority of the sources emphasize that human life has degenerated from an ideal primitive past. The most important myth was Hesiod's age of golden men or golden age. The Israelite traditions and various Middle Eastern cultures possessed their own stories of a fall. In Jewish writers of the Greco-Roman world, accounts of Adam and Eve's transgression and civilization's subsequent decline were often colored by Greek primitivism and the Hesiodic myth.[9] This, for instance, is true of Josephus's account of the period from Adam to the flood (*Ant.* 1.34–79).[10] One misleads, therefore, to facilely contrast Jewish and Hellenistic positions on this subject or to assume the utter uniqueness of the Jewish view of the human condition. Unfortunately, commentators on Romans have been so preoccupied with the so-called Jewish background to 1:18–32 and the parallels in the Wisdom of Solomon that the larger phenomenon of fall stories has been all but overlooked. In fact, the commonly cited Jewish parallels ought to be viewed as peculiar versions of the larger phenomenon of ancient primitivism.

Decline narratives take a variety of forms but widely share a number of characteristics.[11] Accounts depict the earliest humans as living in accord with nature and the gods, in contrast to later ages and the present. People in this golden age lived on a sufficient supply of natural food. They were of high moral character and there was an absence of strife and dissension. The primordial people did not need clothes or arts and crafts and were in harmony with the gods and with the animals of the earth. Ancient writers usually relate the ensuing decline to the gods. Certain traditions associate the fall with the change of divine rule resulting from Zeus's defeat of Kronos;[12] others trace it to Zeus's punishment of Prometheus's treachery.[13] Plato says that humans fell into the present state of quarreling and injustice because Kronos ceased to watch over them and guide their destiny (*Laws* 713C ff).

The Absence of Adam

Tradition reads 1:18–3:19 as Paul's magisterial diagnosis of the human predicament. The empirical rebellion and depravity of Jews and non-Jews are symptomatic of an underlying brokenness or sin. Exposing this sin, according to the traditional reading, constitutes the real point of chapters 1–3. Interpreters can read Rom 1–3 in this way because they assume that the story of Adam and Eve's fall in Genesis 1–3 forms its underlying foundation. These Christian readers also assume that their reading of Genesis and its centrality to religious anthropology are true and obvious: Jews in Paul's time and before would have held the same understanding of Genesis.[14] Moreover, they suppose that this reading came naturally to all early Christian thinkers.

Although Romans and Gen 1–3 provided fertile ground for the elaboration of Christian systems of sin and salvation, these systems are not true to Romans in its first-century context. The supposition of the Adamic fall in Rom 1–3 allows a reading that supports such systems. The reading yields a certain view of the human predicament and doctrines about human nature: The Adamic flaw that Paul supposedly diagnoses in the Jews and gentiles of his day is universal and a necessary rather than contingent fact for each individual. The human plight resulting from this primordial fall can be corrected only by an equally decisive event that reverses its effects. Jesus Christ is the solution to the human problem. Paul in some sense did think Christ the solution to the human problem manifested in the way that the peoples of the earth lived. But Paul's scheme differs greatly from later systems.

Some contemporary scholars believe 1:18–32 to be constructed through allusions to the fall story in Genesis.[15] These attempts are profoundly unconvincing.[16] They fail because they assume the existence and utter obviousness of cultural codes that came centuries later. In Rom 5 and 1 Cor 15, Paul certainly sees Adam as the starting point for sin and death. But interpreters are mistaken when they jump from this to traditional assumptions about the meaning and role of Genesis 1–3. Why? First, the reading of Genesis that interpreters assume is transparent did not yet exist in Paul's time; second, Paul's explicit references to Adam seem to rule out the traditional understanding; third, the absence of the Adamic fall narrative becomes manifest in light of cultural codes and textual readings known to be contemporary with Paul.

John Levison has demonstrated the absence of the later Christian focus on Genesis 1–3:

> The thesis of this book can be stated negatively: the "motifs" of an "Adam speculation" or "Adam myth" which the last generation of scholars discerned in Early Judaism do not exist. This misconstrual of the

data is due to two factors. First, the use of early Jewish texts to provide background material for Paul's letters led to an unwarranted emphasis upon certain dominant Pauline motifs, such as "Adam: the Origin of Sin and Death," or "the presentation of the two Adam-men as contrasting, corresponding universal figures." This approach squeezed the early Jewish data into the mold of Pauline concepts and motifs—the *Tendenz* of Paul and not of individual early Jewish authors became the interpretative key for organizing the ideas of these various texts, leading to a distortion of the meaning of Adam in Early Judaism and a failure to recognize the diversity of interpretations.[17]

Jewish literature before 70 C.E. shows little interest in the effects of Adam's transgression. The Adamic fall does not serve as *the* explanation for *the* human predicament.

A survey of the texts commonly thought to support the traditional view actually belies that picture. The wisdom tradition represented by Ben Sira and the Wisdom of Solomon contains no references to the effects of Adam's transgression.[18] In fact, they want to emphasize that death constitutes a natural phenomenon and that God created humans mortal (*Sir* 17:1–2). As in Hesiod and many versions of Greek creation and fall stories, the mix of good and evil best serves human life in the world to which humans belong. In Wisdom, the very work that most scholars agree Paul echoes in Rom 1–2, Wisdom "protected Adam from transgression" (10:1).[19] The Christian apologist Theophilus of Antioch similarly exonerates Adam, blaming Cain for the spread of death (*Aut.* 2.29). For Philo, Adam was a kind of Stoic sage, the true world citizen who lived according to nature.[20] The curses resulting from his disobedience are not permanently inherent conditions but effects that occur whenever virtue disappears, and that are recoverable for any who choose life according to nature. Philo does, however, read a Greek philosophical anthropology into Genesis that will be a stimulus to later Christian exegesis. The war between body and soul, reason and the passions, the obedient and disobedient represents a discourse from Philo upon which later exegetes and theologians draw heavily. In striking contrast to later Christian interpretations, *Jubilees* exonerates Adam of guilt.[21] Adam continues to serve as true priest and righteous patriarch; he even leaves the garden voluntarily. A couple of decades after the Jewish war, Josephus wrote about Adam in his *Antiquities*. Josephus's Adam, because he listened to a woman, loses his ideal life in the garden but not immortality.[22] Josephus makes him a tragic figure and a lesson for all men.

Adam, as the first human, commits the first sin, and God punishes sin. But extant pre-70 Jewish literature does not make the leap to connect human sinfulness with primeval sin. Fourth Ezra and 2 Baruch, both post-70 writings, display a greater emphasis on the effects of Adam's transgression.[23] But this interest stems from a profound pessimism generated by the catastrophe to Judaism caused by the destruction of Jerusalem. Paul lived on the other side of this divide. The Judaism of 4 Ezra and Baruch would have been unimaginable to the apostle.

The Etiology of Israel and Not Israel

We lack evidence for a Jewish cultural text, a reading of Genesis, available to Paul and his readers that resembles the one traditionally thought to underlie Rom 1–3. Equally important, another way of reading Genesis did exist. Jews, not surprisingly, read Genesis as the story of a chosen nation emerging from among the other nations. For later Christian theology that made Christ the answer to the human problem, the truly vital plot arced from the fall in the garden across to the saving work of Christ. In spite of the enormous variety in Judaisms and of Jewish literature before 70, similarities exist in the treatments of Genesis and Adam. The garden typically appears as but one episode, and by no means the most decisive, in the larger narrative of Genesis. Jewish writings before 70 do not locate the origins of evil in the act of the first man and woman resulting in an ontological flaw which the whole race then inherited. Rather, they account for evil by means of primordial history that becomes ethnohistory, what late twentieth-century people might call cultural history.

Genesis 1–11 lends itself to being read as a series of cycles or ages of human decline ending with the age in which the reader lives. The history of the earth's various peoples explains why the reader lives in the conditions he or she does. Genesis explains how Israel came to differ from the other nations and why other peoples have often endangered Israel's existence. The Hesiodic myth of the so-called golden age and subsequent decline contributed to this way of reading Genesis 1–11 in the Hellenistic and Roman periods, although ancient Near Eastern accounts were crucial in the formation of the Hesiodic myth itself.[24] The main point of both Hesiod's narrative and Genesis is that humans must not presume to transcend their natural earthly existence.[25] In Genesis the attempt to "become like God" results in human life outside the garden. Many Jews read the story of Cain and of Cain's and Adam's descendants as a decline into evil that climaxes in the "sons of God," angelic beings who mate with human women.[26] As a result of this unlawful mixing of the divine and the human, God punishes the race with a flood. Chapter 10 presents a table of the nations, the gentile peoples, who descend from Noah. Jewish and then, later, Christian culture looked to Genesis 10 as the basis of all ethnography.[27] They read chapter 10 together with 11.[28] Once again humans tried to transcend the human sphere and reach to the heavens. Babel showed that, unlike the repentant descendants of Abraham, the various non-Jewish peoples with their own languages and cultures were founded upon rebellion against God.

Far from precipitating a dramatic fall, Adam, Philo explains, was better because he surpassed all who now live; each generation following grew worse as it added yet another remove from the original person (*Opif. Mund.* 140–41). Similarly, *Wisdom* summarizes Genesis as a gradual decline and series of evil generations in which wisdom preserves the future through righteous individuals (10:1–8). Wisdom "saved Adam from transgression and gave him the power to rule all things" (10:1–2). The writer blames the wickedness of the following generations, which ended in the flood on Cain (10:3–4). Abraham stands in contrast to the wicked nations who try to build the tower (10:5). After making Adam into Israel's first great and righteous patriarch, *Jubilees* employs a detailed account of the children and grandchildren of Noah and the nations descended from them in order to explain the current situation of Judea among the other nations. One of the crucial episodes in this decline of the human peoples shares a theme with the Hesiodic tradition: The human peoples sinned by dividing the earth into homelands (*Jub.* 8:8–9:15). The *Biblical Antiquities* falsely attributed to Philo, possibly dating from the first century C.E., passes over Adam with only a mention and tells a story of evil cultures in two stages. Cain is the first to build cities. After the flood, people live in peace until out of evil hearts they build the tower, and God scatters them into the nations of the earth. Only Abraham refuses to participate in the project. The story explains why the Jews are set over against all the other peoples. Josephus also tells the story in two stages: first, the evil of Cain and Cain's descendants leads to the flood (*Ant.* 1.69–100); second, in the period after the flood, humans ignore God and his commandments (1.110) and refuse to acknowledge that their blessings come from God and not themselves (1.111–13). When they build the tower out of hybris (cf. Rom 1:30), God makes them speak different languages and they disperse into the different peoples of the world without repenting. As he enumerates the world's peoples, Josephus, like Paul (Rom 1:14, 16; 2:9, 10), makes Greeks the representative gentiles, noting their insolence and imperialism (1.121).

These Jewish and Greek ethnic writers and their paradigmatic accounts of a decline from a primeval golden age to the current world situation provide the kind of information that Paul and the addressees implied in Rom 1:18–32 shared. As François Hartog writes,

> Between the narrator and his addressee there exists, as a precondition
> for communication, a whole collection of semantic, encyclopedic, and
> symbolic knowledge common to both sides. And it is precisely on the
> basis of this shared knowledge that the text can be developed and the
> addressee can decode the various utterances addressed to him. The
> interpretation of an utterance by the one to whom it is addressed
> demands from the latter not so much a decoding as a "calculation"
> which reconstructs the relationship between the utterance and a certain
> number of points of reference selected from the representations which
> the interlocutor shares, or thinks he shares, with the locutor.[29]

Paul addresses gentiles about the power of the gospel for Jews and Greeks. The
kinds of Jewish, Greek, and Latin writings discussed here allow the modern
reader to imagine part of the larger cultural code implied by Romans. Only
later, I am convinced, did the Christian reading of Romans obscure this code
with the Adamic myth as the paradigmatic narrative.

Except for Genesis 3–11, I am not claiming that Rom 1 draws on any particular decline of civilization narrative, either Jewish or Greek. Rather, Romans
supposes broadly shared cultural knowledge manifested in particular narratives. From the perspective of Christian theology, especially since Augustine
and especially in the West, it is striking that chapter 1 says nothing about
Adam. What has often seemed obvious since the fifth century was not at all
obvious in the first four centuries: the scheme—exalted original state-fall-
restoration—develops surprisingly late in extant Jewish and Christian
sources.[30] Chapter 1 does not describe or even allude to an initial act of disobedience as chapter 5 does. Even more, there is no original sin, prefall par-
adise, state of righteousness, or perfection. It is highly debatable whether any
of these are implied even in chapter 5. In fact, what Paul does say about Adam
in 1 Cor 15:45–49 seems to rule out the later fall/redemption scheme.[31] Christ
brings not a restoration of an ideal earlier state but a new and better state.

Sentences in the present tense bracket 1:18–32: the wrath of God is at
the present time revealed against all those who suppress the truth with their
unrighteousness (1:18), and the gentiles who have in the past fallen into a state
of great wickedness now not only do such evil things but also approve when
others do them (1:32 f.). Paul turns to an account of events in the past to
explain the current situation of those who have refused to recognize God and
instead worship idols in human and animal form.[32] Verses 21–31 describe how
idolatrous and vice-ridden gentile culture became the way it is now (that is,
Paul's time). Such peoples are without excuse and justly subject to God's punishment because God has revealed his true nature to them in the creation of the

world (1:20). An account of their past rejection of God follows this general statement. These people actually did at one time know God and still could know him. Similarly, the Jewish sources discussed above assume various degrees of human communion with God before the tower but then a more consistent turning away. They knew God but did not honor or thank him (1:21). Therefore, their very way of thinking changed (1:21–22, 28) as they turned to the worship of idols (1:23, 25). Adam did not have to deduce God's existence from the creation. He did not lose or pervert his knowledge of God and thereby succumb to sin, and God did not punish him by imposing servitude to passions and desires. Genesis depicts Adam as having a good relationship with God after leaving the garden (4:1, 3–7; cf. 16, 25–26; 5:1–5), and the Jewish sources take their cues from the text in their positive accounts of the first man. Adam and Eve did not fashion images of gods. Rather, Jewish sources associate the various sorts of idols enumerated in 1:23 with various gentile peoples.[33] In 1 Thess 1:9–10; 1 Cor 12:2, and Gal 4:8, Paul writes that his readers formerly served such dumb and lifeless idols.

The shape of 1:18–32 compared with that of 5:12–17 shows that the past turning away from God in 1:20–31 alludes to the gentiles, primarily in the period before the law. Chapter 5 maintains that all those who have lived after the Mosaic law share with Adam the distinction of transgressing God's specific commandments. People between Adam and Moses sinned and were evil, but their error was of a different sort: "Without the law there is no transgression" (4:15). Paul's basic assumption here is that God punished people before the law only in this life, whereas after the law the scales of justice will not be balanced until the last judgment. Those who turned to idols in chapter 1 gave up a basic understanding of god's nature, knowable through the creation, and were punished in this life. Nothing is said of them disobeying commandments, and even their vices are the result not of disobedience to commandments but of passions set out of control as a punishment for rejecting God. When, however, Paul makes his transition to the present-day heirs of these idolators in 1:32f., who live after Moses, he says that gentiles have known God's just requirement that such vices deserve death, supposing that, unlike their ancient ancestors, they live after Moses.[34] These idol worshipers still bear the punishment of enslavement to passions and desires given first to their ancestors but also face a coming judgment (2:1–11). The shape of the narrative implied in 1:18–32 reflects what Romans will labor much to depict as the gentile dilemma under the law. The narrative pattern of 1:18–32 simply does not fit the later Christian Adamic fall.

Chapter 1 argues that the idol-worshiping peoples now justly ("without excuse," 1:20) bear a punishment given to them in the past. The way Paul parallels verses 17 and 18, tying 18 to 17 with *gar* ('for,' 'because'), makes sense on this reading. He will argue that God has indeed made known his justice by demonstrating his impartiality toward all peoples. This demonstration of impartiality involves first justifying the gentiles and freeing them from this ancient sentence of bondage to passions and desires while consigning Jews temporarily also to sin so that the scales of justice might finally weigh in the favor of both. Thus the revelation of God's justice (1:17) is indeed tied to the revelation of God's anger (1:18f.). God punished these idolators by causing or allowing their decline into unnatural sexual practices (1:24–27) and antisocial vices (1:28–31). God allowed them to degenerate into every kind of vice that wreaks havoc with society. Three times the text describes God's "handing over" these peoples to punishments corresponding to their rejection of him.[35] At center, God punished the gentiles by allowing their passions and desires to become dominant, a loss of self-mastery. The Jewish history of the gentiles explains the contemporary judgment of moralists and philosophers about people. Paul describes not a timeless ontological truth but how certain humans created by God became the idolatrous and passion-dominated nations.

A comparison with the Wisdom of Solomon proves illuminating. Scholars agree either that Paul drew on this work in 1:18–2:15 or that he and the writer of Wisdom worked in similar traditions. As discussed above, Wisdom does not attribute evil in the world or human decline to Adam. Like Paul, the work attributes the beginning of vice to idolatry and emphasizes sexual evil: "The idea of idols was the beginning of gender and kinship error (*porneia*) . . . and the corruption of life; for they did not exist from the beginning" (14:12–13). Moreover, Wisdom finds the origins of idolatry in the actions of specific groups and individuals at historical points after the Garden of Eden. The work provides two examples of how idolatry arose. A grieving father made an image of his dead son, and later generations turned it into a cult (14:15–16). Then the custom gradually spread and became a law. Employing a so-called Euhemeristic explanation, Wisdom tells of other people who erected statues of a monarch to honor him in his absence. This too developed into an idol cult (14:17–21). As in Romans 1, a long list of the resulting vices—with a stress on sins that threaten marriage and sexual and gender roles—follows the account of the origins of idolatry (14:22–31). Wisdom's narrative of decline into idolatry and vice unquestionably refers to the non-Jewish peoples.

In recent years, it has been popular to argue that 1:23 contains an allusion to Israel's idolatry with the golden calf at Horeb from Ps 105:20 (LXX).[36] Typically such commentators also point out that Paul does not specifically call the idolators gentiles, and they claim allusion to the Adamic fall in order to argue that 1:18–32 indicts both Jews and gentiles of rejecting God. This account of chapter 1 goes with the currently most popular way of reading Romans as Paul's attempt to heal divisions between Jewish and gentile factions in the church at Rome.[37] This move to include Jews in "Paul's indictment of idolatry" depends almost entirely on the alleged allusion to Ps 105 together with an inattention to audience, argument, and context.

According to 1:23, the idol worshipers "exchanged the glory of the immortal God for the likeness of the image of a mortal human being and of birds and four-footed animals and reptiles." The Septuagint says that Israel made the image of a calf and "exchanged their glory for the likeness of a calf that eats grass."[38] Thus in Ps 105, the Israelites lost their glory, not God's glory, as in Romans.[39] Furthermore, the supposed allusion lies buried in a sentence that clearly refers to gentile practices and to a larger account of gentile decline. The Israelites did not make idols of human beings and reptiles as 1:23 says. Neither do Paul's letters present evidence that God enslaved Israel to passions and desires, as the closely linked verse 24 (dio, 'therefore') would require. Even if some imagined brilliant reader did see an allusion to Ps 105, it cannot have meant to this reader what modern scholars want it to mean. Certainly Paul and other Jews condemned Israelites for the times they lapsed into idolatry. The golden calf is an admonitory tale beloved by Jewish writers. Paul uses the story in this very way, saying that it was written as a warning to his readers (1 Cor 10:7, 11). One of Romans's central points is that God judges all impiety and sin impartially, whether committed by gentile or Jew. But a vague allusion to the golden calf incident would in no way support the claim that Jews have consistently failed to honor God and have instead instituted the worship of idols, the very claim being made about the idolators in 1:18–32.

Interpreters have not placed enough emphasis on God's action in 1:18–32. The passage pivots on God's punishment of the gentiles, a punishment of a quite particular character and one that has consequences for Greeks and other gentiles on both a broadly social and an intimately psychological level. "Handed over" (paredōke) evokes the metaphor of delivering a person into someone else's control or power but in the negative sense that the word very frequently had of handing someone over to be tortured or to be sent to prison, to the police, or to the courts of law. The section begins by talking of God's justice toward the ungodly and of his anger toward them. The specific illustration at the center of 1:18–32 is this handing over of the gentiles that has been in effect from some time in the indefinite past until the reader's present. Rather than into the hands of other people, however, God turned them over to what the ancients considered even crueler masters: "to the desires of their hearts leading to impurity so as to dishonor their bodies among themselves" (1:14); "to dishonorable passions" resulting in the practice of same sex love among both males and females (1:26); "to a base mind so as to do that which is wrong to do" (1:28). Paul separates the sexual sins from the other vices listed in 1:29–31 and adds more detail to the former, thus emphasizing the sexual or gender errors.[40] The vices listed are antisocial acts, habits, and dispositions.

This supposed description of gentile life reflects an ethnic caricature developed by certain Jews that draws on two major cultural codes, the ethic of self-mastery and a Jewish code of purity and pollution.[41] Jews manifested a common cultural milieu with peoples of analogous societies and others in the Greco-Roman world in representing outsiders as less pure and less self-controlled than themselves. These societies share a basic form that centers on the passing of property, power, and status through generations of selected men and on the excluding of women and other categories of men from control of this inheritance. The two codes represent mechanisms for effecting this way of organizing society.

The passage probably highlights gender sins because the two codes overlap and intersect at this point. A sociocultural system must work hard to exclude women from claims to property, power, and status based upon inheritance, as women, the childbearers, play such an obvious and indispensable role in intergenerational continuity.[42] The two codes subordinate women at the point where men and women meet for procreation and at childbirth. These codes have strongly shaped Paul's understanding of the social-moral and theological situation. God punished the non-Jewish peoples by afflicting them with a loss of self-mastery that became a disposition of their very beings. They were enslaved to "the passions of their hearts" (1:25) and to "dishonorable passions" (1:26). The result attributed in the first instance is "impurity consisting of dishonoring their bodies among themselves"; in the second instance, same sex (rather than natural) love, which 1:27 calls shameless, a word associated with gender pollution in Jewish writings. Thus among gentiles loss of self-mastery produced polluting behavior.

Same sex relations constitute a powerful example in the logic of these two codes because such relations can be viewed as gross transgressions of the way the codes would have social relations organized. Using the modern term *homosexuality* would invite serious misunderstanding because the concept implies many things about sex and gender that are utterly foreign to antiquity.[43] Romans 1:26–27 reads, "Their [that is, gentile: note the discourse of otherness] females exchanged their natural use for unnatural; in the same way, the males left the natural use of the female." In the ethic of self-mastery, "natural use of the female" means that a male penetrates a female in an act that signified the subordination of the woman and control by the man over her.[44] Thus the example first implies a confusion of gender that threatens the woman's status as inferior and the man's superiority. As discussed in chapter 2, cultures of the Greco-Roman world understood gender as a sliding scale and maleness as a prize obtained only through self-mastery. Similarly, ancient biological and moral models, unlike the modern idea of two sexes, were based on the idea of one sex but two genders.[45] From the Hippocratics and Aristotle to Galen, biologically and morally a woman was a failed, inferior, or weak version of a man. Writers object to male homoerotic acts because one partner must "play the part of the female." A man could fall into what Philo calls "the disease of femaleness" by losing his male self-mastery and being overcome with passions in "a woman-like way." This loss of the male gender is what Paul means by the "penalty" that such men "get back in their own persons" (1:27); this is something he could not and does not say about women.[46] In the discourse of self-mastery, such men "were burned up with their appetite for one another" (1:27).[47] As this ancient scheme could not conceive of any other possibility, writers speak of subordinate and superior partners, of one woman penetrating another, even in female homoerotic sex.[48] The example of homoerotic behavior, then, illustrates a subversion of both the male and female roles in the organization of that society.

Much has been written in recent years about codes of purity and pollution; this production was inspired by the valuable but inadequate insights of Mary Douglas's early writing.[49] She understands the code as a set of cognitive and social principles for categorizing and organizing the items of the world so as to avoid ambiguity and to create clear-cut boundaries. Thus an impure animal or human act is one that confuses clear categories. But in my view, to end the analysis by merely saying that systems of pollution and purity create order in this broad way is to mystify the problem.[50] The codes of purity and pollution in numerous societies, including the Greek, Roman, Egyptian, ancient Israelite, and second temple Jewish, were intrinsic to systems of animal sacrifice. The codes of purity regulated access to temples and cults, signifying who could participate as well as when and how.[51] The distinctions among classes of people thus established by the sacrificial systems turn out to be the most important social distinctions in the particular societies, for example, male/female, priest/layman, child/adult, elite/common, slave/free, native/foreign.

The most basic distinctions in the Jewish sacrificial system of the second temple period concern gender and priestly lineage.[52] The primary rule says that women can never perform sacrifices. Only males can attain the degree of purity necessary to wield the sacrificial knife. Furthermore, only hereditary priests could perform the sacrifices in the temple, although other Jewish men could perform certain sacrifices outside the temple. The system of purity and pollution sets the purifying, sacrificial blood of men over against the polluting, procreative blood of women, the blood of childbirth and menstruation being especially polluting and central to the way that sacrificial practices organized society. Many rules of pollution affected men and women equally, but in terms of overall effects on the society, the distinctions based on gender and related to procreation were most profound. The focus upon procreation is not surprising in light of the all-important role that it played in determining descent through male lineages. Access to the temple in Jerusalem thus mapped and indexed the social order. The high priest in a state of purity could enter all the way to the Holy of Holies; the ordinary priest (but not Levites) to the inner temple proper (Court of the Priests); Jewish men as far as the Court of the Israelites; women as far as the Court of the Women; gentiles not into the temple proper but only into a portion of the outer courtyard (Jos., *Bell.* 5.194–99, 227–37). Women, "during their impurity" (Jos., *Apion.* 2.102–05), menstruation, and childbirth (or the first stage of childbirth pollution), could not enter even the outer court, where gentiles could go. At the end of the period of birth pollution, forty days for a male child and eighty for a female, the mother was required to make expiatory and sin offerings (Lev 12:1–8; Lk 2:22–24). In this system, bearing a child involved a woman in a type of separation from God that could be cured only when a man who was of priestly lineage rendered the flesh and blood of an animal to God. The most basic distinctions of the sacrificial system center on gender and descent. As Nancy Jay and Howard Eilberg-Schwartz have shown, the system assures the lines of patrilineal descent necessary for a society based on a hereditary caste of men who are priests.[53] Comprehending this social order helps one to understand Paul because it makes sense of his (and other ancient Jews') hypersensitivity to gender errors and of why gentiles, conceived as the social and moral opposites of Jews, were characterized by gender errors. The very idea of people who confused the hierarchy of male and female and who were indiscriminate about sexual activity and thus lines of descent was a threat to the social order and to centuries of cultural values built around that order. Paul was not analytically aware of how his social system worked, for people in a society rarely obtain such distance and perspective. Rather, his reflexes about pollution and purity indicate that he inhabited the social system and its cultural values.

Paul may have been preoccupied with the holiness of gentiles because he assumed that the temple system would continue in the age to come and that gentiles who lived by what he considered a modicum of purity would establish a relation to the cult qua gentiles. The cultic law of the Hebrew Bible has provisions allowing for non-Israelites to participate in the cult and keep a certain level of purity.[54] Thus the cultic system envisioned in the priestly and Holiness sources has a conception of standards for non-Jews in relation to the cult built into it. Moreover, Lev 20:22–26 provides a justification for eliminating the native inhabitants from the land and links this explanation to Israel's separation from other peoples. The Canaanites practiced the polluting sexual abominations of chapters 18 and 20 and therefore deserve expulsion. The caricature of the gentile practicing sexual and gender abominations begins in the ideology of the priestly writer. Thus, a strong link exists between a cultic perspective focusing on purity and the temple and the discourse about gentiles. Gentiles did bring sacrificial offerings in Paul's time.[55] And gentile participation in the cult is a theme in so-called eschatological texts about gentiles.[56] (Paul thought that Jerusalem would play a central role in the eschatological drama to which his mission belonged.) Sexual and gender sins loom large in Paul's conception of and writings to gentiles because the religious system that he inhabited made anxiety about gender hierarchy a basic reflex.

All of Paul's letters, beginning with the earliest one extant, 1 Thessalonians, witness a concern for gentile purity:[57] "For this is what God wants, your holiness, that you abstain from kinship and gender error [*porneia*]; that each of you know how to possess his own wife [lit. "vessel"] in holiness and honor and not with passion of desire like the gentiles who do not know God" (4:3–5).[58] The complex of ideas here comes close to that in Rom 1:18–32. The passage combines the ethnic other (gentiles), ignorance of God, sexual or gender impurity, and loss of self-mastery due to passion and desire; moreover, it expresses anxiety that gentiles, because of their enslavement to passions, will not properly use their sexual property (wives). References to characteristic gentile impurity occur in Rom 1:24, 27 and to the audience's former impurity in 6:19, 21 (1:26–27 may also echo Lev 18:22). Although Romans employs the discourse of Jewish purity codes, the Greco-Roman discourse of self-mastery seems more basic to the discourse of Romans since it explains the impurity.

Rom 1:18–2:16 and the Hortatory Use of Decline Narratives

Fall stories and primitivism became important to ethics and hortatory literature partly through Hellenistic philosophy. The views of the person and society espoused by the Cynics, Stoics, and Epicureans relate to beliefs about ideal human life in earliest humankind.[59] All appealed to a time when people lived naturally, not yet corrupted by unnatural conventions that softened the individual's power to master the passions and appetites. The appeal Romans makes to nature (1:26–27) and other aspects of 1:18–32 may owe something to such philosophical uses of primitivism and would likely have shaped the perceptions of first-century readers. Aristotle's famous exhortation to take up the philosophical life, his *Protrepticus,* may have indirectly opened the way for protreptic appeals to primitive history.[60] There he asks the question first put to Pythagoras, of why God brought humans into existence (frg. 18, Düring). Humans were to live according to nature. Since the work was a very influential model for protreptic literature, its making a place for appeals to primitive history is significant. Posidonius discussed primeval humankind in his *Protrepticus,* employing an account that combined moral decay with technical progress.[61] Seneca, discussing Posidonius's views in letter 90, a hortatory letter, characterizes the earliest human age as a period of virtue, simplicity, and perfect fellowship between humans and the gods. This natural, perfect fellowship lasted until the advent of greed tore it apart.

As in Rom 1:21–22, 28, the practices of this deteriorated life sprang from corrupted reason (90.24). The result was a false wisdom (90.27–31; cf. Rom 1:22). True wisdom should have shown humans the nature of the gods and led to the suppression of human hybris (9.28). Seneca also connects perception of the divine with moral commands and virtuous life (90.34; cf. Rom 1:19 f.). Although such similarities should not be pressed too far, there is a clear genre similarity. Both Paul and Seneca employ decline of civilization narratives for hortatory purposes in protreptic letters.[62]

Paul's use of the decline story resembles Anacharsis letter 9.[63] Anacharsis was a Scythian prince who toured Greece in the sixth century B.C.E. Cynics and others developed him into an ideal model of the primitive or natural life and critic of Greek civilization. The Cynic letters of Anacharsis were written sometime before the second century B.C.E. Letter 9 is a protreptic letter purportedly urging King Croesus to give up his life of vice and luxury and to adopt the simple and virtuous life exemplified by the Scythians. The letter constitutes a call to the Cynic gospel and Cynic life.

The author opens by charging the Greek poets with telling untruths about the gods. They ascribed their pursuit of self-interest rather than of sharing to the gods. The earth was once the common possession of both the gods and humans. Humans, however, transgressed the law (*parēnomēsan*) by dividing the earth among themselves and the gods. The author says, "In return for these [that is, divisions of the earth into private precincts], the gods gave back fitting gifts: strife, pleasure and meanness of spirit." All of the evils afflicting humans come from these vices that the gods bestowed on people for their error. These evils include unnatural activities such as tilling the soil and waging war. Anacharsis continues the account of the fall state in the third person plural, describing the results of the vices given by the gods and the concomitant self-deceit. The style is antithetical: "For though they planted in great abundance, they harvested little, and though they worked at many crafts, their luxury was ephemeral. They sought the riches of the earth in various ways, and came to believe their digging a wonderful thing. They consider most happy the first man who discovered this little undertaking. They remain ignorant of their child-like self-deception."

Anacharsis concludes his account of human decline by turning to address Croesus directly: "I have heard that this evil which has fallen on most men has also fallen on you." In the remainder of the letter, Anacharsis both admonishes Croesus for his particular vice and positively urges him to follow the Cynic way. Anacharsis moves from a general description of the fallen state to direct admonition of Croesus, his epistolary audience. The admonition gets its point and force through the assertion that Croesus participates in this fallen state of civilized culture.

There is no evidence that Paul read or knew Anacharsis 9 or any other Hellenistic degeneration story, but, first, he had assimilated a basic pattern of hortatory discourse and, second, by reading 1:18–2:16 as such one can make better sense of its complexity and detail than does the traditional reading that has been so forcefully criticized.

Clearly Paul and the author of Anacharsis 9 have fundamentally different myths about humanity's fall. Quite possibly, the Hesiodic legends had affected the way that Jews told the Genesis narrative. Nevertheless, the narratives are varying accounts of the primeval decline of humankind. Paul differs most markedly in his tracing of human degeneracy to idolatry, while for Anacharsis decline resulted from humans attributing their selfish division of the earth to the gods in order to justify that division. The Jewish story forms an originary tale of Israel and the other peoples, and the issue of idolatry allowed Jews to differentiate their narratives from other stories. Paul stresses that all unrighteous people (1:18; 2:1) are answerable to the just anger of God. While the punishment of the gods plays a key role in Anacharsis, the letter lacks Paul's emphasis on the justness and inclusiveness of divine punishment. Paul wants to establish God's impartial treatment of both Jews and gentiles.

Although both Paul and Anacharsis presuppose a golden age, a Garden of Eden, neither makes anything of it, partly because both are interested only in the admonitory use of the narrative. Both fall narratives move to direct indictment of their respective epistolary audiences. They begin by asserting that human decline stemmed from false conceptions of the divine. For Paul, people rejected knowledge and worship of the one true God, lapsing into worship of creatures instead (1:18–21); for Anacharsis, humans divided the earth, which was meant to be shared by all, into private precincts owned by men and dedicated to specific gods: "Since they knew nothing of *koinonia* in anything, they ascribed their own evil to the gods."

In the next step, both explain that God or the gods punished people with measure for measure penalties corresponding to their errors. In both cases, the penalties are evil habits of behavior that cause hardship, misery, and social conflict. Anacharsis says that the gods gave fitting gifts in return (*theoi - - - - dōra preponta antedōrēsanto*) for human attempts to divide the earth. The gifts are antisocial vices that divide human society (*eris, hēdonē, mikropsychia*). These vices are in turn at the root of unnatural evils. Paul might have used tilling the soil to illustrate God's punishment of sin (Rom 8:19–22; cf. Gen 3:17–19), for the Hesiodic and Genesis stories have parallels in that respect, but other evils are more central for Romans as it constructs a picture of the gentile. He employs three periods to show that God's punishment of the wicked has corresponded to the crime.[64] Jewish and Greek sources widely assume that measure for measure retribution characterizes true justice.[65] Paul does not just illustrate gentile sin but claims that God deals with it justly (1:22–2:5) and impartially (2:6–16). God allowed those who replaced the glory (*doxa*) of God for idols to dishonor (*atimazesthai*) their bodies (22–24). Those who exchanged (*metēllazan*) the truth about God for a lie, God permitted to exchange (*metēllazan*) natural for unnatural sexual relations (25–27). People (28–32) who did not see fit (*ouk edokimasan*) to recognize God, God gave up to an unfit mind (*adokimon noun*). In each instance, the text emphasizes God's punishing activity (*paredōken ho theos*; 24, 26, 28) and his measure for measure justice.

Both Paul and the author in Anacharsis 9 conclude their accounts by suddenly ending their third person descriptions and addressing individuals in the second person singular. Both accuse this person of practicing the same kinds of evils just described in the account of humanity's decline. The admonition of Croesus combined with an exhortation for him to adopt a more natural way of life occupies the remainder of that letter. The "real" audience intended by the author of this letter was not, of course, Croesus but some unknown readers who the author thought might be open to the Cynic life. When Anacharsis admonishes Croesus for his soft life, he is actually admonishing readers in this audience.

Apostrophe of the Pretentious Gentile in 2:1-16

Paul's shorter apostrophe in 2:1–16 is readily identifiable as speech-in-character used in a hortatory way typical of the diatribe.[66] The teacher or writer in a diatribe will suddenly turn to address an imaginary interlocutor in the second person singular. Paul's use of *anthrōpe* ("O man!"), the indicting-accusatory statement, rhetorical questions, and several other stylistic features is typical of such apostrophes in the diatribe. These apostrophes often have a hortatory function. The teacher or writer characterizes a type of person in addressing the fictitious interlocutor and admonishes or rebukes him. The real objects of the admonition or rebuke, however, are people in the audience whose behavior corresponds to the vices or behavior typified in the characterization of the interlocutor. Paul's characterization in 2:1–5 is clearly recognizable as the "pretentious person" (*ho alazōn*); the one who hypocritically pretends to moral virtue and arrogantly criticizes others even though he does the same kind of things.[67] So Epictetus rebukes the hypocritical student of philosophy (*Diss.* 2.21.11–12; for other examples see chapter 1): "Man (*anthrōpe*), at home you have boxed a prize-fight with your slave, you have driven away your household along with your neighbours' peace; and now do you come to me with quietness, like a philosopher, and sitting down you judge me; how I interpret the reading of the text and the application . . .? You have come with a spirit of envy." There is absolutely no justification for reading 2:1–5 as Paul's attack on "the hypocrisy of the Jew." No one in the first century would have identified the *ho alazōn* with Judaism. That popular interpretation depends upon anachronistically reading later Christian characterizations of Jews as "hypocritical Pharisees" (see chapter 1). The text simply lacks anything to indicate that the person is a Jew. First-century readers might have recognized Paul's characterization of the pretentious person but they, like the students in Epictetus's classroom or the readers of Seneca's letters, would have understood that Paul was admonishing their pretentious attitudes and not thought that he was attacking Jews.

In spite of disclaimers to the contrary, readers usually construe Romans as a theological tractate. Just acknowledging epistolary features does not materially change the traditional ways of reading the letter. Thus interpreters typically treat 2:1–16 as a point in Paul's argument that all humans stand under the power of sin. Commentators then divide over whether Paul is trying to show that the Jews are included or whether he is still speaking of gentiles in 2:1–5 or whether the interlocutor represents humanity.[68] In this reductionistic reading, Paul's apostrophe in 2:1–5 becomes equivalent to the proposition that "even Jews are under the power of sin" or "all men, even those who think that they are morally good, are under the power of sin." But 2:1–5 is much more than a point in an argument or proposition about the doctrine of sin. It is a rich literary text and should not be reduced to a theological proposition. Some of those who have championed the new ecumenical reading, which emphasizes that 1:18–2:16 indicts all humans of sin, want to translate *ō anthrōpe* as "O human." Again, the theological aims of the interpreters have caused them to ignore the Greek language. The expression in 2:1 and 3 is a common, everyday form of address equivalent to "Hey, mister," "fellow," or "sir."

Paul's apostrophe so much resembles speech-in-character in the diatribe that one must begin by assuming that it functions similarly. The burden of proof lies with those who would deny that 2:1–5 functions as an admonition against pretension for the gentile readers encoded in the letter, whose (past) sinful condition Paul has represented in 1:18–32. At the very least, the text serves as a general admonition against pretentious judging that includes the letter's audience. Paul uses the same sort of diatribal apostrophes with the same characterization of pretentiousness in chapters 11 and 14, where they are unmistakably directed at the epistolary audience. After explicitly saying that he is directing his remarks to his gentile readers in 11:13, Paul addresses the personified olive shoot (that is, gentiles) in 11:17–24. He warns this person not to boast about gentile belief and Jewish unbelief. Boasting forms the hallmark of the *alazōn* in the Hellenistic ethological tradition.[69] Paul has the imaginary gentile interlocutor voice an objection that illustrates the nature of the boasting that the apostle wants to censure: "Branches [that is, Jews] were broken off so that I might be grafted on." Then Paul warns against arrogance (11:20). In chapter 14, Paul explicitly gives advice to his audience. In phraseology that re-echoes 2:1 and 3, Paul changes to the second person singular in 14:4 (*su ho krinon* cf. 2:1,3) and 14:10. All commentators agree that Paul directs these admonitions toward those believers in the audience who pretentiously judge others.

Just as the account of humanity's decline in Anacharsis 9 leads to the admonition of Croesus and the inclusion of him in the fallen human situation, so Paul's account in 1:18–32 leads to the admonition of his audience and inclusion of them in the problem of gentile rebellion against God. The peculiar rhetorical dynamic of 1:18–2:16 lies in the way the discourse creates a tension among the past, present, and possible futures of the gentile readers. In spite of having spent their past in an idolatrous and degenerate culture (1:21–31), for which they remain justly accountable (1:18, 32; 2:1–9), the God who is an impartial judge (2:6–16) patiently waits for gentile repentance (2:4–5). The same admonitory tension appears in 11:20–24, which warns the audience that as "unnatural branches," gentile believers stand only because of their faithfulness and God's kindness. Pretentiousness toward Jews could be the gentiles' downfall. God's delay in judgment of the world has meant an opportunity for the gentile mission even as Jews have disbelieved. Romans reminds gentiles that God's delay only means mercy if they are truly repentant and not presumptuous. In parallel language and style, both 2:6–11 and 11:20–24 stress that God expects the same standards from Jews and gentiles.[70] A new dimension does appear in chapter 11: God's impartial treatment of Jews and gentiles has implications for the way they view one another.

The use of "therefore" (*dio*) in 2:1 genuinely draws a conclusion from 1:18–32: "God justly condemns the idolatry and vice of the gentile world; *therefore* you, a gentile who has just emerged from that world, have no right to judge others as if you had attained some special status apart from your actual works (2:6–11); in fact, when you judge others you are manifesting a hybris, arrogance and pretentiousness [*hybristes, hyperēphanos, alazon*; 1:30] that characterizes gentile sin; you are doing the 'same kinds of things' [1:32; 2:1, 3] that I just described." Far from being an abrupt change of subject to "the hypocrisy of the Jews," 2:1 strongly ties together 1:18–32 and 2:1–16.[71] The apostrophe has two major functions. First, by using the imaginary interlocutor, Paul can criticize any readers who have presumptuous attitudes without directly accusing anyone of anything. Second, the technique dramatically represents the precariousness of the gentiles in the face of God's strict impartiality and the impending judgment. Beginning in 2:17 Paul will allow his readers to overhear a discussion between himself and a Jewish teacher about how to deal with this perilous situation of the non-Jewish peoples.

Recent interpreters have claimed that 1:18–2:16 describes and addresses humanity in general and not gentiles. They appeal to the appearance of "all" in 1:18; 2:1, 7. The language of 1:18–2:16, however, is quite precise. Paul does stress the universal criteria for and scope of God's judgment, but he also carefully delimits the address. The speech-in-character of 2:1–6, for instance, is not merely a general condemnation of those who judge others, although a misreading of *pas ho krinon* ("everyone who criticizes/judges") and an oversight of the continuities across the chapter division facilitate such a general reading. The *pas ho krinon* has a parenthetic quality which allows Paul to emphasize that the admonition implied in the characterization applies to all who fit the type (parenthetic as in, "Greetings, Nigel—and to all who celebrate with us tonight—and Nigel, I want to say . . ."). But what exactly is the type? The person here is not condemned simply for criticizing others but for criticizing others even though he does the same things they do. Furthermore, these things are not just any acts that one might choose to criticize but certain specified activities. Paul uses the demonstrative pronoun *toioutos* ("referring to what has been described in the preceding context"—W. Goodwin, *Greek Grammar* [Boston: Ginn, 1958], 86) in order to tie the characterization of 2:1–16 to the specific condemnation of the gentiles in 1:21–32. Verse 32 refers to the list of things that characterize idol worshipers with the expression *hoi ta toiauta prassontes* ("those who do such things"). Moreover, they not only "do such things" (*auta poiousin*), but they also agree with "those who do them" (*tois prassousin*). The language of 2:1–6 pegs the "man" as one who does exactly these things but thinks himself superior to his fellow idolators: "you do the same things" (*ta auta prasseis*). He ought to know that God condemns "those who do such things (*ta toiauta prassontas*), and in v. 3 the apostle reiterates, "Do you think, mister, that when you judge those who do such things (*tas toiauta prassontas*) and you do the same things (*poion auta*). . . ." There is nothing subtle about the man's identity. The text screams that he is one of those people who do the things enumerated in 1:26–31.

Now the traditional reader, armed with the assumption that Paul teaches a doctrine of universal depravity or original sin (of which Paul makes Jews the prime example), will easily sweep over 1:18–2:16 and conclude that 2:1–16 has included all humans in the indictment of idolators. But the text says just the opposite. The person of 2:1–16 is not any person or every person but precisely one of those people who could know the truth about God but who has suppressed the truth by worshipping images of humans and animals so that God decreed an enslavement to passion and desire, resulting in all those unnatural and antisocial activities. The logic of the text is the same as that of the following example: "All who practice child sacrifice have done evil. And you, Sir [anyone who], when you think yourself morally superior, you condemn yourself because you have been practicing child sacrifice." The man in 2:1–16 is just as certainly a morally and religiously pretentious gentile as the man in the example is a child sacrificer.

God's Delay of Judgment and Impartiality toward Jews and Greeks

An indicator of the interlocutor's (2:1–6) identity as a gentile comes when Paul urges him not to despise the "holding back" (*anochē*) and "patience" (*makrothymia*) of God that is meant to lead him to repentance (2:4). By ignoring the opportunity for repentance that God provides out of his goodness, the gentile is accumulating *thesaurizein*, God's righteous anger for the coming day of judgment. Sam K. Williams has discussed the meaning of God's *anochē* (RSV, "forbearance") in 3:25.[72] The same cluster of concepts revolving around God's "holding back" or "restraint" toward the gentiles occurs in 2:3–6. Following Williams's word-syntactical study and his proposed translations of phrases, 3:25–26a can be tentatively rendered thus: (Christ Jesus) "whom God regarded [or 'put forward'] as a means of expiation because of his [Christ's] faithfulness, in his blood, in order to manifest his [God's] righteousness

because of the passing over of previous sins due to God's restraint [*anochē*]."
Williams's exegesis has never been refuted, only ignored.

Williams has shown that the passage speaks about God overlooking gentile sin because of his "restraint" or "holding back." "Passing over" is not to be confused with forgiveness.[73] Rather, God has failed to punish gentiles fully for their sin in the past so that their liability for punishment has accumulated. A long and rich tradition to this conception appears in the Hebrew Bible and later Jewish literature. The words *anochē* and *anechein* frequently mean not forbearance in a positive sense of forgiveness but God's delaying of punishment. Second Macc 6:14 sums up this line of thought:

> I urge those reading this book not to be depressed by such disasters,
> but to realize that these punishments are not for the destruction but
> for the discipline [*paideia*] of our people [that is, Jews]. For not to let
> the ungodly alone for a long time, but to punish them immediately, is
> a sign of great kindness. For with the other nations [gentiles], the Lord
> patiently (*makrothymein*) holds back from punishing them until they
> have attained the full measure of their sins; but he does not see fit to
> deal this way with us, in order that he may not take vengeance on us
> later when our sins have reached their height (*telos*).[74] Therefore he
> never takes away his mercy from us; though he disciplines us with
> disasters, he does not forsake his own people.

God shows his goodness toward Israel by meting out punishment now so that his wrath does not accumulate. But for the gentile peoples, who have entirely rejected him, he patiently overlooks their sin in anticipation of a horrible day of reckoning. Paul expresses the same idea in 1 Cor 11:32: "But when we are judged by the Lord, we are disciplined [*paideuein*], so that we may not be condemned with the world." Romans makes the same assumptions about God's judgment as 2 Maccabees and other Jewish writings but reinterprets these in light of Paul's beliefs about Jesus Christ. In fact, these assumptions form the framework for Paul's beliefs about Jesus.

God will sometime in the future have a great day of judgment in which he will justly mete out reward and punishment to Israel and the other peoples collectively and will also judge individual lives within those collectives. This idea of a judgment day addresses the problem of how those who are wicked (for example, attack, kill, and oppress others, including those who are good) can be allowed to flourish while the good often suffer and live unrewarded. Ancient Jewish writings tend to think of this in collective and concrete terms remote from modern Christian writing about "Jewish beliefs": for example, Babylon and Rome attacked and ravaged Judea. Paul also thinks collectively and concretely in speaking of Jews and Greeks (1:16; 2:10). The collective and the individual do not exclude one another. Both Jewish and Greek writers asked the question Why does God delay punishing the wicked? Plutarch wrote a treatise on the subject.[75] Jews and Greeks gave similar answers. Like other writers, Paul sees two meanings in God's delay, one positive and one negative. For those who open themselves to God's guidance, delay is an opportunity for repentance, atonement, and training. Jews believed that they were attempting to be of this category most of the time. In punishing little by little, God warned those who accepted him and disciplined them as time went on toward the final reckoning. But those who, like the gentile peoples of 1:18–32, refuse to acknowledge God have, since the coming of the Mosaic law, accumulated a huge list of evils for punishment.

In light of God's mercy, his *anochē* in the present is an opportunity for gentiles to repent (2:4). Delay for the sake of providing the gentiles an opportunity to repent forms a significant theme in Jewish writings.[76] This belief forms the basis for Paul's use of the delay motif in 2:4–5 and 3:25–26, and the relation between the delay for the gentiles and the moment of Israel's salvation emerges as the crucial question of chapters 9–11. From another perspective, however, God's patience means that arrogant and unrepentant gentiles are "storing up wrath" (2:5). In 3:25–26, Paul will explain that God has regarded the death of Jesus Christ as an expiation or propitiation for the sins that he has passed over. Paul assumes what is central to the Hebrew Bible and to every known form of Judaism, namely, that Israel has always had means of atonement so that her sins have not been passed over and stored up but forgiven. Paul goes on to make the key affirmation that God will judge the Jew first and also the gentile without partiality, on the basis of works (2:6–11). The concept of impartiality does not negate God's covenant of atonement with Israel. Rather it affirms it: "The doers of the law will be justified" (2:13).

In theory (2:6–16), Jews and the other nations have an equal chance to be righteous before God. Paul's discussion, however, suggests that the gentiles trapped in bondage to passions and desires stand so hopelessly behind that the fictitious gentile in 2:1–16 inhabits an extremely precarious situation. God's justice seems to require a further act of mercy toward the gentiles if the overall course of the world's history is not to seem unfair toward the non-Jewish peoples. That this is indeed Paul's line of thought appears clearly in 3:21–33 and especially in 3:25–26, where he refers back to 2:4; the accumulated sins of the gentiles (1:21–32) that God has held back from punishing. In Paul's story, Jesus Christ means a special twist to the theme of God's delay in judging that will bring about justice for all.

The reading I have urged leads to an identification of genre. Rom 1:18–32 represents a protreptic speech that on one level directs itself to the imaginary gentile of 2:1f. and on another to the letter's larger encoded audience. Protrepsis is a discourse that urges its audience to leave one way of life and to take up another. Aristotle, Posidonius, Seneca, Maximus of Tyre (Or. 36), and Anacharsis 9 used protrepsis to appeal to decline of civilization narratives in order to represent the moral condition of their readers. One need only look at 1 Thess 1:9–10 to see that 1:18–2:16 echoes Paul's missionary preaching. There he summarizes his initial message and its reception: "How you turned to God from idols so as to serve the living and true god, and to await his son from heaven, whom he raised from the dead, Jesus who saves us from the anger which is coming." As in Romans, one finds themes of gentile idolatry versus service to the true god and the impending day of judgment. Rom 1–2 notably lacks reference to Jesus until 2:16, which relates how God will judge according to Paul's gospel and "by means of Jesus Christ." Romans strategically leaves Jesus' role for the discussion (2:17f.) that Paul will have with a Jewish teacher who takes a different approach to gentiles than the one Paul will advocate. 1:18–2:15 provides a piece of common ground regarding gentiles in Paul's discussion with the other Jewish teacher.

To recapitulate, the first half of 1:18–2:16 reflects not the Adamic fall but a Jewish account of human degeneration into the non-Jewish peoples. When these people refused to acknowledge God, he exercised his measure for measure justice by causing enslavement to their own passions and desires that in turn led to gentile impurity and rampant antisocial vices. Chapter 1 emphasizes loss of self-mastery and gender sins. These conditions still mark gentile life, which is now even more precarious as the record of gentile sin accumulates for the coming judgment of God. In 1:18–2:16, Paul pursues a rhetorical strategy that parallels Anacharsis 9. The decline of civilization narrative serves an admonitory function that comes to fruition with the address to the gentile in 2:1–16. Indirectly, Paul warns his gentile readers that they stand acceptable in God's sight only through repentance and illustrates the extreme difficulty of the gentile situation. God is just and therefore impartial. He punishes and rewards both Jews and gentiles on the basis of their works. This admonition parallels Paul's censure of the arrogance of believing gentiles toward Jews in 11:13–32, both formally and functionally. The narrative of gentile degeneration into vice and the warning that the unrepentant gentile is storing up wrath for the day of reckoning anticipate 3:21–26. There the apostle explains that God has manifested his righteousness by regarding Jesus Christ as a solution to the sin of the gentile world that he passed over and allowed to accumulate.

The first two chapters of Romans speak of Jews and gentiles as peoples and not in abstract-individual-universal terms. Salvation does not concern a universal question about human nature. These chapters do not treat the philosophical question of the human condition or the root sin. Instead of an individual-universal perspective of the human essence, Paul's perspective is collective and historical. This kind of discourse can be found in the Hebrew Bible, in other Jewish literature, and in Greek and Roman ethnographers and historians. Israel has a certain basic relation to God by virtue of the covenants. The gentiles have another relation. Both peoples possess a history over which God rules and judges. Salvation is not one thing in a narrowly predefined sense—"restoration of the image of God lost in the garden of Eden" or "God's justifying grace which destroys human self-assertion and creates openness to life." Salvation is salvation from God's anger when individuals and peoples deserve that anger. For Paul, God's wrath, which had long and justly been stored up against the gentiles, was an obvious and acute problem. Paul thought that God was at present also angry with Israel but for different reasons (chapters 9–11). Both peoples need salvation from God's wrath. Rom 1:18–2:16 is not about sin in general or the human condition but about the gentile situation in light of God's impartial judging of both Jews and non-Jews.

The reader should not be tempted by the perspectives of modern abstract individualism: Paul is not saying that every gentile (or every human person) first knows God and then turns away to idolatry and immortality.[77] It has been one of the hermeneutical moves of post-Augustinian and especially post-Reformation interpretation to "de-literalize" and universalize Rom 1–2. This was accomplished by psychologizing: for example, Every human person through self-love sets up himself or herself (or his or her loves or religion or social groups) as an idol in place of God. Rather, the peoples who became the gentile nations knew God and rejected that knowledge until ignorance of the truth became habituated in both their thought and their forms of life. Paul also provides a theological-psychological explanation through the discourse of the passions and self-mastery. The gentile situation is a punishment by God under which he condemns Greeks and barbarians to slavery under the tyranny of passions and desires.

Commentators correctly suppose that here, as so often elsewhere, biblical narratives lie behind Paul's text. The story, however, does not tell about an act of disobedience that plunged the whole race into sin and darkness. The focus on Adam's sin occurred when Christian thinkers, especially stimulated by controversies about the relation between Christ's nature, human nature, and salvation, developed philosophical anthropologies. Then it became important to describe human nature before and after the fall. Paul's perspective, however, is not philosophical anthropology, the human essence, but what moderns would call ethnic cultural stereotype.

Knowledge and Accountability

The much-disputed and crucial question of whether Rom 1–2 contains a doctrine of natural law must be approached with nuance and caution. Roman Catholic scholars (who usually do find the doctrine) and Protestants (who usually do not) have put much passion into the debate, often assuming that a body of weighty laws was at stake. One side fears the loss of moral authority; the other ecclesiastical tyranny and an undermining of scriptural authority. Both sides have assumed that the awesome natural law tradition that emerged in the medieval West could be traced back to the founders of Stoicism and was therefore available to Paul. The institutional authorization given to natural law doctrine in later times does not equip one to grasp the chaotic, contradictory, and often inchoate state of natural law theory in Paul's time and before.

From the pre-Socratics to the Stoics and in Paul's own time there was no agreement about what was meant by *nomos* (law) and *phusis* (nature).[78] The philosophical schools debated vigorously over just these concepts and often came up with contradictory conceptions. Many agreed that one had to look to undomesticated plants and animals to determine what was natural for humans.[79] Bees proved that natural behavior was inherently cooperative and harmonious; lions that natural behavior was competitive and violent. The Stoics first articulated a theory of natural law, but their teaching has been misrepresented.[80] For the Stoics, the goal of life was to live by a set of perfectly consistent principles variously called the Law of Nature, the Common Law, Right Reason, or the will of Zeus.[81] Humans exist to obey these principles and can do so because individuals possess reason that connects them to the Reason which governs the universe according to the perfect principles. By contemplating the world, one can grasp these principles and perfect one's reason until, becoming a sage, one's mind is fully coherent with God's mind.

Thus far the account makes it seem that the Stoics would have been able to set down a body of fixed rules or laws of morality. But this is false because the early, or orthodox, Stoics emphasized that "correct acts" will vary according to circumstances and cannot be determined by fixed rules.[82] This is partly because humans can never know the determined course of events in the universe. The sage's appropriation of the laws of nature takes the form of an insight that allows him to act in harmony with Nature or Reason in particular circumstances. In fact, the Stoics emphasized that following the laws of Nature would tend to make one act counter to the normal laws or conventions of society.[83] Thus the classical Stoic theory of natural law cannot be put to the conservative political and social uses that natural law advocates usually seek. The early Stoics said that following the laws of nature would mean doing away with the family and kinship, slavery, and distinctions between men and women and allowing free sex, including same sex love and even incest, and would lead to the conclusion that there was nothing intrinsically wrong with eating human flesh.[84]

The first two thinkers known to have understood natural law as a conservative body of fixed moral rules are Cicero and Paul's Jewish contemporary Philo.[85] Both drew on later developments in Stoic thought, although it is unclear whether they or later Stoics first made natural law into fixed rules. It is unlikely that Paul knew Philo's writings, and Philo's developments seem to have been largely unprecedented.[86] In Cicero, these natural laws both substantively and functionally turn out to be nearly the opposite of the original Stoic conception. Chrysippus said that all existing laws and constitutions were erroneous (*hēmartēsthai*; *SVF* 3.324) and needed reform.[87] For Cicero, natural law confirmed traditional social, moral, and political standards as understood by elite classes. Self-evident and supposedly universal rules among the "civilized" like the prohibitions of cannibalism, incest, and desertion on the battlefield constituted natural laws.[88]

Natural law theories can be understood only historically in the context of the social and political aims of those who advocated them. The early Stoics were reformers advocating an egalitarian society without slavery and the social hierarchies of the traditional polis.[89] They rejected the traditional ethic of self-mastery with reason ruling over the passions just as they did the rule of monarchs.[90] Both the soul and the state should have an egalitarian harmony of their constituent parts. The chief figures of the middle Stoa, Cicero's mentor Panaetius and Posidonius, reshaped Stoicism so as to accommodate it to Roman rule.[91] In psychology, they brought back reason's mastery over the passions and developed theories to support Rome's conquests and domination. Rome already had an extensive legal tradition and now Rome had to adjust its law to the rule of numerous foreign nations. By modifying the old Stoic theory with fixed rules that turn out to be traditional elite morals, Cicero created or adapted from Panaetius a conception that gave great authority to Rome's international rule and bequeathed the concept to the West.[92] Although "the natural" remained as incoherent as ever, appeal could be made to the law of all humans. In Cicero's *De Republica,* Laelius articulates the central principle of this conception: The basic law of nature is that the stronger should rule the weaker (3:23–33; Lact. *Inst.* 6.8.6–9). Because I have argued that Paul's words about men and women leaving the natural use of each other means overturning the "natural" hierarchy of male dominating female, Paul might seem to have known Cicero. Cicero, however, was merely using one of the oldest and most persistent ideas of what nature taught in order to justify Rome's imperialism.[93] As early as Plato's *Gorgias,* Callicles invokes nature to show that the strong should rule over the weak (483A7–484C3).

There are problems, then, in asking whether Romans appeals to natural law. The example of Callicles points to the fact that writings frequently appeal to nature without having any conception of natural law in the sense that a number of fixed, universally applicable rules could be derived from observing nature. In fact, when ancients appealed to nature they often meant merely that something was appropriate or inappropriate, just as today we often use the term without implying a theory of natural law (for example, "It's natural for John to react so strongly in such circumstances"). Moreover, the orthodox Stoics held a conception of nature's laws that denied they could be fixed rules. Rather, people could develop the capacity to discern what course of action would conform to the patterns of Nature in particular circumstances. This approach emphasizes the complexity and contextual nature of moral choice and the limited knowledge of human observers.

The possible evidence for Paul's use of natural law consists of his statements describing specific actions as natural or unnatural, the statement in 1:32 that gentiles know God's decree, and 2:14–15, which speaks of gentiles "doing the things of the law by nature" and "being a law in [or "among"] themselves" and "showing the work of the law written in their hearts." The claim that gentiles could have learned of God's true nature through perceiving the creation (1:18–20) is natural revelation rather than natural law, but Paul's belief in such knowledge makes it more likely that he believes in natural law.

Paul does not develop a body of moral principles for his gentile congregations based on natural law. If he believed in natural law as Cicero and the later church did, this is precisely what one would expect him to do for his communities of non-Jews. But he rarely appeals to nature and uses other means and authorities in developing an ethic, including the Jewish law.[94] He does, however, advocate a kind of moral discernment based on abilities given by God that seems open to moral criteria of all sorts (for example, Rom 12:2–21; Phil 1:9–10). Thus it is conceivable that he held to some conception of natural law resembling the early Stoic theory. In light of his failure to use natural laws, many scholars have seen Paul employing an appeal to natural knowledge in Rom 1–2 only in a negative way to prove that gentiles are morally knowledgeable and therefore responsible for sin.

Second, if Paul does appeal to natural law in the noted passages, natural law remains a woefully insufficient way of explaining what he says elsewhere about the relation of gentiles to the law. The evidence that Paul spoke of gentiles as being subject to the law of Moses is overwhelming, which means a doctrine of natural law seems irrelevant. Paul depicts the gentile readers of the letter as having been under the law of Moses before coming to Christ. In 6:14–15, baptized into Christ, they are now not under law but under grace. They have also died to the law that formerly held them (7:4–6). Two things make certain the identity of law here as the law of Moses. Verse 2:17 speaks of a Jew himself following and teaching the law with allusions to the Ten Commandments, and from that point onward this identity must be constantly supposed if one allows any continuity to the discourse. Thus, 3:21 casually speaks of the "law and the prophets." Two verses earlier Paul writes, "What the law says, it says to those in the law . . . so that the whole world might be subject to God." Chapter 7 gives as an example of a commandment from this law the tenth commandment (7:7–8). Only 2:12 may create a problem for reading *law* consistently as the law of Moses throughout the letter, but this anomaly is merely apparent (see chapter 4). The case for gentiles being under the law is clear in Galatians. The arguments of Howard, Sanders, and Hübner are conclusive.[95] Paul so obviously places gentiles in a relation to the Jewish law that one has difficulty imagining a role for the law of nature.

Third, the idea that gentiles have always been held responsible to a law of nature contradicts the narrative about human history that 1:18–32 implies (see chapter 5). Rom 5:13–14 insists that those who lived between Adam and the Mosaic law did not have their sin counted because there was no law. The profound change caused by the coming of the law constitutes one of the letter's persistent themes (3:20; 4:15; 5:20; chap. 7). Rom 1:20–21, 25, and 28 speak of a historical time when the gentile peoples knew God but rejected that knowledge (thus the expression "gentiles who do not know God"; 1 Thess 4:5; 2 Thess 1:8; Gal 4:8; 1 Cor 1:21). Chapter 1 does not say that gentiles knew that their actions were against God's law and that he therefore punished them, but that God punished them by means of sinful behavior for failing to acknowledge him and for falling into foolish ignorance. When the apostle mentions gentile awareness of God's condemnation (1:32f.), he tellingly slips into the present tense (2:1f), pointing to contemporary gentiles who unambiguously live after Moses. Paul understands the gentiles as cultures fundamentally marked by a past refusal to acknowledge the true God and yet somehow aware of their error since the giving of the Jewish law. Traditional readings see Paul appealing to natural law in order to make gentiles accountable, and yet such a view flies squarely in the face of Paul's own claims about the period before Moses. Thus, seeing an appeal to natural law in Romans remains dubious on the most basic level because Paul's own account of gentile history excludes it.

Paul's manner of narrative discourse suggests a solution to the problem of law in Romans. In the way Christian interpretation has shaped Romans, chapters 1–3 aim to show that every human individual, unless saved in Christ, has existed in a state of sinful separation from God. But another reading was more likely for first-century readers. The letter does not seek to show that every individual human has been a sinner. Commentators have long puzzled over the explicit claim of 2:14–15, 26–27 that some gentiles fulfill the law. Attempting to find readings that get around "the plain sense of the text" has become a minor industry.[96] Romans is not about salvation in any traditional Christian sense. Paul is literally writing about Jews and Greeks, and the "eschatological sinfulness of all" means these peoples as collectives, not as individuals (see chapter 6). The fact that everyone sins in the ordinary sense is not Paul's concern. If this account holds, Rom 1–2 does not invoke natural law to show that every non-Jew also has had access to God's law and therefore stands guilty of sin. Rather than an account of timeless human nature, Romans assumes a certain reading of Genesis and the rest of the Pentatuch that makes gentiles both ignorant of God and at least potentially knowledgeable of the Mosaic law.

The Hebrew Bible, the LXX, and most later Jewish writings simply assume that the non-Jewish peoples know what God expects *of them* and are responsible for their disobedience. In texts like Ps 48:1 (LXX), the reader hears a "universal" address: "Hear this, all the nations [ta ethnē]; give ear all inhabitants of the earth." Similarly, Psalm 100 addresses all the nations, calling on them to praise the Lord. Time after time in the Hebrew scriptures God holds gentile nations responsible for their actions and punishes them. God punishes the king of Assyria for arrogant boasting (Isa 10:12–13) and the king of Babylon for aspiring to divinity and violence (Isa 14:3–15, 22–23); he calls to account Nebuchadnezzar for not practicing righteousness (Dan 4:27) and Pharaoh for failing to recognize God as creator (Ez 29:3, 9–10). In Amos 6, gentile nations are punished for transgressing God's laws (1:3,13; 2:1). The whole book of Jonah hangs on the explicit premise that God's standards of justice apply to all (see 3:1–10). Leviticus 18 assumes that the gentile inhabitants of the land bear responsibility for their sexual transgressions. A Jew needed only knowledge of the scriptures to assume that gentiles were responsible to the law.

Some Jews equated this knowledge of God's law by gentiles with the general moral sense that they saw among gentiles.[97] Some explained such knowledge as owing to commandments given to Noah for all humans and subsequently included in the Torah of Moses, although this explanation may not go back to Paul's time.[98] Philo appeals to and may have largely created the concept of a universal law of nature that was made into a theological and exegetical cornerstone by Origen.[99] With or without explanations, many Jewish writings assume that the law of Moses was given publicly and continued to be a publicly available body of teachings. Paul assumes this when he says that gentiles in his day know God's moral demands and that some gentiles keep the law. Passages like Deut 4:6–8 made natural law superfluous for Jews unless they wanted, like Philo, to prove the congruence of Greek and Jewish wisdom: "Keep them and do them; for that will be your wisdom and your understanding in the sight of the peoples, who, when they hear all these statutes, will say, 'surely this great nation is a wise and understanding people.'"

Although much later than Paul and not a direct witness to first-century forms of Judaism, so-called Rabbinic literature emphasizes the public nature of Torah and the gentile rejection of it. One account (*Mek. Bahodesh* 1) stresses that Torah was given openly and freely in a public place rather than in the land of Israel so that Israel could not say that the other peoples had no share in the law and gentiles might be responsible to it. The text explains the verse "They have not known his commandments" (Ps 147:20) with "They were not willing to accept them." Like Romans, Rabbinic texts can assert both that the Torah is continually available to all of humanity and that the gentiles refuse to acknowledge and follow it.

Jewish literature from the second temple period widely supports the same assumptions as Paul about gentile access to the law and gentile responsibility. The *Sibylline Oracles* predicts the destruction of the Romans due to their injustice, arrogance, homoerotic acts, and greed (3.182–90). It condemns the Greeks and several other nations for idolatry and for "transgressing the holy law of immortal God" (599–600). Again, a Jewish writer holds gentiles responsible and assumes that they can or do know the law. Again, it would be wrong to force a theory of natural law upon the third *Sibyl*.

Such writers as Aristobulus (Alexandria, second century B.C.E.), Eupolemus (Jerusalem, second century B.C.E.), Philo, and Josephus illustrate another way in which some Jews explained the universal knowledge of God's law. They depict Moses as the original lawgiver and source of gentile wisdom and law,[100] a claim that was known and even plausible to some Greeks (see chapter 2). Christian apologists from the second century onward also adopted this claim. The complex and intensive interaction among peoples in Hellenistic and early imperial times produced a major cultural debate about which people was oldest and which law and wisdom was the source of all others. The Jewish claims in this debate are an essential assumption in Paul's view of the gentile cultures, their culpability, knowledge of the law, and the fact that they sometimes do behave as righteous gentiles in accordance with the law (2:12–16, 26–29). In supposing the law of his own people to be the foundation of truth and reality imperfectly mirrored in other cultures, Paul has entered the larger transcultural exchange of the ancient Mediterranean world.

The Greek ethnological writers were the first to set forth a pan-Greek theory of cultural borrowing and diffusion.[101] From the logographers and Herodotus onward, Greek writers tried to show that barbarians did not understand their own histories and thus should be corrected by Greek history.[102] As Greeks assimilated barbarians to their Greek master narrative, so Jews assimilated gentiles to their master narrative. Hellenized people did not simply capitulate to Greek claims, relinquishing their own identities. Xanthus, a contemporary of Herodotus, set out a pan-Lydian theory. Around 300 B.C.E., Hecataeus of Abdera published his history of Egypt, which held that civilization, including even Greek religion, went back to Egyptian sources. Manetho in turn used Hecataeus as a source for his Egyptian history. Philo of Byblus made similar claims for the Phoenicians. Artapanus, Pseudo-Eupolemus, Pseudo-Hecataeus, Eupolemus, Aristobulus, Philo, and Josephus are Jewish writers known to have claimed Jewish origins for civilization and the truth in gentile wisdom. The most likely explanation for Paul's assumption that gentiles can know the truth about God and are morally responsible to the law comes from a commonsense reading of the Hebrew scriptures and the long-established claims that the gentiles derived their knowledge of righteousness from the Jews. Rom 1–3 treats some such explanation as a basic assumption shared between writer and audience. The letter depicts the gentile followers of Christ in Rome as people who know and accept the Jewish master narrative.

Two additional considerations help to explain the strength of the letter's emphasis on gentile knowledge of the Mosaic law. First, most of Paul's converts and potential converts were probably gentiles who already had established an interest in and knowledge of Judaism. Thus some knowledge of the law on the part of gentiles was a basic reality of his situation. Second, because the letter sets up a discussion between Paul and a Jewish competitor for gentiles, the discourse naturally tends toward "thinking about" the kind of gentiles who would have listened to a teacher of the law like the teacher caricatured in 2:17f. The discourse supposes and focuses upon gentiles who are interested in Judaism.

The preceding considerations allow room for a more judicious reading of 2:14–15. One problem stands out immediately. With a couple of exceptions, all commentators have followed the natural law tradition established by Origen and have read "by nature" (physei) as belonging with the second part of 14a: "They do the things of the law by nature."[103] For several reasons it is more likely that *physei* goes with the first phrase: "For when gentiles, not having the law by nature." Although Greek usage permits the word to be taken with either phrase, placing it with the first phrase is appropriate to standard Greek word order, whereas the other option is awkward. Adverbial modifiers normally follow the verbs or verbal nouns that they modify.[104] If a Greek writer had wanted to modify *ta echonta* with *physei* (that is, "having by nature") he would have written the phrase exactly as Paul did; if he had wanted to modify the second phrase, he would have put *physei* after *poiōsin* ("they do"). The standard reading also destroys the balance of the sentence because it makes the second half redundant. On this reading, "gentiles, although not having the law, they do the things of the law by nature" is virtually repeated by "although not having the law, they are a law to themselves." Taken the other way, the two clauses of the sentence balance nicely in the "when/then" form that one would expect.

Taking *physei* with the first phrase also better fits the context and Paul's usage of "nature." Verses 14–15 introduce the theme—mere outward possession of the books of law versus inward disposition to follow the law's teachings—that Paul exploits in 25–29. In 2:27, "the uncircumcised by nature [*ek physeōs*] who keeps the law will judge you a transgressor of the law who have the books of the law and circumcision."[105] The contrast makes sense because 2:14–15 has already said that gentiles could "do the things of the law" and "be a [or "the"] law to [or "in" or "among"] themselves." Quite strikingly, 2:14–15 and 2:17–29 speak as if there is one law that Jews have in written form to which gentiles have access but in a different way.

The meaning of "nature" is similar in 2:14 and 2:27. The RSV translates the phrase in 2:27 as "physically uncircumcised" but that cannot be right. "Physically" would be *en sōmati* or *en sarki*. *En sarki* in fact appears in 2:28, and the RSV translates it (correctly) as "physical." So what does "uncircumcised by nature" mean? Jews are uncircumcised naturally. We would say that they are circumcised by social convention or religious practice. In fact, however, *nature* almost always means convention in appeals to human behavior.[106] *Natural* refers to a feature of life that the writer regards as self-evident, unarguable, or taken for granted. From Paul's perspective, being uncircumcised belongs to the essential nature of gentiles but not that of Jews. In Gal 2:14, he writes of "we who are Jews by nature and not gentile sinners." Cultures that place great emphasis on birth, as did all those in antiquity, speak as if their cultural characteristics were acquired by birth or were of their essential being. In Paul's thought, just as a gentile was uncircumcised by nature, so also was he without the law by nature (2:14). But Paul also held a Jewish belief that gentiles, who often could be seen living by standards and teachings found in the law, had obtained such moral knowledge from Jews and the law of Moses sometime in the indefinite past. As we have seen, cultural diffusion was the standard way that Greco-Roman thinkers explained cultural similarities. And by Paul's time, Jews had long held Moses to be the earliest lawgiver. Verses 14–15 assume some such account, arguing that this unacknowledged knowledge of the law forms a legitimate expression of the law among gentiles. If they embody such teachings in their lives, God will judge them on that basis, according to works (cf. 2:6, 15, 25–27). As a Jew, Paul has no difficulty in claiming, as he so obviously does, that gentiles can know or do know the law and are held accountable to it. What he does not state but assumes is that certain parts of the law that do not touch on Israel's specific constitution (for example, food laws and temple cult) apply to both Jews and gentiles. I see no evidence that by *law* Paul ever means some kind of cosmic principle, unwritten moral law, or law of conscience. He means the five books of Moses.

Romans, then, makes gentiles responsible in their own way to the law of Moses, and 1:18–2:16 may be seen as a protreptic or missionary sermon to an imaginary gentile. The section represents gentile culture as ignorant of God; yet to some degree it is aware of essential teachings from God's law, and such awareness makes gentiles morally culpable and sometimes even capable of doing what the law requires. But the overwhelming condition of the idolatrous gentile cultures is a state of bondage to their passions and desires, as decreed by God himself. By viewing 1:18–2:16 as a missionary appeal to a gentile, one can understand the tension between saying that gentiles are enslaved to evils and the assertion that gentiles can follow the law. Although 1:18–32 indicts gentile culture generally for idol worship and vice, and 2:1–5 admonishes a listening gentile to repent, 6–16 provide the grounds for God's final punishment or reward of gentiles. The last passage explains that Jews and gentiles will be judged by the same criteria. The argument sets forth in a general way the conditions that would make the imaginary gentile's repentance and salvation possible.

Again, the section reminds one of the allusion to the missionary message in 1 Thess 1:9–10—turn from idols and await salvation from the wrath to come—except that Rom 1:18–2:16 lacks 1 Thessalonians' reference to Christ as the agent of that salvation. The whole section of Romans lacks a discussion of *the means* to the kind of transformation that it demands of the gentile because it serves to prepare for Paul's discussion with the Jewish teacher in 2:17f. That discussion pits against one another two Jews who advocate different means for gentiles to obtain justification: moral education through study of the law versus the effects of Christ's faithfulness. Rom 1:18–2:15 provides basics upon which both teachers agree: the gentiles' condition, the call to repentance in the face of a final judgment, God's impartiality, and the performance of what the law requires of each as the criteria for judgment of Jews and gentiles. In the ensuing discussion, Paul draws heavily on these agreements, particularly on God's impartiality, in his attempt to convince the teacher that Christ forms God's answer to the gentile problem.

Quotations from Another Cultural Code

Scholars speak of the apocalyptic concepts in Rom 1–2 but then so abstract and reorganize discourse from so-called apocalyptic works that they end up with shadows of later Christian theological schemes. An antidote to such synthesizing activity are two texts from the Greek Bible upon which Paul likely drew for narrative patterns, metaphors, and motifs, using the sacred Jewish writings to think about the gentile problem. Texts that reflect the same kinds of discourse found in Romans offer a depth of understanding difficult for the modern reader to acquire.

Allusion to Zephaniah likely played a large part in Paul's writing of 1–2, and that allusion evokes codes upon which the work's intelligibility rests. No one of the echoes of Zephaniah in Romans is a convincing quotation in itself because individual elements of the language appear widely in Jewish literature. But Zephaniah is the locus classicus for much of this language, and the accumulation and combination of features found in Zephaniah make it a work with which Romans connects. New Testament scholars, looking too exclusively for verbal citation, have neglected narrative patterns and configurations of tropes that form a structure for Paul's writing. Zephaniah has been much neglected in Christian traditions of reading Romans because, unlike Isaiah and Zechariah, it lacks passages that can be read messianically. Zephaniah concerns God's judgment and redemption of Israel and the gentile nations.

The ideal first-century reader would have been able to connect Romans 1–2 with three themes in Zephaniah: the wrath of God and the day of God's wrath; the arrogance of Israel and the gentile nations; the repentance, removal of arrogance, and salvation of Israel and the gentile nations. One must imagine a reader like Paul reading the LXX of Zephaniah creatively in terms of contemporary cultural codes. Paul, the narrator, frames the admonition to the gentiles and the discussion of their decline with three references to God's coming judgment: 1:18, 2:5–9, and 2:16. The "wrath of God" in 1:18 and "day of wrath" in 2:5 echo the language of Zeph 1:18, cf. 2:2 (*hēmera orgēs kyriou*). More significant, however, both Zephaniah and Romans begin their oracles of judgment and admonition by proclaiming that God's wrath will soon be poured out on all humankind, both Israel and the gentile peoples (Zeph 1:2 [*panta*]; 1:3 [*anthrōpoi*]; 1:17, 18; cf. Rom 1:18 [*anthrōpoi*]; 2:9–11). The crucial point for reading Romans is that Zephaniah, even while using the language of "all humanity," does not reduce Israel and the various non-Jewish peoples to abstract individuals-in-relation-to-God. Both works view individuals as members of human communities and treat individual relations to God under the larger category.

Those in Jerusalem who are responsible for leading Israel have committed specific transgressions that are seen as breaches of Israel's special mission (Zeph 1:4–13; 2:2–4; 3:1–8). In Rom 2:17–3:8 and chapters 9–11, Paul charges that some contemporary Jews have failed in ways crucial to the nation. In Zephaniah, the gentiles, devotees of other gods (2:11), have committed their own sins. Both Israel and gentiles have manifested hybris in their particular ways. Alluding to Zeph 1:15, Rom 2:9, as part of the admonition of the interlocutor, warns gentiles against arrogance. The day of wrath about which both speak will be a day of "tribulation and distress." Paul replaces Zephaniah's *anagkē* (cf. 1 Cor 7:26) with *stenochōria* (perhaps also suggesting Isa 8:22). gentile nations have "taunted (or reproached) my people and made boasts against my borders." First, Rom 2:1–5 rebukes gentiles for judging others; then in 11:19 Paul places a taunt in the mouth of a gentile, representing gentile arrogance toward Jews: "[Jewish] branches were broken-off so that I might be grafted in." Zephaniah pronounces an oracle of doom against the gentiles "in return for their arrogance [*hybris*] because they taunted and boasted against the people of the Lord of hosts" (2:10). The arrogant gentiles have said, "I am, and there is no longer any one else" (2:15).

Israel has also rebelled against God, but on the day of God's wrath she "will not be put to shame" because God will remove the proud and haughty ones from her (Zeph 3:11–12). In Rom 11:26, quoting Isa 59:20–21, Israel's savior will expel ungodliness from the nation. Rom 2:4 calls for gentile repentance and humility. Zephaniah predicts a day when God will pour out his wrath upon the gentiles (3:8) but also "change the speech of the peoples to a pure speech so that all of them may call upon the name of the Lord" (3:9). This reversal of the confusion of the nations at Babel will lead them to bring an offering to God (3:10). Paul's request that the gentiles in Rome share in the gentile offering to the poor in Jerusalem follows an exhortation for the readers to be reconciled in Christ (15:1–13). Paul also speaks of calling on the name of the Lord and not being put to shame when he argues that God will save both Jews and gentiles (10:11–13; cf. 9:33; 1:16). Paul probably understood the offering brought by the nations to include both the collection of money from the gentiles to Jerusalem (Rom 15:30–32) and, more important, the presentation to God of sanctified gentile communities (Rom 15:16).

How did Paul get the notion that God had punished the gentiles by allowing their enslavement to passions and desires? By reading the scriptures through contemporary lenses. The account of the nations in Genesis certainly forms a general framework and provided many details. Well-known texts about God's future dealings with the gentiles also hold significance. But Psalms 9 and 10 (9, LXX) were also crucial for him. These form an acrostic in the Hebrew Bible and a single psalm in Paul's "Bible," the LXX. Paul would have read Ps 9 as a description of God's righteous judgment against the gentiles. Rom 3:14 cites Ps 9:28 (10:7 Hebrew) as part of the catena on sinfulness in 3:10–18. Other early Christian texts show that the Psalm was used in this way. In Acts 17:31, Paul announces that God will judge the world with righteousness using Ps 9:9.

The first sixteen verses of Psalm 9 establish the framework for the themes of Israel, the gentiles, and God's justice. The poem begins by praising God for saving Israel from its enemies, focusing on God's justice in dealing with the world's peoples: "You the righteous judge have sat on the throne. You have rebuked the gentiles and the ungodly one is undone. . . . He has prepared his throne for judgment. He will judge the world with righteousness and the peoples with honesty. . . . You have not forgotten those who seek you, Lord. . . . Sing to the Lord who dwell in Zion; proclaim his ways among the gentiles. . . . He has not forgotten the prayer of the poor."

In 13–20, the psalmist praises God for saving Israel from its enemies. The following verses describe God's punishment of the gentiles. Paul may not have connected vv. 13–14 with 15–20 because, given his assumptions, 15–20 would have appeared to him to be general statements about the gentiles: "The gentiles were trapped in the corruption which they created. Their foot was caught in the trap where they hid. The Lord is known for making judgments. The sinner is caught by the works of his own hand." Here Paul would find the idea—so important in 1:18–32—of God punishing gentiles by means of evils that they created for themselves (cf. Ps 7:12–16). The Lord judged that the gentile peoples be trapped in their own corruption.

Verses 17–20 introduce the key motif in Romans of the gentile situation under the law: "Let the sinners be turned back to hades; all the gentiles who have forgotten God. For the poor shall not be wholly forgotten; the endurance of the needy will never perish. Arise, O Lord, do not let humans prevail; Let the gentiles be judged before you. Appoint, O Lord, a lawgiver against them; Let the gentiles know that they are humans!" The attack on gentile arrogance in 20–21 is reminiscent of Rom 2:1–6 (cf. Ps 50:6 and Rom 3:4) and may have inspired some of its language. So also both texts share the notion of the gentiles forgetting God (Rom 1:18–23, 28). Most striking, however, the psalm calls for a lawgiver to frame a law so that the gentiles will recognize that they are merely human. The Hebrew text of v. 20 calls upon God to "inspire fear" in the gentiles rather than provide a lawgiver. The translator of the Greek seems already to have had the idea of the law calling the gentiles to account. At any rate, here Paul would have seen vivid confirmation of his idea that the law of Moses served only to condemn gentiles for their rebellion, showing them that they stand outside of Israel's covenant and its atoning grace.

Verses 21–25 introduce two ideas essential for Paul's argument: the hiddenness and delay of God's judgment and the notion that God punished the gentiles by allowing the corruption of their reasoning and bondage to desire: "Why Lord have you stood at a distance: Do you pay no attention in times of distress? When the ungodly acts arrogantly, the poor is set on fire. They are caught in deliberations which they reasoned [*dialogizesthai*]. For the sinner is praised for the desires [*epithumiai*] of his soul and the wicked one is blessed. The sinner has angered the Lord." The question of why God has not already decisively punished the gentiles and why Israel was subject to them lies close to the heart of ancient Jewish discourse about God's judgment. Paul addresses the mystery of God's delay in Rom 2:4–16, 3:21–26, and chapters 9–11. Indeed, 1:18–32 provides a partial answer by saying that the gentiles have already been definitively punished in a bondage to their desires, dooming them to final wrath unless God provides release. The psalm again speaks of gentile arrogance and violence that backfires because of the very corruption of their thinking. Rom 1:21 says that in their refusal to honor God their reasonings (*dialogismoi*) were darkened, and God handed them over to the desires of their hearts (24). Thinking in confused ways, according to the psalmist, gentiles praise one another for the desires of their souls and bless wickedness. At the climax of Paul's indictment, v. 1:32, he says that gentiles not only commit all the evils that he has listed but, worst of all, they approve what they know to be against God's law.

Paul and similarly formed readers read the scriptures in just such ways. One can imagine how readers in Paul's day might have read Romans only if one understands the interplay of scripture and current issues involved in such reading and writing. Writings like Psalm 9 provided Jews and interested gentiles with the basic texts of a discourse about the contemporary non-Jew. But the discourse would have had no power for Jews and gentiles concerned with the relations between the two if these readers had not seen culturally loaded icons like the word *desire. Desire*, for example, allowed entry to all of the issues of self-mastery and the connections with Greco-Roman culture that Jews had forged by representing themselves as a culture of self-mastery. For too long Romans has been read misleadingly as an exercise in reflection on abstract questions of theology or, on the other extreme, as a very long, convoluted, and exceedingly indirect way for Paul to tell Jewish and gentile Christians in Rome that they should accept one another.

World Decline and the Age of Sin in Paul's Era

Rom 1:18–32 contains compressed allusions to Jewish versions of decline narratives. The compressed reference serves larger rhetorical and hortatory purposes. In 1:21 the gentiles refuse to acknowledge God and to rightly glorify and give thanks to him. As in some decline of civilization accounts there is a loss of reason and unnatural behavior.[107] For Paul, this mental disorientation led to the beginning of idol worship (1:21–23; cf. 28). God then allowed these peoples to become enslaved to their passions and desires (1:24–25). The third stage, describing gentile decline, concludes with a long list of vices (1:29–31) that resemble those found in Hesiod (*Erg.* 181–200) and other golden age decline narratives.[108] Almost every vice in Paul's list can be paralleled in Hesiod and in reinterpretations of Hesiod's legend that had gained great cultural and political importance in Paul's day. Fall narratives stress hybris and arrogance. Similarly, Paul stresses the triad of *hybristes, hyperēphanos,* and *alazōn* in 1:30. He concludes by turning to the present tense in 1:32 f. and thus connecting the past fall of the gentiles to the current state of their society. They not only do these evil things but approve of those who do them. Hesiod writes, "Man will praise the evil doer and his hybris" (191).

In some ways the differences between Paul and the Hesiodic accounts are more striking than the similarities. Some of the key themes in Hesiod—for example, the turn to luxury from simplicity—are missing in Paul. And the Hesiodic tradition does not, of course, criticize idolatry. But an either-or contrast would be misleading. The modern reader needs to imagine the cultural codes of the ancient readers that would have constrained their readings. One of the most important aspects of the reading process is genre identification. Believing gentile readers might well have conflated, just as Jews sometimes did, the fall narratives from their Greek cultural codes with the Genesis story of the decline of the nations learned as Jewish sympathizers or converts. This would explain why Paul can so confidently criticize their Greek culture: their cultural codes agree. From the ancient poets down to the present, Greek sages have agreed that life now has greatly deteriorated from its original state close to God and nature.

Myths of degeneration are endemic to patriarchal cultures. You can never be the man your father was. Such cultures trace themselves back to great founding heros (for example, Abraham, Kekrops) or even gods. Genealogy establishes one's place in society, and the greater your ancestors, the greater your place. Thus the patriarchal lense magnifies the past in relation to the present. Paul's assertions that the nations had rejected true piety and had turned to unnatural behavior, lust, greed and insolence would not have struck his contemporaries as shocking new ideas or outrageous claims. In fact, Roman politics had made the idea somewhat of a contemporary obsession: The present age was an age of sin and corruption.

Roman writers and politicians of all sorts seem to have agreed that Rome and civilization in general had declined from a distant and virtuous past.[109] They disagreed about which reformer would return Rome to its ancient virtues and glorious past. The first historian known to have invoked the idea of historical decline is L. Calpurnius Piso, but the laments of Horace, Virgil, Livy, and Sallust are better known.[110] In Paul's era, the myth had been given a particular shape by the Augustan revolution.[111] The best-known golden age text from the Augustan era is Virgil's fourth *Eclogue*, which prophesied the return of Saturn's reign with Virgin Justice and the birth of a miraculous child, all leading to the disappearance of human sin and a paradisal earth. Virgil's vision, drawing on a wide range of somewhat exotic sources, celebrated the truce between Antony and Octavian in 40 B.C.E.[112] One of those sources was the Jewish *Sibylline Oracles*, through which he derived eschatological and paradisal ideas and images from Isaiah.[113] Interpreters often underappreciate the fact that the golden age theme has its corollary in a postdecline age of sin reaching into the writer's present. The *Phaenomena* of the Alexandrian poet Aratus was another of Virgil's sources; this is the same poem that Acts has Paul quoting in the Areopagus speech (17:28).[114] Virgil alludes to Aratus's highly popular account of human degeneration when Justice, the last of the immortals, left the earth (4.5). Horace, Virgil, and other writers of the period came to emphasize the wickedness of the age and Augustus as savior from that evil. In this context, the most important word for sin, wicked deeds, or wickedness is *scelus*.[115] In *scelus* one finds the kind of behavior that brings the wrath of the gods and requires sacrificial expiation (*piaculum*). In a conception reminiscent of the martyr's prayers in 4 Maccabees, Virgil writes (*Georgics* 1.501–02), "O let the blood already spilled atone for the past crimes of cursed Laomedon" and looks to Octavian, just victorious at Actium, as the hope. The gloom about the "godless age" (*Georgics* 1.468) stemmed largely from the darkness of the civil wars, and the Augustan writers interpreted war as divine punishment for sin, including sexual sin (for example, Horace, *Odes* 1.2; 3.24, 25–29; 3.6, 17–48). Having focused on sexual and kinship sin, Horace writes (*Odes* 3.6.45–48), "What does corrupting time not diminish? Our grandparents bore weaker heirs; we have degenerated further and soon will beget offspring more wicked yet." This line of thinking, which emphasized sexual error, further developed in conjunction with Augustus's program of legislation on marriage and morals.[116] The doors of the great temple that Augustus dedicated to Apollo for his victory at Actium featured the theme of divine wrath.[117] The slaying of Niobe's children had become a paradigm for God's punishment of human hybris. The doors portrayed that story together with another of the barbarians being driven from Apollo's sacred Delphi.

By the end of Augustus's reign, the themes of primeval degeneration, the sinful age, and the wrath of God had become established together with expectations of a return to the golden age.[118] Upon the accession of each Julio-Claudian emperor, orators, writers, artists, public works, festivals, and coinage would revive expectations of the golden age.[119] In each case, disappointed hopes soon led to renewed laments that the times yet belonged to the age of degeneration. Suetonius tells of a popular lampoon when discontent set in with Tiberius: "Caesar you have put an end to the Ages of Gold: They will always be Iron until you grow old."[120] Philo speaks in glowing terms of the expectations that the golden age had begun at the beginning of Gaius's rule and the bitter disappointment later (*Leg.* 13). Paul wrote Romans early in Nero's reign, when golden age ideology and hopes may have reached their highest peak since Augustus.[121] About the same time that Paul wrote Romans, Nero's tutor and advisor, Seneca, addressed *On Clemency* to the emperor.[122] Seneca here presents Nero as the one who has the potential to save the empire from sin and usher in the golden age. The great multitude of the people are "unruly, seditious, without self-mastery, ready for mutual destruction if it throws off the yoke of rule."[123] "We have all sinned; some in serious ways, some in less serious ways; some by deliberate intent, some impulsively or led astray by the wickedness of others" (1.6.3–4; cf. 1.22.2).

Part of the historical meaning of Romans comes from imagining how readers in Paul's day would have received his pronouncement of God's judgment with hope of salvation and his account of the sinful degeneration of the Greeks and other nations. The revolution that created the Roman empire witnessed a developing ideology of sin, God's wrath, and hopes of a golden age. These ideas transcended ethnic boundaries of Jewish, Greek, and Roman. The labor of so much New Testament scholarship of attributing to Paul a pure Jewish pedigree falsifies history and is itself an ideological construct. Part of the power in Romans' discourse would have come not from the novelty of the message but from the way in which it played on politically and culturally charged themes that readers met daily on the images of coins, in public monuments, and in everyday discourse. The readers represented in Rom 16 were the kinds of people who were attuned to cultural and sociopolitical trends in the empire concerning the ethic of self-mastery and social mobility. Rom 1:18–2:16, while still fully Jewish, resonates with images and motifs fitting the moral and sociopolitical milieu of the people represented in chapter 16. Rather than having dropped out of heaven or having popped out of a pure stream of religious ideas going back to the "Old Testament," the discourse of Romans is alive with responses to Paul's own world.

Warning a Greek & Debating a Fellow Jew:
Romans 2 as Speech-in-Character

The serious difficulties in the received readings of Romans
show themselves most acutely through a close, critical exegesis of 2:6–16, especially in conjunction with 2:25–29.
Such sharp analysis of the text, however, is unusual.[1] Commentators are so clear about their destination at 3:9 ("all are
sinners in need of Christ") that they tend to fly over chapter
2 quickly and at a high altitude, seeing only the message of
3:9 being worked out. Of course, the seriousness of the
problems has not been overlooked by all. Before Augustine,
the chief problem for interpreters was determining exactly
what kind of law the gentiles were under.[2] In the West, following Augustine and the Pelagian controversy, the chief
problem was reconciling the works of the law according to
which Paul says Jews and gentiles will be punished and
rewarded (2:6–10, 13, 25) with the "works of the Law" elsewhere (for example, 3:20, 27; Gal 2:16; 3:10), which are
said to bring a curse rather than justification.[3]

Origen realized that Paul had contradicted himself, if
2:12 meant that gentiles are not under law in any sense.[4]
He produced what became the classical reading of that text
by introducing the idea of natural law. Thus 2:12 means
only that gentiles are not under the law of Moses. They are
under God's natural law as vv. 14–15 indicate. This reasoning made great sense for Origen, who was heir to an
Alexandrian tradition from Philo and Clement which had
developed the concept of natural law. The later Augustine
solves the problem of our chapter in two crucial moves.[5]
First, he dehistoricizes the law into a fundamental element
in the human condition that makes the individual aware of
sin. To a certain extent this is done by psychologizing a conception of the universal law of nature. Second, Augustine
develops a key principle of interpretation: Negative statements about Jews and gentiles refer to actual unbelieving
Jews and gentiles. Thus Augustine reads 2:17–29 as Paul's

"empirical" description of the ethical depravity of Jews: They are thieves, adulterers, blasphemers, and so on.[6] Above all, they are proud. Because of their pride, even the depraved and idolatrous gentiles keep the law better than Jews. The other side of Augustine's hermeneutical principle is that positive statements about Jews and gentiles refer to Jewish and gentile Christians.[7] Thus the Jew and Greek in 2:10 are believers, and 2:12–15 speaks of Christians who keep the law. Origen has a much more historical understanding of Romans: Paul treats issues regarding the Jewish and gentile peoples, and the Jews and gentiles of chapter 2 are not Christians.[8]

When exegetes have recognized the inadequacy of the Augustinian type of solution or solutions, which claim that Paul speaks hypothetically of fulfilling the law, they have had to fall back on explanations which admit that chapter 2 does not fit "Paul's system."[9] Albrecht Ritschl took 2:6–11 to be the words of a Pharisee that Paul had placed in the text as a foil to his doctrine of justification by faith.[10] J. C. O'Neill has argued that chapter 2 was a Hellenistic Jewish missionary tract added by a later hand.[11] He says that the chapter assumes "that Jews and gentiles can keep the law, and can act in a manner to deserve God's praise by obeying the commandment" and that "on the basis of the present passage [2:1–16], the best way to help gentiles to be righteous would be by preaching the law to them."[12] I find O'Neill's logic compelling except that it leads me to a different conclusion: The *received system* for reading Romans and constructing Paul's thought cannot sustain close, critical questioning of the texts without contradiction. Others have followed O'Neill's type of solution. Sanders argues that chapter 2 is a synagogue sermon that Paul only poorly integrated into his letter.[13] Räisänen has replied that Paul's thought is merely in a state of hopeless contradiction.[14]

The Promise to the Gentile of Impartiality at the Judgment (2:6–11)

Again I must insist that we take account of Paul's continuing address to an imaginary gentile. This admonitory apostrophe began in 2:1 following a passage about the degeneration of gentile culture. The protreptic speech to the gentile warns of his precarious situation in light of God's delay and accumulation of guilt; the dangers of pretentiousness and the need for genuine repentance. God will be fair in judging not only Jews but also Greeks by the applicable standards of the law. Although Paul does not use the second person singular after 2:5 until he turns to a Jew in 2:17, there is no indication of a break in the discourse. The acute reader will imagine Paul continuing to address this gentile in 2:6–16. The statements in 2:6–11 that speak of God's impartial reward and punishment of not only Jews but also Greeks take the form of a promise and a threat addressed to this gentile.

The apostrophe to the person in 2:1f. introduces the future day of judgment into the protreptic speech, and 2:6 puts forward the principle of God's impartial judgment: "He will repay each one according to his works" (Ps 62:13). Scholars have rightly noted that 2:7–16 (or 2:7–29) reads like a commentary on 2:6.[15] The peculiarity of this section derives from the forceful and lucid way in which Paul announces the parity that Greeks will have with Jews at the judgment. Gentiles who keep the law (2:12–16) will be rewarded just like Jews who keep the law (2:25–29). Paul directs the first speech to an imaginary gentile (2:1–16), the second to a Jew (2:17–29). His treatment of the two, however, is not analogous. Romans makes no claim that Jews as a whole have rejected the true worship of God and fallen into false worship, bondage to passion, and desire and vice. Indeed, a striking asymmetry characterizes the descriptions of the religious and moral states of Jews and gentiles in Rom 1–3. No generalizations about Jewish vices appear. The letter nowhere claims that Jews, like gentiles, have been sentenced to slavery under their passions and desires. Paul does argue that God will judge both impartially, and he emphasizes that a wicked Jew is no better in God's sight than a gentile sinner. But these claims are not the same as saying that Jewish culture is vice-ridden, idolatrous, ignorant and dishonoring of God, and enslaved to passions and desires.

Both Jews and Greeks whom God judges righteous at the end will receive glory (doxa), honor (timē), peace (eirēnē), and immortality (aphtharsia).[16] Paul has made the current gentile relation to these eschatological gifts quite clear in 1:20–32, but he says nothing similar about the Jews having lost their basic relation to God. In chapter 1, Paul described how the gentile cultures rejected the truth (1:18, 25; cf. 2:8). They destroyed the relation to God that is the basis for good works and God's eschatological gifts. They traded away the glory (doxa) of God (1:21–23). Therefore God allowed them to dishonor (atimazein) themselves (1:26–27). Gentiles thus earned the anger of God (1:18), bondage to passions and desires, and enmity and strife among themselves (2:28–31). Finally, Paul says that the gentile nations have made themselves worthy of their sentence to mortality (1:32; cf. 5:12; Gen 2:17). The gentiles gave up true worship of the one God, the privilege of being illuminated by God's glory. Without the true worship and glory of God they lost all access to the gifts that God will bring to fruition in the future.

But what about the Jews? Nowhere in the letter does Paul say that Israel has also traded away the worship, glory, and promises of God. Readers, however, usually assume that critique of Judaism by importing a doctrine of sin into the text that goes something like this: Sin is the ontological flaw or state of depravity of all humans that only belief in Christ (read, being a Christian or a member of the Church) can overcome. Paul clearly says that both Jews and gentiles are subject to sin (3:9–20) and fall short of the glory of God (3:23), that God is now angry with the Jews as a whole (not with everyone, chapters 9–11), and that the gospel has the power to save Jews from God's anger. One can affirm these statements by Paul without also assuming the definition of sin given above.

At least since the second century, readers of Paul have come to the texts assuming that God has rejected the Jews and given their prerogatives to the Church, the true Israel.[17] Assumptions are everything when it comes to reading a text. I believe that Paul assumed just the opposite and that he never argues or implies the end of God's covenant with the Jews. Later Christian polemicists saw that the central argument against the Jews would have to revolve around both the inadequacy of the temple cult with its system of atonement and the unrepentance of Israel. This seemed obvious at a time when the temple no longer existed and Judaism was a separate religion from Christianity. But in Paul's day the temple system was still working and Christianity was not a distinct religion. Nowhere does Paul mount an argument about the inadequacy of the covenant and the temple system. To prove that Jews are under sin in the way that gentiles are, Paul would have had to argue that the Law's system of repentance and holiness was not working.

In order to enable a reading of Rom 1–3 based on what I believe to be Paul's assumptions, I will discuss some texts that appear later in the letter but that are usually overpowered by the reading already given to early parts of the letter, especially chapters 1–3. I want to draw trajectories from the latter part of Romans to the earlier that will allow for a different perspective in the earlier. In 9:1–5, Paul, like a new Moses, steps forward in his full persona for the first time since the epistolary introduction and pleads for Israel in the face of God's anger.[18] He proclaims that the Jews still possess the kind of relation to God which 1:20–32 say that the gentiles have lost: "They are Israelites, and to them belongs the sonship [huiothesia],[19] the glory [doxa],[20] the covenants [diathēkai)] the legislation [nomothesia], the temple cultus [latreia], the promises [epangeliai]; and to them belong the patriarchs and from them, Christ according to the flesh. God who rules over all be blessed for ever. Amen."

The concepts of sonship, glory, law, worship, promises, peace, and immortality play important and interrelated roles in the stories of gentile degeneration, the eschatological rewards for righteous Jews and gentiles, and the covenant of election that the Jews have with God. The series of interrelated narratives in which these concepts find their meaning are for the most part implicit and yet manifestly present within Romans' discourse. The most important narrative, the story that stands at the center, is the gospel narrative about God's righteousness demonstrated through Jesus Christ. It lies far beyond the scope of this work to study these narratives in detail. Nevertheless, they cannot be ignored. In tracing the theme of glory, for instance, one will find it interrelated with the other concepts and with the gospel narrative. Furthermore, Paul employs these concepts in implied narratives about the gentiles. The Jews enter the discussion only as their story bears on the story of the gentiles. The only place where Paul describes the fundamental status of the Jews and not just facets of their current relation to the redemption of the gentiles is 9:4–5.

Commentators usually say that *doxa* in 9:4 means the presence, or *shekhinah*, of God without relating it to the use of the concept elsewhere in the letter. The "presence" of God, however, forms a sign of God's continuing relation with Israel and is intimately connected both with right worship and eschatological glorification.[21] Whereas the gentiles exchanged the glory of God for idols and worshiped the creature, Jews worship the one God whose presence is centered and symbolized in the temple in Jerusalem. Thus Paul writes, "To them belong the temple cultus and the glory."

Evidence that Jerusalem and the temple were still significant to Paul serves to counter the individualizing and spiritualizing tendencies of traditional readings. The consensus seems to be that such passages as 1 Cor 6:19 ("body is a temple of the holy spirit") mean that the church is a replacement for the temple in Paul's thought.[22] First, any allusion to the Jerusalem temple in such passages is undetectable.[23] Second, other Jews—those at Qumran, for example—both spoke of the community as a temple while radically criticizing the existing operation of the temple and also held the continuing existence of the actual temple in Jerusalem to be of the highest importance.[24] Ancient Jews may have at times spiritualized their language about the temple and critiqued its current operation, but such an attitude does not logically necessitate the belief that the temple ought to be replaced or abolished.

Rom 9:4 refers to the temple cultus as a central and continuing privilege of the Jews.[25] In 1 Cor 9:13, Paul argues that preachers of the gospel, like priests in the temple, ought to get their living from their work.[26] At the very least, Paul betrays no indication that the priesthood is not a continuing and valid institution. Moreover, he seems to imply that the priesthood in some respects parallels the ministry of the gospel. In 2 Thess 2:3–4, the author speaks of the "man of lawlessness" who will exalt himself in the last days so as to proclaim himself God and "take his seat in the temple."[27] If one believes, as I do, that the arguments against the Pauline authorship of 2 Thessalonians are extremely weak and suspects that these arguments may be motivated by the desire to modernize Paul, then this text provides evidence that Jerusalem and the temple were to play vital roles in the events of the last days.

Rom 11:26–28 contains quotations from Isa 59:20–21; 27:9, and Jer 31:33: "And so all Israel will be saved, as it is written, 'The savior will come from Zion, he will turn away ungodliness from Jacob'; 'and this is my covenant with them, when I remove their sins.'"[28] One can make a good case for associating the struggle in 11:26–28 with the "man of lawlessness" in 2 Thess 2:3–10.[29] The return of unfaithful Jews to a restored Israel would then coincide with Christ's coming to bring God's sovereignty over the rulers of the earth. Thus, 2 Thess 2:8 says, "The Lord Jesus will kill him with the breath of his mouth and destroy him by appearing when he returns." This text has proven extremely embarrassing to the sensibilities of modern exegetes and theologians. Such offensively unmodern conceptions make it easy to deny Paul's authorship. No one, however, denies that 1 Corinthians was written by Paul. There, in what interpreters might consider less crude language, Paul says that Christ will turn the kingdom over to God after he destroys every ruler, every authority and power (1 Cor 15:24–25; cf. 2:6). Again, recent study has provided weighty arguments for considering these to be earthly rulers.[30] In sum, the temple and Jerusalem seem to play important roles in Paul's eschatological scenario.

Johannes Munck argued that Jerusalem was the center of the eschatological drama for Paul and that the trip to Jerusalem which he discusses in Rom 15:19f. was to initiate the final events there.[31] I would modify Munck's scheme by saying that Paul's trip was only a crucial stage on the way to the final events, especially since the apostle looked forward to completing the gentile mission in the west after his trip. Nevertheless, the gospel began in Jerusalem and most likely the city remained the sacred center for Paul. Dieter Georgi has argued that Jerusalem was such a sacred center for Paul early in his ministry but that he later changed his evaluation of the city and Jerusalem.[32] Georgi's second phase in Paul's ministry is highly dependent on his reading of Galatians and Romans. The reading that I am proposing would mitigate against a second phase in which Paul gave up his focus on Jerusalem.

These considerations should warn us against quickly dismissing Paul's statements about Israel's continuing election. Judaism, the religion of the chosen people and their land, continues to be significant for Paul. "Jew and Greek" seems to refer to actual concrete cultures and is not just a cipher for abstract humanity. Since Paul's communities are gentile and the concerns of his letters are gentile, he has little opportunity to mention Jerusalem, the temple, and the Jewish situation. When he does refer to these institutions, however, he assumes their continuing validity. Of all Christian writers, Paul is the only one who lived before the temple's destruction. His statements directed at gentiles who might doubt Israel's status make it difficult to dismiss the claims of 9:1–5. So, for example, concerning the continuing election of the Jews he says, "The gifts and call of God are irrevocable" (11:29). With absolute certainty Paul asserts that the present disobedience of Jews is temporary (11:12, 15, 23, 25–26, 31).

The gentiles, then, have lost God's glory, while Israel enjoys it, and righteous Jews and Greeks both will receive the future glory of the world to come. A text from chapter 15 illustrates another part of the narrative: The gentiles who have failed to glorify God have and will come to glorify him. Rom 15:5–12 forms the conclusion, perhaps even the summary, to the body of the letter:[33]

> May the God of endurance and encouragement give you the ability
> to agree among yourselves, according to Christ Jesus, that you may
> together in one voice glorify the God and father of our Lord Jesus
> Christ. Therefore receive one another, as Christ has received you, for
> the glory of God. For I tell you that Christ became a servant to the cir-
> cumcised on behalf of God's truthfulness, in order to make certain the
> promises to the patriarchs, and in order that the gentiles might glorify
> God for his mercy. As it is written, "For this I will praise you among
> the gentiles, and sing your name." And again it says, "Rejoice, gentiles,
> with his people." And again, "Praise the Lord, all gentiles, and let all
> the peoples praise him." And again Isaiah says, "The root of Jesse shall
> come, he who rises to rule the gentiles in him shall the gentiles hope."[34]

At the very end of the long discourse begun in 1:16, Paul still speaks of Jews and gentiles. The gospel is a power for salvation to the Jews first and also the Greek (1:16).[35] Paul has spoken as if the mission to the Jews is a fact of the past in chapters 9–11, but the good news certainly began with them. Presumably owing to priority of election as God's people, they will also receive the consummation of their eschatological promises first when God judges each person (2:9–10). But 15:5–13 addresses itself to gentiles and their future. Israel warrants mention here only because Christ's ministry to the Jews also forms the basis for the redemption of the gentiles (15:8–9) and because their futures interconnect (15:10). Even here, Paul speaks of two distinct, even if related, episodes: 15:8 calls the reader back to 9:4–5; Christ was a servant to the Jews *not* to establish a relation with God and attendant blessings—*those* they already had—but to "make certain the promises given to the patriarchs": the same patriarchs and promises that 9:4–5 says still belong to the Jews. The promises would, of course, include the promise that interests Paul in Romans, namely, the promise that Abraham would be the father of many peoples so that the gentiles might be blessed. Paul understands the promise of the land in Gen 15:7, 18 to mean that Abraham's descendants will inherit the whole world. Jews and gentiles who can justly claim Abraham as forefather will one day possess the whole world.

The controlling concept of Christianity can easily blind the reader to distinctions that were important to Paul. Only here in 15:8 and in 9:4 does Paul speak of promises in the plural. Elsewhere in the letter (4:13, 14, 16, 20, 21; 9:8, 9) he speaks of *the* promise, meaning the Abrahamic promise concerning the redemption of the gentile peoples. But for Israel, there were many promises, not just the one. Because Romans is about gentiles, the promises peculiar to Jews bear only a mention. Likewise, Abraham is not only the father of Jews but "the father of many nations" (4:17–18; cf. 4:11, 16, 18). But in 15:8 Paul speaks of the fathers (plural), who include Jacob, Joseph, Moses, and many others who are not fathers of the gentiles in the same way as Abraham. Only Abraham received the promise that in his seed the gentiles would be blessed. This promise does not lessen the significance of the other fathers for Jews (9:5). Indeed, when facing gentiles who might say that God has rejected the Jews because many have not accepted the good news (11:13–32), Paul writes, "As chosen [people] they are loved [by God] for the sake of [or "on account of"] their forefathers, for the gifts and call of God are irrevocable" (28). Thus Paul speaks as if there are two separate but interrelated paths; as if Christ were significant for both but in different ways.

The central theme of 15:5–12 concerns gentiles coming to glorify God. After appealing to the example of Jesus' adaptability to the needs of others (15:1–4), the apostle prays that the gentile readers might be united so as to glorify (*doxazein*) God (vv. 5–6). An exhortation again based on the example of Christ follows the prayer. Gentiles are to accept one another as Christ adapted himself in order to accept gentiles in their need, for the glory (*doxa*) of God (v. 7). Paul, then, explains (*gar*) in vv. 8–9 that Christ's mission had the effect (the purpose) of making the gentiles come to glorify (*doxazein*) God for his mercy toward them and his gift of Christ as their ruler. This climax and conclusion to the body of the letter piles up quotations about the redemption of the gentiles (Ps 18:49; cf. 2 Sam 22:50; Deut 32:43; Ps 117:1; Isa 11:10), stressing the praise and glory they owe to God. Verse 10, a quotation from Deut 32:43 (LXX), calls upon the gentiles to "rejoice with God's own people." The gentiles will be enabled to rejoice and glorify God as the Jews already do.

Even in concluding the letter's discourse, Paul maintains a pattern of separating and linking Jews and gentiles. What reader from Paul's time would have guessed that the Jews had not been glorifying God all along? The text proclaims the miraculous change in the gentile attitude toward God and exhorts the readers to exemplify this attitude. This concluding text dramatically underlines the reversal of the gentile failure to glorify God described in 1:18–32. Chapter 8 discusses another change of status for the gentile readers. They have become fellow heirs with Christ and therefore sons of God. A few verses later (9:4), the apostle announces that Jews already possess "sonship" just as they do the temple, the promises, the patriarchs, the law, and the covenants.

To recapitulate, the glory, honor, peace, and immortality that 2:6–11 promises to both Greeks and Jews who do what the law requires are attributes that 1:18–32 describes as being lost to the gentiles in the past. This would ordinarily cause no difficulty to the standard readings because Paul supposedly argues that Jews are just as degenerate and lost as gentiles in 2:17–3:20. In order to raise questions about this reading at the outset, I have discussed the theme of glory in 9:1–5 and 15:5–12. The purpose of this strategy was to enable a different way of reading chapter 2 and the rest of the letter, uncontrolled by concepts of sin, salvation, and Christianity, that overpower the distinctions which Paul makes between Jews and gentiles. The glory texts seem to be dominated by a story that goes like this: The gentile peoples have failed to glorify and worship God and thus have no basis for eschatological glorification. Nevertheless, through Christ, gentiles have come to glorify God and will share in Christ's sonship and glorification. Thus, what heretofore belonged only to Israel has come also to the gentiles.

Making a Conundrum of 2:12

Until a few years ago, the meaning of *anomōs* in Rom 2:12 always seemed obvious and unquestionable to me: The gentiles are not under the jurisdiction of the Mosaic law, they are "without the law." Since they are not under the jurisdiction of the law, they will not be judged by its standards. If any doubt existed about its meaning, 1 Cor 9:21 settled the issue: "To those without the law [*anomois*] I became as one without the law [*anomos*], though not being without the law [*anomos*] of God but within [*ennomos*] the law of Christ, that I might win those who are without the law [*anomous*]." The contrast between "within the law of Christ" and *anomos* seems to make it absolutely clear. Not until I tried to marshal evidence against the view of a lone interpreter who suggested that *anomōs* in Romans 2:12 might be translated as "godlessly" did I begin to see problems with the usual reading of 2:12.[36]

Wilhelm Gutbrod in the *Theological Dictionary of the New Testament* seems to express the general assumption of scholars when he says that *anomia, anomos,* and *anomōs* have two root meanings.[37] The first is "there was or is no law" or "without law"; the second, "against the law," with connotations of disapproval. Aside from Rom 2:12 and 1 Cor 9:21, he provides only three examples of the first meaning. Plato's *Statesman* 302E constitutes Gutbrod's best evidence. There Plato says that "monarchy when harnessed by good written prescriptions, which we call laws, is the best of all six [forms of government]; but without law (*anomos*), it is hard and most oppressive to live." "Without the law" is a fair translation here, but one should be clear about what Plato means. He has discussed the nature of the "legal" (*ennomos*) and "illegal" (*paranomos*) forms of monarchy, oligarchy, and democracy. The point is not that the king who rules *anomos* has no access to law, is not under the jurisdiction of law, or knows no law, but that he has substituted his personal tyranny for the rule of law. He is without law in the sense that he rejects the law's claim on him.

Gutbrod's second example, Oxyrhynchus papyrus 1121, does not support him. The petition of a certain Aurelia Techosis complains that residents in the house of her recently deceased mother "lawlessly carried off" (en *anomiais apēsylēsan*) her mother's possessions. Gutbrod cites Preisigke's translation, "as though there were no legal protection," which is surely wrong. Arthur Hunt's "lawlessly carried them all off" is correct.[38] The woman's point in the petition is the unlawful nature of the men's actions. In fact, she contrasts their unlawful actions with her own legal rightness when she says, "A few days ago she died intestate, leaving me her daughter in accordance with the law."

Gutbrod's final example is Philo, *Leg. All.* 3.79: "A king is a thing at enmity with a despot, the one being the author of laws, the other of lawlessness (*ho de anomias estin eisēgētēs*)."[39] Again the context makes it clear that Philo means the despot's wickedness: He is cruel and harsh, controlled by his passions. It is not that he has no law available or could not be under the jurisdiction of the laws of the city in which he rules.

Aside from his discussion of the two root meanings and later references to Rom 2:12 and 1 Cor 9:21, the meaning "no law," "without law" plays no part in the article on *anomia, anomos, and anomōs*. The completely overwhelming use of these words corresponds to Gutbrod's second root meaning. Commentators are unanimous in simply assuming "without" or "apart from the law" as the meaning of *anomōs* in 2:12. Liddell, Scott, and Jones, *Greek English Lexicon,* the major authority outside of New Testament studies, gives "lawless" and "impious" as the first meaning for *anomos*.[40] It thereby implicitly admits that the Pauline usage is unique. They also equivocate by giving a definition that contains both of Gutbrod's meanings. For *anomia* they first give "lawlessness, lawless conduct, opp. *dikaiosynē*" and then "negation of law," citing only Dem. 24.152. Demosthenes argues, in *Against Timocrates,* against repealing duly enacted laws and replacing them with new ones: "How can we rightly call this [that is, the new law] a law; rather is it not *anomia*?" Demosthenes is being rhetorically cute, playing off *nomos* with and without the alpha privative. The translations "lawless" and "against law" would do well here. The new law is an antilaw.

In Greek literature until 70 C.E., I have found only one instance where *anomia, anomos,* or *anomōs* may possibly mean "without law." Isocrates in *Panegyricus* 39 speaks of Athens as the civilizer of Greece: "For, finding the Hellenes living without laws/lawlessly [*anomōs zōntas*] and in scattered groups, some oppressed by the tyrannies, others perishing through anarchy, she delivered them . . . for she was the first to set down laws and establish a constitution." Isocrates describes a time comparable to Paul's time before the giving of the law (Rom 5:13–4). Here in Isocrates one can indeed use the meaning "without law," but the extraordinary rarity of this meaning, which seems to be confined to only one instance from classical Athens, is overwhelming. Such evidence certainly does not prove that Paul could not have used *anomos* and *anomōs* in this way, but it should make one ask questions about the received reading of 2:12.

I have not identified a single instance in which these terms mean "without law" in the LXX and other Jewish literature before 70, a finding confirmed in an article by James Davison.[41] Even though he cites Gutbrod's two meanings in his study of *anomia* in the LXX, Davison does not give evidence for the first meaning.[42] He also does not find *anomia* to mean "rejection of the law in principle" either in the LXX or in the Matthew where such a meaning has been claimed. In both bodies of literature, *anomia* and its cognates mean rejection of the law only in the sense of behavior that is contrary to the law. The word appears interchangeably with sin (*hamartia*), unrighteousness (*adikia*), and godlessness (*asebeia*). These words and *anomia* translate several Hebrew terms for wickedness, evil, injustice.

A number of scholars claim that *ho anomos* and *hoi anomoi* were common terms for gentiles or technical expressions for gentiles.[43] The evidence does not support this claim. Although Gutbrod and Davison hold to the received view among New Testament scholars that these are technical terms for gentiles, their language reflects the basic problem with that view. Gutbrod writes, "In Judaism *ho anomos* or *hoi anomoi* is a common term for gentiles. Here it is hard to distinguish a mere affirmation that they do not have the law and a judgment that they are sinners. In general the latter view seems to predominate."[44] But I find it impossible to make a generalizable semantic distinction between *anomos* when used for Jews and *anomos* when used for gentiles. I have found no texts in which I could detect the sense, "they do not have the law." Surprisingly, Gutbrod goes on to give examples that only describe gentiles as wicked or as sinners. Similarly, Davison says, "*Anomia* can be used, because of its root meaning of lacking law, as an appropriate designation for the gentiles. There is a note of condemnation and judgment in the application of the term, however. . . .In most cases, the term is employed in the sense of conduct that is opposed to the law of God and meets with his condemnation."[45]

Again we see the conviction that the meaning "lack of law" must be present, although Davison presents no texts that demonstrate such a meaning. I suggest two reasons for Gutbrod's and Davison's positions. First, they employ the misleading concept of "root meaning," which has been discredited by modern semantics.[46] Second, Gutbrod, Davison, and many others assume that *anomos* and *anomōs* must have meant "lacking law" because of the use of the words in the two Pauline texts. That gentiles were not responsible to the Mosaic law has become a tenet of Christian theology. From reading scholars who discuss the terms, one might get the impression that, even if they are not technical terms for "being without the law," they appear so often in conjunction with gentiles in Jewish literature that *hoi anomoi*, for instance, virtually meant "the gentiles." Again the evidence does not support that view. The verbal, adjectival, and adverbial forms of the word occur 382 times in the LXX. In only 22 of these cases are the terms used unequivocally in reference to gentiles. The proportion seems to be roughly the same in other Jewish texts of the second temple period. If there is any characteristic semantic reference in Jewish literature, it is to Jewish transgressors whose behavior stands against what the particular text considers the normative practices and teachings of Israel.

In sum, *anomos* and its cognates almost always mean evil, wicked, or sinful in Jewish literature before 70 C.E., and the vast majority of examples refer to Jews or to the wicked in general and not to gentiles. It comes as no surprise, then, that the *RSV* employs transgressor, lawless men, lawlessness, evildoer, iniquity, and wickedness to translate *anomos* and *anomia*. The exceptions, of course, remain "outside the law" for *anomos* in 1 Cor 9:21 and "without the law" for *anomōs* in Rom 2:12. Judging from pagan, Jewish, and Christian usage, either Paul forged a nearly unique usage in these two texts that is at odds with other Jewish writers or the traditional reading is highly questionable. The accepted reading seems even more problematic on the realization that Paul himself uses these terms in the normal way elsewhere. In Rom 4:7 he quotes Ps 31:1. There the *RSV* translates *hoi anomiai* as "iniquities." In 6:9 the *RSV* renders *anomia* as "iniquity." Both texts parallel the terms with "sin" (*hamartia*).

The accepted meaning of *anomōs* in 2:12 seems to be powerfully supported by 9:21. Here Paul seems to contrast the states of having and not having the law. Thus the *RSV* translates, "not being without law toward God but under the law of Christ." (*mē ōn anomos theou alla ennomos christou*). The seemingly obvious reading, however, is not always the best reading. A text from Heliodorus's *Ethiopian Story* shows that the obvious reading in 9:21 is not the necessary one. In 8.8.57, the author writes, *ouden gar outos ephilei Theogenes ho tos son anomon bouleumaton ennomos huperoptes.* Sir Walter Lamb translates thus: "nothing could be so pleasing to Theogenes, the loyal contemner of your disloyal designs."[47] Moses Hadas renders the text as follows: "such would be the desire of Theogenes, who lawfully despised your lawless intrigues."[48] This text shows that *anomos* can be used in opposition to *ennomon* and "without law" and "under law" need not be the obvious or even plausible translations. On *ennonos*, the Liddell and Scott lexicon again betrays the idiosyncratic nature of the traditional translation. They give "ordained by law," "lawful," "legal," "keeping within the law," "upright," "just." First Cor 9:21 stands as the only exception. Regardless of how exactly one understands 9:19–21, clearly 9:21 provides no compelling evidence for the usual reading of 2:12.

Romans 2:12 in its Context

A central point of 1:18–2:12 further developed in 2:12–3:20 is that God bases his punishing and rewarding of Jews and gentiles impartially on merit in living according to the law. It makes no sense for him to distinguish the situation of Jews and gentiles in 2:12, where he works so hard to show that both will be judged by the same standards. In my reading, 2:12 is fully congruent with 2:6–11 and not a problematic modification, as must be the case in traditional readings. The chief obstacle to my view, however, comes from the Alexandrian insistence on seeing the "law of nature" in 2:14–15. Origen jumped at any opportunity to find philosophical concepts in the Bible.[49] The law of nature quickly became ubiquitous in Christian exegesis of scripture because the concept was necessary for a coherent universal economy of salvation applying to every individual human and because natural law solved the problem of why Christians discarded the so-called ritual law. The typical exegesis proceeds by way of this reasoning: Paul says that gentiles must keep the law, but in 2:14 he also writes that gentiles who do not have the law keep it by nature; therefore gentiles live under a different law than the law of Moses, a universal moral law. My arguments in chapter 3 make it most unlikely that Romans appeals to natural law.

Paul's argument requires that "law" mean the same thing throughout chapters 2–3.[50] Commentators tacitly acknowledge this. They usually read Paul to be saying that the law which divides humans into Jew and gentile can be known and kept by nature among gentiles who do not actually possess it. This raises a host of generally unacknowledged problems for those who believe that

Paul follows a Stoic doctrine. In no sense is the law of nature a "natural" method or capacity for keeping a written code of law as "they do the law by nature" (2:14) would suggest. I have already argued for the improbability of translating 2:14 in this way.

I translate 2:14 as follows: "for when gentiles, who do not possess the [written] teachings of the law by birthright, do what the law teaches, they themselves, though not possessing the law, embody the law in themselves." The verse observes that some gentiles who quite naturally did not have access to Torah scrolls or to the communal training based on such texts, nevertheless live lives in accord with the righteousness that the law demands of gentiles. These non-Jews embody the law's teachings in their lives even though they have no *direct* access to the law. Two different laws are not in view. One law constitutes the criterion for God's judgment. God judges Jews and gentiles on whether they do what the law teaches not merely on the basis of a birthright that may or may not have given an individual the opportunity to explicitly hear the law (v. 13). Paul, however, did not believe that the law expected exactly the same thing for Jews and gentiles. More things were expected of God's chosen people. Romans assumes the existence of righteous gentiles who are so without becoming Jews or quasi-Jews.

With this understanding of 2:14, I propose a reading of 2:6–16 that I believe to be more coherent than the one generally recognized. Commentators read v. 12 as an assertion of universal condemnation for universal sin: The first part of the verse means that gentiles ("those without law") will be destroyed by God's judgment and 12b that Jews will be condemned by the law which they cannot keep perfectly or miserably fail to keep. Verse 12 forms a crucial link in traditional readings of Romans: here Paul supposedly states his double indictment of Jews and gentiles, which leads to the claim that all humans are hopelessly lost in sin without the sacrifice of Jesus Christ. Verses 14–15, 25–29 have, on this reading, seemed an illogical turn of argument in which Paul "entertains" the idea that some gentiles have kept the law and been righteous.

I propose the following translation of vv. 11–14:

God shows no partiality. For all who have sinned in a lawless manner, shall perish in a manner befitting lawlessness. All who have sinned while living within the law, shall have their case judged by the law. For those who (merely) listen to the law are not righteous before God but those who do the law shall be judged righteous. For when gentiles, who do not possess the teachings of the law by birthright, do what the law teaches, they themselves, though not possessing the law, embody the law in themselves.

These verses do not constitute an argument that no one can keep the law, that no Jew or gentile is righteous. Verse 12 is not "in tension with" (read "contradiction") vv. 14–15. Rather, 11–15 argue consistently that God in his impartial justice will judge gentiles like Jews on the basis of whether their lives conform to the law's teachings. In other words, gentiles do not have to become Jews to be righteous. Access to Jewish teachers of the law—like that Paul opposes and like the imaginary one that he introduces in 2:17–29—is not necessary in order to be righteous. If gentiles live the righteousness of the law, then they *are* righteous and embody its teachings even if they have never heard of Genesis, Exodus, Leviticus—or explicitly of the way of life taught in the Jewish writings. By arguing this way, Romans creates an opening for the claim that gentiles can "fulfill the just requirements of the law [8:4]" through the spirit of Christ without "works of the law."

Verse 12 does not distinguish between Jews and gentiles. That would be counter to the preceding and following argumentation about the equality of Jews and gentiles. Instead, Paul makes a distinction basic to the religion of Judaism: the wicked, who make no serious attempt to follow God's law, and those who live, though imperfectly, within its teachings. God will destroy the wicked but he will measure out reward and punishment by degree to each of those who attempt to live within the law. Paul rejects a view that would have all gentiles categorically belonging to the wicked. By the same token, he indicates in 2:17–29 that not all Jews automatically fall into the other category, for some are among the wicked. He never argues that each and every human being is wicked. He does assume that all humans sin and maintains that some Jews as well as gentiles belong to the wicked.

"They shall be judged" (*krithēsontai*) in 12b does not mean that Jews "will be condemned." Paul has an unambiguous belief in the last judgment of every individual, including faithful believers in Christ.[51] He also believes in degrees of sin, reward, and punishment. These beliefs about individual judgment and degrees of reward have a close relation to the distinction between the lawless (*ho anomos*) person and the righteous person (*ho dikaios*). Speaking of the concept of the wicked in the Synoptic gospels, E. P. Sanders writes, "It refers to those who sinned willfully and heinously and who did not repent."[52] These conceptions of the wicked and the righteous have been erased by interpretations which have Paul claiming that it is necessary to keep the law perfectly in order to be considered righteous. Paul neither argues nor suggests that doctrine. Moreover, that teaching was not held by any known form of ancient Judaism. All of this flies in the face of the dominant Western understanding of Paul's doctrine of justification by faith alone. Verse 13 speaks quite unambiguously, however: "The doers of the law shall be justified." For Paul to say that he was "blameless with regard to righteous in the law" before he was in Christ (Phil 3:6) is no anomaly. With respect to his apostolic work among the gentiles, he contemplates the possibility that he may suffer for his failures at the last judgment, although he is certain that he will be saved (1 Cor 3:12–15). His reflections on his life in Judaism both before Christ and after suppose the ready availability of God's forgiveness and means of atonement for sins.

The arguments of 1:18–2:29 do not aim to show the sinfulness of all humans. Rather, they seek to establish that God will accept gentiles, provided they behave toward God and neighbor as the law requires, even if they do not become Jews or live as some sort of God-fearing gentile community that possesses the law. Paul's argument drives toward 3:21: "But now God's righteousness has been manifested apart from the law"; and 8:4, "sending his own son . . . that the just requirement of the law might be fulfilled in us, who walk not by the flesh but by the Spirit"; and 13:8, "he who loves his neighbor has fulfilled the law." Gentiles in Christ can do what the law justly requires of them without becoming people with a constitution explicitly based upon the law.

The best commentary on "all who have sinned in the law will be judged by the law" is 2:15–16. These verses depict a gentile who has lived "in the law" being judged by the law. No known Jewish group in antiquity taught that a person had to keep the law perfectly in order to be acceptable to God. Paul naturally assumes that even law-keeping Jews and gentile believers will sin and be judged by God. Similarly, when God examines the law-keeping gentile's past on the day of judgment, some aspects of his behavior will accuse him, other aspects will excuse him (2:15–16). In 2:26–27, Paul contrasts the gentile who keeps the commandments of the law with a Jew who has the written code but does not keep the law. He says that this Jew is not genuine. Although interpreters often infer the contrary, he does not say that the gentile becomes a true Jew but that God will regard the gentile *as if* he were circumcised, that is, in a covenant relation.

Verse 16 implies an intimate relation between gentiles doing what the law requires of them and Paul's gospel. When Jesus Christ returns, God will judge the world. God will look into the mental records of gentiles and determine to what extent they have lived lives in accord with the law. The criterion for God's judgment will also come from Paul's gospel. One should not dismiss the pronoun "my" in 2:16. Precisely Paul's gospel, as the apostle to the gentiles, proclaims that gentiles can be made right in God's sight through Christ without becoming Jews or adopting parts of the law. In a sense, then, the fact of some gentiles who have lived as the law demands without having the books of law (2:14–15, 26–7), prefigures Paul's gospel that God is in the process of forming the gentiles into communities of the righteous apart from Jewish attempts to make gentiles live by the law.

If ancient readers had ears finely tuned to speech-in-character, then the modern reader must read imaginatively, for that form of speech, above all, called on the dramatic imagination. Rom 1:18–2:16 presented the competent ancient reader with a Jewish teacher's "missionary" sermon spun out of the rhetorical technique of speech-in-character. The ancient reader overhears Paul critique impious gentile culture and depict its dilemma of slavery to passion and desire (1:18–27). Resounding with motifs of sin, impiety (1:18–23, 25, 28), moral degeneration, and the perversion of nature (1:26–27), the passage plays on themes made potent in the Roman empire since the reign of Augustus. Such echoes might make the hearer feel the weight of living at the end of generation upon generation in downward spiral: or would such gloom intimate hope of a coming savior and a golden age? The audience hears a narrative giving a novel but intriguing explanation to the closely felt problem of the passions and the failure of self-mastery. Several men in the audience who rule over substantial households and have a place in the community are especially interested and anxious at the talk of sexual and gender sins. Paul frames this critique with warnings of God's just anger (1:18; cf. 24, 26, 28, 32), another contemporary motif. He saves word of God's impending judgment, however, for 2:1–16, where he picks out of the imaginary audience a particular gentile, a Greek (2:9–10). The warning about pretentiousness (2:1–5) sounds a note Paul will eventually direct explicitly toward the gentile readers encoded in the letter (11:13–25). For now, the admonition remains indirect. The missionary calls for the Greek's genuine repentance in light of a life of unatoned sin stored up for God's final judgment (2:3–5). The rest of the speech (2:6–16) then lays out the basis for the coming judgment with a note of hope. The judge will not favor Jews more than Greeks (2:6–11). The good gentile has her or his own access to the criteria for judgment from the law, even if not to the written words of the law (2:14–15). God will show the full fury of his punishing anger toward the utterly lawless but will mercifully mete out degrees of punishment and reward to those who have tried to conform their lives to the law's teachings (2:12). Thus it comes down to actual thoughts and deeds (2:13). At the point we expect Paul to get to the heart of the matter, he turns away from the Greek. The apostle has just mentioned his good news and Christ Jesus (2:16) when he spots one of his competitors in the crowd, a Jew who has committed himself to teach gentiles about the Mosaic law. Paul knows that many gentiles in the audience have been attracted to such teachers and decides that he can best continue his missionary appeal by provoking a debate with the other Jewish teacher in front of his gentile audience (2:17–4:21).

A Teacher of the Law (2:17-29)

Rom 2:17–29 provides a key to understanding the letter's rhetorical strategy. When one reads the passage in the traditional way, as a polemic against Judaism, the reader's conception of the whole letter must almost inevitably follow a certain course. An alternative conception of the text eschews the polemical model and develops another by recognizing that the passage depicts a particular Jewish teacher through speech-in-character.

The Jew to whom Paul turns in 2:17–29 seems familiar enough to traditional modern readers, especially those who come from a Christian background.[53] The Jew is, of course, the hypocritical pharisee, the legalist who clings to the letter of the law but misses its intent. Such people harshly judge others but do not keep the law themselves. The person depicted in 2:17–29 is supposed to be the Jew who depends on himself, his own works, and his ethnic heritage for justification rather than depending on God. The text supposedly makes the theological point that the law is impossible to keep. Readers have understood this point as part of Paul's larger proof that all people without Christ are hopelessly enslaved to sin. Even if Jews by every observable standard seem to be righteous and good, the external view is an illusion. Jews are inwardly more depraved than gentiles. Pride and self-love, the very essence of sin, motivate all of that good and righteous behavior from deep inside.

Standard commentaries and the writings of important scholars confirm this view of the text. Ernst Käsemann describes the section as "a concrete attack on the Jews" and Gunter Bornkamm as "an extremely sharp attack on the Jews."[54] According to Käsemann, the passage denies the pious pharisee's and rabbinic leaders' claims.[55] The text is also said to be "an elaborate description of Jewish self-understanding."[56] Thus, 2:17–24 in particular supposedly depicts typical Jewish boasting about "Jewish privileges," pride in the Jews' ability to achieve righteousness by works of the law, and arrogance in their proselytizing of gentiles. Paul, then, deflates this supposedly typical self-understanding with a fierce attack on "Jewish hypocrisy." In reality, the Jew cannot save himself by keeping the law or make claims on God. The Jews' inconsistency actually dishonors God. True Judaism is an inward matter, not a matter of outward, formal, and legalistic keeping of the letter of the law.[57] C. E. B. Cranfield believes that Paul here regards hypocritical teachers as "characteristic of Jewish life" and that "all contemporary Jews are guilty" of stealing, adultery, and robbing temples.[58] James Dunn denies such literal wholesale moral condemnation, believing that Paul is "pricking the balloon of Jewish pride and presumption that being the people of God's law puts them in a uniquely privileged position in relation to the rest of mankind."[59]

Rudolf Bultmann and those under his influence have created a new version of the Augustinian-Lutheran theme of pride and self-dependence as the primordial sin that Paul attacks. As Bultmann said, "The attitude of sinful self-reliance finds its extreme expression in man's 'boasting.'"[60] The "typical Jew" epitomizes this attitude of boasting. Käsemann writes that "only from the perspective of the Jew as the representative of the religious person can universal godlessness be proclaimed."[61] The Jew represents the ultimate rebellion against God, "pathological religiousness."[62] The Bultmannian interpretation transforms Paul's statements into timeless principles whereby "works," "law keeping," and "religion" become the ultimate expressions of the human denial of God's sovereignty. Judaism, based on works, becomes the utter antithesis of Christianity, based on faith.

But Paul lived before the Gospel of Matthew, Augustine, the Protestant Reformation, and Rudolf Bultmann. The known beginnings of the polemical stereotyping of Judaism by way of contrast to Christianity may appear in the Gospels. When Matthew was written, believers in certain places were for the first time ranged over against an incipient normative Judaism.[63] Jewish leaders were consolidating and reconstituting the remnants of the varieties of Judaism that had existed before the catastrophe of 70. In this critical period, both Judaism and Christianity were struggling for self-definition. Matthew reflects a kind of Christianity that has emerged from Jewish roots and has painfully defined itself vis-à-vis this incipient Judaism.

Neither Paul's audience in Rome nor anyone else in the Roman empire would have or could have recognized 2:17–29 as a depiction of the typical Jew. The caricature did not yet exist. Moreover, Paul does not speak of Judaism in general in 2:17–29, but rather he addresses an imaginary individual Jew. It is grossly misleading to generalize this fictitious address to a critique of Judaism. In fact, 2:17–29 does caricature a type of person with whom Paul's readers might have been familiar, but that type is not the "typical Jew."

The Pretentious Teacher

Rom 2:17–29, like 2:1–5, employs speech-in-character to create an imaginary apostrophe to a fictitious interlocutor.[64] This device appears prominently in the so-called diatribe, a moral-philosophical lecture and discussion of a philosophical teacher.[65] The diatribe had its own pedagogical tradition of hortatory rhetoric. Scholars have long recognized that Romans exhibits the same kind of rhetoric.[66] As in 2:1–5, Paul suddenly stops speaking directly to his epistolary audience and shifts to the second person singular. He addresses an imaginary individual identified as a Jew. Paul sharply scolds this fictitious

Jew. The irony and rapid-fire rhetorical questions hit hard. The discourse amounts to more than a scolding, however, since the apostle's words also produce a characterization of this unnamed interlocutor.

One familiar with the literature of the Hellenistic moralists can readily recognize Paul's characterization as a certain type. Here, as with the Greek in 2:1–16, he characterizes a pretentious person (*ho alazōn*).[67] The type was made familiar not only by moralists and philosophers but also in the New Comedy.[68] Plautus wrote a play about a pretentious soldier, *Miles Gloriosus,* based on an earlier Hellenistic comedy. In his *Characters,* Theophrastus typifies the pretentious person and defines the vice as "laying claim to advantages a person does not possess." The pretentious person is above all a boaster and someone who pretends to be what he is not.[69] This person strives for the external trappings of wealth, honor, power, or virtue rather than really possessing them.[70] Desire for praise and honor motivates the pretender. The pretentious person is also typically a proud, conceited, or arrogant (*ho hyperēphanos*) individual.[71] The person in 2:17–29 belongs to a well-known type.

One can be even more specific about the characterization, however. In the diatribe, the interlocutor most often appears as the pretentious teacher or student of philosophy. This character type plays a central part in the hortatory rhetoric of the diatribe. Rom 2:17–29 creates a fictitious persona and life situation for the readers. Paul's scolding address in 2:17–29 and the dialogue that follows in 3:1–9 are "philosopher talk." Ancients might have heard such language in a market or stoa as a teacher addressed students. An ancient reader might also meet such language in a popular moral essay that affected the style of the diatribe. Today people who have never seen the inside of a church instantly recognize the comedian's parody of a fundamentalist preacher. Similarly, the writers of ancient satire and comedy could assume that people in the culture would recognize philosopher-talk and stock characterizations. Thus, 2:17–4:23 portrays a situation in which Paul plays the part of a teacher attempting to correct this pretentious fellow Jewish teacher by employing apostrophe and dialogue. The issue is how gentiles are to become righteous before God.

As in 2:17, so in the diatribe, one finds the motif of name versus reality in apostrophes to a fictitious addressee.[72] Thus Maximus of Tyre says that Epicurus "rejects the form [*schema*] of philosophy but sees fit to possess the name." Then Maximus addresses the one who follows the Epicurean principle of pleasure and keeps the name philosopher. "Lay aside the name, O man, together with your claims" (*Or.* 33.2b-c). In a diatribe (*Diss.* 2.19.19) entitled "To those who take up the teaching of the philosophers only to talk about them," Epictetus censures, "Your own evils are enough for you—your baseness, your cowardice, the bragging [*ho alazoneia*] that you indulged in when you were sitting in the lecture room. Why did you pride yourself upon things that were not your own? Why did you call yourself a Stoic?" Epictetus aims at those who want the name, the renown, the external trappings of philosophy but whose actions do not correspond to that calling. He often points to the disparity between word and deed: "If you wish to be a proper sort of philosopher, a perfect one, consistent with your own doctrine. If not you will be no better than we who bear the name of Stoics; for we too talk of one thing and do another" (*Diss.* 3.7.17). Or to another fictitious would-be philosopher he speaks with a Pauline-like irony: "Come now, do you also tell me your style of life . . . eager follower of truth, and of Socrates, and of Diogenes. . . . Why, then, do you call yourself a Stoic? Well, but those who falsely claim Roman citizenship are severely punished, and ought those who falsely claim so great, and so dignified a calling and title get off scot-free?" (*Diss.* 3.24.40–41). Finally, Epictetus tells this false philosopher that he will not escape the divine penalty that comes to the pretentious (*ho alazōn*): Their vices will turn them into pitiful wretches (*Diss.* 3.24.42–43).

The use of these scolding apostrophes and the interest in the pretentious person become intelligible in the context of the psychagogic relation of the student and teacher. In his essay "Progress in Virtue," Plutarch polemicizes against certain Stoic views of character development. In so doing he discusses the things that hinder and promote one's progress in virtue. Much of the work criticizes teachers who are not fit or ready to teach others. At first, training in the philosophical life is a matter of leaving certain things behind (77C). The beginner must desire virtue rather than external things (*ta ektos*; 78E-F). By setting virtue over externals, one expels that which most vexes beginners, that is, envy and jealousy (78E). Furthermore, "practically all beginners in philosophy are more inclined to pursue those forms of speaking which make for repute" (78E). Some because of pride and ambition pursue theoretical and doctrinal studies, while others go in for disputations, knotty problems, and sophistic quibbles (78F). The majority study argumentation and prepare to immediately practice sophistry. Plutarch chides their superficiality (79C). Practice, not theory, constitutes the genuine sign of progress. Typically, however, "those who are still studying busily look to see what they can get from philosophy which they can immediately haul out for display in the market, or at a gathering of youths" (80A). These do not really practice philosophy. Plutarch calls them charlatans. These are teachers who have not assimilated wisdom themselves and yet want to teach others. Desire for repute and ambition motivates such would-be teachers (80B).

Words and actions ought to go together, and usefulness ought to prevail over ostentation. The philosopher should keep his pride in himself hidden and feel no need for the praise of hearers (80E-F). Plutarch urges those who would study wisdom to give up pretentiousness and conceit (81B). They must be certain that they practice what they preach. They should apply their criticism of others to themselves and "cease feeling pride in their philosopher's beard and cloak" (81C). Those who follow this advice will "not arrogate to themselves, as before, the name of philosophy and the repute of studying it, or even give themselves the title of philosopher" (81C-D). The only way that such people can be cured and adopt another manner is to submit to the admonition (*nouthetein*) and censure of a genuine teacher (81E, 82A-B).

Several of Epictetus's diatribes highlight the same problems. *Dissertations* 4.8 bears the title "To those who hastily assume the form of the philosopher." Epictetus worries about the disrepute that such people bring upon philosophy (4.8–9). People too often judge by what is external (*ektos*; *Diss.* 4.10; cf. 4). The true philosopher is known by being free from error in word and action. Epictetus sharply censures the imaginary student who wants to teach before he has learned: "Man, do you also beware: you have grown insolent, you have leaped forward to occupy some petty reputation before its due time; you think yourself somebody, fool that you are among fools" (*Diss.* 4.8.38–39). Would-be philosophers, "when they have taken a rough cloak and let their beards grow, they say, 'I am a philosopher.' But nobody will say, 'I am a musician,' if he buys a plectrum and a cithra" (*Diss.* 4.8.16). The model philosopher Euphrates kept the fact that he was a philosopher secret for a long time. Euphrates says, "I knew that whatever I did well, I did so, not on account of the spectators, but on my own account . . . it was for myself and for God. . . . And what harm was there in having the philosopher that I was, recognized by what I did, rather than by outward signs?" (*Diss.* 4.8.17–20). The sign of a good philosopher comes not from having many pupils or being theoretically precise (*Diss.* 4.8.24). It is not in being a boaster (*ho alazōn*) or in proclaiming (*kēryssein*) that one is a certain kind of person (*Diss.* 4.8.27–28). Rather the true philosopher, like the Cynic "deemed worthy of the sceptre and diadem of Zeus," says, "Behold, I have been sent to you by God as an example: I have neither property, nor house, nor wife, nor children, no, not even so much as a bed" (*Diss.* 4.8.30–31). The true philosopher brings honor upon his profession by being a living example of what he teaches.

Paul was not a philosopher, and the Jew in 2:17–29 does not represent a teacher from some Hellenistic philosophy. Nevertheless, a combination of rhetorical forms and thematic motifs makes it clear that 2:17–29 parodies the philosophical teacher's admonishing censure of a pretentious would-be philosopher. Paul has created an interlocutor who is a fellow Jew and with whom he will conduct a diatribal dialogue. Although the particularity of the characterization in 2:17–29 stands out sharply, the echoes of philosopher-talk and of the pretentious would-be philosopher still break through.

This person "merely calls (*onomazō*) himself a Jew." Paul uses the popular philosophical motif of name (*onoma*) versus deed/reality (*ergon*), as do Epictetus and Plutarch. Paul's indictment, however, has another dimension because he has argued that God will judge everyone according to what they do (*ta erga, ergou agathou*) by the standards of the law. God will measure claims and professions against acts. The discourse of 2:17–29 (cf. 3:27, 4:2) all but flashes red lights to tell the reader that this person is a boaster (*ho alazōn*). He boasts of his learning, his skills in teaching and speaking in the law, and of his relation to God. Paul, perhaps ironically, describes his pretentious claims to knowledge and wisdom: "You know his will and approve what is excellent, being instructed in the law" (2:18). Verses 19–22 emphasize the person's pretensions toward being a teacher and moral-religious model. He claims to be "a guide to the blind, a light to those who are in darkness, a corrector of the foolish, a teacher of children" (19–20). The section employs the popular philosophical motif of the one who teaches others but has not yet learned how to live what he teaches. As in the apostrophes of the diatribe, Paul censures the interlocutor for the disparity between his pretensions and his behavior. Even the patterns of rhetorical questions parallel diatribal patterns (21–23). As the diatribal authors charge pretending philosophers with bringing disrepute on philosophy, so Paul accuses the interlocutor of dishonoring God by his inconsistency. At the admonition's climax, Paul quotes Isa 52:5 and applies it to the interlocutor's behavior: "God's name is blasphemed among the gentiles because of you."

The apostle continues his address in vv. 25–29, expanding on the inner/outer theme. The example of circumcision seems appropriate as the best-known sign of Jewish differentiation from gentiles. Philosophical writers and moralists frequently emphasized that the philosopher's cloak and beard, the outward symbols of the profession, were of no value if he did not live the philosophical life. The true philosopher was a philosopher inwardly. Euphrates was a genuine philosopher even though he did not have any of the outward marks of a philosopher, while numerous pseudo-philosophers went about with beard, cloak, and staff. Paul says, "A genuine Jew is one inwardly, and genuine circumcision is a matter of the heart, in the spirit and not merely following the letter of the law" (2:29). Genuine Judaism, like genuine philosophy, does not derive its legitimacy merely from what is outward (*en tō phanerō*, 2:28). Judaism is first of all an inward (*en tō kpyptō*) matter of the heart (2:29). Plutarch and Epictetus said that pseudo-philosophers want praise from men, but true philosophers like Euphrates desire only to please themselves and God. Paul says that the praise of the genuine Jew comes not from men but from God (2:29).

These parallels do not hide the fact that Paul has adapted the censure of the pretentious student to a Jewish setting. Paul speaks to a Jewish teacher about his work with gentiles. Nevertheless, the meaning of the passage lies partly in its echoes of popular philosophical style and motifs. Because Romans has been abstracted, generalized, and individualized, interpreters have missed this essential point, mistaking the admonition and censure of Paul's diatribal rhetoric for a polemic against Judaism in the form of an attack on "the typical Jew." The traditional reader understands 2:17–29 as an assertion of the proposition that God judges Jews to be as depraved as idolatrous gentiles. Why else the sharpness of the rhetoric? Why else its bitterness and sarcasm? Does Paul not rail against the religion of hypocritical self-salvation and legalistic works of righteousness? Does Paul not attack and destroy false theological positions and religious self-understandings?

In summary, Paul adapts a well-known character type to his own purposes in 2:17–29, a character type that appears as a gentile in 2:1–5. Applying the type to both a Greek and a Jew reinforces the theme of equity. Making the type of the pretentious person into a Jew weds two cultural codes; popular moral rhetoric and Jewish-Christian discourse. The themes of name versus reality, saying rather than doing, inward versus outward, and sincerity of the heart versus merely outward sign have places both in popular moral-philosophical rhetoric and in the Jewish traditions concerning "circumcision of the heart." Paul expresses the Jewish motif in the teacher-talk of the philosopher. Thus in the rhetoric of Romans, Paul the apostle to the gentiles confronts another Jew who is also a teacher of gentiles. Paul tries to persuade this interlocutor of his approach to making gentiles right with God by using the techniques of censure and protreptic. This dialogical fiction, when developed in chapters 3–4, produces contrastive positive and negative models of how gentiles are to become right with God.

In the typical readings of Romans, 2:17–29 bears the burden of proving or showing that Jews, like gentiles, are sinners or are under the power of sin. The weakness of this reading can be exposed on general grounds. For Paul to prove that Jews are no better with regard to sin than gentiles, he would have to argue either that the means of repentance-atonement that Jews believed was taught in the scriptures was nonfunctioning or inadequate or that Jews never repented and sought forgiveness. Paul obviously read his scriptures and knew about God's covenant with Israel and the establishment of the temple. The letter contains no argument about the inadequacy of the covenants, repentance, and sac- rificial cults, institutions that constitute continuing blessings for the Jews (9:1–5). Precisely because the gentiles lack such blessings, they live in idolatry and immorality for which they have no forgiveness, so that their sins are "stored up" (2:5; 3:25–26). If Paul meant to show that Judaism and the law were inadequate to deal with sin and that a new religion of Christ was thus needed, he completely failed.

Neither does Romans argue that keeping God's law is a purely spiritual matter in opposition to any outward signs or acts. Rather, the outward signs of Judaism must be brought into conformity with sincere intention in keeping the law. "Circumcision is of value if you do the law" (2:25). Finally, Paul does not assert that all Jews empirically fail to keep the law and commit transgres- sions like the theft and adultery attributed to the imaginary interlocutor (2:21–22). These interpretations of 2:17–29 have been shaped by a reading of the text through 3:9–20 as a proposition about universal human depravity, an acute ontological flaw fixable only through the incarnation and death of Christ. The apostrophe in 2:17–29 depicts a certain individual. There is no reason to think that he stands for all Jews. If that were the case, Paul would be guilty of a gross and unforgivable exaggeration, not to mention hypocritical. Paul claims that he was blameless with regard to righteousness under the law (Phil 3:6). If we are to take our clue from similar apostrophes in the diatribe, we must conclude that the Jew represents not Jews in general but Jewish teach- ers who behave like the one in 2:17–29.

A Jewish Teacher of Gentiles

To show only that 2:17–29 echoes the rhetoric of the diatribe would be to miss what is important: Paul's adaptation of this rhetoric. The character- ization in 2:17–24 exhibits a highly specific shape. I will argue that the dia- logical features of chapters 3–4 maintain the characterization of 2:17–24 with remarkable consistency. The reader must therefore well understand 2:17–24, since it remains a key to 3–4. Verses 17–29 depict a Jewish teacher of gen- tiles, but the portrait is even more specific: The discourse of 2:17–29 suggests a polemical construction of "missionary" opponents. This Jew is one of Paul's competitors for gentiles. Reading with the Christian tradition's portrait of Jesus' attack on the "legalistic, hypocritical Pharisee," interpreters have seen the pas- sage as being saturated with sarcasm. Karl Barth and Cranfield have rightly insisted that Paul is not merely ironical when he speaks of this person calling himself a Jew, resting in the law, and boasting in God.[73] These are positive things for Paul. The irony and sarcasm enter when Paul suggests that although the Jew knows the law and believes that he is doing God's will, he breaks some weighty commandments. This teacher of gentiles may well be totally sincere (for example, *peithō*, v. 19). Only when he sets himself up as the one having the cure to the moral and religious malaise of gentiles does he appear especially hypocritical and pretentious.

Interpreters will probably only confuse matters by describing the teacher as a missionary. Then one imports the model of later Christianity, a religion of salvation in a sense that the Judaisms of Paul's day were not. Although Jews may have generally welcomed proselytes, they did not typically think that they had to convert gentiles to Judaism in order to save them.[74] More typical is the idea of "righteous gentiles." If gentile peoples live justly and recognize the true God, God will judge them fairly. Verses 17–29 fit this understanding. The three things the Jew teaches are commandments from the Decalogue. Elsewhere Paul says that the sins prohibited by these commandments were characteristic of gentiles before their coming to Christ (1 Cor 5:9–13; 6:9–21). Paul and the Jewish teacher share the same understanding of gentiles as ethnic-religious other. They agree that gentiles need not be made into Jews. Paul's objection to the teacher's moralizing effort is different. Such Jewish teachers think that they can make gentiles righteous before God by teaching them to observe certain works from the law. If one can train gentiles to keep universally applicable ethical teachings like the Ten Commandments, then they will be righteous, and the Jew will have fulfilled his task of being a light to the gentiles. This teacher seems, like Philo, to advocate moral teachings that could be interpreted to gentiles through the ethic of self-mastery. Paul's approach was utterly different. Only God can make a person right with him, and he has chosen to justify the gentiles through Jesus Christ in a way analogous to Israel's becoming a righteous people before God through Abraham's faithfulness. Christ's coming fulfills the expectations that God would gratuitously save the gentile peoples at the end of the age when Israel will be restored (for example, Isa 2:2–3; 49:6; *Sib. Or.* 3.616; cf. Rom 11).

The pretentiousness of the Jewish teacher comes from his thinking that he can transform the gentiles by getting them to do works from the law. The reader risks seriously misreading if she or he does not understand Paul's indictment of the teacher in the context of the larger discourse: 1:18–2:16 stresses God's impartiality in judging Jews and gentiles; 3:1–20 emphasizes that both Jews and gentiles have sinned in apocalyptic proportions and therefore require a special act of God's mercy in the current world crisis. How can the Jewish teacher make gentiles right before God by his efforts when he himself is not righteous? Paul's intimation of the Jewish teacher's own immorality is a way of saying that Jews have enough problems of their own. They, like gentiles, must finally rely on God's mercy, not on their own works. If the Jewish condition makes such moral betterment by Jewish teachers unlikely, the gentile side is even more problematic in Paul's view. According to 1:18–32, God has punished gentiles for their refusal to honor him by allowing them to be enslaved to their passions and desires. Do Jewish teachers think they can overcome God's decree through their feeble pedagogical efforts?

In view of God's impartiality, the need of all peoples for God's grace, and the Jewish teacher's refusal to acknowledge God's way of dealing with gentiles, Paul thinks that the interlocutor's condescending and arrogant attitude of superiority over gentiles is grossly misplaced. Verses 2:19–20 enumerate terms of condescension toward gentiles from biblical and other Jewish sources that speak of Israel's mission of being a light to the gentiles. Paul, of course, agrees that Israel should be a light but identifies that mission with the preaching of the good news about Jesus Christ. The teacher prides himself on being "a guide to the blind, a light to those who are in darkness, a trainer of fools, a teacher of little children." Verse 19 echoes Isa 42:6–7, which speaks of Israel being "a light to the gentiles, to open the eyes of the blind . . . and to lead out . . . those who sit in darkness." The idea that Jews ought to be a light and guide to gentiles appears widely in Jewish and Christian literature (for example, Isa 49:6; 1QSb 4.27; 1 En. 105.1; Sib. Or. 3.195; Wis 18:4; Acts 13:47, 26:23). But in Paul's construction of such Jewish teachers, no light shines for gentiles. All rely on God's grace, even Jewish teachers, and Christ is God's ultimate expression of mercy to the gentile peoples. He quotes Isa 52:2 against the teacher: Because of him the name of God is slandered among the gentiles.

Religions and peoples, for example, Jews, Greeks, and Egyptians, create ethnic-religious others that define them as unitary people over against an ideologically constructed outsider. Individuals, especially leaders who write, also construct individual others who stand over against their own self-image and help to define that for which the leader stands. The teacher forms a version of the Pauline other. Both Paul and his other are teachers of gentiles. According to the Pauline logic, two characteristics, above all, make such teachers into Paul's opposites: unjustified boasting and immorality, that is, failure to keep the law and to be right before God. These characteristics appear clearly in 2:17–29 in conjunction with the Jewish teacher and also with the opponents in Galatians and Philippians (see chapter 2 above). In Gal 6:12, those who urge the gentiles in Galatia to keep the law want "to make a good showing in the flesh" and "to boast in the flesh" (6:13). Paul, on the other hand, boasts only in the cross of Christ (6:14). Those who teach the Galatian gentiles that they must be circumcised do not themselves keep the law (6:13). In Phil 3:2–3, the evil workers who advocate circumcision for gentiles "put their confidence in the flesh," in contrast to Paul, whose confidence rests in Jesus' faithfulness (3:9). These "enemies of the cross," of whom Paul has repeatedly warned the Philippians (3:18; cf. 3:1–2), live base lives and hold their lower appetites as their god (3:19). Remarkably, in one aspect, the opposing teachers as constructed by Paul resemble the gentiles whom they teach: They are controlled by their lower appetites and do not keep the law.

Paul's letters also characterize such teachers as boasters. In Rom 2:17 and 23 the teacher fits this characterization. When Paul explains the sufficiency of Christ's faithfulness for gentiles to the teacher in 3:21–26, the interlocutor asks what then happens to his basis for boasting (3:27). He challenges Paul's teaching about the justification of the gentiles by claiming that Abraham was a gentile who was put right by his works and thus had the right to boast (4:2). Chapter 5 concludes Paul's reply to the teacher by asserting that there is indeed a justified boasting in light of the benefits wrought by Christ (5:2, 3, 11). The letter consistently depicts the interlocutor as a Jewish teacher who views his work with gentiles as the basis for his pride and honor from others, including God.

The letters closely associate boasting with Paul's self-understanding as a missionary and with his polemics against opposing teachers. His boast is in his work as a teacher of the gospel to gentiles (Rom 15:17), and the real ground of his boasting—which he would rather die for than forfeit—is not his preaching as such, since God made him preach, but his self-supported preaching so as to make his message available to all types of people (1 Cor 9:15–17). After the writing of 1 Corinthians, competing Jewish teachers entered the Corinthian community. Paul's response to them in 2 Corinthians revolves around the motif of legitimate and illegitimate forms of boasting (2 Cor 5:12; 10:8, 13, 15–17; 11:12, 16–21; 12:1, 5–6, 9). Again the interlocutor fits the larger pattern. Like Paul's missionary competitors, he boasts illegitimately. The Jew in 2:17–29 appears almost as a mirror image of Paul the teacher of gentiles. He is the image against which Paul partly defines his own gospel.

Reading 2:17–29 as a set of propositions about the sinfulness and depravity of Jews in general or all Jews constitutes an egregious misreading. The text can be clearly identified as a type of *prosōpopoiia* (speech-in-character) frequently employed in the diatribe. One can recognize the characterization in 2:17–29 as that of the pretentious teacher. Paul creates a specific picture of a Jewish teacher from the traditions at his disposal. Thus, 2:17–29 criticizes not Jews or Judaism as such but teachers who in Paul's view stand in antithesis to his own gospel concerning justification of the gentile peoples through the faithfulness of Jesus Christ.

A Lecture to the Teacher on God's Impartiality (2:25-29)

Many interpreters have been certain that Paul effectively annuls Judaism in vv. 25–29. That view, however, requires taking 28–29, which say that true Judaism is a matter of the heart, in the harshest and most extreme sense while disregarding 2:25 and 3:1–2, which proclaim the value of circumcision. The rules of fair exegesis require that we allow both sorts of statements to stand instead of systematically dismissing positive statements about Judaism. Above all, one must be clear about the kind of literature one is reading. The text does not present a series of dispassionate general propositions about the human condition. Paul continues to admonish the imaginary Jewish individual who arrogantly preaches to gentiles while breaking the law himself. Verses 25–29 also maintain Paul's address in the second person singular. The symmetry of 2:17–29 to Paul's earlier admonishing of a pretentious gentile interlocutor in 2:1–16 holds significance. In each case, a little lecture about how the doers of the law, whether Jew or gentile, will be justified by God (2:6–16, 25–29) follows a characterization of the interlocutor through censorious apostrophe (2:1–5, 17–24). Both sections drive home the point that God will judge gentiles who do what the law requires (of them) on a parity with Jews who keep the law. The lectures to both individuals conclude with passages claiming that true justification before God must be an inward matter of the heart, not just of birth and external symbols (2:13–15, 28–29).

Verses 25–29 contain statements about this Jew, Judaism, and gentiles that could seem contradictory. The interpreter's major exegetical challenge is to give all of the apostle's statements their due force without too easily admitting contradiction. I therefore suggest five key points. First, as a Jew, this person possesses the written words of the law in a way that gentiles do not. Thus, 2:27 makes his possession of the written words (*ta grammata*) parallel to his physical circumcision. Second, circumcision and, by extension of Paul's logic, the written words of scripture are indeed valuable if a Jew keeps the law. Paul shows such concern that readers might misunderstand him to imply a denial of God's covenant with the Jews, that he has the teacher ask, "What value does circumcision have?" and "What is the advantage of the Jew?" in 3:1. He answers, "Much in every way."

But how does one relate these positive statements about keeping the law and Judaism to 2:28–29? My third point is that 2:25 and 2:28–29 are parallel and not contradictory. As noted, Paul's use of the inner/outer theme in censuring the pretentious teacher has popular-philosophical parallels. But whereas the philosophical moralists can dismiss the outer signs of the teacher as unessential, Paul cannot. He knows that the law requires circumcision of Jews, although not of gentiles. (He is still arguing that "the doer of the law shall be justified," 2:13; cf. 25–27). The highly elliptical language of 2:28–29 makes it easy to read and translate, as traditional Christian treatments have, in a manner that spiritualizes circumcision and Judaism to the point that they vanish. But 2:25–29 says that the meaning of circumcision lies not in the outward sign itself. The outward sign is the symbol of an inner disposition toward God. In other words, "circumcision is indeed valuable if you do the law" (v. 25). Paul is far from saying that intention alone is enough, but he does stress the inner disposition here. In this regard, Paul was hardly radical or innovative, although his admonitory diatribal language is sharp and forceful. The theme "circumcision of the heart" comes directly from the Jewish scriptures, and many varieties of ancient Judaism emphasized it (Lev 26:41; Deut 10:15, 30:6; Jer 4:4, 9:25–26; Ez 44:7–9; *1QS* 5.5; *1QHab.* 11:13; *1QH* 2:18, 18:20; Philo, *Quaest. Ex.* 2.2; *Spec. Leg.* 1.305). Thus Jews frequently wrote that true circumcision was a matter of the heart without ever supposing an elimination of physical circumcision.

Indeed, in these scriptural texts about true inner circumcision, one meets some of the conceptual world of Romans 2. Deuteronomy 10 holds together loving God with all one's heart, keeping the commandments, God's mercy toward Israel, and Israel's election (vv. 12–15). After, "circumcise therefore the foreskin of your heart, and be no longer stubborn," the warrant for obedience is God's justice: "For the Lord your God is God of gods . . . who does not show partiality and takes no bribes. He effects justice for the fatherless and the widow, and loves the foreigner who lives in the land" (vv. 16–18). The passage holds together God's election of Israel with his mercy toward those outside the covenant and his impartiality as a judge. Paul uses similar conceptions of "doing the law"—sincere Judaism, circumcision of the heart, and God's impartial justice toward both Jew and non-Jew—in order to set up an argument for the justification of the gentiles through the faithfulness of Jesus Christ.

I find it difficult to decide whether the "spirit" in 2:29 means the human spirit or God's Spirit. (It is probably misleading to capitalize "spirit" used of God in this period but since I cannot discuss the matter here, I will bow to Christian convention and capitalize with reservation.) If the former, then the contrast between circumcision of the spirit rather than "mere literal circumcision" simply amplifies "circumcision of the heart." If one decides on God's Spirit (cf. 7:6; 2 Cor 3:6), one should not then jump to the conclusion that the text now refers to Christians who have been suddenly and without explanation thrust into the discourse. Even if Paul believed that Christ had brought a special outpouring of the Spirit on Israel (which is by no means clear) as well as on gentiles, he also knew that the scriptures describe God's Spirit as empowering particular Israelites. Christians after 70 do begin to take over every prerogative and attribute of Israel and apply them exclusively to the church; Paul does not. Jewish sources before Paul had already connected circumcision of the heart with the agency of God's Spirit (Jub. 1:23; cf. Odes Sol. 11:1–3). In spite of what numerous commentators have said, there is no trace of Jer 31:31 in chapter 2. Thus Paul does not describe an eschatological miracle in 2:25–29 that turns Jews and gentiles into Christians. Rather, he uses the concept of circumcision of the heart to argue that gentiles who do the law can be as acceptable to God as Jews, given that both are capable of having the right inner disposition. Indeed, an obedient gentile is more acceptable than a disobedient Jewish teacher of gentiles.

Fourth, the Jew in 2:17–29 who does not keep the law is a "transgressor" of the law, not just an imperfect person, that is, one who sins and repents. As E. P. Sanders has reminded us, a wide variety of ancient forms of Judaism shared a distinction between "the wicked and occasional sinners."[75] The wicked, the lawless, and the sinners are those who have "sinned wilfully, heinously and do not repent."[76] The person in 2:17–29 is hardly one who merely cannot keep the law perfectly. He is arrogant, he dishonors God and commits transgressions like stealing and adultery. In calling him a "transgressor [parabatēs] of the law" (2:25; cf. vv. 23, 27), the letter makes the distinction in question. The discourse also implies that the interlocutor is a sinner (hamartōlos) in 3:7. This person fits into Paul's category of those who "have sinned in an utterly lawless manner" (2:12).

The distinctions made in Gal 2:14–21 concerning Paul's relation toward God as a Jewish missionary among the gentiles repay attention.[77] He and Peter are not "gentile sinners" but "Jews by birth" (2:15). Paul assumes that gentiles normally have the status of sinners (cf. Rom 1:18–32) and that Jews normally do not. In 2:17 he writes, "If seeking to be justified in Christ we ourselves are found to be sinners, is Christ a servant of sin?" As apostles of Christ among the gentiles, Paul believed that he lived lawlessly from the perspective of his Jewish identity. He lived like a gentile. His apostolic self-understanding included the idea of adapting himself to the situation of those to whom he directed his work (for example, 1 Cor 9:19–24). But he was not a sinner outside of God's grace because, in adapting himself to the gentiles he was serving, he sought to be justified by the faithfulness of Jesus Christ (Gal 2:17). He says, "If I build up again that which I tore down, I show myself to be a transgressor" (parabatēs, 2:18). If Paul inconsistently added "works of the law" to his justification in Christ, then he would truly be a transgressor, a sinner. Gal 2:14–21 reveals the depth of Paul's distinction between sinners or transgressors and those who are in Christ or in the law.

Thus, in Paul's understanding, the interlocutor, as a sinner and transgressor of the law, lives as if he were uncircumcised. This portrait of the Jewish transgressor helps us to understand why Paul uses the name versus work motif so prominent in the diatribe and moral-philosophical literature. The Jewish teacher merely calls himself a Jew (that is, 2:17, *su Ioudaios eponomazē*). That Paul can use the same language to describe those whom he considers grossly immoral believers, who are to be excluded from the community, ought to warn us against treating 2:17–29 as Paul's critique of Judaism. In 1 Cor 5:11, he tells his readers not to have any fellowship with such people. He describes such a person as "one who is merely called a brother" (*tis adelphos onomazomenos*). In considering his interlocutor a false Jew, Paul does not introduce some radical new idea that he could have discovered only through his faith in Christ. Again, the theme appears in scripture: for example, "I will punish all those who are circumcised but not truly circumcised—Egypt, Judah, Edom, the Sons of Ammon, Moab . . . for all these peoples are uncircumcised, and all the house of Israel is uncircumcised in heart" (Jer 9:25–26). The impartial God of all will treat Israel as he treats gentiles when Israel acts like gentiles.

Fifth, 2:25–29 implies an overlap but also a difference between the applicable content of the law for Jews and gentiles. How can Paul say that if an uncircumcised man keeps the just requirements of the law, God will consider him circumcised, when he knows that circumcision is itself a requirement of the law for Jews? The best answer seems to be that Paul, along with many other Jews in antiquity, assumed that the law required different (and fewer) things of gentiles than of Jews. The passage simply assumes that the law requires literal circumcision of Jews but not of gentiles. Thus some of the much later so-called rabbinic sources speak of the commandments in the Torah that were given to Noah for all peoples. Paul seems to be alluding to something similar in verse 26 when he speaks of gentiles keeping the "just requirements [*ta dikaiōmata*] of the law."

Paul's extant letters use the word *dikaiōma* five times, and all five instances appear in Romans. In 1:32 he says that the gentiles know God's "just requirement" that those practicing the evils listed in vv. 28–31 deserve death. Christ did what the law could not: He condemned sin in the flesh so that those who walk by the Spirit might fulfill the "just requirements of the law" (8:4). In the first instance, the just requirement is an aspect of God's moral order that the gentiles are said to know. In the second instance, God's Spirit enables the gentile readers to keep the just requirements of the law. From what Paul says in other letters and elsewhere in Romans, this obviously does not mean circumcision, Israel's food laws, and the requirements of the priesthood and temple system. The most economical and least strained solution is to conclude that Paul assumes as axiomatic, and thus not even a matter for discussion, that the law required more general justice, morality, and worship of the one God for gentiles and these plus the more specific requirements of the covenants for Israel. In other words, Paul reflects a commonsense traditional Jewish reading of the LXX or Hebrew Bible.

These five points allow 2:25–29 to be read coherently and in a way that does not have Paul negating or spiritualizing Judaism. Moreover, the movement of the discourse becomes clear. Paul makes two points to the "so-called" Jew who feels superior to gentiles. First, since he grossly and willfully transgresses the law, he is no better in God's sight than a gentile sinner. Second, if the gentiles that he despises as "blind," "foolish," and "childish" (2:19–20) keep what the law requires of them, God will treat them as if they were Jews and not second-class, unelect people, beggars at the door of Jewish wisdom. Paul's thinking in 2:25–29 may not have been convincing to most Jews in antiquity. Nevertheless, the implied argument does proceed from his previous discourse. God expresses his judgment in his impartial punishment and reward of all people. He will show mercy to those who sincerely attempt to follow his law. Thus 2:17–29 amplifies 2:12–16 while introducing the kind of Jewish teacher against whom Paul competed for the hearts and minds of gentiles sympathetic to Judaism.

5 Paul's Dialogue with a Fellow Jew

One's reading of 2:17–29 decisively sets the direction for reading chapters 3–8. The reader who sees a "phenomenological description" of Jewish piety and a universal indictment of Jews as controlled by the power of sin will go on to attribute to Paul one of the traditional economies of salvation. I have insisted, however, that the text depicts an individual who represents not Judaism or the depravity of every Jew but a Jew who is one in name only. In particular, he arrogantly understands himself to be a moral teacher of gentiles and yet causes the name of God to be dishonored among the gentiles because of his failing to live by the law.

The reader must be clear about the progress of the discourse. In 1:18–2:16 Paul discourses to his gentile audience about gentile wickedness and God's impartial justice, which allows mercy for lawkeeping gentiles and promises punishment for all who will not live by the teachings of the law, Jew or gentile. The section begins with a reference to the "good news" and ends at 2:16 with Paul announcing that God will judge the secrets of human hearts according to "his good news." "His good news" is the message God revealed to him and commissioned him to preach. Paul's gospel says that God in his righteousness has provided a way for gentiles to come to him, thereby giving them new life through the faithfulness of Jesus. At this point (2:17), Paul turns to a Jewish teacher who holds out a different approach to gentiles of moral betterment.

In 3:1, this teacher initiates a dialogue by objecting to Paul's insistence on God's impartial judgment. Paul treats him not as an enemy but as a student in need of instruction. The discussion arises (3:1) when the interlocutor reacts to Paul's claim that God will fully accept gentiles—*as if* they were members of God's chosen people—if they do what the law requires of them (*ta dikaiōmata*, 2:26). Furthermore, Jews who do not truly attempt to live the law have no exemption from God's wrath. The teacher's superior attitude toward gentiles and Paul's effort to claim God's righteousness for gentiles motivate the ensuing dialogue. At the same time, the teacher's own character raises the question of God's treatment of unfaithful Jews.

The prevailing explanations of 3:1–9 prove unsatisfactory in several ways. First, current interpretations only inadequately account for the place of the passage in the letter's argumentation. Scholars usually explain the text as some form of digression.[1] A recent commentator has said Paul writes the passage as if he "were taking a breath" before stating his conclusion to 1:18–3:20.[2] Many believe that Paul gets ahead of himself here, briefly raising and summarily answering objections that he will treat in chapters 6–7 and 9–11.[3] Thus, Paul is diverted from his "main argument." This view of 3:1–9 as a digression correlates with another view about the main argument of Rom 1–4: 1:18–3:20 argues that both gentiles and Jews are sinners subject to God's wrath, and 3:21–4:25 proclaims that mankind can be saved by faith rather than by the law. On this reading, 3:1–9 has to be an aside from Paul's argument about Jewish sinfulness.

The second problem with prevailing readings, closely related to the first, is their contention that the passage lacks unity and coherence. C. H. Dodd writes that "the whole argument of 3:1–8 is obscure and feeble" and adds, "The argument of the epistle would go much better if this whole section were omitted."[4] Virtually all commentators divide the text into two parts, vv. 1–4, in which Paul treats Jewish objections, and vv. 5–8, in which he supposedly replies to charges of libertinism. Thus, vv. 5–8 form a further digression from the main argument.[5] Interpreters never satisfactorily explain why Paul jumps to the topic of libertinism.

A third problem is that interpreters prove unable to make sense of the text's dialogical form. A bewildering array of conflicting explanations and observations on this problem confronts the interpreter. Most commentators note that Paul uses the style of the diatribe in 3:1–9 or say that the passage suggests some kind of conversation.[6] Many also agree in calling v. 1 a "Jewish objection."[7] But there the agreement ends. Several exponents think that an objector raises the questions.[8] Some believe that Paul turns to objections from "enthusiasts," "libertines," or gentiles in vv. 5–8, while others see Paul continuing a quasi-conversation with a Jewish interlocutor.[9] M.-J. Lagrange held that the style of the diatribe remains present in the use of rhetorical questions but also said that the text cannot be a dialogue because Paul uses authority, not reason.[10] Lagrange reflects Bultmann's view that Paul is less rational and more intuitive in his use of diatribe style than the pagan authors.[11] Who is the interlocutor? How is he to be conceived? Most agree that in v. 1 he is a Jewish objector. But is he a Jewish Christian or some other sort of Jew? Does Paul turn to gentile objections in vv. 5–8? Again, interpreters offer numerous suggestions, but no clear answers or consensus exists. Some have argued that the text contains "a debate with Judaism itself." The debate symbolizes the dialectical antithesis of the Christian faith to "Jewish Torah-religion." The Jew here represents pathological religiousness. Paul uses the Jew, then, as a type to proclaim "universal godlessness."[12]

The fourth problem shows the degree of incoherence in the accepted reading. This approach, as reflected in the RSV, has Paul using a collective "we" referring to humanity in v. 5, an exemplary or generalizing first person singular in v. 7, a first person plural in v. 9a meaning "we Jews" and another first person plural in 9b read as an authorial "we" and translated as "I." How readers could understand so many shifts in the reference of the first person in such a short space of text has never been explained. In fact, the necessary contextual indicators for those shifts are not present, and only a priori assumptions that certain types of statements could be made solely by or about certain groups of people (Paul, Jews, Christians, Libertines) make the traditional reading possible.

The universally acknowledged difficulties in making sense of 3:9, and especially of how to translate *proechometha,* belong with this larger problem of understanding vv. 5–8. The most widely held way of reading 3:9 has Paul rhetorically asking, "Are we Jews any better off?" and answering, "No, not at all." But this contradicts 3:1, where the same question is asked but answered in exactly the opposite way.

Finally, the fifth problem with the received reading of vv. 1–9 comes as a consequence of the other difficulties: the inability to satisfactorily account for the function of the passage in the letter's rhetoric.[13] Interpreters either forthrightly admit that Paul is obscure, confused, "has got ahead of himself" or try to show how it makes some sense for him to digress and guard himself against possible objections. But if Paul wanted to guard against objections, his way of doing so in 3:1–9 is extremely ineffective. On this reading, what interpreters take as Paul's answers to the objections are so weak that one would do well to agree with Dodd that the passage is an embarrassment to the rest of the letter. To say that Paul raises questions which he will only adequately treat in chapters 6–7 and 9–11 does not help. The interpreter must come to terms with the location of the passage in 3.

One interpretive option is to accept the traditional reading of 3:1–9 and say that Paul had a lapse, that Paul's argumentation is just not effective in 3:1–9. The reader, however, should not too quickly abandon the possibility of finding a way to read the text that allows it to better fit the argumentation and rhetoric of the larger context. A more natural and coherent interpretation of 3:1–9 and its context is possible if one employs models of dialogue from the diatribe to suggest how the text might be read.

Censorious and Protreptic Dialogues in the Diatribe

The diatribal writings employ various methods to give their discourse a dialogical quality.[14] One method involves the simulation of a full-scale dialogue of questions and answers between the author and an imaginary interlocutor. These dialogues often appear in Arrian's diatribes of Epictetus and in certain discourses of Dio Chrysostom. The diatribal writers understand these dialogues as imitations of the Socratic technique of critical questioning (elenchein) whereby a person was led to a realization of his ignorance, lack of virtue, and need to learn wisdom.[15] Dialogues in the diatribe, then, often have a protreptic character, that is, they attempt to convert the interlocutor to the philosophic life as understood by a particular school or teacher.

In chapter 1, I noted that one form of speech-in-character consists of the speaker or writer simulating an imaginary dialogue with a fictitious interlocutor. One finds this technique with great frequency in the diatribal literature. Teles frg. 1.3 provides an example of this method:

Teles: Appearing to be good isn't better than being good, is it?

Interlocutor: Of course not!

T: Well then, do actors act well on the stage because they appear to be good actors or because they are?

I: Because they are. [dialogue continues]

Teles asks questions that the interlocutor can answer only as Teles wishes. Eventually Teles draws out the conclusion toward which he is driving.

In *Dissertationes* 2.12 Epictetus complains about the lack of ability among philosophers to win people to philosophy and advocates the method used by Socrates. Socrates, he says, used to cause the one with whom he was conversing to be his witness. He gives the following example with his parenthetic comments:[16]

Socrates: And so does the person who feels envy enjoy it?

Interlocutor: By no means (*oudamōs*)! But he feels distress rather than enjoyment. (By the contradiction he has moved his partner in discussion.)

S: Very well (*ti de*)! Does envy seem to you to be a feeling of distress at evils? But what envy is there of evils? (Thus he has made the him say that envy is a feeling of pain at good things.) Very well (*ti de*). Would a person feel envyabout something that did not concern him at all?

I: By no means (*oudamōs*)! (And thus he filled out and elaborated the concept . . .)

Epictetus emphasizes the use of absurd or unthinkable false propositions or conclusions stated as questions that the interlocutor must strongly reject, that bring to light contradictions in his beliefs, and that lead him to the right conclusion. The initial function of the questioning is negative; the Socratic censure (*elenchein*) that indicts the person by exposing ignorance and moral inconsistency. Only after this negative process can the positive teaching or exhortation occur.

In *Dissertationes* 2.23.16f. an interlocutor intrudes with an objection. Epictetus then addresses him in a censorious manner and thereby characterizes him as an Epicurean.[17] Epictetus asks,

Epictetus: What then (*ti oun*)? Does a person dishonor his other faculties?

Interlocutor: By no means (*mē genoito*)!

E: Does a person say there is no use or advancement except in the faculty of moral purpose?

I: By no means (*mē genoito*)! That is ignorant, impious, ungrateful towards God. [dialogue continues].

Epictetus states questions representing false reasoning or unthinkable alternatives so sharply that it forces the interlocutor to reject the questions and in fact state the logical alternative toward which Epictetus leads him. Thus, the interlocutor himself provides the evidence or conclusion. Epictetus then elaborates the implications and draws further conclusions.

When a full-scale dialogue occurs and not just occasional objections from an interlocutor, the speaker or writer usually characterizes the imaginary person as a certain type either corresponding to a specific vice or sometimes belonging to a school of thought. Thus, the interlocutor might be the cowardly philosopher, the boaster, or a pleasure-seeking Epicurean. One very commonly meets characterization by means of apostrophe to the imaginary person.[18] As in Rom 2:1–5 and 17–29, the speaker suddenly shifts to the second person singular and addresses the fictitious person in a censorious tone. When at that point a dialogue follows, the listener or reader knows the identity of the interlocutor. These types usually reflect problems that the teacher believes form impediments to progress in philosophy or flaws that characterize competing teachers. Sometimes the interlocutor is an outsider in regard to the teacher's philosophy or not yet fully committed. In that case the nature of the dialogue becomes protreptic, and the teacher seeks to lead him to the philosophical life. Epictetus, for example, depicts the inconsistent Stoic (*Diss.* 3.24.41):

> Epictetus: "Why, then, do you call yourself a Stoic? But indeed, people who falsely claim Roman citizenship are severely punished, and should those who falsely claim such a great and hallowed calling and name go unpunished? . . .
>
> Interlocutor: What then (*ti oun*)? Do you want me to serve so-and-so? go to his front-door?
>
> E: If reason so decides . . . [dialogue continues][19]

Or the one who is a slave to material security and cannot give things up for the philosophic life:

> Epictetus: And this was the gift of the philosopher, yet will you not come boldly, instead of trembling for your measly clothes and silver plate? Wretched man, have you so wasted your life til now?
>
> Interlocutor: What then (*ti oun*) if I get sick?
>
> E: You will endure sickness well.
>
> I: Who will take care of me?
>
> E: God and your friends [dialogue continues] (*Diss.* 3.26.36–37)

When the discourse lacks a characterizing apostrophe, either the context preceding the dialogue identifies the interlocutor or his character emerges gradually in the conversation. Questions and objections especially reveal the interlocutor's character.

Colloquial style and the use of everyday conversational expressions characterize dialogues.[20] Sentences are short and periods rare. Ellipsis and anacoluthon appear frequently. Exclamations such as *ti oun, ti de,* and *ti gar* are common. The authorial voice sharply rejects false conclusions or unthinkable propositions with expressions such as *mē genoito, oudamōs* and *pantōs ou.*[21]

The first person plural appears in the diatribal literature in dialogues.[22] This dialogical "we" refers to the two discussion partners in the dialogue, the authorial voice and the interlocutor. The "we" often points to the discussion itself, as when Dio says (*Or.* 61.2, 3), "Well now, let us examine . . ." or "Are we then to suppose . . . ?" And Musonius Rufus exhorts (8.38.12 Hense), "Let us observe. . . ." These "we" texts often express solidarity, agreement, or some area of commonality. The first person plural may occur in a shared false conclusion, as in Epictetus, *Dissertationes* 3.7.2: "Which is the best? What shall we say (*ti eroumen*) to people? The flesh?" When an interlocutor in Seneca, *Epistulae* 117.3, asks, "What then? Why do we not say that being wise is a good?" the "we" means Seneca and the interlocutor as Stoics. The teacher (authorial voice) especially makes use of undeniable basic principles or beliefs that are axiomatic for both discussion partners. These force the interlocutor to answer his questions in a way that draws out implications supporting the teacher's point of view.

Paul's Use of the Dialogue in 3:1–9

In light of the preceding characteristics of diatribal dialogues, the rhetoric of 3:1–9 gains clarity. To begin with, the phenomenon in 3:1–9 has its beginning in 2:17. There Paul suddenly shifts to the second person singular and begins to address and characterize the Jewish teacher. This address continues until the fictitious Jew interrupts with an objection in 3:1. Dialogues from the diatribe suggest that 3:1–9 should be read as follows:

Interlocutor: Then what (*ti oun*) advantage does the Jew have? Or what good is circumcision? (A)

Paul: Much in every way! Above all, the Jews were entrusted with the words spoken by God himself. For how else could it be (*ti gar*)? If some Jews were unfaithful, their unfaithfulness doesn't nullify God's faithfulness, does it? (B)

I: God forbid (*mē genoito*)! Let God be true and every man a liar, as it is written, "so that you may be justified in what you say and win when you are challenged." (C)

P: But if our unrighteousness demonstrates the righteousness of God, what shall we say (*ti eroumen*)? Is God unrighteous when he expresses his anger? (I am speaking in a human way.) (D)

I: God forbid (*mē genoito*)! For then how will God judge the world? (E)

P: But if the truthfulness of God is magnified by my falsity and increases his glory, why should I still be judged a sinner? And shall we then say (as certain people also slanderously charge us with saying), "Let us do evil that good may come"? (Those who slander us in this way are justly condemned.) (F)

I: What then (*ti oun*)? Are we [as Jews] at a disadvantage? (G)

P: Not at all (*ou pantōs*)! For we have already charged that both Jews and Greeks are all under sin. (H)

The text overflows with the characteristic expressions and stylistic traits of the diatribal dialogue. The passage abounds with the various types of questions and the rejection of false conclusions with *mē genoito* and *ou pantōs,* the typical exclamations *ti oun* and *ti gar,* and so on. More important, however, the text genuinely holds together and makes sense. Many commentators recognize the style of the diatribe in 3:1–9, but their readings make little sense because they understand the questions in vv. 1, 3, 5, and sometimes 7 and 8 as objections from the interlocutor. Read in this way, the dialogue simply does not work. Furthermore, dialogue in the diatribe is not typically conducted in that way; the teacher asks the questions or guides the discussion. Rom 3:1–9 is not a series of relatively unrelated questions or objections. In fact, the five problems characterizing the traditional reading of the text can be solved if one reads 3:1–9 as a diatribal dialogue.

Paul begins to address a fellow Jewish teacher in 2:17 and in 25–29 argues that the criterion for acceptability by God applies equally to Jew and gentile. If gentiles somehow conform to the law, though not having the law, then they are just as acceptable to God as Jews. The Jewish teacher then asks the logical question: What is the advantage of being a Jew? As in the diatribe, *ti oun* clarifies the inferential nature of the question. Based upon what Paul has said in 2:25–29, it might seem possible to conclude that membership in the Jewish community provides no advantage and is of no value. But Paul strongly resists this conclusion in B and, as if beginning a list of advantages, mentions that the Jews were entrusted with, according to several translations, "the oracles of God."

The meaning of "oracles of God" (*ta logia tou theou*) has been problematic for modern commentators. When scripture was read openly in the context of dogmatic systems, the expression meant scripture as a whole or the Bible. Read in Paul's context, however, this meaning becomes implausible. Whatever the reading, one must argue from the discourse of the letter, not from some system imagined to be in Paul's head. Sam K. Williams's scholarly discussion of *ta logia tou theou* consistently works from the letter's context.[23] Williams in turn builds on the philological work of T. W. Manson, who had concluded that *logia* in 3:2 meant "the promises of God."[24] Williams shows that "they were entrusted with" (*episteuthēsan*) in 3:2 can be used to further delimit the meaning of *ta logia*.[25] Each time Paul employs the passive form of *pisteuein*, it is in reference to his or someone else's responsibility for preaching the gospel, for example, he and Peter were "entrusted with the gospel" (Gal 2:7; cf. 1 Thess 2:4, 1 Cor 9:17). Paul places much importance on the claim that this good news was promised beforehand in Israel's scriptures. In the very opening sentence of the letter he speaks of "God's good news that he promised before through his prophets in the holy scriptures." Williams also cites Gal 3:8: "The scripture, foreseeing that God would make the gentiles righteous on the basis of faithfulness, preached the good news beforehand to Abraham, saying, 'In you shall all the gentiles be blessed.'" Williams concludes that *ta logia tou theou* in 3:2 means specifically the promise given to Abraham and confirmed by the prophets that God would bless the gentile peoples through Abraham's seed (Christ).[26]

Williams, however, does not recognize the significance of Paul's dialogue with his Jewish competitor for gentiles. Paul criticizes him for his arrogance toward gentiles and for his moral failure. This teacher is not the light to the gentiles (2:19) that he pretends to be. The apostle sums up his rebuke by quoting Isa 52:5: "Because of you the name of God is slandered among the gentiles." It comes as no surprise, then, that Paul answers the teacher's question about the Jewish advantage by retorting that God has entrusted Jews with the good news to the gentiles. This amounts to another deep rebuke: Precisely the project at which this particular Jew has most miserably failed ought to have been his greatest honor, blessing, and responsibility. The meaning remains much the same even if *ta logia* means "God's promises" in general. The area of failure relevant to the teacher still concerns the Abrahamic promise to the gentiles (Rom 4).

One further clue adds weight to this understanding of "God's oracles." Philo (*Somn.* 2.220) speaks of "the unfalsifiable witnesses of the holy oracles [*chrēsmoi*]." Philo's word for oracles was used interchangeably with *ta logia* in Greek culture for oracular pronouncements of the gods. Philo goes on to explain that these are words from scripture of which God himself is speaker and cites the example of Ex 17:6. This meaning fits 3:2 perfectly because Paul goes on in his discussion with the teacher to focus on words of God spoken to Abraham (Rom 4).

This reading explains the traditionally puzzling logic of discourse in 3:1. Paul does not begin to list the advantages of Israel and then forget to go on to the second one. His answer is a dismissive rebuke, although he is quite serious about Jewish priority. Many interpreters understand 3:3 as a second objection from the interlocutor. Rather, 3:3 constitutes a form of the diatribal teachers' leading question: The teacher raises the objection (A), but Paul answers him sharply and assumes the role of a questioner. The apostle not only answers with a strong "no" (B) to the interlocutor's implication (A) that God might fail to give the advantages he had promised to the Jews but turns the question of failure toward his partner in discussion. Just because "some Jews," like the Jewish teacher, have been unfaithful to God does not mean that God will be unfaithful to Israel as a whole. Paul's language belies the universal indictment of Jews supposed to be the point of 2:17–3:8. Only some Jews are unfaithful. Moreover, Paul does not say that all Jews are morally depraved or fail to live by the law. The failure under discussion is the failure to be a light to the gentiles.

The "some" (cf. 11:17) in 3:3 is the first place in the letter where Paul suggests that more than one Jew, the interlocutor, has been unfaithful. Such language next appears in 11:20, 23. Ancient and medieval commentators, anxious to pounce on "the Jews," usually understood "unbelief/unfaithfulness" in both chapters as "unbelief," "failure to believe in Christ as personal savior." Most modern commentators have seen that the immediate context makes that translation highly unlikely in 3:3 but have used it for chapter 11. Paul in fact plays on the word's root when he speaks of Israel being "entrusted" (episteuthēsan with the oracles of God and then of some being "unfaithful" (episteuthēsan, apistia). Furthermore he contrasts this unfaithfulness with the faithfulness (pistis) of God. Surely he is not talking about an act of mental assent on God's part, God's faith. Rather, as C and F show, he means his loyalty and truthfulness to his promises. In 11:17f. the olive tree is Israel. Some of the tree's branches have been broken off because of their apistia, their unfaithfulness (vv. 17, 20). This group of Jews will be grafted back on if they do not persist in their unfaithfulness (v. 23).

Anticipating later discussion, I suggest that Paul's dialogue in 2:17–5:11 relates in important ways to chapters 9–11.[27] The teacher forms a caricature, an extreme example of Jews who, in Paul's eyes, have radically failed in their mission to the gentiles. The similarity in language between chapters 3 and 11— both speak of "some" who have been unfaithful—is not an accident. An example of who such Jews might have been appears in 15:31 when Paul asks his readers to pray that he might be delivered from "the disobedient ones in Judea" (tōn apeithountōn; cf. 11:30–32). If the teacher represents or at least includes opponents of his mission to the gentiles, then Paul's use of the interlocutor assumes a clearer significance. Romans allows gentile believers to overhear a discussion in which Paul argues for gentile justification through Christ against a Jew who opposes righteousness for gentiles apart from works of the law. In this way, he can dramatically argue both for his own gospel and against its most threatening alternative.

In 3:3 (B), Paul begins to question the teacher and will lead him not only to answer his own objection but also to admit the apostle's basic claims. Paul's

Jewish discussion partner can only deny in the strongest terms the suggestion that the unfaithfulness of some of God's people (for example, the teacher himself) means that God would fail to uphold the covenant (3:4). The interlocutor not only rejects this false conclusion with *mē genoito* but also proclaims God's truthfulness even if all humans are false and backs this up with a citation from Ps 51:4. As in Epictetus's explanation of how such dialogue works, Paul has led his discussion partner "to be the witness," to provide the evidence. God's steadfast faithfulness to his word and gracious activity on behalf of his people is an axiomatic premise for both Paul and his discussion partner. The question of 3:3 answers the objection of 3:1 on the most basic level: The God who made his covenant with Israel remains true to his promises and will continue to pursue the best interests of the Jewish people. The teacher has affirmed exactly what lies at the heart of Paul's argument: Whatever happens in history, God is faithful to his promises.

The teacher's admissions in 3:4f. about God's trustworthiness have an even closer connection to 2:17–29 than I have suggested above, and that connection contains an even sharper irony. Paul has accused the teacher of causing gentiles to slander God's reputation (2:24). Verse 4 speaks about the justification of God's word and his vindication in the face of criticism; v. 5 of confirming his justice and v. 7 of his truthfulness; vv. 21–26 speak seven times of God now demonstrating his justice or righteousness through Christ. The argument of Rom 1–3 takes a motif that earlier Jewish writings applied to Israel and extends it to the gentiles. God will bring about justice, restoring Israel, in order to vindicate his reputation among the nations. Paul adds that since God does not make unfair distinctions among peoples, he will also act equitably toward the gentile peoples. The teacher's hypocritical pose as a moral teacher of gentiles only further sullies God's reputation among the other peoples. Paul will tell him that God has now used Jesus' faithfulness to deal with gentile sin so as "to demonstrate his righteousness at the right time in history in order that he might be just" (3:26). God's reputation is at stake.

The dialogue of 3:1–9 leads the teacher to admit that the unfaithfulness of some Jews in communicating God's promises will not prevent God himself from faithfully fulfilling his promises. God will vindicate his name by restoring Israel and redeeming the gentiles as he has promised. The discourse with the teacher echoes texts like Ez 36:17–36. Some commentators believe that 2:24 alludes to Ez 36 in addition to Isa 52:5. Ez 36:17–21 speaks of God exercising his anger against Israel for her sins by dispersing her among the nations. But wherever they went, the people of the nations say, "These are the people of the Lord yet they had to go out of the land" (20). Verse 23 continues:

I will vindicate the holiness of my great name, which has been defiled among the gentiles, which you defiled among them; and the gentiles will know that I am the Lord when through you I vindicate my holiness before their eyes. And I shall take you from among the gentile peoples . . . and bring you into your land . . . and I will purify you from all uncleanness . . . and I will give you a new heart and a new spirit . . . and cause you to walk in my rulings . . . and the gentile peoples who remain round about you shall know that I, the Lord, have restored the ruined places. . . . I, the Lord, have spoken and I will do it. (36:23–26 LXX)

Jewish writings that develop the idea of a day when gentiles repent and acknowledge God treat this gentile turning as a reaction to God vindicating his reputation by restoring Israel in fulfillment of his promises. Similarly, 1 Cor 14:25 cites Isa 45:14 to describe the repentance and conversion of gentiles in the community assembly. Isa 45:14–25 announces gentile repentance as a consequence of God saving Israel in his righteousness and faithfulness to his promises. Israel's restoration will precipitate and therefore must precede gentile repentance. The firm logic of this order causes Paul, in chapters 9–11, to wonder at the amazing mystery of God's surprise in allowing the gentile mission to precede Israel's restoration. As I will argue below, Paul believes that the meaning of Jesus' life and death is intimately connected with this reversal.

In D (3:5), Paul drives the point further, drawing attention to the discussion itself with the dialogical "we." Again, Paul's question leads the teacher to answer with *mē genoito* and to affirm that God is the judge of the world, another shared axiomatic belief that received special emphasis in 1:18–2:29. Tradition has taken 3:5 as a general affirmation of human sinfulness and guilt in contrast to God's righteousness, but that reading does not fit Paul's discussion with the Jewish teacher. Thus I want to look more closely at 3:5: "If our unrighteousness confirms (establishes) God's righteousness (justice), what shall we say? Is God who inflicts anger unjust?" If we make the letter itself, rather than some later scheme of Christian theology, the context for reading the verse, what could "our unrighteousness," "God's righteousness," and "our unrighteousness confirming God's righteousness" mean ?

Broader theological implications do mark 3:5: for example, that the one side of God's righteousness, namely, his grace toward the house of Israel, does not negate the other side of his righteousness, his right "to inflict wrath upon us (Jews)." The teacher's response implies that if God showed his righteousness only by affirming his people, then his place as just judge of the whole world would be called into question. Paul drives the interlocutor toward an admission of God's impartiality and of his own culpability as a lawbreaker who has caused God to be blasphemed among gentiles. But too many arrows from 3:5 point the reader to places earlier and later in the discourse to stop at such a general level of meaning.

The much-disputed expression "the righteousness of God" appears for a second time in the letter at 3:5. Rather than studying the concept in other Jewish literature and bringing its meaning to the text, one should ask what an ancient reader of the letter might have learned about God's righteousness up to this point. The good news, which Paul defines (1:1–3; Gal. 3:8) as the Abrahamic promise to the gentiles, reveals God's righteousness. God's righteousness somehow also concerns the salvation of Jews and gentiles, and it has something to do with someone's faithfulness (1:17–18). No person in the Greco-Roman world, pagan or Jew, would have begun reading 1:18f. ("For the anger of God is revealed from heaven against all ungodliness and wickedness") and *not* have assumed that chapters 1–2 were in some sense discussing God's justness or righteousness in his relations to the world's peoples and specifically to the non-Jewish peoples. Verses 18–32 of chapter 1 stress God's measure for measure punishment of gentile vice. Chapter 2 labors the theme of God's impartiality in judging, punishing, and rewarding and highlights the precarious situation of the gentiles. Williams has shown that "God's righteousness" in Romans is, above all, his just settlement of the situation of the gentiles.

The specificity of the context confirms Williams's conclusion. The topic of Paul's discussion with the Jewish teacher is how gentiles are to be made righteous and Jewish responsibility for that mission. The teacher belongs to a group of Jews who have, in Paul's view, failed their trust in communicating God's promises to the gentiles (3:2). Paul claims that God's reputation among the gentiles has been harmed by the teacher's approach (2:24). The teacher himself admits that God's reputation for keeping promises must be vindicated (3:4). Then Paul suggests that Jewish unrighteousness is somehow actually working to confirm, show, or establish God's righteousness.[28] Thus Jewish failure in conveying God's promises to the gentiles somehow actually supports God's plan to bring about justice for the gentiles. Paul postpones telling the reader just how Jewish unrighteousness supports God's justice until chapters 9–11. There he climactically reveals the mystery that God has brought about a temporary hardening of Jewish attitudes, delaying Israel's restoration and the world's judgment in order to allow an opportunity for the gentile mission. The disobedience of Jews like the teacher has delayed Israel's salvation so God can be merciful to both Jews and gentiles. Although the section certainly makes sense on its own terms, the ancient reader would be able to understand the full significance of 2:17–3:9 only in retrospect after reading chapter 11. Postponing the final key to Paul's account of God's ways and plans constitutes one of the letter's central rhetorical strategies.

The question of whether God can justly punish those he has hardened for the sake of the greater good disturbs the apostle. Thus chapter 9 elaborates the issue of justice raised in 3:5. "Is there injustice with God?" 9:14 asks. Paul then uses the example of God hardening Pharaoh's heart. What purpose do God's hardening and punishing serve? The apostle quotes Ex 9:16: "I raised you up for this very reason; to show my power by you so that my name may be proclaimed in the whole world." Again we encounter the theme of God vindicating his reputation among the nations. Similarly, 9:22–24 speaks of God expressing his anger, making known his power, and patiently enduring vessels of anger in order to make known the riches of his glory for vessels of mercy, those called from not only the Jews but also the gentiles. Again the letter's characterization of the Jewish teacher fits. The dialogue defines him as belonging to "some Jews" who have failed in Israel's mission to the gentiles.

At the end of chapters 9–11, Paul breaks into a doxology: "O the depth of God's riches, wisdom and understanding! How unsearchable are his judgments and unknowable are his ways! For who has known the Lord's mind, or who has been a counselor to him, or who has given a bribe to him in order to get something in return." According to Paul, Jewish opposition to his mission to the gentiles and God's anger with these Jews was part of God's larger plan. The result would be to demonstrate God's justice and mercy to the whole world, both to the Jews and the other nations. The doxology emphasizes not only the mysteriousness of this plan but also God's justice as a judge and particularly his impartiality. These are precisely the themes of 1:18–3:26, God's righteousness.

Paul is not a radical innovator in all of this. Although the specific role of his gospel is new, much of the discourse about God, Israel, and the gentiles appears prominently in ancient Jewish writings. The *Psalms of Solomon* 9 begins by bewailing Israel's plight. When exiled they turned away from God so that he punished Israel by dispersing the nation among the gentiles. Why did God punish Israel in this way? The author, like Paul, alludes to Psalm 51: "That your righteousness might be proven right, O God, in our lawless actions. For you are a righteous judge over all the peoples of the earth. For none that do evil shall be hidden from your knowledge, and the righteousness of your devout is before you, Lord. Where, then, will a person hide himself from your knowledge, O God?" *Psalms of Solomon* 9.2–3 and Rom 3:1–9 (also 2:1–3:31) share a similar complex of ideas. Israel, like the other nations, has also sinned. God justly punishes her. His punishment shows that he is a righteous judge of all the nations and that none can escape his judgments. God's actions all ultimately serve Israel's good. She is beloved by him. Paul, however, pushes these ideas by insisting that God's righteousness means equality not only in punishment but also in reward for gentiles (2:6–16, 25–29). Thus the teacher wants to know what advantage the Jew has (3:1) and if Jews do not actually end up at a disadvantage (3:9).

Verse 7 continues to push the teacher. The rhetorical first person singular aims to highlight the absurdity of someone like the teacher questioning God's plan to use the sinfulness of Jews in order to promote his larger purposes. The teacher's failure to acknowledge the good news for the gentiles in the oracles of God does support God's larger plans, but the teacher must still bear responsibility for his sinfulness. Again 15:8 forms the best commentary on the "truthfulness of God": Christ's ministry was to secure God's promises to Jews and gentiles and thus "on behalf of God's truthfulness."

To most interpreters, F (vv. 5–8) has seemed to be a digression in which Paul gets ahead of himself and anticipates chapter 6: "Are we to continue in sin that grace may abound?" Commentators usually say that Paul takes this "unexpected turn" in order to guard himself against an antinomian misunderstanding of his doctrine of grace.[29] But it simply makes no sense for the discourse to suddenly jump forward to an entirely different subject. Such an interpretation makes little sense even on a traditional Western reading but no sense at all in the context of my reading. Rather, the saying embedded in 3:8 ("Let us do evil that good might come") is the logical objection that a competitor like the teacher might make to Paul's explanation for the widespread Jewish failure to recognize the gospel of Jesus Christ. "If you are saying, Paul, that our unfaithfulness to God's oracles helps to bring about his righteousness and the fulfillment of his promises, then why should we not just sin all the more and further support God's plans." Paul admits that he has actually met such objections as he dismissively anticipates that argument (3:8).

The question of how to take *proechometha* in 3:9 is one of the more vexing problems in the letter. In the dialogical reading that I am proposing, the only way of taking *proechometha* that is without serious grammatical and philological problems is also contextually plausible. Modern interpreters have usually taken the verb as a middle used as *proechomen* the active.[30] Although the middle is used for the active, it is never attested for *proechō*, and I find it difficult to understand why Paul would not just use the active.[31] If one understands the word as a genuine middle, the meaning would be "do we offer something as a defense?" This will not work, however, because there is no direct object for the verb in the text. If, instead of taking *proechometha* as a separate question, one joins it with *ti oun*, then *ti* could be the object; but in that case the answer would have to be *ouden* instead of *ou pantōs*.[32]

Interpreters have been driven to the desperation of taking *proechmetha* as a middle used as an active because reading it as a passive does not fit the usual understanding of 3:1–8. If Paul assures Jews of God's faithfulness in 3:1–4 and then turns to the problem of libertinism is vv. 5–8, why would he use the passive and say, "Are we Jews at a disadvantage?" in 3:9? The customary interpretation also poses the serious problem of having Paul restate the question of 3:1 in 3:9 and yet give the opposite answer.[33]

If, on the other hand, we understand Paul as asking questions in vv. 5–8 which lead to the conclusion that the teacher cannot escape responsibility for what he does in spite of God's faithfulness, then it makes good sense for him to ask whether he as a sinner stands in a worse position than gentiles. Paul strongly affirms the justness of God's wrath against the unfaithfulness of some Jews in 5–8 and might seem to eliminate God's mercy and forgiveness toward Israel. While emphasizing the positive possibilities for gentiles in 2:14–16 and 26–29, he warned the teacher of his condemnation for failure to keep the law (2:17–24, 27). Chapter 2 contrasts gentiles who keep the law with Jews who do not. The interlocutor thinks that Paul has eliminated God's mercy toward Israel, although Paul only opposes a one-sided, partial mercy toward Jews alone. On this reading, 3:1 and 3:9 are parallel: both texts affirm that God's impartiality does not create a disadvantage for his people, the first text with respect to promise or covenant and the second with respect to judgment. In 3:9, Paul replies, "Not at all" and again using the dialogical "we" supports his answer by reminding the interlocutor of what has already been established in their discussion: "For we have already charged that both Jews and Greeks are all under sin." In 3:4, the teacher answered Paul's question by quoting scripture. Now Paul overwhelms him with a chain of quotations in 10–17.

This reading of vv. 5–9 solves another serious objection to the customary interpretation, the five different uses of the first person, the changing references of the "we" that I listed above. How the original readers could have known to make all of these shifts remains a serious problem for traditional interpretations. The dialogical "we," meaning Paul and his discussion partner, on the other hand, makes sense consistently for the whole text.

My first and fifth objections to the prevailing understanding of 3:1–9 were the inability to adequately relate the passage to its context and to account for its function in the rhetoric of the letter, respectively. The proposed reading permits a more coherent understanding of the argumentation of chapters 1–3, one that accounts for aspects of that argumentation which have generally been overlooked. Traditionally Paul's accusation in 3:9 that "both Jews and Greeks, all are under sin," has been viewed as the purpose and theme of 1:18–3:20. Jouette Bassler has shown that this emphasis on the negative function of 1:16–3:20 is one-sided and reductionistic.[34] I would go further. Chapters 1–2 do not aim at proving that all are sinners. Rather, they depict the desperate situation of gentiles owing to their idolatry and God's punishment of enslaving them to passions and desires; Paul mounts an argument that God will accept gentiles as gentiles if they behave toward God and neighbor as the law requires. Chapter 2 first dramatically addresses a gentile, then a Jewish teacher who represents a certain kind of Jewish competition for gentiles and an approach to the gentile dilemma that Paul wants to criticize. The argument of 1:18–2:29 being understood in this way, my reading of 3:1–9 fits the context very well indeed. The passage does not form a digression but a continuation of the discussion with the Jew introduced in 2:17–24.

In the traditional reading, 3:21f. begins a distinctly new phase in the argument, one having little connection with what precedes except that 1:18–3:20 has established universal sinfulness as the problem for which 3:21ff. is the answer. That reading cannot stand if one takes Paul's dialogue with his fellow Jew seriously. Paul not only continues to direct his remarks in 3:21–26 to the fictitious interlocutor, but again resumes their dialogue in 3:27–4:2. Moreover, the groundwork for what Paul announces to the teacher in 3:21–26 has already been laid in 3:1–9. On this reading 3:1–8 no longer seems to be a digression with its own parenthetic digression. Rather, 1:18–3:9 and, as I will argue, 3:10–4:25, fit tightly and flow smoothly in a complex and powerful rhetoric constructed with speech-in-character. Instead of forming an appendix or an afterthought on Jewish unbelief, on this reading chapters 9–11 become a climactic resumption of issues already raised in 2:17–3:9 that touch the very heart of Paul's message and ministry.

6 Paul on Sin & Works of the Law (3:9-20)

"Paul conclusively establishes the wickedness of all humanity in Rom 1:18–3:20."[1] By such statements, which are
amazingly sure and frequent, interpreters do not usually
mean that no one is perfect or that everyone fails to live up
to moral standards. Rather, they mean that every human
being has existed in a qualitative state of wickedness and
separation from God. In some versions of this interpretation, relative goodness or wickedness does not matter.[2]
There is no difference between Moses and Adolf Hitler.
Without faith in Christ, both are sinners totally separated
from God.

The reading I propose stands in clear contrast to this
powerfully influential Western understanding. Rom 1:18–
2:5 announces that God is angry with the gentile nations
and has punished them justly with bondage to their own
passions, and it warns gentiles that they must repent lest
they face God's terrible day of judgment with all of their
sins stored up before God; 2:6–16 argues that God is just
and impartial in his punishment and reward of both Jews
and gentiles. The important distinction upon which judgment will be made is between wickedness and living as
God's law teaches. In fact, gentiles can know the law, and
some even live by it. On the other hand, some Jews, like the
arrogant teacher of gentiles (2:17–29), miserably fail to
keep the law. God will judge the lawkeeping gentile as if he
were a faithful Jew, while he will condemn the Jew who
lives like a wicked gentile. This, however, does not mean
that being a Jew is not of enormous value (3:1–9). Even
though some Jews have failed in their primary trust of bearing God's oracles to the world, God has been and will continue to be faithful toward his chosen people. He will bring
about their good, but he cannot ignore the wickedness of
some.

The classical Western doctrine of sin cannot be found

in 1:18–3:8. If contained at all in Romans 1–3, it must be found in 3:9–20. Yet 1:18–3:20 has been made to bear enormous weight in the classical Western conception of Paul on sin. The paucity of texts on sin in the letters (other than Romans) makes a rapid survey of the evidence possible. The earliest is 1 Thess 2:13–16. Birger Pearson has argued that the text is an interpolation from a period after 70 C.E.[3] Pearson has argued as well as one can for this view, and he has convinced a number of scholars. Nevertheless, weaknesses in his argument make his position ultimately unpersuasive. Strong arguments against Pearson's view and for the "authenticity" of the text have been made by John Hurd.[4] Furthermore, the text can be shown to fit both the hortatory discourse of the letter and classical hortatory patterns in paraenetic letters that contain calls to imitation.[5] Finally, the persuasiveness of typical arguments for interpolations has been greatly reduced by a new candor in literary studies. Literary theory associated with the New Criticism demanded that all literary texts have coherence and integration; that they be at some level fully self-consistent. Whatever else one's judgment of poststructural literary theory, it has shown that degrees of incoherence and contradiction play a part in every text.[6] Therefore, it is no longer so clear that anomalies in Paul's letters are inauthentic.

I translate 1 Thess 2:14–16 as follows:

> For you, brethren, became imitators of the communities of God in Judea, those in Christ Jesus; for you suffered the same things from your own people as they did from the Judeans, who killed both the Lord Jesus and the prophets, and expelled us, and are not pleasing to God and oppose all people, hindering us from speaking to the gentiles that they may be saved. Thus as a result they are continually filling up the measure of their sins. But God's wrath has overtaken them at last!

This earliest extant Pauline reference to sin bears language similar to what we have seen in Romans. The text does not describe sin as some universal ontological state but as specific behavior by specific groups of people at historical times and places.

Some gentiles at Thessalonica and some Jews in Judea have actively opposed the new believing communities and Paul's mission to the gentiles. According to Paul, these Judeans stand in the tradition of Jews who killed Jesus and persecuted the prophets. Now God's wrath has come upon these Jews at last. Paul gives no hints to help us identify that display of God's wrath. But elsewhere he can attribute various kinds of natural, historical, or moral catastrophes to God's wrath (for example, Rom 1:24–28; 13:4–5; 1 Cor 10:6–12; 11:30–32). Unfortunately, recent discussions of early Christian anti-Judaism have tended to read the text in a more generalizing sense than it can bear. Later

Christian interpretation certainly read the text as a universal condemnation of Jews and Judaism, but that makes little sense in Paul's context. It makes as little sense to read this as a general condemnation of Jews and Judaism as it does to take verse 14 as meaning that all gentiles or even all Thessalonians were guilty of persecuting the community in that city. Here, as elsewhere, Paul's condemnation of fellow Jews falls upon those who have actively opposed his law-free mission to gentiles.

Second, I find significant the "apocalyptic" context of the reference to sins. The result of the opposition from those Judeans is that "they continually fill up their sins" or, as the RSV renders, "so as always to fill up the measure of their sins." The passage contains conceptions about God's justice and history that play significant roles in Jewish literature before Paul. The basic idea seems to go back to Gen 15:16 (cf. Jub. 14:16), which explains that the Amorites cannot be driven out of the land until their iniquities are complete (cf. 9:25; Lev 18:24–25). God's judgment against these gentiles will not be exercised until their sexual immoralities have reached a cumulative level of evil that merits their destruction. Dan 8:23 provides the classic apocalyptic instance: "And at the end of the kingdom, when their sins have reached their full measure, a king . . . shall arise." God has used the gentile nations as instruments to chastise his people. At the end of this "period of God's indignation," Antiochus, the enemy of Israel, will arise (8:19; 11:36). Israel, however, will be punished, will repent, and will be restored when the period determined by God concludes (9:24). On the other side, the transgressions of Antiochus and his predecessors have built up with prosperity instead of punishment (11:36). When the period of God's anger against Israel has ended and the sins of the gentiles reach their full measure, God will exercise his terrible judgment against Israel's oppressors. Second Macc 6:12–16 sums up this philosophy of history: "With the gentile nations God waits patiently to punish them until the complete measure of their sins has been reached." With Israel, however, God mercifully punishes them as they sin so that their transgressions do not build and reach a measure deserving of God's vengeance.

Paul's belief that Jews suffer for evil they do is no innovation; it is common to the tradition.[7] In 1 Thessalonians, those "Judeans who killed both the Lord Jesus and the prophets and expelled us and displease God and oppose all people by hindering us from speaking to the gentiles" are filling up the measure of their sins so that God's wrath has come upon them. Paul applies this language often used for gentile oppressors to Jews who have oppressed those in Jesus' "prophetic" tradition. In Romans, at least, applying the charge to some of his Jewish kin follows from his doctrine of impartiality.

Other texts about sin fall into clear categories: gentiles are sinners (1 Thess

4:5; 1 Cor 5:1, 9–11; 12:2; Gal 2:15); sin in the believing community (1 Cor 6:17; 7:1–8; 2 Cor 12:21); Christ died for sins (1 Cor 15:3; 2 Cor 5:21; Gal 1:4). Gal 3:22 appears almost as an anomaly: "But scripture consigned all things under sin in order that the promise might be given on the basis of Jesus Christ's faithfulness to those who are faithful/believe." First, except for Romans, only here among Paul's letters does such universal-sounding language appear in reference to sin. Second, as in Romans, the context in Galatians is explicitly a discussion of gentile redemption, the Abrahamic promise concerning the gentile peoples. By clarifying what Paul has to say about sin in Romans, one will also clarify Gal 3:22.

The noun *hamartia* (sin) appears forty-eight times in Romans and only ten times in the other letters. In Romans, it appears thirty times in chapters 6–7. In 1:18–3:20, the very argument in which Paul supposedly proves that all people are sinners, it occurs only at 3:9 and 20: for the first time at 3:9! Moreover, *hamartia* is found another eleven times in chapters 5 and 8, resulting in forty-one instances throughout 5–8. Something about this picture subtly belies the traditional reading of Romans. In light of the reading I am arguing, the statistics come as no surprise. Rom 1:18–3:20 is not about human sin as such but plays a part in the argument about God's impartiality and Paul's reading of the current world crisis. Sin looms so large in chapters 5–8 because there Paul discusses the transformation of gentiles, by definition sinners. Precisely when the letter again turns to the subject of self-mastery, sin becomes the major topic together with discussion of the law.

The discussion of sin in Paul (actually Romans) has been confounded by the following recent modern scholarly formulation: "Paul treats sin as a trespass and as a power."[8] According to a prominent scholarly consensus, chapters 1–4 of the letter primarily discuss sin as transgression while 5–8 discuss sin as a power. This widespread scheme for constructing "Paul's theology" was developed in an influential way by Martin Dibelius and then popularized by Rudolph Bultmann and his students.[9] In a vague way, scholars claim that Paul's notion of sin (especially in chapters 5–8) is analogous to so-called apocalyptic or Gnostic notions of world domination by demonic spiritual beings. Paul supposedly radicalized "the Jewish concept of sin" by proclaiming universal enslavement to the power(s) of sin.[10] But "sin as power" in this modern formulation hides a version of the Augustinian bondage of the will doctrine (*non posse non peccare*).

The twentieth-century scholarly tradition tends to treat the issue as one of deciding to which cultural code Paul's language belongs, for example, gnostic, Jewish apocalyptic, orthodox Judaism. Links to these supposed cultural codes, however, have been made only in the vaguest way and add virtually

nothing to the reading and interpretation of the texts in question. The vague-
ness of the approach can be revealed by asking what it meant for Paul to think
that sin was a power. Did he intend an ontological predicate? Is sin a personal
being like Satan? Did he mean only that everyone sins? If one goes with a psychological or a demonological meaning, then how does one reconcile this with
Paul's seeming supposition of human freedom and his discussion of "sin as
transgression"?

The real issues, however, concern reading and interpreting particular texts.
The sin as power construction seems to break the most basic rules of reading
and interpretation. How does one answer the question about meaning? What
is the context? Everyone seems to agree that sin as transgression dominates
chapters 1–4. Does anything in the other texts in question, 3:9; 5:12, 21; 6:16,
21, 20, 23; 7:9, 11, 14, 17–20, indicate that "sin reigned in death" (5:21) is not
metaphorical, like "The ship mastered the storm"? In fact, if these texts do contain some trope about sin as a power, the larger context shaping that trope is
the language about sin as trespass that dominates 1–4 and continues in 6–8.
Even in 6, sin stands in contrast to obedience. A case similar to the one I am
suggesting has been argued by Bruce Kaye and reaffirmed by Heikki Räisänen.[11] In my later discussion of chapters 5–8, I will provide an explanation
for the language about sin in these texts

In sum, the classical Western doctrine of sin cannot be found in 1:18–3:8.
Its absence also marks Paul's other letters, of which the only universalist text
appears to be Gal 3:22. Other texts about sin concern sin in the community or
describe gentiles in contrast to Jews as sinners. The earliest text about sin,
commonly read as a statement about Jews and Judaism, turns out to be about
some Jews and to be a variation on a well-known apocalyptic tradition. The
passage in 1 Thessalonians, moreover, shares an apocalyptic cultural code
found in Romans. Sin in Rom 1–4 means trespass against God's law. Many
have argued that Paul shifts to the idea of sin as power in 5–8, but I have
called this view into question. The next step requires engagement in a critical
inquiry concerning the reading and interpretation of 3:9–21.

If one is certain that 1:18–3:8 has demonstrated that all humans are hopelessly enslaved by sin, then the meaning of 3:9 stands clear: "I have already
charged that all men, both Jews and Greeks, are under the power of sin" (RSV).
The RSV's interpretation, first of all, renders Paul's "we have already charged"
(proētiasametha) as a first person singular, "I have already charged." This constitutes an impossible reading for an ancient audience. Rather, the plural is a
dialogical "we," that is, "I, Paul, and you, the interlocutor, in our discussion
have already concluded." If indeed a reference to the discussion itself, the particular charge to which Paul refers in 3:9 should probably be found in Paul's

discussion with the teacher in 2:17–3:8. It should not be made a general reference to all of 1:18–3:8, as the *RSV* translators have done. Second, the *RSV* adds the word "power" to the text and thus introduces the sin as trespass and sin as power interpretation. Third, in addition to begging the question of gender, the *RSV* interprets *pantas* along the line of abstract universal individualism by adding "men," that is, "all men, both Jews and Greeks."

If my reading of 1:18–3:8 holds, 3:9 does not constitute the section's climactic conclusion. In that case its meaning is open to various possible interpretations. To whom does the subject refer? Does "all, both Jews and Greeks" mean each and every individual who has lived and will ever live? Does it mean that Jews and Greeks as peoples are under sin but that not every individual is a sinner? Often the Hebrew Bible and Jewish literature describe Israel as turning away from God, but at the same time they say that many faithful individuals remain. In 4 Maccabees, for example, the high priest Jason "altered the nation's way of life and changed its constitution in complete violation of the law," and some of the people joined in his wickedness (4:15–20). Because of this, "the divine justice was angered," and God used Antiochus to punish that nation. On the other hand, many of the people resisted and endured death and torture in order to remain faithful (4:24–27). It required the heroic endurance and death of Eleazar, the mother, and her seven sons in order to propitiate God's anger for the nation's sin. As I have suggested, assuming abstract universal individualism endangers good exegesis in Romans. A more collective sense should at least be a consideration for the subject in 3:9. The Greek of 3:9 allows two possibilities that amount to a collective sense. First, the statement might be rhetorical hyperbole for emphasis, as when Acts 17:21 says that "all the Athenians and resident foreigners spent their time in nothing else than telling and hearing the latest opinions." Second, the phrase can mean "Jews and Greeks as a whole," reminding one of 11:26, which speaks of Israel as a whole being saved.

Interpreters have often taken this alleged universal indictment as the climactic and dramatic conclusion to Paul's earlier argument. Ancient readers, however, would have more likely greeted the statement with a yawn than a gasp. That all people are evil or sinners was a commonplace in Jewish, Greek, and Roman culture. In fact, one has to ask why Paul would have to argue such a thesis at all in a world in which people generally assumed that the human moral condition had drastically declined from the time of a distant golden age. The "age of sinfulness" became a theme of the early empire (see chapter 3). Horace wrote, "What does corrupting time not diminish? Our grandparents bore weaker heirs; we have degenerated further and soon will beget offspring more wicked yet" (*Odes* 3.6.45–48). Cynics and Stoics went about proclaiming that virtually all people were fools totally trapped by vice. Stoics might admit that there had been a few truly virtuous wise men in history: They were as rare as the Phoenix, which rose once every six hundred years. Some Cynics were only a bit more optimistic. Lucian's gentle Cynic, Demonax, "thought that it was human nature to sin but godlike or nearly godlike to restore that which had fallen" (*Demon.* 7). The urbane Roman gentleman Pliny the younger quotes the Stoic Thrasea Paetus approvingly: "He who hates vice, hates mankind" (8.22.3). Seneca confesses, "We have all sinned" and reasons that babies are different from others in that they are merely destined to sin (*De Clem.* 1.6.3; *De Ira* 2.10.1; cf. *Ep.* 70.3). Philodemus admits that even the sage "is not perfect and . . . all people habitually sin" (*P. Parr.* 46:5–11). The list could go on and on, but one point is sobering: Augustine drew heavily on Cicero, especially the *Hortensius*, for his doctrine of original sin and a primeval fall.

Varying conceptions of sin existed in the Greco-Roman world, yet the mere statement that all are under sin would be neither surprising nor anything to argue about because almost everyone would agree. Some would say that Paul's version is more profound (extreme!) and more universal. But as I have shown, that is not the case in 1:18–3:8. gentiles on the whole and a certain Jew are, to be sure, described darkly. But what a strange way to argue for universal depravity, however, to allow that some gentiles live by the law (2:14–15, 27) and to say only that some Jews have been disobedient (3:3).

What does "under sin" (*hypo hamartian*) mean? It does not express a universal demonological or bondage of the will doctrine. Paul could have written that humans are under Satan's power or that they are inherently idolatrous and wicked by nature in 1:18–3:8, but he does not. Nevertheless, I do think that Romans employs a kind of metaphor about power. The interpreter, however, should resist over-reading the metaphor and importing an alien doctrine. Rom 7:14 ("I am sold under sin"), Gal 3:22 ("scripture consigned all things under sin") and 3:25 ("we are no longer under an overseer"; cf. 4:2–3) are enough to show that "under sin" means something like "subject to sin" or "under sin's dominion."

The power in Gal 3:22 is not Satan but God (scripture); and this in the only universalizing text outside of Romans. Moreover, its language echoes in Romans 11:32: "For God consigned all to disobedience, so that he may show mercy to all." The preceding verses explain how all Israel will be saved. Paul speaks to the gentiles at Rome and says, "Just as you were at one time disobedient to God but now have obtained mercy because of their [the Jews'] disobedience, so they are now disobedient so that by the mercy shown to you, they may now also obtain mercy." Galatians 3 discusses the promise to Abraham. In Abraham and his seed (Christ), God will bless all the gentiles. Verse 22 explains why God consigned all things under sin: "Scripture consigned all things under sin in order that the promise might be given to those who believe/are faithful on the basis of Jesus Christ's faithfulness." The gentiles were put under sin so that God could bless them on the basis of Jesus' faithfulness and not on works of the law. What else would this "placing the gentiles under sin" be except their enslavement to passions and desires? In other words, the punishment of the gentiles depicted in 1:18–32 had a larger and constructive purpose in view.

The Greek verb *synkleiō* ("to consign") means to lock up, to shut up, to enclose, to confine. Gal 3:23 illustrates the meaning well. Verse 22 parallels *synkleiō* with *phroureō*, which in the passive means to guard or imprison someone. Gal 3:22 and Rom 11:30–32 explain that God has planned the course of history so that in Paul's own time the Jews as a people, as well as the gentiles, would be trapped in sin of their own making. Furthermore, God planned this circumstance so that all the peoples of the world could be shown mercy and blessed equally. God has made sin into the great equalizer of nations. When Paul says that "scripture consigned all things under sin," he means that scripture describes and predicts this plan of God. Paul's own gospel announces the sinful state of idolatrous gentile culture (1:18–2:5). This critique of gentile culture echoes Genesis 1–11. In Rom 9:25–29, 10:21, and 11:7–10, Paul quotes what he understands to be biblical prophecies of Israel's temporary sinfulness and disobedience at the current penultimate point in world history. After quoting a string of scriptural texts in 3:10–18 that either testify to the universal tendency toward sin or more likely prophesy a moment of universal sinfulness, the apostle writes, "Whatever the law says to those in the law, it says in order that every mouth might be shut and the whole world might be subject to God."

Thus in 3:9 we should understand "both Jews and Greeks, all are under sin" to refer to a current state of affairs planned by God whereby not only the gentile peoples like the Greeks (3:9) are in a general relation of sin toward God but also the Jewish people. Paul knows that this belief can raise questions about God's justice and so discusses the hardening of Pharaoh's heart in chapter 9. No wonder Paul uses language suggesting control by a power. The power is God himself. Paul says (3:9) that he has already discussed this charge with the teacher. This, I think, refers at least primarily to 2:17–3:8. On the one hand, it is a basic assumption of the discussion that gentiles are generally sinners and transgressors of the law, and 2:25–29 concerns whether any exceptions to this rule exist. On the other hand, vv. 25–29 not only charge that the Jewish teacher is a transgressor, but suggest a general principle applicable to other Jews as well. Finally, 3:3 alludes to a specific historical circumstance in which an unspecified number of Jews have been disobedient in a way that threatens Israel's basic mission, and 3:4–8 argues that God justly condemns this sin. At this moment in history, both Israel and the other nations stand disobedient before God. Paul's deep conviction holds that all of the peoples have been prepared to seek God's mercy in the current generation. His discussion of God's justice and impartiality leads to the conclusion that all of the nations need and deserve God's mercy; Jews have not escaped this time of sin. As he says in 3:22–3, "For there is no distinction, because all have sinned and come short of God's glory."

Rom 3:9 does not present an exception to the present tense mode of 1:18–3:26. The wrath of God is being revealed against a present historical situation (1:18f.), and the righteousness of God is revealed "now" (3:21). Verses 9 and 10–18 of chapter 3 do not mean that all humans, including Enoch, Moses, and Elijah, have been horrible sinners, no better than the worst gentiles. Rather, at the present moment in history, God has brought about what for Paul is a mysteriously strange and wonderful equalization of Jews and gentiles as peoples standing before their creator (see 11:25–36). A God-wrought, worldwide humiliation will lead to repentant self-understanding by all the peoples.

Commentators usually take vv. 10–18 as a string of scriptural proofs that clinch the timeless universal indictment of 3:9. Another way of reading 3:10–18 begins by looking closely at the content and composition of the text, as Leander Keck has done.[12] Verses 10–12 and 18 assert the universality of sin while 13–17 describe sin's character. If one reads 10–12 and 18 traditionally as literal, timeless statements about the condition of every human person apart from Christ, then, as I have argued, 1:18–3:20 becomes hopelessly contradictory. Keck has shown that this catena of freely edited scriptural texts resembles similar texts in apocalyptic literature. He believes that Paul used a preexisting text, probably borrowed from another source. I would emphasize two points in addition. The verses are examples of invective and display the exaggeration typical of that genre. And the parallel texts that Keck cites were meant to savage contemporary historical situations, individuals, and groups, for example, the wicked priesthood and followers who have corrupted Israel. If Paul employs the catena for current historical circumstance in which all the nations have been consigned to sin, then, his use of the form fits an apocalyptic literary tradition.

In the trivial sense, Paul believes that all humans sin, but that is far from saying that all are unrighteous, all fail to understand, all fail to seek God, all have turned away, and not a single person fears God (3:10ff.). These failures, however, accord with his descriptions of gentile culture in general, with the killers of Jesus and persecutors of his followers, and with his missionary opponents like the teacher. Verses 10–18, in fact, address the boastful teacher and are examples of scripture prophetically consigning all things to sin (Gal 3:22). Paul has already spoken so as to show the reader that "in the law" is not simply a Jew/gentile division. Gentiles are also under obligation to the law, and some gentiles live in the law (2:6–16; cf.1:32; 2:25–29). In 3:19, however, Paul continues speaking to the teacher, who, by definition as a Jew, should be in the law. If he represents Jews whom Paul believes have radically failed in their mission of illuminating the gentiles, and if he is among some Jews (3:3; 11:17) whose disobedience (2:17–24; 3:3; 10:21; 11:30–32) has placed Israel under sin, then 3:19 makes excellent sense. He considers himself to be in the law. Thus he and Paul, as Jews, know (*oidamen*) that the law uncovers and exposes sin in the time of sin, both Jewish and gentile, as the string of scriptures illustrates.

Paul's language about the times being sinful (for example, "The wrath of God is revealed against"; "God has consigned all to sin"; "no one is righteous") fits within that broad and varied Jewish discourse known as apocalyptic. In this literature, one finds widespread belief in a time of crisis and tribulation before the arrival of the new age.[13] The extant texts reveal broad agreement on general characteristics but diverse specific scenarios. One frequent characteristic of these times is that sin and wickedness will multiply and reach horrific proportions. Sometimes the writer understands this to be the current situation and not just a future episode. At Qumran the current period was called the time of wickedness, and the writers of this literature believed that these evil times were already upon them (*CD* 6.10, 14; 15.7–10).[14] According to the *Commentary on Habakkuk,* the gentiles have signaled the end by their wickedness in the worldwide violence of the Roman empire and the Jews by their rampant apostasy, denial of the law, and general wickedness. *Fourth Ezra,* in a text about the tribulations of the end time resembling the little apocalypse of Mark 13, says, "And unrighteousness shall be increased beyond what you yourself see, and beyond what you heard formerly" (5:6); "And one country shall ask its neighbor, 'Has righteousness, or anyone who does right, passed through you?' And it will answer, 'No'" (5:11). *Jubilees* 23:16–17 predicts a future evil generation: "And in this generation children will reproach their parents and their elders on account of sin, and on account of injustice, and on account of the words of their mouth, and on account of great evil which they will do, and on account of their forsaking the covenant. . . . For they all did evil and every mouth speaks of sin and all of their deeds (are) polluted and abominable. And all of their ways (are) contamination and pollution and corruption."[15] Again its language fits the tradition by its harsh, universal description of depravity. This passage compares well to Rom 3:10–18.

Illuminating parallels exist not only for the form and function of vv. 10–18, but also for what seems to be the capstone of the statements about sin in the quotation of Ps 143:2 (LXX 142:2) in 3:20 (cf. Gal 2:16). Indeed, Paul seems to belong to a tradition of Jewish writers using Ps 143:2 to characterize the apex of sinfulness at crucial points in the historical drama. Chapter 80 of *1 Enoch* concerns the cosmic tribulations of the end time including allusions to the error of sinners. It also contains several parallels to Mark 13 and other early Christian apocalyptic texts. In chapter 81, Enoch is commissioned to tell his children what he has learned about the course of the generations: "Show to all your children that no one of the flesh can be just before the Lord; for they are merely his own creation" (81.5).[16] Like Paul, the writer has replaced "no living person" of the Hebrew and LXX with "no flesh." Although the text does allude to future generations of wickedness, it does not literally mean that every person is unrighteous. Indeed, Enoch assumes and often iterates common Jewish belief that humans as God's creatures are righteous only through God's grace and mercy. Thus the *Hymns* (XVI.11; cf. XV.12) from Qumran cite Psalm 143 and add "righteous except through you [God]." All are unrighteous except by God's mercy. Never for a moment does either writing suggest that Israel is therefore lost or that the law is useless. In the *Ps. Sol* 17:19–20, the gentiles (Romans) have laid waste to the land and corrupted the nation. Even in Jerusalem "there was no one among them doing righteousness or justice: From their ruler to the least of the people, they did every sin; The king was lawless, the judge disobedient, the people sinners." The first two lines are reminiscent of Rom 3:20 and especially 3:10 (Ps 14:1–2): "No one is righteous, not one." The psalmist's statements are just as bold and exceptionless as Paul's, but interpreters have learned to provide historical contexts for such statements in *1 Enoch,* the Qumran writings, and the *Psalms of Solomon,* while in Paul interpreters read them as the most literal universal philosophical propositions about human nature. The writer of the *Psalms of Solomon* did not think that every single inhabitant of Jerusalem or the land of Israel was totally evil but only that the representatives of the nation had been co-opted and that unfaithfulness had reached unheralded proportions.

Scholars know about the time of tribulation and sinfulness in apocalyptic texts. In Romans, however, although many would readily admit that such thinking occurs in chapters 9–11, 1–8 have been typically read as if Paul speaks from the Archimedean point of the philosopher. Even in recent years when scholars have recognized that apocalyptic conceptions appear in 1–8, they have failed to connect them with the historical contextuality and particularity of 9–11. An unacknowledged wall separates the two. But Paul's discussion with the Jewish teacher in 2:17–3:20 repeatedly anticipates what he will say about Israel in 9–11. Recognizing the existence of the Jewish teacher makes the numerous parallels between the two parts of the letter salient. The earliest Christians, including Paul, understood Jesus' resurrection to have signaled the last days and in various ways connected these events to the time of the great tribulation, when sinfulness would abound mightily and God's wrath would be imminent. Paul gave his own peculiar interpretation to this period of sin. At the end of the present age God would dramatically show that all depended on his righteousness, mercy, and impartiality, thereby reconciling the world.

Verse 20 contains three major difficulties: the meaning of "works of the law," the adaptation of Psalm 143, and the reference to knowledge of sin. Lloyd Gaston's challenge, in his searching attempt to understand "works of the law," is important because it strikes at the heart of the dominant understanding of Paul since the Reformation: Paul was the one who preached salvation by faith as opposed to works.[17] Thus, for instance, Ernest de Witt Burton defined "works of the law" in a way characteristic of the tradition: "By *erga nomou* Paul means deeds of obedience to formal statutes done in a legalistic spirit, with the expectation of thereby meriting and securing divine approval and award."[18] "Works of the law" meant trying to earn one's own salvation, making a claim on God, trying to pull oneself up without God. In contrast to this supposedly Jewish gospel, Paul preached that God would give salvation to anyone who had the mental act of will and assent called faith. The tradition was quick to realize that such a formulation made faith into another sort of work by which one obtained salvation. The classical way out of the dilemma goes back to Augustine, who said that even the act of believing is a gift from God. So the loss of human freedom became the price paid for consistent theology. Another solution was to say that Paul's formulation was a contrast between the active life, which was supposedly frantic, self-seeking, corporate, and Jewish, and the passive-contemplative-individual religious life of which God approved. The eastern theologians used this version of Paul for importing the Platonic virtues of solitude, quietness, and inwardness into Christianity. But especially the Western tradition made Judaism into the antithesis of Christianity. Judaism was the concrete historical expression of everything religiously hateful summed up in the expression "works of the law," for example, self-striving, legalism, piety, pride. The Paul who founded a religion that is the antithesis of Judaism is not historically plausible.

In an earlier article, Gaston followed the researches of Markus Barth on "works of the law."[19] Barth concluded that "works of the law" was never a Jewish term used of Judaism but rather means "the adoption of selected Jewish practises on the part of gentiles." Gaston cites evidence of judaizing gentiles, sometimes called godfearers, who adopted certain parts of the law but did not follow the "whole law" and become Jews. Thus Paul tells the Galatians that if they receive circumcision, the sign of Israel's peculiar covenant, they must follow the whole law and not just selected bits and pieces (Gal 5:3). Gaston argues that corresponding to this socioreligious situation of judaizing gentiles is the theological problem of the righteous gentile in widely diverse kinds of Jewish literature. What does a gentile have to do in order to be considered righteous by God? Which parts of the law must the gentile observe? On this understanding of 3:20, Paul would be telling the teacher that the moral precepts of the law that he teaches (2:19–22) gentiles cannot make them righteous before God. In this case, justification would be what E. P. Sanders calls transfer terminology: To justify or make someone righteous means to get them into a relation with God when they previously had none.[20] The argument of chapters 1–4 means that only God can make a people righteous by establishing some normative relation with them as he did for Israel with her covenants. In 3:21, Paul announces a new way for gentiles as gentiles to be made righteous through Jesus Christ. This reading of the text, with Barth's and Gaston's earlier interpretation of "works of the law," deserves to be taken seriously. As far as I know only John Gager has done so in publication.[21]

The traditional understanding of the phrase leads to various interpretive dilemmas that have no satisfactory solution. Usually commentators take "works of the law" as equivalent to doing the law or living by the law. Often they further abstract "works of the law" to mean human effort, activity, or achievement. But Paul assumes that activity, religious achievement, and good works are both proper and essential (for example, 1 Cor 15:58; 16:10; Phil 2:12; Gal 6:4).[22] The very foundation of his argument in the first three chapters of Romans arises from the conviction that God judges according to deeds (2:6–16; cf. 2 Cor 5:10). As Räisänen has put it, "That is in accord with the general Jewish view that election and salvation are by God's grace, while reward and punishment correspond to deeds."[23]

Räisänen, Joseph B. Tyson, Sanders, and others have rightly rejected the view that "works of the law" reflects a critique of "Jewish boasting" or legalism.[24] Instead, they have argued that it represents one side of Paul's supposed antithesis between the religious systems of Judaism and Christianity: Christ, grace, Spirit, promise, and faith oppose the law and works of the law. Speaking of Galatians 3, Räisänen writes, "Paul thus assumes a priori that faith and law exclude each other."[25] Even though Räisänen admits that Paul's argument concerns the inclusion of the gentiles, on a very basic level he reads the texts as discussions of two mutually exclusive systems of salvation; one attained by doing the law, the other by having faith. Barth's and Gaston's proposal, that works of the law means specifically things in the law that gentiles must do to be righteous, would seem to have the advantage of more closely fitting Paul's argument about gentile "inclusion." Paul does oppose works of the law to faith or faithfulness (*pistis*). But does *pistis* mean an act by which the lost may attain salvation or receive grace? Comprehending "works of the law" hinges upon the meaning of *pistis*, but I must postpone a discussion of *pistis* until the next chapter.

Gaston's and Gager's understanding of "works of the law" advances exegesis considerably by providing a much more historically and contextually plausible reading. Their proposal, however, still involves interpretive problems and a rather abstract theological quality that makes difficult imagining what significance "works of the law" could have had for Paul's ancient readers. In chapter 2 I described a phenomenon of Jewish moralizing directed at gentiles. Jews like Philo thought that following parts of the law was a superior means to self-mastery of passions and desires. Such writings also connect gentile righteousness before God with the achievement of self-mastery. I have tried to illuminate the appeal and psychological power of this ethic, so closely connected with ambition to rule, gender identity, and prestige. Romans 1 reflects the discourse of this ethic in representing the gentile dilemma as a loss of self-mastery. The letter depicts the Jewish interlocutor as teaching gentiles moral principles from the Decalogue (2:18–24) in a way reminiscent of Philo. Therefore when Paul tells the teacher, in the context of discussing how God will make gentiles righteous, that no one will be made righteous by works from the law, we are justified in associating works from the law with a Jewish ethic of self-mastery for gentiles. The association only implied here becomes quite explicit in Romans 6–8. Paul uses "works of/from the law" as a shorthand for a certain approach to gentiles on the part of some Jews. This approach presents the law as a solution to the gentile moral weaknesses that keep them from being acceptable to God.

Why the Law Cannot Justify

Romans 3:20 gives a reason why works of the law cannot provide justification: "For by the law comes knowledge of sin." With the exceptions of George Howard, Gaston, and Gager, exegetes read 3:20 as a universal statement about humanity. The above scholars have argued that close attention to the context reveals a discussion of "gentile inclusion." My reading, which recognizes the role of Paul's discussion with the Jewish teacher, adds support to that conclusion since the question in view is God's equal acceptance of gentiles.

Certain negative reasons also lead to the conclusion that 3:20 regards gentiles. In Paul's mouth, that "they cannot be righteous under the law because the law brings knowledge of sin" becomes an inconsistent, incomprehensible statement about Jews. Paul knew better. Traditionally, he has been understood to say that the law of Moses had only the negative functions of pointing to and increasing sin. First, Paul read his Bible and knew that its writings depicted the law as a positive gift that, as part of the covenant, was a blessing essential to the constitution of Israel as a people. Could the apostle have forgotten about the central institutions of repentance and atonement that were meant to keep Israel right with God? In later Christian theology, in which "the law" generally means something like the principle of right and wrong, the traditional readings of 3:20 seem possible. But the minute one begins to imagine the books of Moses concretely and to think about how these writings functioned among Jews in Paul's time, the idea of Paul saying that the law, with its divinely ordained institutions, cannot make Jews acceptable to God becomes absurd.

Second, Paul must have known that the major Jewish groups constituting the Judaism of his day considered the law to be a positive expression of God's grace. Third, he reflects such a positive evaluation several times in his letters.[26] Fourth, as Räisänen insightfully points out, the idea of God giving a weak or insufficient law is fraught with problems of theodicy.[27] It would be strange for Paul to create such a sharp problem of defending God's justice when he is so concerned with theodicy in Romans. Origen could not bring himself to accept the view that the law brought an increase of sin and attributed the idea to Marcion.[28] No wonder Räisänen suggests there is an implicit cynicism in Paul's view.

The reading for which I have been arguing requires that 3:20 be primarily about gentiles and that *dikaioō* ("to justify," "to make righteous," "to show mercy") be a transfer term. It has reference only to those who are outside of a positive relation with God. As such, it could refer only to gentiles or perhaps to extremely wicked and unrepentant Jews. God "makes righteous" when he provides a way for people who have no positive relation to have a relation. Thus 3:20b would mean that the law only informs gentiles about their degenerate state. Is this not exactly the case? Genesis contains the story of the progressive decline and formation of the other nations. Even after Israel receives the law, wicked Egyptians, Canaanites, Assyrians, and others oppose God's people at every turn. For Paul, the Bible contains two stories about the peoples of the earth. The one story concerns an often-wayward but also repentant people who worship God, and the other concerns the usually wicked and idolatrous gentile peoples. The law does not show how the gentile peoples can become an elect people like Israel, it only chronicles their sin.

I believe this reading to be correct but incomplete. The statement in 3:20

is not qualified by "only"; that is, "the law *only* brings knowledge of sin." More-over, other texts speak even more strongly about the law's negative role for gentiles (Rom 4:15; 5:13, 20; 6:14; 7:5, 7–11; Gal 3:19; 1 Cor 15:56). In 4:15, "the law brings about [God's] anger; but where there is no law, there is no transgression." Interpreters have, I think rightly, associated this passage with 5:13: sin was a part of life before the law, but it was not registered by God. Again the text forces the reader to infer a narrative. Before the law, God punished sin in the lives of those who sinned, but after the law, he also registered sin for the final judgment. The implication seems to be that the law meant a more systematic and strict condemnation and punishment of sin. For Israel, following the law as its light and finding mercy through repentance, the law is a gift. Paul does not explicitly discuss this narrative role of the law for Israel in Romans because his subject, God's justification of the gentiles, is different.

For the gentile peoples, the law brought to light their ungodliness and started that process of registering sin for the final judgment (cf. 2:5, 3:25–26).[29] The dual effects of the law's coming are nicely illustrated in the *Biblical Antiquities*, falsely attributed to Philo. As the children of Israel reach Sinai, God says, "I will give light to the world and illumine their dwelling places and establish my covenant with the sons of men and glorify my people above all nations. For them I will bring out the eternal statutes that are for those in the light but to the ungodly a punishment." To Moses God says, "I will put my words in your mouth, and you will enlighten my people, for I have given an everlasting Law into your hands and by this I will judge the whole world. For this will be a testimony. For even if men say, 'We have not known you, and so we have not served you.' therefore I will make a claim upon them because they have not learned my Law."[30] The writer of the *Biblical Antiquities* could say with Paul that the law brought knowledge of sin and God's anger against gentiles who have rejected that knowledge. The law increased God's judgment against the gentiles.

But Paul goes beyond these negative roles for the law. The law "increased" the transgression (5:20). This might be taken as describing no more than 3:20 and 4:15 do, but 7:5–11 clearly goes beyond them. Thus 7:5 links the law with arousing evil passions: "For when we were in the flesh, the passions of sins by means of the law worked in the parts of our body so that we bore fruit for death." Chapter 7:7–11 seems to provide some sort of explanation for 7:5. Somehow the commandments of the law make sin alive. Here the law actively promotes rather than just providing a knowledge of sin and increasing accountability for it.

Anticipating my discussion of chapter 7, I suggest that the explanation for the law's stimulation of sin lies in God's punishment of the gentiles. Chapter 1 explains that the nations other than Israel refused to acknowledge and worship God but instead glorified idols. God punished them by delivering them over to the desires of their hearts so that they dishonored their bodies (1:24); to dishonorable passions resulting in sexual sins (1:26); and to a base mind so that they practice all sorts of vice (1:28). God said, "I condemn you gentiles to obey the evil impulses of your passions and lusts." In 1:32 he explains that this means a blatant and knowing disregard for God's law in spite of the sentence of death. The law can be said to stimulate sin in this way. Because God has put the gentiles in bondage to their evil impulses, when the law says "Do this" or "Do not do that," gentiles are typically bound to obey their passions, which command the opposite. Thus the inner struggle which Paul depicts in chapter 7.

Now it is clear why for Paul, the teacher cannot succeed by saying to gentiles, "Keep these commandments from the law and you will become righteous." Works of the law typically cannot be done consistently by gentiles because God has consigned them to sin as a punishment for their rejection of him. At most, the law gives them only a knowledge of their bondage to sin and their culpability. The law cannot serve to make the ungodly and unrighteous righteous because God did not intend for the law to function that way.

Recent critics have been insightful in concluding that Paul's argument about universal human depravity in 1:18–3:20 miserably fails to persuade. Rom 1–3 "fails," however, not, as these critics believe, because of Paul's ineptitude but because 1:18–3:20 does not attempt to argue for the sinfulness of every human. These scholars are judging Paul for something he does not attempt. Rather, he assumes gentile sinfulness with exceptions and Jewish righteousness with significant lapses but argues that God will, out of his justice, provide an active remedy that treats both with parity. For Paul, the teacher represents Jews who have actively opposed God's plan for making gentiles righteous with a plan of their own; a plan that cannot possibly bring gentiles into the kind of relation to God that Israel possesses. In chapters 9–11, Paul will gradually elaborate his belief, already asserted obliquely in 3:3–19, that not only gentiles as a whole but also large numbers of Jews have been temporarily consigned to disobedience by God so that the gentile peoples can be saved. Romans displays a vision of history rapidly moving to a point at which all humans will with sparkling clarity witness the glory of God's righteousness in his magnificent justice toward all peoples.

To summarize 3:1 (where the conversation between Paul and the teacher begins) through 3:20, Paul first asserts the failure of Jews like the teacher to responsibly witness concerning God's promises. On the basis of axiomatic beliefs that Paul and the teacher share about God's character, Paul gets his partner in discussion to make some admissions that prove fundamental to his gospel. God justly condemns Jewish unfaithfulness to the promises even though that very failure by some Jews mysteriously supports God's plans for justice and the fulfillment of his promises (3:3–8). The teacher wants to know whether Paul's hard line toward his fellow Jews means that they have now fallen to an even worse state than gentiles (3:9). Paul responds that neither Jews nor Greeks stand in an inferior or superior position to one another because both peoples now live in equally deep enthrallment to sin. To support his claim, the apostle pulls out a string of scriptural quotations and allusions that evoke an apocalyptic vision of sin's high point (3:10–18). Paul has reinterpreted apocalyptic traditions of the great tribulation to serve his beliefs about God's rectification of the world situation through Christ. The law's condemnation of the world's peoples equalizes all because all together have been brought to trial before God (3:19). God has chosen this approach rather than the teacher's attempt to instruct gentiles in the law because the law was never meant as a way to redeem the peoples who have rejected God. The law only informs these people of their captivity to sin (3:20).

God's Merciful Justice in Christ's Faithfulness (3:21-33)

Rare are the occasions when the weight of scholarly argument on a subject shifts decisively and probatively. But recently such a shift has taken place in the understanding of the word *pistis* (faith, faithfulness) in Paul's letters. In particular, the evidence and arguments for reading *pistis Iēsou* as the "faith" or "faithfulness of Jesus" rather than as "faith in Jesus" have proven decisive.[1] Similarly, it is now clear that *dikaiosynē tou theou* means God's own righteousness, not the alien righteousness that he imputes to those who have faith.[2] These two shifts mean a dramatic change in the way one reads 3:21–26, Romans as a whole, and the entire Pauline corpus. In light of these modifications, "the center of Paul's thought" no longer concerns how the individual gets the gift (that is, by the believer's faith) but rather the gift itself (the benefits of Christ's faithfulness) and the giver of the gift (God).[3] This shift in understanding moves the reader away from the characteristically Western fixation on the subjectivity of the individual. Paul no longer appears to be the modern man whom interpreters have been depicting for the last 150 years. In addition to these major shifts, the traditional understanding of Jesus' atoning sacrificial death forms an inadequate basis for interpretation. I will suggest a reappraisal of Jesus' death in Paul's letters.

The traditional reading of Rom 3:9–26 has made the passage into a syntactical muddle that is literally impossible to construe intelligibly according to the rules of Greek grammar.[4] The reading advocated here transforms that muddle into a smooth and nearly seamless discourse that connects tightly with what precedes and follows. In the first sentence I summarize 3:9–19 and then render 3:20–26:

> Since at the present crisis in history, all nations are
> under sin, the law sends the whole world, both the
> Jews and the gentile peoples, to court before God.

Therefore, none of those who stand outside of a right relation with God will be made right by doing works of the law, for, in fact, the law itself shows that these people have joined the ungodly. But at this time in history, God has made known his loving justice meant to rectify the dilemma of the world's peoples; a plan based not on lawkeeping but promised and outlined in the law and the writings of the prophets. God's plan to make things right has come by means of Jesus' faithfulness, intended to elicit an appropriate faithfulness (like Jesus') among all peoples (and not the Jews only), since Jews and gentiles have been equalized and shown lacking [when God consigned all to sin]. All the ungodly, then, are made right as a gift through God's graciousness by means of the deliverance in Jesus Christ whom God intended (accepted) as a solution to the problem of his anger [against the gentiles] by means of the faithfulness manifested in Jesus' death. God brought this about to prove his loving justice since he passed over the previous sins of the gentile peoples when he held back punishment. He did this to prove his own loving justice at this crisis in history so as to be just and to make right the person whose status springs from Jesus' faithfulness.

Richard Hays rightly says, "Romans is from start to finish theocentric. Nowhere is there any statement . . . which unambiguously presents Christ as an object of faith." He then cites 4:24, in which righteousness is reckoned "to those who believe in the One who raised Jesus."[5] As I have already argued, the discussion of God's justice and mercy (that is, his righteousness) forms the centerpiece for Paul's justification of gentile salvation in 1:18–3:26. My chief question, then, is how *pistis* and Christ, which are at the center of 3:21–26, relate to God's righteousness and to gentile redemption.

God's Righteousness

Exegetes have taken 1:16–17 and 3:21–26 as the primary texts for understanding "the righteousness of God." The dominant traditional Protestant readings have found almost nothing about "the righteousness of God" in 1:18–3:20. The latter portion of the letter was understood only in a negative way as proof of universal sin. But 1:18–3:20 argues that God's impartial justice (that is, his righteousness) requires equal treatment of gentiles. Verses 21–33 of chapter 3 form the climax of the argument, not a new phase or sudden shift from talk of sin to talk of salvation. God's impartiality as a judge of peoples and individuals emerges as the major theme of chapters 1–2. Paul suggests to the Jewish teacher that God is now taking advantage of an equalizing disobedience on the part of certain Jews in order to justly rescue the gentiles. In the midst of this discussion, Paul makes quite explicit the meaning of "the righteousness of God." By the time the reader reaches 3:21, the problem of gentile alienation and the solution of divine justice have become so specific that "God's righteousness" implies a plan that will equalize the standing of Jews and gentiles before God.

In 3:3–7, the apostle parallels God's faithfulness (*pistis*), his truthfulness, and his righteousness. Not only do these three terms appear in a larger discussion about God's impartial mercy toward gentiles, but also, as we have already seen, Paul engages the teacher precisely about the "oracles of God" (3:2), which point toward God's promises to Abraham that he would someday bless the gentiles. Thus, righteousness here does not signify strict justice but quite specifically a redeeming merciful justice. In some places, the phrase could be translated as "the merciful justice of God." Romans associates this merciful justice with a promise to Abraham and the good news. "God's righteousness" becomes almost synonymous with God's plan to save the world's peoples from his just anger. Because the letter uses the expression in this concrete way, Paul can speak of God's righteousness as something revealed, made known, and demonstrated (1:17; 3:5, 21, 25; 10:3).[6] A close reading of the context, then, can delimit the meaning of the expression with some precision. Depending on the local context, the accent in "righteousness of God" might be on God's own just and merciful character or on the plan or activity that is a specific expression of his just and merciful character.

The whole of 1:18–5:11 concerns God's righteousness. Thus, although the letter, in good rhetorical fashion, catches the reader's interest initially by introducing the deeply felt issues of the passions and self-mastery, it soon shifts the discourse to God's character and activity. Paul employs this strategy to decenter the issue of self-mastery. Romans sets up the discussion so as to focus on God's righteousness and on how God, not gentile ethics, Jewish work with gentiles, or human activity, makes gentiles righteous . Only after radically shifting the perspective toward divine activity does he refocus on human activity in chapters 12–15.

God's *pistis* in 3:3 cannot be his faith in the sense of his belief. God's *pistis* is his faithfulness toward his promises to Abraham even if some Jews have failed to carry the good news to gentiles. *Pistis* means his "truthfulness" (3:4, 7) in regard to his promises. God's righteousness consists of his punishment of human evil together with faithfulness and truthfulness in regard to his promises of mercy and blessings for all nations. Chapter 15:8–9 connects Christ's role with God's truthfulness. There Paul writes that Christ became a servant to the Jews on behalf of God's truthfulness. This confirmation of God's truthfulness consists in two things, the securing of God's promises to the Jewish patriarchs and the showing of mercy to the gentiles.

· Sam K. Williams and Richard Hays have been almost alone in strongly emphasizing the continuity between 3:1–20 and 21–26.[7] Both stress the concept of God's righteousness in Psalm 143 (142 LXX), to which Paul alludes in 3:20 ("no flesh shall be justified before him"). In 143:1, just before Paul's allusion in 143:2, the psalmist cries out to God in his "truthfulness" and "righteousness," asking for God's aid. The close parallel between the language of Ps 143:1–2, to which Paul alludes in 3:20, and the language of God's righteousness in 3:3–7 supports a stress on continuity into 3:21–26 with its declaration of Christ as a demonstration of God's righteousness. Hays argues for the following structure to Paul's argument: God's faithfulness and righteousness are called into question (3:3–5); Paul responds with "a crushing indictment of humanity's unrighteousness" (3:9–20, that is, man, not God, is unrighteous); 3:21–26 declares how God has shown his righteousness by overcoming human unrighteousness.[8]

I agree with Williams's and Hays's argument for continuity but with a major exception. Both scholars treat what Paul says about sin in 3:1–21 as universal philosophical statements about human nature. I have made the case that they are not and have tried to show the clarity that recognition of Paul's discussion with the teacher brings. At the present historical moment both Israel as a whole and the other nations stand equally before God as disobedient peoples (not every individual member). Paul's words to the teacher mean that Jews cannot say, "We are better than the gentiles; they do not deserve a special manifestation of your mercy." On my reading, the "now" (nyn) of 3:21 does not come as a new turn in the tense of the discourse. Hays agrees with others who have recently emphasized that chapter 3 treats God's integrity.[9] In other words, this first part of Romans contains a defense of God's justice, a theodicy. Although I do think that Paul is arguing from God's integrity, I do not believe that a defense of God provides the object of the argument. Paul did not sit down to write a general theological treatise on theodicy and decide to send it to Rome. Rather, Rom 1–3 sets out to show that God's character as revealed in scripture and history leads to the conclusion that he will provide a just and merciful deliverance for the gentiles. In the dialogue of 3:3–8, Paul admits that God's use of Jewish unfaithfulness for his salvific purposes could be construed as unjust but insists on God's justice and faithfulness to his promises.

Psalm 143 dovetails with the letter's description of both Israel and the gentiles as disobedient at the present moment. The psalmist, severely beset, desperately needs God's help. Unlike the speaker in Psalm 17, this psalmist cannot appeal to his innocence. He can only confess his inability to stand before God, appealing to God's righteousness and truthfulness, God's promises of mercy and forgiveness. The psalmist can only appeal for God to manifest his own righteousness in his own way. In the sixth decade after Jesus' birth, Paul believed that Israel (in general) and the gentile peoples (in general) stood in exactly the same desperate situation before God. Paul read history through scripture, and scripture told him of a day when God would manifest his righteousness to the gentiles. He would have read Isa 51:4–6 (LXX) as an announcement to Israel of God's salvation of the gentiles: "Hear me, my people, and listen to me you kings for the law shall go forth from me and my judgment as a light to the gentiles. My righteousness draws near quickly and my salvation shall go forth as a light and the gentiles will hope on my arm." Isa 45:22–25 connects God's truthfulness to his word, his righteousness, and the salvation of "those who are from the end of the earth" (that is, gentiles). Paul weaves a section of v. 23 into Phil 2:10–11. Interpreters of Paul rarely look closely at the Isaiah passage: "Turn to me and you shall be saved, those who are from the end of the earth. I am God and there is no other. I swear by myself. Truly righteousness shall proceed from my mouth. My word shall not return. For every knee shall bow to me and every tongue confess to God, saying, righteousness and glory come to him and all those who separate themselves shall be shamed. They shall be justified by the Lord and they shall be glorified by God, every offspring of the sons of Israel." Paul is emphatic. The question of God's righteousness that he has been dealing with in 1:16–3:20 has been answered in the recent events surrounding Jesus Christ. God's righteous mercy toward the gentiles foretold in scripture has been "demonstrated in the present time" (*pros tēn endeixin tēs dikaiosynēs autou en tō nyn kairō,* 3:26) and will involve gentiles becoming offspring of Israel.

A Reading of 1:16-17

The theme of God's righteousness first appears in 1:16–17. The traditional view that this text concerns how the individual receives the gift, is justified, is saved is well represented by the *RSV*: "For I am not ashamed of the gospel: it is the power of God for salvation to every one who has faith, to the Jew first and also to the Greek. For in it the righteousness of God is revealed through faith for faith; as it is written, 'He who through faith is righteous shall live.'" The *RSV* translators give "the righteous shall live by faith" as an alternative rendering of the quotation from Habakkuk.

So profound is the hold of the Western paradigm that focuses everything on the individual's quest for salvation that the *RSV* translators almost certainly saw none of the different possibilities reflected in the following translation: "For I am not ashamed of the good news, because it is a power which God has to save all who are faithful, the Jew first and afterwards also the Greek. For it [the good news] makes known God's merciful justice as a consequence of [Jesus'] faithfulness which leads to faithfulness [like Jesus']. As it is written, "The righteous one [that is, Jesus] shall live as a consequence of faithfulness."

Like all words, *pistis* had a range of meanings in ancient usage: loyalty, honesty, good faith, faithfulness, trust, trustworthiness, belief, proof, and confidence. It has no Platonic root meaning or essence. The practical social and linguistic contexts of its usage by speakers and writers—Paul included—provided ranges of possible meanings for hearers and readers. How one renders the term in English will be determined by the translator's larger understanding of Paul's thought, his or her reading of the particular letter, and the immediate context. The Western readings of Paul have focused on the question of what the sinner need do or be in order to be saved. The traditional reading has presented *pistis* as the answer to this question, construing it as a mental "act of believing in spite of evidence" or an "attitude of trust in Christ." This view has often been critiqued, but not thoroughly enough.

I have chosen "faithfulness" as the most satisfactory translation for many texts, although I am often not entirely happy with any English word. Paul associates *pistis* with obedience to God, and "trusting obedience" is sometimes a possible translation. At other times, the emphasis lies on confidence in God's promises, and "trust" makes a good translation. Used of God, as in 3:3, it means his faithfulness to his commitments and "obligations." Used of Abraham and Christ, it describes their confidence in God's promises and faithful action in view of those promises despite hardship and suffering that would have caused most people to act unfaithfully.

Hab 2:4 is a key to the meaning of *pistis* in Romans. The quotation serves as the scriptural warrant for the thematic sounding statement about the gospel in 1:16–17. In 1:1–3, Paul had spoken of the good news about God's Son announced beforehand by the prophets in the holy scriptures. According to the traditional reading as reflected in the RSV, Paul says that God has revealed "righteousness" or "his righteousness" by justifying or declaring righteous the one who believes in Christ. Hab 2:4 provides scriptural warrant and prophetically foretells of this new way to be righteous. On this view, the mental act or disposition of having faith replaces the old Jewish way of living by the law as a precondition for salvation. Christ serves the passive role of being the object of belief.

A different way of reading the quotation was first proposed independently by J. Haussleiter and A. T. Hanson and recently refined by Richard Hays.[10] Exegetes have argued endlessly about whether the quotation should be rendered "the righteous one shall live by faith" or "the one who is righteous by faith shall live." A better starting point is to ask about the identity of "the righteous one." In the traditional view, "the righteous one" is generic, anyone who believes. Thus the *KJV* boldly mistranslated *ho dikaios* by "the just" ("the just shall live by faith"), as if *dikaios* were plural.[11]

The Masoretic tradition of the Hebrew text supports the conventional reading. Thus the *RSV*'s translation of Hab 2:4: "Behold, he whose soul is not upright in him shall fail, but the righteous shall live by his faith (or faithfulness)." But Paul did not use the Hebrew text. He used the Septuagint. Most LXX manuscripts have "The righteous one shall live by my faithfulness." The pronoun refers to God. Hab 2:4 in the LXX concerns God's faithfulness. Two important manuscripts of the LXX, however, differ from the majority and agree with the citation in Heb 10:38: "My righteous one shall live by faithfulness." In these manuscripts "the righteous one" probably already refers to the messiah or a messiah-like deliverer. As Hanson and Hays point out, it is difficult to imagine that Paul would not have understood Hab 2:3–4 to be about Christ. I have attempted to translate correctly according to grammatical possibilities but with the assumptions that Paul and the author of Hebrews brought to scripture: "For the vision yet awaits its proper time, and will come to be at last and will not be in vain. If he delays, wait for him, for a Coming One will arrive and will not be long; if he were to shrink back in fear, my soul would have no pleasure in him but the Righteous One will live as a consequence of [his] faithfulness." Here Paul would read a prophecy of a long-awaited Davidic messiah who will come but also be involved in some sort of delay that the readers of the prophecy must endure. The messiah will not be overcome by fear but instead will please God by being just/righteous and will be made to live as a consequence of his faithfulness to his mission. Hab 2:3–4 became the locus classicus in Jewish literature for the idea that the final age would be prolonged and the final time of reckoning delayed and in early Christian literature for the delay of Christ's return.[12] Thus, for example, the *Commentary on Habakkuk* from Qumran interprets 2:3 as encouragement for the faithful to endure even though the end of the age has been delayed (*1QpHab*). Paul, as I shall argue below, associated the spread of the gospel with a delay of the end and with Christ's faithfulness. Indeed, I shall argue that Paul understood Jesus' faithfulness as a kind of delay.

Heb 10:37–38 displays a messianic understanding of Hab 2:3–4, although it does not take "the just one" as a messianic title. Other New Testament texts, however, do employ "the just one" (*ho dikaios*) as a designation for Jesus (Acts 3:14; 7:52; 22:14; 1 Pet 3:18; 1 Jn 2:1).[13] Paul either used an LXX text that did not have the pronoun "my" (*mou*) or omitted it himself. At any rate, that version permits the messianic reading, "the righteous one shall live by his own faithfulness," as well as the meaning, "by God's faithfulness."

This messianic comprehension of Hab 2:4 coheres with Paul's exegesis of Gen 17:8 in Galatians 3.[14] Chapter 3 argues that God made the promise to Abraham and his seed. The seed, Paul insists, is one individual whom God would make heir of this blessing. Nils Dahl has shown that Paul bases his exegesis here on an analogy with 2 Sam 7:12–14, which was regarded as messianic even in pre-Christian times.[15] There "seed" (*sperma*) is both messianic and singular.[16] Paul argues as follows: The Christ is the single biological descendant of Abraham who inherits the promise to Abraham. Others only share in this blessing by being "in Jesus Christ" (Gal 3:14). Thus Paul says that he no longer lives but that he now lives in Christ "by faithfulness" (*en pistei*). Paul does not live by his own means but by means of the faithfulness of Christ, who was the righteous one delivered up on Paul's behalf (Gal 2:20). Others have a right status before God as a consequence of whatever Jesus did that Paul represents when he speaks of Jesus' *pistis,* his faithfulness.

Paul would have probably read Isa 53:10–12 as associating "the seed," "the righteous one," and the "heir." Hays writes, "What Paul has done in Gal 3:6–18 is to bring this cluster of messianic themes into conjunction with Hab 2:4, interpreted messianically, so that the Messiah's faith becomes the key to his inheritance of life and the promises."[17] Only a more precise grasp of Paul's story about Christ can further clarify the phrase "out of faithfulness." Unfortunately, this meaning, so essential to Paul's argument in Galatians and Romans, has been hidden by the translations. Thus the RSV grossly distorts the Greek of Gal 3:22: "But scripture consigned all things to sin, that what was promised to faith in Jesus Christ [*ek pisteōs Iēsou Christou*] might be given to those who believe." The phrase *ek pisteōs Iēsou Christou* cannot mean "to faith in Jesus Christ." Rather, the promise was "on the basis of Jesus Christ's faithfulness."

Similarly, the RSV, following the KJV, translates Rom 3:26 as follows: "to prove . . . that he himself [God] is righteous and that he justifies him who has faith in Jesus" (*ton ek pisteōs Iēsou*). The translation "faith in Jesus" goes against Greek grammar in general, LXX and New Testament usage, and Paul's own usage elsewhere.[18] The phrase *ek pisteōs Iēsou* is either a metaphor of source and origin or instrumental and means "out of" or "as a consequence of" or "by" or "on the basis of Jesus' faithfulness." Thus God "justifies the one who lives on the basis of Jesus' faithfulness." The impossibility of reading the traditional idea of "faith in Christ" into *ek pisteōs Iēsou* is brought home dramatically by notice of an exact parallel nearby in 4:16. There Paul speaks of *tō ek Abraam,* "the one who is out of Abraham's faithfulness" or "the one who lives on the basis of Abraham's faithfulness." There is no question of one having faith in

Abraham. Rather, Abraham's faithfulness was the basis for a covenant in which all of his descendants live. They share in its blessings not because of faith in Abraham or their own faithfulness but because of what Abraham did, his faithfulness.

If *ek pisteōs* in 1:17 means "on the basis of Christ's faithfulness," then we can clarify the heretofore mysterious *ek pisteōs eis pistin* ("through faith for faith," *RSV*) in the same verse. "God's righteousness is revealed as a consequence of Jesus' faithfulness." This makes much greater sense than the usual reading: God's righteousness is revealed in that the believer's faith has now become the precondition for salvation. But what does *eis pistin* (into faith) mean? Notice that these prepositions are metaphors of physical movement: out of something and into something.[19] The first metaphor implies origin, agency, or instrumentality, that is, "out of," "on the basis of," or "by means of Jesus' faithfulness." The second implies movement into a state, into faithfulness. This makes sense if the key question is not the believer's faith but Jesus Christ's faithfulness in which the believer shares. Thus *eis pistin* parallels the phrase "to be baptized into Christ" (Rom 6:3: Gal 3:27). The phrase could then be rendered, "The righteousness of God is revealed in it [the gospel] by means of [Jesus'] faithfulness resulting in faithfulness."

Both 1:16–17 and 3:21–26 probably contain allusions to Ps 98:2, 9 (LXX 97:2, 9). All three speak of God revealing his righteousness by bringing righteousness and salvation to the gentiles. Paul, of course, adds to the Psalm his belief that the faithful Jesus, obedient to the point of death, was the means by which God brought about the fulfillment of his promises to the gentiles. "The Lord has made known his salvation. He has revealed his righteousness before the gentiles. He has remembered his mercy to Jacob and his truthfulness to the house of Israel (LXX)." If we believe what we read in his letter to the Romans, Paul's confidence in his own people and in God's commitment to them never wavered. But he was also convinced that the God of the whole world had acted decisively to embrace the other peoples. The God who chose one of the world's families could not be worthy unless he also demonstrated his love toward the other humans on the planet.

God's Justice toward the Gentile Peoples (3:21–26)

The tradition and its translations have conditioned moderns to read Romans in a flat, universalistic way as an answer to the question, "How can the sinner be saved?" But Paul's focus on the gentiles is thereby lost and with it a nuanced reading that fits Paul's context. Context and cultural codes determine meaning even for sentences that use the words "all" or "every." "Penicillin is effective for everyone" presumably does *not* mean that every person on earth should be taking the antibiotic all of the time. Normally people would suppose the statement to mean that penicillin is effective for anyone who has a bacterial infection. The phrases, "for all who believe/are faithful" (3:22) and "all have sinned" (3:23) should not become signals that automatically force a later Christian scheme of salvation upon the text. The significance of even these phrases should be delimited and specified by a well-argued reading of Romans.

In his epistolary prescript, Paul presents himself as the apostle to the gentile peoples, writing to a community of gentiles about their situation as gentiles. The purpose of his apostleship is to bring about the "obedience of faithfulness among all the gentile peoples" (1:5; cf. 15:15–18; Gal 1:15–16; 2:7, 9). Even though he proclaims that the good news about Jesus Christ is a power to save the Jew first and also the Greek, presumably meaning that Israel will be vindicated first at the great judgment, 1:18–4:25 attempts to argue both the necessity and manner of gentile salvation. His big secret about Jewish salvation in chapter 11 turns out to be the opposite of what readers have tended to think. Chapter 11 announces the mystery of the interrelatedness of Jewish and gentile salvation. In 1:18–2:16, the apostle uses the principle of God's impartiality to argue that God is bound to reward gentiles who keep the law's just requirements. Then, in 2:17–3:21, Paul converses with a Jewish teacher of gentiles and continues to argue for God's impartiality. In the current critical moment, a part of Israel has been disobedient so that all, both Jew and Greek, stand in the clearest equality of sinfulness before God. Chapters 1–4 never lose their focus on the gentile peoples.

Rom 3:21–26 should be taken together with 3:27–4:25 as the climax of the argument in 1:18–3:21. Whereas 1:18–3:21 argues *that* God by his nature must treat gentiles equally, 3:21–4:2 announces *how* God has now in fact acted impartially toward gentiles and thus made known his righteousness. The oracles of God (3:2) containing the Abrahamic promise that the gentiles would be blessed have been fulfilled in Jesus Christ. This fulfillment of God's promises demonstrates his truthfulness and faithfulness to his word.

The theme of God's impartiality continues in 3:21–4:2.[20] God's righteousness has been manifested through the faithfulness of Jesus Christ for *all* who are faithful (3:22). The warrant for God manifesting his righteousness to all, that is, also gentiles, is "there is no distinction [between Israel and the gentiles] because all have sinned and fallen short of God's glory" (3:23). Being a just judge, God has no basis for showing mercy to Israel only, as if one nation had been consistently faithful.

Significantly, 3:21–4:2 continues Paul's discussion with the teacher of gentiles that began with Paul's apostrophe in 2:17–29 and opened into a dialogue in 3:1–9. I provide an unorthodox working division of the "section" at 4:2 because the dialogue picks up again in 3:27–4:2. Paul had earlier characterized the teacher as a boaster (2:17, 23) in light of the teacher's attitude of superiority toward gentiles (2:19–20). In 3:27f., the apostle censures his boasting. Christ's faithfulness removes any basis for the Jewish teacher's boasting because it renders his ethical program for gentiles irrelevant. In 3:29–30, Paul explicitly appeals to God's impartiality: Because God is the God of all peoples, he will treat all on the same basis.

Some specific themes from Paul's Jewish heritage also show that 3:21–26 concerns the gentiles. Syntactically, all of 3:21–26 depends upon and explicates "now God's merciful justice [righteousness] has been made known" in v. 21. Verses 25b-26 explain why the redemption provided through Christ's death was necessary to effect God's merciful justice: "in order to demonstrate his [God's] merciful justice because of passing over of previous sins when God held back punishment." Verse 25b recalls 2:5, in which Paul warns the presumptuous gentile of the wrath stored up for the day of judgment. Sam K. Williams has shown that "passing over" (*paresin*) does not mean forgiveness and that God's "restraint" or "holding back," his *anochē*, is frequently a negative concept used for his judgment of gentiles.[21] Thus 2 Macc 6:14 explains that the calamities that have befallen Israel are a sign of God's kindness. Instead of allowing sin to accumulate until it reaches its full measure, God disciplines his people continually. But, "in the case of the other nations, the Lord waits patiently to punish them until they have reached the full measure of their sins." Since God has not continually dealt with gentile sin as he has with the sin of his chosen people, the gentiles face a terrible day of wrath (cf. Rom 2:4–9).

Rom 3:21–26 assumes fundamental Jewish ideas about sin, punishment, repentance, and atonement. Unfortunately, these ideas have been badly distorted in traditional readings of the letter and in Christian depictions of ancient Judaism. The myth has two forms (which interpreters sometimes combine) and goes as follows: Jews believed that they were saved by their mere status as Jews who possessed the law and so believed that they did not truly need to live repentant lives, or, alternatively, the law taught that a person had to keep it perfectly in order to be saved, and Jewish striving for this perfection constantly ended in either false arrogance or despair. The myth is from beginning to end a polemical Christian fabrication. First, it wrongly assumes that ancient Judaism was a religion of salvation. No form of ancient Judaism, except perhaps certain forms of Christianity, viewed salvation as a goal of the Jewish way of life. Second, the myth grossly misrepresents common Jewish understandings of the law, repentance, and atonement. To make the kind of case often read into chapters 1–3, Paul would have to argue either that the law's provisions for repentance, forgiveness, and atonement were flawed or that Jews as a whole failed to take advantage of them. He does not. Rather, both as a people and individually, ancient Jews accepted sin as human but believed that God in his covenant and law allowed means of mercy through which both (what we distinguish as) ritual impurity and moral sin could be corrected and forgiven. In times when Israel or individual Israelites were sinful and unrepentant, God would punish in order to return the wayward to justice and holiness. Forgiveness did not mean cheap grace; sometimes punishment was required.

The gentiles stood in an entirely different relation. Thus 2:4–5 warns gentiles that by lack of repentance they are storing up God's wrath for the day of judgment. From Paul's Jewish perspective, the gentile peoples had cut themselves off from a relation with God that could allow for regular means of healing acts of alienation from him. Paul came to believe it unjust for God to allow gentiles to persist in this unequal relation resulting from their original rejection of God. Therefore, in his righteousness, being faithful to his ancient promise to Abraham, God had provided the faithfulness of Jesus as a means by which the long accumulation of gentile sins could be forgiven.

But what of the Jewish relation to Christ's faithfulness? Here Paul's letters provide only hints. One can understand this lack of clarity because he writes his letters to gentiles, about the gentile situation. Discussions of Israel appear only incidentally. Evidently, however, Israel does have a relation to Christ's faithfulness, although Paul speaks as if it differs from that of the gentiles. "The Jew first and also the Greek" is not merely Paul's way of saying "humanity." Although they share in the blessings of Abraham brought about by his heir, Christ, Paul does not assimilate the two into a single scheme of sin, salvation, and community. When he speaks of their relation to Christ's faithfulness, he avoids language that assimilates the two. The language of 3:30 and 4:11–12, 16 reveals the separate but related ways of Jews and gentiles (see chapter 8). Paul assumes that Israel continues to live by the law. Righteous life in the law, however, also somehow seems to proceed out of Christ's faithfulness. Once the interpreter sees that Paul did not spiritualize religion, that is, translate it into Platonic philosophical conceptualities, then Paul's language of separate but interrelated destinies for Jews and gentiles makes sense. His language betrays the belief that though the peoples are intimately interdependent, the promises are not the same for both. When arguing the case for gentiles as co-heirs in chapter 4, the text speaks of "the promise" singular (4:13, 14, 16, 20) because only the promise of Gen 17:5 (cf. 22:17; 18:18; 12:3) is relevant to gentiles. In 9:4, however, when enumerating the gifts and prerogatives of Israel, he speaks of their promises. Likewise, Christ secured the promises given to the patriarchs in 15:8. These promises might include the covenant promises, especially those concerning the land of Israel, and promises relating to national autonomy and Davidic rule (cf. Rom 1:3).

The meticulously crafted assemblage of quotations (Isa 59:20–21; Ps 14:7; Jer 31:33; Isa 27:9) in 11:26 contains one of the few places in the letters affording a hint about end-time events for Israel. The texts serve as a warrant for saying that all Israel will be saved when the full number of gentiles has come in. "The deliverer will come from Zion" means that Christ, at his coming from heaven, will play some role in the holy city. At Christ's return, ungodliness will disappear from Israel, and God will honor his covenant with his people when he removes their sins. The whole discussion of Rom 9–11 has its premise in the assumption of separate but interrelated end-time destinies for Jews and gentiles.

The Inadequacy of the Sacrificial Explanation

Rom 3:24–25 has been the most important Pauline and one of the most important New Testament texts for interpreting the meaning of Jesus' death. Even today scholars and readers suppose that these verses describe a doctrine of sacrificial and vicarious substitutionary atonement for human sinfulness.[22] But this reading is like a house of cards, which collapses when one card is removed. Following are outlines of major criticisms of the traditional sacrificial interpretation.[23] These considerations indicate that even if there is some sacrificial language or allusion in 3:21–26—and that is far from certain—one cannot move easily from such language to a conception of Jesus' death as a sacrifice of vicarious atonement analogous to the sacrifice of animals in the Jewish cultus.

1. The anthropological and history of religions study of animal and human sacrifice impedes analogizing sacrificial practices, including Jewish sacrificial practices, and the death of Jesus.[24] In fact, a deepening scholarly appreciation of ancient animal sacrifice has revealed that later Christian conceptions of sacrificial atoning death have been systematically projected back onto Judaism. From Hebrews and Barnabas to Origen and beyond, Christian exegetes made the Jewish scriptures conform to Christological and cultic fulfillment. The process reached its zenith during the fourth century, when Christianity became the religion of the empire and sought to systematically appropriate both the holy land and the Old Testament cultus from the Jews.[25] But Paul lacked one of the presuppositions for this kind of exegesis: The temple and the temple system still existed and operated during his life. When the historian permits Jewish practices of the second temple to stand in their own

right, in their own cultural and historical context, the similarities with Christian ideas melt away. In ancient Jewish and ancient Mediterranean animal sacrifice and in the rites of numerous other cultures the death of the animal was an incidental prelude to the ritual.[26] Strange as it may seem to readers steeped in the legacy of Christianity, these sacrificing cultures attach no special significance to the death of the animal itself. The sacrifice was a ritualized use—disorganization and reorganization of the animal's body—that took place after the killing.[27] Sacrifice is not about death or ritual killing.

Unlike the later forms of Christianity, the Jewish temple system was not premised on the assumption of an essential brokenness in divine/human relations and the solution to sin and death that would lead beyond this world. Scholars have been so desperate to discover an "Adam theology" at the base of Jewish thought precisely because they have needed to make ancient Judaism like later Christianity. The Jewish temple religion rested on an assumption that humans were essentially at home in and made for this world. Such locative sacrificial systems treat the problems and limitations of human life as natural.[28] In fact, sacrificial practices in their connection with systems of purity and pollution set the human over against the divine and men over against women by defining and regulating the divinely ordained order of the world. Humans could live happily in a cosmic, natural, and social order for which they had been made to fit perfectly, if they maintained that order. The sacrificial practices of the temple were a means of keeping the order finely tuned and in balance. The ancient meanings of animal sacrifice simply do not lend themselves to the interpretation that Christian interpreters want. New Testament scholars cannot take for granted that ancient readers would have understood sacrifice as it has been radically redefined by Christian ideas about atonement for sin and Christ's death.

2. The purpose of the sacrificial system both as represented in the priestly sources of the scripture and as instituted in the second temple period was not to atone for personal sin or to provide a means for dealing with human alienation from God; these ideas have been projected onto the temple system by Christian and later Jewish theology. Traditionally, interpreters believed that the so-called sin offering of the Levitical cult and the second temple was a means of removing personal moral or ontological sin. In some places, the LXX translated ḥaṭṭā't by hamartia, which in its lexical meaning signifies error in a wide sense. But interpreters commonly read Leviticus with specific Christian conceptions of sin that suppose some idea of a fall or original sin. The sacrifice in question would more accurately be called a purification offering. In the priestly literature, such sacrifice cleanses not the one offering the sacrifice but the temple of impurity carried by the offerer.[29] Num 15:22–29 says that sacrifices deal

only with the impurity of unintentional error and denies that they deal with the intentional acts that Christians associate with sin (Num 15:30–31).[30] For sacrifice to cure the human tendency to sin or death or both would violate the very premises of the system. Contact with the dead, childbirth, menstruation, and various discharges make one impure and unfit to come into contact with the divine precisely to show the natural mortality and fragility of humans in relation to God and to indicate that men stand closer to the divine than women.[31]

In terms of the cult's ideology, failure to keep the temple pure meant to risk God's anger and the loss of his presence. At the same time, the rules of purity indexed and mapped the Jewish social order (see chapter 3). Paul and his readers may have understood the cult either through their own reading of the scriptural sources or through a knowledge of the temple cult as it operated in the first century or through a combination of scripture and current practice. Jacob Milgrom, David Wright, and others have shown that the scriptural sources understand the so-called sin offering to be for the purification of the temple.[32] In the sin offering, the blood of the animal was the purging agent that was applied to various parts of the temple and removed the *consequences* of sins and impurities (that is, the pollution of the temple). The person did not receive forgiveness for a sinful act itself but dealt only with the consequences of such acts on the temple. The so-called guilt offering worked in a similar way.[33] Forgiveness for intentional sins came when the sinner repented and made any required reparation. On the Day of Atonement priests purified the entire temple, including the Holy of Holies, by means of sacrifices. In another ritual of that day, the sins of the people were transferred to a goat, which carried the sins away from the temple and the habitation of the people. It is difficult to read Rom 3:25 by analogy to the sacrifice of animals in the cult: "whom God purposed [or 'set forth'] as an act of propitiation [or 'conciliation'] by means of [Jesus'] faithfulness in his blood." The scapegoat might seem to offer better analogies because it could be viewed as a means to atonement for the sins of the people, but it is not a ritual of blood or death and was not offered by God.

Writings from the period of the second temple generally follow the understanding of the cult found in Leviticus and Numbers but with a tendency toward the moralization of the sin offering in Josephus and especially Philo. Josephus (*Ant.* 3.230–32) conflates the sin and the guilt offering and makes the latter apply to conscious violations. Owing to the generality of Josephus's discussion, one cannot determine whether he thought that the sin offering dealt only with the consequences of the violations on the temple or also with the sin itself. Discussing the Day of Atonement (*Ant.* 3.240–43), he first mentions the sin offerings and then says that, in addition, a goat is sent out to serve as an aversion (*apotropiasmos*) and a pardon or supplication (*paraitēsis*). Josephus uses *hamartēma* for the sins pardoned by the scapegoat, but the Ionic *hamartas* with cultic connotations (Herod. 1.91) for the sin offering. His discussion leaves the impression that the scapegoat, in pardoning sin, served a function distinct from the sin offering. Philo interprets the sacrifices in his usual way of systematic moralizing with Greek philosophical conceptions. He makes sin offerings apply to unintentional violations, and guilt offerings to intentional offenses. He treats the guilt offering from the perspective of the sinner's psychology of repentance. Inner conviction and repentance will lead to reparation of damages, propitiation (*hilaskomai*) of the person who has been wronged, and then to the temple, where the offender, armed with his convicted conscience, will ask for forgiveness of sin (*Spec. Leg.* 1.235–38). Here Philo leaves unclear the relation between the actual sacrifice and the request for forgiveness. Philo describes (*Spec. Leg.* 1.186–88; 2.193–96) the Day of Atonement as a festival of self-mastery and abstinence. He emphasizes that it is a day of repentance and prayer to God for pardon. When he gets to the cultus, he distinguishes the sacrifices for purification from the scapegoat bearing the curses that had been upon transgressors who have now converted to a better life (*Spec. Leg.* 1.187–88). Philo's moralizing places the emphasis on the sinner's prayer and repentance but provides little evidence for viewing the sacrifice of animals in the temple as a system for dealing with human sinfulness. Other sources from the period of the second temple agree in emphasizing the Day of Atonement as an occasion for repentance and pardon but agree with the scriptures in associating atonement with the scapegoat and not with sacrifice (*Jub.* 34:18–19; Sir 50:5–21; 11 Q*Temple* 25:10–27:10; *Ps. Philo* 13.6).

3. The least plausible reading of *hilastērion* (*RSV*: "expiation"; *KJV*: "propitiation") in Rom 3:25 is as a reference to the so-called mercy seat. The LXX translators used *hilastērion* for the Hebrew *kapporeth*, the golden covering of the ark in the temple's Holy of Holies. Those who favor this interpretation of *hilastērion* have imagined 3:25 saying that God put forth Christ as a once-and-for-all place where atonement is made: Christ replaces the temple cult.[34] But this reading fits neither the Jewish institutions in question nor Paul. First, this interpretation requires Paul and his readers to have a kind of typological understanding of the Hebrew scriptures based on the premise of Christianity superseding Judaism. Paul shows no signs of such supersessionism and the comprehensive typological reinterpretation of the Jewish cultus as a shadow made to fit the reality of Christ. Hebrews, written after the destruction of the temple and reflecting a Platonic ethos, does make these assumptions. Second, the mercy seat interpretation wrongly imagines that the sprinkling of blood on the *kapporeth* denoted the atonement of personal and moral sin rather than

purification. What I said above about sin offerings applies also to the sacrifices for the priest and people on the Day of Atonement. The sacrifices on that day provide a complete purification of the temple, not an atonement or forgiveness of the people's sin. Lev 16:20 is explicit: "When he has ended the atoning for the holy place and the tent of the meeting and the altar, he shall show forth the live goat." The *kapporeth*, or mercy seat, is an item of cultic furniture, not a symbol of God's dealing with the problem of sin, except in later Christian typological imagination. Proponents of this reading talk as if the image of the high priest sprinkling blood on the *kapporeth* each year for the atonement of their sins would have been vivid in the minds of Jews in Paul's time. But these interpreters fail to mention that there had never been a *kapporeth* in the second temple. Third, proponents of the mercy seat interpretation cannot explain how readers would have recognized a reference to the *kapporeth* in 3:25. The translators of the LXX got the word *hilastērion* from ordinary Greek usage, where it could be used, like the verb form *hilaskomai,* in both cultic and noncultic contexts.[35] Even though *hilastērion* does not seem to have been a common word, there is nothing mysterious about its meaning in everyday speech. In fact, the use of its word group was part of everyday language.[36] Its relation to the more common cognate forms would be clear even for a Greek speaker who had never heard the word before; either an adjective meaning propitiatory/conciliatory or, when used as a substantive, a conciliatory/propitiatory thing, place, or act.[37] There is nothing sacrificial about the concept of propitiation or conciliation that the hilask- words denote, although the words had associations with the divine and cultic activity. People in everyday speech could use *hilaskomai* in reference to appeasing another person's anger or conciliating someone (for example, Philo, *Spec. Leg.* 1.237; Plato, *Phd.* 1C; Plut., *Cat. Mi.* 61).

Scholars sometimes argue that the phrase "by his blood" in 3:25 would make clear to readers that Paul was alluding to the *kapporeth* or to sacrifice.[38] Paul's usage of "blood" elsewhere shows that it means Christ's death, not the blood in itself.[39] In sacrificial practice the blood itself was a significant and effective ritual symbol, but the death had no atoning/purifying power.[40] I can see no reason why even Jewish readers steeped in the LXX would see a reference to the mercy seat in 3:25. The context does not fit. By referring to Jesus' death through "blood," Paul underlines the violent nature of his death, the readers knowing that Jesus died by crucifixion. Paul can describe Jesus' death in horrific imagery from the scriptures as an accursed death (Gal 3:13; Deut 21:23) and Christ as suffering and becoming sin.[41] Paul's whole conception of Jesus' death projects an image utterly antithetical to Jewish sacrifice. For the latter, enormous emphasis and symbolic import lie in the bodily perfection and purity of the sacrificial animal, which must die quickly and easily. The sacrifice is the gift to God and the precise symbolic rendering (burning some parts and eating others, uses of blood, and so forth) of the animal's body that took place after the killing. It does not work to say that Christ's death for Paul was a paradoxical sacrifice because the problem posed by 3:25 remains how readers could have recognized a reference to sacrifice at all, much less a theology of sacrificial atonement.

Early Christian writings do of course employ the language of sacrifice for Christ's death. Paul can say that "Christ, our paschal lamb, has been sacrificed" (1 Cor 5:7). But interpreters must recognize the limited nature of such analogies and not read a theory of atonement into them. "Bob is a real tiger" does not mean that Bob walks on all fours, hunts animals, and eats raw meat. Should we develop a theory about how Bob can have a human nature and an animal nature at the same time? Rather, the metaphor means that Bob is a competitive or a powerful and energetic personality. Similarly, sacrifice was so commonly described as a gift or service or thank-offering that it was natural to use the language for the benefits of Christ. Other limited analogies also drew on the language of sacrifice.[42] When Paul speaks of Christ as the paschal lamb, he evokes an image of "the Christ event" as a liberation from bondage. The enormous difficulty the church had in developing a theory of Christ's sacrificial atoning death—beginning with Eusebius and Athanasius in the fourth century—should warn us against assuming such a reading of Rom 3:25.[43]

4. With one possible exception, the traditions of ancient Israel and Judaism in the second temple period lack the idea that a person could vicariously atone for others. Furthermore, atonement and atonement for others are conceptually distinct from sacrifice. Several scholars have shown that the idea of a person suffering or dying on behalf of others in order to expiate sin is utterly alien to Jewish sacrificial ideas of the second temple.[44] Fourth Maccabees (first or second century C.E.), which adapts the theme from Greek literature, may be the exception to the absence of vicarious atonement in Jewish literature. The earliest extant Christian writings, including the New Testament, share with 4 Maccabees exactly the language of "death on behalf of" from the Greek tradition of noble death. In works like Euripides' *Iphigenia at Aulis* (especially 1383–84, 1420, 1472–73), *Heraclidae* (especially 499), and *Phoenician Women* (948, 952, 997–98) others' heroic deaths save people from threatening situations. These writings describe such heroic deaths as acts of deliverance and salvation. This includes virtuous death in order to propitiate a god (*Iphigenia at Aulis*, 1553–55; *Heraclidae*, 532; *Alcestis*, 154–55) and such expressions used by early Christian writers for Christ as "death on behalf of" (*hyper auton*), "satisfaction" (*arkestheis*), and death as a "ransom" (*antipsychon auton*; cf. *Alcestis* 340–41, 434; *Heraclidae* 580). H. S. Versnel has shown that "death on

behalf of" does not usually imply vicarious or substitutionary death.[45] His work points to a lack of clarity and precision in the way writers facilely speak of vicarious suffering and death. The tradition of noble death for others appeared widely in Greek literature and rhetoric and had many branches, including the noble martyrdom of philosophers on behalf of truth or justice, Socrates being the most famous example.

Scholars have long known that the closest parallel to the language of Jesus' death in Rom 3:24–25 comes from 4 Maccabees. It uses exactly the language mentioned above concerning the effects of the martyr's endurance in suffering unto death. So, for example, Eleazar cries out to God as he is being put to death (6:28–29), "You know God that although I could save myself, I die in fiery torment for the sake of the law. Be merciful to your people, and let my punishment be a satisfaction on their behalf. Make my blood a purification for them and take my life as a ransom for theirs." The language of 4 Macc 17:22 shares the words *hilastērion* ("propitiation") and "blood" with Rom 3:25: "Through them [the martyrs] our enemies did not prevail against our nation and the tyrant was punished and our land purified, since they as it were became a ransom for the sin of the nation. It was through the blood of these righteous ones and the propitiation [*hilastērion*] through their death, that divine Providence saved Israel."

The martyr's death for others here has nothing to do with sacrifice or the temple cult.[46] Like Paul's talk of Jews and gentiles in the present historical moment, the situation depicted in 4 Maccabees lacks universalist abstraction. The Jewish people find themselves in a particular historical crisis that threatens the nation's very existence. The Syrian Greek king Antiochus has deposed the legitimate high priest, Onias, and appointed Jason, who "changed the nation's way of life and its constitution in total rejection of the law" (4:19). Because of this apostasy, God in his justice was angered, sending Antiochus to punish his people (4:21). Many Jews, however, have not been unfaithful and resist Antiochus's attempts to Hellenize the nation. The seven martyrs endure unspeakable physical and psychological tortures in order to remain faithful to their God. On one reading, the martyrs' extraordinary endurance and faithfulness move God to end his anger at the nation's unfaithfulness. The martyrs' endurance serves as a *hilastērion*. On another reading, they indirectly bring an end to God's anger with his people because their endurance and example for other Jews lead to Antiochus's defeat and the nation's return to God (17:20–24; cf. 7–19; 1:11; 18:4–5). The martyrs' example leads to national repentance and Antiochus's defeat, and thus to the propitiation of God's anger. It would be a misinterpretation of 4 Maccabees to think that some mysterious blood rite by martyrdom had produced atonement. The faithful resistance (not their deaths) of the martyrs certainly wins God's favor, but at the same time the effects of their examples on other Jews and on Antiochus bring about the salvation of the nation from Antiochus.[47] Later Christian sacrificial theology should not be read into the story. Fourth Maccabees shows that the language of Rom 3:25 could be used without sacrificial connotations.

5. Cilliers Breytenbach has shown that the language of reconciliation should not be associated with sacrificial atonement as it did not carry such connotations in Jewish and Greco-Roman literature.[48] The LXX does not associate with or use the reconciliation word group (di-/katalassein) for atonement/propitiation. In fact, Breytenbach shows that the language of reconciliation came from secular relations between people and the concept of friendship. Thus Rom 5:1–11 speaks of God using Christ to bring about a new relation of friendship with himself.[49] Later tradition has woven these separable conceptions into plans of salvation and theologies of atonement. Christian tradition has shown the right instinct in supposing that a particular unifying story lies behind the varied figures and concepts Paul uses to talk about the meaning of Jesus Christ. But careful historical-philological analysis of Paul's language also shows that the traditional unifying stories supplied by later Christianity do not fit his figures, concepts, cultural codes, and historical context.

6. In all of Paul's writing, only Rom 3:25 speaks of atonement, and atonement (that is, "conciliation," "appeasement") need have no connection with sacrifice.[50] If the key to Paul's thought about Christ rests in the idea of his death as a sacrifice of vicarious atonement for sin, then why does the only plausibly arguable evidence for that conception depend on the meaning of one word in Paul's last extant letter? The sacrificial interpretation simply proves insufficient to do the interpretive work that exegetes want it to do and therefore is not able to provide the most historically plausible reading of 3:21–26.

Even considering the objections, one might still argue that some readers from Paul's time might have seen a vague allusion to propitiatory sacrifice in 3:25. If one were to grant this possibility, it would signify only that Jesus' faithful death had averted God's anger toward the gentiles. The objections raised above show that any closer or more detailed analogy with sacrifice would be incoherent. The logic of sacrifice is not the structure that gives coherence to Paul's understanding of Christ's death. In fact, numerous passages in the letters invoke a narrative that does make sense of Jesus' life and death.

The Messiah Who Delayed: A Hypothesis

My hypothesis is as follows: Paul believed that God commissioned the man Jesus, chosen descendant of Davidic lineage, to be his messiah. Jesus was sent with a mandate to rectify the domination of the wicked over the right-eous and to restore God's people, the Jews, by overthrowing unfaithful Jews and the Roman oppressors. God gave Jesus Christ his Spirit and divine powers to accomplish this task of judging (that is, of bringing justice), punishing the wicked, and protecting and rewarding the faithful. In other words, Jesus had been granted the authority and power to bring about God's righteousness in fulfillment of God's promises. Jesus, however, out of faithfulness to his man-date, chose not to exercise the awesome divine powers available to him. Jesus did not exercise the powers given to him because if he had, much of Israel and most of the gentiles would have been lost. Jesus died and postponed the world's judgment out of love for the ungodly. In accord with God's purposes and out of faithfulness to God's promises and believing that God would vindi-cate him and allow him to fulfill his messianic role in the future, Jesus refused to use his divine powers to the point even of not escaping capture and execu-tion by the Romans. In forgoing his messianic prerogatives, Jesus was allowing Jews and gentiles an opportunity to repent and trusting that God would delay his mission until God's righteousness could be effected. Jesus' refusal to take the easy way out was an act of faithfulness to God's commission and God's pur-poses. He died on behalf of others. God vindicated Jesus by raising him and making him the pioneer of the world's renewal. Jesus, like Abraham, was not just a passive object of faith but one whose faithfulness actually effected the merciful justice toward the world's peoples that God intended.

This account allows us to see why Paul admits to traditional messianic beliefs about the earthly Jesus in passing but places no weight on them or on the specifics of Jesus' career. Instead, the apostle focuses everything on Jesus' faithful death and God's vindication of Christ's faithfulness. All of the promises that he believed God had been bringing toward fulfillment since Jesus' death were a result of Jesus' willingness to postpone the time of messianic reckon-ing by dying. The successful conversion of the gentiles and the future repen-tance of unfaithful Jews are made possible only by virtue of Christ's death. In Paul, Christ's messianic duties of judging and subduing the world's hostile forces have moved to the time of his return.

Paul undoubtedly understands Jesus Christ as Israel's messiah and attrib-utes messianic functions to him in the future but describes the present and past significance of Christ to his gentile audiences in terms that are mostly alien to those messianic traditions. The way he uses "Christ" epitomizes the problem. In Paul's letters, *Christos* can be read almost as a surname of Jesus. But Nils Dahl has subjected Paul's usage to careful philological analysis and shown that *Christos* is not completely fixed as a proper name.[51] In the best-known case (Rom 9:5), after enumerating blessings given to the Jews, one reads, "and from them is the Christ according to the flesh." "According to the flesh" implies that the Christ ought to be evaluated from two perspectives with regard to status and identity. Spirit ranks higher than flesh. Messiah according to flesh does not cease to be important but becomes subordinated to messiah according to Spirit.

Paul clearly understands a concept of "the anointed one" that bears continuity with certain earlier Jewish conceptions of a messiah ("anointed one"), and yet that understanding has faded into the background for Paul.[52] Instead, the faithful death, resurrection, present lordship, and future coming, which play no part in Jewish messianic beliefs, have come to define and give significance to *Christos*. The best explanation lies in the narrative sketched above: Jesus' act of forgoing messianic powers and privileges meant, for Paul, that although Jesus was the messiah, his all-important act was his dying for the ungodly and his assumption of the status and role given to him when God approved his faithful act by vindicating him in the resurrection.

Jewish expectations about the future were extremely varied and fluid in the first century C.E.. Even those few texts that speak of an anointed one vary considerably and fall into distinguishable beliefs and traditions. Nevertheless, some descriptions of Paul's Christ fit certain traditions.[53] Thus in 1 Cor 15:24–25, "then comes the end, when he will hand over the kingdom to God the father after destroying every sovereignty, every authority and power. For he must reign until he has placed every enemy under his feet."[54] Here Christ assumes the role of the royal messiah as warrior and temporary ruler—but in the future. In the *Psalms of Solomon* God sends a Davidic ruler and gives him the strength to defeat the unrighteous rulers and purify Jerusalem of the gentile oppressors (17:21–22). He will condemn sinners and "destroy lawless gentiles by the word of his mouth" (17:23–24). His power comes from the holy Spirit that God gives to him (17:37). This one who is anointed, a son of David, will restore Israel and judge the nations justly, but only God is truly king (17:34, 46).

Paul's traditional messianic understanding of Christ as worldly ruler, warrior, and judge has been an embarrassment to theologians and biblical scholars, who marginalize such beliefs by attributing them to quotations of primitive traditions, suggesting that they are vestiges that Paul quotes but does not really believe. But I take it as certain that Jesus was executed by the Romans as a messianic pretender, even if he did not proclaim himself messiah, and as likely that Paul persecuted Jesus' followers as obstinate preachers of a failed messiah. At some point, however, Paul came to believe that Jesus was the messiah, but a messiah who had acted in an unexpected although divinely approved way. The Christ was now waiting in heaven in order to allow unfaithful Jews and the other peoples to repent. The various messianic and royal pretenders of the period that Josephus writes about add to the plausibility of this picture.[55] Such leaders drew popular followings but were quickly crushed by the nervous Roman governors. Some Jews in the first century stood ready to believe in and die for those who claimed to be messiahs and Jewish kings.

Nowhere does Paul place more emphasis on this messianic tradition than in Romans. Toward the end of the letter (15:12), Paul cites from Isaiah 11 about the root of Jesse, who will rise to rule the gentiles and upon whom the gentiles will hope. The string of quotations to which v. 12 belongs gives support to an exhortation for the readers to accept one another after the model of Christ, who adapted himself to the needs of Jews and gentiles. The traditional Davidic connotations of Isaiah 11 belong to Paul's larger story of Christ's adaptability: He is the august, powerful Davidic messiah, but he adapted to the needs of Jews and gentiles rather than please himself (cf. 15:1–3).

The letter opens with a notable messianic reference that summarizes the gospel message preached by Paul: "the good news concerning his Son who was born from the seed of David with regard to the flesh and who was appointed Son of God in power with regard to the Spirit of holiness by the resurrection from the dead" (1:3–4). Scholars have written an enormous amount about these lines.[56] Much of the ink has amounted to thin speculation about the original form of this supposedly primitive Christian confession. I do not know the origin of the lines, but I see no reason to doubt that they belong fully to Paul and to the letter. Rom 1:3–4, on the one hand, speaks of Jesus as the Davidic Son of God and messiah according to the flesh and, on the other hand, of his appointment by God as his Son in power by the Spirit of holiness in the resurrection. "Son of God" was a designation closely associated with David and hoped-for kings of the Davidic line.[57] Verses 3–4 suggest that the power and significance of Jesus Christ were raised to a higher level by the resurrection. He was no longer merely God's Son in the Davidic line but Son of God in the power of the resurrection. If my hypothesis is correct, the hierarchy and juxtaposition of Christ the traditional messiah and Christ exalted by the resurrection reflect the story of a messiah who delayed the exercise of his powers only to receive greater powers after submitting to death.

The passage may help to explain Paul's Spirit/flesh dichotomy. Christ forfeited the rightful honors and powers due to him as the anointed son of David out of trust that God would do even more for Israel and the world's peoples than traditional expectations and the world's situation would allow. When Paul came to this understanding, his whole vision was refigured. The messiah according to traditional fleshly expectations had been superseded by the messiah who trusted that God would fulfill all of his promises to the whole world.

Flesh came to stand for all of those unacceptable conditions that would have held if Jesus had chosen to follow the expected role in the expected way. The new age began not with Jesus' birth but with his death and resurrection. Paul writes in 2 Cor 5:14–17: "For Christ's love controls us, having judged this, that one died for all; therefore all have died. And he died for all in order that those living might no longer live for themselves but for the one who died on their behalf and was raised. Thus, from now on we do not know anyone according to the flesh; even if we once knew Christ according to the flesh. Therefore, if anyone is in Christ he is a new creation; the old has passed away, behold, the new has arrived." Paul once viewed Jesus' messiahship in a traditional way, but he no longer does. Moreover, the new comprehension, focused on Jesus' willingness to forgo the traditional prerogatives, has become the central moral and religious paradigm that Paul follows and promotes. In vv. 18–21, Paul celebrates his role as ambassador of God's plan to reconcile the world to himself through Christ. Paul's Christ does not give up inherited messianic roles as warrior, judge, protector of the righteous, restorer of Israel's life, and agent of God's promises, but these roles are projected into the future and reoriented around the theme of God's love and Christ's willingness to die for the sake of the ungodly.

Paul's letters never detail the message that he preached, but they frequently allude to it. When he wants to distill the good news, he uses the image of Christ crucified (for example, Gal 3:1). A central part of that message was to explain the meaning of Jesus' death and of God raising him by reference to Christ's faithfulness. This faithfulness to God's true purposes meant that Christ temporarily renounced and delayed his exercise of power. At the end of Rom 11, Paul reveals a mystery: God has hardened a portion of the Jewish people toward the new movement until the full number of the gentiles turn to God (11:25). Then Christ will appear in Jerusalem, and the disbelieving Jews will repent (11:26–27). According to a basic assumption for Paul, God's people, the Jews, will experience God's judgment and salvation first at the final reckoning (for example, Rom 2:10; 1:16). Only then will God turn to the other peoples. Rom 11:11–12 (cf. 28–32) indicates that the final events (resurrection) will occur when the Jews as a whole repent and that gentile salvation and Paul's mission have been made possible only by God's act of hardening the Jews. Jewish disobedience has allowed time for the mission to the gentiles. Scholarship has tended to treat these ideas as speculations that Paul throws out toward the end of his career; speculations inspired by his disappointed realization that his own people have not believed. I do not find this reading credible. Paul certainly knew that his people as a whole and its leadership had from the beginning rejected belief in Jesus and in the crucified messiah. He himself was a persecutor in those very early days! Paul had no illusions about the nature of Jewish response to Jesus. The revelation in 11:25, to a church that he did not found, refines an understanding that he had had since his calling by the risen Christ to preach to the gentiles. Paul's scenario in Romans has its basis in the idea that Jesus had delayed his messianic mission to provide an opportunity for the ungodly to repent. If Jewish repentance would bring the final events, then that repentance had to be delayed if God were to be just and allow an opportunity for the gentiles also. This belief forms a premise of Paul's gospel.

Paul's language about Christ's forbearance also points to my hypothesis. According to the *RSV*'s translation, 2 Cor 10:1 refers to the "meekness and gentleness of Christ." The translation is misleading. *Epieikeia* ("gentleness" [*RSV*]) is the kind of clemency that kings and generals show.[58] *Prautēs* ("meekness" [*RSV*]) has similar associations. *Epieikeia* describes the king who defeats a rebellious city and has every right to sack it but does not, or the ruler who could execute his political opponents but instead shows leniency. The concept implies power over others that one does not exercise. The context of 2 Cor 10:1f. confirms this meaning.[59] In 10:1, Paul implicitly compares his behavior with Christ's. When Paul worked face-to-face with the Corinthians he acted humbly for their sakes, but when away he indirectly corrected them boldly by letter. Paul here turns his opponents' criticisms of him into something positive (cf. 10:10). He implies that he has acted like Christ, who could have exercised the powers that God had given him when he was on earth but held back out of *epieikeia*. Paul's boldness from a distance suggests a parallel with Christ's resurrection power and authority at the right hand of God. Paul goes on in 3–6 to develop the metaphor of laying siege and taking a fortress with captives. Only he will not use worldly means in taking captive for Christ the rational deliberations of the enemy. In other words, he will follow the model of Christ, who renounced powers of destruction for persuasion. The central motif of the whole section hinges on an allusion to the story of Jesus Christ's holding back and forgoing out of care for those who are hostile.

Much of 1 Cor 1–2 develops the theme of God's unexpected and paradoxical wisdom in exercising his power through the one crucified. This surprising wisdom of God was hidden from the rulers of this age, who are destined to lose their power and who would not have crucified Jesus if they had understood who he was. The rulers are the historical authorities who crucified Jesus and not cosmic powers.[60] If the Romans and their Jewish collaborators had understood that Jesus was actually God's messiah who could call down armies of angels or exercise other awesome powers and who would return to defeat and judge them, they would not have crucified him. Again, the story suggests the Christ who held back by submitting to the very rulers he had come to defeat.

One of the features that makes the hypothesis so compelling is the way that it seamlessly integrates ethics and Christology in Paul's thought. The theme of Christ's, Paul's, and the believer's adaptability to the needs of others appears as a constant. In other words, Paul distilled his central moral and social principle from the idea that Christ, instead of saving the few and using violence against those who did not come up to his level, the righteousness demanded by the law, saved the many by lowering himself to the level of those in need. Thus he can talk about Christ coming to know sin, although not being sinful, and even dying like a cursed criminal (2 Cor 5:21; Rom 8:3; Gal 3:13). The theme of Christ's willing loss of power and status, then, goes together with the moral theme of adaptability to others.[61] Though Christ was rich, he became poor so that others could become rich on account of his poverty (2 Cor 8:9). It is highly implausible that Paul or his readers would see a reference to "the incarnation" here.

The most crucial passage on the theme of adaptability and loss of power and status is the much-controverted so-called Christ hymn of Phil 2:5–11.[62] If it is a hymn that Paul quotes, he has completely integrated it into his thought, into the letter as a whole, and into the immediate moral context. Scholars like to remove the hymn from its context, but both flow together so completely that separation seems violent and pointless.[63] The passage directly presents Christ as a model for the exhortation "Do not look out only for your own needs but also for the needs of others" (2:4) and implies that Christ's actions are also a model for love, compassion, mercy, the like-mindedness of friends, and humility (2:1–3).[64] Later (3:1–11), Paul will present his own act of leaving behind the true and great blessings in his Jewish way of life in order to adapt himself to the needs of the gentiles as a parallel model in imitation of Christ. The passage may be translated as follows: "Have the attitude among yourselves which Christ Jesus had, who being in the form of God, did not regard being Godlike as something to exploit for himself, but made himself powerless, taking the form of a slave, having become like [mere] human beings. And by appearance having been encountered as a man, he humbled himself, becoming obedient to the point of death, even death on a cross. Therefore, God lifted him high and gave him a name that surpasses every name so that in the name of Jesus every knee should bow . . . and every tongue confess that Jesus Christ is Lord, for the glory of God the father." My translation for the most part reflects the consensus with regard to exegetical decisions about the Greek. As scholars widely recognize, *Isa theō* cannot possibly mean "equality with God," as most translations, dutifully following orthodox dogma, have rendered the words in 2:6. *Isa* means "similar in some respects" or "like."[65] Thus in a passage that must have been almost paradigmatic for Greeks, the people of Ithaca look on Eurymachos "as a god" (*isa theō*) in *Odyssey* 15.520. Paul's wording quite precisely says that Jesus was godlike or Godlike but not equal to God. The hymn agrees with the strict subordination of Christ to God in 1 Cor 15:28, in which Christ at his second coming exercises the powers of God to subject the world, in the end submitting himself to God after completing his messianic task. The words *isa theō* (Godlike) clarify *morphē theou* (form of God) and have even been considered epexegetic of the first phrase.[66] The text no more makes Jesus literally God than it makes him literally a slave in v. 7 (that is, *morphē doulou*). But by the same token, the passage makes Jesus' slavelike loss of rights, even of power over his own life, as real as the Godlike power and authority that were his to use.

I follow R. W. Hoover in taking *harpagmon hēgēsato* as an idiom meaning "to regard something as a thing to be taken advantage of." As N. T. Wright has especially reclarified Hoover's discovery, the object in the idiom is something already possessed, not something to be grasped; and the expression seems to assume that the subject will continue to possess that object which he/she might use for his/her own advantage.[67] In Paul's story, Jesus was endowed with God's powers, authority, and wisdom as Israel's Christ. Jesus Christ possessed this likeness to God and could have used it at any time. But out of compassion for the ungodly and in faithfulness to God's promises, he renounced the use of his godlikeness. He allowed himself to be captured and executed by the authorities in order to delay the messianic conquest, creating a time during which the ungodly could repent. In Paul's view, Jesus could, in theory, at any time have decided to wield his powers and will actually do so at his return.

In the economy, coherence, and historical fit of this reading, the preexistence and incarnation of Christ vanish. Since James Dunn's book on Christology, scholars can no longer easily assume a doctrine of preexistence in Paul.[68] The case has not been closed, but the genuine difficulties with that view cannot be ignored. Whatever conception of preexistence, if any, might be salvaged, it will not resemble any orthodox doctrine of preexistence and incarnation. Further, one of the greatest difficulties with reading these ideas into Paul's letters results from their superfluity. The doctrines simply have no role to play in his thought.

The hypothesis of the messiah who delayed allows a reading of passages about Christ's mission and death for which ideas of a vicarious substitutionary sacrifice or the incarnation of God in human form are unnecessary and distorting. For example, one of the essential ingredients of the context of Gal

4:4 comes in the dominating themes of lineage, inheritance, and family. The later Christian readings, with their categories of sin and salvation, have obscured the issues of ethnic lineage and inheritance that would have appeared central to Paul's ancient readers. Paul writes about gentiles who, being outside of the fleshly lineage of Abraham and its sonship, find only condemnation under a law that they cannot fully keep because only a part of it applies to them. Thus in 4:4–5, God commissioned ("sent out") his (Davidic, messianic) son, who had the necessary fleshly and spiritual prerequisites, to redeem the gentiles from their slave status under the law. Slaves are subject to the rule of the family but do not share in the family's rights or future because they lack a biological relation to the family. The central blessings and institutions of the law apply only to descendants of Abraham. God's son was an Israelite by nature ("born of woman, born under the law"), and the descendant (seed) of Abraham prophesied in the promise to Abraham that the gentiles would be blessed through a descendant (3:15–18): "If you are of Christ, then you are a descendant of Abraham and inheritors according to the promise" (3:29). Thus God commissioned his son, who was the chosen descendant of Abraham, to free those who were slaves without any rights of lineage under the law, adopting them as sons and bringing God's Spirit to them (4:5–7). Christ created a new line of descent based on both fleshly lineage *and* spiritual adoption. In Paul's view, works of the law have nothing to do with gaining either status.

How did God accomplish this redemption of the ungodly through Christ? First, Christ brought about a reprieve from certain punishment, since the gentiles stood condemned under the law. According to my hypothesis, he brought this reprieve by dying as a messianic pretender rather than by exercising his messianic powers. Thus Jesus manifested faithfulness to his own mission and to God's promises to Jews and gentiles (cf. Rom 15:8–9). Without his act in accordance with God's purposes, the gentile peoples would have been condemned and the Abrahamic promise void. Second, in Paul's understanding, God had not only vindicated Jesus in a marvelous and unexpected way but had made the "reversal" of his death the beginning of the general resurrection of the dead and outpouring of God's Spirit that was to come at the end of the age.[69] The messiah had renounced his campaign, allowing himself to be captured and executed, and God had turned his death into the beginnings of world redemption, with the messiah nowhere in sight except to those who had experienced the power breaking in through his resurrection. Paul taught his gentile communities that this end-of-the-ages manifestation of God's Spirit, introduced by Christ, was the fulfillment of God's promise of a blessing for them through Abraham's descendant (Gal 3:14).

The uniquely Pauline stamp to these beliefs comes from the way in which the letters focus on Jesus Christ's faithfulness to death on behalf of the ungodly and the way in which he makes this focus into a moral and social model through the concept of adaptability. Clarence Glad has shown how Paul borrowed from Greco-Roman culture the controversial ideal of adapting himself to the needs of the many.[70] Greek and Roman writers extensively discuss how and to what extent the psychagogue ("leader of souls") should adapt himself in his teaching and educational activities. Abraham Malherbe has shown that in 2 Cor 10:1–6, discussed above in relation to Christ's *epieikeia* ("gentleness" [*RSV*]), Paul employs imagery, terminology, and issues about the form of life and approach to others that the Cynic philosopher should adopt.[71] The discussion can be traced back to Antisthenes, who with later teachers and philosophers invoked Odysseus as a model of the adaptable philosopher. In this view, Odysseus proved willing to humble himself if circumstances required and adapt his manner for the benefit of his friends and associates. To Paul's critics in Corinth, his adaptability appeared as duplicity, inconsistency, and weakness; to Paul himself, it meant embodying the very form of the gospel.[72] Scholarship has not appreciated the centrality of this issue to the apostle who became all things to all people (1 Cor 9:19–23). Paul's genius was in his using this concept of adaptability to interpret the meaning of the crucified messiah, to define his self-understanding as an apostle, and to provide a paradigm for social relations in his gentile communities.

Paul tells others to imitate his adaptability, as he imitates Christ's: "Give no reason for stumbling to Jews, to Greeks or to God's assembly, just as I [seek to] please all people in whatever I do, not seeking my own advantage but that of the many that they might be saved. Become imitators of me as I am of Christ" (1 Cor 10:32–11:1). He can exhort the Galatians to become like him because he has become like them (4:13). This pattern of coming to know and share the circumstances and problems of the other so as to benefit the other appears with dizzying repetition in Paul's letters, most notably in language about Christ's significance. Thus, as we have seen, Christ made himself powerless, becoming like a slave (Phil 2:7). Even though he was not a sinner, he experienced the role of a sinner for the sake of sinners (2 Cor 5:20; Gal 3:13; cf. Rom 8:3), and so on. Paul speaks of three categories of people to whom he has adapted himself: Jews, gentiles, and the weak (1 Cor 9:21–23). All three appear prominently in Romans.

Paul focuses so intently on interpreting Christ's significance in general patterns of faithfulness to God's purposes and his adaptation to save others that the details of the historical Jesus disappear. Thus I cannot prove my thesis that the saving act for Paul was Jesus' decision not to exercise his messianic mandate. But those who explain Paul's conception of Christ by means of an incarnation or a sacrifice of atonement also cannot prove their cases. My hypothesis, however, brings sense to Paul's language with more economy and more coherence and with a sense that more plausibly fits Paul the Jew of the first century. My proposals about Paul's understanding of Christ have many implications for the reading of Rom 3:21–4:25.

The reading that I am proposing for 3:21–26 means a definite shift in emphasis from traditional conceptions. The text does not reveal what the sinner has to do in order to be saved (that is, have faith). Rather, it tells how God has shown himself to be righteous by justifying the gentile peoples through Jesus' faithful death. I want to compare the *RSV* with a translation of mine.[73] To facilitate comparison with standard versions, my translation here is conservative in the sense of retaining as much as possible of the traditional phraseology and wording from the major tradition of English translation. First is the *RSV*, followed by my translation:

> But now the righteousness of God has been manifested apart from law, although the law and the prophets bear witness to it, the righteousness of God through faith in Jesus Christ for all who believe. For there is no distinction; since all have sinned and fall short of the glory of God, they are justified by his grace as a gift, through the redemption which is in Christ Jesus, whom God put forward as an expiation by his blood, to be received by faith. This was to show God's righteousness, because in his divine forbearance he had passed over former sins; it was to prove at the present time that he himself is righteous and that he justifies him who has faith in Jesus.

> But now God's [own] righteousness has been made known apart from the law, the law and the prophets bearing witness to it. It is God's [own] righteousness [effected] by means of Jesus Christ's faithfulness for all who are faithful. For there is no difference [which makes Jews alone worthy of God's mercy] since all have sinned and are in need of God's glory. They [the ungodly/gentiles] are made right freely by his grace through the redemption in Jesus Christ, whom God purposed as an act of conciliation by means of [Jesus'] faithfulness in shedding his blood. This was to demonstrate God's own righteousness because he passed over previous [gentile] sins when he held back punishment; it was to demonstrate his own righteousness at this time in history so as to be righteous himself and to make righteous the person who lives on the basis of Jesus' faithfulness.

Above all, 3:21–26 is about God and what God has done in order to be true to his promise to Abraham about the gentiles. The passage does not treat the Christian subjectivity of faith. The text also deals with how God has effected his justice through Jesus' faithfulness even to death. A reading appropriate to Paul's context and cultural codes will not result in a description of how the believer receives salvation on the condition of faith in Christ. Belief in what God has done through Christ certainly forms a part of sharing in Jesus' faithfulness but that is not the point. Sam K. Williams writes,[74]

> My contention is that we do not find the expression *pistis en Christō* in Paul's letters because Paul was not accustomed to thinking of Christ as the "object" of faith. Whether one stresses faith as a response to the gospel (see *akoē pisteōs* at Gal 3:3,5), faith as confession (Rom 10:9–10), faith as trust (Romans 4), or faith as obedience (see *hypakoē pisteōs* at Rom 1:5), the person of Christ is not faith's object. *God* is. In committing themselves to the truth of the gospel, believers confess what *God* has done by raising Christ from the dead and making him Lord (Rom 10:9; Phil 2:9–10). Believers trust *God,* for it is God who gives life to the dead and justifies the ungodly (Rom 4:5,17; cf. 4:24). Nor, surprisingly, does Paul write that believers are to obey Christ. Christ himself was obedient to *God* (Philippians 2, Romans 5), and so, like Christ, is the Christian. To summarize the point being stressed here: Christians confess what God has done through the death and resurrection of Christ, and, like Christ, they obey unstintingly Him whom they can trust unwaveringly. God, not Christ, is the "object" of the Christian's faith, although, of course, it is through Christ that God has made himself known and has taken the initiative for human salvation.

Paul seems far more monotheistic and far more Jewish than traditional readings of his letters have allowed.

In Rom 3:21–25, Paul explains to the teacher how God has effected his merciful justice by conciliating his anger toward the idolatrous gentiles. This release of God's long and just anger occurred when Christ acted faithfully in accord with God's purposes by dying and thus delaying the imminent punishment of the gentiles and when God vindicated Jesus' faithfulness by making him the firstborn of a new "race" created (or born) "out of his faithfulness" (*ek pisteōs*). Thus God demonstrates his merciful justice by forgiving the sins "stored up against" gentiles (2:5), who now find their origin in Jesus' faithfulness (3:25b-26). Later, Paul will explain how these gentiles liberated "out of Jesus' faithfulness" have, like Christ, died to the law that marked their transgressions (7:1–6; cf. 3:20; 4:15; 5:20). On this reading of 3:21–25, the content of Paul's gospel gives lucid meaning to "as an act of conciliation" (*hilastērion*) and "redemption/liberation" (*apolutrōsis*). The redemption, however, is not universal in the sense that all humans apart from all historical particularity are shown to be of one moral-ontological status in sin curable only by Christ's death. The latter scheme assumes a dehistoricizing, individualizing, and departicularizing of religion that came from the wedding of Christianity and Greek philosophy and from social developments in late antiquity.

The issue Paul discusses with the Jewish teacher involves a case of undeserved leniency: God has justified the ungodly, accepting the gentiles on the basis of Christ's faithfulness. Chapter 4 will explain that Jews and gentiles participate in the blessings given to Abraham and his heir Christ not because they have kept certain works of the law but solely on the basis of Abraham's and Christ's faithfulness resulting in God's pure graciousness. When a Jew is born into the community of Israel or a gentile baptized into Christ, the blessings of the lineages that they receive have nothing to do with their merit. God pronounced the blessings in which later Israelites, including Christ, participate solely because of Abraham's faithfulness to the point of having a child in old age that would continue the lineage. God has shown an undeserved leniency toward the gentile nations solely because of Christ's faithfulness as an expression of his own loving justice. God has provided a new way for them to live on the basis of Christ's faithfulness, not of their own faith or works. In the thought of Romans, those who say that gentiles must do certain works of the law as a prerequisite for justification have misunderstood God's actions. The letter's rhetoric creates a boastful interlocutor with such views and then pulls the rug out from under him so that he can no longer claim a role in making gentiles righteous by teaching the law.

This understanding illuminates much of the language in Paul's letters that commentators have long held to be most obscure. Gentiles are justified "out of [*ek pisteōs*] of Jesus' faithfulness" (3:26). The promise is a matter of grace depending solely on God's integrity because it comes to the one who shares in it "out of Abraham's faithfulness" (4:16). The preposition *ek* can express descent or origins. Paul's language about the faithful being "out of" Christ's or Abraham's acts of faithfulness makes little sense on traditional readings. But if the letter concerns the relation of ethnic peoples who define themselves by descent, then the connotations of *ek* having to do with lineage and paternity/maternity make sense. Gentiles are justified "in" Abraham (Gal 3:8). Those who live on the basis of faithfulness are blessed "together with the faithful Abraham" (Gal 3:9). Gentiles are justified and receive the blessing to Abraham "in Christ." The obedience of a single individual brings about righteousness for many, and this is a free gift of God's grace (Rom 5:19 cf. 17). In all of these cases and many more, whole peoples become the heirs to blessings of God occasioned by the faithful acts of individuals who establish new lines of family. Not until chapter 8 does the reader hear how God has adopted the gentiles as sons together with and through Christ, but the language of gentile redemption "out of Christ" and the way Christ parallels Abraham make descent a central issue.

8 One God & One Father Abraham (3:27-5:11)

Romans 4 read as a discussion based on the logic of patrilineal descent from the founder of a lineage reveals that the
letter indeed treats the relations of ethnic peoples. Paul's
resumed dialogue with the teacher in 3:27–4:2 establishes
the issues for the discussion of Abraham: The one impartial
God of the whole world has employed the faithfulness of
chosen individuals to effect his merciful justice for all peoples. Abraham serves as a model not of the believer's saving faith but rather of how God brings to pass his promises
by founding lineages that incorporate whole peoples into
the blessings made possible by the founding ancestors.

Romans does not wrestle with the problem of how God
goes about saving the generic human being. Rather, it asks
how families of people establish a kinship with God and
with one another. Jews inherit a status as God's children (literally "sons") from generation to generation; other peoples
do not. How do the gentile peoples get into a family relation so that they can stand righteous before God rather than
as enemies and aliens? Paul's thinking is sure to remain
opaque insofar as one equates his world and ours. The great
enemy of strong, extended webs of kinship is the modern
state.[1] The corollary of the modern state is the individual in
whom rights reside (rather than kin groups) and the small-
est socially and culturally feasible form of family, the nuclear
or single-parent family. Modern Western states encourage
the nuclear family but vigorously and often violently suppress larger kinship groups. In Paul's world, kinship largely
subsumed both individual and state. The ancient person's
life was overwhelmingly determined by parentage. One
simply misses the point by branding Paul a mean-spirited
opponent of liberal values. Those values were not known.
As Greeks and Romans began to share power and culture
they instinctively reworked myths of kinship in the process
of forging and conceptualizing these ties. Paul, like other

Jews who thought about such problems, just as naturally turned to the law, with its origins of the world's peoples and stories of the patriarchal families who had founded Israel, in order to rethink Israel's relation to the world's peoples.

Owing to his reading of Genesis and his convictions about Christ, Paul rejects the teacher's suggestion that God constitutes his people(s) on the criteria of lawkeeping (4:1–2). Abraham neither became righteous nor won the right to found the Jewish people by keeping the law or even a select set of commandments, for example, circumcision. Two things seem decisive for Paul's position here. First, Paul understood the law as coming later than Abraham and found a passage (Gen 15:6) that he read as explicitly denying that God accepted Abraham on the basis of righteousness according to law. Second, Paul's understandings of Abraham and Christ influenced each other. The gospel was a message of Christ adapting himself to raise people rather than requiring people to lift themselves up to him. Abraham had come out of ungodly idolatry (cf. 4:5, 7). God did not require Abraham to keep a code of specific commandments as a prerequisite for accepting him. God's approach required Abraham's trust in the divine promises in a way that ensured Abraham's faithfulness to the hopes embodied in the promises. Specifically, in spite of his being too old to procreate, Abraham was circumcised, and Abraham and Sarah had sexual intercourse because of God's promise. This was Abraham's faithfulness: Not lawkeeping but acting as circumstances required in light of God's promises.

In Paul's view, the essential ingredients of the relation between God and Abraham, those that ensured the intended results and that made Abraham righteous, were added when God promised and Abraham put his trust in what God had said. The fact that Gen 15:6 has God accepting Abraham as righteous when the patriarch first hears the promise and before he could act out his faith meant that trust/faithfulness toward God was the primary generative act that ensured Abraham's paternity, making him father of Jews and gentiles. Romans 4 does not put Abraham's trust and his circumcision into opposition but simply stresses that the trust came first. In this way, Paul makes God's miracle and Abraham's commitment to God's promise generative of Abraham's work of circumcision rather than making the circumcision the basic generative act.

At this point, the traditional reader is apt to make some false assumptions. Abraham's initial trust upon hearing God's promise should not be separated from his continuing faithfulness, which allowed him and Sarah to conceive and bear Isaac. The faith has no independent status in isolation from the faithful acts. Rather, by pointing to the way in which Abraham's trust/faith preceded the works that God required, Paul shows God adapting to Abraham's level rather than having Abraham first come up to God's standards. Thus, one should not read the chapter as presenting a model for the attitude of true religion—faith—versus false religion—works, lawkeeping—but as God's way of adopting whole peoples as his own by using the generative trust of Abraham and Jesus to work procreative miracles that founded new families. Thus the descendants, all those in Abraham and Christ, find themselves born into blessings and covenants with God that they have not earned and whose continuance depends on their acting faithfully in view of the promises. Paul assumes that Jews and gentiles must live by requirements of the law. But gentiles cannot earn their way into God's graces through works. They must be born (Jews) or adopted (gentiles) into the lineages begat by the generative faithfulness of Abraham and Christ.

The Reformation understanding of faith reflects Western Christendom and modernity, in which religion marks off a personal sphere of sentiment and spirituality. Faith affects primarily the interiority of the individual. How different Abraham's faithfulness in Romans 4! God provided the miracle of restoring the life principle to Abraham's seed and the nurturing capacity to Sarah's womb, but Abraham in faithfulness planted his seed. If Abraham had not acted as if he would have offspring and planted his seed, trusting that God would somehow bring about his promise of offspring, there would have been no Isaac, no Moses, no Israel, and no Jesus Christ. The descendants come from Abraham's seed and share his characteristics, including his faithfulness. If Jesus Christ had not chosen passiveness at the right moment, trusting in God, but had acted as the Messiah should, multitudes of gentile peoples and a great number of Jews would have been destroyed. Abraham's and Christ's faithfulness actually effected events in the world. In this kind of *pistis* no place exists for contrasts between belief/faith versus action, spiritual versus physical, inner versus outer, faith versus reason. Not Paul's doctrine of faith, but his conviction that the Christ had stepped onto a new level of existence as the pioneer of a new age (through the resurrection) is what produced his own Spirit/flesh dichotomy.

How does Abraham's faithfulness affect and benefit others? Here Paul employs the logic of unilineal descent groups. The promise was made "to Abraham and to his seed" (Rom 4:13). In Gal 3:8, citing Gen 12:3, perhaps modified by Gen 18:18 ("gentiles" replacing "tribes of the earth"), Paul claims that the gospel is God's promise that the gentiles would be blessed "in Abraham" (that is, *en soi*). The next verse describes "those who are out of faithfulness" (that is, gentiles) being blessed "with the faithful Abraham." Here Paul envisages all of Abraham's future descendants already being present in Abraham's seed and being blessed with him. Genesis 25:23 illustrates this conception, widespread in societies based on unilineal descent, of all descendants being present in the ancestor: "Two nations are in your womb and two peoples shall be separated out of [*ek*] your womb." Hebrews 7:9–10 is even more graphic: Levi paid a tithe to Melchizedek because Levi, like all of Abraham's descendants, was "still in the loins of his forefather when he met Melchizedek." One of those in Abraham's seed was Jesus Christ. (Or, in Gal 3:16–17, Christ is the seed.) Owing to Jesus' own generative act of faithfulness, God incorporated the gentiles into him. Thus Paul speaks of the believer being "in Christ" and of the gentiles being "sons of God through faithfulness; in Christ Jesus" (Gal 3:26). If they are "of Christ," having been baptized "into" him, they are Abraham's seed and heirs by God's promise (Gal 3:29). In Rom 4:16, all of Abraham's seed (literally, his "entire seed") includes both those who are "from the law" and those who are "from faithfulness." In a classic essay on unilineal descent groups, Meyer Fortes describes a lineage as a single legal and political personality.[2] The Ashanti in West Africa call a lineage "one person."[3] Gentiles have kinship with God and with the lineage of Abraham by incorporation into Christ by his generative faithfulness. Paul's language of belonging to Christ, being in Christ, and belonging to his body treats Christ and his family as one entity.

Romans and Galatians argue that one can become a descendant of Abraham by incorporation into a descendant of Abraham who reenacted Abraham's lineage-founding faithfulness. Both founders trusted in God's promise that he would produce offspring when that hope seemed impossible. Abraham's act of faithfulness was, first, simply to trust in the promise and then to have sexual relations with Sarah; Jesus' faithfulness lay in allowing his execution to occur rather than judging and subduing the world, trusting that God would bring life and the promises out of death. God's responding generative miracle was, one the one hand, live seed containing all of Abraham's progeny and, on the other hand, raising Jesus Christ from the dead as the first fruits of immortal sonship by the Spirit (cf. 8:29–30, 9–17). In connecting Christ's generative faithfulness with Abraham's, Paul retains the principle of descent while subordinating it to procreation by the Spirit of God. Both ascription (inheritance, God's gifts) and achievement have a place in Paul's thought. His thought deals with tensions between ascription and achievement that were central to Jewish culture throughout the second temple period.[4] For a priest, one's role, status, and power depended largely upon one's lineage, one's parents and purity of descent. For other Jews, however, descent meant little and achievement a great deal.[5] Achievement in the study and observation of the law increasingly became an alternative to ascribed status by birth and would become central to the kind of Judaism represented in the Mishnah and Talmuds. Since the tension between birth and lawkeeping had become so central to Jewish identity, Paul naturally thinks about the gentile problem in these terms. Paul takes a complex middle road between making birth the only significant criterion for divine peoplehood and making achievement the criterion.

Structure and Rhetoric: 3:27–4:2 as Dialogue

The tradition has made divisions in chapters 1–5 according to topics in "the Christian system of salvation":

- 1:18–32—The gentile is a hopeless sinner.
- 2:17–29 (or 2:1–29)—The Jew is also a hopeless sinner.
- 3:1–8—Digression
- 3:9–20—Conclusion: Every human is hopelessly trapped in sin.
- 3:21–26—Faith in Christ is the only means of justification/salvation.
- 3:27–31—Digression
- 4:1–25—Abraham as an example of how faith justifies
- 5:1–11—The benefits of justification

Paul did not write in paragraphs, and paragraphs should not be assumed as the only way to arrange the sense of an ancient prose text. The traditional reading of Romans as a theological treatise made it difficult to construe 3:27–4:2 as a dialogue between Paul and a Jewish teacher. This approach treats the passage as a digression after the letter's so-called thesis in 3:21–26; or, according to Ernst Käsemann, as a "polemical development" in the style of the diatribe, an attack on the Jew whose lawkeeping epitomizes human boasting.[6]

Romans 2:17–5:11 reads best if one places a premium on its unity. I have argued that the traditional breaks at 3:1 and 3:21 do not make much sense. I will urge the same for 3:27, 4:1, and 5:1. The argument and discourse of 2:17–5:11 fit together so tightly that any division poses difficulties. Paul's discussion with the fictitious Jewish teacher about the fate of the gentiles unifies the section. Even though the style of discourse changes—from apostrophe (2:17–29), to dialogue (3:1–9, 27–4:2), to scriptural chain (3:10–19), to announcement (3:21–26), to exegetical argument and *exemplum* (4:3–5:11)—the discourse is tightly woven. My approach takes seriously the dialogical nature of the texts and the role of the teacher constructed with speech-in-character. Numerous obscurities, then, such as the self-referential nature of the discourse that one would expect in a dialogue (for example, 3:9, 4:1, 9), become clear. Moreover, 3:1–8 and 27–31 no longer appear to be digressions but directly fit the movement of discourse. Furthermore, long-standing difficulties that show themselves even in the ancient textual variants at 3:9 and 4:1, making these texts only half intelligible, resolve themselves with ease.

Two major arguments for the unity of 3:21–31 recommend themselves.

The first comes from content. As I and others have shown, 3:21–26 concerns the redemption of the gentiles.[7] Verses 27–31 also explicitly discuss God's way of redeeming the gentiles. The second argument proceeds from style, although form and content cannot be easily separated. Verses 21–31 sit in the middle of a dialogue between Paul and a fictitious interlocutor. Here I face the difficulties of scholarly unwillingness to question the flat, discursive reading of the text as a theological essay and of centuries of textual editing and arranging to support that reading. Unfortunately, I do not believe that the issues have been clearly formulated.

In order to sharpen the issues, let me respond to an appreciative critic of my approach. Richard Hays writes, "Both Stowers and Malherbe refer to these false inferences as 'objections.' This is an appropriate term if one thinks of the text as a dialogue between Paul and an imaginary interlocutor. In the absence of specific indicators in the text (as in a Platonic dialogue), however, it would seem preferable not to posit an actual change of speakers. Even though Paul states in the form of a rhetorical question a view which is opposed to his own, *Paul* remains the speaker; even though there are two points of view, there is only one *voice*. Stowers' otherwise excellent study fails to make this distinction."[8] The interpreter must be clear about the form of the ancient texts and the implications thereof for interpretation. As noted in chapter 1, the Greeks and Romans never considered punctuation and reading aids to be a necessary part of written texts. They wrote their manuscripts in *scriptio continua* with infrequent punctuation.[9] Plato, of course, had some of the most highly developed characterization in antiquity, and change of speakers is sometimes made explicit, as when the speaker addresses his partner by name. A great amount of dialogue from antiquity, however, is not so highly developed. Arrian's diatribes of Epictetus, for example, abound with dialogue that does not have the "specific indicators" that Hays seeks.[10] Manuscripts of Plato usually (but not always) indicate change of speaker by means of the *paragraphus*, a horizontal line under the beginning of the first word, or, less frequently, the *dicolon*, similar to a colon.[11] Scholars are uncertain about when these aids were introduced into Plato's works. Much rarer are *notae personarum*, names of the speakers written in the margins (for example, *POxy* 1083). It is unlikely that any of these go back to Plato: they seem to have been added by the Hellenistic scholars who edited the Platonic canon.[12] The case proves similar for dialogue in dramatic texts. Most of the papyri, for example, have only the minimal help of the *paragraphus* to indicate change of speaker, even though it commonly also had several other functions and was never used consistently. Ancient editors provided far more aids for the Platonic and the dramatic texts than was the case for most dialogical texts. These were the writings with the most editorial markup in Paul's time!

Ancient readers, then, faced texts containing dialogues that had no punctuation, no word division, and nothing to indicate change of speakers. Yet this does not mean there were not textual indicators. Ancient readers seem to have gotten along just fine with such texts. They read aloud and had ears well trained for the rhythm, rhetoric, and sense of their language. In previous work, I have extensively documented the extraordinary degree to which the features of diatribal dialogues appear in Romans and the role of speech-in-character. The claim of Hays, Ulrich Wilckens, and others that Paul keeps his voice, rhetorically asking and answering his own questions, does not come to terms with the phenomenon of Romans.[13] First, as I have shown, Paul does develop a characterization of an individual using speech-in-character. The individual Paul addresses and characterizes in 2:17–29, using the second person singular, becomes a speaker in 3:1–9 and 27–4:2. This phenomenon cannot be wished away by treating the text as a vivid illustration of universal propositions about the degenerate nature of all Jews. Second, as I have shown extensively, the texts in question slavishly follow the idioms of everyday conversation and diatribal dialogue; for example, characteristic use of particles, exclamations, questions and answers, elliptical expressions, negatives, interrogatives. Third, there is evidence that some ancient Greek editors and commentators understood the texts as dialogues with imaginary interlocutors.[14] Codex *Ephraemi rescriptus* arranges 3:27–31 with conventions used to indicate dialogue in drama. The uncial Greek and Latin codeces *Boernerianus* (*G*) and *Augiensis* (*F*), the old Latin witnesses, the *Vulgate,* and a few other Greek manuscripts have *sou* ("your" singular) after *kauchēsis* in 3:27: "Where then is *your* reason for boasting?" No one thinks that this reading goes back to Paul. It does reveal, however, that an ancient editor recognized Paul as speaking with the teacher introduced in 2:17–29. Finally, 2:17–29, 3:1–9, 3:27–4:2 simply make better sense understood as I am urging. Interpreters have become far too tolerant of difficulties in sense, difficulties often relieved by a dialogical reading.

I propose the following reading of 3:26–4:2:[15]

Paul: This was to demonstrate God's own righteousness because he had passed over previous [gentile] sins when he held back punishment; it was to demonstrate his own righteousness at this time in history so as to be righteous himself and to make righteous the person whose origin lies in Jesus' faithfulness. (A)

Interlocutor: Then where does that leave the basis for boasting? (B)

P: It has been cut away! (C)

I: By what teaching from the law? Works? (D)

P: No, but through the teaching about faithfulness. For we consider a person to be justified by faithfulness without works of the law. Or is God the God of Jews only? Is he not God of the gentile peoples also? (E)

I: Yes, also of gentiles. (F)

P: If indeed God, who will justify the circumcised out of faithfulness, is one, he will also justify the uncircumcised by means of faithfulness. (G)

I: Are we then subverting the law through faithfulness? (H)

P: God forbid! Rather, we are supporting the law. (I)

I: What then will we say? Have we found Abraham to be our forefather by his own human efforts [that is, according to the flesh]? For if Abraham was justified by works, he has a reason for boasting. (J)

P: But not before God. For what does the scripture say? "Abraham trusted [or "was faithful toward"] God, and it [his trust] was counted as righteousness." (K)

Verse 27a, "Then where does that leave the basis for boasting?" is the voice of the teacher and a direct response to what Paul has just said in 21–26. His response to Paul remains completely in character with his depiction in 2:17–29. There he twice receives the label of "boaster" (2:17, 23). The significance of this boasting becomes clear in 2:19–22. As any ancient moralist could tell you, boasting is comparative.[16] The boaster has pride in being wiser, stronger, wealthier, or more pious than others. In this case, the teacher has convinced himself that he is "a guide of the blind, a light to those in darkness, a teacher of fools, an instructor of children." In short, Paul pictures a Jewish teacher characterized by a condescending pride over against gentiles. He will teach them how to become righteous before God. After Paul's claims in 3:21–26 that God has made the gentiles righteous through Jesus' faithfulness, it comes as no surprise when the teacher says, "Where does that leave the basis for boasting?" As Paul indicates by *exekleisthē*, God has taken away the objective basis for his boasting.[17] If God has justified the gentiles on the basis of Jesus' faithfulness, then the proud teacher has lost his students. If God has forgiven their sins and made them right with him "in Christ," then teaching gentiles to do certain works from the law in order to be acceptable is superfluous.

Unfortunately for the self-esteem of numerous generations, the Western reading understood Paul to be talking not about an imaginary teacher's attitude toward gentiles but about the basic human sin. Augustine is the first we know to have read Romans as an attack upon and antidote for pride.[18] Pride is the most subtle of sins and to even think for a moment that you do not have it is to have it. In reflecting upon the famous pear stealing incident of the *Confessions* (2.4–6), Augustine finds its cause in a mysterious idolatrous pride, the foolish attempt of the creature to be like God. To this day, major scholarly interpretations construe Rom 1:18–4:25 as a critique of just such idolatrous pride or boasting. This is not surprising since pride was the key to the West's psychologizing of Paul and the Christian scheme of salvation. Augustine said, "Pride is the beginning of all sin; and the beginning of man's pride is a falling away from God"; and "whence doth iniquity abound? From pride. Cure pride and there will be no more iniquity. Consequently, that the cause of all diseases might be cured, namely, pride, the Son of Man came down and was made low."[19] Origen also called pride (*hyperēphania*) the greatest sin (*Hom. Ezech.* 9.2; cf. *Hom. Gen.* 5.6; *Hom. Jude* 3.1–2; *Hom. Num.* 12.4). Origen's and Augustine's thought on this subject was shaped by later Platonism's myth of the soul's turning and fall from a higher realm into individual material bodies.[20] Both the pagan Plotinus and Augustine speak of this turning as a kind of audacity or pride. For Paul, however, pride or boasting could hardly be cut out "once and for all" through human faith in Christ. Paul's aorist in 3:27 means that the teacher's reason for boasting has been decisively "cut away."

The phrases *poiou nomou, ton ergon* ("what sort of law, of works"), and *nomou pisteōs* ("law of faithfulness") are vexing. Some have translated *nomos* as "principle" (for example, RSV). In that case *nomos* does not refer to the scriptures at all, and the latter expression is equivalent to just saying "faith." The fact that Paul uses *nomos* for the Jewish law in 3:19, 20, 21, 31, and throughout chapter 4 is an insuperable difficulty for this reading. Recently, a number of scholars have argued that *nomos* means the Jewish law and that *nomou pisteōs* means something like "the law as understood from the perspective of faith."[21] In other words, 3:27 implies that Jews as a rule were never able to bring the right attitude to bear on their use of the law but that Christians can rightly use the law by having faith. Similarly, some have suggested that the expression means bringing a Christological reading to bear on the Hebrew Bible.[22]

A more satisfactory solution begins with a critical perspective on the English word "law" as a translation for *nomos*. Jewish scholars have long complained that "law," meaning legal code, does not have the semantic range of *torah* and is therefore an inadequate translation.[23] Something like "divine teaching" seems to be better. The Greek word itself can variously mean legal code, custom, usage, tradition, teaching. We could fairly consistently translate *nomos* as "divine teaching(s)" or "the divine teaching(s)," and we would get, "Through what sort of divine teaching? Works? No, but through the divine teaching about faithfulness." According to context, *nomos* can refer to the whole of scripture, the books of Moses, portions of the scriptures, or teachings, laws, and practices discovered in scripture, including narrative portions. For the sake of consistency, I have rendered "divine teaching" as "teachings of the law" in 3:27.

The teacher's question, then, "through what sort of teaching from the law? works?", is a challenge hurled back at the apostle to justify his assertion in C with scripture. "Works?" also carries the implication that Paul cannot justify his claim about faithfulness because the law itself teaches that gentiles can be right only if they are trained to do a list of things from the law. This is just the sort of challenging response for which interlocutors in diatribal dialogues are famous. On this reading, one can see that the text already has the discussion of Abraham in view. Indeed, Paul's claim that "the law and the prophets" (3:21) witness to God's just mercy is not a throwaway sentence but rather signals a major concern of Paul to justify himself by interpreting the scriptures. The dialogical rhetoric has the teacher push the same issue of scriptural justification in H and J. What else would one expect from a Jewish teacher of the law?

In E, Paul responds to the teacher's challenge: The law, Paul claims, teaches that the way people who are ungodly come into a relation with God is through faithfulness. "For we consider" is the dialogical "we." As in 3:9 and 4:1, Paul, in the fiction of the dialogue, refers to what he and the teacher have discussed earlier (that is, in 3:19–26). The following paraphrase captures the sense: "No, it is the law's teaching about faithfulness. For remember we have said that the law and the prophets witness to a justification of the gentiles by Jesus' faithfulness, not works of the law."[24] In a way typical of the diatribe, Paul now takes the offensive by asking incisive questions that will push the teacher toward the conclusion that Paul desires: "Or is God, the God of the Jews only? Is he not God of the gentile peoples also?" The teacher can only answer in the affirmative. Both Jews, Paul and the teacher, share fundamental assumptions about God's creation and rule over the whole world.[25] Notice how little sense all of this makes in the traditional reading, with Paul directly arguing theology to Christians in Rome. The discourse works perfectly, however, as an inner Jewish discussion whereby Paul tries to persuade a fellow Jew by using axioms of Jewish belief. The law itself teaches that God is sovereign creator, sustainer, and judge of all the nations and not just Israel. Paul's questions suggest that if God made justification of gentiles depend upon the law, then Jews would have all the advantage and gentiles only condemnation. God would be acting like a local tribal deity instead of like Lord of the universe.

I have been persuaded by Hays to take 3:30 (G) as a fully developed conditional sentence.[26] Reading 3:30 as a conditional sentence emphasizes that Paul speaks as if justification by faithfulness were an obvious point to which his kinsman would agree if shown the evidence from scripture. If the teacher grants Paul's understanding of Abraham and also agrees that God is the one God of the whole world, then, he will concede that God will justify gentiles through faithfulness. God's impartiality forms the unstated premise.

Christ, Jews, and Gentiles: Clues from Prepositions

Paul's language shows him assuming that Jews and gentiles have similar but different relations to Christ, Abraham, and the law. The language of chapters 3–4 belies traditional Christian formulations even if it does not tell us all that we would like to know about Paul's thought on these issues. An analysis of the language in 3:30 provides a point of entry for a reading that finds Abraham, founder of a blessed lineage, analogous to Christ rather than an example of saving faith.

The use of *ek pisteōs* ("out of faithfulness") for Jews and *dia tēs pisteōs* ("through the faithfulness") for gentiles in 3:30 has provoked two reactions in the history of interpretation.[27] The vast majority have followed Augustine in viewing the variations as "merely" stylistic or rhetorical (*Spirit and the Letter* 29.50). A minority have held that Paul makes some distinction between Jews and gentiles in varying the prepositions.[28] That small minority, however, includes the venerable and erudite scholarship of Origen and Theodore of Mopsuestia.[29] What makes their discussions particularly worthy of attention is that both go against their own strongly universalizing tendencies in reading Paul and note that the apostle's language indicates a distinction between Jews and gentiles with regard to *pistis*. Both are ancient native speakers of Greek who may have caught a subtlety of grammar that eludes modern exegetes.

Characteristically, Theodore's comment is brief and Origen's prolix. Theodore writes, "Concerning the Jews, he has written 'out of faith', as if, on the one hand, they have other opportunities in regard to justification, but on the other hand, they are not able to share in it except 'out of faith'. But concerning the Greeks he has written 'by means of faith'."

Origen explicitly treats the meaning of the prepositions in 3:30: "It would appear to indicate that, if they believe in Jesus, both the circumcised and the uncircumcised are saved, the former when they do the law of Moses according to their ability, the latter when they live as citizens according to the freedom of Christ." Origen goes on to say that Paul makes a distinction between Jews and gentiles by using the different prepositions.[30] He then cites two other passages in which he says Paul makes a similar distinction.[31] His initial example is 1 Cor 11:12, in which woman was created *ek tou andros* ("out of man") and man is born *dia tēs gunaikos* ("through" or "by means of the woman"). The second text is Rom 11:36, which speaks of God: *dia autou kai ex autou kai eis autou ta panta* ("all things are through him and out of him and in him). This theological formula came from Stoicism as adapted by Hellenized Jews like Philo.[32] The *dia* refers to God's agency and the *ek* to the origin of all things in the divine. Origen observes that *ek* indicates something that comes from something, while *dia* indicates something done by someone.[33] Since *ek* means a direct relation, Origen concludes that Paul's words show that the Jew, being justified *ek pisteōs,* is more noble than the gentile, whereas being justified *dia pisteōs* reveals the inferiority of the gentile.[34]

Theodore and Origen are far from vilifying Judaism here and recognize that Paul gives a place of honor and even priority to Israel. Both, however, show hesitancy and some tentativeness about their reading: Theodore says that Paul writes "as if" and Origen that the text "appears to indicate." Both must have felt pressure to overlook Paul's positive statements about Jews and distinctions between Jews and gentiles.[35] Yet both feel obliged to note that Paul's different prepositions indicate a distinction. I propose that the intuitions of Origen and Theodore about the language of 3:30 were basically correct but that their assumptions about the meaning of *pistis* and the point of Paul's argument in 3:21–26 kept them from seeing the full significance of their observations. The two ancient commentators, like most since, have assumed that 3:30 deals with the believer's saving faith in Christ, reading chapters 3–4 through a spiritualizing lens that filters out Paul's issues of kinship and descent. They did not see that Paul's distinctions reflect a conception of two different lineages sharing a common ancestor and his messianic descendant, Christ, with blessings defined by the distinctive Jewish and gentile places in these genealogies.

These ancient readers make an observation that would be natural to Greek speakers since the two relations indicated by the words were commonly contrasted in Greek thought. Sources commonly employ *ek* and *dia* in two spheres of discourse relevant to the distinction in question, namely, discussions of lineage and paternity and philosophical discussions that employ metaphors of human descent and procreation for physical theories. In both popular thinking and in the dominant theories of procreation and descent, fathers were thought to provide the generative spark, individual form, and essential substance that was passed on from generation to generation through a particular line of fathers going back to a progenitor like Abraham. Thus a descendant was from the seed (that is, sperm) of the line's founding patriarch. Women provided only supportive nutrients and a place for the father's seed to grow. Father provided the seed; mother the soil.[36] The Pauline examples that came to Origen's mind epitomize the way that Greeks used *dia* and *ek* to distinguish the essential generative from the instrumental supportive role. In this patriarchal conception, women are *from* or *out of* men in the sense that the man passes on the essential generative substance/seed, but men are born *through* the supportive role of women in carrying the seed. In the creation story to which Paul refers, woman was created *from* or *out of* man (1 Cor 11:8). God is the ultimate father and progenitor (1 Cor 11:12).

Aristotle's discussion of *aitiai*, "essential conditions of a thing being," is illuminating in that it reflects Greek assumptions about men as creators and procreators. Thus "the father begetting the child" stands as a prime example of *aitiai* (*Physics*, 194b 29–31, 195a 22; cf. 194b 14–15) together with the results or products produced by a "professional man" (195a 30–31). Here *ek hou* ("from which" or "out of which") is Aristotle's category for the material cause, such as the clay from which the pot is made, and he illustrates the efficient cause with the father's generative seed (*Physics*, 195a 15–26). Adapting Aristotle's categories, Philo (*Cher.* 125–26) chides Eve for saying, "I have begotten a man through God [*dia tou theou*]." The expression *di' hou* represents instrumentality, but according to Philo, God is the creative cause, not the instrument. The ordinary Greek use of *ek* in expressions concerning descent and paternity makes the philosopher's distinctions possible.

In the LXX of 1 Chron 5:2, for example, David is "from" (*ek*) Judah. He is from Judah's seed, that is, Judah's patriline. Jn 1:13 speaks of "those who are not born out of [*ex*] bloods, nor out of [*ek*] the will of the flesh, nor out of [*ek*] the will of a man but out of [*ek*] God."[37] Jos. *Ant.* 12.226–27 and 1 Macc 12:20 give versions of a letter purportedly sent from Areios, king of Sparta, to Onias the high priest, referring to documents proving that the Jews and the Spartans "are of one people" (*ex henos eien genous*; *Ant.* 228) since they are "from a common descent relationship by virtue of Abraham" (*ek tēs pros Abramon oikeiotētos*; *Ant.* 228–29). Jews and Spartans are brothers "from the lineage of Abraham" (*ek genous Abraam*; 1 Macc 12:22). For Paul, Jews and gentiles are now related because Christ has made Abraham father of gentiles, so that the two sets of peoples share the same progenitor. In Areios's letter also, the two peoples share kinship through Abraham. The use of *ek* in Rom 3–4 finds no exact parallel in any of the instances I have discussed, but I believe that Romans cannot be understood as ancient readers might have understood it in the absence of the interpretation that such instances suggest. Paul's expression *ek pisteōs* ("from" or "out of faithfulness") plays on the *ek* of expressions regarding descent and thus creates a discourse for depicting a new kinship for gentiles that relates them to Jews.

The very first lines of the letter signal the motif of descent when they contrast Christ "from the seed of David" (*ek spermatos Dauid*) to Christ son of God "from the resurrection" (*ex anastaseōs*) by the Spirit of holiness. This perspective suggests implications for reading the quotation of Hab 2:4 in 1:17. If the reader takes "the righteous one" as Jesus Christ, then, "The righteous one's life will spring from faithfulness rather than from the messianic lineage" might be understood. Christ brought an end to his Davidic line and to a messianic dynasty when he allowed his death but founded a new form of kinship through the resurrection. Paul frames his own life by the same contrasts when he writes of his call to imitate Christ's adaptation to the ungodly by going to the gentiles. He has great reason to boast in the flesh, including circumcision, descent from the family or lineage of Israel (*ek genous Israel*), from the tribe of Benjamin, and from being a Hebrew out of Hebrews (Phil 3:4–5). Instead of retaining these blessings, he identifies with the gentiles and their salvation. Leaving life in the law, he has a righteousness "through Christ's faithfulness, from God on the basis of faithfulness" so as to share in Christ's suffering and death and attain the resurrection (Phil 3:9–11).

In light of the understanding of Rom 1–4 for which I have argued and of the recognition that *pistis* in 3:22, 25, and 26 refers to Jesus' faithfulness, an interesting pattern emerges in Paul's use of the prepositions: *dia* appears when the gentiles are in view and *ek* when either or both Jews and gentiles are under discussion. *Dia* first occurs in 3:22, when Paul announces that God has shown his impartial righteousness by "including" gentiles *dia pisteōs Iesou Christou*. Verse 25 gives further explanation when it speaks of a conciliation *dia [tēs] pisteōs en autou haimati* (through the faithfulness in his blood). Considering 3:21–26, 3:30 provides no surprise when the apostle writes that God will justify the gentiles *dia tēs pisteōs*. On my reading, 3:31 is the teacher's objection. By repeating Paul's phrase, he asks specifically about the justification of the gentiles: "Are we then subverting the law *dia tēs pisteōs*?" The article *tēs* refers back to Paul's earlier statements about *pistis*: "Are we subverting the law through *this* faithfulness?" Paul strongly rejects his false inference and asserts that justification of the gentiles *dia tēs pisteōs* supports the law.

If *dia pisteōs* in Rom 3 represents God as agent and Christ as means, then, *ek pisteōs* focuses on *pistis* ("faithfulness," "trust") as Abraham's and Christ's generative activity. Unlike *dia pisteōs*, which Paul applies specifically to the solution of the gentile problem, *ek pisteōs* is generative for both Jews and gentiles. These various translations of *ek pisteōs* suggest the possible nuances of Paul's play with the generative metaphor. In 3:26 *ek pisteōs* refers to the gentile. The article with *ek* is well known in Greek as a way of denoting origins, participation, and membership. Thus Lucian speaks of the Peripatetic school as *hoi ek tou peripatou,* "those who are from the Peripatos." (*Vit. Auct.* 43). But 3:26 does not denote membership or participation in the same way, since *pistis* does not constitute a group of people. As the discussion of chapter 4 progresses, Paul's use of *ek pisteōs* as a generative metaphor will become evident. At this point, I propose the following translations: "the person whose status springs from Jesus' faithfulness" or "the person who finds his/her source in Jesus' faithfulness."[38] The *RSV*'s "him who has faith in Jesus" is a gross mistranslation.[39]

In 4:14, Paul speaks of *hoi ek nomou,* "those who are of the law" or "those whose status (basis or source) is from the law." Verse 16 has the expression *dia touto ek pisteōs,* "for this reason [the promise] has its origin (or basis) from faithfulness." The second part of the verse illuminates the issue even further: *Ou tō ek tou nomou monon alla kai tō ek pisteōs Abraam.* Why does the promise "spring from faithfulness"? So that it might be a matter of pure grace—what Abraham and Christ did and God accepted for others—and thus secure "not only for those whose status comes from the law" (that is, righteous Jews, the circumcised) but also for "those whose status springs from" Abraham's and Christ's faithfulness (Jews and gentiles). These phrases with *ek* play on a spatial metaphor of origin or source (that which is "out of") and echo the language of lineage from a founding progenitor. The promise of a blessing for the gentiles "springs from" both Abraham's (4:16) and Jesus' (Gal 3:22) faithfulness. The use of different prepositional phrases with *pistis* for Jews and gentiles in 3:30 is neither accidental nor merely stylistic. In the context of 3–4, the phrase *dia tēs pisteōs* refers very specifically to Jesus' "atoning" death for the redemption of the gentiles, saving them from God's wrath and giving them a share in the benefits of that faithfulness. Paul sums up God's just and merciful action through Jesus with *dia pisteōs.* How Jews relate to this, he never says. He writes to gentile churches about the gentile situation, and his mostly incidental remarks about Israel are fragmentary and unclear. It is clear, however, that he does not assimilate the two into a generic Christianity. Jews and gentiles alike share in blessings *ek pisteōs* of Abraham and Jesus, although not in identical ways. Thus Paul applies *ek pisteōs* to Jews in 3:30 but not *dia pisteōs.* Origen's and Theodore's intuitions about Paul's language were correct even if their particular economies of salvation prevented them from drawing fully Pauline implications.

The redemption of the gentile peoples apart from works of the law through Christ's faithfulness actually establishes or supports the law (3:31).[40] By this response to the teacher, Paul means something specific: The law teaches that the ungodly cannot be made righteous by works of the law but only on the basis of God's grace in response to human faithfulness. Thus Paul introduces the scriptural warrant of Abraham in 4:1 in the teacher's voice. The teacher still wants to claim a right to boast and appeals to the example of Abraham: "What shall we say? Have we found Abraham to be our forefather by his own human efforts? For if Abraham was justified by works he has a reason for boasting."[41] If Abraham can rightly serve as a warrant for the justification of gentiles by moral betterment through the law, then the interlocutor can rightly boast in his own teaching activity.

Making good sense of 4:1 involves enormous difficulties, manifested by the attempts of scribes and editors to improve and correct the verse. A dialogical reading that attributes the verse to an interlocutor eases some but not all of these problems. Hays has advanced grammatical considerations that also help alleviate certain problems.[42] His reading of the text, however, has its own difficulties. Hays proposes a rendering of the verse as translated above except that he understands *kata sarx* to mean "physical descent": Abraham is forefather by virtue of physical descent from him.[43] That idea, however, is entirely unmotivated. The teacher does not advocate that only those born of Jewish blood can be righteous. He advocates attempting to reform non-Jews. Rather, the issue is whether gentiles can enter into a right relation with God by doing works of the law. "Works of the law" is explicitly the issue in 3:20, 21, 27–28; 4:2, 4–6. Paul shifts to other issues in 4:9–25. Hays wants to explain 4:1 by reference to this latter section while overlooking the immediate context of 4:1. But "according to the flesh" is better understood as "by human efforts" and thus as cohering with the issue of justification by works and reflecting the characterization of the interlocutor as a teacher of the law to gentiles.

Paul responds to the teacher's claim that Abraham warrants boasting: "But [*alla*] not toward God! For what [*ti gar*] does the scripture say?" The apostle cites Gen 15:6. What does this text show? According to Paul, God's way of bringing wayward peoples into a relation with him is not to demand that they first keep the commandments of his law. Rather, it comes from God's initiative in adapting his approach to humans when he makes promises to a chosen person who will respond with trust and allow himself to become an instrument for including others. Thus through Abraham, God made an eternal covenant with his descendants. Part of that process was the giving of the law, including the special teachings and statutes for Israel. Paul considers justification to be not the end but only the beginning of a developing relation with a people. Abraham was ungodly (*asebēs*, v. 5), but God accepted him and forgave him (6–8) on the basis of his trusting loyalty, not his past record of righteous deeds. It was a matter of God's grace and Abraham's faithfulness that allowed Israelites to be a people right with God. Paul's gospel (2:16) proclaims that God has done the same for the gentile peoples through Abraham and Jesus.

The reader grossly distorts any reading possible in Paul's time by construing the issue as a religion of a grace versus a religion of good works. Paul's language of being made righteous is what E. P. Sanders has called transfer terminology.[44] It concerns how one gets into a relation with God. It is misleading to think of this primarily from the perspective of the individual person. Abraham and Jesus Christ are essential for Paul precisely as individuals who have made possible divine benefits inherited by whole peoples. Paul's letters evince no thought that keeping the law, which means doing what is good and right, is problematic. The problem rather lies in the fact that more than a thousand years of a gentile world confronted by the law have produced little more than condemnation. In 9–10, Paul argues from scripture that Abraham was a gentile at the time God reckoned his faithfulness as righteousness. Circumcision came later, also as part of God's response to Abraham's faithfulness (11–12). Thus, both the ancient covenant with the Jews and the recent redemption of the gentiles rest ultimately on Abraham's faithfulness (*pistis*) and God's graciousness. Participants share in these blessings by having the trusting faithfulness that Abraham had.[45] Each individual will be judged at the last day according to the works that they have done, but life within the covenant comes as an inheritance.

The language of Rom 4 carefully distinguishes Jews and gentiles and yet provides them with a common basis in two ways. First, Abraham is the father of both the descendants by his blood and also those by adoption through incorporation into Abraham's blood descendant, Christ. Second, both peoples are expected to share in and live out of Abraham's faithfulness. For Jews this means continuing to have Abraham's trust in God's promises and to keep the covenants (including the law) established by Abraham and his descendants. Paul thinks that much of Israel has failed to trust in the Abrahamic promises because they have not accepted Christ as a fulfillment/fulfiller of them (3:2; chapters 9–11). Paul writes that Abraham was first justified by his faithfulness and then circumcised, "so that he might be father of all who trust while uncircumcised, so that they might be reckoned righteous, and father of circumcision to those who are not out of circumcision only but also [those?] who walk in the steps of the trust of our father Abraham when he was uncircumcised." These lines (11–12) do not square with traditional schemes of Christian salvation, although translations have made the text as compatible as possible with traditional understandings. The *RSV*'s translation of 11 suggests that it is the believer's faith that justifies: "father of all who believe without being circumcised and who thus have righteousness reckoned to them." The "and thus" is an extremely unlikely way to construe the Greek and makes the sense problematic. The Greek indicates a relation of purpose or result between Abraham's faithfulness signified in the covenant and his fatherhood, which in turn results in the justification of gentiles (11c) and fatherhood of Jews (12). The *RSV* obscures this relation of Abraham's faithfulness resulting in gentile justification and introduces the extraneous idea of justification by the individual believer's faith. The *RSV* also translates *monos* as "merely" instead of "alone" or "only." "Merely" makes it sound as if Paul is giving a negative connotation to circumcision, but the Greek text implies just the opposite. Similarly, 4:16 speaks of the promise being given "not only to the one whose source is the law but also to the one whose source is Abraham's faithfulness." Paul is far from depreciating circumcision or the law for Jews. Rather, he argues that these are themselves founded on a yet more inclusive act of God's grace toward Abraham based on Abraham's faithfulness.

In response to the teacher and to the apostle's judaizing opponents, Paul writes (13), "The promise to Abraham and his seed that he would inherit the world is not by means of the law but by means of the righteousness of faithfulness." The law/faithfulness contrast seems clear, but to what promise does the verse refer and what does it mean to inherit the world? Christian commentaries get fuzzy and spiritualizing on these questions or simply forget to ask them. The priestly writer responsible for so many of the passages containing the promise makes its center the promise of fertility in Abraham's lineage, for example, "Behold my covenant with you: you shall be the father of very many nations. And you shall no longer be called Abram, but your name shall be Abraham, for I have made you the father of many nations. And I will increase you very exceedingly and I will make you into nations, and kings will come from you" (Gen 17:4–6). Paul quotes from this passage in 4:17: "I have made you the father of many nations." Howard Eilberg-Schwartz has shown just how circumcision, a rite of male fertility in many cultures, is a symbol of the covenant. The male organ is symbolically readied for procreation in light of God's promise. The penis serves as the instrument of a covenant that has to do with fertility and intergenerational continuity between lines of males. Paul understood all of this but had come to believe that the male act of procreation could not and was not meant to do the job of making the nations of the earth Abraham's offspring. Circumcision alone would not secure the promise.

Paul conflated the promise of descendants encompassing very many peoples with the promise of the land understood in a particular way. Before Paul, Jewish exegetes had interpreted the promise of the land (for example, Gen 15:7) as Israel's dominion and God's rule over the whole world.[46] This interpretation comes easily for Paul because he also has in mind the promise of Gen 17:5 quoted in v. 17: "I have made you the father of many nations." Paul connects the universal inheritance with bringing the gentile nations into obedience to God.

Paul neither excluded the "political eschatology" found in Jewish exegesis nor eliminated the promise of the land. Paul's eschatology is a peculiar reformulation of a widespread collection of related beliefs found in many Jewish sources; it is not a rejection of these beliefs or a totally new departure.[47] To be sure, Jesus the risen Christ, who now dwells with God, will be the chief warrior and political officer for God. The readers of the letter are fellow heirs with Christ (8:17), and in spite of the final apocalyptic strife will be victorious with him (8:31–39). When the defeat of the evil rulers comes about, those in Christ will rule and judge with Christ (for example, 1 Cor 6:2–3). This victory can be nothing other than Christ's destruction of the rulers of this earth who oppose God's kingdom (1 Cor 15:24–27).[48] Every knee will finally bow in subjection to Christ (Phil 2:10). The last battle, however, will be only a final roundup of the utterly recalcitrant. The apostle understood Christ's death as a renunciation of force for persuasion as the preferred means of extending God's sovereignty. Through the preaching of the good news, gentiles come into Christ and receive adoption into Abraham's lineage. Paul identifies this adoption with a promise that the gentiles would receive empowerment from God's Spirit.

Jews understood the land as being central to the Abrahamic promises. By at least the second century B.C.E., some Jews had interpreted the promise of the land as the promise that Abraham's descendants would possess the world.[49] Thus the famous text in Sirach 44:19–21:

> Abraham was the great father of very many nations, and no one was found like him in glory. He kept the law of the Most High and entered into a covenant with him. He established the covenant in his flesh and was found faithful when he was tested. Therefore the Lord certified to him by an oath that the nations would be blessed in his seed, multiplying him like the dust of the earth, raising up his seed like the stars, and causing them to inherit from sea to sea and from the River to the ends of the earth.

Paul gives every indication of falling into this broad tradition. Just as the heirs of Abraham consist of Jews and gentiles, so also the heritage consists of the land of Israel and the lands of the gentiles. Thus in 4:13, Paul speaks of the promise that Abraham's heirs would inherit the world (*kosmos*). One has to be committed to a spiritualizing exegesis in order to find an otherworldly or symbolic reference here.[50]

Paul alludes to a particular version of the promise in 13 when he writes of "the promise to Abraham and his seed" (cf. Gal 3:16). In both Gen 13:15 and 17:8, God tells Abraham that he will give the land of Canaan *to him and to his seed*. Paul apparently understood the *gē* (land/earth) in these texts as a type for the whole world because he speaks of the kosmos in 4:13. The apostle likes this formulation of the promise because it contains the idea of descendants and heirs being incorporated into the ancestor who founded the lineage. Thus the promise was made to Christ, who was present in Abraham together with his fellow adoptees, sons of God by the Spirit. Christ is both a descendant by blood and an adoptee by the Spirit in the resurrection (1:3–4). Paul's language of "predestination" seems also to come from the logic of patriliny: "Those whom he foreknew he also designated beforehand [cf. horizein in 1:4] to be conformed to the image of his son, in order that he might be the first born among many brothers" (8:29). God gives and knows all of the line's offspring because they are already in the founder's seed. Thus, Abraham's gentile heirs "in Christ" were already "designated beforehand" in Abraham. Just as each generation passes on and shares the "image" of the ancestor, so also those in Christ are brothers sharing with Christ and each other the image of God the father.

Interpreters have seen v. 14 as a definitive rejection of the law or "salvation by the law." But 14 means, "If only those whose status springs from the law are heirs, Abraham's faithfulness has been made useless and God's promise is unkept." If gentiles are excluded, God has not kept his promise. Verse 16 says plainly that both those of the law and those of faithfulness are recipients of the promise. Origen saw that verse 16 would make lawkeeping Jews equal with Christians and therefore claimed that Paul in v. 16 meant only the natural law.[51] Verse 15 shows that the problem in view remains gentile redemption because it provides a reason (gar) the heirs cannot be only those who live in the law. The law contains a covenant with Israel but only promises and condemnation for the gentile nations. Abraham has fathered all, not just Israelites (16). (The "us" at the end of v. 16 shows Paul continuing to address the teacher.) One simply loses the argument of chapters 1–4 when the English versions render ethnē in 17–18 as "nations" while they translate the same word in 1:13; 2:14, 24; and 3:29 as "gentile[s]." The translations also render most of the twenty-one instances of ethnē in chapters 9–16 as "gentile[s]." For Paul, Gen 17:5 is proof that Abraham is the father of gentiles also. He assumes that Abraham is the father of Jews. While "nations" fits the original meaning of Gen 17:5, it can lead readers to the wrong conclusion if they think that it means something different from "gentiles." For Paul, the ethnē are "the other nations," the gentile peoples, and he is the apostle to the "other nations."

Commentators, Greek texts, and English translations treat the text violently when they mark v. 18 as a new section. Readers of the English would never know that 16–22 are one sentence in the Greek. Translators cannot be faulted for breaking such an unwieldy unit into several English sentences. The division between 17 and 18, however, reflects a reading of the text: 1–17 show that faith has priority over works and the law; the law cannot justify, only faith can; 18–25 illustrate the character of justifying faith. But Paul neither shows the superiority of faith to law nor recommends Abraham as a model of Christian faith. Verse 16 explains that the promise was based on Abraham's faithfulness so that the blessing might be a gift guaranteed solely by God for Jews and gentiles. The end of v. 16 and the beginning of 18 begin two relative clauses that modify "Abraham."[52] The first cites Gen 17:5 and the second 15:15 with an allusion to 17:5. Both then connect the merit of Abraham's trust in God's promising with God's pronouncement of the promise that he would be father of the gentiles. The description "God who makes what is dead come to life and calls what does not exist into existence" (17) already alludes to God empowering Abraham and Sarah for the birth of Isaac, while suggesting similarity to Christ's resurrection. Verses 19–22 then expand on the quality of Abraham's and Sarah's faithfulness as they trusted in God's willingness and ability to provide them with a child.

Beginning at 4:23, a new element enters the discourse. For the first time since the prescript (1:1–15), the epistolary audience comes explicitly into view. The "we" here is clearly "me, Paul" and "you gentile believers at Rome." The Jewish teacher has faded from view, although the final answer to his boasting will be provided—to the letter's audience—only in 5:1–11. So even though the address shifts in 4:23–5:11, it proves misleading to begin a new chapter at 5:1. It is likely that 4:23–5:11 forms the hortatory conclusion to the first four chapters. The fact that it mentions themes that will reappear in chapter 8 has significance but should not cause the reader to lose sight of its crucial role in the letter's unfolding discourse.[53] After announcing in 3:21–26 that Jesus Christ is the answer to the question of God's impartial righteousness toward all nations (that is, the gentiles have been redeemed), Paul claims that the interlocutor's basis as a teacher of the law to gentiles is excluded (3:27). He supports this claim by first arguing from the *Shema* (Deut. 6:4) in 3:28–31 and then from the story of the promise to Abraham. No direct reference appears in these sections to Christ or Christian faith. This makes sense only because Paul is trying to convince a Jewish teacher. Without leaving the issues that he has discussed with the teacher, he turns in 4:23–5:11 to the audience of the letter and draws implications for them.

Richard Hays has shown that what the traditional reading finds in 4:23–25 is a later importation.[54] Paul does not say that the principle of being justified by faith exemplified in Abraham also applies to believers in Jesus. If believers in Jesus Christ can be justified in the same way as Abraham, that would be a dramatic departure from 4:1–23, which argues that Jews and gentiles receive their justification by sharing in Abraham's righteousness rather than by establishing a righteousness of their own through works of the law. Verses 22–25 mean that God's pronouncement reckoning Abraham righteous comes as a gift also to those who are heirs of Abraham. This passage connects Jesus' generative trust in dying for the ungodly and God's gift of life with Abraham the forefather and prefiguration of the faithful Christ. At the last judgment, God will vindicate "us" gentiles who share in the blessings of Abraham's heritage. Those blessings of Abraham have been actualized for the gentile peoples through the Jew Jesus Christ, who was killed for "our" transgressions and raised for "our" justification. Paul writes of "us" who trust in the one who raised Jesus from the dead (4:24). There is no question that Jews and gentiles are expected to trust in or be faithful to God. But Paul does not draw an analogy between Abraham's justification by his faith and the follower of Christ's justification by his or her faith. Rather, the progeny share the characteristics of their ancestors and forefathers. Paul certainly preached that gentiles should believe in the one true God and what he had done through Jesus Christ, but he did not proclaim that their salvation hinged on their own act of believing.

A number of writers assuming the traditional reading have honestly pointed out that Paul makes Jesus Christ unnecessary for justification in Romans 4. If Abraham was justified by his faith in God, why is Christ necessary at all? As Hendrikus Boers writes, in using Abraham to discover the essence of justification by faith, Paul "could not prevent the reference to Christ in the justification of the believer from becoming an accidental in the definition of justification by faith."[55] But Paul does not speak of the believer's justification by his or her faith, but of covenants and promises that God established in response to the faithfulness of certain individuals.

Rom 5:1–11 announces the reconciliation of the gentiles. One finds terms here that Paul, the Pauline school, and other Jewish sources use for gentiles: ungodly (6); sinners (8); enemies (10). More important, as I have argued, Romans characterizes only the gentiles as fundamentally (rather than occasionally) sinful and unrighteous peoples. Now Paul proclaims their justification and salvation from the wrath of God first announced in 1:18 (cf. 5:9–10).

Most modern commentators have taken *echō* in v. 1 as an indicative ("we have") rather than a subjunctive ("let us enjoy"), although the ancient manuscript evidence overwhelmingly supports the subjunctive. An argument swaying recent commentators holds that Paul speaks in the indicative of a fact accomplished by God and that it would be strange for Paul to jump suddenly to a hortatory subjunctive. That argument, however, flies in the face of a pattern that Romans establishes. I have argued that 2:1–5 is hortatory. It warns gentiles against arrogance and pride. That text is immediately preceded by a section (1:18–32) in the third person indicative. Likewise in 6:11–13, after describing the death to sin of those who are in Christ, the apostle breaks into exhortation. Exhortations appear just as suddenly in 8:12 and 9:17–24. Romans does not consist of a theological argument (1:18–11:34) followed by ethical exhortations (12:1–15:13). Chapters 1–11 have a strongly argumentative character, but the letter is hortatory throughout.

How then explain the role of 5:1–11? First, one does better to speak of 4:23–5:11 because something new happens in the discourse at 4:23, when Paul, the authorial voice, returns explicitly to his readers for the first time since 1:15. Second, 4:23–5:11 reads well as a section that draws conclusions from the preceding argument and provides hortatory application for the letter's audience. If *echō* is subjunctive in v. 1, then so also is *kauchōmetha* in 2 and 3 (that is, "let us boast in hope of glory"; "let us boast in afflictions"). The appearance of the same word in v. 11 in the form of a participle that probably has imperatival force (cf. 12:9f.) closes the section.

Unfortunately, the translations have entirely hidden the crucial connections in the text. The major versions render *kaukasthai* either as "exult" (*NEB*) or "rejoice" (*RSV; KJV*). But "boasting" constitutes a major theme of 2:17–5:11 and a concern of the whole letter. Earlier in the letter (2:17, 23, 3:27; 4:2), English versions translate the word and its cognates differently, usually as "boasting," and therefore hide the crucial connections with 5:1–11. We first meet the word in 2:17 and 23. Employing speech-in-character, Paul characterizes "the braggart" (*ho alazōn*), a Jew who arrogantly boasts as he hypocritically presents himself as a teacher of gentiles. The section, 2:25–4:22, constitutes a debate between Paul and the teacher in which the apostle tries to establish that he has no ground for boasting. The teacher himself invokes boasting in 3:27 and 4:2. To ignore the motif of boasting in 5:1–11 cuts the conclusion from 2:17–4:22.

All along, the fictitious discussion with the Jewish interlocutor served the letter's audience of gentile believers. Romans aims to persuade them not to seek justification from works of the law and to dull the allure of Judaism as a school of self-mastery. Paul wants them to understand their security as gentiles in Christ apart from Judaism and yet to know their kinship to Abraham's lineage. He rejects the teacher's claim that the gentiles, like Abraham (4:1–2), are justified by works of the law and that such justification provides a warrant for boasting. Paul provides a corresponding counterclaim in 4:23–5:11. Gentiles share in Abraham's righteousness as his progeny "in Christ" through the death and resurrection of Jesus Christ (4:23–5:2, 6–11). Those in Christ do have reasons for boasting but not because they have earned righteousness by feats of obedience to the law. The grounds for boasting are hope in the glory that awaits those in Christ (5:2), the honor of enduring the final time of testing before the new age (5:3), and God's work of reconciliation through Jesus Christ (5:11).

The teacher's appearance raised the question of Israel's mission as a light to the gentile nations. The apostle charges that he (2:24) and some Jews (3:3) have failed in that mission because they have preached that the gentiles can be made righteous by doing works from the law. In Paul's view, the teacher's effort disregards the grace of God manifested through the promise to Abraham (4:2–22). The apostle reasserts divine impartiality: At the very time the promise has been kept through the redemption in Jesus Christ's faithfulness, both Israel and the gentile peoples stand helplessly before God in sin (3:9–26). Neither can claim righteousness on their own. The credit goes to Abraham and his descendant, Jesus Christ, who founded lineages carrying God's grace and promises. Both the teacher and the gentiles hold the status of heirs. They should receive the gift and recognize their kinship by manifesting the characteristics of their ancestors. The section attempts to refigure the genealogy of ethnic peoplehood for Jews and gentiles. The final answer to the teacher's boast comes as an exhortation to the gentile audience: Boast not in works of the law but in the reconciliation and hope that God has wrought for you through Jesus Christ! (5:1–11).

9

The Gentile Share in Christ's Obedience & Life (Chapters 5–8)

In this chapter I will not enter into a comprehensive exegetical discussion of Romans 5–8 but intend to show that 5–8 stand in continuity with the reading that I have proposed for 1:1–5:11. These chapters attempt to show how gentiles obtain obedience and life in Christ and do not propose a scheme of sin and salvation for humanity. The argument in this section of the letter develops in opposition to the view that works of the law provide a route for gentiles to attain self-mastery. Given that Paul did not know the concept of Christianity, he could not have anticipated the later reading but assumed that his readers would continue the line of his earlier (1:18–5:11) discourse on the justification of the gentiles.[1]

Perhaps the most prominent traditional way to conceive the role of these chapters is to say that 1–4 are about sin and justification, whereas 5–8 treat Christian sanctification. There has been much debate about whether chapter 5 or sections thereof belonged to the first or second part. Since the later nineteenth century, some scholars have spoken of two relatively independent but parallel lines of thought in the supposed forensic or juristic language of 1–4 and the mystical or participatory language of 5–8.[2] In at least one respect, what I have argued goes against this second scheme. If 3 and 4 speak of sharing in Christ's and Abraham's faithfulness rather than justification by the believer's faith, those texts are just as participatory as 5–8, which also contain so-called juristic language.

A more helpful way to penetrate 5–8 is to ask what is new and what continues from 1–4. One thing that does not continue is dialogue with the teacher. He does not reappear in 5–8. In fact, 4:23–5:11 mark a change of address. Paul for the first time since the prescript speaks directly and explicitly to the encoded readers. A theme that does not continue is discussion of *pistis* (faithfulness). Traditional readings of the letter find this fact difficult to explain. If 3–4 treat faith, the fundamental stance of the Christian toward God and Christ, why does the word disappear after 5:1? Furthermore, why does it reappear in chapters 9–11, which discuss not the Christian life but the future of the Jews? These problems solve themselves when one recognizes that 3–4 speak not of the Christian's justifying faith but about Jesus' and Abraham's conciliating and covenant-founding faithfulness. Moreover, the argument about faithfulness develops over against claims that gentiles can become righteous by following certain teachings from the law. The same issues reappear in 9–11, where Paul plays with the prejudices of presumed readers by again raising the question of Jewish responsibility in relation to the gospel. Chapter 5 gives more content to Jesus' "faithfulness" by speaking of his adaptation to the ungodly in 5:6–10 and of his justifying obedience in 5:12–20. Chapters 6–8, then, explain how gentiles can attain obedience by relating themselves to Christ's obedience. Chapter 7 attempts to show that this obedience cannot come about through gentiles adopting works from the law. Rom 6–8 also return to the ethic of self-mastery after 1–5 have established a Pauline discourse for thinking about the law, passions, and desires and the gentile situation before God. The apostle puts on a brilliant display of speech-in-character in 7:7–8:2 by depicting the conflicted gentile talking about the inner struggle announced in chapter 1.

Some themes continue prominently in 5–8. The theme of righteousness appears at 5:17, 21; 6:13, 16, 18, 19, 20; and 8:10. If the central theme of 1–4 is that God has shown himself to be just/righteous by making the gentiles righteous, then 5–8 elaborates the motif of gentile righteousness by incorporation into Christ. Chapters 5–8 closely relate obedience and righteousness. Even though the teacher disappears, the questions that his appearance raised about gentiles and the law remain. The issues concerning the law of 3:20, 31 and 4:13–15 receive further development in 5:13, 20; 7:1–25; and 8:1–8. The central and normative role of the law as part of God's gracious covenant with the Jews never comes into view in 5–8.

Several themes in 5–8 appear to be new except for brief but important anticipations in chapters 1–2. This feature of the letter's organization tellingly reveals that 5–8 deal with the transformation of the gentiles. Chapter 1 explains that because of their refusal to acknowledge God, he sentenced them to enslavement under their desires (*epithumiai*) and passions (*pathē*). This, of course, is a well-known characterization of gentiles from widely varied texts of Jewish literature. Can it be mere coincidence that 6–8 explain how freedom from desires (6:12; 7:7, 8, 13) and passions (7:5; 8:18) becomes possible for those who are in Christ? The law cannot free a person from this slavery; only the Spirit of Jesus Christ can. The Spirit of God reverses the sentence pronounced against the gentile peoples in chapter 1. There is no place whatsoever for including Jews here. Nowhere does the letter claim that Jews also were given over into slavery under their desires and passions. They alone of all the nations have acknowledged and rightly worship the one God.

Similarly, the theme of obedience/disobedience belongs primarily to the gentiles in Romans; Israel's obedience awaits a dramatic act of God in the unspecified future (11:26–27). In 1:5, Paul announces that God has appointed him an apostle of Jesus Christ to win "obedience of faithfulness [hypakoen pisteōs] among all the gentiles." Likewise, 16:26 speaks of the mystery from the prophetic writing now being made known to all the gentiles, resulting in the obedience of faithfulness. He also speaks of Christ working through him to win the obedience of the gentiles in 15:18.

On the other side, what else does 1:18–23 describe but the fundamental disobedience of the gentile peoples who refuse to recognize God and disobey his laws (1:32)? At the climax of his censorious address to the gentile interlocutor in 2:1–16, Paul warns that God impartially punishes those who disobey the truth (2:8; cf. 1:18, 25) and obey wickedness (2:8; cf. 1:18, 29). Is it then only an accident that the theme of becoming obedient looms so large in chapters 5–8? Jesus Christ introduced an obedience affecting all, as Adam's disobedience affected all (5:19). Chapter 6 describes how those in Christ are free from slavery to passions and can thus become obedient (6:12, 16, 17). Freed from the condemnation of the law, gentiles can, through God's Spirit, fulfill the just requirements of the law (8:4).

Israel, to be sure, is also disobedient. This disobedience, however, does not fundamentally characterize Jews but stems from a recent turn in history brought about by God himself: "Just as you [that is, you = gentiles] once were disobedient to God, but now have been shown mercy due to their [the Jews, Israel] obedience, so also they have now been disobedient so that by the mercy shown to you, they also may receive mercy" (11:30–31). Paul unambiguously assumes obedience to be typical and normative for Jews and disobedience so for gentiles. Chapters 6–8 tell how gentile sinners appropriate the faithful obedience figured forth in Jesus.

The Place of 5:12-20 in the Discourse

Just as the example of Abraham supported the argument of 3:21–31 by showing how one person's faithfulness could effect a right relation with God for the many, so the example of Adam in 5:12–20 supports 5:1–11 by showing how Christ faithfully adapting himself to the situation of the ungodly affected "all" and "the many." Ever since the so-called debate about Gnosticism in the second century, the role of Genesis 1–3 has loomed so large in Christian theology that it remains difficult to approach Paul's analogy between Christ and Adam without anachronism. The interpreter must be clear about what the text *does not* say in 5:12–20. Paul shows no interest either here or elsewhere in developing a timeless psychology or anthropology of sin from the story of Adam's fall. His main concern consists in showing how the actions of one person can affect many. The passage nearly assaults the reader in stressing that the analogy between Adam and Christ is limited, underlining the dissimilarity of the two with loud qualifications in 15–17.[3] Paul never finishes verse 12 but goes immediately into explanations and qualifications because he wants to make it clear that his point is limited.[4] His most important qualification explains that the relation of Adam and Christ to the many is analogous only in the period from Adam to the law.[5] Only before Moses did everyone die merely as a result of the sentence passed on Adam for his disobedience (5:13–14). After the giving of the law, people became accountable for their own transgressions. Verse 16 could not be clearer: "And it is not a matter of [the effects of] one man's sin being like the gift: The judgment resulting from [the sin] of one person resulted in condemnation, but the gift following many transgressions resulted in acquittal." Christ's faithful obedience covered the transgression of the many who were disobedient so that all could be righteous.

Paul's discussion of Adam and Christ raises a host of questions that have provided endless room for speculation. But for my purposes, the reader must understand what Paul *does* say and how 5:12–20 advances the letter's discourse. We learn several new things: The letter now describes Christ's conciliating faithfulness, which is discussed in 3:21–31 as his obedience: "By one man's obedience many will be made righteous" (5:6).[6] Phil 2:8 speaks of Christ becoming obedient unto death on a cross. Furthermore, Christ's obedience effects not only justification but also eternal life (5:17, 21). Christ's obedience affects the many in a way analogous to the effect of Adam's disobedience in the period before the giving of the law. Adam disobeyed, and all until Moses subsequently shared in his tendency to sin, and all shared in his sentence of a limited life span merely because the punishment was passed on from Adam. The law permitted renewed possibilities for obedience and disobedience. Christ's obedience canceled the sentence of death and produced the possibility of righteousness for all after him. But then the analogy breaks down because Christ's obedience canceled not only these inherited liabilities but also the debt created by the sin of all those who explicitly disobeyed God by transgressing his law. This latter disobedience chosen by the gentiles when they rejected the law was possible only after Moses.

The apostle knows that Israel received the law as part of a covenant that included forgiveness and atonement for trespasses. Indeed, he knows that Moses was also a representative figure in whom Israel had unique blessings and responsibilities and a justified relation with God. Just as he can speak of the gentile readers having been baptized into Christ and thus having received the benefits of righteousness, obedience, and life (6:3f), so also he can speak of the fathers in the wilderness having been baptized into Moses (1 Cor 10:2). But Paul ignores the positive role of the law for Israel because it has no relevance to his discussion of gentile redemption. For them the law meant only that God began to keep track of the good and evil of individuals (v. 13) in view of the world to come and thus law increased their liability (v. 20).[7]

The Role of Chapter 6

The voice of chapter 6, unlike that of 1–5, speaks in the first and second persons plural.[8] Exegetes and commentators unanimously recognize that Paul is speaking with ("we") and to ("you") and about his "Roman audience." The letter represents the readers as gentiles. Not a shred of sound evidence exists to indicate that he directs himself to Jews or so-called Jewish Christians. Paul tells us how he regarded the preconversion lives of these gentiles: "you were once slaves of sin" (6:17 cf.6:6); "you once yielded your members to impurity [akatharsia] and lawlessness for the purpose of lawlessness" (6:19); "when you were slaves of sin . . . what fruit did you get? Things of which you are now ashamed!" (6:21). There is no justification for the traditional view that sees chapter 6 as describing pre-Christian human life, including faithful Jews.

We must continually ask how we know what we know. Imagine an ancient reader of Greek who knew nothing of Christian schemes of sin and salvation; whose only knowledge of "Christianity" was from reading Romans. Having read 1:1–14 and 15:13–16, she would know that the audience consisted of converted gentiles in Rome. Chapter 6 addresses these people and discusses their lives before and after coming to Christ. What resources would the letter give her for understanding the description of the preconversion life in chapter 6? Paul criticizes a particular Jew in 2:17–29 for being a hypocritical, arrogant teacher of gentiles. But even his sins do not correspond to the sin of chapter 6. In chapters 9–11, Paul generalizes about a segment of Jews, but the charges have nothing to do with what we find in chapter 6. They concern some sort of disobedience toward God in light of the preaching of the gospel. The description of the gentiles in 1:18–32, however, would provide this reader with what she needed to make sense of the preconversion state described not only in chapter 6 but also in 7–8.

Verse 13 exhorts the audience not to present the parts of their bodies as instruments of injustice (*adikia*). Verses 18–32 of chapter 1 describe gentile *adikia* (1:18, 29). Chapter 6 tells of a time when the audience was in bondage to sin. The apostle urges them to no longer allow sin's rule, which makes them obey the desires (*epithumiai*) of their mortal bodies (6:12). Formerly, when enslaved to sin, the bodily parts of these readers served impurity (*akatharsia*) and lawlessness (6:19). Romans 1 speaks of God punishing the gentile peoples by causing their bondage to lusts and desires: "Therefore God handed them over to the evil desires [*epithumiai*] of their hearts for impurity [*akatharsia*] so that they dishonored their bodies" (1:24). Both chapters describe this conduct as shameful (6:21, 1:27). In chapter 1, God handed the gentiles over (*paradidōmi*) to their evil desires. In chapter 6, God reverses the state by handing them over (*paradidōmi*) to a type of teaching that frees them from bondage (6:17). Paul brings his invective against the gentile cultures to a climax in 1:32 (cf. 2:1–11) by saying that such wickedness constitutes willful disobedience of God's requirements, which the gentiles know carries the penalty of death. As I argued earlier, this can be nothing other than gentile knowledge of the law, which brings a terrible indictment against their sin. Earlier in 5:20, law increased the trespass, and 6:14–15 reminds the gentile readers that they are no longer under the law. The law's condemnation of them as peoples has been replaced by God's grace. Our ancient reader could conclude only that chapter 6 describes gentiles who had formerly tried to obey the law but have now discovered a new way to overcome their passions and desires through Christ.

Chapters 6–8 develop a series of claims that Paul has made in conversation with the Jewish teacher, but now Paul directs his voice toward the letter's encoded readers. He has claimed that the gentiles can be redeemed through Christ but not by the teacher's attempts at moral betterment through the law. He has also claimed that gentiles must do what the law requires of them (2:12–29). God himself, following an ancient pattern and plan going back to Abraham, has made Jesus an instrument for gentile reconciliation. Their redemption is a matter of pure grace stemming from Jesus' faithfulness. Chapter 4 explains gentile justification as entrance into a type of kinship. A person does not earn admittance into a family but inherits kinship and its blessings. Chapter 6 both exhorts the readers to the new life and explains how the gentile life described in 1:18–32 is transformed by sharing in the benefits of Christ's faithful obedience. They have been baptized into Christ (6:4). They have been buried with him. The old character has been crucified with Christ (6:6). They will therefore live with him (6:8).[9]

The apostle's positive message shapes part of the discourse in 5–8, but rebuttal of the teacher's appeal to gentiles also constrains the rhetoric. Paul strongly rejects his solution. The situation of gentiles cannot be ameliorated by training them to do works of the law; a Jewish ethic of self-mastery for gentiles. According to the apostle, this approach not only lacks realism and threatens his mission, but also denies what God has done for the gentile peoples. Thus his rhetoric attempts to persuade his readers that living by a code from the law for gentiles is and has been primarily a negative experience; bondage under the law versus freedom in Christ. Verses 1–13 of chapter 6 contrast death and life, sin and justification, appealing to the warrant of the audience's own experience of coming into the new community. In 6:14–23, however, the teacher's position comes into view, and Paul slides into the metaphor of slavery and freedom, paralleling slavery to sin and desire with slavery to the law. This begins a major argument, continuing through chapter 7, against gentile adherence to the law. The pairing of law with slavery and desire implies a particular grasp of the gentile relation to the Jewish law. Philo, Josephus, 4 Maccabees, and other sources provide a context for construing Paul's discourse about passions, desires, the law, and self-mastery. Chapters 6–8 present the benefits of Christ as a way to the goal of gentile obedience but without a law-centered regimen of practices aimed at subduing the passions. Those who have reenacted Christ's death have simply died to bondage under passions and desires. Identification with Christ lifts God's sentence of gentile slavery under the passions and desires.

Interpreters have puzzled over the relation between ethics and Christ in chapter 6. The connection does not consist of imitating Christ's sufferings. The passage gives no reason to think that Christ-like suffering is therapy for the passions. In fact, Paul seems purposely to avoid an approach that might encourage Christ to become the model of self-mastery. The text simply does not present him as a model for ethical behavior. The key lies in Paul's focus on Christ's death as a voluntary forfeiture of a whole way of life as messiah according to the flesh; a loss of a life that God replaced with life on a new plane. The old life was not so much left behind, however, as lifted up and reconstituted without its worst liabilities. Jesus was raised and remained the Christ but with a whole new meaning, taking up the old meaning but transforming it. In baptism, Paul is asking his gentiles to imagine making that break from the fleshly level to the life of the world to come. Even if Christ alone has arisen from the dead, the Spirit of God and of Christ will allow a foretaste of the life to come. Since sin and slavery to passion characterized the old, in identification with Christ's breakthrough, these gentiles are to imagine themselves living lives free of sin's domination, obedient to God. But Paul defines gentile obedience through his concepts of faithfulness and adaptability. When he develops a concrete ethic, he takes a completely different tack that presents Jesus' adaptability as a model (especially chapters 12–15).

Adaptability to the needs of others rather than mastery of emotion and desire becomes the paradigm for the ethic.

The expression *eis hon paredothēte typon didachēs* ("the type of teaching to which you were handed over") has perennially troubled modern interpreters (6:17). Rudolph Bultmann even wanted to excise it as an interpolation.[10] It seems to come out of nowhere, at least on traditional readings of the letter. I have already suggested, however, that *paradidōmi* forms a contrastive allusion to the "handing over" of gentiles to evil desires in chapter 1. Protestant exegetes often fear that 6:17 will be read as a reference to the handing down of tradition, but Paul's language makes that impossible. These gentiles did not hand down a teaching, but rather they were handed over to a teaching by God. Moreover, it was one type of teaching rather than another. What could that other kind of teaching be? Interestingly, the only references to teaching in the previous discourse occur in Paul's initial address to the teacher. He is an instructor (*paideutēs*) of fools and a teacher (*didaskalos*) of children (2:20). Verses 17, 18, and 20 mention the knowledge of the law that he proudly teaches to gentiles. With sarcasm Paul writes, "You who teach others, do you not teach yourself?" The gospel of Jesus Christ, a teaching to which God delivered these gentiles, not the teaching of works from the law, has freed them from "the pagan life of sin."

Arguments against Gentile Subjection to the Law (7:1–25)

One might reasonably consider Chapter 7 the key to the Western understanding of Romans, going back to Augustine but with roots also in Origen. Peter Gorday writes, "This entire section of Rom. 7:14–25 is absolutely omnipresent in Augustine's work, and is linked with every other passage in the epistle where the concern is to reinforce the complex interplay of grace and law that Augustine saw in Romans."[11] Romans 7 facilitated the development of a psychologizing interpretation of Paul's statements about sin, law, boasting, and grace. It provided interpreters with a supposed analysis of the human predicament to which Christ was the solution. That reading still dominates the interpretation of Romans. In his influential commentary, Ernst Käsemann writes,

> The experience which Paul envisions consists in the fact that the pious, who alone come into the picture here, do not succeed in realizing the will of God as the true good so long as the Spirit of Christ is not given to them. Instead, in their very acts they give a place and reality to evil, although that is not their intention. Their helplessness in face of this

perversion of their intentions shows that they are in fact oriented to the good, that they feel themselves to be under obligation to the will of God, and that they accept it as the norm of their existence. Obviously this is in the first instance a depiction of the situation of the Jew who is faithful to the law. The situation is present among the gentiles only in the shadow of 2:14ff.[12]

Interpreters in this tradition have placed much weight on Romans 7 as they make Pauline Christianity the antithesis of an imagined Jewish religiosity. Ironically and unfortunately, Romans 7 became a most important text for the Christian understanding of "Jewish religiosity." On this reading, Judaism forms not only the antithesis to Christianity but also the necessary prelude to Christian existence because the supposed archetypical Jewish struggle with pride and lawkeeping occurs on some scale in every person as they seek to do the good.

The editorial tradition has set off chapter 7 as a unit because the section encompasses a discussion of bondage to and freedom from the law. The theme, however, already receives development in 6:14–23. The tradition has also made certain divisions within the chapter. Verses 7–25 stand apart stylistically owing to their special use of the first person singular. Verses 7 and 13 introduce new topics and make transitions in the discourse through the use of rhetorical questions in the form of false conclusions. Thus commentators usually treat 7:7–12 and 13–25 as units. Verses 1–6 also have their stylistic peculiarities. Paul first turns to his epistolary audience in 4:23 by using the first person plural. In chapter 6, he reaches a new level of immediacy with the readers by addressing them directly and speaking about their experience. This gradual development in Paul's relation to the literary audience reaches its apex in 7:1 and 4 with the address "brethren." Verses 4–6 also focus intensively on the experience of the readers both under the law, in the life of the flesh, and also free from that bondage in Christ. The rhetoric changes entirely in 7:7–25 as the audience disappears. This section is personal in an entirely different way, as it seems to depict the inner struggle of an individual.

It is necessary first to get behind the Augustinian tradition of reading 7:7–25 and especially 14–25.[13] When Augustine retrospectively reinterpreted his conversion in light of the Platonic myth of the soul's falling, alienation from the Good, and return to it, he created a model of religious experience that would become characteristic of the West, especially in late medieval piety and the individualism of Protestantism. So, for instance, the eighteenth-century conversion of Isaac Backus would not have been possible without Augustine's reinterpretation of Paul and, above all, chapter 7 of Romans:

As I was mowing alone in the field, August 24th, 1741, all my past life was opened plainly before me, and I saw clearly that it had been filled up with sin. I went and sat down in the shade of a tree, where my prayers and tears, my hearing of the Word of God and striving for a better heart, with all my other doings, were set before me in such a light that I perceived I could never make myself better, should I live ever so long. Divine justice appeared clear in my condemnation, and I saw that God had a right to do with me as He would. My soul yielded all into His hands, fell at His feet, and was silent and calm before Him. And while I sat there, I was enabled by divine light to see the perfect righteousness of Christ and the freeness and riches of His grace, with such clearness, that my soul was drawn forth to trust Him for salvation. And I wondered that others did not also come to Him who had enough for all. The Word of God and the promise of His grace appeared firmer than a rock, and I was astonished at my unbelief. My heavy burden was gone, tormenting fears were fled, and my joy was unspeakable.[14]

What elements, if any, of the Western theology of conversion and struggle with sin are attributable to the text read historically in the context of Paul's time? In what sense is Paul the source for this sort of piety?

A Greek Tradition in 7:14-24

Fortunately, there is a solid place to stand in trying to contextualize chapter 7 and treat it in a nonanachronistic way: 7:15 and 19 contain a ubiquitous Greek saying that is central to the Greco-Roman ethic of self-mastery. Some scholars have noted this fact but usually dismiss it because the saying is supposedly trivial while Paul's antimoralistic (that is, Augustinian-Lutheran) "transformation" of it is supposedly profound.[15] In other words, interpreters have judged the historical fact by the ideology of that Christian tradition.

The text remembered as the starting point for this tradition is Euripides' *Medea* 1077–80: "I am being overcome by evils. I know that what I am about to do is evil but passion is stronger than my reasoned reflection and this is the cause of the worst evils for humans." These words of Euripides' Medea became the classic text for the long and varied ancient discussion of *akrasia,* lack of self-mastery. It represents what can be described as the tragic position in literary depictions and philosophical discussion of "the will," or self-mastery in moral psychology. The tragic tradition emphasizes that the good of the human life is vulnerable to luck, conflict of values, and the passions as structures of perception that allow humans to be deeply affected by situations and powers they do not control.[16] Tragedy emphasizes the often evil consequences of these limitations, but it also claims that what is good and beautiful about human life is intrinsically bound to this vulnerability. Just before the text quoted above, Medea, driven by anger and the thought of revenge, determines to follow a terrible plan that includes killing her children. Twice she wavers as she reflects that another course of action would be better (1040–48; 1056–58). Finally, in our text she recognizes how evil her deed will be but says that her desire for revenge is stronger than her reasoned reflections.[17]

The ancients also remembered Phaedra's monologue in Euripides' *Hippolytus* in connection with the failure of self-mastery (377–83):

> I do not think people do evil by nature, for many are good
> But one must consider that though we know and understand what is good
> We don't act on what we know—some through laziness,
> Others through preferring pleasure more than goodness.

Not only emotions and drives but other habits of character prevent people from doing the good that they know and recognize.

In the Protagoras 352 D, Socrates refers to this view in Euripides as the understanding of the masses: "Most people say that . . . while knowing what is best they do not will to do it although they could do it but instead they do something else. And when I have asked why, they say that those who act this way are acting under pleasure or pain or the power of the things I just mentioned." The other side of the debate was begun by Socrates, who in contrast to the popular view held that akrasia, acting against what one knew was right, was impossible. Plato too, partly under the influence of Socrates and partly for other reasons, opposes the popular view in some of his writing. Plato also opposed the larger tragic perspective. Through ascetic suppression of desire and passion and by valuing the abstract and universal rather than the vulnerable and changeable particular, Plato sought to find a way for humans to become godlike and avoid the limit and vulnerability of human life.[18] Thus in several respects, he sets or anticipates the agenda of the Hellenistic philosophies with which Paul had at least indirect contact. Aristotle, on the other hand, affirmed the tragic and popular view.[19] Book 7 of his *Nicomachean Ethics*, devoted to the discussion of akrasia, distinguishes between lack of self-mastery that is impulsive and lack of self-mastery that is deliberate and fully aware of itself.[20] Later debates focused on whether weakness of will (that is, lack of self-mastery) stemmed from ignorance and false beliefs, the Stoic position, or from inherently rebellious passions, the popular and Platonic position.

The Stoics developed a sophisticated version of the Socratic position that passion and weakness of the will were due to ignorance or false belief. Chrysippus reinterpreted the *Medea* from this perspective: "Medea declared before her infanticide: 'I know what evil I intend to commit, I see it well; but passion is stronger in me than reason.' But this passion is not a sort of foreign power, which wrests dominion from the mind; it is Medea's mind, which in unhealthy agitation chooses the bad. It turns away from itself and from every reasonable reflection. Precisely this conscious turning away from calm reflection and from the mind itself is the essential characteristic of emotion."[21] The early Stoics denied the existence of a distinct, irrational part of the soul, instead arguing for the soul's unity. The passions were disturbed or diseased states of the soul engendered by false beliefs. To be healthy is to have no contrast in the personality between reason and emotion. What most people think of as reason and emotion harmonize in the healthy person.[22]

Chrysippus is said to have studied the *Medea* zealously.[23] Later Stoics showed continued interest in Euripides' tragedy. Paul's nearly exact contemporary Seneca wrote a *Medea* of his own based on Euripides' work. Paul's near contemporary Epictetus has an imaginary interlocutor cite Medea's words to represent the popular view of reason and emotion (*Diss.* 1.28.6–8):

> Interlocutor: Can't a person believe that something is profitable for him, and yet not choose it?
>
> Epictetus: He cannot.
>
> I: What about she [Medea] who said, "Now I understand what evils I intend: But passion overpowers my reasoned reflection?"
>
> E: It is because she regards the very indulgence of her passion and the vengeance against her husband as more profitable than saving her children.
>
> I: Yes, but she was deceived [cf. Rom 7:11].
>
> E: Show her clearly that she is deceived, and she will not do it; but until you show it, what else has she to follow but that which appears true?[24]

Epictetus elsewhere uses a version of the nearly proverbial saying that we find in Rom 7:15 and 19: "For since he who does wrong [*hamartein*] does not want to, but to be right, it is clear that he is not doing what he wants to do [*ho men thelei ou poiei*]. . . . He, then, who can show to each person that which[25] causes him to do wrong, and can clearly demonstrate to him how he is not doing what he wants, and is doing what he does not want to do [*ho thelei ou poiei kai ho mē thelei poiei*], is strong in argument, and also in both exhortation and moral criticism" (*Diss.* 2.26.1–4). Platonists followed a more popular view in opposing the Stoics and in emphasizing that reason, emotion, and appetite are distinct powers that do battle in the soul. So, for example, Plutarch, with his typical eclecticism, draws heavily on both Plato and Aristotle, quoting Medea's famous words in attacking the Stoics in *On Moral Virtue* (446A). In the following passages, Galen attacks the early Stoics and in the first text specifically Chrysippus's interpretation of Medea's words. According to Galen, the soul consists of distinct powers that can never be completely harmonized. Notice how what one knows or understands about the good or evil of one's actions is an issue in the debate as it also is in Romans 7 (cf. 7:7, 11, 15). Galen writes,

> If Euripides were supporting the teachings of Chrysippus, he would not have said that she understands but just the opposite, that she is ignorant and does not understand what evils she is about to do. But to say, on the one hand, that she knows and, on the other hand, that she is overcome by anger—what else is that but a person introducing two sources for Medea's impulses, one by which we perceive things and come to know them, which is the rational power, and another irrational, whose work is anger? This [anger], then, forced Medea's soul. (*Hippoc. et Plat.* 4.274.15–22)

> But Medea was not only not persuaded by any reasoning to kill her children but on the contrary, as for reasoning, she says that she understands the evil of the deeds that she is about to commit, but her anger is stronger than her reasoned deliberations; that is, her passion has not been brought into subjection and does not obey and follow reason as if it were a master, but throws off the reins and bolts and disobeys the command, so that it is some other act or passion or power than the rational. For how could anything disobey itself or run away from itself or not follow itself?[26] (*Hippoc. et Plat.* 4.244.2–9)

Finally, the famous Medean saying occurs not only in drama and philosophers' debates, but also in such contexts as letters and public orations.[27] The famous parallel to Paul's words in Ovid *Met.* 7.17–21, for example, are the words of Medea dialoguing with herself: "Oh wretched one, drive out these flames that you feel from your maiden breast if you can. If I could, I would be more reasonable. But some strange power holds me back against my will. Desire impels [or "counsels"] me one way, my mind another. I see what is better and approve it, but I follow the worse. Why do you, a royal maiden, burn for a stranger, and think about marriage in a foreign world?"[28]

These texts illustrate how versions of the saying found in 7:15 and 19 played a central role in the Greek moral tradition. The words of Euripides'

Medea were widely cited in this connection. In philosophy and literature alike the words were variously interpreted in discussions about the roles of the emotions, deliberation, and knowledge of good and evil in moral psychology. Most aspects of Paul's discussion in 7:7–25 can be paralleled with language from this tradition. No one, however, would deny that Paul's text has its own character. In order to get at Paul's use of the tradition it is first necessary to discuss the style and rhetoric of 7:7–25.

The Style and Rhetoric of 7:7-25

Since W. G. Kümmel's monograph, most scholarship on Romans 7 has agreed that the first person singular in 7:7–25 is the fictive "I."[29] The technique dramatically presents a general idea. In Romans 7, the fictive I is not autobiographical, and it does not include Paul. Kümmel based his argument about the fictive I primarily on examples from Paul's letters. Instances such as 1 Cor 10:29–30 supported Kümmel's case: "For why should my liberty be determined by another man's scruples? If I partake with thankfulness, why am I denounced because of that for which I give thanks?" This is the fictive voice of the strong person who protests against Paul's admonitions about displaying deference to the weak. Kümmel gathered only a few examples of the fictive I from outside the New Testament. Aside from their lateness (some are medieval), the Rabbinic examples lack value because they are narrative texts in the first person and thus not at all parallel.[30]

Fortunately, Paul's rhetoric in chapter 7 can be identified and explained.[31] The texts in question are a type of *prosōpopoiia,* speech-in-character. Both Kümmel and recently Gerd Theissen have concluded that the phenomenon of 7:7–25 was not discussed in ancient rhetoric.[32] Amazingly, Kümmel followed his conclusion with the statement (relegated to a footnote) that the phenomenon in chapter 7 might be related to prosōpopoiia.[33] He defined prosōpopoiia as follows: "where the speaker places a speech in the mouth of another person or where inanimate things can speak."

In contrast to modern interpreters, ancient students of Paul, who were native speakers and had varying levels of Greek education, as a basic reflex recognized speech-in-character in chapter 7. Celsus's polemic against Christianity, the *True Discourse,* extensively employed prosōpopoiia, and Origen's reply to Celsus includes a helpful critique of his prosōpopoiia. Celsus employed a number of different characters and forms of speech-in-character in his polemic. In one instance, he seems to have imitated a child having his first lesson with an orator (*C. Cels.* 1.28).[34] Twice Celsus introduces general types of people: the person who has difficulty seeking God and the fleshly person, and suggests that Christians are like these people (6.66; 7.36.17). Most important, however, Celsus employs an imaginary Jew through major portions of the work who first addresses himself to Jesus, then carries on a dialogue with Jesus that Origen explicitly describes as prosōpopoiia. In another part of the work Celsus has the Jew (or a Jew?) speak to caricatured Christians.[35] In all, Origen explicitly refers to Celsus's prosōpopoiia using either the noun or the verb some twenty-six times.

Origen complains that Celsus does not create characterizations that fit the persons being described and that he fails to keep his characterizations consistent (1.28.1). Not only must characterizations fit the person or type, but each time the character speaks or is reintroduced into the discourse, what the person says must be consistent with what the person said before or what was said about the person. Here Origen reflects the critical use of speech-in-character of the grammarians and exegetes that I discussed in chapter 1. In 1.43, Origen criticizes Celsus for ideas and words that might be appropriate to Epicureans, Peripatetics, or Democritus—that is, to skeptical philosophers—but not to a Jew. Origen himself then uses speech-in-character to address an imaginary Jew. Elsewhere Origen points out Celsus's ignorance of Judaism when Celsus has the imaginary Jew speak as if there were only one prophet who foretold. Origen says that such words might fit Samaritans or Sadducees, who hold only to the books of Moses, but not the typical Jew that Celsus wants to portray because they believe in other prophets (1.49). Elsewhere Origen points out that the imaginary Jew's words are fitting for address to imaginary gentile Christians but not to the Jewish Christian audience that Celsus depicts (2.1).

Most of 7.36–37 constitutes an extended critique of Celsus's speech-in-character. Origen first cites a passage from the *True Discourse* in which imaginary Christians speak and Celsus replies to them in his own person. Origen next levels some criticisms: "It is a virtue in a writer who portrays a person by speech to keep consistency in the meaning [*boulēma*] and character [*ethos*] of the person to whom the words are attributed; and it is a vice when one creates words which do not fit [*mē harmozein*] the imaginary person's character. Equally at fault are those who, in putting words into the mouth of an imaginary person, impose philosophy which the author has learned to barbarians and uneducated people or slaves, who have never heard philosophical arguments and could never say such things properly." Origen then notes that people praise Homer for the aptness and consistency of his characterizations but that Aristophanes ridiculed Euripides for giving barbarian women and slave girls philosophical sounding lines (cf. Aristophanes, *Ach.* 393ff.). Theon makes the same comparison and refers to Euripides attributing inappropriately philosophical lines to Hecuba (2.60.27–32). Others in antiquity criticized Homer for inconsistency in characterization (Ps. Plut., *Vit. Hom.* B66). Origen's discussion makes clear that ancient readers often read with strict, stereotyped ideas about characterization. Certain attributes were deemed consistently true of men, women, barbarians, and so forth. Paul's characterizations must be read with close attention to form and consistency.

Finally, Origen's understanding of divine prosōpopoiia in scripture can help one grasp the relation of the technique to an author's adaptability in speaking and use of the authorial voice. Celsus charged the scriptures with crudeness and bad theology for attributing to God passions like love and anger (4.71). Origen replied that God sometimes spoke from his own person in scripture but when addressing the weak, used speech-in-character appropriate to their fleshly level of understanding (4.71): God spoke in fleshly terms to the fleshly. Origen's doctrine of revelation through the logos here fits with what moralists and rhetoricians said about the authorial adaptability of speakers and writers.[36] In light of Origen and the general rhetorical attitude toward adaptability, one should take seriously the implications of Paul's claim of adaptability toward Jews, gentiles, and the weak (1 Cor 9:19–22).

Several fragmentary sources have survived for Origen's commentary on 7:7–25.[37] Greek fragments from the *Philocalia* and the *Catenae* show that Rufinus's Latin translation has abbreviated the section and not without distortion.[38] Jerome's *Epistle* 121 also depends on Origen's commentary and can be used but only with caution. Origen says that Paul does not speak of himself alone in 7:7–8 but of every person. He then gives his famous interpretation of the passage as a reference to the time in childhood before rational accountability, when the natural law teaches right and wrong to each individual. Origen may have referred to prosōpopoiia here. The fragments make it difficult to be certain what Origen thought about the rhetoric of 7:7–13, although the principles that he lays out in his discussion of 7:14–25 seem to apply to 7:7–13. Clearly, for Origen the speaker of 7:7–25 does not speak autobiographically of Paul. Among other objections to an autobiographical interpretation, Origen points out correctly that Jews do not speak of a time in their life when they live "without the law," as 7:9 would indicate on this reading (*ComRm.* 6.8 [1082]).

The Greek fragments, Rufinus, and Jerome agree that Origen's main topics for 14–25 were the identity of the speaker(s) and the type of experience described (Ruf. 2.51.8–53.10; *cat.* xli; Jer. 34.14–22). He begins by pointing to the contradiction between what the person speaking says of himself and the way Paul describes himself elsewhere. The Greek fragments have examples from 1 Cor 6:19 and Gal 3:13 and 2:20 of Paul speaking in his own persona in words that contradict the self-description in chapter 7. Rufinus in addition has 2 Cor 10:3; Rom 8:11; and 1 Cor 6:19. Jerome has Acts 9:15; 1 Cor 6:19; and

2 Cor 13:3. I suspect that Jerome has added the texts from Acts and 2 Corinthians, but the other sources may have abbreviated. Origen goes on to say that the reader faces contradiction "unless we should say that the discourse has different characterizations [prosōpopoiiai] and the sections conform to various qualities of characters [prosōpa]."[39]

Origen's key to understanding the content of speech-in-character in 7:7–25 is his conception of moral progress. Technical Stoic language and philosophical koine regarding moral psychology and ethics occur densely throughout his discussion. Origen wants to see in the chapter persons speaking who represent different stages. According to the *Catenae* (41.4–5), Origen places all of the character types represented in the section under the category of the unwise who act against their own intentions and purposes, the problem of akrasia. If Origen had not been so intent on seeing degrees and types of moral progress or lack thereof, he might have more simply described the whole text as a characterization of the *akratēs*. The catenist understood prosōpopoiia and has selected the fragments that introduce the characterizations, for example, "The present discourse is appropriate to be said by . . ." (41.6–7); "These words are appropriate for one to say who . . ." (42.1).

According to the *Catena* fragment, v. 14 is said by "those who have learned concerning the law that it is divine and seen that its commandments are good, but nevertheless do not understand how they fall under sin since they are sold under sin and fleshly" (41.6–7). Origen probably distinguishes the person represented by 14–15 from the characterization of 17–25 because the former seems to be in a state in which he recognizes the good but does not understand the evil powers of the passions and desires, whereas the latter fully understands the battle within. The person in 14 has just learned about the law.[40] According to Rufinus, Origen referred to 1 Cor 9:22 in order to explain Paul's speech-in-character (*ComRm.* 6.9 [1086A]). Paul adapts himself to the condition of the weak by speaking the words of the weak.

The *Catena* extract on 7:15 (42) "fits the words" of "those who wrestle with their desires but who fall due to the weakness of their reason, and those who are conquered by anger and fear and who do what they do not want and what they hate. And also when having been overcome by the elation of reason we are conquered by that which seems to be good but is not truly, we agree with the law that it is good but we act according to [the demands] of pleasure." Origen recognizes that Paul is discussing akrasia and explains the state with technical Stoic concepts. Here Rufinus agrees with the Greek, although he is unable to convey Origen's technical language.[41]

According to extract 43, Paul depicts in 22–23 "those who have not yet strengthened their habituation toward that which is best. Just as if a soldier having defeated enemies parades captives, so in regard to the characters set forth, the law of their [bodily] parts wages war against the law of their mind, taking captive the wretched soul and parading it before the law [of sin in their bodily parts]."[42] Origen seems to have read 17–25 as coming from the mouth of the same imaginary character who represents the new convert. Paul interjects the cry of thanksgiving in 25a, but otherwise the words represent the person newly come to Christ who has not yet overcome his former habits (*ComRm.* 6.9 [1089A-1091B]; *Catena* 44).[43] Again, the Greek fragments show that Origen understands the passage to be discussing akrasia but here for the situation of the new Christian.[44]

Origen shows us how and why an ancient reader would have understood 7:7–25 as prosōpopoiia. He reads the text just as grammar school teachers taught their pupils they should and employs the technical vocabulary that philological scholars and rhetoricians used in exegesis.[45] He employs the criteria of appropriateness and discusses change of speaker, characterization, and authorial versus imaginary personae. Origen assumes as patently obvious that the general subject of the characterization is akrasia. But he does not try to imagine historically what this might mean for Paul the Jewish missionary to gentiles living before the destruction of the temple. Instead, he sees types, ranging from the person who has just come to accountability under the natural law of reason, to the *akratēs* who does not understand the causes of his condition, to the new convert who knows his condition but still struggles for self-mastery. In other words, Origen adapts the characterization to the pedagogical progress emphasized in the philosophically informed Christianity of his time.

Origen is not the only ancient interpreter of Romans to read chapter 7 as speech-in-character. Rufinus and Jerome, at least at the time they wrote the texts cited above, seem to accept Origen's approach. Didymus of Alexandria vigorously argues an interesting reading of 7 as prosōpopoiia, denying that Paul speaks of himself. Nilus of Ancyra follows the terminology of the later rhetorical tradition, describing the "I" in chapter 7 as *ēthopoiia*. This shows that his judgment came independently of Origen. In a letter to a certain Olympius, who in Nilus's view seriously misread chapter 7, Nilus writes, "God forbid! The divine apostle does not say concerning himself that, 'I see another law in my members taking me captive through sin.' Rather these things are uttered by a person [*ek prosōpou*] representing those who are troubled by fleshly passions" (*Ep.* 1.152 [*PG* 79, 1.145]). In a subsequent letter, Nilus adds, "It is easy to grasp that the apostle is employing characterization [*ēthopoiia*] when a voice says, 'But I was once living without the law.' And truly there is never any time when a person has respite without the law of Moses; for from a young age he was closely brought up in the law by Gamaliel. Moreover, the person [*to prosōpon*] is to be understood as belonging to those who have lived outside the law of Moses" (*Ep.* 1.153 [*PG* 79, 1.145]). Nilus understands the passage as speech-in-character but in the terminology of a different rhetorical tradition from Origen's. Nilus saw 7:7–24 as depicting one person, someone not a native to the law who came under the law but who is nevertheless mastered by passions and desires. If Nilus had had a historical perspective, he would have said that the passage depicted the gentile under the law or the gentile who keeps works from the law.

The work of the ancient commentators should be evaluated critically. Fortunately, their theological and ethical systems stand out so that it proves easy to evaluate their readings of Romans historically. They have no interest in consistently setting Paul the first-century Jewish apostle to the gentiles into his own context. But even if their interest lies in expounding their own theological-philosophical and moral issues, they, as native speakers, still show sensitivity to Paul's style and rhetoric and often make valuable insights regarding Paul's own context. That Rom 7:7–25 is speech-in-character depicting a person who lacks self-mastery strikes these ancient commentators as obvious. But they have little interest in or understanding of Paul's world of gentile godfearers drawn to Judaism as a school for self-mastery.

Toward a Historical Reading with Speech-in-Character

The difficult task of imagining a reading possible for readers in Paul's time must preclude Christian assumptions and readings that make sense only in epochs later than Paul's. The interpreter can neither presuppose the introspective Christian conscience of late antiquity or the middle ages nor assume the much later Christian stereotype of the legalistic Jew who attempts the impossible task of keeping the law. The picture of Paul the Pharisee, who attempted that impossible task, clearly comes from reading the narratives of his conversion in Acts through the lens of later Christian constructions of Judaism and the law.[46] Types and assumptions for reading will have to be those that readers in Paul's time could have made.

The section begins in v. 7 with an abrupt change in voice following a rhetorical question that serves as a transition from Paul's authorial voice, which has previously addressed the readers explicitly described by the letter in 6:1–7:6. This constitutes what the grammarians and rhetoricians described as change of voice (*enallgē* or *metabolē*). These ancient readers would next look for *diaphōnia*, a difference in characterization from the authorial voice. The speaker in 7:7–25 speaks with great personal pathos of coming under the law at some point, learning about his desire and sin, and being unable to do what he wants to do because of enslavement to sin and flesh. If one asks whether Paul gives his readers any clues elsewhere in the letter that this might be his autobiography, the answer is clearly no. And this picture does not fit what he says about himself in other letters.[47] The passage seems to present a distinctive, coherent ethos with a particular life situation. As the handbooks recommend, the person speaks of his happy past before he learned about the law (7:7b–8 and especially 9), his present misery, and his future plight (7:24). Since this tragic characterization also centers on self-reflection and takes the form primarily of a monologue, the passage fits the classic models of speech-in-character. The text portrays emotion, moral-psychological disposition, "inner thoughts," and "complaint" (Quint. 9.2.30–33).

Dividing the character's speech into parts according to the tense reflects different temporal standpoints on the character's life or circumstances. Hermogenes recommends that the order be present, past, and future, and Apthonius's example follows this order. It is clear, however, both from Hermogenes' reasons for this order and from practice that various purposes of the speaker and subjects of characterization could call for different orders of the tenses. Apthonius's example has Niobe speaking in a monologue after discovering the death of her children. She begins in the present tense bemoaning her loss. Then there is a transition to the past—"Woe is me! The misfortune I bear is like that of the one from whom I descended"—in which she explains the origin of her present tragedy. In her final words she reflects on her future fate and on the possibility of receiving help from the gods. Paul also uses all three tenses, although he begins with the past (7:7–11) and moves to the present (7:14–24a, 25) and the future (7:24b).[48]

In accord with a form of the technique discussed in the handbooks, Paul's authorial voice does not explicitly introduce the person. In comparison with the preceding context in 6:1–7:6, in which Paul's voice addresses "brothers," the addressee/s of the voice in 7:7–25 is either ambiguous or only Paul. The explicit audience of the letter addressed in its prescript disappears, as it does in 1:18–4:23, which I have elsewhere argued is also dominated by speech-in-character. At one point (7:25–8:2), again fitting prosōpopoiia, dialogue between the speaker in 7:7–25 and Paul occurs. The characterization of 7:7–25 reads like someone personally witnessing to the statement "when we were in the flesh, our sinful passions worked in our bodily parts through the law (7:5)," after the false conclusion and its rejection in 7:7a, "What shall we say? Is the law sin? By no means!" I find the identity of the speaker at 7:7a unclear: perhaps it is Paul, perhaps the person characterized in what follows, perhaps an anonymous objector.

Tragic characters or newly created characterizations of people in emotionally laden tragic situations were favorite subjects of prosōpopoiia.[49] One finds a remarkable intersection of style and content in Romans 7, an intersection of the techniques of prosōpopoiia and motifs and style of the tragic monologue as mediated by the tradition of moral psychology. As we saw in the tradition of Medea's words, such tragic speeches are often in the form of monologues or soliloquies. They usually employ the first person singular. The tragic speeches were models for the teaching of soliloquy in the *progymnasmata* and rhetoric. Ovid, another near contemporary of Paul, not only wrote a *Medea* but also the *Heroides*, which are letters written by means of prosōpopoiia imagining what legendary women might have written. These include letters from Medea to Jason. When Paul wrote Romans, Ovid's works were popular reading in Rome.

One reason the figure of Medea gained such continuing popularity appears in connection with purity of citizenship and ethnicity ("nationality").[50] Medea stood for foreigners who corrupted the purity of the citizen body, and her saying about akrasia connoted the moral degeneracy that mixing with foreigners would supposedly bring. I find great irony in the fact that Paul the Jew resonates these allusions back to Greeks and Romans who apparently now see themselves as gentiles, outsiders to Judaism described as immoral foreigners. The figures of Medea and other passion-bound barbarian women from Greek tragedy became important in imperial Rome. As early as Cicero, the type becomes a prominent oratorical slander (*Pro Cael.* 7.18; *Leg. Man.* 8.21). But the theme rose to a height of public consciousness during the struggle between Antony and Octavian and the early years of the empire. The propagandists for Augustus depicted Antony as a man dominated by passionate foreign women and compared Cleopatra to Medea, Omphale, and Semiramis. Niobe, whom we have already seen recommended as a model for prosōpopoiia, paralleled Medea as a type of the degenerate foreign woman. On the doors of the temple to Apollo in Rome, erected as a votive for the victory at Actium, stood the scene of Niobe slaying her children. This not-so-subtle allusion to the defeat of Antony and Cleopatra used Niobe as the paradigm of God's wrath against barbarian hybris. All of this helps us to fathom how the Medean saying might have played in the public consciousness of Paul's time.

Rom 7:7–25 resembles tragic soliloquy and prosōpopoiia of the person in a tragic situation in several ways. It reveals the conflict of inner thoughts and feelings using the first person singular. The exclamation "wretched man that I am!" (*talaipōros egō anthrōpos*) reads almost as a parody of the tragic outcry. In Seneca's *Medea*, Medea cries "What, wretched woman, have I done?" as she reflects on how her will to do the good has been overpowered by anger. In the *Metamorphoses* (7.18), just before she speaks the famous words about akrasia, Medea calls herself "wretched" (*infelix*). The Vulgate uses the same word to translate *talaipōros* in Rom 7:24. Just before he introduces the example of Medea, Epictetus uses the fictive I: "Who is more wretched than I?" (2.17.18; cf. 26). In 1.4.23–26, Epictetus says that tragedies in which people say "wretched man that I am" are the depiction of people suffering because they admire external things.[51] The cry of despair "oh wretch that I am" is first made prominent in literature by the tragedians and comedians themselves.[52]

Another important feature that Romans 7 shares with the tragic monologue and the soliloquies of prosōpopoiia is the language of external power for moral and psychological states. I have already discussed the importance of "sin as a power" for traditional readings of Romans, and I have argued that one should not take Paul's language as more than rhetorical and metaphorical except in one regard. Now I can be more specific about the tradition of this rhetoric. Such language is not typical of the Hebrew Bible/Old Testament (for example, the Psalms) or earlier Jewish literature but rather of what scholars often call the fragmented personality of Homer and the Greek poets.[53]

Greek polytheism facilitated expression of the common human dilemma of conflicting goods and obligations.[54] Different gods corresponded to different impulses and demands of human life. So, for example, in the *Hippolytus,* Euripides explores the conflicting demands of Aphrodite, goddess of love, and Artemis, goddess of virginity. As her nurse reflects upon Phaedra's dilemma of knowing what she ought to do but yielding to the power of love, she blames Aphrodite (358–59): "The modest forced against their wills to lust after evils! Aphrodite is no god!" Hippolytus's Phaedra speaks of being unable to subdue the goddess by self-mastering mastery (401). The language of outside powers shows itself in the tradition of Medea's saying and the broader discussion of willing and doing. Plutarch quotes from Euripides' lost *Chrysippus:* "Wretched I am, this evil comes to men from God, when one knows the good but does it not."[55] In Hellenistic and Roman times, philosophers and moralists usually rationalized that language. The powers were not really external but internal. Epictetus said, "When a man does something contrary to his opinion under the compulsion of love, while seeing the better thing but lacking the strength to follow, one might think him worthy of being excused, because he is in the power of something violent, and, in a manner of speaking, godlike" (*Diss.* 4.1.147). I find it no surprise, then, that Rom 6–7, with part of its subject matter from Greek moral psychology, uses the language of external power.

Thus in 7 one meets a well-known and highly developed kind of rhetoric that was employed by moralists and philosophers to treat the very issues that Paul discusses.

Gentiles in Chapter 7

Paul uses prosōpopoiia in chapter 7 to characterize not every human or every human who is not a Christian but rather gentiles, especially those who try to live by works of the law. Paul has already introduced and explained the character depicted in the prosōpopoiia of 7 from a historical point of view in chapter 1. Chapter 1 introduces the gentile mind as a motif that reappears at crucial points in the letter's discourse. When the gentile peoples rejected the true God and adopted polytheism, their reasoning became vain and their hearts became senseless and darkened (1:21). The true God, who has been unjustly rejected, now enters the story. He punishes these peoples in a fitting way by handing them over to slavery under a cruel tyrant. They are allowed or caused (which is not clear) to be under the mastery of their appetites and passions. As we saw in chapter 6, Romans treats its audience as having been enslaved to these masters before their baptisms. God handed these gentiles over to the lusts (epithumiai) of their hearts so as to practice impurity (akatharsia) and dishonor their bodies (1:24). God also handed them over to dishonorable passions (pathē), which resulted in perversions of nature and self-deceit (1:26–27). Paul sums it up by saying that God handed these gentiles over to a "base mind" (nous). He explains what this means by giving a long catalogue of characteristic vices. Chapter 7 speaks of bondage to both the passions (ta pathēmata) and desire (epithumia). The law made this bondage to desire known but also increased its hold (7:7–12) on the persona of 7:7–25. This person has been deceived by sin (7:11) and has a mind (nous) that is captive to sin and the flesh (7:23, 25). Paul uses the traditional language of external power for these inner forces. But God is the one who has handed the gentile peoples over to the powers, so that even God's law only witnesses to the bondage.

This view of gentiles enslaved to their appetites and passions appears elsewhere in Paul's letters. In 1 Thess 4:4 he writes, "Each man should know how to possess his own wife in holiness and honor, not in the passion of desire [en pathē epithumias] as the gentiles who do not know God."[56] The Thessalonians themselves had just recently turned from idols to the true God (1:10). Paul characterizes the preconversion life of Corinthians with a mind-boggling list of vices (1 Cor 6:9–11). Nowhere in the letters is there comparable generalizing about Jews. In fact, defining gentiles as captive to their appetites over against Jewish freedom from such captivity constitutes a fundamental feature of self-definition for Paul.

Paul's view of gentiles is, of course, not unique to him but widespread in Jewish sources. The view of gentiles as morally degenerate must be considered a fundamental feature of Jewish self-definition in antiquity.[57] Whether the authors believed what they were saying is a different matter. A few illustrative examples will suffice. The letter of Aristeas contrasts Jewish with gentile sexual practices (152): "For the vast majority of humans pollute themselves by promiscuous intercourse, committing great wickedness, and entire countries and cities pride themselves on such things. For they not only have intercourse with men, but they pollute the mothers who bore them and even their daughters. But we have kept our distance from these sins." Such texts attribute all kinds of abuses of appetites and desires to gentile peoples, but those concerning kinship taboos and relations with the same sex, especially between adults and children, are most prominent. These constitute the great sins against patriliny and patriarchy. An example from the Sibylline Oracles (3.591–99) illustrates the assumption that by such actions the gentiles were transgressing the law of Israel's God to which they were in some unspecified way responsible: "But [the Jews] raise holy hands toward heaven, rising early from their bed and continually purifying their body with water, and they honor Him alone who rules forever, the eternal One, and then their parents; and far more than any other people they remember the purity of the marriage bed. Nor do they hold unholy intercourse with boys, as do the Phoenicians, Egyptians, and Latins and spacious Greece and many other peoples, Persians and Galatians and all Asia, transgressing the holy law of immortal God." Finally, such texts often find the cause of gentile degeneracy in their worship of idols.

This picture of non-Jewish cultures is such a great distortion that it is natural to ask why and how it was maintained. The representation clearly has something to do with Israel's master narrative, which in turn became the mainspring of Jewish social and cultural integrity. Group boundaries of a constantly threatened people may have been a factor, but one must turn to Jewish society's internal organization to understand the role of the representation. The master narrative centers on a certain reading of the books of Moses. The gift of the land to Israel came about because of the perversions of the peoples who occupied it. When Noah curses Canaan, he proclaims that his descendants will be enslaved to the descendants of his brothers because of his sin (Gen 9:24–27). In Gen 15:16 God promises Abraham that his descendants will inherit the land when the "wickedness of the Amorites is complete." After a list of "abominations," Lev 18:24–25 continues: "Do not pollute yourselves by all of these things, for by all these the peoples I am casting out before you polluted themselves; and the land became polluted, and I paid back their wickedness on account of it, and the land was greatly angered with those who inhabited it." The "peoples of the land" and later "gentiles" more broadly exhibit practices that are opposite to the rules of genealogical purity and inheritance of property and status from father to son. The ascendancy of the hereditary priesthood during the second temple supported by a centralized cult with a powerful written discourse of purity and pollution promoted an almost obsessive consciousness of sexual and kinship rules. Deut 7:1–5 provides the mandate for Israel to erase the other nations from the land and forbids intermarriage and dealings lest "they turn away your sons" from following God. The representation of the lustful gentile who is promiscuous about matters of paternity and ignorant of lawful kinship relations developed from patriarchal and patrilineal ideology and served as a foil to those ideals.

It is not the later Christian focus on Adam and Eve's moment of disobedience in the garden that stands behind chapters 1 and 7 of Romans, but the story of the gentile peoples as a part of Israel's story. In Romans, this view of gentiles has been Hellenized by a retelling of the narrative in terms of the inner mythology of moral psychology. This was not a unique way of conceptualizing the other in the Greco-Roman world. A most fascinating parallel comes to us through Diodorus of Sicily. He draws on the Egyptian historian Hecataeus of Abdera for the following and precedes the passage with a discussion of how even Egyptian kings had to follow the law (*nomos*):

> And in doing what custom required in these matters, they did not become indignant or take offense in their souls, but rather they believed that they lived a most happy life. For they believed that all other men, in irrationally gratifying their natural passions, do many things which bring them injuries and perils, and that often some who know [*eidotas*] that they are about to sin [*hamartein*] nevertheless do base acts when overpowered by love or hate or some other passion, while they, on the other hand, by virtue of their having followed a manner of life which had been chosen before all others [or "judged superior to all others"] by the wisest of men, fell into the fewest faults. (1.71.3)

Here Egyptians prove superior to all the other peoples because they are able to do what they know is right by following their law rather than be overcome by their passions. Hecataeus characterizes the non-Egyptians with the Medean saying, They know what is right but are not able to do it because of their passions. But how is it that the Egyptians are morally superior in such a basic way? Their superiority results from their having a superior politeia, a better social, political, and cultural constitution. Jewish apologists like Philo and Josephus claimed exactly the same for Judaism: Its superior constitution, the divine law, made Jews typically more self-controlled, just, and humane than non-Jews. Jews could better control their passions.

Not only Jews and Egyptians related moral psychology to culture, but also Greeks and Romans.[58] The Greek equivalent of Jew/gentile is Hellene

(Greek)/barbarian. The latter classification was made with far wider criteria of taxonomy than just language. The taxonomic indicators for "barbarian" often included much of what we moderns mean by morals and culture. Even Galen, that sophisticated and most educated Greek in the center of the Roman world, has a Greek view of the other. After citing the famous words of Euripides' Medea about akrasia, Galen writes, "Taught by reason, doubtlessly she knows the greatness of the evils she is about to do, but she says that her anger gets the better of her reason, and therefore she is forcibly led by anger to commit the act. . . . Euripides has used Medea as an example of barbarians and uneducated people, in whom anger is stronger than reason; but among Greeks and educated [read Hellenized] people . . . reason prevails over anger" (*Hippoc. et Plat.* 3.189.20–190.1). Elsewhere (*Hippoc. et Plat.* 3.214.10–20) Galen explains that children, wild animals, and barbarians are often slaves of their desires (*epithumiai*).

Rom 1 and 6–7 draw on a Jewish version of a widespread Greco-Roman way of portraying the other. The free adult male of your own people constitutes the norm. As the scale moves away from him, the other becomes less rational and more emotional on the scale of self-mastery. A foreign woman like Medea is doubly dangerous. Jews, Greeks, Romans, and Egyptians all had their own frames of reference, which in Paul's time had been made somewhat ambiguous because of the political dominance of Rome and the cultural dominance of the Greeks. Sexual transgressions and rules of purity and pollution loom large in such conceptions of the other to the extent that the societies are patrilineal or otherwise constructed around lineage and descent. Such societies practice animal or some other form of sacrifice. Since the patrilineal principle of earlier times had been modified and weakened among Greeks, Romans, and Jews, a new order arose that is reflected in the ethic of self-mastery. In Paul's time both codes coexisted and competed. The centrality of the one temple with its hereditary priesthoods, however, reinforced the principles of birth and purity of descent for Jews. The very fact that the Judaism which emerged after the end of the temple so radically moved the focus from ascription by descent to achievement in studying Torah serves as a measure of how important pure blood had been in Paul's time. On the other hand, certain strains of Judaism and Israelite religion that downplayed blood and stressed achievement had always existed.[59] Adaptation to the complexities of the Greco-Roman world made the tension between the two principles even more complex. Thus Paul's talk of gentile immorality, mastery by sexual passions, the theme of works versus adoptive kinship, and his very mission is concerned with working out tensions inherent in Judaism and in similar societies in which purity of birth had been central but achievement had gained a major role.

Ambiguity lay in Paul's own situation. His basic categories for humans are Jew and gentile. He recognizes the dominance of Greek culture in the Roman East by interchanging "gentile" and "Greek." At the same time, however, he views the world from a Greek perspective. The non-Jewish part of humanity, the gentiles, can be divided into two parts, Greeks and barbarians (Rom 1:13–14). His native language is also Greek. Someone who does not speak Greek is for him a barbarian (1 Cor 14:11). Whatever Paul's Greekness, and the evidence seems to be that it was great, in his self-conception he has assimilated it to his Jewishness.

If we understand the anachronism of introducing a third term, "Christian," then the persona of Romans 7 can only be a gentile. Some have claimed, however, that it is precisely in 7:1 that Paul turns away from gentiles when he says, "Or are you ignorant, brothers—for I am speaking to those who know the law—that the law rules over a person for as long as he lives?" In fact, 7:1 turns out to be one of the most widely mentioned pieces of evidence for the existence of Jews in the Roman church. The weight of scholarly opinion, however, sees gentiles, who know something about the law, at least included in 7:1.[60] But Paul allows no entry into the discourse for this phantom Jewish audience. If the Roman church was made up of Jews and gentiles, we would never know it from reading Romans. It is most important to pay close attention to Paul's construction of the letter's audience throughout its discourse. As I have shown, 1:18–4:22 lacks explicit recognition of the epistolary audience. There the fiction of imaginary interlocutors takes the place of the epistolary audience, but the first-level readers encoded in the discourse remain gentiles or Greeks. From 4:23 through 6:23, Paul more and more identifies himself with the gentile readers by use of the first person plural. In chapter 6 he addresses them directly with the second person plural, including imperatives. The apex of this development occurs in 7:1–6. Paul addresses his audience as brothers in 7:1 and 4. The last time he did that was at 1:13, where he describes his epistolary audience as gentiles at Rome. The only other places in the letter where Paul addresses his audience so intently are in chapters 9–11, where his own persona both changes and becomes much more vivid. There he shifts from identifying himself with gentiles to identifying himself as a Jew.

All of Paul's rhetoric, including his concern to argue for gentile equality and to argue against gentile judaizing, makes sense if we suppose that Paul's literary audience represents something like those who have traditionally been called godfearers in modern scholarship.[61] From beginning to end, Romans presupposes an audience that consists of gentiles who had or still have a lively interest in Judaism. Such people existed and most likely made up the bulk of the early gentile converts to Christ. Those who know the law in 7:1 were for-

merly enslaved to their passions and desires while they submitted to the law
(7:4–6). Paul supposes that all gentiles are in some sense "under the law" and
responsible for teachings that apply to gentiles. The *person* in 7:7–25 whom
Paul so carefully constructs by means of prosōpopoiia, however, seems more
specific. That person represents those caught between two cultures. Like
Medea, he cannot submit to a foreign law because his gentile passions will not
allow it. Rom 7:7–25 represents the judaizing gentile's ambiguous status. Neither fully Jew nor fully Greek, he is torn between the passions of an idolator
and the law of the one true God.

According to a long, influential line of Western interpretation, Rom 7 and
8 contrast the Jewish and Christian self-understandings. I believe it a great
tragedy that generations of Christians have seen Jews through these dark
lenses. The currently most influential commentator has written of 7:7–13,
"First, it is to be maintained under all circumstances that the apostle is speaking of mankind under the law, or specifically of the pious Jew."[62] In a recent
study, Gerd Theissen unfortunately falls into this Western reading.[63] He even
makes the chapter autobiographical, a description of Paul's struggle as a Pharisee from the later Christian perspective.[64] In this Western reading, the linchpin is usually pride. The human or the Jewish crime is pride. Jews may be
outwardly virtuous and good but their good behavior is at the base evil because
it is motivated by pride. Again the ghost of Augustine lives on. But Paul says
nothing about pride or anxiety or overachievement. These interpreters have to
argue that the concepts are hidden but assumed in the concepts of "sin" and
"doing the law."

The ten commandments must have been basic to what gentiles who
wanted to identify with Judaism were taught. When Paul caricatures the works
of the law that a Jewish teacher taught to gentiles, he cites three commandments from the Decalogue (2:21–22). The gentile *persona* in 7:7 gives the commandment against covetousness as an example of what he was taught. This
prohibition was given a special significance by Jews who wanted to show the
correspondence of Jewish teaching and the Greco-Roman ethic of self-mastery
(see chapter 2 above). The LXX's use of *epithumia* to translate the Hebrew
allowed Jews like Philo and the author of 4 Maccabees to claim that the Jewish
law agreed with Greek moral psychology in its emphasis on the passions as
the source of evil impulses. Furthermore, following the appropriate commandments from the Jewish law was an extraordinarily potent therapy for the
ravages of rampant desire. Translations introduce an entirely alien idea when
they render *epithumēseis* in 7:7 as "you shall not covet," rather than "you shall
not desire," hiding the connections with the motif of gentile desire and Paul's
Hellenistic conceptualities.

The dilemma of the gentile who tries to base his life on works of the law appears in 7:8–11. Although the law reveals that desire is sin, it can do little to change the fact that *epithumia* forms a fundamental aspect of his character. The gentile ruled by his God-ordained slavery to the desire arising from passions experiences the law against desire as a deceitful, almost teasing condemnation (7:8–11). Instead of controlling excessive desire, the commandment stimulates desire in accordance with God's punishment and adds a knowledge of God's condemnation. Perhaps Paul thought that the gentile was definitively socialized in one way, the Jew in another or that each carried the characteristics of his ancestors. He definitely believed that lifting a few commandments out of the Jewish politeia could only lead the gentile to a knowledge of his bondage to sin and the penalties of God's wrath. Behind Paul's caricature may lie sociological realities. Gentile godfearers may have aspired to live by certain Jewish teachings, but they still lived in gentile society. Could a gentile living in such circumstances really be expected to forge for himself a life truly pleasing to God? The attendant schizophrenia might even make matters worse.

Rather than merely repeat and elaborate the mythological discourse of Hellenistic moral psychology and its ideology, one must understand the social constructions indicated in such discourse. Paul, of course, employs the Hellenistic discourse and not social analysis. Indeed, the discourse often functions to mask these realities. Romans 7 stands forth as a Jewish Christian adaptation of Greco-Roman discourse about the problem of akrasia, in service of an argument against gentiles attempting to gain self-mastery by following the law. Rom 6–8 uses "sin" in a way similar to the concept of *akolasia,* a set disposition to do wrong. Paul adds the assumption that sin is wrongdoing offensive to God and his law. In Hellenistic moral thought, habitual akrasia becomes *akolasia.* Ancient moralists debated as to whether akrasia, weakness of will or lack of self-mastery, was caused by ignorance and false belief or by passions inherent in human nature. In light of modern study, both approaches vastly oversimplify the problem, but the Stoics had the most sophisticated analysis, attributing akrasia to false beliefs and ignorance.[65] Paul in crucial respects sides with the popular and Platonic view against the Stoics. Knowledge alone cannot cure gentile akrasia. Merely knowing the teachings of the law fails to solve the problem. Using the popular view, Romans explains akrasia in terms of desire arising from passions (similar to our emotions and appetites).

Again using the popular and Platonic view, Romans 7 divides the person between a true self identified with the mind or rationality and a lower or false self identified with the body or the flesh. According to Paul, the passions and desire reside in the flesh or the body and its parts (Gal 5:16, 24; Rom 6:12–13, cf. 1:26–27; 7:5, 18, 22; 8:3). The mind rationally apprehends and wills to do the law (7:22), but since it has been corrupted by the turn to idolatry (1:21–22, 28), the desires of the flesh overcome it. Only a mind renewed by infusion with God's Spirit can enable the gentile to resist the flesh and act according to God's law (8:5–8). Thus the law is not the problem but also not the answer (7:9–13, 16; 8:3a). The problem stems from God withholding his divine Spirit from gentiles who are thus not related to him as children (8:12–30) and cannot master the flesh (8:2–11). God effected gentile redemption from the flesh by making his son the pioneer of the movement from life dominated by the flesh to life dominated by the Spirit. Redeemed gentiles do not leave the body for a spiritual existence but are incorporated into Christ's mode of life by infusion with God's (also called Christ's) life principle (spirit/*pneuma*).

At some points in 7:14–25 the person seems not to understand what is happening to him and to be acted upon instead of acting (15, 17). One need not appeal to demons, spiritual powers, or external forces to explain this. As I have shown, this language comes from the tradition of the fragmented personality. Paul unsurprisingly uses Greek traditions to convince Greeks. The akrasia depicted here can be partially explained as a conflict between incidental, fragmentary, fluctuating, transitory desires and long-term desires.[66] The latter are relatively constant, long-term projects and commitments around which people organize their lives and their identities. Part of what the imaginary gentile voice is saying is this: "I want to live an overall plan of life like the Jewish law teaches, but my habitually overpowering but transitory desires consistently frustrate that larger goal." The Greek tradition about akrasia dramatically represented such moral schizophrenia by speaking as if there were distinct agents in the soul. One agent could even deceive the other (Plautus, *Trinum.* 658; cf 7:11). Desire resembles giving birth to flames of fire in one's breast: It is a strange power that holds down the will (Ovid, *Met.* 7.17–19). Owing to the conflict between long-term desires or volitions and transitory desires the gentile does not understand his behavior (v. 15). At the same time he knows the right and knows that the right is God's law, even if he does not do it.

The passage suggests not only a matter of conflict between short-term desires and long-term desires but also between irreconcilable long-term desires. In other words, the conflict could not be adequately described as one of nature versus norm.[67] The first clue comes from an allusion to Paul's paradigmatic story of the gentiles denying God. The person says that he is "sold under sin" (14). The word *piprasko* is of interest here. Writers frequently use it as a metaphor for betrayal and disloyalty, as, for instance, in 1 Macc 1:15: "They [the Jewish Hellenizers] joined with the gentiles and were sold to do evil."[68] One also frequently encounters the word in connection with selling people into slavery.[69] But who sold this gentile into slavery? In one sense it would obviously be his own betrayal, since Paul assumes responsibility for sin. The answer appears in the language of chapter 1, which speaks of God "handing over" the gentiles to their evil passions and desires. The word *paradidōmi*, much like *pipraskō*, was very frequently employed of handing someone over as a captive or prisoner. Thus the language alludes to God's punishment of gentile disloyalty by allowing or causing them to become enslaved to their own passions and desires. Romans depicts this slavery to desire as a consequence of a more fundamental decision of the gentile peoples to ignore the one God and to commit themselves to polytheism. In other words, their dilemma goes back to a long-term desire/volition.

A second clue suggesting a conflict of long-term volitions is the talk of two laws in 21–25. The metaphor of another law has its basis in the dual allegiance of the judaizing gentile that he portrays in 14–20. On the one hand, such a person resolves to keep certain parts of God's law, Israel's scriptures. Thus when he hears, "You shall not satisfy desire," this agrees with some of the long-term volitions of his mind. On the other hand, he has been socialized as a gentile under God's decree of bondage to passion and desire. The chapter implies that emotions, appetites, and desires are at least partly moldable, perhaps even constituted by socialization into particular cultures, different constitutions. But Paul believed that the law by itself could not deeply affect the person's gentile character. Treating similar issues in Galatians, he warns that if a man is circumcised he must follow the whole law (5:3). He seems to conceive of Judaism and gentile life in Christ as religious systems that work for individuals only if the systems are allowed to keep their integrity. Thus when the gentile hears the command of God's law, he also hears an analogous but more powerful antithetical voice of his gentile passions and desires, a different law. This is the law of sin (23, 25). The power of both laws on the person is possible only because the person has some basic but conflicting long-term desires or volitions in relation to each.

The gentiles need a new mind to replace the mind corrupted by idolatry (1:21, 22, 28). The gentile who is torn between his will to follow the law of God and the life of the flesh cries out in 7:24 asking for a savior. Verse 25 is best read as a parenthetic interjection of the authorial voice within the speech of the imaginary persona. The person's speech continues and concludes in v. 25. Paul then ends his prosōpopoiia by addressing the imaginary gentile in 8:1–2. The apostle tells him that he is freed from condemnation and from the law of sin and death through the Spirit of Jesus Christ, which will effect a renewed mind (8:1–11).

This way of reading the text resolves a long-standing textual dilemma. A textual variant generally ignored because it does not fit traditional ways of reading Romans indicates that Paul addresses the person of 7:7–25 as a conclusion to the passage. Earlier and better witnesses give strong force to reading *se* ("you," singular) in 8:2 rather than *me* ("me").[70] The "me" became the standard reading and the reading of most English translations, even though the Nestle-Aland critical Greek text reads "you" singular.[71] This contradictory state of affairs came about because the prosōpopoiia in 7:7–8:2 (the imaginary speaker in 7:7b-25 plus Paul's address to him in 8:1–2 and 7:25a) became unintelligible to later readers, who were far removed from Paul's historical and rhetorical context. The imaginary dialogue was lost. The first person reading came about when Paul's imaginary discussions with Jews and gentiles was no longer comprehensible and the categories of interpretation became humanity and Christianity. But in light of ancient prosōpopoiia and the sense of the passage, the "you" fits well indeed. The character's speech ends when Paul addresses him in words of encouragement.

Verses 3–8 provide an explanation for what Paul has said to the person in 1–2 and a transition to his epistolary audience, which he once again addresses in v. 9. This movement of the discourse supposes that the characterization of the person in chapter 7 sheds light on the experience of the letter's gentile readers. If 7 provides dramatic arguments against gentile believers mixing their life in Christ with forms of Judaism, then, chapter 8 explains how a reformed gentile politeia based on a new lineage comes about through the Spirit of Christ.

In my earlier discussion of 2:12–29, I showed that Paul actually upholds the principle of judgment according to the law for gentiles. They will be judged by how well they live by what the law requires of them. Paul supposes that the law requires other things of Israel (for example, circumcision, purity laws, festivals) and that the law is Israel's constitution as a people in the way that it is not for gentiles. Nevertheless, the law also contains the story of how the gentile peoples originated, then rejected God and shows what God expects of them. After extensive arguments against gentiles attempting to adopt parts of the law, chapter 8 finally explains how gentiles can "fulfill the just requirement of the law" (*to dikaiōma tou nomou*; cf 1:32; 2:26; 8:4).

Through Jesus Christ, "who was appointed son of God in power by the holy Spirit" (1:4), God enacted the destiny of others, including the gentile peoples (8:3). Jesus Christ's life figured forth what God had planned for the gentiles and presumably, but on a different track and schedule, for Jews. Christ reversed the curse on the gentiles, which made their flesh weak, being particularly vulnerable to sin (8:3) and not able to do what the law requires (8:4). As the Spirit empowered Jesus Christ, so also the Spirit gives the gentiles a new mind (8:5–6), allowing them to submit to God's law (8:7). Paul does not speak of this new mind as something that eliminates their freedom as agents. Indeed, he exhorts them to cooperate with this power (8:5–8). In Gal 5:17–21, he describes this new mind as a disposition toward certain social virtues and away from antisocial vices. That text provides a somewhat different description characterizing the new mind as a new set of desires (*epithumiai*), desires of the Spirit. In other words, the new empowerment enables virtues that reverse the state of gentile society described in 1:29–32.

Now enabled to submit to God's law, gentiles are reconciled to God (8:7). As Christ's body was raised by the power of the Spirit to new life (1:4), so also those in Christ will experience new life in their bodies (8:10–11). As Christ was appointed "a son of God" or "the son of God" (Paul's language is ambiguous), so also gentiles in Christ will be designated sons of God. Jesus is the "first born from the dead" (8:29) who "was appointed son of God, coming forth from the [general] resurrection of the dead" (1:3–4).[72] Paul understands Jesus' suffering to have been the beginning of the time of troubles that are a transition to God's redemption of the world.[73] Jesus' resurrection is the first instance of the general resurrection. As fellow heirs with Christ (8:17), Paul's gentile communities will share in the recent turn of events inaugurated by him. They too will share in the sufferings and testing of the period of transition (8:17–25) but will also be glorified as he has been glorified. God planned this boost for the whole world since the beginning of his creation. But he has for a time subjected that creation to decay and futility in order that his ultimate goal of glory might be achieved (8:19–22). The gentile communities that are thus "conformed to the image of his [God's] son" (8:29) have been destined, called, and justified as part of God's plan to reconcile the world.

Paul sums up all that has happened to these gentiles when he explains that they have been "adopted as sons" or have received "sonship."[74] As sons they become heirs of God's promises. Paul has already explained that the redemption of the gentile nations forms part of God's promise to Abraham that he would inherit the world (4:13). Paul conceives of world reconciliation as a kind of ethnic unification. Only Abraham's line has maintained the kinship with God that God intended for all. Through Christ's faithfulness to the patriarchal promises, all of the peoples will now be adopted into the one faithful family. But the principle for the inclusion of the other peoples is not blood or the seed passed down from the patriarch but infusion with the life-giving, creative power (God's Spirit) directly from God. Jews and the other peoples come to share in a principle of kinship prefigured in the miracle of Abraham's and Sarah's fertility and Jesus' resurrection.

Just what this means concretely is notoriously fuzzy. I think it certain, however, that it will not do to make Gal 3:28 the key and then to construe that text in terms of liberal individualism and the premises of the modern nation-state. The promise that Abraham's seed would inherit the world means that all will be adopted into Abraham's families through the Spirit and that there will be an organization of one government under Christ, who will finally turn things directly over to God. Abraham ends up having many peoples descended from him, all of whom have been infused with a higher level of life. Paul's gentile assemblies seem to be vanguards and beachheads of gentile renewal planted at strategic locations in various parts of the empire. They are in preparation to serve with Christ at his return. The Jewish family of Abraham maintains its integrity. To what extent Greeks, Romans, and others reformed "in Christ" maintain distinct identities remains unclear to me. It may not have been clear to Paul either. After laboring through the eight chapters, Paul has finally explained how the gentile peoples can attain the privileged status of sonship that Israel already has (9:4): They are sons and heirs when they receive the Spirit of Christ and live as communities participating in the paradigmatic narrative of renewal that Jesus Christ has already pioneered. All of this radically reinterprets the goal of self-mastery that drew many gentiles to works from the law.

Finally, comparing Paul to Philo on the topic of kinship allows a helpful perspective, illustrating that both were working out similar problems. Philo gives a novel reading to Deut 13:18: "These kinships as they are called from our forefathers based on blood and those based on intermarriage and other similar causes, let these relationships be thrown away if they do not aim at the same goal, namely, to honor God. Such honor is the unbreakable bond of all the fellow feeling which unites us. Those who so honor God will receive in exchange kinship of greater sanctity and holiness. The law confirms my promise when it says that those who do what is pleasing to nature and what is noble are sons of God. For it says, 'you are sons of your Lord God.'" Philo certainly does not attack ascribed "blood kinship," but he ranks a kinship based on ethical and religious achievement higher. Paul denies that kinship can be achieved by ethical attainment while ranking adoptive kinship by God's plan higher than blood kinship, although he incorporates the blood lineage of Abraham into the higher and more encompassing principle of kinship by God's creative plan and power.

10 A Warning & a Promise to Gentiles
(Chapters 9-11)

Chapters 9–11 have often been an anomaly in traditional understandings of Romans. F. W. Beare's evaluation of 9–11 reflects the position of many interpreters: "We have left out of consideration three chapters (9–11) of this letter, chiefly because they do not form an integral part of the main argument. They are a kind of supplement in which Paul struggles with the problem of the failure of his own nation. We cannot feel that the apostle is at his best here, and we are inclined to ask if he has not got himself into inextricable (and needless) difficulties by attempting to salvage some remnant of racial privilege for the historic Israel—Israel 'according to the flesh'—in spite of his own fundamental position that all men are in the same position before God."[1] The view of Romans as a treatise about justification by faith (1:18–8:39) with one appendix about Israel's unbelief (9–11) and another on ethics (12–15:13) has begun to lose adherents in recent years. Only a few, however, have been so bold as Krister Stendahl and J. Christiaan Beker, who argue in different ways that 9–11 constitutes a climax to the letter.[2]

Most commentaries outline chapters 9–11 according to the following scheme described but not approved by Nils Dahl:

1. The failure of Israel is not incompatible with God's promises because in his absolute sovereignty God is free to elect and to reject whomever he wills. (Romans 9)

2. The "hardening of the hearts" is due to the Jews' own guilt; their lack of faith is at fault. (Romans 10, or 9:30–10:21)

3. The current situation, the Jewish rejection of Christ, will not last forever; at the end, God will show mercy and save all Israel (Romans 11).[3]

Paul is thus understood to provide three basically independent answers to the problem of Jewish unbelief in Christ.[4]

Both the place of 9–11 in the letter as a whole and the relation of the three chapters to each other have become key questions in scholarship on Romans.

I have argued that Rom 1–8 does not treat the source and psychology of sin and salvation for a human being but rather God's gracious redemption and sanctification of the gentile peoples, who have become heirs to ancient promises made through Israel (for example, Abraham, Jesus, Paul). While developing this positive argument, Paul also opposes Jews who would attempt to redeem gentiles by teaching them parts of the law. Even in this broad generalization, 9–11 fits with the earlier chapters. Both parts speak of God's punishing, rewarding, promising, and choosing of peoples, Israel, and the gentile peoples. The two parts also cohere in much more specific ways. Above all, Paul's discussion with the Jewish teacher in 2:17–4:23 anticipates chapters 9–11. In 2:17–4:23, the apostle explains how God has extended his righteousness to the gentile nations. The teacher's presence in the discussion raises the question of Israel's role in his extension of mercy to the gentiles. He is a caricature and the most extreme example of that for which Paul criticizes his fellow Jews in 9–11. Paul clearly does not generalize one element of the characterization in 2:17–29 to a larger number of Jews in 9–11. He does not accuse "disobedient" Jews of immorality and moral inconsistency as he does the teacher.

In other ways, however, 2:17–5:11 anticipates 9–11. Paul's kinsmen have a true zeal for God (10:2) and the law (9:30–31). The interlocutor knows and teaches the law proudly, (2:17–23) boasting in God (2:17). Instead of accepting God's way of extending his righteousness on the basis of Abraham's and Jesus' faithfulness, Jews have insisted that gentiles perform works of the law (9:30–32; 10:3–4). The teacher seeks to save gentiles by instructing them in certain works from the law (2:19–23) but succeeds only in causing gentiles to blaspheme God (2:24). Rom 9:30–10:21, like 2:17–3:9, contains one basic criticism of some Jews: They have failed in their mission as a light to the gentiles.[5] Prefaced by 2:6–16, 2:25–29 warns the teacher that God treats Jews and gentiles impartially. Paul reiterates the principle of impartiality to the teacher in 3:9–20, 22–23, 29–30 and uses it as a basis for arguing that God has extended his righteousness to the gentiles. Similarly, in 10:11–13, Paul says that God will bless all who call upon him and not Jews alone, since God is impartial.

The teacher, worrying over the implications of God's strict impartiality, asks about the value of circumcision, of being a Jew (3:1). Paul answers, "much in every way." Chapters 9–11 are prefaced by a list that displays the value of Israel's relation to God (9:4–5). If God will punish and reward Jews and gentiles impartially, what will happen to Israel when some have been unfaithful

(3:2–4)? First, God will be faithful (*pistis*) to his promises in spite of human unfaithfulness. Israel will flourish and be blessed as God has promised. Second, God must continue to punish those Jews who sin. Otherwise he would not be just (3:5–9). Chapter 9 raises the question, "Has the word of God failed?" (9:6). The whole of 9–11 treats this question. The answer is the same as in 3:2–9: "The gifts and the call of God are irrevocable" (11:29); "All Israel will be saved" (11:26). God nevertheless breaks off some branches because some Jews have been disobedient (11:17, 19–24). In 3:2, some Jews have been unfaithful because they have failed their trust in regard to the "oracles of God" (3:2). I will argue that 9:30–10:21 also criticizes Jews for failing in this responsibility toward gentiles. Paul's contrast between justification by faithfulness and justification by works of the law should be understood in the context of this criticism. Many Jews have offered gentiles works of the law rather than the good news of Christ's faithfulness. In this light, it should come as no surprise that the language of works, faithfulness, and justification is concentrated in the discussion with the teacher (3:3, 4, 20, 21–31; 4:2–6, 9, 11, 13–25; 5:1, 9) and in 9:30–10:17. Similarly, the language of promise and covenant occurs only in chapters 4 and 9–11 (4:11–12, 13–14, 16, 20–21; 9:4, 8, 9; 11:27). A massive correspondence of arguments, themes, vocabulary, and concerns occurs between 2:17–5:11 and 9–11. Paul does not think that the gentile future can be divorced from the Jewish future. By presenting gentile salvation in a discussion with the teacher and then returning to Jewish unbelief in 9–11, Paul interrelates the two without eliminating the difference. In addition, believing gentiles must learn the correct attitude toward Jews.

The Literary Audience

Romans discusses the salvation of Jews and gentiles alike. Yet the whole letter, even 9–11, directs itself toward gentile readers. In contrast to what we might suspect was in Paul's mind or deduce from the supposed composition of the Roman church, the audience constructed by the text itself is gentile. Paul speaks so explicitly on this point that there should be no need to argue it. Chapters 1–8 provide no place for the introduction of Jewish Christians or generic Christians, and Paul again makes his audience explicit in 11:13: "Yes I am speaking to you gentiles; yet inasmuch as I am the apostle to the gentiles, I glorify my ministry, that somehow I might make my kinsmen jealous." Paul here does not turn to address a portion of the church. Rather, 11:13 describes the audience as a whole. Readers have been poorly served by translations which make it appear that Paul turns from the church as a whole or from Jewish Christians to gentile Christians. The *RSV* has, "Now I am speaking to you gentiles" and makes verse 13 begin a new paragraph. The Greek, which has *de,* does not justify the idea, "now at this point in the discourse." Liddell and Scott's second meaning for *de* clearly holds also for 11:13: "It often serves merely to pass from one thing to another, when it may be rendered *and, further.*"[6] In good diatribal style, vv. 11, 12, and 13–14 contain three closely related thoughts which, however, are not well coordinated or subordinated grammatically. The verses read almost like a list of related ideas. This is the classical condition for the appearance of the *de* about which Liddell and Scott speak. Thus 12 and 13 begin with the same particle.

Translators and commentators have frequently failed to show that "I am speaking to you gentiles" relates closely to the rest of v. 13 and to v. 14. Here the significance of the combined particles *men oun* has not been properly understood. Most commonly, translators and commentators treat the words as so-called colorless connective particles that do not affect the reading.[7] Others take *oun* in its typical sense of "therefore" and explain *men* by suggesting that a coordinate *de* is missing owing to some sort of anacoluthon. But lacking a *de* to answer the *men,* the two particles should coalesce, as they do in 9:2 and 10:18. Then *men oun* must be taken adverbially with an adversative or corrective force, as it has elsewhere in the New Testament. Indeed, *menoun* reads most naturally in 11:13 in the context of the paratactic diatribal style in which Paul asks and answers questions (11:11; cf. 11:1, 2, 4, 15) and provides affirmations and replies. A very important use of *menoun* occurs in dialogue and the imitation of conversational style: in these contexts, *menoun* indicates an adversative or corrective reply to something that has just been said.[8] Paul uses it exactly in this way in 9:20: "You will say to me, 'why does he still blame us?' . . ." "But [*menoun*] who are you, mister, to talk back to God?" In chapter 11, Paul asks and answers his own questions without creating another persona until 17–24, when he speaks to the personified olive branch. The meaning of 11:13–15 may be paraphrased as follows: "Yes, I am addressing you gentiles in this letter *but* you should understand that my very ministry to the gentiles has direct relevance to the salvation of my fellow Jews and their salvation to your own." The part of the sentence set in contrast by *menoun* corrects any mistaken impression that the discussion of Israel's future has no place in this letter so wholly addressed to gentiles and the gentile situation. Paul goes on to argue that the futures of Israel and the gentile peoples are interrelated (11:15–16, 30–32; cf. 11:12). At the same time, 11:13 makes it transparently clear that the letter addresses itself only to gentile believers.

This explicit statement indicating the letter's gentile audience seems to have caused difficulties for ancient editors. The *menoun* with *de* after *hymin* makes it almost impossible to understand Paul as turning to one group within the letter's audience (the gentile portion) rather than to the letter's audience as a whole. And yet some ancient interpreters, with their exclusivistic and universalistic understanding of the church, persisted in seeing Paul now turning to the gentile component of the church or in assuming that Christianity was in fact, if not in theory, a gentile phenomenon. Numerous variant readings for the particles in v. 13 reflect this difficulty.[9] These readings are too varied and too complex to discuss in detail, but I can mention one instance. Some manuscripts read *gar* instead of *de* and omit *menoun* altogether (DEFG and some minuscules).[10] This variant suggests that someone tried to read 13 as an explanation for verses 11–12. Paul could more easily (but still with difficulty) be understood to say that he speaks to the gentile part of the congregation. If Rufinus's Latin translation accurately reflects the Greek, then both Origen and Chrysostom read *gar* and *men* but have no *oun* (PG 14.14.1187; PG 60.9.587). For Origen, the whole letter frequently alternates between addressing Jewish and gentile Christians or even unbelieving Jews and gentiles. Thus he reads 11:13 as another turning to gentile Christians. For Chrysostom, on the other hand, Christians are in fact gentiles, the Jews having rejected Christ and been rejected by God, although in theory there could be Jewish Christians. Chrysostom explains that Paul employs a rhetorical play with a consolatory purpose in chapter 11. Even as he expresses Jewish guilt and rejection by God in contrast to gentile acceptance, he wants to keep the Jews from being utterly crushed. Chrysostom reads Romans in a strikingly anachronistic manner, supposing the gentile triumphalism of his own day.

Even commentators who note that Paul speaks of Jews only in the third person while addressing gentiles directly equivocate. Typically, they say that 11:13 and similar texts show that the Roman church had a gentile majority. W. Sanday and A. C. Headlam write, "This verse and the references to the gentiles that follow seem to show conclusively that St. Paul expected the majority of his readers to be gentiles."[11] But could the supposition of a Jewish Christian minority be made on the basis of Romans alone? I think not. Buried in that supposition lies the belief that Jews can find salvation only in the Christian church. The great historical challenge to exegetes comes in finding a way to read chapters 9–11 that takes the text's literary audience seriously and does not import anachronistic understandings of the church and Jewish Christians.

The Literary Author

Not only the literary audience or implied reader but also the authorial persona demands attention. The authorial voice takes a dramatically new form in 9–11. One must recognize that author and audience are rhetorical strategies. No one will ever know how much the Paul of the letter corresponds to the mind of the real Paul or how much the audience of the letter corresponds to the real audience. Even if Paul knew the believing gentile community at Rome intimately, which is unlikely, the audience in the letter is a rhetorical construction, a textual strategy meant to persuade and affect.

The author and audience (or reader) show two faces of the same rhetorical strategy in traditional epistolary literature. In order to understand 9–11, the interpreter should have a good sense of this strategy unfolding in 1–8. Romans displays a first-level audience that always remains plural, an implied community of reader-hearers. We naturally equate this audience with those who will hear the letter read in Rome. I call it first level because the inscribed authorial voice addresses itself to these readers, even if only by implication, throughout the letter. The whole letter addresses the first-level reader-hearers, but in many places the text also inscribes another addressee, such as one of the imaginary interlocutors.

The salutation and thanksgiving thrust the first-level audience into the foreground. Here the apostle to the gentiles speaks to a certain community of gentiles, sounding the voice of divine authority and care for the audience he will also visit in person. After the transition in 1:16–17, the voice of friendly ethos disappears and the voice of authority remains. The first-level audience fades into the background and reemerges only in 4:23–8:39. The style of impersonal pronouncement about gentile civilization causes the first-level audience of the prescript to disappear and opens the way for a clearly defined second-level audience in the person of the gentile interlocutor in 2:1–16. The authorial voice becomes that of a messenger from God admonishing gentiles. The color of the apostolic persona also fades into an impersonal voice of authority, except for 2:16, where "my gospel" appears. The same proves true for the author's voice in 2:17–4:22, where the second-level addressee is a Jewish teacher. The authorial persona remains that of the apostle who speaks of "my gospel" but stripped of the epistolary ethos. In 1:18–5:22 as a whole, the authorial persona is not that of a Jew or a gentile but of a prophetic admonisher of Jews and gentiles and a spokesman for God's righteousness and gentile rights. Only in 3:5–9 is there some suggestion that the author identifies himself with Jews. Here Paul plants seed that will explode fully into life when Paul the Hebrew of the Hebrews steps out, stripped of all masks, in chapters 9–11. In 4:23–5:11, the discourse begins to change from earlier in the letter. The authorial voice includes itself with the first-level gentile audience as it addresses that audience. The next section, 5:12–20, forms another impersonal interlude, but the authorial voice of the prescript and the first-level audience begin to come more strongly to the foreground in 6–8 as the author continues to identify himself with the experience of the gentile who is in Christ. Whereas the first-level audience only overhears "Paul the apostle" speaking to others in 2:1–4:22, in chapters 6–8 he speaks directly to them as one who identifies with their experience. The exception is 7:7–25, in which an anonymous voice of gentile experience speaks from the first-level audience. This soliloquy ends in 8:1–2 when the apostle steps forward to address the anonymous gentile persona.

An adequate reading must include the realization that the most fully developed authorial persona appears in chapters 9–11. Here the reader meets Paul the apostle to the gentiles speaking to gentile believers. Chapters 9–11 richly inscribe both the first-level audience and the author of 1:1–15. Instead of the rather remote, abstract voice of authority found in many earlier parts of the letter, one hears the voice of epistolary friendship first constructed in 1:1–15. Dahl has demonstrated that the "epistolary style" shows itself more clearly in 9–11 than in 1:17–8:39.[12] By epistolary style, Dahl means the letter's conventions of writing as if friends were conversing in each other's presence. Dahl's points include the following:

1. Chapters 9–11 are characterized by personal address from Paul to the Romans. He addresses them as "brothers" (10:1; 11:25), using even an epistolary disclosure formula (I want you to understand, brothers) at 11:25.[13]

2. The statement that he does not lie (9:1) and the oathlike assurances of his conscience in the Spirit correspond to "epistolary sections" in his letters (2 Cor 11:10; Gal 1:20; Rom 1:8; 2 Cor 1:12, 23; Phil 1:8).

3. Parallels to his assurances and his intercession in 9:1–5 are to be found in opening sections of his letters.[14]

4. "I bear witness to them" in 10:2 is a common expression of recommendation for a third party in letters.[15]

5. Paul speaks of his vocation in 9–11, and elsewhere he mentions it only in the "epistolary opening and conclusion of the letter" (1:1–6, 9–15; 15:15–21; cf. 10:15, 17; 11:13f.).

One could add to Dahl's observations. Greek letter writing theory taught that friends should share their whole personalities, including their emotions, in letters. As Paul's ethos comes to life in 9–11 so does his pathos.[16] The highly charged introduction in 9:1–5 sets the tone for the whole section and for the rest of the letter. Friends were also supposed to be frank in criticizing others but to soften admonition by making it indirect.[17] Indirect admonition played an important role in letter writing.[18] Paul follows just such conventions in 11:13–32 when he criticizes his gentile audience.

The frequency of usage of the first person in 9–11 shows just how much the authorial voice changes there. The first person used of Paul, the first-level speaker, appears fifteen times in 1:1–17. It occurs only seven times in 1:18–8:39 (2:16; 3:5, 7; 6:19; 7:1, 4; 8:18), and two of these are asides in which Paul comments that he is speaking in human terms (3:5; 6:19). In chapters 9–11, the first person refers to Paul twenty-seven times.[19] As striking as these numbers are, they do not reveal the significance of the authorial persona developed in 9–11. The authorial voice of 4:23–8:39 differs from the voice of 1:18–4:22 that is dominated by discussions with fictitious interlocutors. In 4:23–8:39, the first person plural predominates. Here the speaker identifies with the first-level epistolary audience (especially in 4:23–5:11; 6:1–7:6; 8:3–39). The speaker is Paul, the writer introduced in 1:1–16, but that persona is minimally developed, with one exception: Paul identifies himself with the religious experience of the gentile audience. He has had the same kind of experiences in Christ that they have had. It is "we who are justified" (5:1), "we who have been baptized into Christ" (6:2), "we were living in our passions of sin" (7:5), and "we who walk by the Spirit" (8:5). To the gentile, Paul has become a gentile (cf. 1 Cor 9:19–23). Paul's gentile identification proves understandable in light of his doctrine of adaptability.[20]

The unexpectedness and pathos of the new authorial persona in 9–11 strikes as a rhetorical tour de force. When Paul returns to the first person singular and fills out the authorial ethos and pathos, he turns out to be a Hebrew of the Hebrews. Even his mission to the gentiles turns out to be an episode in the self-story of an Israelite acting for the sake of his people. Here the importance of Paul's expression of willingness to give up his life in Christ for the sake of the Jewish people has been vastly underrated by Christian exegetes. Commentators who customarily read the apostle's words with literal credulity now see a slightly cynical exaggeration or have him making a totally empty wish.[21] The ancient reader could not have missed the powerful theme of self-sacrifice for one's people so ubiquitous in the literature of Greece and Rome and so vital in later Judaism. As most commentators have noticed, the passage sounds a paradigmatic echo of Moses pleading with God to have his name erased form the book of life in exchange for the salvation of the people of Israel (Ex 32:32; Num 11:15). Nothing in the Pauline corpus prepares the reader for this. Paul often speaks to his gentile communities about his suffering for their benefit in the likeness of Christ's suffering.[22] But here he would forfeit life in Christ for the sake of his fellow Jews.

At crucial points, the author punctuates the discussion with self-references that develop this persona. The voice that identified with gentile experience in chapters 5–8 now even more powerfully identifies itself as Jewish, as if Paul were saying, "Yes, I, the apostle to the gentiles, am truly as a gentile in Christ and have shared their experience but you must understand that the irreducible core of my identity making my apostleship a reality is that I am a Jew, a member of God's people Israel." Thus in 10:1, he renews the petition of 9:1–3, "Brethren, my heart's desire and prayer to God for them is that they may be saved." He also stands as a witness to their zeal (10:2). In 10:19 one meets an expression unprecedented in the letter. Instead of the voice of an interlocutor or of Paul and an interlocutor (for example, "what shall we say?"; "you will say"), the apostle introduces rhetorical questions with "I say" (*lego*) in 10:19; 11:1; 11:11; 11:13:

- But I say, did Israel not understand? (10:19)
- I say, then, has God rejected his people? Not at all! I myself am an Israelite . . . (11:1)
- I say, has their stumble resulted in a fall? Not at all!
- Yes I am speaking to you as gentiles but however inasmuch as I am an apostle to the gentiles I glorify my ministry hoping somehow that I might make my own kinsmen jealous, and I might save some of them (11:13–14).

The "I" here is the person in 9:3 who would be cut off from Christ for the sake of his fellow Jews. Paul impersonally joins gentile believers in the first person plural in chapters 5–8, but here a bold and forceful ego appears. That ego remains at the core Jewish. His words leave no doubt about his ultimate commitment to the Jewish people and his confidence in their future. He indeed is an instrument in their salvation. The reader meets one kind of Jew in 2:17–29 and another kind in chapters 9–11. As it turns out, the letter does not contrast Jews and gentiles but Jews who represent opposing solutions to the gentile problem. Chapters 9–11 contain the climax, in terms of both ethos and pathos, of the authorial persona in the letter. To ignore this is to risk an egregious misreading of the letter. Paul recognizes (15:15) that he has forged a bold rhetorical strategy in first arguing for gentile rights against a Jewish interlocutor (1:18–5:11) and identifying with the experience of gentile redemption in Christ (6:1–8:39) but then revealing that the heart and soul of this man for the gentiles is Jewish. No matter how much Jonah might commit himself to the reformation of the Ninevites, his heart lies with the people of Israel, and his work would lack sense if that people were destroyed.

Strategies for Reading Chapters 9-11

Ecumenically minded Christian interpreters of today argue for better Jewish-Christian relations by stressing Paul's unambiguous statements about

Israel's election and salvation in chapter 11.[23] By various strategies they subordinate chapters 9 and 10 to chapter 11. Good reasons exist for not subordinating chapter 11 to chapter 9 in the way that traditional readings do, but the ecumenists prove too facile and jump too easily from the text to the valorization of normative ecumenical theologies. Other scholars continue to advance and elaborate the traditional Christian readings. Typically they ignore the plain sense of 9:1–5 and use 9:6–10:4 to explain away Paul's insistence on Israel's continuing election in chapter 11. Although few maintain the grossly artificial attempts to spiritualize the term "Israel" to mean the "church" or the "truly elect" in chapters 10 and 11, many still read the references to Israel, Pharaoh, and the patriarchs allegorically or typologically in chapter 9. This move is absolutely necessary. The traditional readings cannot be sustained without introducing the distinction between the empirical or physical Israel and the true or spiritual Israel. For these interpreters, 9:6–18 serves to introduce this crucial distinction. Most readers, including ecumenists, suppose that Paul has already critiqued Judaism in chapters 2, 3, and 7. Many assume that he has already denied the validity of Judaism as a religion in these chapters. On my reading, no such critique is to be supposed as one begins to read chapter 9. If one does not assume this challenge to Israel's validity from earlier in the letter, chapter 9 reads quite differently from traditional interpretations.

Heikki Räisänen has skillfully exploited this division among interpreters that has placed too much tension on the integrity of 9–11.[24] Räisänen defends the traditional, orthodox reading, but with a twist. First, he provides the nuances and qualifications that modern biblical and theological scholarship has applied to the traditional reading. Second, he highlights the striking contradictions intrinsic to but suppressed in traditional readings. The major contradiction is that in chapters 9 and 10 Paul supposedly denies Israel salvation because it fails to believe in Christ, while in 11 he holds that all Israel will be saved because of God's promises. Because Räisänen's discussion constitutes a spirited defense of the most up-to-date version of the traditional reading, I will compare his with mine at a number of points.

Like all traditional readings, Räisänen's is blind to the letter's rhetorical audience, imagining a primitive version of "the church" consisting of Jewish Christians and gentile Christians that resides both out there in Rome and in the letter. Also typically, the exhortations to gentile readers not to become arrogant in light of Israel's misstep (11:17–25) virtually disappear in Räisänen's reading. He says nothing about Paul's warnings against arrogance over against Jews but only that "gentiles are admonished to remain in faith so that they will not be broken off too."[25] In light of Paul's heightened persona and epistolary address, which draws the reader's attention vividly and concretely to the audience (11:13–25) for the first time since the prescript, I take the admonition to be a climactic moment in the letter's rhetoric. The importance of 11:13–25 increases with the realization that 2:1–5 anticipates its warning.

Räisänen's approach to chapter 9 can stand in illuminating contrast to Lloyd Gaston's. Gaston writes,

> How is it that people can say that chapter 9 deals with the unbelief of Israel when it is never mentioned, and all human activity, whether doing or believing, whether Jewish or gentile, is expressly excluded from consideration? How can people say that Paul teaches the divine rejection of Israel in chapter 9 when he later expressly says the opposite (11:1)? How can people say that the purpose of 9:6–13 is to declare that Israel is not defined by physical descent from the patriarchs when Paul later says that "as regards election they [= all Israel] are beloved for the sake of the patriarchs" (11:28)? How has Romans 9 been turned into an anti-Jewish polemic?[26]

Surely no one can doubt that 9–11 has been used to beat Jews over the head. Readers suppose that the section not only describes God's rejection of the Jews but also denounces the depravity of Jewish religion. Traditional readings often hit Judaism with a catch-22. On the one hand, they condemn Jews for being people who think they can live purely on God's grace based on his word of election without regard for the weightier matters of religion (9:6–29). On the other hand, Jews are deprecated for supposedly believing that they can earn God's reward by their good works and religious effort (9:30–10:4). Gaston rightly rejects such nonsense.

For Gaston, 9:6–30 treats the inclusion of the gentiles (9:24–25) and not the rejection of any Jews. It contains a critique of the church. According to Gaston, Paul makes the point that Israel's election does not find its basis in works or faith but only in God's call, while the gentiles were, in the past, the people not called. Gentiles have no right to voice complaint about not being called in the past. Gaston reads chapter 9 with the statements about Israel's irrevocable call in view from chapter 11 but unlike traditional readers deemphasizes the statements in chapter 11 about Israel's disobedience.

Räisänen does just the opposite: "In v. 6a, Paul undertakes to refute the claim that God's word should have failed. Such an allegation must somehow result from what Paul says in vv. 1–5. What else could have caused it, except the fact that Israel has rejected the gospel and thus forfeited salvation?"[27] The last sentence proves to be the key to Räisänen's and the tradition's construction. "Salvation" is a track that carries a freight load into the text. Salvation, however, can imply quite different narratives of human dilemma and divine activity. The following are three of the possibilities:

1. All humans, Jews, and gentiles have a moral-ontological flaw. Humans can be saved from this sin only by believing in Jesus Christ, who was incarnated or died or both in order to make possible a remedy to sin and death.

2. God has sent Jesus Christ to be Israel's king or prophet or priest (or all three) in order to save her from the oppression and corruption brought about by foreign domination and her own failures. Only those Israelites who are loyal to God's agent will be saved from God's wrath and included in Israel's restoration. [Israel's renewal signals the end of this evil age when God will also turn the gentiles to him through his agent Jesus Christ and bring about blessings that belong to the promised age.]

3. In the current generation, a substantial portion of God's chosen people (that is, Israel) as a whole, although not every individual, has been unfaithful and disobedient to God and can find salvation from God's just anger only if they repent and once again become faithful to him. [To be specific they have rejected God's plan for restoring Israel and making the gentiles into a holy people.]

Räisänen implies something like the first option when he says that Israel has "forfeited salvation." This narrative approximates the traditional orthodox economy of salvation. I have argued that one misreads to find this economy of salvation in chapters 1–8. The other two options, I believe, come closer to the mark. If we omit the bracketed sentence from the third option, we have words that Elijah, Isaiah, Jeremiah, or Ezekiel could have uttered. The Hebrew Bible tells many stories about times when the leaders and a large number of the people acted unfaithfully under particular conditions. These are always stories of salvation. Some of the faithful remain, and God finds a way to use the remnant to bring Israel back to him. There is never a serious question of God abandoning the covenant and revoking his promises to Israel.

Paul casts his persona so as to echo two of these paradigmatic narratives of Israel's salvation. In 9:1–5, he likens himself to Moses after the golden calf incident. Because of Moses' faithfulness, God saves Israel as a whole after meting out punishment for her unfaithfulness. Paul belongs to the remnant, in 11:1–6, like the seven thousand who remained faithful when Israel turned to Baal worship under Ahab and Jezebel. The remnant in the thought of the Hebrew Bible and later Judaism is often understood as God's way of guaranteeing that Israel will be preserved.[28] One introduces an anachronism by equating the remnant with Jewish Christians, if by the latter one supposes the first scheme of salvation. In the first scheme of salvation, Jewish Christians are people who have abandoned one religious system for another, even if they remain ethnically Jews and keep customs that have nothing to do with their salvation. Rather, the remnant much more resembles Israelites who rallied around Elijah and his movement to restore Israel to the true worship of God. The idea of the salvific remnant allows Paul to present himself to his readers in such a bold and startling fashion as a leading agent in Israel's salvation (11:11–15). If these gentiles had entertained any mistaken notion that Paul's law-free gospel implied the abolition of Judaism, then 9–11 would have sharply dashed such misapprehensions.

Räisänen reads chapter 9 as a version of the traditional allegory of gentile Christianity replacing Judaism. Pharaoh, Ishmael, and Esau represent the majority of Jews who find out that they never were elected by God. For Gaston these represent gentiles. Gaston refuses to go along with the tradition in seeing a correlation between statements about Israel's disobedience in chapter 11 and statements about God's right to elect some and reject others in 9. Truly, chapter 9 says nothing explicit about God not electing the majority of Jews. The discussion in 9:6–23 occurs on a fairly high level of generality, with broad principles about God's sovereign will, hardening of some, and electing of others. Perhaps it does go too far to make Pharaoh and Ishmael types of Israel in Paul's day. Räisänen, however, makes strong criticism of Gaston's view that 9:1–29 does not criticize Israel at all and that 9:30–11:36 criticizes Jews only for failing to support the gentile mission:

> All commentators note that Paul does not explicitly mention the unbelief of Israel with regard to the gospel as the reason for his sorrow and anguish. Lloyd Gaston lays great weight on Paul's silence. Nevertheless, no other reason makes sense. If Israel merely lacks understanding or faithfulness "with respect to the gentile mission," why should Paul have such deep sorrow in his heart? Paul goes even further. In v. 3 he expresses the unreal wish that he could be "accursed [*anathema*] and cut off from Christ" for the sake of his kinsmen. This implies that they must be "in a plight as serious as the one he is willing to enter for their sake." They are anathema. This can only be due to their unbelief when faced with the gospel. Israel's *apistia* is in fact mentioned in 3:3 and 11:20, 23, and her disobedience with respect to Christ is described in 9:30–10:21. In 10:1, Paul refers to his prayers for the salvation of Israel. This presupposes that his kinsmen are for the moment outside the sphere of salvation. Paul's pathos shows that very much is at stake.[29]

Paul's anguish in 9:2, the concept of the remnant in 9:27–28, and the question about Israel not attaining the law (9:30–32), which arises from the preceding discourse, all make it impossible to deny that 9:6–25 has some application to Israel's problem, whatever exactly it is.

Israel's Problem and the Gentile Reader

Just what does 9–11 say in criticism of Paul's contemporary fellow Jews? To avoid begging the question in 9:6–25, I will bracket that text until I have asked the question more broadly of 9–11. Two features of the discussion should not be bracketed. First, one should not ignore the fact that Paul treats Israel's problem as part of a paradox. Jews have not merely disobeyed but gentiles have obeyed; a reversal of all expectations! That 9:6 points to this paradox can be seen from the way in which Paul's broad theological-exegetical discussion in 9:6–23 prefaces a section about the calling of both Jews and gentiles and Israel's failure to attain the law (9:24–33). One who reads with an awareness that Jews and gentiles alike are under discussion throughout 9–11 will be not only better able to relate 9–11 to 1–8, but also not so apt to suppress the theme of God's judgment of both followed by his mercy on both. Paul's formulation is not that gentiles have succeeded where Jews have failed but that the rise and fall of both are interrelated.

Second, Paul often immediately qualifies references to Israel's problem. In chapter 11, he treats the view that God has rejected Israel as a misunderstanding to be corrected. The rhetoric of 11 plays on the assumption that what he has said in 9–10 might lead the reader to the false conclusion that God has rejected Israel, the people called in the promises to the patriarchs. The move of Räisänen, Sanders, and others which contrasts 9–10 to 11 and explains the contradiction as the result of Paul's loss of logical consistency due to his anguish over conflicting convictions fails. It fails utterly because the rhetoric of the text does not bear it out. Chapter 11 is not blind to 9–10, and it does not contain a displacement of logical consistency. Rather, the basic rhetorical pattern repeated on many levels of discourse works through a logical formulation that is roughly as follows: Yes, God's way of acting is X and Israel is Y, while the gentiles are X, *but do not conclude Z*. The admonition in 11:13–32 is not gratuitous. Even the fundamental structure of 9–11 forms a warning to gentiles. This rhetorical structure, with its razor sharp admonitory edge, beautifully mirrors the rhetorical structure of 1:18–2:16 in one important way. The design of both 1:18–32 and 9:6–10:21 invites the proud gentile believer to arrogantly laud the condemnation of those other people who are sinful. Then in the first instance, Paul hits such readers with 2:1–5: "When you judge another, you judge yourself . . . do you despise the richness of God's goodness and forbearance of your own evil . . . if you are not repentant you can still suffer God's just anger."

Chapter 11 functions in a similar way in relation to 9–10. Verses 6–23 of chapter 9 lay out the ways of God's electing, hardening, and showing mercy in a general way. Paul carefully fails to draw explicit links to the current status of Jews. The ambiguity of 9:6 seems calculated. He leaves it to the reader to draw his or her own connections. 9:24–10:21 baits the trap by raising questions about present-day Israel. The remnant becomes a remarkably ambiguous concept in the setting of Paul's trap. Does the remnant mean that only a few "Jewish Christians" like Paul will be saved and the vast majority damned? Has God forever rejected the historical people of Israel? Did the gentiles attain righteousness and Israel fail to attain it (9:30–33)? To what does Paul's prayer "that they might be saved" point? (10:1). He seems to say that they have failed with regard to the gospel (10:2–21). Paul, then, states in his own words just what he has tempted his gentile readers into thinking: "I ask, then, has God rejected his people? By no means!" (11:1). "Have they stumbled so as to fall? By no means!" (11:11). Chapter 11:1–16 makes the gentile reader aware of the presumption of his arrogant and hasty conclusions; 11:17–32 describes and addresses his conceit: "Do not boast over Jews who have been broken off the tree of God's Israel!" (11:18); "remember that the tree's root supports you!" (11:18); "Do not be arrogant about the broken Jewish branches and your own grafting (11:19–20)." "Do not become arrogant but stand in awe"(11:20); "They were broken off by unfaithfulness, you stand by faithfulness. If God did not spare the natural branches, he will not spare you. Recognize God's kindness and severity . . . you too may be cut off. Indeed, those Jews who were broken off will be grafted back, if they do not remain unfaithful" (11:20–23). Here we have the warning given in 2:1–5 except the letter now explicitly reveals the object of gentile superiority: Jews who have in some sense rejected Jesus Christ or the plan to which Jesus Christ is central. In each case, an imaginary interlocutor who represents gentile presumption and arrogance becomes the object of a warning. Even the final mystery that Paul announces in 11:25–36 is not just information but given "lest you be wise in your own conceits." Generations of Christian readers have taken the apostle's bait without ever feeling the spring of the trap.

Interpreters from the second century onward have read chapter 9 in light of the historical knowledge that the vast majority of Jews rejected the supposed new religion of Christ and that the church had become gentile. Paul, on the other hand, views his contemporary situation, in which many Jews have actively opposed the new movement and many more have simply failed to join in its mission, from the perspective of paradigmatic narratives about Israel in the scriptures. In times when Israel was on a course diametrically opposed to God's will, what happened? Paul tries to answer this question from the perspective of God's agency. Not how have the people of Israel acted so as to be faithful, unfaithful, repentant, recalcitrant? But what are the patterns of God's activity whereby he directs history and uses historical forces and actors? The discussion in 9:6–18 takes care of the idea that there is any simple formula for predicting who will be used for what purpose or who will come out on top at what point.

A central point of 9:14–29 is that God's positive and negative choosing should not be judged as unjust because the agents and groups chosen serve God's larger purposes of mercy. The chosen part serves the good of the whole. Pharaoh was hardened so that God's name might be glorified in all the earth (9:17). Paul probably suggests here that without the miracle of the Exodus and the establishment of the land of Israel, the other nations of the earth would not have heard the good news (cf. 15:9–12). Paul does not raise the questions about God's justice in 9:14 and 19 in order to theoretically defend God or even less in order to say that God acts arbitrarily in his sovereignty. On the contrary, the whole discussion in 9–11 supposes that God consistently acts for the greater good of those (Israel and the gentile peoples) to whom he has committed himself by promise. But human observers stand in no position to judge why God acts in the way he does (cf. 11:33–36). Paul connects this theme of God's inscrutable ways to the theme of human works. In the doxology that concludes 9–11, he follows scriptural passages about human inability to know God's purposes with Job 41:3 (LXX): "Who has given a gift to him that he might be repaid." Even the righteous with their best intentions cannot use their own good efforts as a guarantee that God will do things the way that seems best to them. God cannot be bribed, even with works of righteousness. God's choice of Isaac rather than Esau for the Israelite lineage was not made on the basis of their works. Rather he acted in the way that would best fulfill his promises and enact his mercy. Do Jewish teachers and gentile pupils really believe that they can win God's approval and change gentile nature with their lists of works from the law! How dare gentiles think that their faith in Christ and Jewish refusal to believe can change God's mind about his promises to Israel, beloved for the faithfulness of Abraham, Sarah, Isaac, and Jacob (11:28b)!

Paul can tread these murky theological waters so confidently because of his universalism. He himself as the apostle to the gentiles was God's chosen instrument for "the reconciliation of the world." One of Paul's most fundamental convictions was that God had through Jesus Christ at long last revealed his impartial justice by extending his mercy to all the peoples of the earth. In light of that conviction, he confidently views God's seemingly unjust decisions to choose one and harden another as divine acts in service of the future good of all peoples.

It is not a question of ecclesiology: Who belongs to the saved group?

Paul's point is not that Ishmael and Esau were damned. They were not. Rather, Isaac and Jacob were made instruments "so that God's purpose of election might continue" (9:11). God chose one particular lineage for a special task. Paul's logic parallels what anthropologists and natives alike know about unilineal descent groups and to some extent all societies based on lineage. Such lines are never natural or biological but are human creations that must be sustained by adoption and creative genealogy. Offspring of a couple quickly branch into immense trees but never of themselves according to the principles of descent and inheritance that the society follows. Thus reckoning a lineage resembles drawing a straight line through the stars of the night and excluding large numbers whose kinship might have been recognized if the dots had been connected differently. For Paul, of course, God, not humans, draws the lines. And God has the advantage of knowing all the stars and their fates. Thus chapter 9 tells us that one cannot find membership in a lineage by works. Rather, God decides on the lines of descent, and membership in the lineage comes by birth. God can play creative genealogy as he wills, but he does stick to his promises.

Paul admits that the process of making one descent group into God's own family seems unjust. But Paul, unlike many Christian readers, did not think that those outside the chosen group were headed for damnation. They were just members of other families not chosen for a certain relation to God. Moreover, on Paul's reading, one of the chosen family's very purposes was to serve as an instrument through which all families might become children of God. Part of the difficulty in sorting out the sense of 9 stems from the way that the chapter mixes talk of chosen families with talk of chosen individuals. Individuals like Pharaoh or Isaac may serve positive or negative purposes and be praised or condemned. Paul believes that God punishes and rewards individuals by merit. But I see nothing here of whole peoples damned because God so chooses. Chapter 9:24–28 emphasizes that God in the present time has raised instruments of mercy not only from Israel but also from the gentiles. Thus, even if it appears that Israel's future is as dim as that of Sodom and Gomorrah, such destruction will not come to pass (cf. 9:29). "And so all Israel will be saved" (11:26) does not come as a surprise or, as Räisänen would have it, as a shocking contradiction to chapter 9. Rather, that claim forms a neat deduction from the logic of divine purpose and human instruments in chapter 9. Räisänen cannot see this because he, along with most, assumes that Paul taught a new system of salvation for humans.

The crucial texts about the call of the gentiles and God's use of remnants in 9:24–29 have been turned on their head in Christian exegesis. Recent work has shown that Paul was presenting no novelty in viewing the remnant as an instrument of Israel's salvation, but that he was following patterns typical of later Jewish scriptural interpretation.[30] The translations, however, subtly slant the text toward the traditional reading. In introducing Isa 10:22 (9:27), for instance, the *RSV* reads, "Isaiah cries out concerning Israel." The informed reader supposes that "concerning" translates *peri*; a very neutral description of what Isaiah is doing. But Paul's Greek is *hyper* with the genitive. The lexicon yields as appropriate translations, "for, in defense of, on behalf of." One would never know from the *KJV*, *RSV*, or *NEB* translations that Isaiah speaks an oracle of God's ultimate mercy. The fact that *hyper* can on very rare occasions be used in a way that seems to approximate *peri* should not rule against the larger context of 9:27, which makes natural the normal use of *hyper*.[31] The parallel quotation from Isa 1:9 makes it clear that the message is "judgment followed by restoration." The few now will lead to the survival of the whole. The LXX translator of Isaiah goes so far as to identify the remnant as all those Jews in the whole world who are the audience of God's word.[32] The conclusion drawn in Isa 10:24–25 is, "Therefore says the Lord of hosts, do not fear, my people . . . for my anger will cease in a little while." Yes, God is angry with Israel, but because the covenant depends on God's promise and not on Israel's works, the days of anger and punishment will be followed by the salvation of all Israel. The quotation from Isaiah evokes images and narratives of God's past deliverance of Israel in times when the nation went astray.

Again, the English translations proffer a misreading when they add "only" to Paul's citation of Isa 10:22: for example, "only a remnant of them will be saved" (*RSV*). One finds no "only" in Paul's Greek text. The traditional understanding of Paul's scriptural usage has been decisively shaped by Christian ecclesiology and soteriology. But attempts to make Paul's language of remnant become the category "Jewish Christians" misconstrues the discourse. In the apostle's hands, "the remnant" becomes a trope for signs of Israel's salvation in times of doom. Thus Paul can speak as if he himself is the final guarantee that the Jews have a future with God: "I myself am an Israelite" (11:1). Case settled! This is a hard saying for the traditional reader: "If I am genuine, then no doubt can exist; Israel will be saved." When God called Abraham, God's promise guaranteed the future of a people.

The next section, 9:30–10:4, introduces one of the letter's overriding concerns: Jews like the teacher of gentiles in 2:17–29 have misunderstood the goal of the law and tried to substitute their own way of making things right for God's way. The Jew in 2:17–29 believes that he can make the gentiles into righteous people by teaching them to follow commandments from the Decalogue. Paul replies, "You cannot even make yourself righteous." Israel has enough problems of her own. As the patterns of God's activity recounted in

9:6–29 show, Israel's own future cannot be guaranteed by her works but only by God's grace. How much less ought Jews think that they can transform the gentile peoples by means of their own works. What made this situation so tragic for Paul was that, in his view, God had extended the very righteousness or justice for which Jews were working as a gift in the faithfulness of Jesus Christ: "They have a zeal for God but it is unenlightened" (10:2).

Recent scholarship has shown the lack of justification for treating 9:30–10:4 as a contrast between the legalistic religion of Jewish lawkeeping and the spiritual religion of faith in Christ.[33] Sam K. Williams has shown that the "righteousness of God" is not used in Romans as either a broad concept of God's own righteousness or of the righteousness that God gives to humans.[34] Rather, it specifically concerns God being faithful to the Abrahamic promise that the gentile nations would be blessed. Moreover, "faith" in 9:30, 32 is not the believer's but Christ's faithfulness, on which God based the fulfillment of his promise.[35]

Somewhat inchoate agonistic imagery underlies the discussion in 9:30–10:4.[36] The development of the metaphor lacks just enough clarity that reading the text variously exercises the imagination. Is the metaphor of an athletic competition, perhaps a race with two contestants? Is it some other form of struggle or competition? The obscurity of the imagery stems partly from the paradoxical nature of the analogy. Israel "chased after" (*diōkein*) righteousness, but the gentiles, who did not even enter the contest, "were first to arrive" (*phthanein*) at the goal. At some points, the language also suggests two lovers and their beloved. Hosea and the Song of Songs come to mind, and the language epitomizes Greek love poetry and romance. Israel is "zealous" for its "ultimate objective," God (10:1–3), and "chases after" God and God's law but does not "obtain" its object. Instead, God takes another for himself, the gentiles. In 11:11 (cf. 10:19) Paul will bring the gentile reader back to earth by revealing that God chose the gentiles in order to make Israel jealous. Although writing on a different topic, Anne Carson pinpoints the dynamics of the metaphor:

> The word 'jealousy' comes from Greek *zelos* meaning 'zeal' or 'fervent pursuit.' It is a hot and corrosive spiritual motion arising in fear and fed on resentment. The jealous lover fears that his beloved prefers someone else, and resents any relationship between the beloved and another. This is an emotion concerned with placement and displacement. The jealous lover covets a particular place in the beloved's affection and is full of anxiety that another will take it. Here is an image of the shifting pattern that is jealousy, from more modern times. During the first half of the fifteenth century a type of slow pacing dance called the *bassa danza*

became popular in Italy. These dances were semidramatic and transparently expressive of psychological relationships. "In the dance called *Jealousy* three men and three women permute partners and each man goes through a stage of standing by himself apart from the others" (Baxandall 1972, 78).[37]

According to Paul, God turned to the gentiles in order to stir up Israel's jealousy for God. The gentiles have stood alone; now Israel stands alone. It is a story of passion and desire.

The race metaphor, however, proves crucial for understanding the argument. Christ, the *telos* (10:4), is the victory line, the goal, as Robert Badenas has argued, not the termination of the law.[38] I have tried to show that Paul consistently distinguishes Jews from gentiles in Romans. In 9:30–31 he differentiates the goal of the race: gentiles, who did not actually pursue "righteousness," reached that goal first; Jews who ran toward the "law of righteousness" have stumbled and fallen behind the gentiles, not yet reaching their goal. "Law" here means Torah, Israel's constitution, paradigmatic narrative, and body of divine legislation. The text gives not the slightest hint of anything negative about the law, Israel's goal.[39] It is parallel to the gentile goal of righteousness without the law. Paul asks why Israel did not get there first (9:32). It appears that Israel will come in second (11:25–32; cf. 11–15) because she ran believing that her running and winning depended upon her human works. Instead, the Jewish people should have realized from the law itself (cf. 4:1–23; cf. 10:4) that the running and winning of this race depended upon God's and the Messiah's faithfulness.

After fifteen hundred years of Christian theology, we tend as modern readers to overgeneralize the meanings of "works" and "faithfulness" here. The discourse in chapters 3–4, however, bounds their meanings in a quite specific particularity. There the Jewish teacher (2:17–29; cf. 3:1–4:22) tries to please God and fulfill his mission of being a light to the gentiles. He understands the promise to Abraham, "In you shall all the gentiles be blessed" (Gen 12:3), to mean that Jews, as the descendants of Abraham, were to make the gentiles righteous by their own pedagogical efforts. "Works of the law" refers to injunctions that would make gentiles righteous if observed. In 9:32, "works" may mean both the things gentiles were taught to do and the belief that Jews could be faithful to their mission only by working at the education of gentiles. According to Paul, however, the law itself taught that gentiles would be redeemed not by being made to observe the law, but by God's gracious mercy in response to and by means of Jesus Christ's faithfulness (*ek pisteōs*, 9:32).

Romans treats the redemption of the gentiles in light of what Paul perceived as Jewish opposition and indifference. Paul's complaint about his fellow Jews is not that they have depended on ancestry. The principle of ancestral religion is not criticized even in 9:6–13. Interpreters forget that in choosing Isaac over Esau, God was committing his blessings to Isaac's descendants as an act of pure grace. The question concerns only whose descendants will receive the blessing. Neither does he criticize lawkeeping as such. Keeping the law constitutes Israel's relation with God in the covenant. The question in chapter 9, however, concerns the election of peoples by God and the surprising response of Jews and gentiles to God's election of gentiles. "Works of the law" cannot bring about the election of a people. Only God's merciful will can do that. Israel has stumbled but is still in the race. Why did God's people stumble? Because of ignorance (10:2–3). Israel's heart was right (10:2) but her thinking confused. Instead of recognizing God's plan to make the world right through Jesus Christ, Jews have proceeded as if they could bring the world to God through their own plans and efforts.

Paul goes even further in diminishing Jewish culpability for this stumble caused by ignorance.[40] In 11:8, he quotes Deut 29:3 in order to show that God himself has hardened Israel for providential purposes. "Israel failed to reach what it sought after" owing to God's hardening of her heart (11:7). Just in case someone might misunderstand the use of the race metaphor, Paul asks, "Have they stumbled so as to fall? By no means!" Rather, God caused Israel to stumble and the gentiles to overtake her in order to stimulate her to even greater zeal for the competition (11:11 cf. 10:19).

Paul entirely subverts the logic of his own metaphor. Races are about will, effort, achievement, and well-earned rewards. But 9:16 says, "so it depends not on a person's will or a person's running but on God who shows mercy." The race is fixed. God has predetermined the outcome and made the winner someone who did not even enter the contest. Furthermore, he has tripped up the runner who has been out there doing her best all along. The subversion of the metaphor strikingly reveals that Israel's dilemma is tragedy. The subverted metaphor makes it silly or perverse to ask, "How could Israel have run the race so as to have won?"

Those like Räisänen who want to say that chapter 11 contradicts 9–10 have not seen the impact of the fixed race. An appropriate commentary could well be 11:31–32: "So they [Jews] have also now been disobedient in order that by the mercy shown to you [gentiles] they also may receive mercy. For God has imprisoned all in disobedience, that he may show mercy to all." Whatever the identity of the stone of stumbling in 9:33, it is paradoxical. The stone has been put there to trip one of the runners so that both can be declared winners. Paul's warning to gentiles (11:13–32) only makes the implicit explicit.

Gentile believers must not misunderstand the current unresponsiveness of Jews by concluding that there will be only one winner. God is in control, and he will make certain that his righteous mercy, as manifested in his promises to both Israel and the gentiles, prevails. Obedient and disobedient individual actors and groups play roles in the interrelated stories of both peoples, Jews and gentiles. Individuals and groups may rebel and fall, but God will make a future for both peoples as peoples of God.

Does Paul say that the disobedience of Jews consists in their failure to believe in Christ as their personal Lord and Savior? Traditionally the answer is yes. But I believe this traditional affirmation to be a misreading of the first-century historical and literary context of the letter. A good example of the differences between the interpretive tradition and Paul's context can be seen in the case of the expression "the righteousness of God." In 10:3 Paul says, "For being ignorant of God's righteousness and seeking to set up their own righteousness, they did not submit to God's righteousness." "Righteousness" is one of those words that evokes whole economies of salvation for traditional readers. In the West's introspective reading of Paul, "God's righteousness" ultimately became the righteousness that God requires of humans and gives to sinners in his act of forgiving grace. "Righteousness" implies human unrighteousness, humanity's original sin or the sin that humans can overcome only through Christ. The next step is the idea of an adequate satisfaction or expiation for universal sin and so on. At the beginning lies the fall from angelic to human existence.

Strict observance of the principles of modern semantics that James Barr explained for biblical scholars nearly thirty years ago reveals a more specific and more Jewish denotation of "righteousness" and its conceptual associations.[41] The interpreter must begin by realizing that Galatians and Romans consist of narratives, arguments, and figures constructed from webs of intertextual connection. The meaning of each instance of the word "righteousness" is to be determined by the way these narratives, arguments, and figures impinge on the word and its immediate context. All recognize that 1:16–17 constitutes a key text for understanding righteousness in Romans: The righteousness of God is being revealed in the gospel on the basis of faithfulness. The verb *apoka-lyptetai* is the present tense. God's righteousness is being revealed when Paul preaches his law-free gospel to gentiles. The letter makes it clear that Paul really means *his own* gospel, for example, "I am not ashamed" (1:16); God will judge according to "my gospel" (2:16; cf. 1:1–7, 14–15; 15:15–24). Unlike Galatians, which mentions Peter's gospel to the circumcised, Romans is written as if Paul's gospel to the gentiles were the whole ministry of the good news. The verb is also a "divine passive."[42] When Paul goes about preaching this good news to gentiles, God is making his righteousness known through that preaching. We get the English word "apocalyptic" from the Greek word Paul uses. In apocalyptic literature, sages receive visions and revelations of God's plans for the world. As Paul preaches his gospel to the gentiles, God makes known his plans for the world to those who hear. The plan is revealed "out of" or "on the basis of faithfulness" (*ek pisteōs*). As I have shown in discussing 3:30, *ek pisteōs* refers to the covenant-founding faithfulness of Abraham and Jesus. If one could be sure of a messianic reference to the righteous one who lives on the basis of faithfulness in the Habakkuk text (1:17b), the meaning would be even clearer. Verses 16–17 point the historically sensitive reader forcefully toward 3:21–4:22. Again, I appeal to my reading: That section tells of how God has demonstrated his impartial righteousness by redeeming the gentiles.

The point that seals the case is the observation that Paul repeatedly explains the "righteousness of God" by referring to scriptural texts that he believes point to the redemption of the gentiles. In 3:21, "God's righteousness" is explicitly "manifested by the law and the prophets," and chapter 4 shows how the story of Abraham and the promise concerning the gentiles manifests God's righteousness. The long sentence that includes 1:1–5 speaks of the gospel being proclaimed beforehand by the "prophets in the holy scriptures" and explains that Paul has been set apart as an apostle for this gospel to the gentiles. What could be clearer than Gal 3:8: And scripture, having foreseen that God would justify the gentile peoples on the basis of faithfulness, preached the good news beforehand to Abraham, saying, "In you shall all the gentiles be blessed"? Gen 12:3 is the good news! It reveals God's plan to bring the other nations into covenant with him. For Paul, it shows that God is not and has never been prejudiced and unjust in his dealings with the peoples of the world. God has always been working on a plan that would effect his righteousness in spite of human unrighteousness.

How different 10:4–21 reads if we delimit the meaning of "righteousness" by context rather than import an orthodox economy of salvation. Even 1:16 reads differently. Yes, the gospel is the power of salvation for all who believe, for the Jew first and also the Greek (1:16). But for the chosen and the newly chosen, the salvation differs because their historical relation to God differs. If "God's righteousness" means fulfilling the promise to Abraham (Gen 12:3) and thus redeeming the gentiles, then 10:3 says that Jews have failed to understand (*agnoein*) God's plan for the gentiles and have substituted a plan of their own making. Paul's discussion with the Jew in 2:17–4:22 portrays an attempt to dispel his ignorance of God's plan, a plan for which this teacher has substituted works of the law.

"Christ is the goal of the law, for all who believe." But that is not what Paul says in 10:4. He says, "Christ is the goal of the law *with respect to righteousness, for all who believe.*"[43] In other words, "Christ is the goal of the law with respect to God's plan to redeem the gentiles." This meaning should come as no surprise because Paul repeatedly explains the gospel and God's righteousness by referring to the law and its story of the Abrahamic promise to the gentiles. The text that has been thought so unambiguously to proclaim the termination of Judaism and the law actually affirms their continuity together with a scriptural plan for the other peoples through Jesus Christ.

Verses 5–8 offer scriptural witness to Paul's statement in 4: Christ is the fulfillment of the law's promise of God's righteousness toward gentiles. At the cost of enormous exegetical difficulties, 10:5–8 has been read as depicting the opposition between two ways of righteousness; The legalistic works right-eousness of Judaism (characterized in 10:5 by the quotation of Lev 18:5) and the true religion of righteousness by faith (pictured in 6–8 by creative allu-sion to Deut 30:12–14). Commentators have read the verses as a contrast between doing and believing. All exegetes face a major textual problem in verse 5. The reading that places *hoti* after *nomos* is transparently an early attempt of editors to conform Paul's text to Lev 18:5 and Gal 3:12. The majority of recent commentators seem to agree.[44] Verse 5 could then be translated, "For Moses writes, that 'the man who does' the righteousness of the law, 'shall live by it.'"

Paul likely read the words of Moses here as a messianic prophecy.[45] The text predicts that a certain man will have life because he has fulfilled the right-eousness of the law. Paul would then read the second verb, *zēsetai,* as a refer-ence to the resurrection life of Jesus that God bestowed on him because of his faithfulness (*pistis*).[46] Jesus' "righteousness of the law" is another way of describing his faithfulness. Similarly, Phil 2:7 speaks of his "obedience to the point of death." Rom 5:19 explains how "many will be made righteous by the obedience of one man." Paul retains *anthrōpos* in 10:5, as he does not in his use of the quotation in Gal 3:12, because he wants to point to the messianic obe-dience of the one man. Did Paul ever doubt that Jesus' faithful obedience was obedience in conformity with the law? I see no evidence that he did. This read-ing makes 10:5–8 a strikingly apt confirmation (cf. *gar,* v. 4) of 10:4. The law itself points to Christ as the linchpin of God's plan to extend his righteous mercy to the whole world. What makes this reading even more likely is the messianic understanding of the Hab 2:4 quotation in 1:17: "The righteous one shall live on the basis of faithfulness." Paul would have read both Hab 2:4 and Lev 18:5 as prophecies about one man who is truly righteous and faithful. Both texts, using *zēn* (to live) in the future tense, speak of this one receiving "life."

Interpreters usually understand 10:6–8 in contrast to 10:5; the word of Moses versus the word of righteousness by faith.[47] In my reading, 10:6–8 supports and complements 10:5. If 10:4 proclaims that the law points to Christ as the agent of God's righteous plan, and 10:5 provides a supporting prophecy from the law about the Messiah's righteousness, then 10:6 creatively incorporates Deut 30:12–14 into Paul's writing by trope and metonymy. The text contrasts God's plan of righteousness through Christ's faithfulness to the efforts of people who want to do it their way. The phrase "do not say in your heart" from Deut 8:17 and 9:4 signals the theme by allusive intertextual comparison between the situation of ancient Israel and Paul's time: "Do not say in your heart, 'My might and the strength of my hand have gotten me this great power' (Deut 8:17). Do not say in your heart, when the Lord your God has destroyed these gentile peoples from before you, 'It is because of my righteousness that the Lord has led me in to inherit this good land; while it is because of the impiety of these gentile nations that the Lord will destroy them out before you'" (Deut 9:4). It is easy to imagine the way Paul read the story of Israel here so as to see figures of Israel and the gentiles in his own day. In Deut 8:17 and 9:4, the Israelites are warned not to claim that God's gifts were obtained by their achievement or power or were owing to their righteousness. This, of course, recalls 9:30–10:3 and especially "seeking to establish a righteousness of their own, they were not subject to the righteousness of God" (10:3). Paul's writing is a reading of scripture, and, as Robert Scholes says, "Comparison and contrast is not just some sort of academic reflex but a fundamental part of the reading process."[48] The scriptural texts contain metaphors and narratives for thinking about the present and future of Jews and gentiles.

Paul again makes use of prosōpopoiia, personifying righteousness in 10:6. The "righteousness based on faithfulness" speaks the word of warning from Deuteronomy. The prosōpopoiia of abstract concepts was a favorite device among moralists. The *de* in v. 6 is connective, not adversative. Verse 5 describes the Messiah's faithfulness, and 6 extends the discourse by personifying the righteousness that results from the Messiah's faithfulness, warning that the Messiah is not apprehended by great plans and efforts of human design. Paul transposes the words of Moses in Deut 30:12–14 into a lesson about contemporary Israel. The original text reads: "This commandment which I command you today is not too great for you, nor is it far off from you. It is not up in heaven, that you should say, 'Who will ascend for us to heaven, and bring it to us; and we may hear it and do it?' Nor is it beyond the sea that you should say, 'Who will cross the sea for us, and bring it to us; and we may hear it and do it?' The word is very near you; it is in your mouth and in your heart and in your hands, so that you can do it." God has not made the law difficult to keep, an accomplishment achievable only by dint of human sweat and strain. God made his word easily apprehensible so that it can be embodied by the people of Israel. In contrast to what the dominant interpretive tradition has supposed, I am convinced that in 10:4–8 Paul is paralleling and even at points identifying the law with the gospel of God's acts in Jesus Christ.

Verses 6–8 are a way of saying that God's character remains the same as in the time of Moses. If he made the law apprehensible by hearing and open receiving, he also makes the gift of the Messiah promised in the law apprehensible by hearing and receiving. While Jews like the teacher of 2:17–29 are set on bringing about God's righteousness by a massive educational program for the heathen nations, God's own righteousness finds its human agency in the faithfulness of Abraham and Jesus. God has said, "In honor of these faithful servants I will freely extend my transforming mercy to the whole world." Again Paul explains, citing Deut 30:14 with commentary that the giving of the gospel resembles the giving of the law: "'The word of God is near you, in your mouth and in your heart' (Deut. 30:14); that is, the word about [Jesus'] faithfulness which we preach; so that if you confess 'with your mouth' that Jesus is Lord and if you believe 'in your heart' that God raise him from the dead, you will be saved."

The good news that Paul and his associates ("which we preach") bring to gentiles (15:15–24; 11:13; 1:1–7, 13–14) announces the benefits brought about by Jesus' faithfulness. The message requires that gentiles acknowledge God's act of mercy and look to the one who figured forth their new life through his faithful obedience. Paul's allusion to Deut 9:4 suggests that he also saw another parallel. This lesson is implicit in his understanding of the gospel. God tells Israel that he did not bless her because she was righteous and the other nations wicked. Yes, the other nations were indeed wicked, but Israel was not righteous herself. This is the same argument given in the address to the teacher, 2:17–29; 3:1–19. Rather, Israel is blessed with the land because God made promises to Abraham, Isaac, and Jacob (Deut 9:5). The faithfulness of these patriarchs and God's grace have made Israel secure, not her own righteousness. Paul deduced that God would act in the same way when he made the other nations into peoples of his own. What puzzled and troubled Paul was how Jews, the graced people of Israel, could fail to read in scripture and life as he did that God had now acted toward the gentiles as he had once acted toward them. To paraphrase Paul's thought: Why do they act as if they have to climb up to heaven in order to bring the Messiah down, when he is apprehensible in the message about Jesus' faithfulness? "They have a zeal for God but it is unenlightened," he writes in 10:2.

A perusal of the commentaries, I believe, makes it clear that the traditional Christian frame of reference has made a mess of 10:1–13. This, in part, results from an attempt to force its richly figural and playful intertextual allusion into

Christological and soteriological proofs and, in part, from failing to understand the argument: Christ is the law's own answer to how God will "make things right" by showing mercy to the gentile peoples. The following paraphrase, which contains parenthetic pointers to Paul's intertextual allusion to scripture and to aspects of his rhetoric, illustrates the coherence of this reading:

> I pray to God that my fellow Jews might be saved from God's anger. They want to do God's will but they are ignorant about God's plan for making things right. They have tried to work out a plan of their own for making things right instead of accepting God's plan. For Christ is the law's goal with respect to God's plan for making things right, for *all* who believe [not just Israel]. Thus [even in the giving of the law at Sinai] Moses writes [in a figure for Christ] that, 'The Man who has enacted the righteousness which the law teaches will live by it,' (Lev 18:5) And the way of making things right based upon [Christ's] faithfulness says, 'Do not say in your heart, [as in the warning to Israel at Sinai against presuming her own power and rightness instead of God's grace; Deut 8:17; 9:4] who will go down into the underworld' (Deut 30:13) to bring the Christ back from the dead. Rather, what does Moses say in the scriptures, 'The word is near you, on your lips and in your heart' (Deut 30:14). This is a figure for the word about Christ's faithfulness which we [apostles from Israel] preach [to the gentiles]. Namely, Moses' words figure forth our call to confession with the mouth that Jesus is Lord and belief in the heart that God raised him from the dead so that the one who confesses and believes might be saved. For in the heart one believes with respect to things being made right and by the mouth one confesses with respect to salvation. [We know this] because scripture says, "*No one who believes in him shall be put to shame*" (Isa 28:16). For [the basic principle upon which I have argued for gentile equality stands, that is, 2:11; 3:22, 29–30], God makes no distinction between Jew and Greek since he is Lord of *all* and bestows his generosity on *all* who call upon him. For [again scripture says] '*Everyone* who calls upon the name of the Lord will be saved' (Joel 2:32 LXX).

The Christian reading goes in a different direction from Paul's reading because he assumed that God's covenants and promises to Israel were valid, while the traditional Christian reader assumes that they have been annulled and superseded. When it says, "God bestows his generosity on all who call upon him," Paul construes this to mean that the gentiles have now *also* been chosen by grace. For the Christian reader, it means that all Jewish and gentile individuals stand equally before God with all covenants and promises stripped of any salvific significance. All are abstractly naked individuals whose only truly significant characteristic is the stain of primordial sin. Everyone stripped to this equality of sameness, equally has the opportunity to decide for or against salvific belief in Christ. Yet the traditional Christian reading comes hard to chapters 9–11, and critical scholars like Beare are quick to see inconsistency on Paul's part (see above).

In light of what I have argued about the rest of chapter 10, the reading of 14–21 follows with ease. Verses 1–4 suggest Israel's responsibility to preach as a light to the nations. Verses 18–21 raise the historical irony that indeed the gospel has been preached but the nation chosen to preach it did not even understand the message. The gentiles have turned to God without Israel's lead. Verse 19 introduces the jealousy motif so crucial in chapter 11. All of the components for Paul's rebuke of the gentiles and affirmation of Israel's future are to be found in chapters 9 and 10. These chapters project a dark and complex riddle. Chapter 11 solves the riddle and brings light out of darkness. The dark riddle is a snare designed to catch gentiles in their own arrogant presumption. Paul tells them bluntly that the disobedience of Israel arises from God's own plan. The gentile upsurge is a ploy to make Israel jealous, to spur her on even faster toward the finish line. Paul has no doubt that both will celebrate together after the race: "Christ became a servant to the circumcised to demonstrate God's truthfulness, in order to confirm the promises given to the patriarchs, and in order that the gentiles might glorify God for his mercy. As it is written . . . 'Rejoice, O gentiles, with his people' (Deut 32:43).

Reading Chapter 11 with a Foot Race

What has become in traditional Christian exegesis a story of the Jews' hard-hearted disbelief and even, for some, their damnation was for Paul a different story. The story narrated a kind of divine pedagogy. The theme of envy as a stimulus to imitation in Greek literature is too well known to detail. Plato explains why children study the heroic characters of the poets: "Here they meet with many admonitions, many descriptions and praises and eulogies of good men in times past, that the boy in envy [*zelōn*] may imitate them and desire to become even as they" (*Prot.* 326). When Paul asks whether Israel's stumble in the race has caused a fall (11:11), he is suggesting that the gentiles have shockingly misconstrued (*mē genoito*, 11:11) the story. Rather, through Israel's "false step" (*paraptōma*) salvation has come to the gentiles for the purpose of (*eis to -sai*) making Israel jealous. Exegetes have failed to notice that the race metaphor reappears in 11:11–12. Here Paul asks if the stumble, described in 9:32–33 with texts from Isaiah, has caused Israel to fall. This is a significant question. The one who falls down in a race loses. The one who merely stumbles may be able to continue. The quotation from Isa 28:16 makes it clear that God himself laid down the "stone of stumbling in Zion." God caused the stumble in order to make Israel imitate the gentile's zeal and run even harder.

In addition to "tripping" and "falling," other language in 11:11–12 belongs to the race metaphor. Commentators divide over the meaning of *paraptōma*. Some argue that Paul's typical use of it elsewhere for "transgression" must hold for 11:11–12.[49] Others, noting the metaphor of tripping and falling, advocate the more literal meaning of "false step."[50] Apparently no commentators understand that the race metaphor continues from 9:30f. Surely, however, *paraptōma* in 11–12 worked well for the ancient reader both because it commonly meant the misstep that a runner makes in a race and was also a common word for a transgression against God. Neither should the race be suppressed nor *paraptōma* forced into a monovalency that ill suits the context.[51] The imagery of the footrace would have been unmistakable to the ancient reader. At the same time the "misstep" of the race serves as a trope for "transgression" against God's plan.

The uncovering of the imagery in 11–12 solves what has been a nasty problem for exegetes: the meanings of *to hēttēma and to plērōma*. It is an understatement when Ernst Käsemann says that, "the meaning of *hēttēma* is the subject of a lively debate."[52] "Failure to meet demands," "deficit," "overthrow," "loss," "reduction" are some of the commonly proposed meanings. C. K. Barrett's translation follows a venerable exegetical tradition and illustrates its interpretive method:[53] "the cutting down of their numbers" ("But if their stumble has thus come to mean the wealth of the world, and the cutting down of their numbers has led to the wealth of the gentiles, it will mean so much more when their numbers are again brought up to full strength").[54] A certain story controls Barrett's reading, the narrative of gentile Christianity's supersession of the Jews as the people of God. Barrett and the traditional reader discover what became the case only later, in Paul, through the concepts of the true Israel and the remnant. *Hēttēma,* then, refers to the reduction of saved Jews to the small remnant of Jewish Christian believers like Paul, and *plērōma* refers to the eschatological salvation of Israel when Jews finally convert to Christianity.

But the neat scheme of the old Israel being superseded, salvation passing to the gentiles, and the small remnant of Jewish Christians surviving does not appear so neat if one notices the texture and shape of the metaphors instead of suppressing them with anachronistic clarities. I find great irony in all of the debate about *hēttēma* because its most common meanings are well known, as are those of its cognates. *Hētta* is the normal word for defeat or failure in an athletic contest. Philo, another Jew, describes how athletes that he himself has seen have transcended bodily weakness and trauma by means of the mind's zeal for victory and fear of defeat (*hētta*).[55] Polybius provides the telling phrase *ton ton hēttomenon zēlon* (9.10.6): One should not imitate the loser, the implication being that it is natural to imitate the winner. *Hētta and hēttasthai* frequently occur not just to denote the final loss of a race or contest but to indicate any sort of failure or mistake in a competition. The race imagery makes the meaning of the troublesome 11:12 transparent: If Israel's misstep (that is, tripping, stumbling) in the race resulted in wealth for the world and her loss of the race in wealth for the gentile competitor, how much more will her completion (*plērōma*) of the race mean? The metaphor implies that Paul expects Jews to make an about-face rather soon. How many steps behind could Israel be? After all, she only stumbled, she did not fall.

A truly historical reading of a text requires two separate acts of informed imagination. The reader must imagine both the intentions of the author and also the possible and probable readings of the author's contemporaries who share in her or his cultural codes.[56] Greeks who were likely to have read Paul's letters would have felt the resonance of a story similar to Paul's in meeting Paul's foot race imagery. Athletic competition in Greek culture was elemental. Modern scholars and ancient readers have recognized that Paul's letters abound with athletic imagery.[57] He thinks in athletic imagery, as a Greek is apt to do or even a Greek-speaking Jew.[58] One of the paradigmatic narratives of Greek culture is the funeral games for Patroclus in book 23 of the *Iliad*. The Greeks read this narrative as the originary myth of the Olympic games and all athletic competition. Paul's Greek readers would have known this story. The structure of Paul's story echoes Homer's tale of the footrace in the funeral games and then diverges in equally significant ways. The athletic story of Rom 9–11 cannot but have evoked a rich play of comparison and contrast in ancient readers.

The race in the funeral games has three contestants—Antilochus, Ajax, and Odysseus—instead of two. In Homer's race too, a god trips a runner. As the runners reach the homestretch, Ajax is in the lead with Odysseus on his heels. Approaching the finish line, Odysseus prays to Athena for greater speed. The goddess answers not only by giving the second place runner additional speed but also by causing Ajax to slip and fall into the disgusting filth left from a cattle sacrifice made by Achilles. Although Odysseus passes Ajax and takes first prize, Ajax manages to get up and finish ahead of Antilochus. The god trips the runner who is on the verge of winning; the second place runner unexpectedly comes in first, but the runner who was tripped manages to finish the race and share in the prize.

The shift to direct address of the gentile audience and a series of admonitions toward them comes in 11:13. Here a series of extremely complex figures that speak of the temporary rejection of some Jews replace the race metaphor. At the same time, Paul sternly warns the gentile audience not to be arrogant toward those Jews (11:18) and not to be overly proud of the temporary gentile superiority (11:19–20, 25). Pride is properly due the winner of a contest! Something makes this contest different. As in the case of Odysseus, the winning runner did not win by his own strength. Like Ajax's, Israel's stumble was ordained by the divine will. Who can resist? Unlike the gods of the *Iliad*, who patronize their human favorites, Paul's God of Jews and gentiles does not play favorites (2:6–11; 3:23, 29–30; 4:16; 10:11–13; 11:32, 34–35). Paul's problem is this: How can God, who has so long seemed to have favored his chosen people Israel, honor commitments to her, judge the failings of both peoples fairly, and bring about equality by also giving the gentiles a privileged status before him? Paul thinks through this problem in figures and tropes that allude to both Jewish and Greek texts.

At the center of Paul's answer is the tripping and speeding of the two runners at various times. One might think of the process as a series of games. The contestants have virtues and vices as athletes that contribute to the winning or losing of this or that contest. But overall, God watches the games and makes sure that the competitions come out even in the end with a trip here and a push there. If one translates 11:28–32 into this metaphor, the logic of Paul's use of athletic imagery in 9–11 becomes apparent. Having a winner, with all of the glory that winning entails, requires having a loser. The reciprocity described in 11:28–32 suggests that at the conclusion of the games each competitor will be able to appreciate that both have won and both have lost, and they will be able to appreciate the fact that the other's losing allowed the glory of their own winning. The limits and dangers of this metaphor as a way of thinking about the problem of Jews and gentiles are easy to find. A better, yet more complex reading of 9–11, however, requires that this twine of figures be threaded into the complex weave of these chapters.

Again, the logic motivating the metaphors of the race and the branches broken off that will be grafted back comes not from a radically new insight but from assumptions Paul shared widely with other Jews. Jewish writings generally agreed that Israel's final vindication would coincide with the universal judgment. When Israel finally repented and God decided to mete out rewards and punishments to the world (both corporately and individually), the time for repentance would be ended. If Jesus' mission had succeeded in bringing about the renewal of Israel, then the gentiles would have had no hope. Again, as in chapters 2–3, the race metaphor plays with the concept of God delaying his judgment. Israel's disobedience was God's plan to allow time for the mission to the gentiles. The race ends when Israel crosses the finish line. In the logic of this race, all who finish before the pacesetter win; all who finish after that runner lose. God had to trip the Jews in order to provide opportunity for the gentiles and show that he is a just God.

Finally, the race metaphor provides a way to illustrate something about how Paul's intertextuality works and about the perils of making Jewish or Hellenistic influence mutually exclusive. Paul thinks—that is, writes—in both kinds of cultural discourse. He privileges the scriptures and situates his Greek texts in the background. Ironically, however, the Greek texts often control the scriptures. New Testament scholars should abandon the fantasy that Paul had some biblical doorway into the culture of ancient Israel and a super culture-blocker that prevented him from inhabiting even his own language. Paul reads scripture in terms of his own experiences and of the cultural codes of the Jewish-Greco-Roman society of which he was a member.

These generalizations can be illustrated by Paul's use of the jealousy motif. Paul finds the jealousy scenario in Deut 32:21, which he cites in 10:19: "I will make you jealous [*parazēlosai*] of a nonpeople; I will make you angry with a foolish people." Paul reads this as a clue to Israel's situation during the gentile mission. The motif reappears, picked up in 11:11 and 11:14. Paul himself, through his ministry to the gentiles, makes his fellow Jews "jealous" or "zealous," that is, to vie with the gentiles. The essential point is this: The jealousy motif obtains its sense within the structure of the footrace metaphor. Israel already has zeal but does not know how to run the race (10:2). Jews do not understand that God has used Christ to train gentiles into fully equipped runners. Jews like the teacher want to condescendingly feed pablum to gentiles, whom they suppose to be foolish and immature (2:20) when they are really, owing to God's grace, competitive runners. God's answer is to bring Israel to a sudden awakening by tripping her in the race and allowing the gentile runner to fly past her toward the goal. The shocking realization that she has been passed by "ungodly gentiles" will fill her heart with a competitive zeal to catch the leader. As a result, both will end the race running well. Paul finds a bit of the sacred Jewish writings (Deut 32:21) meaningful because it fits within an illuminating scenario derived from a most essentially Greek practice. Deut 32:21 says that God will make Israel jealous of gentile nations. Because the same word is central to the Greek conception of athletic competition, Paul can interpret Deut 32:21 through the athletic metaphor. Paul explicitly cites the scriptural text, appealing to its authority, but the allusive background metaphor from the discourse of Greek culture provides the framework of meaning for Deut 32:21.

11 Faithfulness as Adaptability: An Ethic of Community for Gentiles (Chapters 12-14)

The work of this chapter will be to defend the claim, in view of 12:1–15:14, that my reading unifies the letter. I will approach this task by briefly outlining the reading's implications for 12:1–15:14. Conventional readings have construed 12 and 13 as collections of general moral exhortations, either entirely unrelated to 1–11 or only indirectly related to Paul's earlier theology.[1] Scholars have divided over whether 14:1–15:13 (the conventional division) continues the general moralizing or gives advice aimed at correcting the conflict between groups at Rome implied by the terms the "weak" and the "strong." In recent years, it has become fashionable to read 14–15 as a Christian model for ecumenical and irenical relations, with "the weak" being understood as Jewish Christians and "the strong" as gentile Christians. Maintaining this view has been tricky business because what the chapters say about the weak does not fit any known Jewish practices in Paul's time. But, as I will show, the compelling case against the Jewish interpretation comes from the fact that the concepts of the weak and the strong and other language of 14–15 is well known and well understood from a different arena in Greco-Roman moral literature.

Romans Chapters 12-13

Chapters 12–13 reveal their implied gentile readers in the way they serve as a positive reversal and counterpoint to the programmatic criticism of the gentile peoples in 1:18–32. I will draw attention to some of the most important connections between the two. The first verse of 12 urges the readers to offer their bodies to God as holy, living sacrifices, of acceptable and rational worship (*latreia*). Verse 1 draws on philosophical and Jewish language developed in criticism of popular religion and idol worship.[2]

Chapter 1 tells of the ungodly and unacceptable worship of idols. These people worshiped (*latrein*) the creation instead of the creator (1:25). They thus "dishonored their bodies" (1:24). The readers in 12:2 are to renew their minds. In the first chapter, gentile minds became base (28), their reasonings confused, and their sense darkened (21). Verse 3 of chapter 12 exhorts to a realistic humility as a basis for behavior, while 1:22 and 30 accuse gentiles of false claims to wisdom, hybris, arrogance, and pretentiousness. As 1:28–31 lists a long string of antisocial vices, so 12:4–13:10 spells out a counter list of social virtues. The first chapter speaks of enslavement to desire and sexual passion; 13:8–14 elicits a freedom from sensual gratification. The latter chapters call for a reversal of precisely the degeneracy depicted in 1:18–32.

The opposition to chapter 1 only partly explains the construction of 12–15. The best traditional accounts have 12–15:13 exhorting readers to the new life described in 1–11 and thus connect the parts of the letter only in the most superficial and abstract way. I, however, want to argue for a genuine internal coherence between the discourse and thought of the two sections. If 1–11 finds its focus on God's righteousness being made good through Christ's faithfulness and understands Christ's faithfulness as his generative adaptation to the needs of others, then 12–15 sketches an ethic of community based on the principle of faithfulness as adaptability to others.

Verses 3–6a of 12 sketch the basic social conception and in so doing tie it to the theme of faithfulness (v. 3): Based on his grace as the apostle to the gentiles, Paul begs his readers "not to think higher thoughts than one ought to think but to think with *sōphrosyne,* each person [to reach self-understanding] as God has measured him or her a measure of faithfulness [*pistis*]." Paul then goes on to the metaphor of members as parts of a body, each having contributions, and to gifts as varied abilities to help others. Verse 3's idea of members sharing in faithfulness recalls the expression *ho ek pisteōs,* the one whose origin, life, or basis springs from or shares in Christ's faithfulness and the language that describes gentiles finding their new life by participating in Christ's life. Jesus Christ, characterized by his faithfulness, pioneered a mode of life that God has enabled the readers to share. Paul avoids direct calls to the imitation of Christ because he does not want his readers to do just what Jesus did but to adopt the basic principle of faithfulness as adaptability.

The explicit analogy between Christ and the reader appears at the end and climax of the section. The strong are to adjust themselves so as to aid the weak, to build them up rather than to please themselves (15:1–2). "For Christ did not please himself" but (quoting Ps 68:10 LXX) allowed himself to be attacked for being faithful to God's promises. The same language appears in 1 Cor 10:31–11:1, in which Paul picks up on his words about becoming all things to all people and speaks of imitating Christ by pleasing others instead of himself. The example again becomes specific in 15:7–12, where Christ serves as a model for the readers' taking one another into friendship and mutual assistance. The word for actively taking someone into friendship (*proslambanein*), often translated limply as "to welcome," is what the strong are to do for the weak (14:1). Christ manifested this behavior of going to someone's assistance and initiating a relation by becoming a servant to Jews so as to bring about the patriarchal promises, including the redemption and adoption of the gentiles (15:7–9). As I argued in chapter 7, Paul understood Christ's unexpected adaptation, even to the point of suffering dishonorable death on a cross, as his peculiar and exemplary faithfulness to God and his promises. Rom 12:3 makes such faithfulness into a principle for a particular kind of community.

Paul does not name Christ in 12:3, but after 3:25–8:39, readers could hardly hear about faithfulness and not think of Christ's and their share in it. Moreover, God gives manifestations of this faithfulness to each person so that all the diversely equipped members form "one body in Christ" (12:4–5). Verses 6–8 then provide examples of varied gifts that constitute abilities to contribute to the good of others and of the social whole. The passage presents an ethic that balances individual difference and social unity. At center stands an idea of social interrelation in which each person in the community maintains a social identity partly constituted by her or his abilities to benefit others.

The series of exhortations and gnomic-like sayings in 12:9–21 have been considered miscellaneous and unrelated to the specifics of Paul's thought. Although one must admit a certain miscellaneousness to the section, it nevertheless fits the ethos and even, at times, the particulars of faithfulness as adaptability. The most important Greco-Roman discussions of adaptability concern a certain type of friendship (see further on 14:1–15:14). Several of the sayings in 9–21 are about friendship and its ethos (9–10, 13, 15). Some verses urge meeting other people on their level rather than being distant and haughty, enjoining the addressees to share in the emotional experiences of others (15–16).

The principle of adaptability meant that one acted so as to benefit not only those who were alike but also those who were different. A few philosophers even advocated adapting oneself to benefit enemies. In this light, the turn in the discourse from the community to enemies and outsiders (14, 17–21) makes sense, as does Paul's discussion of relating to ruling authorities (13:1–7). After discussing enemies, he needs to address the question of whether the rulers ought to be treated as friends or enemies. Rom 13:8–10 uses the love command to sum up the principle of adaptability. Here one sees more of how Paul's moral thought relates to the theme of gentile redemption in chapters 1–8. That part of the letter insists that gentiles are accountable to the law but have overwhelmingly failed to live by the teachings applicable to gentiles. The teacher of 2:17–25 would solve the problem by instructing gentiles to keep the Decalogue. Paul argues that gentiles cannot find righteousness by works from the law because the law was not designed to bring the ungodly to God, and God himself has enslaved gentiles to their own passions and desires. Thus gentile attempts to observe the tenth commandment against desire prove futile (7:7–25). But in Christ, the Spirit of God empowers gentiles with the powers of the new age that Christ pioneered through his faithfulness. Thus by adoption into the new family generated by God out of Jesus' faithfulness and by following the new mode of life exemplified by Christ, gentiles can fulfill the "just requirements of the law" (8:4) without being tutored in the law or becoming quasi-Jews. In 13:8–10, Paul implicitly identifies the principle of adaptability with the love command, which fulfills the other commandments applicable to gentiles, including the commandment against desire. Again, as if in agreement with the Jewish teacher, Paul assumes that the Decalogue epitomizes the teachings in the law pertinent to gentiles. The teacher, understood in the context of 1:18–32 and 7:7–25, represents those who presented the law as a regimen for gentile self-mastery. Paul opposes this approach and demotes self-mastery to a minor role. This demotion appears clearly in 13:8–14. Unlike Philo and 4 Maccabees, Romans does not give the commandment against desire as the chief commandment. Instead, the injunction to love the neighbor becomes the key and the tenth commandment only one among all the others.

Romans 14:1–15:14

Commentators usually struggle to find a relation between chapters 12–13 and 14–15. Chapters 14–15 also concern the principle of adapting to the needs of others. Clarence Glad has demonstrated the centrality of the concept of adaptability in Paul's letters and the great extent to which he drew on areas of Greco-Roman culture for his discourse about adaptability.[3] The discourse about adaptability comes from discussions of friendship by philosophers, social theorists, and moralists. (Even to use the English word "friendship" invites misunderstanding because the Greco-Roman concept differs greatly from the modern—but no good alternative exists.) Plutarch, for example, discusses the often close similarities and key differences between flatterers and true friends.[4] The true friend will praise and encourage when appropriate and at times give frank analysis and criticism of his comrade's weaknesses. As Paul knew only too well from his experience at Corinth, adapting one's speech and life-style to the needs of various people could be interpreted as inconsistency and duplicity.[5] Philosophically informed friendship focused on therapy of the soul. The Hellenistic philosophies taught that virtually all people were dominated by passions, which promoted vice. Philosophy provided therapy for the passions through rational arguments and spiritual disciplines that could produce self-mastery. True friends would provide such therapy, including mutual criticism and encouragement. Some groups, such as the Epicureans, formed themselves into communities of friends that focused on intensive mutual therapy. The Epicurean teacher Philodemus has left us parts of a handbook, *Concerning Frank Criticism*, on how to apply frank criticism in such communities: when to be gentle, when to be harsh, the roles of the weak and of the strong. Such psychagogic activity required relative categories for the more mature members who guided and for the less mature who were led. The most important terminology for the less mature was *asthenēs, astheneia* (weak, weakness), the ordinary term in the New Testament writings and common speech for illness.[6] This term thus fit the therapeutic or medical metaphor of Hellenistic philosophy. Human beings were infected by diseases or passions of the soul and needed strong therapy from a reliable guide who would adapt his therapy to each person's condition.

Paul wedded some of these concepts and practices to his understanding of Christ, to his role as an apostle and his conception of renewed gentile communities. But he also manifests a critical stance, not accepting the basic therapeutic model as a whole.[7] Glad and Abraham Malherbe have discussed Paul's "borrowings" and adaptations in great detail.[8] I shall make only a few remarks pertinent to Rom 14–15. First, Paul employed the categories of the mature and immature, the weak (or sick) and the strong in his communities.[9] These are not fixed roles but relative categories that would differ for an individual at various times and in regard to the particular behavior or aspect of character in question. Thus the weak and the strong (or mature or wise and so on) are not groups or parties or theological positions, as New Testament scholars have thought, but dispositions of character.

Individuals at Corinth who considered themselves wise were following "rational beliefs" about the nature of the one God and the nonexistence of idols just as a Hellenistic philosophy or a philosophically minded Jew might teach.[10] They were either arrogantly ignoring or insensitively attempting to lead by example their weak fellow members, who had irrational false beliefs and passions (that is, fears) about the pagan gods and meat offered to such gods.[11] In 1 Cor 8:1–11:1 Paul acknowledges that the strong are right in having true beliefs that allow them to act without superstitious fear but charges them with grossly failing to follow Christ in adapting to the level of the weak. You do not cure a cold by amputating a limb. Love requires that the cure be adapted to the patient's illness. It thus comes as no accident that Paul presents himself as a model of adapting to others: he adapts to Jews, gentiles, and the weak in order to benefit each (9:19–21).

Although Paul's gentile communities seem to have been eager to take up such practices and although he was quick to correct abuses, Paul encouraged the use of such psychagogic activities if they fit what he understood as the model of Jesus Christ's faithfulness. Gal 6:1–2, for example, instructs that "if a person is anticipated in some fault, those of you who are spiritual ought to correct such a one in a spirit of gentleness [cf. 2 Cor 10:1] . . . bear the burdens of one another and you will in this way fulfill the law of Christ." Here and elsewhere (for example, 1 Thess 5:12–14; 1 Cor 2:14–16; 5:1–13; 2 Cor 2:5–10) Paul institutes and encourages practices of mutual evaluation and criticism. A superficial reading of Rom 14–15 might lead one to conclude that Paul had come to oppose any such activity, but as Glad has shown, that conclusion is premature.[12] Rather, from his missionary experience, Paul had come to expect that many of the gentile converts were very keen on such psychagogic practices. Either from popular moral philosophy or from kinds of Judaism like Philo's they had come to view these practices as a means to personal self-mastery and moral achievement. In 14:1–15:14, he seeks to correct abuses that he finds typically connected with psychagogic practices and to recast them according to his ethic of adaptability to the needs of others.

Paul's injunction in 14:1 introduces the section and signals its overriding concerns. As elsewhere, he places the primary responsibility on the strong because they are not the ones with an illness. The whole of 14:1–15:14 shares this emphasis (especially 14:13b ff.), although he also has words for the weak. The word *proslambanein* (to take someone into a relation of mutual assistance, that is, ancient friendship) signals the section's chief theme: "Take into friendship those who are weak in faithfulness but not for judgments about reasonings" (14:1).[13] Commentators tend to read the section in terms of modern liberal individualism and to have Paul saying that each person is to evaluate and criticize only herself or himself. That, of course, would put an end to the kind of mutual correction and encouragement that Paul's letters consistently advocate. Moreover, it would make Paul egregiously inconsistent given that he has practiced such criticism in the letter itself and encourages his readers to do the same in his conclusion to the section and transition to the next (15:14–15). In 15:14, he expresses his confidence that the addressees can admonish one another responsibly (*nouthetein*). Admonition is a particular kind of constructive criticism important in psychagogy; ancient moralists wrote much about it, and Paul frequently uses and reflects upon it in his letters (for example, in 1 Cor 4:14–16).[14] As he indicates in 15:15, Paul himself has used admonition earlier in the letter. Most notably, 2:1–16 and 11:13–35 use admonition primarily by means of speech-in-character to indirectly warn the readers against presumption and arrogance toward Jews.

Paul does not urge an end to this kind of criticism and mutual psychagogy. Rather, the major problem in view comes when the weak and the strong will not accept one another into the relation of mutual aid and friendship indicated by *proslambanein*. The weak hold to false beliefs about things like food and special days that they would use as criteria for not accepting others in the community who act more in line with the boldness and freedom of Jesus' faithfulness. The strong are inclined to accept the weak only in order to attack their superstitious beliefs with rational arguments, acting like philosophers subjecting the foolish to therapy of the passions with reason.[15] Paul did not consider the church a school for self-mastery. In the apostle's understanding, God and Christ in concert had accepted the gentile readers into a relation of help and friendship when they were ungodly (God and Christ being the subject of *proslambanein* in 14:3 and 15:7, respectively; cf. 5:6–11). Paul draws two points from this basic conviction of his gospel. God has accepted the weak and the strong alike. Who are they not to accept one another! Christ's acceptance of the ungodly meant adapting himself to their level to meet their needs (for example, in 5:6–8; 8:3–4). The weak and the strong must adapt themselves to one another in the same way.

On this reading, 14:1–15:14 does not just display superficial connection with chapters 1–11 but absolutely depends on those earlier chapters for its sense. God's way of accepting the gentiles through Christ's way of being faithful gives logic to the ethic of 12:1–15:14. Moreover, the letter's concern with addressing and criticizing an approach centered on the ethic of self-mastery reappears in terms of concrete community practices. Talk of gentile passions and desires and works of the law as a way to self-mastery might seem remote from the everyday concerns of the community, but 14:1ff. shows how such issues impinged on the basic conception of the community itself in very concrete ways. The Pauline ethic, or more correctly Pauline social thought, does indeed have an intimate and internal connection to Pauline theology.

Conclusions

I will not repeat the summary of my reading that can be found at the conclusion to chapter 1. Instead, I will briefly note some ways in which this reading provides advantages for the interpreter. The cogency of a reading lies both in the detail and in the larger, interpretive issues. I have discussed some of the most important details at points throughout this book. Here I will confine myself to the broadest issues.

1. Coherence of the reading. Throughout I have claimed that my approach gives a coherence to the letter that solves perennial difficulties faced in traditional readings. The traditional Western readings, which have focused, with some success, upon joining 1:18–3:20, 3:21–5:22, and 6:1–8:39, rely heavily on a framework of broad motifs external to the discourse of the letter to produce coherence. Thus a certain conception of human sinfulness and its universality that cannot be gotten from the details holds together the traditional reading of 1:18–3:20. A conception of Christ as the answer to this sinfulness ties 1:18–3:20 to 3:21–5:22, but the internal connections are very weak. Much of 2:1–29 and 3:1–8 actually belies the reading on a rather overt level and must be ignored or explained away. The larger external motifs warrant holding 3:21–5:22 together with 6:1–8:39 as the relation between theology and the moral life or justification and sanctification or numerous variations of these motifs, but internal coherence largely fails. Even if we posit the legitimacy of the external motifs, their lack of internal connection is striking. If salvation from sinfulness rests on God's gracious forgiveness and the believer's act of faith, Christ becomes an object of faith without internal connection to the salvation and moral life that spring from God's justification and the believer's faith.

The traditional way of making chapters 9–11 cohere with 12:1–15:13 is very weak indeed, and I need not labor a fact that has long stood at the center of Pauline scholarship. The recent trend in scholarship has viewed Romans as an "ecumenical" writing to unite Jewish and gentile Christians in Rome or as a missionary tractate laying out Paul's gospel and missionary strategy in light of likely misunderstandings. While the latter formulation, I believe, comes closer to the mark, the actual readings under its rubric have proven to be only modifications of the traditional reading that add external reasons related to Paul's missionary strategy to account for 9–11 and 12:1–15:13. This, indeed, is an advance because such readings allow a greater appreciation for Paul's language of Jews and gentiles. Nevertheless, this approach does little to improve internal coherency because the letter becomes a miscellany of topics and strategies put together for reasons that must be explained by considerations external to the letter itself. An outline of arrangement derived from the ancient rhetorical handbooks can be used to describe these readings, as has become popular of late. But they can also be placed on virtually any reading without essentially changing the reading.

I have argued that the theme of the gentile dilemma and God's merciful and impartial justice unites 1:18–3:20, even making difficult a strong division from 3:21–5:11. This theme cannot be properly abstracted from its rhetorical presentation through speech-in-character. An apostrophe to an imaginary gentile (2:1–16) establishes the letter's admonitory edge to be developed primarily in chapters 9–15. The Jewish teacher allows Paul to argue his gospel against a "gospel" that must have been his greatest challenge as he went from city to city preaching to gentiles who had already found a connection with Judaism. This discussion with the teacher not only ties together the details of 2:17–4:22 but also establishes Paul's mode of arguing for his gospel against works of the law in chapters 5–11. By understanding the specific shape of gentile unrighteousness as the loss of self-mastery and bondage to passions and desire, 1:18–32 and chapters 6–8 can be seen to relate intimately to the issue of gentiles following works from the law. Christ's faithfulness then has a crucial internal connection to the gentile dilemma of a condemnation even increased by attempts to follow parts of the law. Christ's decision to adapt himself to the place of the ungodly instead of exercising his messianic powers delayed the punishment of the gentiles, allowing the Abrahamic promise to be fulfilled. God's response to Jesus in the resurrection created a new family of God's people sharing in the sonship of the Spririt already won by Christ. Thus the new life described in chapters 6–8 finds its basis in the faithfulness of Abraham and Jesus discussed in 3:21–5:11, and that faithfulness was God's way of manifesting his justice toward all of the world's peoples. Again, all of this is argued as an alternative to the approach of Jews like the teacher. Thus all of 2:17–8:39 has the failure of Jews as a light to gentiles in the background and sometimes in the foreground.

Chapters 9–11, then, come as no surprise but treat a problem that has nagged the whole discourse in light of the opening claim that the good news would save both Jews and Greeks. In 12:1–15:14 Paul urges that the ethical virtues, the social form and practices of gentiles in Christ, follow the pattern of Christ's faithfulness as adaptability to the needs of others. Thus even 12–15 connects internally with earlier parts of the letter, especially since it presents the paradigm of adaptability as an alternative to an ethic of self-mastery.

Read in this way, Romans appears similar to protreptic writings in which teachers presented their messages and introduced themselves to new audiences.[1] Philosophers claimed that protreptic that was more than a flattering invitation should be marked by admonition. Teachers should discover and criticize the particular vices of their hearers. Romans fits this pattern in making a warning against gentile presumption central to its message. As a protreptic letter, Romans also serves the plans Paul announces in 15:14–33, including support for his trip to Jerusalem and preparation for work in Rome and the west.

2. Explanation of later readings. My reading can account for the way in which Romans and Paul's letters were interpreted in the ancient and later church far better than the dominant understandings. Here, eastern and western Christianity differ, although not as much as scholars have often thought. In the western account that has prevailed, Paul arose out of Judaism with a message about law's inability to enable goodness and the impossibility of attaining moral virtue by human effort. In fact, such efforts offended God and his grace. As the account goes, Paul's message was essentially antimoralistic but virtually no one in the ancient church understood the message until Augustine. The ancient church largely read Paul as a kind of moralist concerned with both God's grace and moral self-mastery. According to some versions of this account, thinkers in the (western) church after Augustine until Luther more or less understood Paul, but even those who mostly understood him, like Thomas Aquinas, were tempted into compromising and watering down his radical message.

The reading for which I have argued helps us to see that all of the interpreters both understood and misunderstood aspects of the letters. In each case, loss of Paul's historical and cultural context and the concerns of later Christianity led to a different Paul. The church before Augustine rightly saw that he was concerned about the passions, virtues, self-mastery, and keeping of God's law. But they did not have available Paul's context of the gentile as the ethnic-religious other of Jews and Christ's faithfulness as an answer to that problem. Instead, they used Paul's discourse to create a theological philosophy of human nature, making Christianity a therapy for the passions and other evils without Paul's critical stance toward such therapy of the passions. Augustine and those who followed him focused upon texts in which Paul argued that Christ's faithfulness as a free gift from God had saved the gentiles rather than Jewish-led efforts to get gentiles to keep parts of the law. But Augustine, in the heat of the Pelagian controversy, made Paul's argument about God's plans for the gentiles into a timeless theology that placed human agency in opposition to divine agency. This made doing good or keeping God's law into a complex religious and psychological problem that doing the good and keeping the law was not for Paul himself.

3. Paul's relation to Judaism. The Christian Church has loved the idea of finding its origins in Judaism and ancient Israel but has generally hated Jews. Paul, read as the critic of "Jewish legalism" and the law, has served as a model for that love/hate relation. The tradition has read him as a continuator of the true biblical and Jewish religion of the prophets, a spiritual religion of faith but not of temple, people, and law. To the historian, this Paul comes out of nowhere. To pit divine agency against human agency in a basic way and to make this into the fundamental principle of religion simply makes no sense for a Jew in Paul's era. Judaism without the law is like Christianity without Christ. The more we have learned about Judaism as it actually existed rather than the Judaism of Christian imagination, the more impossible it has become to give a historical account of the traditional Paul.

The Paul of the reading advocated here makes sense as a complex person fully understandable in the context of the Judaism of his day. He neither converted to a new religion replacing Judaism nor radically revised Judaism as a personal religion of faith. Rather, he, like a number of other Jews, came to believe that Jesus of Nazareth had been God's messiah who had made an unexpected decision to die that could be understood as an act of ultimate faithfulness to his messianic mandate. God had begun the end-of-the-ages resurrection of the dead with Jesus, thus vindicating Jesus' act and making him the pioneer of the age of the Spirit when God would bring to pass all of his promises to both Jews and gentiles. He did not preach a radical doctrine of sin or of evil that was either ahistorically cosmic and personal or that posited a primordial angelic-like existence and fall. Like other Jews, he believed that the gentile nations had rejected God and were typified by certain evils. Like other Jews, he also believed that Israel as a whole sometimes drifted or fell into disobedience and had to be judged and redeemed by God. This Paul seems plausible as a former Pharisee. Paul fully accepted the temple and other Jewish institutions, although he, like most other Jews, may have at times criticized their current administration by those who were in power. Paul most distanced himself from other forms of Judaism in his devotion to Jesus Christ and in his beliefs about Christ's divine empowerments as God's agent. The apostle was nevertheless as fully monotheistic as other Jews; and not monotheistic as monotheism was radically redefined by orthodox Christianity.

4. Paul's relation to Greco-Roman culture and the Roman Empire. Jewish and Christian ideology has made Paul and other Jews into ghosts walking through their world without belonging to or being touched by their "pagan environment." Such oppositions create ideologies that exert powerful social control over people who serve such beliefs, but the historian who truly desires to understand must resist these powerful patterns of thinking by mutually exclusive categories. Asking whether Paul is Jewish or Hellenistic is like asking whether a certain rabbi from Boston is Jewish or American; Jewish or western. The question is silly. Paul was both fully Jewish, absolutely dedicated to his people, and fully a person of Hellenistic culture inhabiting the life of the early Roman empire.

The correlate to Paul's theological problem of God's justice toward Jews and the other peoples is the sociological problem of Jews relating to non-Jews in the highly interactive polyethnic environment of the early empire. Paul's problem in Romans, his way of treating the problem, his dialogue with the ethic of self-mastery in relation to themes connected with imperial rule and his known social connections suggest a certain social location. He might be imagined to have moved in the interstice between two larger overlapping circles or interconnected networks. On the one hand were gentile households in cities of the Greek east and in Rome who had contacts with Jews. This included connections with the imperial household. Paul's specific contacts here may often have been with slaves and freedpersons, but he had significant contact with the kind of people who found new ways to move in a new social space opened up by the creation of the empire and its tensions with and manipulation of the traditional aristocracies. These circles would often include people who, as Wayne Meeks has shown, were characterized by status inconsistency. On the other hand, Paul had significant contact with the traditional ruling classes in Judea and the Jewish communities of the Greek east. Again, Paul's contacts were probably for the most part not with those at the top but with members of their households and retainers. These Jewish elites and their responsible dependents must have been constantly faced with questions of how to relate to and deal with gentiles.

Paul's location was that of a former retainer who continued to move in parts of his network. As a Pharisee, he belonged to a class of retainers who were lower-level administrators, knowledge producers, and problem solvers ultimately dependent on the hereditary landed aristocracy but having a semi-independence through their authority in regard to traditional forms of Jewish knowledge, for example, as interpreters of the law. Thus Paul felt the "gentile problem" acutely in many personal and theoretical forms. Having lost his legit-imacy as a Pharisee because of his convictions about Christ, he nevertheless continued as a maverick knowledge producer, problem solver, and expert on the law. Perhaps the closest Greek counterpart to Paul's role and social loca-tion was the philosopher. This helps to explain his reception by and appeal to gentiles and why so many popular philosophical themes and issues appear in his letters.

This scenario helps us to understand Paul's interpretation of Christ and his doctrine of adaptability. Christ brought about a new arrangement that would make gentiles into decent people by Jewish standards, ultimately defeat hostile and recalcitrant gentile rulers, create ties of kinship between Jews and the other peoples, and usher in the new age marked by the empowerments of God's Spirit. The new arrangements would require a new ethic to inform the interaction of Jews and gentiles. This constitutes the meaning of Paul's doc-trine of adaptability. This idea shaped his understanding of Jesus Christ and his self-understanding as an apostle of Christ to the gentiles and served as a paradigm for social and ethical relations in his gentile communities. He prob-ably expected this idea to also inform Jewish believers, although just how is unclear. Paul probably saw his role as the apostle to the gentiles as unique. When working with gentiles, he would live as a gentile in Christ. But Romans 9–11 leaves no ambiguity about the unchanging foundation that prevented his adaptability from being lack of stable character. He is a Jew who has under-taken his calling to the gentiles to help his own people.

If this account of Paul through a reading of Romans has substantial merit, then E. P. Sanders's view, that Paul discovered his solution in Christ and then tried to formulate the problem, will not work. Paul most likely faced problems concerning Jew/gentile relations all his life. But most of all, Sanders's formula-tion fails because Paul's gospel never addressed the abstract problem of the human plight. Paul's letters reveal a kind of Christianity that existed before Christianity became a religion of an intrinsically sick human nature and its cure.

Notes

Chapter 1. Toward a Rereading of Romans

1 For a brief survey, see John Godsey, "The Interpretation of Romans in the History of Christian Faith," *Interpretation* 34 (1980): 3–16.

2 Krister Stendahl, "The Apostle Paul and the Introspective Conscience of the West," *HTR* 56 (1963): 199–215, reprinted in *The Writings of St. Paul,* ed. Wayne A. Meeks (New York: Norton, 1972), 426.

3 Albrecht Dihle, *The Theory of Will in Classical Antiquity* (Berkeley: University of California Press, 1982), 123–44. Dihle must be corrected by Ch. Kahn, "Discovering the Will: From Augustine to Aristotle," in *The Question of "Eclecticism,"* ed. J. M. Dillon and A. A. Long (Berkeley: University of California Press, 1988), 234–44, and Jaap Mansfield, "The Idea of the Will in Chrysippus, Posidonius, and Galen," in *Proceedings of the Boston Area Colloquium on Ancient Philosophy*, 7th ed., ed. J. Cleary (New York: University Press of America), 107–57.

4 Peter Brown, *Augustine of Hippo* (Berkeley: University of California Press, 1967), 104–27, 158–81. I follow Paula Fredriksen in "Paul and Augustine: Conversion Narratives, Orthodox Traditions, and the Retrospective Self," *JTS* 37 (1986): 3–34.

5 For an account and bibliography, see Brigitte Berger and Peter L. Berger, *The War over the Family* (Garden City, N.Y.: Doubleday, 1983), 85–127.

6 *Paul's Letter to the Romans* (Pelican NTC; Baltimore: Penguin, 1975).

7 *PLJP* and the second part of *PPJ*.

8 *PLJP* 125.

9 PPJ 552.

10 "Paul's Theological Difficulties with the Law," *Studia Biblica 1978: III Papers on Paul and Other New Testament Authors* (JSNT Suppl. 3; Sheffield: JSOT Press, 1980), 301–20; *Paul and the Law.*

11 "Paul's Difficulties," 314.

12 Roland Barthes, *Image, Music, Text* (New York: Hill and Wang, 1977) 146, 148.

13 Richard Hays, *Echoes of Scripture in the Letters of Paul* (New Haven: Yale University Press, 1989). Unfortunately, Hays proceeds as if one can understand the letters adequately through the scriptural allusions and quotations that the letters and Christian tradition have privileged without recourse to other "sources."

14 Richard Bernstein, *Beyond Objectivism and Relativism: Science, Hermeneutics, and Praxis* (Philadelphia: University of Pennsylvania, 1983).

15 F. C. Burkett, "Response" to "The Punctuation of the New Testament Manuscripts" by C. Lattey in *JTS* 29 (1927–28): 397–98; Donatien DeBruyne, *Sommaires, divisions et rubriques de la Bible latine* (Namur, 1914); Bruce Metzger, *The Text of the New Testament* (Oxford: Clarendon Press, 1964), 22–25; *Manuscripts of the Greek Bible* (Oxford: Oxford University Press, 1981), 32, 40–44.

16 Nils A. Dahl, "The Particularity of the Pauline Epistles as a Problem in the Ancient Church," *Neotestamentica et Patristica* (NovTS 5; Leiden: E. J. Brill, 1962), 261–64; Harry Gamble, *The Textual History of the Letter to the Romans* (Grand Rapids, Mich.: Eerdmans, 1977), 117; Krister Stendahl, "The Apocalypse of John and the Epistles of Paul in the Muratorian Fragment," *Current Issues in New Testament Interpretation,* ed. W. Klassen and G. F. Snyder (New York: Harper and Row, 1962), esp. 243.

17 Dahl, "Particularity," 261–67; Gamble, *Textual History,* 115–29.

18 Gamble, *Textual History*, 129.

19 David Trobisch, *Die Entstehung der Paulusbriefsammlung* (NTOA 10; Göttingen: Vandenhoeck and Ruprecht, 1989), 84–100.

20 Ibid., 12–61.

21 Ibid., 89–96.

22 Literary works do not seem to have been divided into chapters and paragraphs until the second century C.E. and then only gradually. The origin of such editing appears to have been in legal documents whose chapter and article divisions were used for reference. Reference was probably the major reason for their later use in the New Testament (H. K. McArthur, "The Earliest Divisions of the Gospels," *Studia Evangelica* 3.2, ed. F. L. Cross [Text u. Unters, 88; Berlin: Akademie, 1964], 266–72).

23 J. A. Kleist, "Colometry and the New Testament," *Classical Bulletin* 4 (1928): 26; Albert Debrunner, "Grundsätzliches über Kolometrie im Neuen Testament," *Theologische Blatter* 5 (1926): 231–33; Roland Schutz, "Die Bedeutung der Kolometrie fur das Neuen Testament," *ZNT* 21 (1922): 161–84; Metzger, *Manuscripts,* 39–40.

24 *Diatribe and Romans*, 78–118.

25 Jouette Bassler (*Divine Impartiality: Paul and a Theological Axiom* [SBLDS 59; Chico, Cal.: Scholars Press, 1981]) argues against the division at 2:1 on other grounds.

26 Sanday and Headlam, *Romans,* 54.

27 Bassler has shown the centrality of the theme in *Divine Impartiality.*

28 *PG* 14, 873f.

29 *PG* 60, 423.

30 Alexander Souter, *Pelaguis' Expositions of Thirteen Epistles of St. Paul* (Texts and Studies 9; Cambridge: Cambridge University Press, 1931), 2:24, on Romans 2:21.

31 Jacob Neusner, "Pharisaic-Rabbinic Judaism: A Clarification," *History of Religions* 12 (1973): 250–70; id., "The Formation of Rabbinic Judaism: Yavneh (Jamnia) from A.D. 7 to 100," *ANRW* 2, 19.2, 3–43; id., "The Use of the Mishnah for the History of Judaism prior to the Time of the Mishnah," *JSJ* 11 (1980): 1–9.

32 Stendhal, "Introspective Conscience," 199–215.

33 *Luther's Works*: Vol. 25: *Lectures on Romans, Glosses and Scholia,* ed. Hilton C. Oswald (Saint Louis: Concordia, 1972), 15. In contrast to Luther, Bullinger's view is interest-

ing. He wrote that 2:1–5 was a response to pagan philosophers and moralists who might claim exemption from 1:18–32.

34 Ibid., 16.

35 Ibid., 136.

36 *Diatribe and Romans,* chap. 4.

37 See, for example, Origen on Rom. 3:1–8; 7:14f., and 9:14–19: *PG* 14, 839–1291; *Le Commentaire d'Origène sur Rom. III. 5-V.7 d'après les extraits du papyrus No. 88748 du Musée du Caire et les fragments de la Philocalie et du Vaticanus Gr. 762,* ed. Jean Schérer (Cairo: Inst. Franc. D'Arch. Orient., 1957); Chrysostom on Rom 7:7; *Hom. in Rom* 12–4 (500).

38 *Codex Ephraemi Syri Rescriptus,* ed. Constantine Tischendorf (Leipzig, 1843).

39 Thomas H. Olbricht, "The Historical Awareness of Informative Communication," Paper presented at the Colloquium in Philosophy and Rhetoric, Pennsylvania State University, February 1964.

40 I owe the translation "speech-in-character" to James R. Butts ("The Progymnasmata of Theon: A New Text with Translation and Commentary" [Diss., Claremont Graduate School, 1986], 459–60). For discussions of *prosōpopoiia,* see the following in addition to Butts: Josef Martin, *Antike Rhetorik* (Munich: C. H. Beck, 1974); George A. Kennedy, *Greek Rhetoric under Christian Emperors* (Princeton: Princeton University Press, 1983), 64; D. L. Clark, Rhetoric in Greco-Roman Education (New York: Columbia University Press, 1959).

41 The standard critical edition for Theon has been L. Spengel, *Rhetores Graeci* (Leipzig: Teubner, 1854; repr. Frankfurt am Main: Minerva, 1966); for Hermogenes, Hugo Rabe, *Hermogenes Opera* (Leipzig: Teubner, 1913; repr. Stuttgart, 1969), 1–27; for Aphthonius, Hugo Rabe, *Aphthonii Progymnasmata* (Leipzig: Teubner, 1926).

42 Butts, "Progymnasmata," 457–59: Kennedy, *Greek Rhetoric,* 64.

43 See my "Romans 7:7–25 as Speech-In-Character," *Paul in His Hellenistic Context,* ed. Troels Engberg-Pedersen (Minneapolis: Fortress Press, forthcoming), and chap. 9 below.

44 Kennedy, *Greek Rhetoric,* 64.

45 This tradition defines *prosōpopoiia* as Theon defines it and includes the invention of both ethos and person under the figure. The most likely common source is Aristarchus and the Alexandrian grammarians. For Cicero and Quintilian, see Quint. *Inst. Orat.* 9.2.29–32.

46 On Paul's educational level, see Abraham J. Malherbe, *Social Aspects of Early Christianity* (Baton Rouge and London: Louisiana State University Press, 1977), 29–59. For education in antiquity, see, H.-I. Marrou, *Histoire de l'education dans l'antiquité,* 6th ed. (Paris: Edition du Seuil, 1965); M. L. Clarke, *Higher Education in the Ancient World* (London, 1971); S. F. Bonner, *Education in Ancient Rome* (Berkeley: University of California Press, 1977); A. Quacquarelli, *Scuola e cultura dei primi secoli cristiani* [Brescia, 1974]). The preceding accounts must be modified with the cautions about diversity, dual educational tracks, and social status of A. D. Booth "Elementary and Secondary Education In the Roman Empire," *Florilegium* 1 (1979): 1–14; Robert Kaster, *Guardians of Language: The Grammarian and Society in Late Antiquity* (Berkeley: University of California Press, 1988); "Notes on 'Primary' and 'Secondary' Schools in Late Antiquity," *TAPA* 113 (1983): 323–46.

47 D. L. Clark, *Rhetoric,* 201, 208–09.

48 Theon 2.115.22; Joseph Felton, *Nicolai Sophistae Progymnasmata* (Leipzig: Teubner, 1913), 66–67.

49 Marrou, *Histoire,* chap. 7, esp. 165–66.

50 Dionysius Thrax, *Ars Grammatica,* ed. Gustav Uhlig (Leipzig: Teubner, 1883), esp.
    1–5; *PBerlin* 13839.

51 Still basic is chapter 3 of Ulrich von Wilamowitz-Moellendorff, *Einleitung in die
    griechische Tragödie* (Berlin: Weidmann, 1907); also Denys L. Page, *Actor's Interpola-
    tions in Greek Tragedy* (Oxford: Clarendon Press, 1934), chap. 1.

52 A. Roemer, *Die Homerexegese Aristarch in ihren Grundzügen* (Paderborn: E. Belzner,
    1924), 223, 253–64.

53 Heinrich Dachs, *Die LUSIS EK TOU PROSVPOU* (Erlangen, 1913).

54 Cf. Virgil, *Aen* 2.29.

55 *Emporii Oratoris, De ethopoeia,* in *Rhet. Lat. Min.,* ed. K. Halm (Leipzig: Teubner,
    1863), 561–63.

56 E.g., *The Reader in the Text,* ed. Susan Suleiman and Inge Crosman (Princeton: Prince-
    ton University Press, 1980).

57 *Word Biblical Commentary: Romans 1–8* (Dallas: Word Books, 1988).

58 Ibid., xliv.

59 Ibid.

60 Ibid.

61 *PLJP,* 172.

62 *PPJ,* 552.

63 *PLJP,* 98.

64 In spite of the great progress that has been made in New Testament studies, I believe
    that the field is still fundamentally shaped by apologetic concerns, especially in the
    scandalous misuse of the Mishna, Talmuds, and "haggadic literature" for Jewish
    "backgrounds" and the isolation (from its Near Eastern and Greco-Roman context) of
    a "Jewish backgrounds" for the N.T. that shapes Judaism according to the concerns of
    orthodox and modern Christianity instead of allowing it an integrity of its own. I
    would not be so arrogant as to claim that I have fully escaped the grip of this power-
    ful paradigm. For insights along the lines of my criticisms, see Shaye J. D. Cohen,
    "The Modern Study of Ancient Judaism," *The State of Jewish Studies* (Detroit: Wayne
    State University Press, 1990), 55–73; "Jews and Judaism in the Greco-Roman World,"
    in *Early Judaism and Its Modern Interpreters,"* ed. R. Kraft and G. Nicklesburg (Atlanta:
    Scholars Press, 1986), 33–56; John J. Collins, "Judaism as *Praeparatio Evangelica* in
    the Work of Martin Hengel," *RSR* 15 (1989): 226–28.

65 See recently, Frank E. Manuel, *The Broken Staff: Judaism through Christian Eyes* (Cam-
    bridge: Harvard University Press, 1992).

66 Stanley K. Stowers, "Greeks Who Sacrifice and Those Who Do Not: Toward an
    Anthropology of Greek Religion" in *The First Christians and Their Social World: Studies
    in Honor of Wayne A. Meeks,* ed. L. M. White and O. L. Yarbrough (Minneapolis: Augs-
    burg Fortress, forthcoming).

67 Review of *Paul and Palestinian Judaism* in JBL 98 (1979): 300.

68 Bernard McGrane, *Beyond Anthropology: Society and the Other* (New York: Columbia
    University Press, 1989), 55–61.

69 G. B. Caird, *The Language and Imagery of the Bible* (Philadelphia: Westminster, 1980),
    209.

70 W. D. Davies, *The Gospel and the Land* (Berkeley: University of California Press, 1974), 169.

71 Ibid., 165.

72 Dunn, *Romans*, 51.

73 Ibid., 89–90.

74 Ibid., 56.

75 Ibid., 77.

76 Ibid., 80.

77 Ibid., 78–82, 89–93.

78 Ibid., 81.

79 Ibid., 81–82, 90–91.

80 Ibid., 84.

81 Ibid., 86.

82 E.g., Isa 5:13–16; 10:20–23; Lam 1:18; Ezek 12–14; *Pss. Sol.* 13:6–11; 16:14–15; 18:4; Jdt 8:24–27; Wis 3:5–7; 2 Macc 6:14.

83 Johannes Munck, *Paul and the Salvation of Mankind* (Richmond: John Knox, 1959).

84 W. G. Kümmel, *Introduction to the New Testament,* 17th, rev. ed. (Nashville: Abingdon Press, 1975), 309–10.

85 Ibid., 307–09.

86 Edith Hall, *Inventing the Barbarian: Greek Self-Definition through Tragedy* (Oxford: Clarendon Press, 1989).

87 Ibid., 19–100.

Chapter 2. Readers in Romans

1 Western interpreters have described this as the moralism of the ancient church and have seen Augustine as the one interpreter who is free of "moralistic distortion of Paul."

2 E.g., the commentaries of Dunn, Cranfield, and Schlier.

3 Cranfield, *Romans,* 1:68.

4 "Use and Abuse of Reason," 253–86, esp. 276–86; Clarence E. Glad, "Adaptability in Epicurean and Early Christian Psychagogy: Philodemus and Paul" (Ph.D. diss., Brown University, 1992), 162–72.

5 "Use and Abuse of Reason," 276–84; Glad, "Adaptability," 388–403.

6 Themistocles Adamopoulo is preparing a dissertation at Brown University on the concept of endurance in Paul's letters.

7 E.g., Galen, *Hippoc. et Plat.* 189.20-190.1; 214.10-20; Hall, *Inventing* the Barbarian, 80–84, 125–33.

8 John J. Winkler, *The Constraints of Desire: The Anthropology of Sex and Gender in Ancient Greece* (New York: Routledge, 1989), 50.

9 "Use and Abuse of Reason," 276–81.

10 Ibid., 280.

11 *Honor and Shame: The Values of Mediterranean Society*, ed. J. G. Peristiany (London: Weidenfeld and Nicolson, 1966); James C. Scott, *The Moral Economy of the Peasant* (New Haven: Yale University Press, 1976); Bruce J. Malina, *The New Testament World: Insights from Cultural Anthropology* (Atlanta: John Knox, 1981), 71–90.

12 Cited by Winkler, *Constraints*, 47.

13 Ibid.

14 Michel Foucault, *The Use of Pleasure* (New York: Vintage Books, 1986), 66–67.

15 Marcel Detienne and Jean Pierre Vernant, *The Cuisine of Greek Sacrifice* (Chicago: University of Chicago Press, 1989), esp. 1–86. The following account is from Vernant.

16 Ibid., 62–78.

17 Both texts cited from ibid., 60.

18 *A Greek-English Lexicon*, H. G. Liddell, R. Scott, and H. S. Jones (Oxford: Oxford University Press, 1968).

19 I have avoided the term "homosexuality" because it is now broadly agreed among scholars of Greco-Roman antiquity that homosexuality is a different and modern concept (see chap. 3 below).

20 See the important discussions by Winkler in *Constraints of Desire and Before Sexuality: The Construction of Erotic Experience in the Ancient Greek World*, ed. D. Halperin, J. Winkler, F. I. Zeitlin (Princeton: Princeton University Press, 1990).

21 One such source of evidence is Artemidoros's *Dream Analysis* (see Winkler, *Constraints of Desire*, 17–44).

22 I have cited the full saying from Menander; Philo's version is abbreviated.

23 "Late Antiquity," *The History of Private Life: From Pagan Rome to Byzantium*, ed. P. Veyne (Cambridge: Harvard University Press, 1987), 246–47.

24 Kenneth Scott, "The Political Propaganda of 44–30 B.C.," *Memoirs of the American Academy in Rome* 11 (1933): 7–49; id., "Octavian's Propaganda and Antony's *De Sua Ebrietate*," CP 24 (1929): 133–41.

25 Subordination to a woman was considered the worst degree of moral degradation and was a common theme of invective in oratory: e.g., Cicero, *Verr.* 2.1.140; *Philipp.* 6.4; *Pro Caelo* 32, 67; *Pro Clu.* 18. Plutarch (*Ant.* 10.3) writes of Antony's wife Fulvia: "She did not concern herself with spinning or housekeeping . . . she wished to rule a ruler. . . . Cleopatra was indebted to Fulvia for teaching Antony to endure a woman's sway, since she got him fully tamed and trained to obey women." The dominant women of Greek myth, Medea, Omphale, and Semiramis, played an important part in the invective both in literature and art. See Jasper Griffin, "Propertius and Antony," *JRS* 67 (1977): 17, nn. 3–5; 23, n. 79; Paul Zanker, *The Power of Images in the Age of Augustus* (Ann Arbor: University of Michigan Press, 1988), 59–60.

26 Lucy Hughes-Hallett, *Cleopatra: Histories, Dreams and Distortions* (London: Bloomsbury, 1990), 36–69. Josephus presents Antony as enslaved to a woman (*Ant.* 15.93).

27 *Poetry and Politics in the Age of Augustus*, ed. T. Woodman and D. West (Cambridge: Cambridge University Press), 19; Jasper Griffin, "Augustus and the Poets: Caesar qui cogere possit," in *Caesar Augustus: Seven Aspects*, ed. F. Millar and E. Segal (Oxford: Oxford University Press, 1984), 189–218.

28 On the iconography, see Zanker, *Power of Images*.

29 Dietrich Mannsperger, "Apollon gegen Dionysos: Numismatische Beiträge zu Octa-

vians Rolle als Vindex Libertatis," *Gymnasium* 80 (1973): 381–404; Zanker, *Power of Images*, 57–65.

30 Scott, "Antony's *De Sua Ebrietate.*"

31 For Octavian's identification with Apollo, in addition to Mannsperger ("Apollon gegen Dionysos.") and Zanker (*Power of Images*), see the literature in Dietmar Kienast, *Augustus: Princeps und Monarch* (Darmstadt: Wissenschaftliche Buchgesellschaft, 1982), 192–202.

32 Gianfilippo Carettoni, *Das Haus des Augustus auf dem Palatin* (Mainz: Philipp von Zabern, 1983); Paul Zanker, "Der Apollontempel auf dem Palatin," *Cittá e Architettura nella Roma Imperiale: Anal. Rom. Suppl.* 10 (1983): 21–40.

33 Zanker, *Power of Images*, 79–333; see also nn. 30, 32 above.

34 Kienast, *Augustus*, 185–202.

35 Zanker, *Power of Images*, 101–238; Richard Gordon, "The Veil of Power," in *Pagan Priests: Religion and Power in the Ancient World*, ed. M. Beard and J. North (Ithaca: Cornell University Press, 1990), 209–12; Andreas Alföldi, *Die Monarchische Repräsentation im römischen Kaiserreich* (Darmstadt: Wissenschaftliche Buchgesellschaft, 1970).

36 Zanker, *Power of Images*, 239–63.

37 For art and architecture, Zanker (*Power of Images*) with up-to-date bibliography on many aspects of the phenomena. For religion, see Gordon ("Veil of Power") and S. R. F. Price, *Rituals and Power: The Roman Imperial Cult in Asia Minor* (Cambridge: Cambridge University Press, 1984).

38 Price, *Rituals and Power.*

39 Gordon, "Veil of Power," 209–13.

40 Andrew Wallace-Hadrill, "The Golden Age and Sin in Augustan Ideology," *Past and Present* 95 (1982): 19–36; Kienast, *Augustus*, 99, 187; Zanker, *Power of Images*, 167–210.

41 Zanker, *Power of Images*, 156–59; Leo Ferrero Radista, "Augustus' Legislation Concerning Marriage, Procreation, Love Affairs and Adultery," *ANRW* 2.13 (1980): 278–339.

42 Andrew Wallace-Hadrill, "Family and Inheritance in the Augustan Marriage-Laws," *Proceedings of the Cambridge Philological Society* 27 (1981): 58–80.

43 Ibid.

44 Brown, *History of Private Life*, 248.

45 J. R. Fears, "The Theology of Victory at Rome," *ANRW* 2.17.2 (1981): 827–948.

46 Eugenio La Rocca, *Amazzozmachia* (Rome: De Luca Editore, 1985), 21–46.

47 Rolf Michael Schneider, *Bunte Barbaren* (Worms: Wernersche, 1986), 64, 161–65.

48 Tonio Hölscher, *Victoria Romana* (Mainz: Philipp von Zabern, 1967).

49 M. Reinhold, "Roman Attitudes toward Egyptians," *Ancient World* 3 (1980): 97–103.

50 Naphtali Lewis, *Life in Egypt under Roman Rule* (Oxford: Oxford University Press, 1983), 31–35.

51 Cicero probably derived this argument from the revisionist Stoic Panaetius, who joined the Scipionic circle in Rome in the second century B.C.E. Panaetius not only went against Stoic teaching in accepting monarchy rather than democracy but also

denied the unitary Stoic psychology, replacing it with a soul divided between an inherently rebellious irrational part and the ruling rational part.

52 Sacrifices were offered for, but not to, the emperor at the temple in Jerusalem.

53 Hall, *Inventing the Barbarian*, 80–84, 124–33.

54 Elizabeth Rawson, *The Spartan Tradition in European Thought* (Oxford: Clarendon Press, 1969), 339–43, 365.

55 Ibid., 21.

56 Ibid., 30–32.

57 *Ibid.*, 110.

58 Ibid., 96.

59 David Whitehead, *The Ideology of the Athenian Metic* (Cambridge Philological Soc. Suppl. 4: Cambridge, Cambridge Philological Society, 1977).

60 Shaye J. D. Cohen, "Respect for Judaism by Gentiles according to Josephus," *HTR* 80 (1987): 409–30.

61 Ibid., 416–25.

62 For additional examples of self-mastery in Jewish writings, see *Ep.Arist.* 221–24; *Ps. Phoc.* 36, 59–69, 76; *Jos. Asen.* 4.9(7); *Sib. Or.* 3.242; *Wis* 8:7; Marinus De Jonge, "Rachel's Virtuous Behavior in the Testament of Issachar," *Greeks, Romans and Christians*, 340–52.

63 Scot McKnight, *A Light among the Gentiles* (Minneapolis: Fortress Press, 1991).

64 On the supposed problems with this "abrupt warning," see A. J. M. Wedderburn, *The Reasons for Romans* (Edinburgh: T. and T. Clark, 1988), 15.

65 For my reading, see, "Friends and Enemies," 105–21.

66 See my "Fourth Maccabees," in *Harper's Bible Commentary*, ed. J. L. Mays (San Francisco: Harper and Row, 1988), 922–34.

67 David E. Aune, "Human Nature and Ethics in Hellenistic Philosophical Traditions and Paul," in *Paul in His Hellenistic Context*, ed. Troels Engberg-Pedersen (Minneapolis: Fortress Press, 1994).

68 On this difficulty, see Richard B. Hayes, "Christology and Ethics in Galatians: The Law of Christ," *CBQ* 49 (1987): 268–72; J. C. Beker, *Paul the Apostle* (Philadelphia: Fortress Press, 1980), 272–301.

69 An approach of older commentators, recycled as "the relation between *kerygma* and *didache*" or " indicative and imperative" or "theological basis and practical conclusions." See further Victor Paul Furnish, *Theology and Ethics in Paul* (Nashville: Abingdon, 1968), 98–99; Dunn, *Romans*, 2.705–06.

70 *Die Formgeschichte des Evangeliums*, 3d rev. ed. (Tübingen: J. C. B. Mohr, 1959), 139; *From Tradition to Gospel* (New York: Scribners, 1935), 238.

71 Abraham. J. Malherbe, "Hellenistic Moralists and the New Testament," *ANRW* 2.26 (forthcoming); *Paul and the Popular Philosophers* (Minneapolis: Fortress Press, 1989), 49–66; *Letter Writing*, 23, 94–106.

72 For 1 Thessalonians, see Malherbe, "Hellenistic Moralists"; for Romans, Furnish, *Theology and Ethics*, 98–111, and generally, 92–98.

73 For a critique of this method, see my " Friends and Enemies."

74 For the mind-boggling variety of "opponents" and "theologies," see Jerry L. Sumney,

Identifying Paul's Opponents: The Question of Method in 2 Corinthians (JSNTS Suppl. 40; Sheffield: JSOT Press, 1990); B. H. Brinsmead, *Galatians-Dialogical Response to Opponents* (SBLDS 65; Chico, Cal.: Scholars Press, 1982).

75 Richard B. Hays, *The Faith of Jesus* (SBLDS 56; Chico, Cal.: Scholars Press, 1983), 143–49.

76 Wayne A. Meeks, *The First Urban Christians: The Social World of the Apostle Paul* (New Haven: Yale University Press, 1983), 55–63; Gerd Theissen, *The Social Setting of Pauline Christianity* (Philadelphia: Fortress Press, 1982); Peter Lampe, *Die stadtrömischen Christen in den ersten beiden Jahrhunderten* (WUNT 2, 18; Tübingen: J. C. B. Mohr, 1989), 124–296.

77 Meeks, *Urban Christians*, 73.

78 Numerous studies have settled the issue of the Roman address of chapter 16 in the positive: e.g, Harry A. Gamble, Jr., *The Textual History of the Letter to the Romans* (Grand Rapids: Eerdmans, 1977); Kurt Aland, *Neutestamentliche Entwürfe* (Munich: Kaiser, 1979), 284–301; Wolf-Henning Ollrog, "Die Abfassungsverhältnisse von Röm 16," *Kirche: Festschrift für Günther Bornkamm zum 75. Geburtstag,* ed, D. Lührmann and G. Strecker (Tübingen: J. C. B. Mohr, 1980), 221–44; Lampe, stadtrömischen Christen, 124–35.

79 Maria in 16:6 is unlikely to be Jewish and probably is a child of a freedperson from the *gens* Marius (Lampe, stadtrömischen Christen, 146–47).

80 *Meeks, Urban Christians,* 59. Lampe's attempts to downplay their higher economic (and probably social) level are completely unconvincing, relying on elite stereotypes of artisans and failing to detect Paul's own social attitudes (stadtrömischen Christen, 159–64, 451–52).

81 Cranfield, *Romans,* 2:784; Sanday and Headlam, *Romans,* 418–20.

82 Meeks, *Urban Christians,* 59. Lampe employs anachronistic and naive arguments, claiming that Paul shows no regard for "status in pagan society," in order to deny Prisca's prominence (ibid., 158–64).

83 Lampe, *stadtrömischen Christen,* 7.

84 P. R. C. Weaver, *Familia Caesaris: A Social Study of the Emperor's Freedmen and Slaves* (Cambridge: Cambridge University Press, 1972); F. G. B. Millar, *The Emperor in the Roman World* (London, 1977), chap. 3.

85 Meeks, *Urban Christians,* 63; John T. Fitzgerald, "Philippians," *Anchor Bible Dictionary,* ed. D. N. Freedman (New York: Doubleday, 1992), 322–23.

86 Stowers, "Friends and Enemies"; and especially the dissertation in progress at Yale by Ken L. Berry, "The Function of Friendship Language in Paul's Letter to the Philippians"; Fitzgerald, "Philippians," 320–22.

87 *Corpus Inscriptionum Latinarum,* vol. 6, 17577, 29104 (Lampe, *stadtrömischen Christen,* 136).

88 J. B. Lightfoot, *St. Paul's Epistle to the Philippians* (London: Macmillan, 1878; rprt. 1908), 172–73; Cranfield, *Romans,* 791–92.

89 Lightfoot, *Philippians,* 173.

90 On the imperial house under Claudius, see Arnaldo Momigliano, *Claudius: The Emperor and His Achievement* (Cambridge: Cambridge University Press, 1961).

91 *CIL* 6.4016, 4032, 4035; Lightfoot, *Philippians,* 173.

92 Anthony J. Saldarini's (*Pharisees, Scribes and Saducees in Palestinian Society* [Wilming-

ton, Del.: Michael Glazer, 1988]) description of the Pharisees as retainers aptly characterizes their social location.

93 Lightfoot, *Philippians,* 173; Cranfield, *Romans,* 2:792 n. 6.

94 Concluded by Lampe (*stadtrömischen Christen*), who overdraws the picture of Roman Christianity as a "slave religion." Meeks (*Urban Christians,* 51–73) has a more nuanced reading of the evidence, but both support the picture of the persons in chapter 16 as mostly slaves and freedpersons.

95 P. R. C. Weaver, "Social Mobility in the Early Roman Empire: The Evidence of Imperial Freedmen and Slaves," in *Studies in Ancient Society,* ed. M. I. Finley (London, 1974), 121–40.

96 Elizabeth Schüssler Fiorenza, *In Memory of Her: A Feminist Theological Reconstruction of Christian Origins* (New York: Crossroads, 1986), 160–204.

97 For Felix's life, see Emil Shürer, *The History of the Jewish People in the Age of Jesus Christ,* rev. ed. G. Vermes and F. Millar (Edinburgh: T. and T. Clark, 1973), 460–66.

98 Loveday Alexander, "Paul and the Hellenistic Schools: The Evidence of Galen," in *Paul in His Hellenistic Context,* ed. Engberg-Pedersen.

99 Translation adapted from Richard Walzer, *Galen on Jews and Christians* (Oxford: Oxford University Press, 1949), 65.

Chapter 3. Gentile Culture and God's Impartial Justice

1 *PLJP,* 125.

2 *Paul and the Law.*

3 *PLJP,* 124.

4 Ibid., 125.

5 *PLJP,* 124; cf. Räisänen, "Paul's Theological Difficulties with the Law," *Studia Biblica* (1980): 301–02.

6 Hilary Putnam, *Reason, Truth, and History* (Cambridge: Cambridge University Press, 1981), 215; also Richard Bernstein, *Beyond Objectivism and Relativism* (Philadelphia: University of Pennsylvania Press, 1983).

7 *Paul and the Law,* 97–109; *PLJP,* 123–36.

8 A. O. Lovejoy and A. G. Boas, *Primitivism and Related Ideas in Antiquity* (Baltimore: Johns Hopkins University Press, 1935); W. K. C. Guthrie, *In the Beginning: Some Greek Views of the Origins of Life and the Early State of Man* (Ithaca: Cornell University Press, 1957).

9 Isaak Heinemann, *Philons Griechische und Jüdische Bildung* (Hildescheim: Georg Olms, 1962), 142–54. Whether Philo's primitivism is to be traced specifically to Cynic sources, as Heinemann claims, is open to question.

10 Louis H. Feldman, "Hellenizations in Josephus' Portrayal of Man's Decline," in *Religions in Antiquity,* ed. Jacob Neusner (Numen Suppl. 14; Leiden: E. J. Brill, 1968), 336–53.

11 For these characteristics, see Guthrie, *In the Beginning,* Lovejoy and Boas, *Primitivism,* and Feldman, "Hellenizations."

12 Guthrie, *In the Beginning,* 70–73; Lovejoy and Boas, *Primitivism,* 24–25.

13 Hesiod, *Erg.* 7.1.42–105; Lovejoy and Boas, *Primitivism,* 196.

14   For examples of this uncritical assumption, see John R. Levison, *Portraits of Adam in Early Judaism: From Sirach to 2 Baruch* (Sheffield: JSOT Press, 1988), 1–31.

15   M. D. Hooker, "Adam in Romans 1," *NTS* 6 (1959–60): 297–306; id., "A Further Note on Romans 1," *NTS* 13 (1966–67): 181–83; A. J. M. Wedderburn, "Adam in Paul's Letter to the Romans," *Studia Biblica* 3, ed. E. A. Livingstone (JSNTS Suppl. 3; Sheffield: JSOT Press, 1980), 413–30, and many others.

16   See Levison's (*Portraits of Adam*, 20–21) sharp critique of Dunn's claims for Adam in Paul.

17   Ibid., 13.

18   Ibid., 33–62.

19   Ibid., 60.

20   Ibid., 63–68.

21   Ibid., 89–97.

22   Ibid., 99–111.

23   Ibid., 113–44.

24   Bodo Gratz, *Weltalter, goldene Zeit und sinnverwandte Vorstellungen* (Spudasmata 16; Hildesheim: Georg Olms, 1967), 1–27; Arthur Droge, *Homer or Moses?: Early Christian Interpretations of the History of Culture* (HUT 26; Tübingen: J. C. B. Mohr, 1989), 12–47, esp. 36–41; Feldman, "Hellenizations."

25   Claus Westermann, *Genesis* (BKAT; Neukirchen-Vluyn: Neukirchener, 1974).

26   Paul D. Hanson, "Rebellion in Heavan, Azazel, and Euhemeristic Heroes in 1 Enoch," *JBL* 96 (1977): 195–233.

27   Westermann, *Genesis,* 662–63 (bibliography).

28   Ibid., 707–14.

29   F. Hartog, *The Mirror of Herodotus: The Representation of the Other in the Writing of History* (Berkeley: University of California Press, 1988), 7.

30   John A. Ziesler, "Anthropology of Hope," *Expository Times* 90 (1979): 104–09; N. P. Williams, *The Ideas of the Fall and of Original Sin* (London: Longmans, Green, 1927), 1–35, 93–390. Excepting the gnostics, Christians sources of the first two centuries are stunningly silent about the Adamic fall; e.g., *1 Clem.*, *Barn.*, *Herm.*, Ignatius, Justin, *Ap.* (but see *D. Trypho* 88.4, in which he says no more than Paul). The later Christian exaltation of the prefall state, and thus the emphasis on the depth of the fall, is certainly related to the platonization of Christianity. Origen believed that rational souls that were originally in fellowship with God turned away and fell. For their punishment and education they fell into a gross material world and bodies. Augustine posited a heavenly precreation soul that fell into bodies. Thus man's true nature is that of an exalted heavenly soul equal to the angels. A precipitous fall indeed! Hal Koch, *Pronoia und Paideusis: Studien über Origenes und seun Verhältnis zum Platonismus* (Berlin: De Gruyter, 1932; reprt. New York: Garland, 1979); Robert J. O'Connell, *St. Augustine's Early Theory of Man* (Cambridge: Harvard University Press, 1968); id., *St Augustine's Confessions: The Odyssey of Soul* (Cambridge: Harvard University Press, 1969). For an important platonizing reading of Rom 1:18–32 and Gen 1–3, see Athanasius, *Against the Gentiles*, 1–9.

31   Ziesler, "Hope," 106.

32   David M. Coffey, "Natural Knowledge of God: Reflections on Romans 1:18–32," *TS* 31 (1970): 674–83; André Feuillet, "La connaissance naturelle de Dieu par les hommes,

d'apres Rom. 1," *Lumière et Vie* 14 (1954): 63–80. Coffey provides a reading of the passage as past historical time. I agree with Feuillet only on this point. Most commentators ignore the tenses in 1:18–2:16.

33 Greeks and Romans were associated with anthropomorphic gods; Egyptians and sometimes Canaanites with animal gods (Wis 15:18f.; Philo, *Decal.* 76–80; *Vit. Cont.* 8f.).

34 My argument is that Paul would apply 1:32 only to gentiles living since the Mosaic law but that in his sweeping style here he leaves out the details and qualifications. Paul strongly links 1:32 to 2:1ff. The emphatic linkage shows that 1:32 speaks of gentiles in Paul's own day because 2:1–16 has present-day gentiles in view.

35 E. Klostermann, "Die adäquate Vergeltung in Rom 1:22–31," *ZNW* 32 (1933): 1–6; Jouette Bassler, *The Impartiality of God: Paul's Use of a Theological Axiom* (Chico, Cal.: Scholars Press, 1982), 128–34.

36 Bassler, *Impartiality of God,* 122, 195–97. Bassler's claims are more careful and nuanced than those of most scholars; Cranfield, *Romans,* 1:119; Dunn, *Romans,* 1.61, and many others. Writers also often cite Jer 2:11 as a possible double for the allusion, but the difficulties with Jer 2:11 are even greater than for Ps 105:20 and the criticisms of the latter also apply to the former.

37 A. J. M. Wedderburn, *The Reasons for Romans* (Edinburgh: T. and T. Clark, 1988), 119–20.

38 Codex Alexandrinus has *doxa autou* instead of *doxa auton,* clearly an assimilation to the Hebrew in keeping with its assimilationist tendencies.

39 The Masoretic text speaks of God's glory, but there is no reason to think that Paul's readers would have any acquaintance with the Hebrew.

40 As I have argued in chapter 2, the issues here are actually those of gender, not of what we think of as biological sex.

41 One might also recognize a code of honor and shame: Halvor Moxnes, "Honor, Shame and the Outside World in Paul's Letter to the Romans," *The Social World of Formative Christianity and Judaism: Essays in Tribute to Howard Clark Kee,* ed. P. Borgen, E. Frerichs, et al. (Philadelphia: Fortress Press, 1988), 207–18.

42 Nancy Jay, *Throughout Your Generations Forever: Sacrifice, Religion and Paternity* (Chicago: University of Chicago Press, 1992).

43 So, for example, "homosexuality" contains the very modern idea of "sexuality," a stable disposition toward one of two sexes that is central to one's identity, psychology, and gender. As far as I can tell, evidence for anything like this is lacking from Greco-Roman antiquity. For scholarship on this question, see chapter 2 above.

44 See chapter 2 above.

45 Thomas Laqueur, *Making Sex: Body and Gender from the Greeks to Freud* (Cambridge: Harvard University Press, 1990).

46 To the expression in 1:27, compare Aiskhines (155–57) speaking of *pornoi* "sinning against their own persons" (*eis heautous exhamartanontas*).

47 Verse 27 does not imply the stable preference for the same sex that is part of the modern concept of homosexuality but rather loss of the power to resist the desire for the same sex. Ancients generally considered the desire for the same sex naturally present in all. The debate was about whether that passion should be resisted or not.

48 John J. Winkler, *The Constraints of Desire: An Anthropology of Sex and Gender in Ancient Greece* (New York: Routledge, 1990), 38–40.

49 Mary Douglas, *Purity and Danger* (London: Routledge, 1966).

50 Douglas does argue that the code reinforced the boundaries between Israelites and non-Israelites but largely ignores Israelite social structure (see Eilberg-Schwartz, n. 53 below).

51 "Greeks Who Sacrifice and Those Who Do Not: Toward an Anthropology of Greek Religion," in *The First Christians and Their Social World: Studies in Honor of Wayne A. Meeks*, ed. L. M. White and O. L. Yarbrough (Minneapolis: Fortress Press, forthcoming).

52 See ibid for a discussion of the characteristics of such sacrificial systems. Although my article treats the Greek sacrificial order, similar principles apply to the second temple in Jerusalem. See also Jay, *Throughout Your Generations*, 94–111.

53 Jay, ibid.; Howard Eilberg-Schwartz, *The Savage in Judaism: An Anthropology of Israelite Religion and Ancient Judaism* (Bloomington: Indiana University Press, 1990), 174–94.

54 Num 15:14–15; Lev 16:29; 17:8–13; 18:26; 19:10. Gentiles seem to have been increasingly kept at further distance from the cult, e.g., Ez. 44:9; Jos., *Ant.* 12.145–9; *Bel.* 194.

55 E. Shürer and G. Vermes, *The History of the Jewish People in the Age of Jesus Christ* (Edinburgh: T. and T. Clark, 1973–86), 1:176, 378; 2:222, 284f.

56 Isa 2:2–4; Mic 4:1–5, cf. Isa 56:6; Tob. 13:11; Ps. Sol. 17:31; *Sib. Or.* 3.710–20, 772f.

57 All of the letters use the language of saints or holy ones. On impurity, see 1 Cor 7:1; 2 Cor 6:17–7:1, 12:21; Gal 5:19; Rom 6:19, 21.

58 For *skeuos* as "wife," see O. Larry Yarbrough, *Not Like the Gentiles: Marriage Rules in the Letters of Paul* (SBLDS 80; Atlanta: Scholars Press, 1985), 65–87.

59 Many of the sources are found in Lovejoy and Boas, *Primitivism*.

60 Werner Jaeger, *Aristotle: Fundamentals of the History of His Development*, 2d ed.(Oxford: Oxford University Press, 1948), 76.

61 Wilhelm Gerhäusser, *Der Protreptikos des Poseidonios* (Munich: C. Wolf and Sohn, 1912), 18–31. Gerhäusser's reconstruction is on the whole much too speculative, but he is convincing on this point.

62 Cf. Maximus of Tyre's 36th *Oration*, in which he employs an account of the golden age and of the fall into unnatural vices, including false conceptions of the gods.

63 F. H. Reuters, *Die Briefe des Anacharsis* (Schriften und Quelle des Alten Welt 14; Berlin, 1963). For a translation and brief introduction, see *Letter Writing*, 118–21.

64 Klostermann, "Die adäquate Vergeltung," 1–6; Bassler, *Impartiality*, 128–31.

65 Bassler, *Impartiality*, and *passim*.

66 *Diatribe and Romans*, 79–118.

67 Ibid., 101–10; Otto Ribbeck, *ALAZON: Ein Beitrag zur antiken Ethologie* (Leipzig: Teubner, 1882).

68 For the various positions, see Dieter Zeller, *Juden und Heiden in der Misson bei Paulus*, 2d ed. (Stuttgart: Katholisches Bibelwerk, 1976), 149 and n. 36; Dunn, *Romans*, 79.

69 *Diatribe and Romans*, 108–09; Ribbeck, *ALAZON*. In fact, *ho alazōn* is often translated as "the braggart" or "the boaster."

70 God punishes those who disobey the truth from "selfish ambition" (2:7–8). The gentile only stands by his faithfulness and ought to stand in awe instead of becoming proud (11:17–24). Paul tries to instill awe in the arrogant man of 2:1–5, threatening

God's punishment and accusing him of possessing a hardened heart. The apostle warns him not to despise God's goodness (*chrēstotēs*) and forbearance. Similarly 11:22 reminds the gentile of God's goodness (*chrēstotēs*) and severity, urging him to remain in God's goodness.

71 Bassler (*Impartiality,* 123–37) demonstrates the unity of the discourse most powerfully.

72 Sam K. Williams, *Jesus' Death as Saving Event: The Background and Origin of a Concept* (HDR 2; Missoula, Mont.: Scholars Press, 1975).

73 The N.T. writings never use *paresis* (3:25) to mean forgiveness but rather *aphesis.*

74 First Thess 2:16 contains a similar constellation of ideas about Jews who have violently opposed the followers of Christ and the gentile mission. The basic idea here is of a limit to God's patience.

75 Plutarch, *On the Delays of Divine Punishment, Moralia* 548–68.

76 E.g., Wis 11:23; 12:2, 10; Bertil Gaertner, *The Areopagus Speech and Natural Revelation* (Uppsala: Gleerup, 1955), 239f.

77 For a brief sketch of "abstract individualism," see Steven Lukes, *Individualism* (Oxford: Basil Blackwell, 1973), 73–78; cf. 94–98; L. Dumont, "The Modern Conception of the Individual: Notes on its Genesis and that of Concomitant Institutions," *Contributions to Indian Sociology* 8 (1965): 24–41.

78 G. E. R. Lloyd, *Methods and Problems in Greek Science* (Cambridge: Cambridge University Press, 1991), 417–34.

79 Urs Dierauer, *Tier und Mensch im Denken der Antike: Studien zur Tierpsychologie, Anthropologie und Ethik* (Amsterdam: B. R. Grüner, 1977).

80 Gisela Striker, "Origins of the Concept of Natural Law," in *Proceedings of the Boston Area Colloquium in Ancient Philosophy,* vol. 2, ed. J. Cleary (Lanham, Md.: University Press of America, 1987), 79–94; Brad Inwood, "Commentary on Striker," ibid., 95–101; Gerard Watson, "The Natural Law in Stoicism," in *Problems in Stoicism,* ed. A. A. Long (London, 1971), 216–38.

81 *SVF* 1.162, 3.314, 613, 614; D. L. 7.87–88.

82 Inwood, "Commentary," 97–99; *Ethics and Human Action in Early Stoicism* (Oxford: Oxford University Press, 1985), 105–11, 205–15; Andrew Erskine, *The Hellenistic Stoa: Political Thought and Action* (Ithaca: Cornell University Press, 1990), 16, 22–23; Watson, "Natural Law," passim; I. G. Kidd, "Moral Actions and Rules in Stoic Ethics," in *The Stoics,* ed. J. M. Rist (Berkeley: University of California Press, 1978), 247–58; N. P. White, "Two Notes on Stoic Terminology," *AJP* 99 (1978): 111–19.

83 Erskine, *Hellenistic Stoa,* 68–70, 207–08.

84 Ibid., 15–74.

85 Watson, "Natural Law"; Inwood, "Commentary," 96–98; Helmut Koester, "NOMOS PHYSEOS: The Concept of Natural Law in Greek Thought," in *Religions in Antiquity: Essays in Memory of Erwin Ramsdell Goodenough,* ed. Jacob Neusner (Leiden: E. J. Brill, 1968), 521–41.

86 Koester, "NOMOS PHYSEOS."

87 Similarly also Zeno (*SVF* 1.226).

88 Inwood, "Commentary," 98; Watson, "Natural Law," 225–36.

89 See Erskine, *Hellenistic Stoa,* with extensive bibliography on the aims of the early Stoa.

90 Ibid., 31–32, 60–67, 73–78, 195–96.

91 Ibid., 103–10, 154–61, 192–214; Watson, "Natural Law," 224–25.

92 Watson, "Natural Law," 224 f.

93 Erskine, *Hellenistic Stoa*, 193; Watson, "Natural Law," 226–27.

94 "Nature" appears in Rom 1:26; 2:27; 11:21, 24; 1 Cor 11:14; Gal 2:15; 4:8. Only 1:26 and 1 Cor 11:14 support standards of behavior. Other uses vary. In Rom 11:21, 24, for instance, grafting branches is unnatural. *Para physin* is used of grafting here and of homoerotic behavior in 1:26.

95 George Howard, *Paul: Crisis in Galatia* (SNTSMS 35; Cambridge: Cambridge University Press, 1979), esp. 66–82; *PLJP*, 81–86; *Paul and the Law*, 18–23; also Heinrich Schlier, *Der brief and die Galater*, 5th ed. (Göttingen: Vandenhoeck and Ruprecht, 1971), 136–38. Recently James D. G. Dunn has claimed that Paul did not consider gentiles to be under the law on the basis of Rom 2:12 ("Works of the Law and the Curse of the Law: Galatians 3:10–14," *NTS* 31 [1985]: 529).

96 I speak of "the plain sense of the text" here because, in spite of all the efforts to find "Jewish Christians" or hypothetical gentiles here, most scholars have declared the attempts artificial and hold that the verses speak of gentiles. See *Paul and the Law*, 101–09.

97 For several formulations of gentile knowledge and status, see E. P. Sanders, *Paul and Palestinian Judaism*, 206–12, 331.

98 W. D. Davies, *Paul and Rabbinic Judaism*, rev. ed (Philadelphia: Fortress Press, 1980), 114ff.; K. Hruby, "Le concept de Revelation dans la théologie rabbinique," *Orient Syrien* 11 (1966): 17–50, 169–98; S. S. Schwarzschild, "Do Noachites Have to Believe in Revelation?," *JQR* 52 (1961–62): 297–308; 53 (1962–63): 30–65.

99 Koester, *NOMOS PHYSEOS*; Richard Horsley, "The Law of Nature in Philo and Cicero," *HTR* 71 (1978): 35–59; W. A. Banner, "Origen and the Tradition of Natural Law Concepts," *DOP* 8 (1954): 49–82.

100 Arthur J. Droge, *Homer or Moses*, 1–48; "The Interpretation of the History of Culture in Hellenistic-Jewish Historiography," in *Society of Biblical Literature 1984 Seminar Papers*, ed. Kent H. Richards (Chico, Cal.: Scholars Press, 1984), 135–59; John G. Gager, *Moses in Greco-Roman Paganism* (SBLMS 16; Nashville: Abingdon, 1972), 25–79.

101 Elias J. Bickermann, "*Origenes Gentium*," *CPhil.* 47 (1952): 65–81.

102 Ibid., 68.

103 The exceptions are Cranfield, *Romans*, 1:156–57; Paul J. Achtemier, *Romans* (Interpretation; Atlanta: John Knox Press, 1985), 44–45. Cranfield also refers to Bengel, whose work I have not been able to consult. On Origen's reading, see Riemer Roukema, *The Diversity of Laws in Origen's Commentary on Romans* (Amsterdam: Free University Press, 1988), 21–23.

104 E.g., Nigel Turner, *A Grammar of the Greek New Testament* (Edinburgh: T. and T. Clark, 1963), 227–29.

105 It is difficult to find a translation of *grammati* and *pneumati* in v. 29 that does not impose some scheme of spirituality foreign to Paul. "Books of the law" is an overtranslation but helps one grasp the meaning of the verse.

106 Winkler, *Constraints of Desire*, 17f., 62 (with reference to Bourdieu).

107 Gratz, *Weltalter*.

108 Gratz (ibid.) discusses both Hesiod's account and the tradition that followed him into the early empire.

109 Edwin Judge, "The Roman Theory of Historical Degeneration," *Hermes: The Magazine of the University of Sydney* 58 (1961): 5–8.

110 On Piso, see ibid.

111 Andrew Wallace-Hadrill, "The Golden Age and Sin in Augustan Ideology," *Past and Present* 95 (1982): 19–36.

112 R. G. M. Nisbet, "Virgil's Fourth Eclogue: Easterners and Westerners," *BICS* 25 (1978): 59–78.

113 Valentin Nikiprowetzky, *La troisième Sibylle* (Paris: Mouton, 1970); Gratz, *Weltalter*, 79–83.

114 Gratz, *Weltalter*, 58–63, 64–70.

115 Wallace-Hadrill, "Golden Age," 24–27.

116 J. H. W. G. Liebeschuetz, *Continuity and Change in Roman Religion* (Oxford: Oxford University Press, 1979), 92–100.

117 Paul Zanker, *The Power of Images in the Age of Augustus* (Ann Arbor: University of Michigan Press, 1988), 85–87.

118 Zanker, *Power of Images*, 88–89, 167–92.

119 Gratz, *Weltalter*, 138–39; for coinage, see H. Mattingly, "Virgil's Fourth Eclogue," *Jl. Warburg and Courtland Inst.* 10 (1947): 14–29.

120 Suet., *Tib.* 59; cited by Wallace-Hadrill, "Golden Age," 22, n. 26.

121 Calp. Sic., *Ec.* 1.20f.; Seneca, *Apoc.* 4; *De Clem.* 2.1.3; Lucan, *Phar.* 1.45–62. The great majority of commentators date the letter between 54 and 58. Nero ruled from 54 to 68. On the various possibilities for dating Romans, see Cranfield, *Romans*, 1:12–16.

122 Miriam Griffin, *Seneca: A Philosopher in Politics* (Oxford: Oxford University Press, 1976), 129–34.

123 1.1.1; Wallace-Hadrill, "Golden Age," 30–31.

Chapter 4. Warning a Greek and Debating a Jew

1 Klyne R. Snodgrass, "'Justification by Grace' to the Doers: An Analysis of the Place of Romans 2 in the Theology of Paul," *NTS* 32 (1986): 72–73.

2 Ibid., 72, and notes 4–8; see below on Origen.

3 Ibid., 72–75, and notes 5–8; see below on Augustine.

4 *Comm. in Rom.* 2:8–11 (891D-894C); Riemer Roukema, *The Diversity of Laws in Origen's Commentary on Romans* (Amsterdam: Free University Press, 1988), 21–23; Georg Teichtweier, *Die Sünderlehre des Origenes* (Regensburg: Friedrich Pustet, 1958), 67ff.; Peter Gorday, *Principles of Patristic Exegesis: Romans 9–11 in Origen, John Chrysostom, and Augustine* (New York: Edwin Mellen, 1983), 55ff.

5 *Contra Jul.* 4.3.25; n. 7 below.

6 Gorday, *Principles*, 155; *The Letter and the Spirit* 26:44.

7 Gorday, *Principles*.

8 Ibid., 43–102.

9   For the major options, see Snodgrass, "Place of Romans," 73–77; *Paul and the Law,* 97–113; *PLJP,* 123–35; Käsemann, *Romans,* 53–68.

10 Wilhelm Schmidt, *Der Brief des Paulus an die Römer* (THNT; Berlin, 1962), 287.

11 J. C. O'Neill, *Paul's Letter to the Romans* (Baltimore: Penguin, 1975), 48.

12 Ibid.

13 *PLJP,* 123–35.

14 *Paul and the Law,* 76–113.

15 Eberhard Jüngel, "Ein Paulinischer Chiasmus: zum Verständnis der Vorstellung vom Gericht nach den Werken in Rom 2, 2–22," *Unterwegs zur Sache* (Munich: Christian Kaiser, 1972), 173–74; Kendrick Grobel, "A Chiastic Retribution-Formula in Romans 2," *Zeit und Geschichte,* ed. Erich Dinkler (Tübingen: J. C. B. Mohr, 1964), 255–61; cf. Snodgrass, "Place of Romans," 80–81.

16 Explicit in 2:10 and implied in 2:7. On the parallel between 2:10 and 1:18f., see Snodgrass, "Place of Romans," 80–81.

17 Marcel Simon, *Verus Israel* (Paris: E. de Boccard, 1948, with postscript, 1964, 1983; English transl., Oxford University Press, 1986).

18 Exodus 30:31–32; Johannes Munck, *Paul and the Salvation of Mankind* (Richmond, Va.: John Knox, 1959), 43.

19 Brendan Byrne, *Sons of God—Seed of Abraham* (Analecta Biblica 83; Rome: Biblical Institute, 1979), 127–39.

20 Ibid., 82, n. 12; Otto Michel, *Der Brief an die Römer* (KEK 4; Göttingen, 1978) on 9:4; Lucian Cerfaux, "Le privilege d'Israel selon Saint Paul," *ETL* 17 (1940): 5–26.

21 Thus sources equate the loss or desecration of the temple with the loss of God's presence (e.g., Ezek 9:3; 10:4–5; 11:23; 1 Sam 4:21; cf. H. G. May, "The Ark—A Miniature Temple," *AJSL* 52 (1936): 215–34.

22 R. J. Mckelvey, *The New Temple: The Church in the New Testament* (OTM; London: Oxford University Press, 1969), 92–107; and more cautiously W. D. Davies, *The Gospel and the Land* (Berkeley: University of California Press, 1974), 164–220; also 2 Cor 6:14–7:1; 1 Cor 3:16–17.

23 Davies, *Gospel and the Land,* 190.

24 Ibid., 188–89.

25 For the tactic used to dismiss Paul's statement in 9:4–5, see Lloyd Gaston, "Israel's Enemies in Pauline Theology," *NTS* 28 (1981): 411–12.

26 Davies, *Gospel and the Land,* 191.

27 Ibid., 193–94; Ernest Best, *A Commentary on the First and Second Epistles to the Thessalonians* (HNTC; New York: Harper and Row, 1972), 281–307.

28 On the complex issues, see Cranfield, *Romans,* 2:577–78; Schlier, *Römerbrief,* 453.

29 Davies raises this as a possibility (*Gospel and the Land,* 195).

30 Wesley Carr, *Angels and Principalities* (SNTSMS 42; Cambridge: Cambridge University Press, 1981).

31 Munck, *Paul and the Salvation of Mankind.*

32 Dieter Georgi, *Die Geschichte der Kollekte des Paulus für Jerusalem* (Hamburg-Bergstedt: Reich, 1965).

33 "Righteousness of God," 285.

34 On the grammatical difficulties, see ibid.; Cranfield, *Romans,* 2:740–43; Käsemann, *Romans,* 385.

35 Nils A. Dahl, *Studies in Paul* (Minneapolis: Augsburg, 1977), 87.

36 "Paul and Torah," 71, n. 60: "The phrase (i.e., "under law") does not appear in the Greek of Roman 2:12, which should be translated: 'Those who have sinned godlessly will perish godlessly, while those who have sinned in (the status of) Torah will be judged on the basis of the Torah.' cf. James 2:12."

37 *"anomia" TDNT* 4, 1085–87.

38 *Oxyrhynchus Papyri* (London: Egypt Exploration Society, 1911).

39 Trans. F. H. Colson and G. H. Whitaker, *Philo* (LCL; Cambridge: Harvard University Press, 1929) 1:53.

40 Liddell, Scott, and Jones, *Greek-English Lexicon* (Oxford: Oxford University Press, 1968).

41 James Davison, *"Anomia* and the Question of Antinomian Polemic in Matthew," *JBL* 104 (1985): 617–35.

42 Ibid., 619.

43 Ibid., 625; Gutbrod, *"Anomia,"* 1087.

44 Gutbrod, *"Anomia,"* 1087.

45 Ibid.

46 James Barr, *The Semantics of Biblical Language* (London: Oxford University Press, 1961).

47 Heliodorus, *Ethiopian Story* (London: J. M. Dent, 1961).

48 *Heliodorus: An Ethiopian Romance* (Ann Arbor: University of Michigan Press, 1957), 203.

49 W. A. Banner, "Origen and the Tradition of Natural Law Concepts," *DOP* 8 (1954): 49–82.

50 *Paul and the Law,* 26.

51 Karl P. Donfried, "Justification and Last Judgment in Paul," *Interpretation* 30 (1976); Nigel M. Watson, "Justified by Faith; Judged by Works—An Antimony?" *NTS* 29 (1983); *PLPJ,* 105–09; Snodgrass, "Place of Romans," 72–77.

52 E. P. Sanders, *Jesus and Judaism* (Philadelphia: Fortress Press, 1985), 177.

53 Käsemann's description of "Jewish nomism" exemplifies the picture of Judaism read into 2:17–29: "What does the Jewish nomism against which Paul fought really represent? And our answer must be: it represents the community of 'good' people which turns God's promises into their own privileges and God's commandments into the instruments of self-sanctification." *Perspectives on Paul* (Philadelphia: Fortress Press, 1971), 72. Against such views, see Bernard Jackson, "Legalism," *JJS* 30 (1979): 1–22.

54 Käsemann, *Perspectives on Paul,* 68; Gunther Bornkamm, *Paul* (New York: Harper and Row, 1969), 6.

55 Bornkamm, *Paul,* 68–69.

56 Heinrich Schlier, *Die Zeit der Kirche* (Freiburg: Herder, 1956), 38–47; Käsemann, *Romans,* 68–77; Keck, *Paul and Letters,* 67. Against the whole scholarly picture of "Jewish self-understanding," see *PPJ,* esp. 419–28.

57 Victor Paul Furnish, *Theology and Ethics in Paul* (Nashville: Abingdon, 1968), 192.

58 Cranfield, *Romans,* 1:168.

59 Ibid., 1:108.

60 Bultmann, *Theology of the New Testament* (New York: Scribners, 1951), 1:241. According to Bultmann, boasting is characteristic of both Jew and Greek. The Jew boasts of the law and the Greek of wisdom, but Bultmann places far greater stress on Jewish boasting.

61 Käsemann, *Romans,* 85.

62 Ibid.

63 Jacob Neusner, *From Politics to Piety: The Emergence of Pharisaic Judaism* (Englewood Cliffs, NJ: Prentice-Hall, 1973), 67–80.

64 *Diatribe and Romans* 79–97.

65 Ibid., 7–78

66 Ibid., 115–18, 152–54, 174, 175–84.

67 Ibid., 108–15; Otto Ribbeck, *ALAZON: Ein Beitrag zur antiken Ethologie* (Leipzig: Teubner, 1882).

68 Ribbeck, *ALAZON,* 55–191.

69 Theophrastus, *Char.* 23.1; cf. Xen. *Cyrop.* 2.2.12; P. Steinmetz, *Theophrastus: Charaktere* (Munich: Huber, 1962), 2:262–76.

70 *Diatribe and Romans,* 221, nn. 114–15; cf. 108–09.

71 Ibid., 108–10.

72 See the examples in *Diatribe and Romans,* 96.

73 Cranfield, *Romans,* 164; Karl Barth, *A Shorter Commentary on Romans* (London: SCM, 1959), 37.

74 Scott Mcknight, *A Light among the Gentiles* (Minneapolis: Fortress Press, 1991).

75 Sanders, *Jesus and Judaism,* 176–79.

76 Ibid., 177.

77 My reading is indebted to *Paul and Torah,* 64–79.

Chapter 5. Paul's Dialogue with a Fellow Jew

1 C. H. Dodd, *The Epistle of Paul to the Romans* (New York: Long and Smith, 1932), 48; M. Black (*Romans* [Grand Rapids, Mich.: Eerdmans, 1981], 62) says, "His mind is typically diverted . . ." Käsemann (*Romans,* 78) thinks that Paul gets carried away into a side debate that he did not plan and that he has to cut short.

2 Käsemann, *Romans,* 78. Recently the importance of 3:1–8 has been emphasized by Käsemann (ibid., 78–85) and his students, who have argued that Rom 3 contains an astoundingly subtle critique of covenant theology which Paul replaces with a universalistic theology of "creation-faithfulness." See P. Stuhlmacher, *Gerechtigkeit Gottes bei Paulus* (FRLANT 87; Göttingen: Vandenhoeck and Ruprecht, 1965), 85–90; C. Müller, *Gottes Gerechtigkeit und Gottes Volk* (FRLANT 86; Göttingen: Vandenhoeck and Ruprecht, 1964), 108–13.

3 W. S. Campbell, "Romans III as a Key to the Structure and Thought of the Letter," *NovT* 23 (1981): 23.

4 Dodd, *Romans*, 46

5 Black, *Romans*, 62–63; Cranfield, *Romans*, 1:140, 183.

6 E.g., R. Harrisville (*Romans* [ACNT; Minneapolis: Augsburg, 1980], 5): "There is the slightest hint of conversation here"; C. K. Barrett, *A Commentary on the Epistle to the Romans* [HNTC; New York: Harper and Row, 1957], 61) says, "The style of this paragraph is again that of the diatribe"; Käsemann, *Romans*, 78; Dodd, *Romans*, 43.

7 Dodd (*Romans*, 43) speaks of the "Jewish objector"; Barrett, *Romans*, 61–62; Sanday and Headlam, *Romans*, 68–70; O. Michel, *Der Brief an die Römer* (MeyerK; Göttingen: Vandenhoeck and Ruprecht, 1955), 80; O. Kuss, *Der Römerbrief* (Regensburg: Pustet, 1957), 1:99; J. Jeremias, "Zur Gedankenführung in den paulinischen Briefen," *Studia Paulina in honorem Iohannis de Zwaan septuagenarii* (Haarlem: Bohn, 1953), 146–54.

8 Käsemann, *Romans*, 78–83.

9 Cranfield, *Romans*, 1:183; R. Cornely (*Commentarius in S. Pauli Apostoli epistolas I* [Paris: Lethellieux, 1896], 164–65) says that vv. 7 and 8 are Gentile objections. On libertines, see Kuss, *Römerbrief*, 1:102. On the supposition of a libertine group at Rome, see P. Minear, *The Obedience of Faith* (SBT 19; Naperville, Ill.: Allenson, 1971), 61–62; cf. 8–10.

10 M.-J. Lagrange, *Saint Paul: Epître aux Romains* (EBib; Paris: Gabalda, 1950), 61–62.

11 R. Bultmann, *Der Stil der paulinischen Predigt und die kynisch-stoische Diatribe* (FRLANT 13; Göttingen: Vanderhoeck and Ruprecht, 1910). Against Bultmann, see *Diatribe and Romans*, 176–77, and A. J. Malherbe, "*Mē Genoito* in the Diatribe and Paul," *HTR* 73 (1980): 231–40.

12 R. Bultmann, *Theology of the New Testament* (New York: Scribners, 1951) 1:108–09; Käsemann, *Romans*, 83–85. Similarly, G. Bornkamm, *Paul* (New York: Harper and Row, 1969), 90.

13 The most valiant and imaginative attempt to give 3:1–9 a reasonable function is that of Campbell, "Romans III as a Key."

14 *Diatribe and Romans*, 48–75, 85–110, 125–47, 158–64.

15 Ibid., 56–57, 59–60, 61, 75–78, 105–10, 138–40.

16 On Epictetus, *Diss* 2.12, and dialogues, see ibid., 158–64; cf. 56–57, 138–40.

17 Ibid., 106–10.

18 Ibid.

19 Stowers, ibid., 101–04, cf. 86–92.

20 Bultmann, *Der Stil*, 10–63; Stowers, ibid., 158–64.

21 *Diatribe and Romans*, 130; Malherbe, "*Mē Genoito*."

22 Examples of the first person plural: Sen., *Ep* 5.6; 65.12; 60.3; Max. Tyr., *Or.* 31.3a; 5.4e; 6.2a; Mus. Ruf., 8.64, 35; Epict., *Diss* 1.4, 8; 1.22, 17; 2.11, 15; cf. 2.11, 17; 2.24, 9; 3.7, 2; 1.4, 5.

23 "Righteousness of God," 241–90.

24 Appendix "*LOGIA*," *Studies in the Gospels and Epistles* (Manchester: Manchester University Press, 1962), 87–104.

25 Ibid., 266–68.

26 Ibid., 269.

27 I share a limited agreement on some points of comparison with "Righteousness of God," 280–81.

28 All three meanings are possible for *sunistemi* in 3:5. Hesychius gives *bebaioun* as a synonym. In 15:8, Christ became a servant to the Jews in order to confirm (*bebaioun*) the promises. See J. A. L. Lee, "*sunistemi*: A Sample Lexical Entry," in *Melbourne Symposium on Septuagint Lexicography* (SCS 28; Atlanta: Scholars Press, 1990), esp. II.1 and 2, p. 3.

29 Cranfield, *Romans*, 1:183, and many others.

30 Cranfield (*Romans*, 1:187–91) is especially clear and complete. He, like Lagrange, Barrett, Käsemann, Harrisville, Nygren, Dodd, and most other commentators, the *RV*, *RSV*, Goodspeed, and the *NEB* take the verb as a middle used as an active.

31 Black, *Romans*, 63; Barrett, *Romans*, 67; Cranfield, *Romans*, 1:189.

32 Cranfield, *Romans*, 1:188–89.

33 Thus the *RSV* translates 3:1, "Then what advantage has the Jew? Much in every way" and 3:9, "Are we Jews any better off? No, not at all."

34 *Divine Impartiality: Paul and a Theological Axiom* (SBLDS 59; Chico, Cal.: Scholars, 1982) 121–70.

Chapter 6. Paul on Sin and Works of the Law

1 See, for example, the comments cited in *PLJP*, 124–25.

2 Günther Bornkamm, *Paul* (New York: Harper and Row, 1971), 123.

3 Birger Pearson, "I Thessalonians 2:13–16: A Deutero-Pauline Interpolation," *HTR* 64 (1971): 79–94.

4 John Hurd, "Paul Ahead of His Time: I Thess. 2:13–16," in *Anti-Judaism in Early Christianity*, vol. 1, ed. Peter Richardson (Waterloo, Ontario: Wilfred Laurier University Press, 1986), 21–36. Hurd's article, however, suffers from an ahistorical positivism.

5 Abraham J. Malherbe, "Exhortation in First Thessalonians," *NovT* 25 (1983): 243–56; *Letter Writing*, 94–106; George Lyons, *Pauline Autobiography* (SBLDS 73; Atlanta: Scholars Press, 1985), 177–218.

6 Terry Eagleton, *Literary Theory: An Introduction* (Minneapolis: University of Minnesota Press, 1983), 47–53, 127–50.

7 E.g. Dan 9:16: 2 Macc 7:38 and examples in chapter 1, above.

8 *PPJ*, 547. According to Sanders, "sin as power" distinguishes Paul's views on sin from Judaism.

9 Martin Dibelius, *Die Geisterwelt in Glauben des Paulus* (Göttingen, 1909).

10 J. Christiaan Beker, *Paul the Apostle* (Philadelphia: Fortress, 1980), 215–18.

11 Bruce N. Kaye, *The Thought Structure of Romans with Special Reference to Chapter 6* (Austin: Schola Press, 1979). Räisänen (*Paul and the Law*, 99, n. 29) writes as follows: "Romans 3.9 might suggest that sin is viewed as something more than doing sinful acts, i.e., as a demonic power; thus e.g. Dibelius, *Geisterwelt* 122f.; van Dülmen, *Theologie* 158–168; Hübner, *Gesetz* 63; Schottroff, 'Schreckenherrschaft' 497 ff.; cf. Rom 5–7. But throughout the section in question the condition of men is seen as 'a matter of their own deliberate and informed choice and action.' The citations in 3.10–18 'show, not that man is under demonic power, but that men do wicked and sinful things': Kaye, *Thought Structure* 40."

12 Leander Keck, "The Function of Rom 3:10–18—Observations and Suggestions," in *God's Christ and His People: Studies in Honour of Nils Alstrup Dahl*, ed. W. A. Meeks and J. Jervell (Oslo: University of Oslo, 1977), 146.

13 Dale C. Allison, *The End of the Age Has Come* (Philadelphia: Fortress Press, 1985), 62–29.

14 Ibid., 9–11.

15 Trans. O. S. Wintermute in *OTP* 2:101.

16 Trans. E. Isaac in *OTP* 1:59.

17 "Paul and Torah," 15–34. Gaston developed another understanding of the expression in a later article ("The Works of the Law as Subjective Genitive", *Sciences Religieuses/Studies in Religion* 13 (1981) 39).

18 Quoted from Gaston, "Subjective Genitive," 39.

19 "Paul and Torah."

20 *PPJ*, 470–72, 501.

21 John Gager, *The Origins of Anti-Semitism* (Oxford: Oxford University Press, 1983).

22 *Paul and the Law*, 184; Karl P. Donfried, "Justification and Last Judgment in Paul," *ZNW* 67 (1976): 9–110; and esp. Klyne R. Snodgrass, "'Justification by Grace' to the Doers: An Analysis of the Place of Romans 2 in the Theology of Paul," *NTS* 32 (1986): 72–93.

23 *Paul and the Law*.

24 For the references and bibliography, see ibid., 177–85.

25 Ibid., 163.

26 Ibid., 150–54.

27 Ibid., 153.

28 *PG* 14,1032B; *Paul and the Law*, 156.

29 I do not think it helpful to say, with Gaston ("Paul and Torah," 56–67), that Paul uses "law" in two different senses, "Torah," which includes the idea of covenant, and "law," which does not.

30 *Biblical Antiquities*, 11:1 and 2. Trans. Daniel J. Harrington in *OTP* 2:318.

Chapter 7. God's Merciful Justice in Christ's Faithfulness

1 Richard B. Hays, *The Faith of Jesus Christ* (SBLDS 56; Chico, Cal.: Scholars Press, 1983); M. D. Hooker, "*PISTIS CHRISTOU*," *NTS* 35 (1989): 321–42; Sam K. Williams, "Again *Pistis Christou*," *CBQ* 49 (1987): 321–42; Luke T. Johnson, "Rom. 3:21–26 and the Faith of Jesus," *CBQ* 44 (1982): 77–90; George Howard, "On the 'Faith of Christ,'" *HTR* 60 (1967): 459–65. Williams responds to Arlen Hultgren's attempt to defend the traditional objective genitive ("The Pistis Christou Formulation in Paul," *NovT* 22 [1980]: 248–63). I find the ease with which Williams demolishes Hultgren's arguments a telling sign. Most recently see Richard B. Hays, "PISTIS and Pauline Christology: What Is at Stake?" and James D. G. Dunn, "Once More Pistis Christou," in *Society of Biblical Literature 1991 Seminar Papers*, ed. E. Lovering (Atlanta: Scholars Press, 1991), 714–29, 730–44.

2 The bibliography on the "righteousness of God" is enormous. For bibliographies, see Cranfield, *Romans*, 1:92–93; Dunn, *Romans*, 1:36–37; M. T. Brauch, "'God's Righteousness' in Recent German Discussion," in *PPJ*, 523–42; Peter Stuhlmacher, *Gerechtigkeit Gottes bei Paulus* (FRLANT 87; Göttingen: Vandenhoeck and Ruprecht, 1965), 11–73; John Reumann, *Righteousness in the New Testament* (Philadelphia:

Fortress Press, 1982). These discussions of scholarship and bibliography focus on German scholarship and its theological preoccupations. The only scholar of whom I am aware who seriously keeps the crucial semantic distinction between the lexical meaning of the phrase and the contextualized meaning of particular "performances" is Williams, "Righteousness of God."

3 My language here has been suggested by Johnson, "Faith of Jesus," 78–79.

4 Among the many syntactical problems of the traditional reading, I judge the following to be particularly important: 3:22 is redundant, mentioning faith in Christ twice with a bizarre awkwardness that leaves no purposive direction for the *eis* clause; the traditional reading cannot make sense of the main verbal clause that governs the whole section (*pephanerōtai* . . .) unless one makes the believer's faith into what reveals God's righteousness; *dia tēs pisteōs* is a grammatical anomaly or an awkward insertion into its context; *haima* makes no sense in the dative; *ton ek pisteōs Iesou* cannot possibly mean "the one who has faith in Jesus." Howard, Johnson, Williams, and Hays (n. 1 above) discuss additional difficulties.

5 Hays, *Faith of Jesus Christ*, 170–71.

6 "Righteousness of God," 259.

7 Ibid., 270–71; Richard B. Hays, "Psalm 143 and the Logic of Romans 3," *JBL* 99 (1980): 107–15.

8 Hays, "Psalm 143," 112–14.

9 Ibid., 115; *Faith of Jesus Christ*, 172.

10 Johannes Haussleiter, "Der Glaube Jesu Christi," *NKZ* 2 (1891): 109–45, 205–30; A. T. Hanson, *Paul's Understanding of Jesus* (Hull: University of Hull, 1963); Hays, *Faith of Jesus Christ*, 151–57; id., " 'The Righteous One' as Eschatological Deliverer: A Case Study in Paul's Apocalyptic Hermeneutics," *Apocalyptic and the New Testament: Essays in Honor of J. Louis Martyn*, ed. J. Marcus and M. Soards (JSNTSS 24; Sheffield: JSOT Press, 1989), 191–216. I have not seen Haussleiter and have depended on others for reference to his work. At most points my account follows Hays.

11 Hays, *Faith of Jesus Christ*, 151.

12 August Strobel, *Untersuchungen zum Eschatologischen Versögerungsproblem auf Grund der spätjudisch-urchristlichen Geschiche von Habakuk 2,2 ff.* (NovT Suppl. 2; Leiden: E. J. Brill, 1961).

13 Hays, "Righteous One," 194–206.

14 Hays, *Faith of Jesus Christ*, 152–53.

15 Nils Dahl, *Studies in Paul* (Minneapolis: Augsburg, 1977), 130–31.

16 Max Wilcox, "The Promise of the 'Seed' in the New Testament and the *Targumim*," *JSNT* 5 (1979): 2–20.

17 Hays, *Faith of Jesus Christ*, 154.

18 Gerhard Kittel, "*Pistis Iesou Christou* bei Paulus," *TSK* 79 (1906): 424; Johnson, "Faith of Jesus," 80; [on the *kai*] C. Blackman, "Romans 3:26b: A Question of Translation," *JBL* 87 (1968): 203–04; Hays, *Faith of Jesus Christ*, 171.

19 Williams, "*Pistis Christou*," 442.

20 Bassler, *Impartiality*, 156–60.

21 Williams, *Jesus' Death*, 19–34.

22 Up-to-date access to the enormous bibliography on the subject of atonement in Paul

can be had from Cilliers Breytenbach, *Versöhnung: Eine Studie zur paulinischen Soteriologie* (WMANT 60; Neukirchen-Vluyn: Neukirchener Vlg., 1989); "Versöhnung, Stellvertretung und Sühne: Semantische und traditionsgeschichtliche Bermerkungen am Beispiel der paulinischen Briefe," *NTS* 39 (1993): 59–79

23   In addition to Breytenbach and the work cited below, see especially Williams, *Jesus' Death*; David Seeley, *The Noble Death* (JSOT Suppl. 28; Sheffield: JSOT Press, 1990).

24   The most important work on sacrifice is Nancy Jay, *Throughout Your Generations Forever* (Chicago: University of Chicago Press, 1992). For Greek sacrifice and the problem of reading back Christian anachronisms, see Marcel Detienne and Jean-Pierre Vernant, *The Cuisine of Sacrifice among the Greeks* (Chicago: University of Chicago Press, 1989), 88–89 and *passim*. For my contribution, see "Greeks Who Sacrifice and Those Who Do Not: Toward an Anthropology of Greek Religion," in *The First Christians and Their Social World: Studies in Honor of Wayne A. Meeks*, ed. L. Michael White and O. Larry Yarbrough (Minneapolis: Fortress Press, forthcoming).

25   Robert Wilken, *The Land Called Holy: Palestine in Christian History and Thought* (New Haven: Yale University Press, 1991); Jonathan Z. Smith, *To Take Place: Toward Theory in Ritual* (Chicago: University of Chicago Press, 1987), 74–117.

26   Vernant, *Cuisine*, 9, 90–91; Stowers, "Greeks Who Sacrifice," 4; Royden Yerkes, *Sacrifice in Greek and Roman Religions and Early Judaism* (New York: Charles Scribner's Sons, 1952), 5.

27   Stowers, "Greeks Who Sacrifice," esp. 25–27, 37–38

28   Jonathan Z. Smith, *Drudgery Divine: On Comparison of Early Christianities and the Religions of Late Antiquity* (Chicago: University of Chicago Press, 1990), 121–25 and n. 13; id., *Map Is Not Territory: Studies in the History of Religions* (Leiden: E. J. Brill, 1978), xi–xv, 67–207.

29   J. Milgrom, "Sin-offering or Purification-offering?" *VT* 21 (1971): 237–39; "The Function of the *hattāt* Sacrifice," *Tabriz* 40 (1970): 1–9; Bradley H. McLean, "The Absence of an Atoning Sacrifice in Paul's Soteriology," *NTS* 38 (1992): 534; Francis M. Young, *The Use of Sacrificial Ideas in Greek Christian Writers from the New Testament to John Chrysostom* (Philadelphia: Philadelphia Patristic Foundation, 1979), 40–43. McLean gives evidence for the continuation of these priestly sacrificial conceptions in the practices and beliefs of Jews in the first century C.E.

30   Jacob Milgrom, *Cult and Conscience* (Leiden: E. J. Brill, 1976), 3–12. Forgiveness for deliberate sins came through repentance and once a year at the festival of the Day of Atonement. The latter was accomplished by nonsacrificial, even antisacrificial, means through the scapegoat, which was impure and not killed.

31   Jay (*Throughout Your Generations*) and Valerio Valeri (*Kingship and Sacrifice: Ritual and Society in Ancient Hawaii* [Chicago: University of Chicago Press, 1985]) have shown that sacrifice above all concerns gender. Their findings apply extremely well to Jewish sacrificial practices and thought (see Jay, ibid., 94–111).

32   Jacob Milgrom, *Studies in Cultic Theology and Terminology* (SJLA 36; Leiden: E. J. Brill, 1983), esp. 67–95; David Wright, *The Disposal of Impurity* (SBLDS 101; Atlanta: Scholars Press,1987). See Wright for further bibliography and reactions to Milgrom's work.

33   On the guilt offering and the concept of repentance, see Milgrom, *Cult and Conscience*.

34   Arland J. Hultgren, *Paul's Gospel and Mission* (Philadelphia: Fortress Press, 1985), 59–69; Dunn, *Romans*, 1:172.

35   G. H. R. Horsley, *New Documents Illustrating Early Christianity* (North Ryde, Australia:

Macquarie University, 1983), 25. Horsley underlines the misguided assumptions of past word studies which have assumed that the *hilas-* word group's New Testament usage must have come from the LXX. Breytenbach's semantic investigations stand above those of others in their linguistic sophistication and care. On the word group, see *Versöhnung,* 84–100, 40–44 for methodological considerations.

36 Horsley, *New Documents,* 24–26.

37 Two examples (*Inscr. Cos* 81.347; Jos. *Ant.* 16.182) illustrate the usage of *hilastērion* that is probably most frequent. Both refer to propitatory monuments. Greco-Roman monuments like that erected by a certain Meidon after Zeus Trosos struck him dumb when his slaves ate unsacrificed meat are quite common, merging with votive offerings, but, of course, do not usually explicitly describe themselves with *hilastērion* even though that is how they would have been commonly described. For the Meidon inscription, see Peter Hermann and Ziya Polatkan, *Das Testament des Epikrates und Andere Inschriften aus dem Museum von Manisa* (Vienna: Hermann Böhlaus, 1969), 58–62. Josephus tells of Herod desecrating David's tomb and building a "propitiatory monument of marble" to conciliate the "terror" he experienced upon robbing the tomb.

38 Hultgren, *Paul's Gospel,* 59; Dunn, *Romans.*

39 Schlier, *Römerbrief,* 154–55.

40 The blood of animals has significance in sacrificial systems because it symbolically acts as men's blood (women never wield the sacrificial knife) over against the procreative blood of women. The practice of men sacrificing produces lines of descent reckoned through males over against lines that could be drawn through the women who gave birth. In the case of the second temple, the most important male lines created by sacrifice were those of the priesthoods. See Jay, *Throughout Your Generations,* 17–29 (esp. 28–29), and *passim;* Howard Eilberg-Schwartz, *The Savage in Judaism: An Anthropology of Israelite Religion and Ancient Judaism* (Bloomington: Indiana University Press, 1990), 115–240. On the interesting evidence of Greek medical writers comparing sacrificial blood to women's procreative blood, see Stowers, "Greeks Who Sacrifice," 6–8.

41 McLean, "Absence of Sacrifice," 548; cf. 538–39.

42 The extremely varied examples in Young (*Sacrificial Ideas,* 97–221) are instructive regarding the loose and indeterminate nature of early Christian sacrificial language.

43 Ibid.

44 Williams, *Jesus' Death;* H. S. Versnel, "Quid Athenis et Hierosolymis? Bemerkungen über die Herkunft von Aspekten des 'effective death.'" *Die Entstehung der Judischen Martyrologie,* ed. J. W. van Henten (Stud. Post-Biblica 38; Leiden: E. J. Brill, 1989), 162–96; "Jezus Soter-Neos Alkestis? Over die niet-joodse achtergrond van een christelijke doctrine," *Lampas* 22 (1989): 219–42; Seely, *Noble Death,* 39–66, 83–99; Breytenbach, "Versöhnung, Stellvertretung," 77–78; McLean, "Absence of Sacrifice," 548–53. I suspect that the avoidance of vicarious atonement by humans and of human sacrifice in the literature of the second temple period is due to the struggle with and elimination of child sacrifice in ancient Israel.

45 Versnel, "Athenis," esp. 182–83.

46 Even the most careful and critical treatments (Williams, *Jesus' Death,* 177–78; Seely, *Noble Death,* 97–98) have assumed that the work employs some sacrificial metaphors in connection with the martyrs' deaths but show how the work specifically draws attention to the limited metaphorical nature of the analogies. In light of a more accurate understanding of sacrifice, however, even this may concede too much. Both scholars seem to assume that sacrifice is about death and suffering and that *hilaterion*

carries an intrinsically sacrificial meaning. The strongest case for sacrificial imagery comes in 6.28–29, which speaks of purification by blood.

47 Williams, *Jesus' Death,* 165–82. For issues from a more traditional and apologetic angle, see, K. T. Kleinknecht, *Der leidende Gerechtfertigte: Der alttestamentlich-judische Tradition vom "leidenden Gerechten" und ihre Rezeption bei Paulus* (WUNT 2.13; Tübingen: J. C. B. Mohr, 1984). Kleinknecht cites extensive bibliography on the "Jewish background" of Jesus' death: a whole industry of splicing snippets of scripture and later Jewish writings together so as to produce a proto-Christian Jewish tradition that prefigures later theology and protects the New Testament from pagan influence.

48 *Versöhnung;* "Versuohning, Stellvertretung."

49 *Versöhnung,* 159, 169.

50 On nonsacrificial atonement for sin, see Marinus de Jonge, *Christology in Context* (Philadelphia: Westminster Press, 1988), 240, n. 26; Breytenbach, "Versöhnung, Stellvertretung," 75–77.

51 Nils Dahl, *Jesus the Christ: The Historical Origins of the Christological Doctrine,* ed. Donald H. Juel (Minneapolis: Fortress Press, 1991), 15–25

52 Ibid., 15–80; id., *The Crucified Messiah and Other Essays* (Minneapolis: Augsburg, 1974).

53 A Davidic messiah can be found in *1QS* 9:11; *1 QSa* 2:14, 20; *4 Q Partiarchal Blessing* 3; *1QSb* 5:20–29 (Davidic prince is subordinate to the high priest); *Parables of Enoch* 48:10; 52:4; *4 Ezra* 12:32; *Syr. Baruch* 29:3; 30:1; 39:7; 40:1; 70:9; 72:2. The last two works come from the end of the first century and have a Davidic messiah but without the language of kingship. The messiah's judging function is most prominent (as also in 1 Enoch) and his rule temporary as in 1 Cor 15:23–28. See the chapters by George Nicklesburg, Shemaryahu Talmon, and Michael Stone in *Judaisms and Their Messiahs at the Turn of the Christian Era,* ed. J. Neusner, W. S. Green, and E. Frerichs (Cambridge: Cambridge University Press, 1987).

54 For the defeated as earthly rulers, see Wesley Carr, *Angels and Principalities* (Cambridge: Cambridge University Press, 1981). In my view, the spiritual powers interpretation, canonized for later Christianity by Origen, has little to commend it.

55 Richard A. Horsley, "Popular Messianic Movements around the Time of Jesus," *CBQ* 46 (1984): 471–95.

56 Martin Hengel, *The Son of God* (Philadelphia: Fortress Press, 1976), 61.

57 Second Sam 7:12–14; Pss 2:7, cf. 89:3–45; 1 Chron 17:13; 22:10; 28:6; *4Q Flor.* 1:7–11; *4Q246*; de Jonge, *Christology,* 167–69. On *4Q246,* which speaks of a king who will be called Son of God and Son of the Most High, see Joseph A. Fitzmyer, "The Contribution of Aramaic to the Study of the New Testament," *NTS* 20 (1973–74): 382–407, = *A Wandering Aramean: Collected Aramaic Essays* (SBLMS 25; Missoula, Mont.: Scholars Press, 1979), 90–94, 102–07; Dunn, *Romans,* 1:11–12.

58 Joanne A. Barnett is currently writing a Brown University dissertation, "*Epieikeia:* The Bridle of Power and Authority in Superior-Subordinate Relationships in Greco-Roman and Early Christian Society."

59 Abraham J. Malherbe, "Antisthenes and Odysseus, and Paul at War," *HTR* (1983): 143–73; "Use and Abuse of Reason," 266–76.

60 See Carr, *Angels and Principalities.*

61 On adaptability to others, see Clarence E. Glad, "Adaptability in Epicurean and Early Christian Psychagogy: Paul and Philodemus" (Ph.D. diss., Brown University, 1992).

62 R. P. Martin, *Carmen Christi: Philippians ii.5–11 in Recent Interpretation and in the Setting of Early Christian Worship* (SNTSMS 4; Cambridge: Cambridge University Press, 1967; 2d ed. Eerdmans: Grand Rapids, 1983). The second edition contains a new preface, pp. xi-xxxix.

63 For appropriate skepticism about the passage being a hymn or a non-Pauline composition or both, see N. T. Wright, "*Harpagmos* and the Meaning of Philippians 2:5–11," *JTS* 37 (1986): 352 and n. 109.

64 Following Ernst Käsemann ("Kritische Analyse von Phil 2:5–11," *ZTK* 47 [1950]: 313–60), many scholars have been persuaded that the passage treats the "mechanism of salvation" and does not present Christ as a moral exemplar. I strongly disagree with Käsemann and would here only point to a marked movement in favor of the exemplar reading in the last twenty years or so. Most recently, see L. Michael White, "Morality between Two Worlds: A Paradigm of Friendship in Philippians," *Greeks, Romans and Christians*, ed. D. Balch et al., 201–15.

65 E.g., Num 12:12; Job 5:14; 10:10; 11:12; 13:28; 15:16; 24:20; 27:16; Isa 53:23; Wis 7:3; Pierre Grelot, "Deux Expressions dificiles de Philippiens 2, 6–7," *Bib* 53 (1972): 495–507.

66 Wright, "*Harpagmos*," 344.

67 Ibid.

68 James D. G. Dunn, *Christology in the Making: A New Testament Inquiry into the Origins of the Doctrine of the Incarnation* (Philadelphia: Westminster Press, 1980). In reviewing the scholarly reaction to Dunn, I was amazed to note how often the response took the form of a confession-like affirmation of belief in the incarnation rather than of substantive arguments against him.

69 Note esp. Rom 1:4; 1 Cor 15:20; Dale C. Allison, *The End of the Ages Has Come* (Philadelphia: Fortress Press, 1985), 62–69.

70 Glad, "Adaptability."

71 Malherbe, "Antisthenes and Odysseus."

72 Glad, "Adaptability," 63–118, 139f., 456f.; "Use and Abuse of Reason," 266–76.

73 I am indebted here to the work of Johnson, Williams, and Hays, although none of the three would, I suspect, agree with all of my decisions.

74 Williams, "*Pistis Christou*," 434.

Chapter 8. One God and One Father Abraham

1 Robin Fox, *Reproduction and Succession: Studies in Anthropology, Law and Society* (New Brunswick, N.J.: Transaction Publishers, 1993), 144, 183–86. I have drawn on Fox in what follows but strongly disagree with his almost magical and mystical appeal to physiology and genetics in certain parts of the book.

2 Meyer Fortes, "The Structure of Unilineal Descent Groups," *American Anthropologist* 55 (1953): 25–26.

3 Meyer Fortes, "Kinship and Marriage among the Ashanti," in *African Systems of Kinship and Marriage*, ed. A. R. Radcliffe-Brown and Daryll Forde (London: Oxford University Press, 1950).

4 Howard Eilberg-Schwartz, *The Savage in Judaism: An Anthropology of Israelite Religion and Ancient Judaism* (Bloomington: Indiana University Press, 1990), 195–216, 191–94.

5 Eilberg-Schwartz (ibid.) illuminatingly compares the attitudes reflecting the roles of

ascription and achievement of the priestly writer, the Qumran writings, early Christianity, and the Mishna.

6 Käsemann, *Romans,* 102 (*polemische Zuspitzung,* "a polemical sharpening" [*An die Römer,* 94]).

7 Williams, *Jesus' Death as Saving Event* (HDR2; Missoula, Mont.: Scholars Press, 1975); "Righteousness of God," 241–90; Krister Stendahl, *Paul among Jews and Gentiles* (Philadelphia: Fortress Press, 1976); George Howard, "Romans 3:21–31 and the Inclusion of the Gentiles," *HTR* 63 (1970): 223–33.

8 Richard B. Hays, "Have We Found Abraham to be our Forefather According to the Flesh?': A Reconsideration of Rom. 4:1," *NovT* 27 (1985): 79, n. 13.

9 See chapter 1 above. E.g., the fragment of Aeschylus's *Distylci, P. OXY.* 18.2161, does not use *notae personarum,* contrast *P. OXY.* 8.1083 for the use of the latter. On the *paragraphus,* E. G. Turner, *Greek Manuscripts of the Ancient World* (Princeton: Princeton University Press, 1971), nos. 19, 24, 27, 28, 29, 30, 31, 32, 33, 34, 40, 41, 42, 43, 52; for the *dicolon,* 14, 19, 41, 42, 43.

10 On codex *Bodleianus Gr. Misc.* 251, see Heinrich Schenkl, *Epicteti Dissertationes Ab Arriani Digestae,* 2d ed. (Stuttgart: Teubner, 1916), liv–cxv.

11 E.g., the fragment of the *Phaedo* from the late first or early second century C.E., *P. OXY.* 15.1809.

12 See chapter 1 above.

13 See Hays, "Have We Found Abraham?" 79, n. 13, in which he cites Wilckens (*Römer,* 1.244).

14 See Origen on 3:27, *CatRm* 6.20–25 in Jean Scherer, *Le Commentaire d'Origène sur Rom. iii. 5-v. 7 d'après les Extraits du Papyrus no. 88748 du Musée du Caire et les Fragments de la Philocalie et du Vaticanus gr. 762: Essai de Reconstitution du Texte et de la Pensée des Tomes V et VI du 'Commentaire sur l'épûtre aux Romains'.* (Institut Franáais d'Archéologie Orientale, Bibliothäque d'Etude, xxvii; Cairo, 1957), 168 and chapter 9 below on 7:7–25.

15 *Diatribe and Romans,* 158–64.

16 Otto Ribbeck, *ALAZON: Ein Beitrag zur Antiken Ethologie* (Leipzig: Teubner, 1882).

17 Cranfield, *Romans,* 1:219.

18 On pride and idolatry in Augustine, see Robert J. O'Connell, *St. Augustine's Early Theory of Man* (Cambridge: Harvard University Press, 1968), 87–111; esp. 94–96, 110.

19 *Hom. John* 25.15–16, trans. John Gibb and James Innes in *The Nicene and Ante-Nicene Fathers,* vol. 16, ed. W. Schaff (Edinburgh, 1886).

20 For Origin's classic statement, *On First Principles,* esp. chap. 8. On Augustine, Platonism, and Plotinus, see Robert J. O'Connell, *Early Theory of Man; St. Augustine's Confessions: The Odyssey of the Soul* (Cambridge: Harvard University Press, 1969); id., *The Origin of the Soul in St. Augustine's Later Works* (New York: Fordham University Press, 1987).

21 Peter von der Osten-Sacken, *Römer 8 als Beispiel paulinisher Soteriologie* (GRLANT 112; Göttingen: Vandenhoeck and Ruprecht, 1975), 245; Hans Hübner, *Das Gesetz bei Paulus* (FRLANT 119; Göttingen: Vandenhoeck and Ruprecht, 1978), 119–22; similarly, Cranfield, *Romans,* 1:219–20.

22 On various interpretations, see Heikki Räisänen, "Das 'Gesetz des Glaubens' (Röm. 3.27) und das 'Gesetz des Geistes' (Röm. 8.2)," *NTS* 26 (1979–80): 101–17. Räisänen's

critique of previous attempted solutions is sharp, but I obviously do not support his own.

23 E.g., H. J. Schoeps, *Paul: The Theology of the Apostle in Light of Jewish Religious History* (Philadelphia: Westminster Press, 1961), 213–18.

24 *Gar* is clearly the better attested reading in contrast to *oun*; it also perfectly fits the sense of my interpretation. *Oun* reflects a struggle to understand the text when the sense of a dialogue with the interlocutor had been lost. Paul is not drawing a new inference but pointing to what has already been said. The assertions in 3:19–26 serve as a reason to support his rejection of the teacher's implied exegesis about works in 27.

25 Nils A. Dahl, "The One God of Jews and Gentiles," *Studies in Paul* (Minneapolis: Augsburg, 1977), 178–91.

26 Hays, "Have We Found Abraham?" 84–85; for my earlier view, *Diatribe and Romans,* 166–68.

27 Käsemann, *Romans,* 104, and bibliography, 101–02. Bruno Corsani ("*ek pisteos* in the Letters of Paul," in *The New Testament Age: Essays in Honor of Bo Reicke,* ed. W. C. Weinrich [Macon, Ga.: Mercer, 1984], 87–105) assumes the traditional readings and does not treat the issues raised here.

28 The strongest modern statement of the minority opinion is by John Gager (*The Origins of Anti-Semitism* [Oxford: Oxford University Press, 1983], 251, 262, 305, n. 1), who follows Lloyd Gaston. His translation of *dia* in 3:30 as "because of" is misleading. That is a good translation of *dia* with the accusative but not of *dia* with the genitive. Others who argue for a distinction: Adolf Schlatter, *Gottes Gerechtigkeit* (Stuttgart: Calwer, 1952), 155–56; Theodore Zahn, *Der Brief des Paulus an die Römer* (Leipzig; G. Boehme, 1925), 205–06.

29 For the text on 3:30, see Scherer. *Le Commentaire d'Origène;* for Theodore, *PG* 66, col. 796.

30 170.10–13 (Scherer).

31 170.14–172.11 (Scherer)

32 Philo, *Spec. Leg.* 1.208; *Cher.* 125–27; Cranfield, *Romans,* 2:591–92.

33 172.12–174.3 (Scherer)

34 Ibid.

35 Roger Brooks shows that Origen's knowledge of and benevolence toward Judaism has been exaggerated: "The Problem of Scholarly Ecumenism: The Rabbinic Background for the Study of Origen," in *Origen in Cultural Context: Proceedings of the University of Notre Dame Colloquium at the 18th Centenary of Origin's Birth* (Notre Dame: Notre Dame University Press, 1988).

36 There were ancient theories that gave women a greater role but the seed/soil view certainly dominated: E. Lesky, *Die Zeugungs- und Vererbungslehrn der Antike und ihr Nachwirken* (Mainz: Akademia der Wissenschaften und der Literatur, 1951), 125–59; Page duBois, *Sowing the Body* (Chicago: University of Chicago Press, 1988); J. Morsink, "Was Aristotle's Biology Sexist?" *Journal of the History of Biology* 12 (1979): 83–112. For evidence that Jews prior to the rabbinic writings held the dominant view, see Pieter W. Van Der Horst, "Sarah's Seminal Emission: Hebrews 11:11 in Light of Ancient Embryology," in *Greeks, Romans and Christians,* 296–301. Van Der Horst shows that rabbinic writers adapted the *epikrateia* theory from Hellenistic sources. One could add that this greater role for the mother goes along with a new Judaism not centering on the priesthood and patriliny.

37 For the seed/soil Aristotelian theory implied by the language of Jn 1:13, see H. J. Cadbury, "The Ancient Physiological Theories Underlying John 1:13 and Hebrews XI 11," *The Expositor*, ser. 9, 2 (1924): 430–39.

38 Hays (*Faith of Jesus*, 150–74) renders *ek pisteos* as "on the basis of [Jesus'] faithfulness."

39 Hays, ibid. 139–77, and esp. 170–74; Williams, "Again *Pistis Christou*," *CBQ* 49 (1987): 431–47; Johnson, "Romans 3:21–26," 77–90.

40 C. Thomas Rhyne, *Faith Establishes the Law* (SBLD555; Chico, Cal.: Scholars Press, 1981).

41 I have been convinced by Hays ["Have We Found Abraham?"] (cf. my earlier construal of 4:1 in *Diatribe and Romans*, 155–74) except that I still attribute it to the voice of the interlocutor.

42 Hays, "Have We Found Abraham?"

43 Ibid., 87–92.

44 *PPJ*, 470–72, 501, 544.

45 Thus the use of *pistis* for Jesus' or Abraham's faithfulness and the participle for those who participate, e.g., 3:22; Williams ("Again *Pistis Christou*," 437–47), who is too quick to give a double meaning, which includes not only Jesus' faithfulness but also the faith of the believer, to *pistis Christou* and *pistis* used absolutely.

46 Dahl, *Studies in Paul*, 129.

47 Dale C. Allison, *The End of the Ages Has Come* (Philadelphia: Fortress Press, 1985), 62–69.

48 Wesley Carr, *Angels and Principalities* (Cambridge: Cambridge University Press, 1981), 115–24.

49 *LXX* Ps 36:9, 11, 22, 29, 34; *Jub.* 14–15, 29–30; 32:18–19; *1 Enoch* 5:6–7; Sir 44:21; *4 Ezra* 6:55–59; Käsemann, *Romans*, 120.

50 Unfortunately, W. D. Davies succumbs to traditional spiritualizing in *The Gospel and the Land* (Berkeley: University of California Press, 1974), 161–220; he is corrected by Walter Brueggemann, *The Land* (Philadelphia: Fortress Press, 1977), 170–83.

51 *Comm. in Rom.* 4.5 (976–77); Peter Gorday, *Principles of Patristic Exegesis: Romans 9–11 in Origen, John Chrysostom, and Augustine* (New York: E. Mellen, 1983), 63–64.

52 For this observation, see Hays (*Faith of Abraham*, 90, n. 44), who arranges the Greek in parallel.

53 For parallels with chapter 8: Dahl, *Paul*, 88–90; *ST* 5 (1951): 37–48.

54 *Faith of Abraham*, 93–95. Earlier (*Diatribe and Romans*, 168–74) I described 4 as an *exemplum*. I would now place less emphasis on the exemplary character of the *exemplum*. Hays is rightly critical (ibid, 91) of treating the chapter as an example of faith. The *exemplum*, however, as an ancient form of rhetorical argumentation is much broader and means more than the English word "example."

55 *Theology out of the Ghetto* (Leiden: E. J. Brill, 1971).

Chapter 9. The Gentile Share in Christ's Obedience

1 Cf. *Paul and Torah*, 31–32.

2 Nils A. Dahl, *Studies in Paul* (Minneapolis: Augsburg, 1977), 81, n. 20; *PPJ*, part 2.

3 Cranfield, *Romans*, 1:284.

4   Ibid., 272.

5   Dahl, *Studies in Paul,* 91.

6   Luke T. Johnson, "Romans 3:21–26 and the Faith of Jesus," *CBQ* 44 (1982): 85–90.

7   *Paul and the Law,* 145. Räisänen's initial explanation is correct. The problems that he raises against it derive from imposing a universalist Christian reading on 2:12 and on Romans as a whole.

8   The exceptions in 1:18–5:21 are primarily in 4:23–5:11, a transitional section.

9   For identification with Christ, see Sam K. Williams, "Again *Pistis Christou,*" *CBQ* 49 (1987): 441; Robert C. Tannehill, *Dying and Rising with Christ* (Berlin, 1967).

10 Rudolph Bultmann, "Glossen im Römerbrief," *TLZ* 72 (1947): 197–202.

11 Peter Gorday, *Principles of Patristic Exegesis* (New York: Mellen, 1983) 164.

12 Käsemann, *Romans,* 203.

13 Augustine's views on 7:7–25 changed during his career.

14 Quoted in William G. McLoughlin, *Isaac Backus and the American Pietistic Tradition* (Boston: Little, Brown, 1967), 14.

15 Rudolf Bultmann, *Theology of the New Testament* (New York: Scribners, 1951), 1:248; Käsemann, *Romans,* 193. The tradition has been most thoroughly discussed by H. Hommel, "Das 7. Kapitel Des Römerbriefs im Licht Antiker überlieferung," *Theologia viatorum* 8 (1961–62): 90–116; Gerd Theissen, *Psychological Aspects of Pauline Theology* (Philadelphia: Fortress Press, 1987), 211–19.

16 Martha C. Nussbaum, *The Fragility of Goodness* (Cambridge: Cambridge University Press, 1986).

17 William W. Fortenbaugh, "On the Antecedents of Aristotle's Bipartate Psychology," in *Essays in Ancient Greek Philosophy*, vol. 2, ed. J. P. Anton and A. Preus (Albany: State University of New York, 1983), 303.

18 Nussbaum, *Fragility of Goodness,* 85–195.

19 Fortenbaugh, "Antecedents of Aristotle," 303–20.

20 Anthony Kenny, *Aristotle's Theory of the Will* (New Haven: Yale University Press, 1979), 62–63.

21 Quoted from Theissen, *Psychological Aspects,* 14–15.

22 It is misleading to overstress the cognitivist character of early Stoic thought. See John Rist, *Stoic Philosophy* (Cambridge: Cambridge University Press, 1969), esp. 22–36, 256–72. Theissen very badly misunderstands Stoic thought, caricaturing it after the manner of its ancient detractors. For a widely regarded understanding of Chrysippus's position on *akrasia,* see Christopher Gill, "Did Chrysippus Understand Medea?" *Phronesis* 28 (1983): 136–49.

23 *SVF* 2.1.

24 Discussed by Theissen, *Psychological Aspects,* 215.

25 Schenkl, following Wolf, supplies *machē* ("the contradiction") here.

26 My translation from the Greek text edited by Phillip DeLacy, *Galen on the Doctrines of Hippocrates and Plato* (Berlin: Akademie Verlag, 1978), 1:274, 244. I have cited Galen's work by book and DeLacy's page and line numbers.

27 Plautus, *Trinum.*, 657–58; Albinus, *Ep.* 243; Aelius Aristides, *Or.* 50; Lucian, *Apology,* 10.

28 I have translated from *P. Ovid Naso Metamorphosen*, 10th ed., ed. Rudolf Ewald (Zurich: Weidmann, 1966).

29 *Römer 7 und die Bekehrung des Paulus* (Leipzig: T. G. Hinrichs, 1929); repr. in *Römer 7 und das Bild des Menschen im Neuen Testament* (TBNT 53; Munich: Kaiser, 1974).

30 Ulrich Wilckens, *Der Brief an die Römer* (EKKNT 6; Zurich: Neuchirchen, 1978), 1:77, n. 293.

31 The weakness of Theissen's interpretation lies in his failure to understand both the rhetoric of chapter 7 and the different ancient constructions of the person; he thus imposes anachronistic "autobiographical" readings.

32 Kümmel, *Römer 7 und das Bild*, 132, n. 2; Theissen, *Psychological Aspects*, 192.

33 Kümmel, *Römer 7 und das Bild*.

34 It is unclear whether this child represents an independent person or whether Origen means that Celsus represented Jesus or the Jew as if they were beginning students.

35 According to Karl Pichler (*Streit um das Christentum: Die Angriff des Kelsos und die Antwort des Origenes* [Frankfurt am Main: P. Lang, 1980], 124–33), the fragments from Celsus in 1.28–71 come from the Jew's first speech and those in 2.1–79 from the second speech, while from 3.1 Celsus speaks in his own person.

36 Clarence E. Glad, "Adaptability in Epicurean and Early Christian Psychagogy: Philodemus and Paul" (Ph.D. diss., Brown University, 1991), 119–72.

37 C. P. Hammond Bammel, "Philocalia ix, Jerome, Epistle 121, and Origen's Exposition of Romans vii," *JTS* 32 (1981): 50–81; *Der Römerbrieftext des Rufin und seine Origenesübersetzung* (AGLB 10; Freiburg: Herder, 1985).

38 On the abbreviation, see Hammond Bammel (*Römerbrieftext*). *The Philocalia of Origen*, ed. J. A. Robinson (Cambridge: Cambridge University Press, 1893); for the *catenae*: A. Ramsbotham, "The Commentary of Origen on the Epistle to the Romans," *JTS* 13 (1912): 209–24, 357–68; 14 (1913): 10–22.

39 Hammond Bammel is mistaken in saying that Origen is guarded and tentative about *prosōpopoiia* in chapter 7 because of the expression *ei mē pou eipomen* and Origen saying that the words are "appropriate" for the characters speaking ("Origen's Exposition," 68). The first expression is due to the condition set up with the preceding section so that Origen speaks of a contradiction "unless." In the second case, she does not understand that *harmozein* is a technical term used by the rhetoricians and grammarians to indicate criteria for *prosōpopoiia*.

40 Rufinus says (*ComRm.* 6.9 [1085AB]) that 14a is spoken with apostolic authority but 14b by one sold under sin. This contradicts the Greek fragments, which make no such distinction. Hammond Bammel ("Origen's Exposition," 68) thinks that both may have come from Origen but that Rufinus and the catenist selected from different parts of his discussion. I think it more likely that Rufinus has tried to improve on Origen.

41 Hammond Bammel, "Origen's Exposition," 69.

42 The brackets enclose a difficult reading not found in the *Munich Codex*.

43 Rufinus and the Greek cannot be fully reconciled on 17–25, but Origen's basic approach is clear. Hammond Bammel ("Origen's Exposition," 69–72) seems to me to assimilate Origen's clear approach to the passage through speech-in-character to Jerome's Western theology of human frailty, seen also in Ambrose, Augustine, and Ambrosiaster on Rom 7.

44 Here I would point to Origen's talk of human *astheneia* explained in terms of constraints against reason and compulsion toward the opposite (*Cat.* 44).

45 On Origen and the philologians, see Bernard Neuschäfer (*Origenes als Philologe* [Basel: F. Reinhardt, 1987], 263–76).

46 Paula Fredriksen, "Paul and Augustine: Conversion Narratives, Orthodox Traditions, and the Retrospective Self," *JTS* 37 (1986): 3–34.

47 The position of Krister Stendahl is still entirely persuasive ("The Apostle Paul and the Introspective Conscience of the West," *HTR* 56 [1963]: 199–215; repr. in *Paul among Jews and Gentiles* [Philadelphia: Fortress Press, 1976]).

48 In light of the change of tenses inherent to *prosōpopoiia,* Theissen's (Psychological Aspects, 195–99) discussion of the change of tenses is beside the point.

49 Aphthonius, for instance, suggests the examples of Hecuba and the speech of Achilles to Patrocles. His illustration is Niobe's speech.

50 John K. Davies, "Athenian Citizenship," *CLJ* 73 (1977): 111–12.

51 On the expression *talas egō,* see *Diss* 1.12.28; 3.13.4.

52 In addition to texts already cited, see Aristophanes, *Thes.* 1039, and Plautus, *Trin.* 657.

53 A. W. H. Adkins, *From the Many to the One* (Ithaca: Cornell Unviversity Press, 1970), 1–126.

54 Nussbaum, *Fragility,* 25, n. 3.

55 My translation of Euripides frg. 841 (*Trag. Grace. Frag,* ed. Nauck). The Plutarch citation is in *Moralia* 33F (cf. 446A).

56 The translation of v. 4 has been a matter of much debate. The word *skeuos* may mean one's own body rather than wife, but I think "wife" more likely. The language of possession actually argues for "wife" given that women were thought of as being property of men. See O. Larry Yarbrough, *"Not Like the Gentiles": Marriage Rules in the Letters of Paul* (SBLDS 80; Atlanta: Scholars Press, 1985), 7.

57 Yarbrough, *"Not Like the Gentiles."*

58 J. P. V. D. Balsdon, *Romans and Aliens* (Chapel Hill: University of North Carolina Press, 1979).

59 So, for instance, Isa 56:1–8 defines Jewish identity so much by lawkeeping that even foreigners can become Israelites.

60 Dunn, *Romans,* 1:359.

61 Scott McKnight, *A Light among the Gentiles: Jewish Missionary Activity in the Second Temple Period* (Minneapolis: Fortress Press, 1991), chaps. 6, 7.

62 Käsemann, *Romans,* 195. Käsemann does recognize that Jews did not understand their own experience in this way.

63 Theissen, *Psychological Aspects.*

64 Ibid., 241–42.

65 Justin Gosling, *Weakness of the Will* (Routledge: London, 1990).

66 Anthony Kenny, *Aristotle's Theory of the Will* (New Haven: Yale University Press, 1979); A. Van Den Beld, "Romans 7:14–25 and the Problem of Akrasia," *Rel. Stud.* 21 (1985): 495–515. I do not want to suggest, as Kenny does, that volitions are not desires.

67 So Van Den Beld, "The Problem of Akrasia."

68 It is also used for political leaders selling themselves for bribes (Demosth. 10.63, cf 17.13; 18.28, 46; Dinarch. 1.71).

69 Cranfield, *Romans,* 1:357.

70 *Se* is supported by Sinaiticus B F G 1506*.1739*.a b sy(p); Tert Ambst; *me* by A D byzantine majority lat sy(h) sa; Cl.

71 The *RSV, NIV, TEV,* and *KJV* use "me." The *Jerusalem Bible* chooses "you."

72 On the reasons for my translation, see Käsemann, *Romans,* 11–13.

73 Dale C. Allison, *The End of the Ages Has Come* (Philadelphia: Fortress Press, 1985), 67–68, 80–82.

74 Brendan Byrne, *"Sons of God"—"Seed of Abraham"* (Analecta Biblica 83; Rome: Biblical Institute, 1979), 79–81.

Chapter 10. A Warning and Promise to Gentiles

1 F. W. Beare, *St. Paul and His Letters* (London: A. and C. Black, 1962), 103–04. I have taken this reference from J. C. Beker ("The Faithfulness of God and the Priority of Israel in Paul's Letter to the Romans," in *Christians among Jews and Gentiles,* ed. G. W. E. Nickelsburg and G. W. MacRae [Philadelphia: Fortress Press, 1986], 11).

2 Krister Stendhal, "The Apostle Paul and the Introspective Conscience of the West," in *The Writings of St. Paul,* ed. W. A. Meeks (New York: Norton, 1972), 426; repr. from *HTR* 56 (1963): 199–215; J. Christiaan Beker, *Paul among Jews and Gentiles* (Philadelphia: Fortress Press, 1976), 3–5, 25–30; *Paul the Apostle: The Triumph of God in Life and Thought* (Philadelphia: Fortress Press, 1980), 87. Beker speaks of "a climactic point." Also, John Koenig, *Jews and Christians in Dialogue* (Philadelphia: Westminster Press, 1979), 53.

3 Nils A. Dahl, *Studies in Paul* (Minneapolis: Augsburg, 1977), 142–43.

4 Ibid., 143.

5 "Paul and Torah," 66. Gaston, however, goes too far in denying that Jesus was Israel's messiah for Paul.

6 *A Lexicon Abridged from Liddell and Scott's Greek-English Lexicon,* ed. H. G. Liddell, R. Scott (Oxford: Clarendon Press, 1966), 151. The *RSV's* "now" in 11:13 is unclear. It is set off by a new paragraph and most easily read as "now at this point in the discourse." The *de* in verse 12, however, is also rendered "now" so that one could imagine the meaning cited by Liddell and Scott.

7 Cranfield (*Romans,* 2:559) and Sanday and Headlam (*Romans,* 322–24) are exceptions.

8 J. D. Denniston, *The Greek Particles,* 2d ed. (Oxford: Oxford University Press, 1954), 475–78; M. E. Thrall, *Greek Particles in the New Testament* (NTTS 3; Leiden: E. J. Brill, 1962), 35.

9 Sanday and Headlam (*Romans,* 324) point to the textual variants wherever *menoun* is found. The variants for 13, however, markedly exceed the typical variants caused by ambiguity over whether *men oun* should be taken separately or adverbially and coalesing. Early Pauline manuscripts did not separate words at all. Therefore it is anachronistic to speak of *men oun* being written together in New Testament times (*Contra* Thrall, *Greek Particles,* 34).

10 Although this reading involves the Western text, it should not be thought that all of the variants for 13 involve Western versus non-Western readings. The Western text does seem to "dislike" the adverbial *menoun.*

11 Sanday and Headlam (*Romans,* 324) cite approvingly a statement by Hort along these lines.

12 Dahl, *Studies in Paul,* 139–41.

13 Ibid., 140. Cf. Rom 1:13; 1 Cor 10:1; 12:1; 2 Cor 1:8; 1 Thess 4:13. J. L. White, "Body-opening Formulae in the Pauline Letter," *JBL* 89 (1970): 91–92; T. Y. Mullins, "Disclosure: A Literary Form in the New Testament," *NovT* 7 (1964): 44–50; "Formulas in the New Testament Epistles," *JBL* 91 (1972): 380–90.

14 Dahl, *Studies in Paul,* 140, n. 10.

15 Ibid., 140, n. 13.

16 On ethos and pathos, see Folker Siegert, *Argumentation bei Paulus* (WUNT 34; Tübingen: J. C. B. Mohr, 1985), 230–31.

17 *Letter Writing,* 125–32; Abraham J. Malherbe, *Paul and the Thessalonians* (Philadelphia: Fortress Press, 1987), 68–78.

18 Ibid.

19 Rom 9:1(4), 2(2), 3(4), 4; 10:1, 2, 18, 19; 11:1(3), 11, 13(4), 14(3), 25.

20 Clarence E. Glad, "Adaptability in Epicurean and Early Christian Psychagogy: Paul and Philodemus" (Ph.D. diss., Brown University, 1992).

21 Chrysostom argues that Paul proposes self-sacrifice not out of love for Jews but to defend God's honor so that God will not be accused of breaking his promises (*Hom. Rom.* 16:1; *PG* 549.50). For a discussion of issues and interpretations, see Cranfield, *Romans,* 2:454–58.

22 See chapter 7 above; Morna D. Hooker, "Interchange and Suffering," in *Suffering and Martyrdom in the New Testament,* ed. W. Horbury and B. McNeil (Cambridge: Cambridge University Press, 1981), 70–83.

23 For an excellent summation of this perspective, see Mary Ann Getty, "Paul and the Salvation of Israel: A Perspective on Romans 9–11," *CBQ* 50 (1988): 456–69. For bibliography containing representatives of the ecumenist position, see 457, n. 5.

24 Heikki Räisänen, "Paul, God, and Israel: Romans 9–11 in Recent Research," in *The Social World of Formative Christiantity and Judaism: Essays in Tribute to Howard Clark Kee,* ed. J. Neusner, E. Frerichs, et al. (Philadelphia: Fortress Press, 1988), 178–206.

25 Ibid., 188. On 181, however, Räisänen says the following: "He has to face the worries of Jewish Christians about the implications of his gospel. Roman gentile Christians would not have cared, at least not if they had to be warned against a boasting attitude toward Jews (11:18, 20)."

26 *Paul and Torah,* 92.

27 Räisänen, "Paul, God, and Israel," 180.

28 Paul E. Dinter, "The Remnant of Israel and the Stone of Stumbling in Zion according to Paul (Romans 9–11)" (Ph.D. diss., Union Theological Seminary, 1980).

29 Räisänen, "Paul, God and Israel," 180.

30 Dinter, "Remnant of Israel."

31 The case for *hyper* as *peri* in 9:27 rests entirely on a strong version of the traditional reading. For that case, see Cranfield, *Romans,* 2:501; F. Blass, A. Debrunner, R. Funk, *A Greek Grammar of the New Testament and Other Early Christian Literature* (Chicago: University of Chicago Press, 1961), par. 231(1); C. F. D. Moule, *An Idiom Book of New Testament Greek* (Cambridge: Cambridge University Press, 1959), 65.

32 Dinter, "Remnant of Israel," 208.

33 George Howard, "Christ the End of the Law," *JBL* 88 (1969): 331–37; Robert Badenas,

Christ the End of the Law: Romans 10:4 in Pauline Perspective (JSNT suppl. 10; Sheffield: University of Sheffield, 1985).

34 "Righteousness of God," 241–90.

35 For opinions about *pistis* in 9:30–32, see Badenas, *End of the Law,* 238, n. 129.

36 Badenas, *End of the Law,* 101, 237, n. 116.

37 Anne Carson, *Eros the Bittersweet* (Princeton: Princeton University Press, 1986), 14.

38 Badenas, *End of the Law.*

39 Ibid., 104–05.

40 Badenas (*End of the Law,* 109) falls into Christian anti-Jewish polemic when he follows interpreters who claim that "knowledge" is not intellectual knowledge but willfulness.

41 James Barr, *The Semantics of Biblical Language* (Oxford: Oxford University Press, 1961). Williams ("Righteousness of God") goes far toward properly contextualizing "Righteousness."

42 "Righteousness of God," 256.

43 The meaning of *eis dikaiosynē* is the crux here. The *RSV* transforms it into a verbal clause so as to introduce the doctrine of justification by faith: "that everyone who has faith may be justified." *Eis dikaiosynē* is best taken with the main clause rather than with *nomos* or *Christos* (Badenas, *End of the Law,* 115–16).

44 A. J. Bandstra, *The Law and the Elements of the World* (Amsterdam: Kampen, 1964), 101–02; Badenas, *End of the Law,* 118–20; Cranfield, *Romans,* 1:520.

45 So Cranfield (*Romans,* 2:521–2), who refers to Karl Barth. See further Bandstra, *Elements of the World,* 104–05.

46 Abraham in 4:17–22 is a type of Jesus. Abraham's procreative powers were "made alive" because of his faithfulness.

47 Badenas (*End of the Law,* 118–25) has argued forcefully against setting the two in opposition.

48 Robert Scholes, *Protocols of Reading* (New Haven: Yale University Press, 1989), 80.

49 Cranfield, *Romans,* 2:555–57.

50 C. K. Barrett, *Romans,* 213; Räisänen, "Paul, God, and Israel," 187.

51 Schlier (*Römerbrief,* 327–28) comes the closest to recognizing the dual-sidedness when he describes *paraptōma* as like *ptaiein* "in der Schwebe zwischen bildhafter und übertragener Bedeutung."

52 Käsemann, *Romans,* 304.

53 Ibid., 213.

54 Ibid.

55 *Omn.* 110. Lucian employs the verb in a text that has a statement about the one winner similar to that in 1 Cor 9:24 (*Anach.* 11.22–25).

56 Scholes, *Protocols of Reading,* 50–88.

57 V. C. Pfitzner, *Paul and the Agon Motif* (NovT Suppl. 16; Leiden: E. J. Brill, 1967).

58 Michael Poliakoff, "Jacob, Job, and Other Wrestlers: Reception of Greek Sport by Jews and Christians in Antiquity," *Journal of Sport History* 11 (1984): 54.

Chapter 11. Faithfulness as Adaptability

1 For issues and positions, see Walter T. Wilson, *Love without Pretense: Romans 12:9–21 and Hellenistic-Jewish Wisdom Literature* (WUNT 2.46; Tübingen: J. C. B. Mohr, 1991); Robert J. Karris, "Romans 14:1–15:13 and the Occasion of Romans," and Francis Watson, "The Two Roman Congregations: Romans 14:1–15:13," both in *The Romans Debate*, rev. ed., ed. Karl P. Donfried (Peabody, Mass.: Hendrickson, 1991), 65–84, 203–15, respectively.

2 Wilson, *Love without Pretense*, 137–38.

3 Clarence Glad, "Adaptability in Epicurean and Early Christian Psychagogy: Paul and Philodemus," (Ph.D. diss., Brown University, 1992).

4 Plutarch, *How to Tell a Flatterer from a Friend*; Glad, "Adaptability," 83–103.

5 "Use and Abuse of Reason," 266–86; Glad, "Adaptability," 104–18, 477–98.

6 Stowers, "Use and Abuse of Reason," 276–84.

7 Ibid.

8 Abraham J. Malherbe, *Paul and the Popular Philosophers* (Minneapolis: Fortress Press, 1989); id., *Paul and the Thessalonians: The Philosophic Tradition of Pastoral Care* (Philadelphia: Fortress Press, 1987).

9 Glad, "Adaptability," 355–85, 388–438.

10 "Use and Abuse of Reason," 276–83.

11 Ibid.; Glad, "Adaptability," 504–21.

12 Glad, "Adaptability," 388–96.

13 On the term, see Glad, Ibid., 398–99.

14 *Letter Writing*, 125–32.

15 "Use and Abuse of Reason," 276–84.

Conclusions

1 On protreptic, see the important article by David E. Aune, "Romans as a *Logos Protreptikos* in the Context of Ancient Religious and Philosophical Propaganda," in *Paulus und das antike Judentum*, ed. M. Hengel (Tübingen: J. C. B. Mohr, 1992), 91–24.

Indexes

Index of Ancient Authors

Index of Selected Subjects